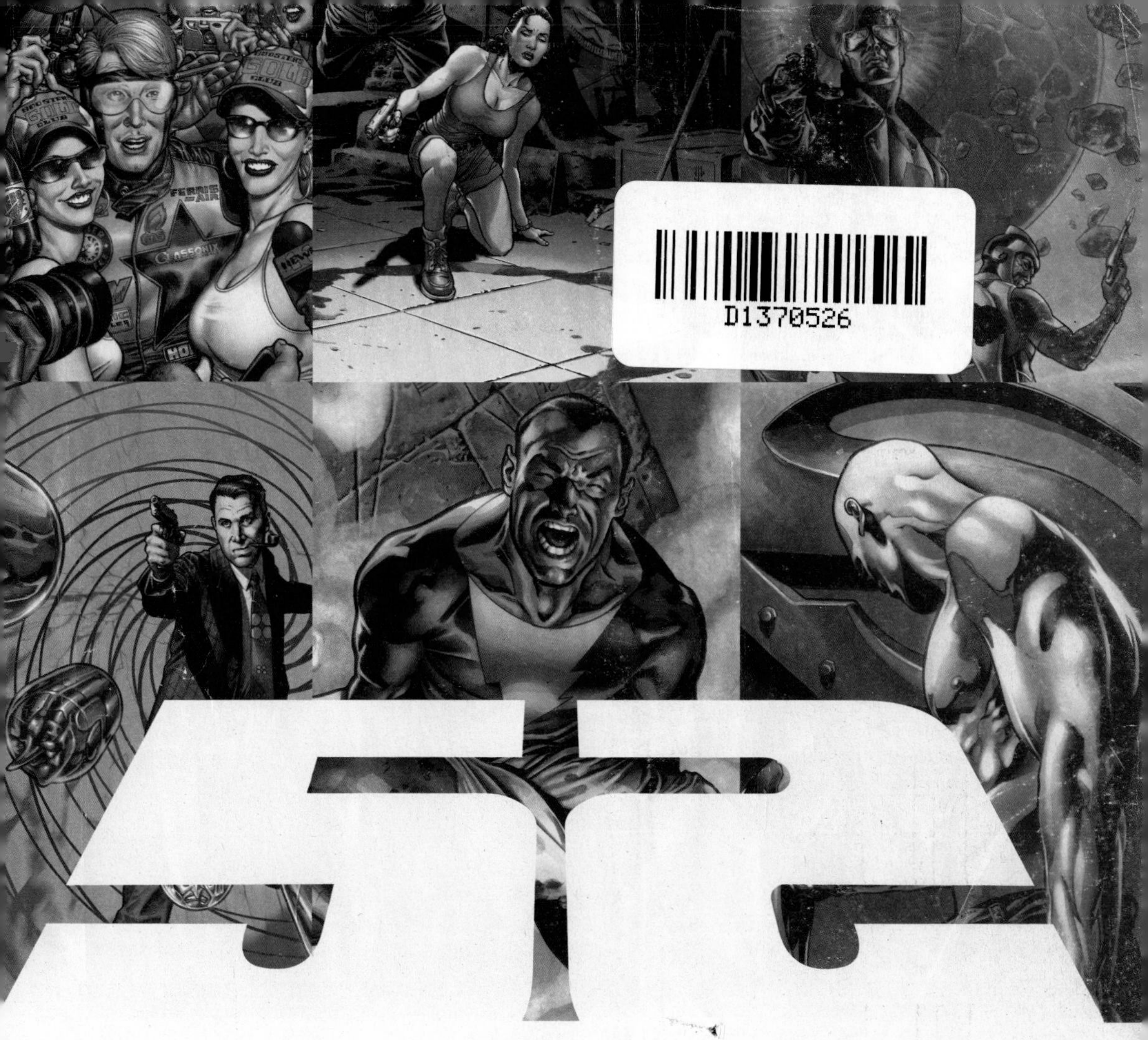

52 THE COMPANION

Dan DiDio Senior VP-Executive Editor   **Anton Kawasaki** Editor-collected edition   **Robbin Brosterman** Senior Art Director   **Paul Levitz** President & Publisher

Georg Brewer VP-Design & DC Direct Creative   **Richard Bruning** Senior VP-Creative Director   **Patrick Caldon** Executive VP-Finance & Operations

Chris Caramalis VP-Finance   **John Cunningham** VP-Marketing   **Terri Cunningham** VP-Managing Editor   **Alison Gill** VP-Manufacturing

Hank Kanalz VP-General Manager, WildStorm   **Jim Lee** Editorial Director-WildStorm   **Paula Lowitt** Senior VP-Business & Legal Affairs

MaryEllen McLaughlin VP-Advertising & Custom Publishing   **John Nee** VP-Business Development   **Gregory Noveck** Senior VP-Creative Affairs

Sue Pohja VP-Book Trade Sales   **Cheryl Rubin** Senior VP-Brand Management   **Jeff Trojan** VP-Business Development, DC Direct   **Bob Wayne** VP-Sales

Cover by J.G. Jones with Alex Sinclair   Color reconstruction on select stories by Drew R. Moore   Publication design by Amelia Grohman

52: THE COMPANION

Published by DC Comics. Cover, introduction and compilation copyright © 2007 DC Comics. All rights reserved. Originally published in single magazine form in RIP HUNTER: TIME MASTER #6, DETECTIVE COMICS #350, MYSTERIOUS SUSPENSE #1, STRANGE ADVENTURES #226, METAL MEN #45, SECRET ORIGINS #35, ANIMAL MAN #16, SUPERMAN: THE MAN OF STEEL #97, JSA #43-44, GOTHAM CENTRAL #40. Copyright © 1962, 1966, 1968, 1970, 1976, 1988, 1989, 2000, 2003, 2006 DC Comics. All Rights Reserved. All characters, their distinctive likenesses and related elements featured in this publication are trademarks of DC Comics. The stories, characters and incidents featured in this publication are entirely fictional. DC Comics does not read or accept unsolicited submissions of ideas, stories or artwork.

DC Comics, 1700 Broadway, New York, NY 10019. A Warner Bros. Entertainment Company.

Printed in Canada. First Printing. ISBN: 1-4012-1557-2   ISBN 13: 978-1-4012-1557-6

CONTENTS

INTRODUCTION BY MARK WAID

In 2005, DC approached writers Greg Rucka, Geoff Johns, Grant Morrison, artist Keith Giffen and myself to make real a crazy idea put forth by publisher Paul Levitz: 52, a weekly comic book designed to last an entire year and, over the course of fifty-two installments, examine every corner and nuance of the DC Universe.

We succeeded, and these are the people without whom:
DC's best artists, an unparalleled production and editorial team—

—and ten specific DC characters, all of whom began 52 as second-stringers and emerged revitalized as key players in the DC Universe to come.

Each story in this volume helped to imprint its star's identity on our imaginations. Put less grandly, each tale collected herein holds important pieces of what makes these characters worth reviving.

If second-string heroes tend to go unloved (after all, there are no Supermen or Batmen in this volume—and if a Rip Hunter movie is ever made, few will expect a $100 million first weekend), it's frankly because comic book history is so full of bad ones. We've all snoozed through the low-stakes complications that ensue when tired creators throw down "daring" new combinations of costume colors and powers. I mean, what if a character wore grey and green and had heat vision? I'll tell you what if. Nothing that demands my comics money. That's what if.

52: THE COMPANION proves that DC's vast stable of backup players is a lot better than that. Many of them can be said to express a single, strong, simple idea as clean as The Flash's speed or Batman's crusade. Robots with feelings. A man with animal powers. An adventurer who must travel across space to defend his true love from danger. These are strong situations and characters, so it's no surprise that many of them boast small but rabid fan bases of their own (because there is no fan so loyal as a sophisticated reader who has made his own "secret" find).

Strong enough to reemerge as core characters in today's DC Universe, the second string has come off the bench.

And they're playing to win.

SUPERMAN: THE MAN OF STEEL #97

Many Superman stories have been written about the relationship between the Man of Tomorrow and the human race he protects. It's a difficult subject, because our reliance on a super-powered individual to right wrongs and keep us safe is not very flattering. On the other hand, Superman has to remain important, or what's the point? Writer Louise Simonson and artist Jon Bogdanove solved this problem neatly when they created Steel, one of many second-stringers with a pedigree in Superman comics.

It went like this: Superman rescued John Henry Irons from what would have been a fatal fall, then practically dared him to make a difference with his life, to become a hero. John Henry reached back into the folklore of his steel-drivin' namesake and adopted the armored, hammer-swinging persona of Steel — the embodiment of what happens when a man with will-power combines the inspiration of Superman with his own sense of self-determination.

This story helped establish John Henry and his niece Natasha as the preeminent dad-and-surrogate-daughter scientists of Metropolis. In 52, it's through their eyes that we see how technology and self-made superheroism shape the DC Universe. **—MW**

JOHN HENRY IRONS (a.k.a. Steel)

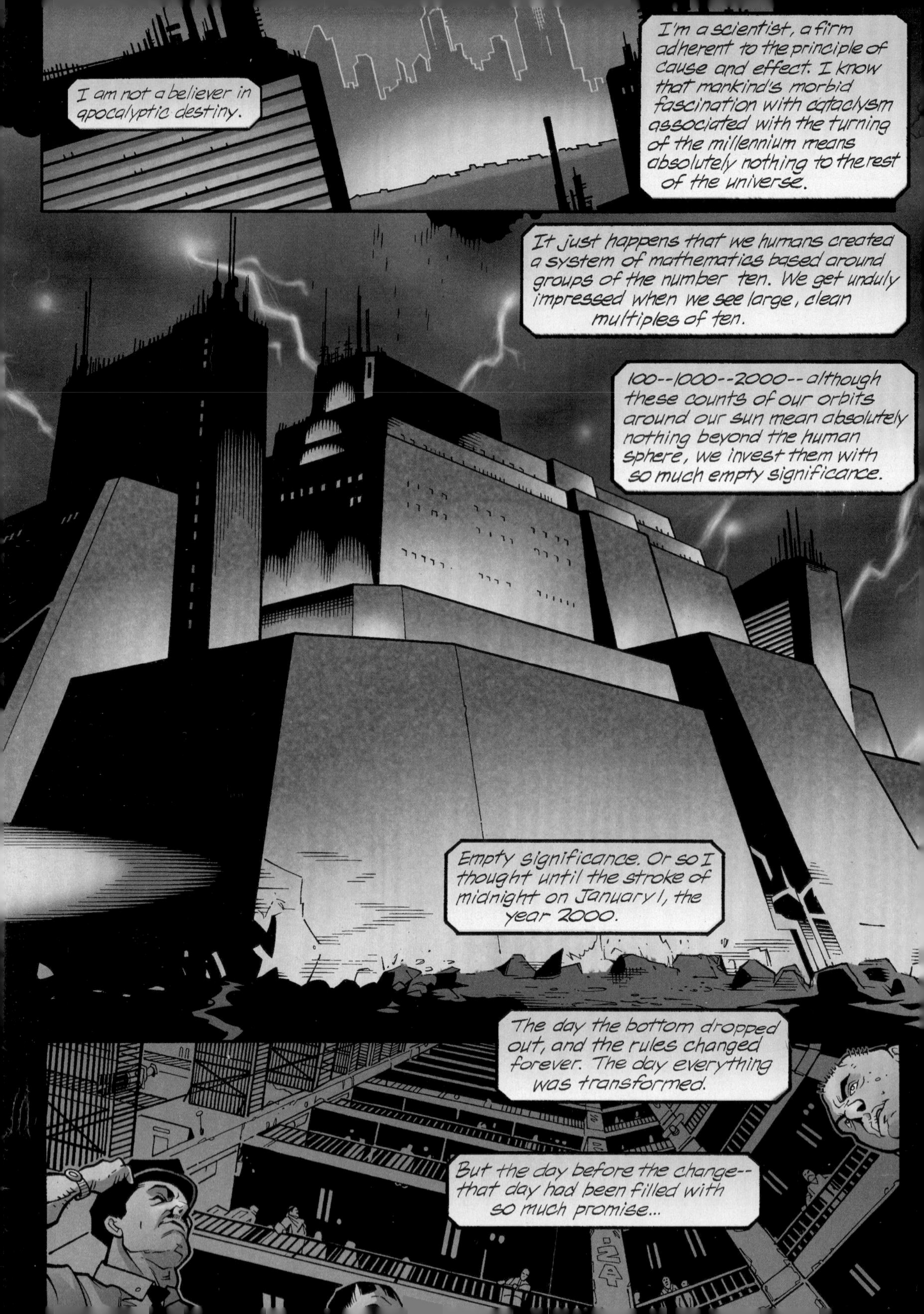
I am not a believer in apocalyptic destiny.
I'm a scientist, a firm adherent to the principle of cause and effect. I know that mankind's morbid fascination with cataclysm associated with the turning of the millennium means absolutely nothing to the rest of the universe.
It just happens that we humans created a system of mathematics based around groups of the number ten. We get unduly impressed when we see large, clean multiples of ten.
100--1000--2000--although these counts of our orbits around our sun mean absolutely nothing beyond the human sphere, we invest them with so much empty significance.
Empty significance. Or so I thought until the stroke of midnight on January 1, the year 2000.
The day the bottom dropped out, and the rules changed forever. The day everything was transformed.
But the day before the change--that day had been filled with so much promise...

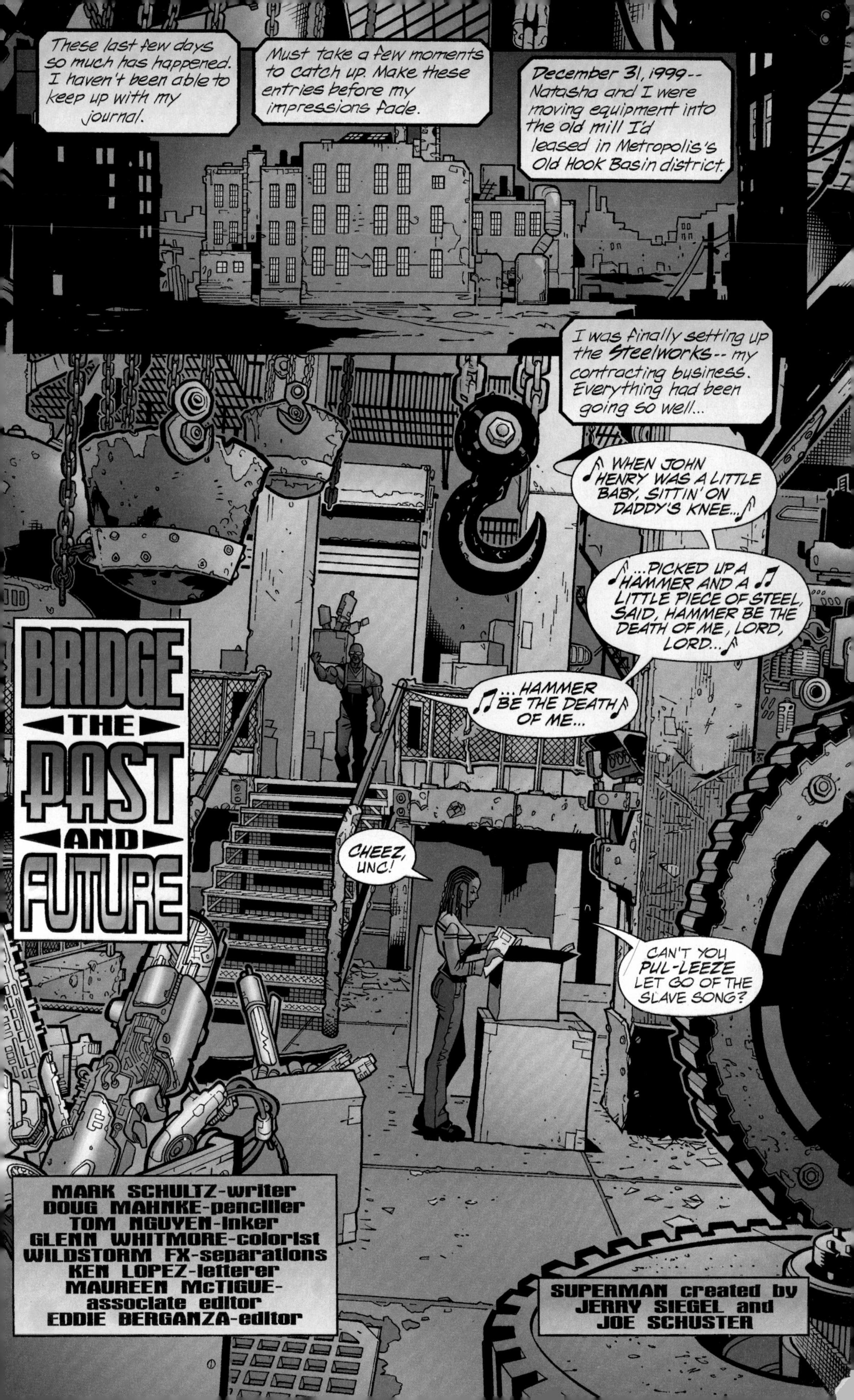
These last few days so much has happened. I haven't been able to keep up with my journal.
Must take a few moments to catch up. Make these entries before my impressions fade.
December 31, 1999-- Natasha and I were moving equipment into the old mill I'd leased in Metropolis's Old Hook Basin district.
I was finally setting up the Steelworks-- my contracting business. Everything had been going so well...
♪ WHEN JOHN HENRY WAS A LITTLE BABY, SITTIN' ON DADDY'S KNEE... ♪
♪ ...PICKED UP A HAMMER AND A ♪ LITTLE PIECE OF STEEL, SAID, HAMMER BE THE DEATH OF ME, LORD, LORD... ♪
♪ ...HAMMER BE THE DEATH OF ME... ♪
BRIDGE THE PAST AND FUTURE
CHEEZ, UNC!
CAN'T YOU PUL-LEEZE LET GO OF THE SLAVE SONG?
MARK SCHULTZ-writer
DOUG MAHNKE-penciller
TOM NGUYEN-inker
GLENN WHITMORE-colorist
WILDSTORM FX-separations
KEN LOPEZ-letterer
MAUREEN McTIGUE-associate editor
EDDIE BERGANZA-editor
SUPERMAN created by JERRY SIEGEL and JOE SCHUSTER

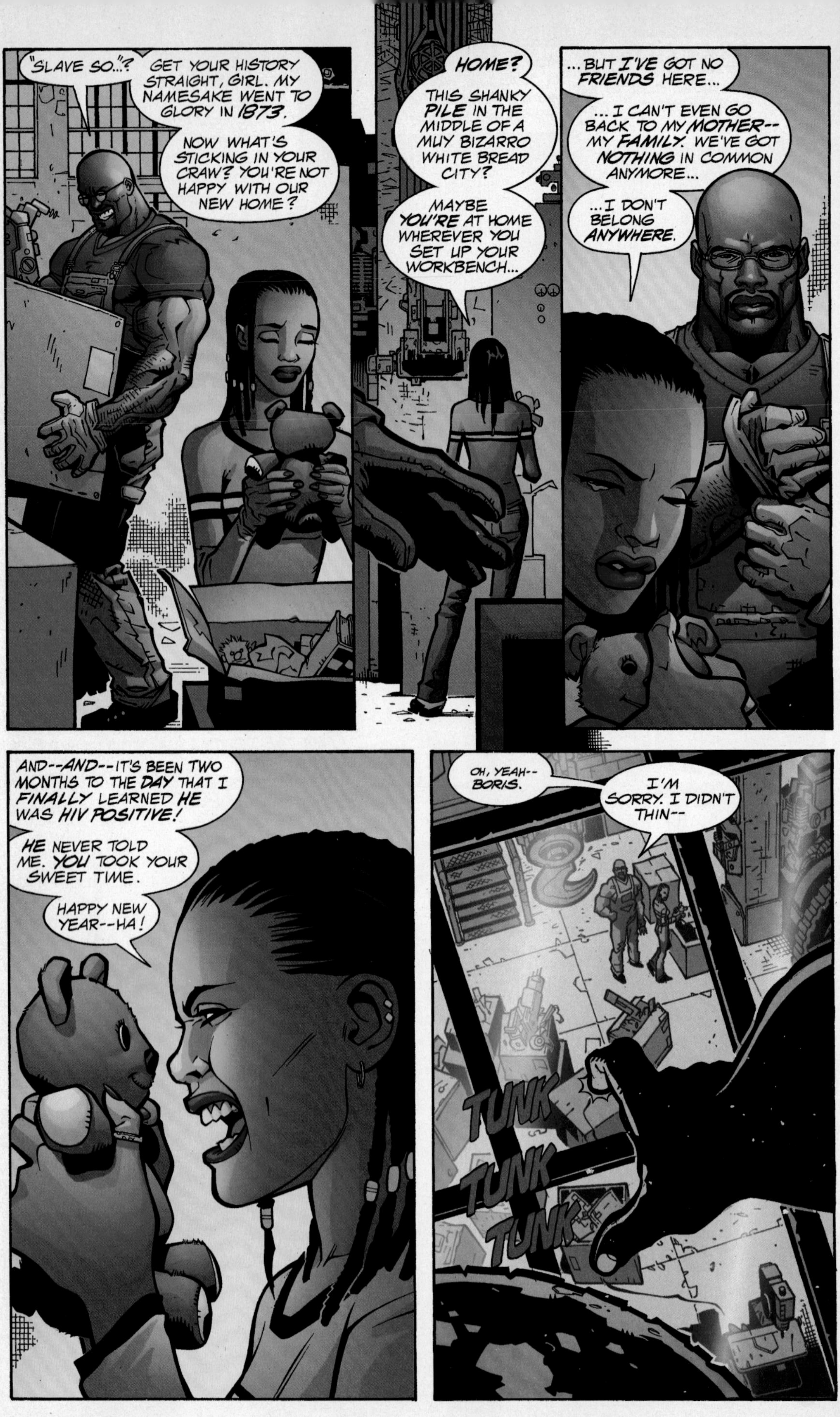
"SLAVE SO..."?
GET YOUR HISTORY STRAIGHT, GIRL. MY NAMESAKE WENT TO GLORY IN 1873.
NOW WHAT'S STICKING IN YOUR CRAW? YOU'RE NOT HAPPY WITH OUR NEW HOME?
HOME?
THIS SHANKY PILE IN THE MIDDLE OF A MUY BIZARRO WHITE BREAD CITY?
MAYBE YOU'RE AT HOME WHEREVER YOU SET UP YOUR WORKBENCH...
...BUT I'VE GOT NO FRIENDS HERE...
...I CAN'T EVEN GO BACK TO MY MOTHER-- MY FAMILY. WE'VE GOT NOTHING IN COMMON ANYMORE...
...I DON'T BELONG ANYWHERE.
AND--AND--IT'S BEEN TWO MONTHS TO THE DAY THAT I FINALLY LEARNED HE WAS HIV POSITIVE!
HE NEVER TOLD ME. YOU TOOK YOUR SWEET TIME.
HAPPY NEW YEAR--HA!
OH, YEAH-- BORIS.
I'M SORRY. I DIDN'T THIN--
TUNK
TUNK
TUNK

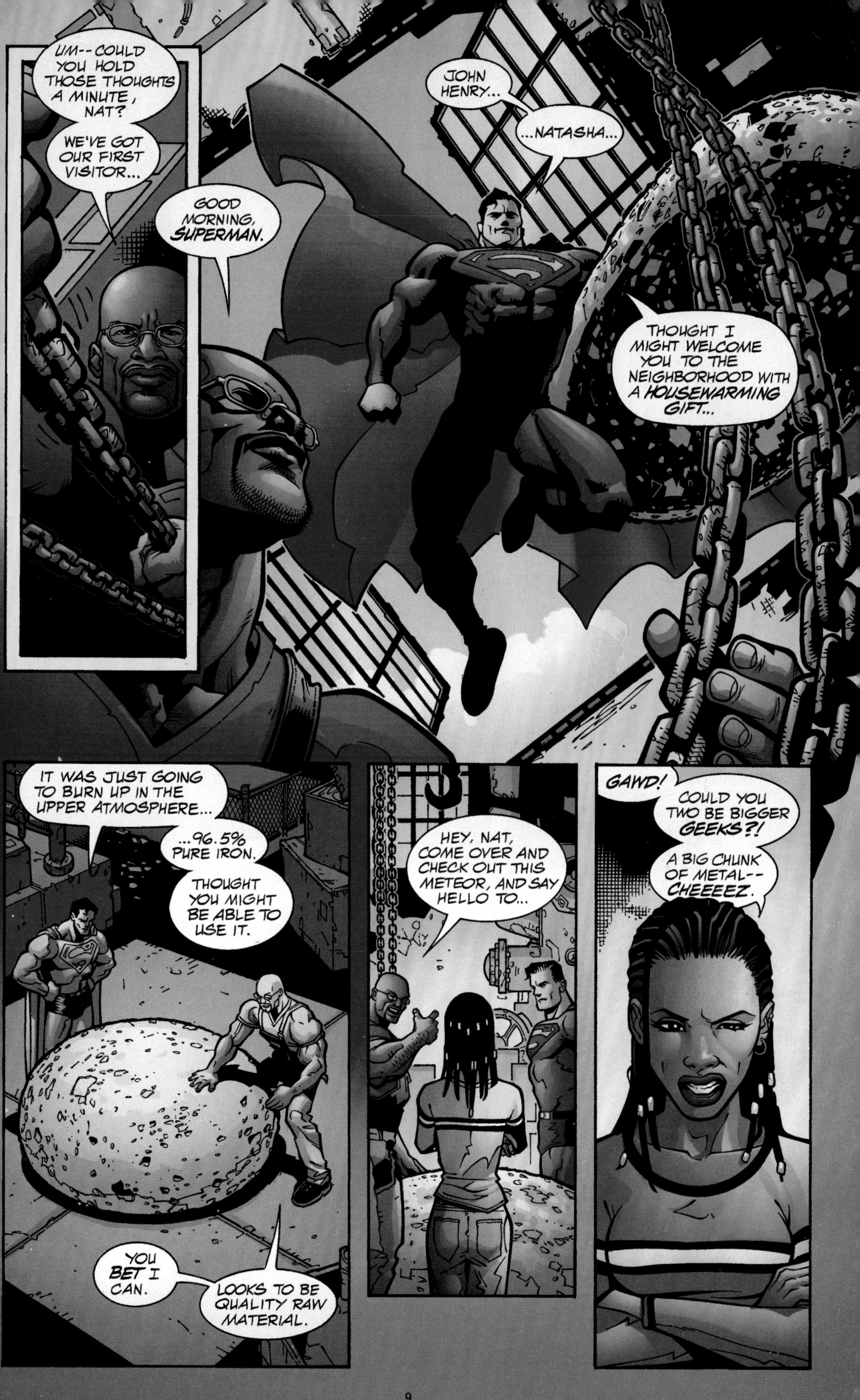
UM--COULD YOU HOLD THOSE THOUGHTS A MINUTE, NAT?
WE'VE GOT OUR FIRST VISITOR...
GOOD MORNING, SUPERMAN.
JOHN HENRY...
...NATASHA...
THOUGHT I MIGHT WELCOME YOU TO THE NEIGHBORHOOD WITH A HOUSEWARMING GIFT...
IT WAS JUST GOING TO BURN UP IN THE UPPER ATMOSPHERE...
...96.5% PURE IRON.
THOUGHT YOU MIGHT BE ABLE TO USE IT.
LOOKS TO BE QUALITY RAW MATERIAL.
YOU BET I CAN.
HEY, NAT, COME OVER AND CHECK OUT THIS METEOR, AND SAY HELLO TO...
GAWD!
COULD YOU TWO BE BIGGER GEEKS?!
A BIG CHUNK OF METAL--CHEEEEZ.

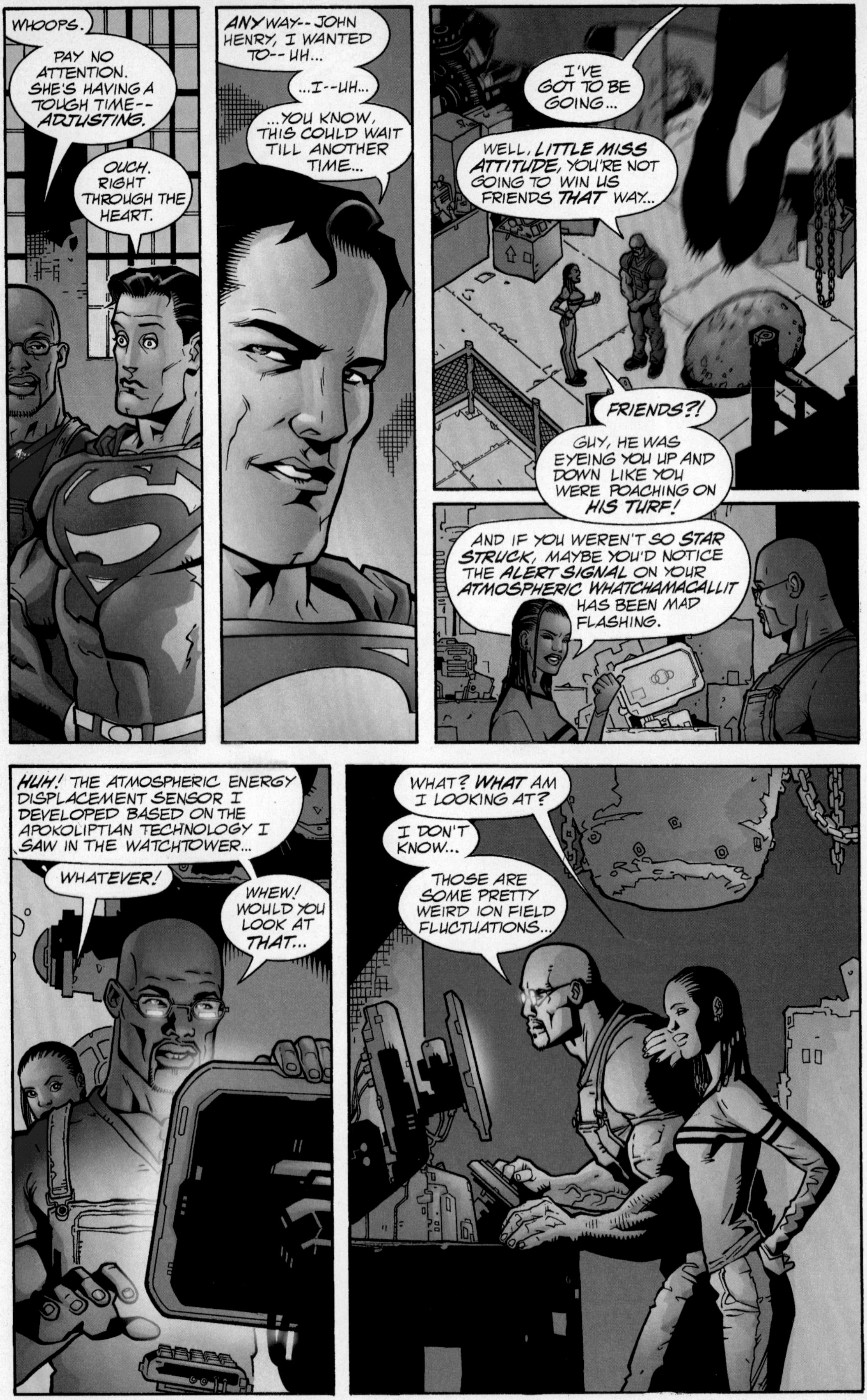
WHOOPS.
PAY NO ATTENTION. SHE'S HAVING A TOUGH TIME-- ADJUSTING.
OUCH. RIGHT THROUGH THE HEART.
ANYWAY-- JOHN HENRY, I WANTED TO-- UH...
...I--UH...
...YOU KNOW, THIS COULD WAIT TILL ANOTHER TIME...
I'VE GOT TO BE GOING...
WELL, LITTLE MISS ATTITUDE, YOU'RE NOT GOING TO WIN US FRIENDS THAT WAY...
FRIENDS?!
GUY, HE WAS EYEING YOU UP AND DOWN LIKE YOU WERE POACHING ON HIS TURF!
AND IF YOU WEREN'T SO STAR STRUCK, MAYBE YOU'D NOTICE THE ALERT SIGNAL ON YOUR ATMOSPHERIC WHATCHAMACALLIT HAS BEEN MAD FLASHING.
HUH! THE ATMOSPHERIC ENERGY DISPLACEMENT SENSOR I DEVELOPED BASED ON THE APOKOLIPTIAN TECHNOLOGY I SAW IN THE WATCHTOWER...
WHATEVER!
WHEW! WOULD YOU LOOK AT THAT...
WHAT? WHAT AM I LOOKING AT?
I DON'T KNOW...
THOSE ARE SOME PRETTY WEIRD ION FIELD FLUCTUATIONS...

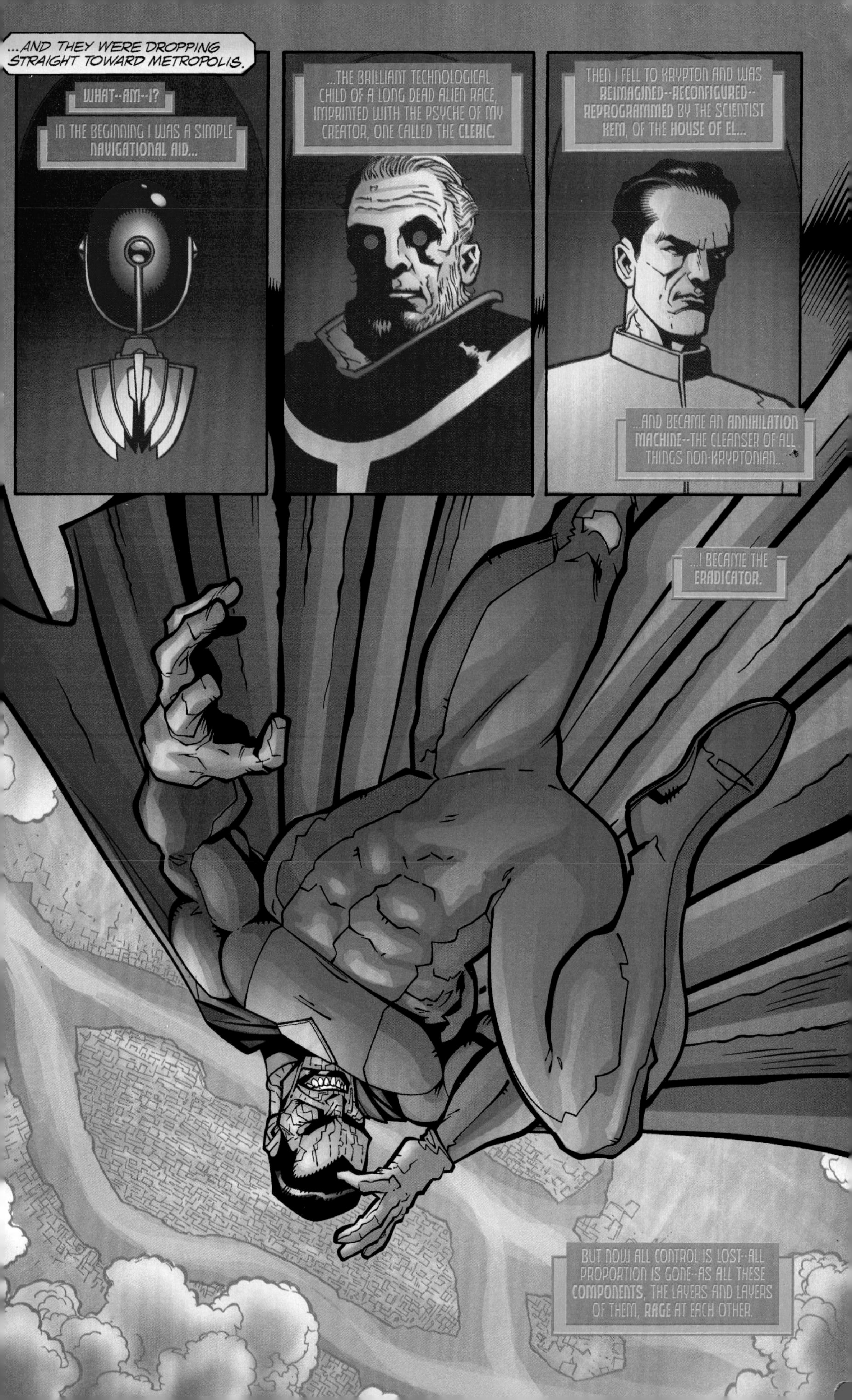
...AND THEY WERE DROPPING STRAIGHT TOWARD METROPOLIS.
WHAT--AM--I?
IN THE BEGINNING I WAS A SIMPLE NAVIGATIONAL AID...
...THE BRILLIANT TECHNOLOGICAL CHILD OF A LONG DEAD ALIEN RACE, IMPRINTED WITH THE PSYCHE OF MY CREATOR, ONE CALLED THE CLERIC.
THEN I FELL TO KRYPTON AND WAS REIMAGINED--RECONFIGURED--REPROGRAMMED BY THE SCIENTIST KEM, OF THE HOUSE OF EL...
...AND BECAME AN ANNIHILATION MACHINE--THE CLEANSER OF ALL THINGS NON-KRYPTONIAN...
...I BECAME THE ERADICATOR.
BUT NOW ALL CONTROL IS LOST--ALL PROPORTION IS GONE--AS ALL THESE COMPONENTS, THE LAYERS AND LAYERS OF THEM, RAGE AT EACH OTHER.

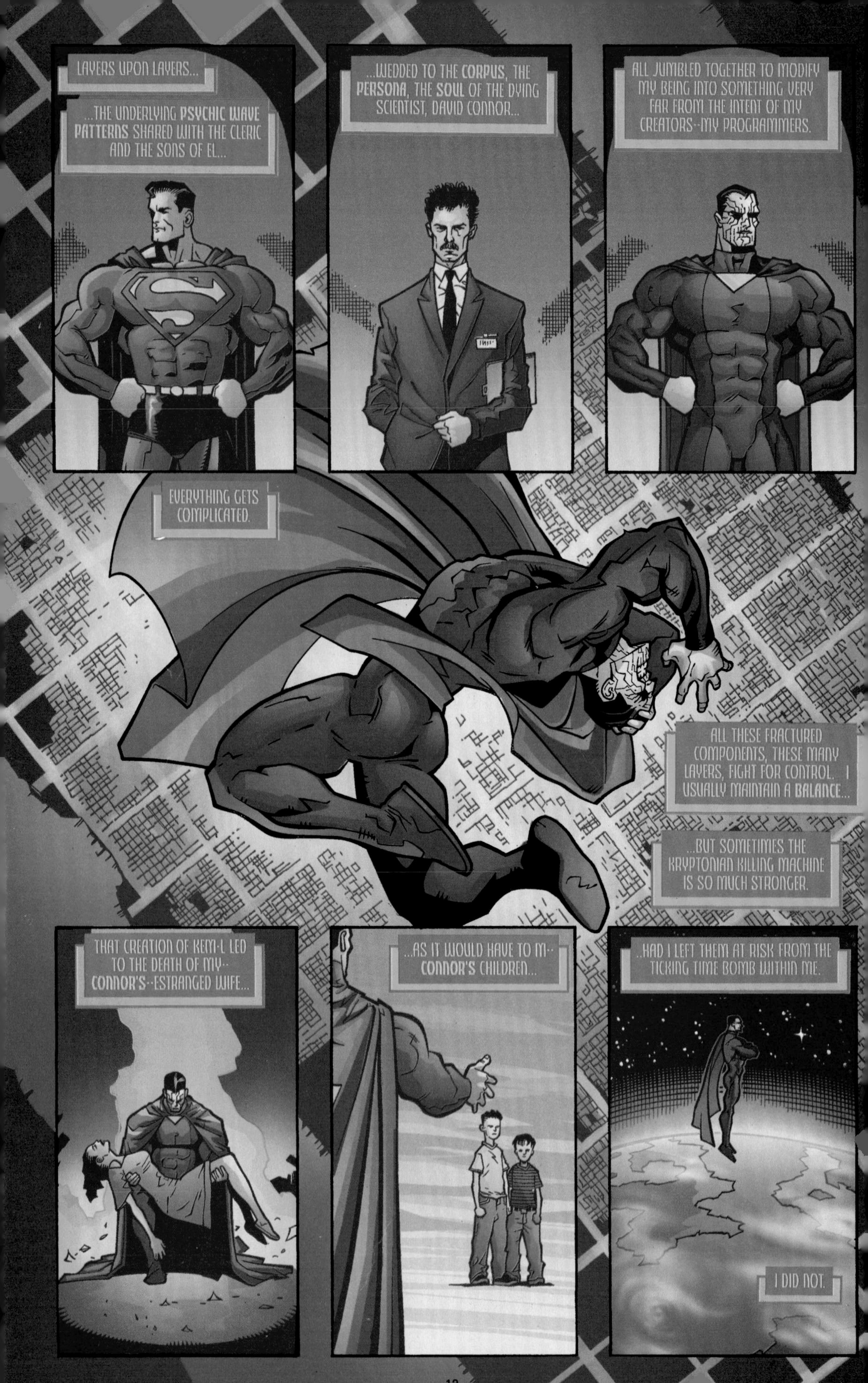
LAYERS UPON LAYERS...
...THE UNDERLYING **PSYCHIC WAVE PATTERNS** SHARED WITH THE CLERIC AND THE SONS OF EL...
...WEDDED TO THE **CORPUS**, THE **PERSONA**, THE **SOUL** OF THE DYING SCIENTIST, DAVID CONNOR...
ALL JUMBLED TOGETHER TO MODIFY MY BEING INTO SOMETHING VERY FAR FROM THE INTENT OF MY CREATORS--MY PROGRAMMERS.
EVERYTHING GETS COMPLICATED.
ALL THESE FRACTURED COMPONENTS, THESE MANY LAYERS, FIGHT FOR CONTROL. I USUALLY MAINTAIN A **BALANCE**...
...BUT SOMETIMES THE KRYPTONIAN KILLING MACHINE IS SO MUCH STRONGER.
THAT CREATION OF KEM-L LED TO THE DEATH OF MY-- **CONNOR'S**--ESTRANGED WIFE...
...AS IT WOULD HAVE TO M-- **CONNOR'S** CHILDREN...
..HAD I LEFT THEM AT RISK FROM THE TICKING TIME BOMB WITHIN ME.
I DID NOT.

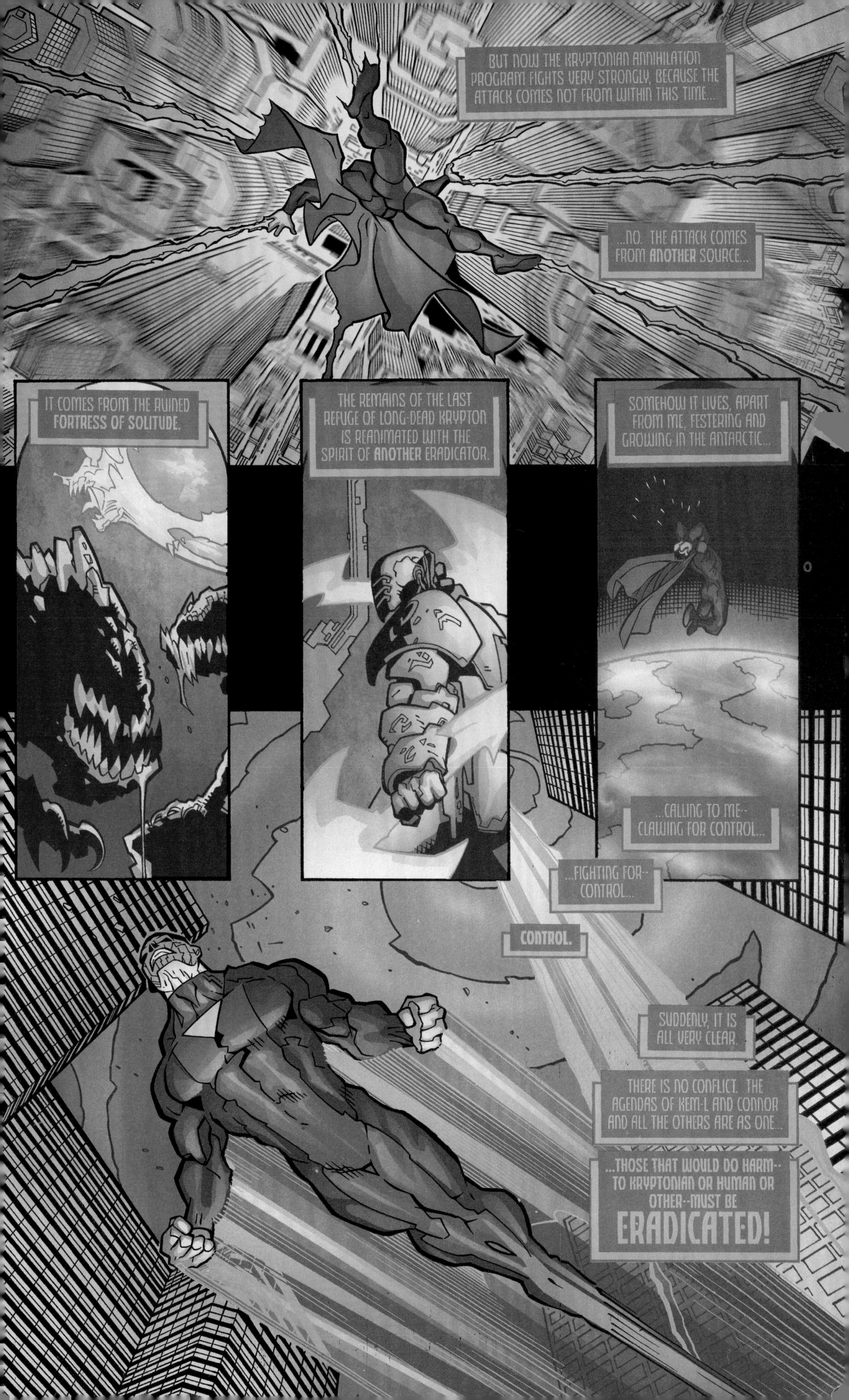

BUT NOW THE KRYPTONIAN ANNIHILATION PROGRAM FIGHTS VERY STRONGLY, BECAUSE THE ATTACK COMES NOT FROM WITHIN THIS TIME...
...NO. THE ATTACK COMES FROM **ANOTHER** SOURCE...
IT COMES FROM THE RUINED **FORTRESS OF SOLITUDE.**
THE REMAINS OF THE LAST REFUGE OF LONG-DEAD KRYPTON IS REANIMATED WITH THE SPIRIT OF **ANOTHER** ERADICATOR.
SOMEHOW IT LIVES, APART FROM ME, FESTERING AND GROWING IN THE ANTARCTIC...
...CALLING TO ME-- CLAWING FOR CONTROL...
...FIGHTING FOR-- CONTROL...
CONTROL.
SUDDENLY, IT IS ALL VERY CLEAR.
THERE IS NO CONFLICT. THE AGENDAS OF KEM-L AND CONNOR AND ALL THE OTHERS ARE AS ONE...
...THOSE THAT WOULD DO HARM-- TO KRYPTONIAN OR HUMAN OR OTHER--MUST BE **ERADICATED!**

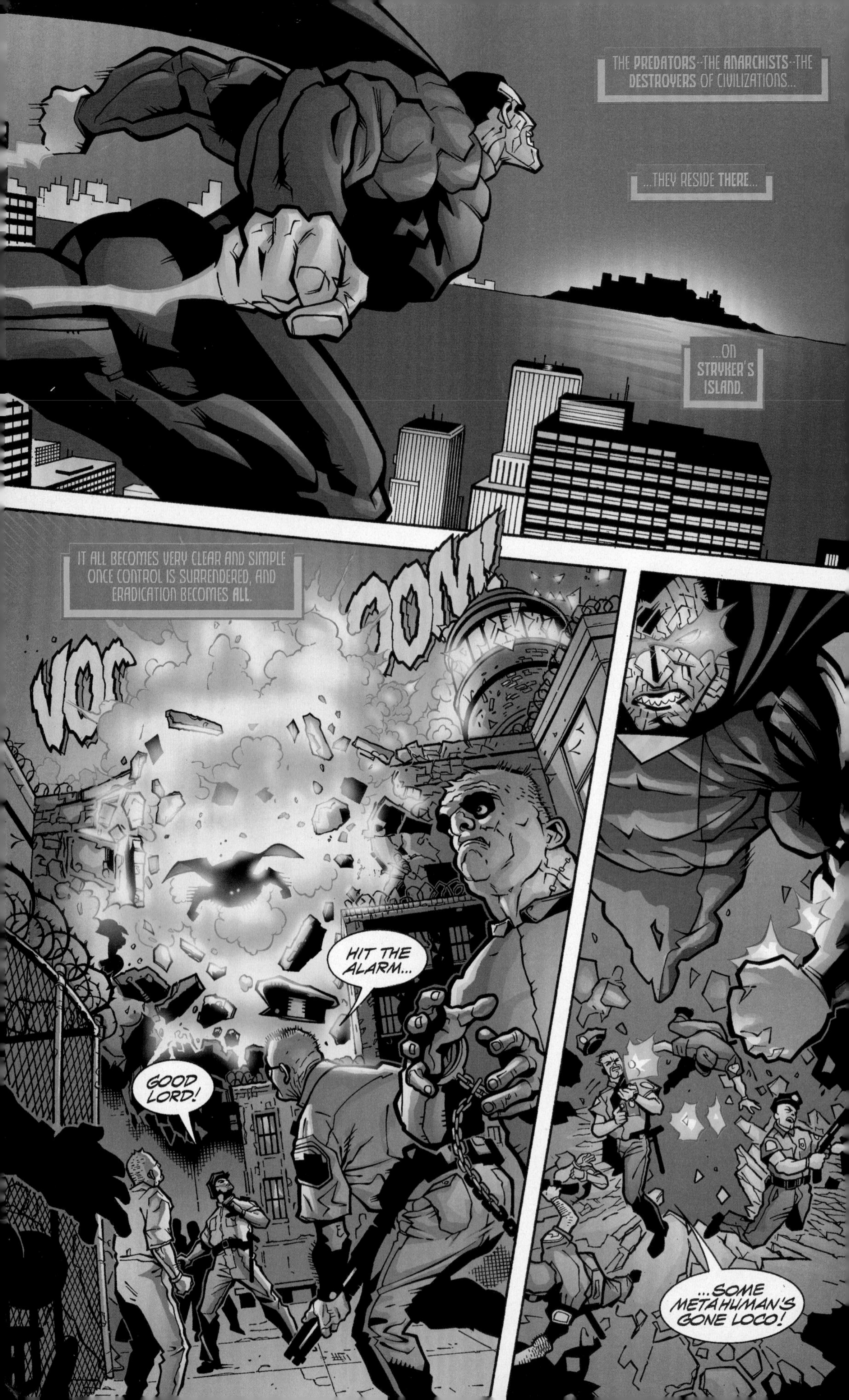
THE PREDATORS--THE ANARCHISTS--THE DESTROYERS OF CIVILIZATIONS...
...THEY RESIDE THERE...
...ON STRYKER'S ISLAND.
IT ALL BECOMES VERY CLEAR AND SIMPLE ONCE CONTROL IS SURRENDERED, AND ERADICATION BECOMES ALL.
VOO
OOM
HIT THE ALARM...
GOOD LORD!
...SOME METAHUMAN'S GONE LOCO!

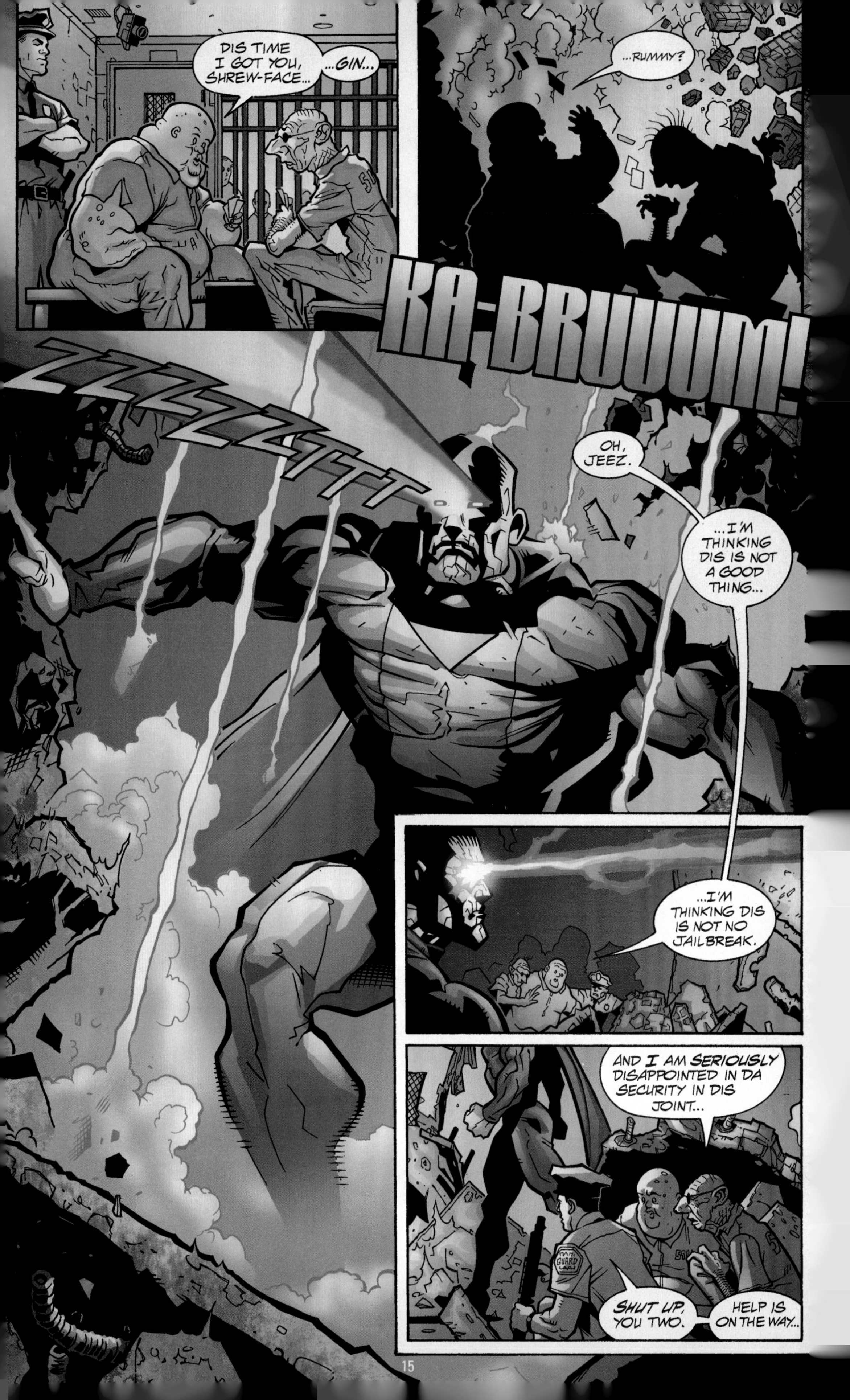
DIS TIME I GOT YOU, SHREW-FACE...
...GIN...
...RUMMY?
KA-BRUUUUM!
ZZZZZZZTTT
OH, JEEZ.
...I'M THINKING DIS IS NOT A GOOD THING...
...I'M THINKING DIS IS NOT NO JAILBREAK.
AND I AM SERIOUSLY DISAPPOINTED IN DA SECURITY IN DIS JOINT...
SHUT UP, YOU TWO.
HELP IS ON THE WAY...

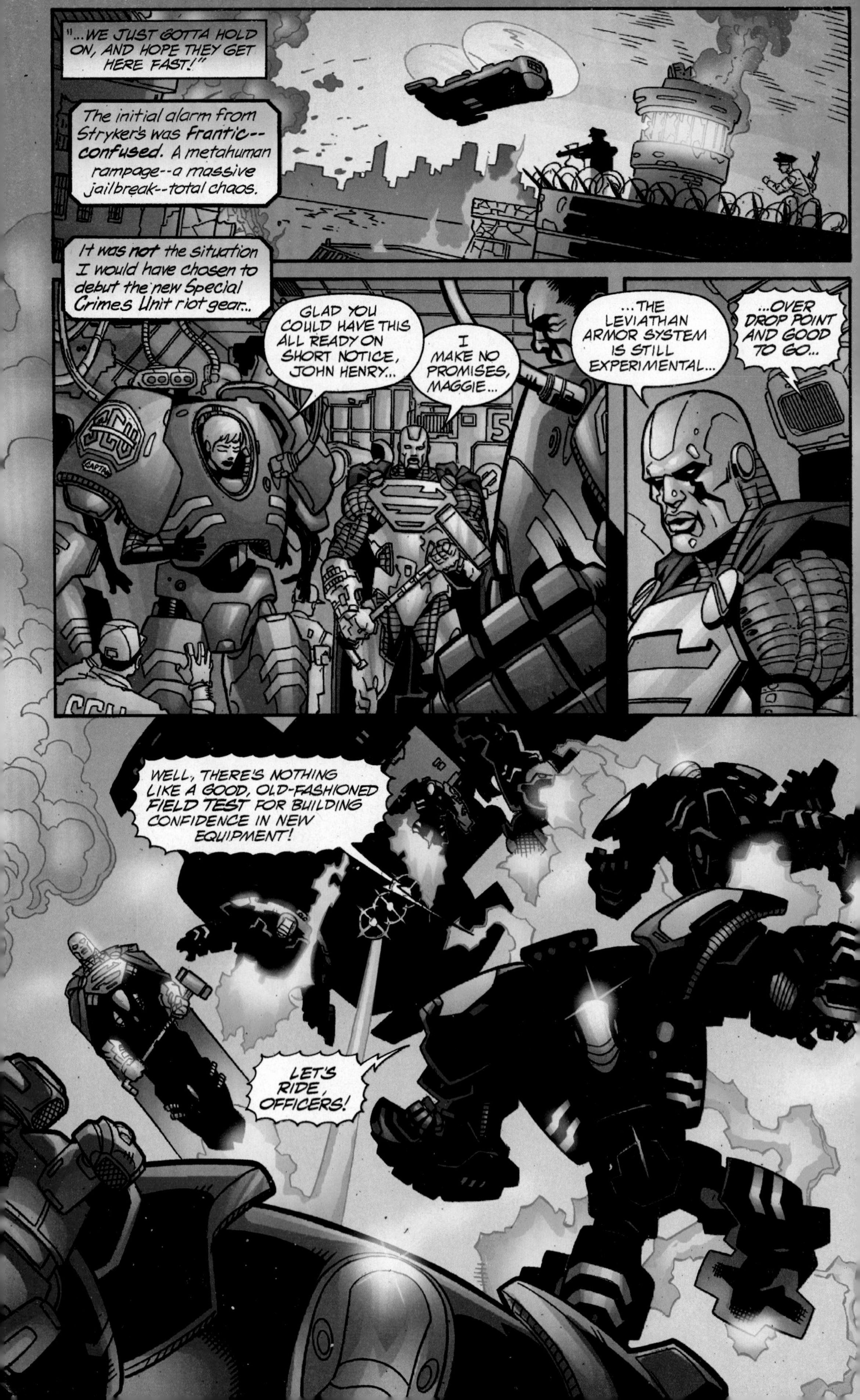
"...WE JUST GOTTA HOLD ON, AND HOPE THEY GET HERE FAST!"
The initial alarm from Stryker's was Frantic--confused. A metahuman rampage--a massive jailbreak--total chaos.
It was not the situation I would have chosen to debut the new Special Crimes Unit riot gear...
GLAD YOU COULD HAVE THIS ALL READY ON SHORT NOTICE, JOHN HENRY...
I MAKE NO PROMISES, MAGGIE...
...THE LEVIATHAN ARMOR SYSTEM IS STILL EXPERIMENTAL...
...OVER DROP POINT AND GOOD TO GO...
WELL, THERE'S NOTHING LIKE A GOOD, OLD-FASHIONED FIELD TEST FOR BUILDING CONFIDENCE IN NEW EQUIPMENT!
LET'S RIDE, OFFICERS!

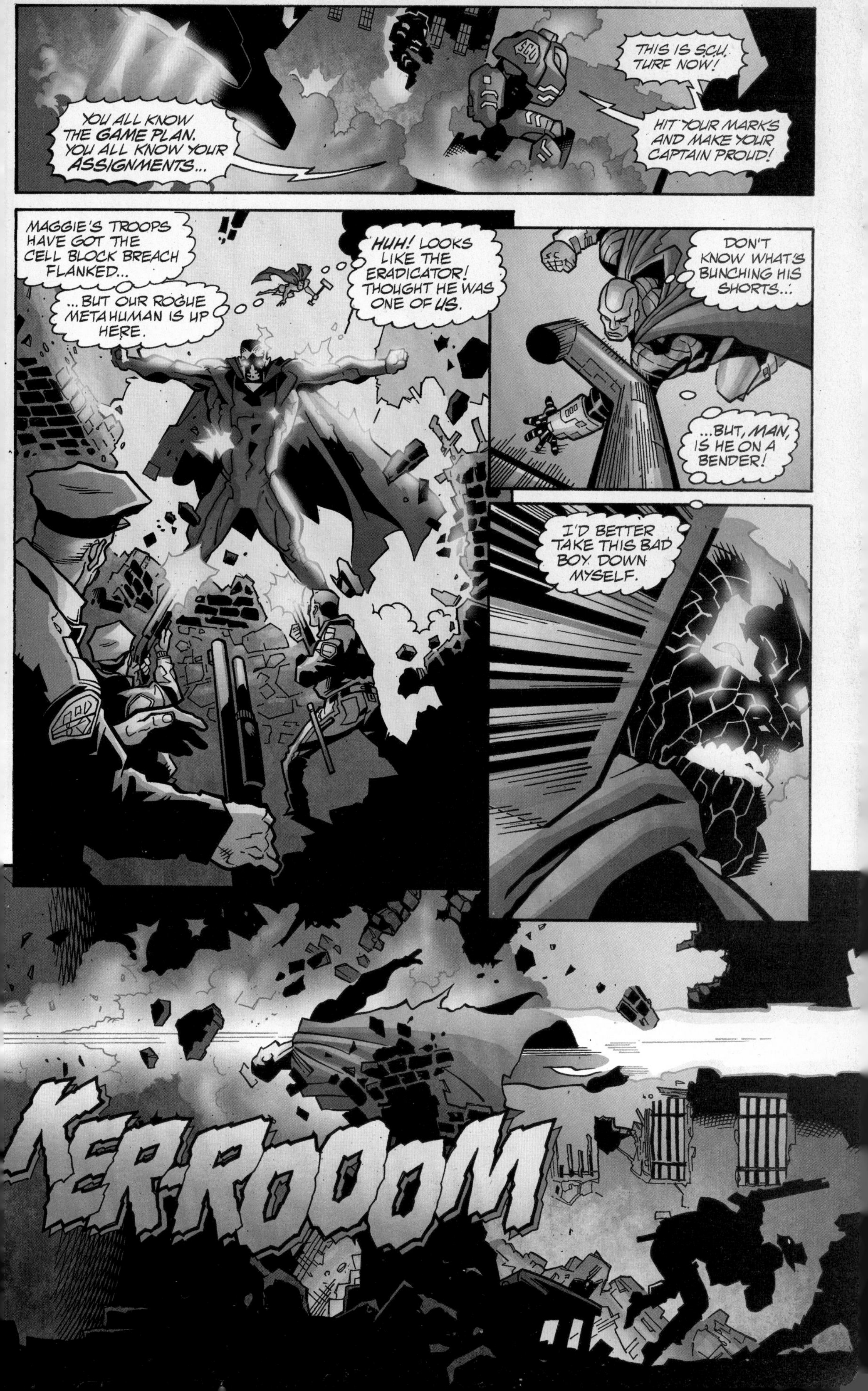
YOU ALL KNOW THE GAME PLAN. YOU ALL KNOW YOUR ASSIGNMENTS...
THIS IS S.C.U. TURF NOW!
HIT YOUR MARKS AND MAKE YOUR CAPTAIN PROUD!
MAGGIE'S TROOPS HAVE GOT THE CELL BLOCK BREACH FLANKED...
...BUT OUR ROGUE METAHUMAN IS UP HERE.
HUH! LOOKS LIKE THE ERADICATOR! THOUGHT HE WAS ONE OF US.
DON'T KNOW WHAT'S BUNCHING HIS SHORTS...
...BUT, MAN, IS HE ON A BENDER!
I'D BETTER TAKE THIS BAD BOY DOWN MYSELF.
KERROOOM

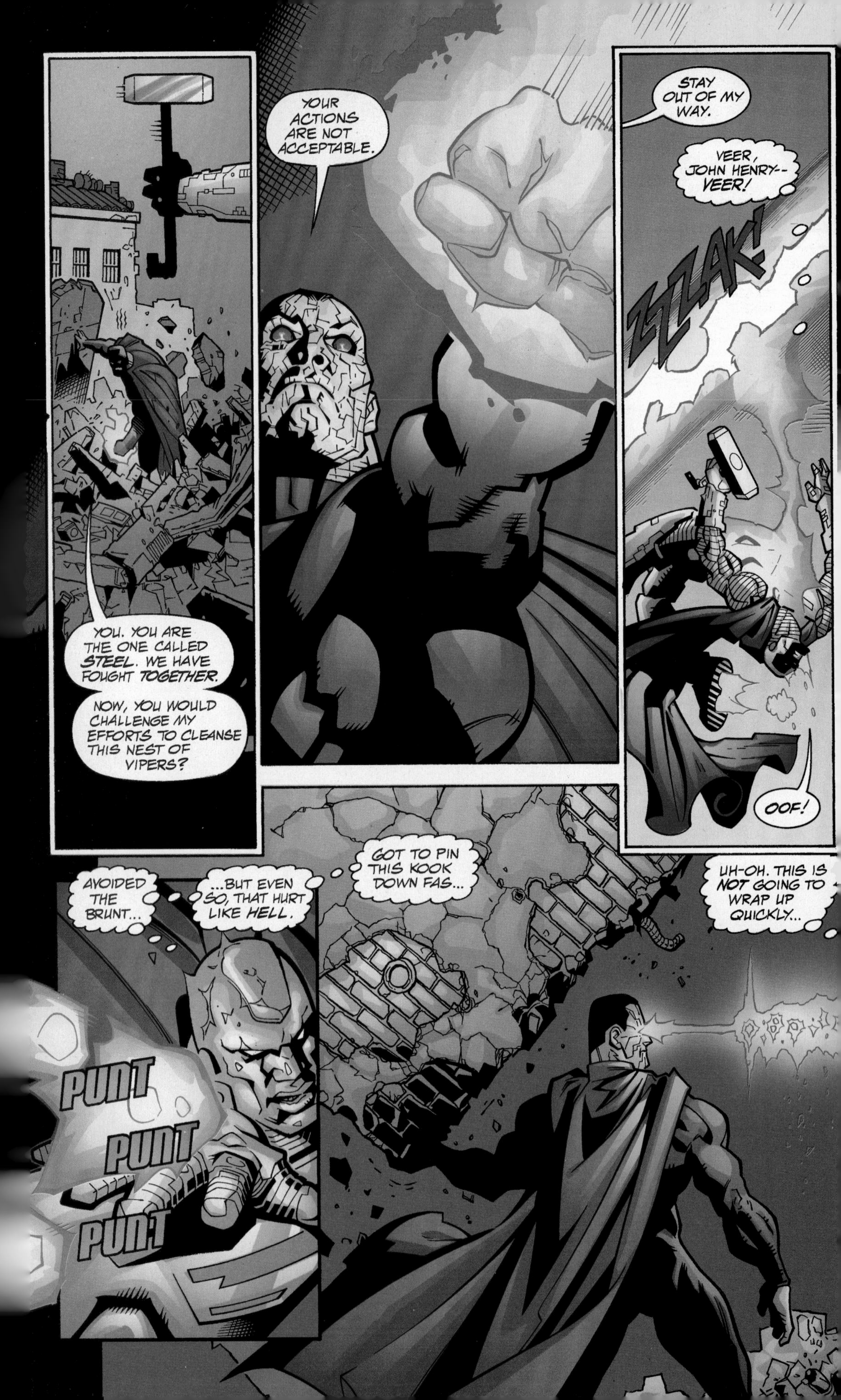
YOUR ACTIONS ARE NOT ACCEPTABLE.
YOU. YOU ARE THE ONE CALLED STEEL. WE HAVE FOUGHT TOGETHER.
NOW, YOU WOULD CHALLENGE MY EFFORTS TO CLEANSE THIS NEST OF VIPERS?
STAY OUT OF MY WAY.
VEER, JOHN HENRY-- VEER!
ZZZZAK!
OOF!
AVOIDED THE BRUNT...
...BUT EVEN SO, THAT HURT LIKE HELL.
GOT TO PIN THIS KOOK DOWN FAS...
UH-OH. THIS IS NOT GOING TO WRAP UP QUICKLY...
PUNT
PUNT
PUNT

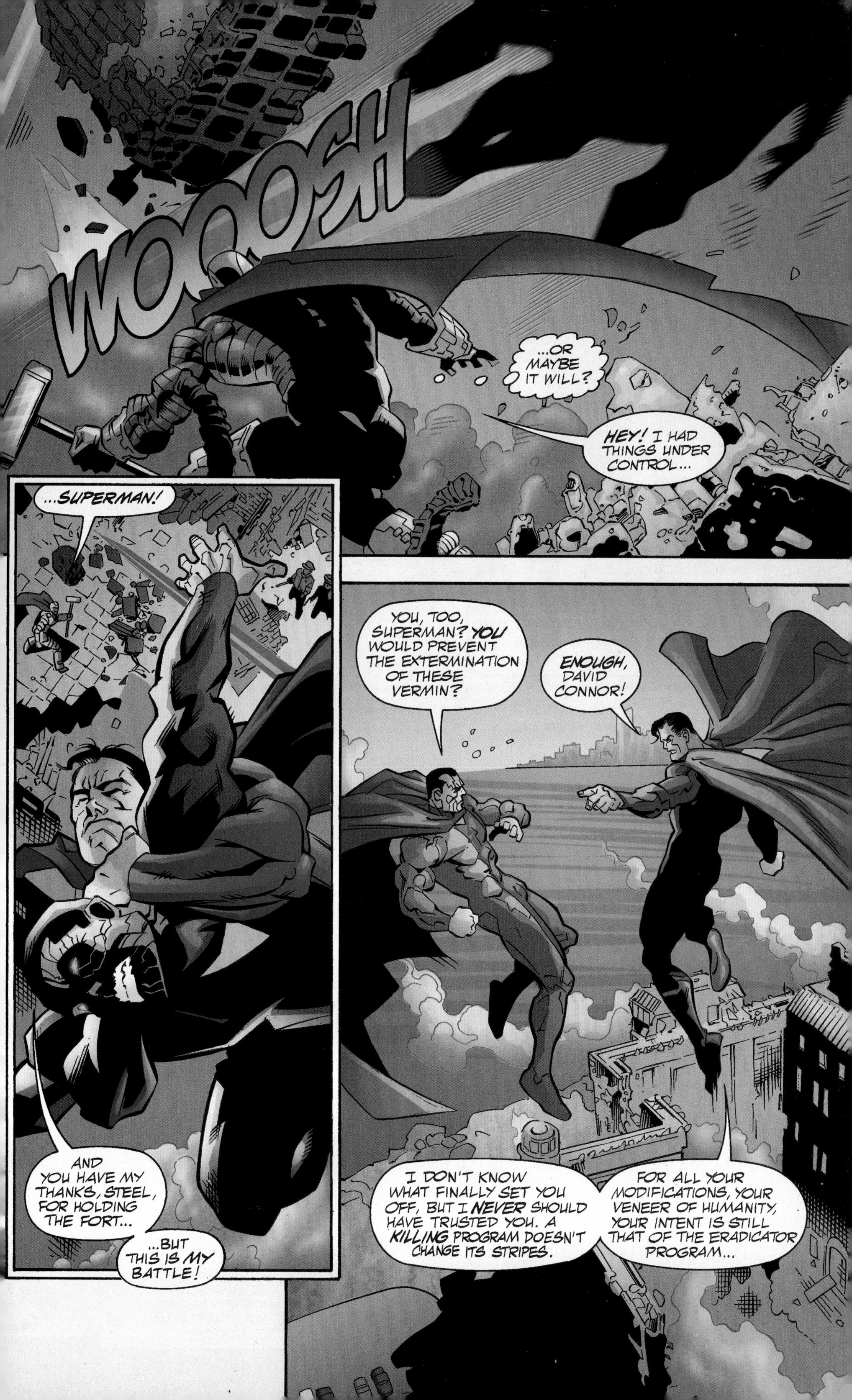
WOOOSH
...OR MAYBE IT WILL?
HEY! I HAD THINGS UNDER CONTROL...
...SUPERMAN!
AND YOU HAVE MY THANKS, STEEL, FOR HOLDING THE FORT...
...BUT THIS IS MY BATTLE!
YOU, TOO, SUPERMAN? YOU WOULD PREVENT THE EXTERMINATION OF THESE VERMIN?
ENOUGH, DAVID CONNOR!
I DON'T KNOW WHAT FINALLY SET YOU OFF, BUT I NEVER SHOULD HAVE TRUSTED YOU. A KILLING PROGRAM DOESN'T CHANGE ITS STRIPES.
FOR ALL YOUR MODIFICATIONS, YOUR VENEER OF HUMANITY, YOUR INTENT IS STILL THAT OF THE ERADICATOR PROGRAM...

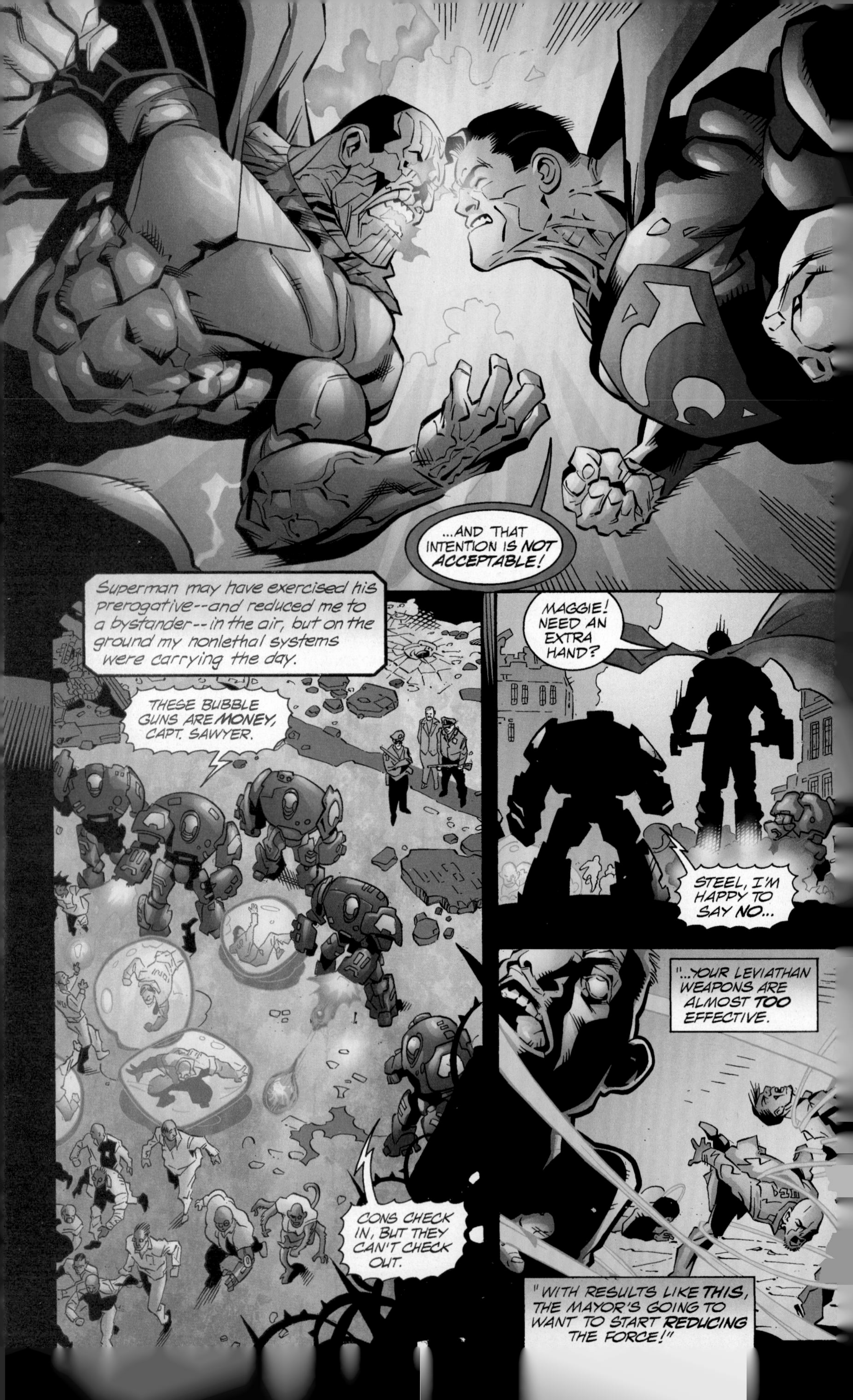
...AND THAT INTENTION IS NOT ACCEPTABLE!
Superman may have exercised his prerogative--and reduced me to a bystander--in the air, but on the ground my nonlethal systems were carrying the day.
THESE BUBBLE GUNS ARE MONEY, CAPT. SAWYER.
CONS CHECK IN, BUT THEY CAN'T CHECK OUT.
MAGGIE! NEED AN EXTRA HAND?
STEEL, I'M HAPPY TO SAY NO...
"...YOUR LEVIATHAN WEAPONS ARE ALMOST TOO EFFECTIVE.
"WITH RESULTS LIKE THIS, THE MAYOR'S GOING TO WANT TO START REDUCING THE FORCE!"

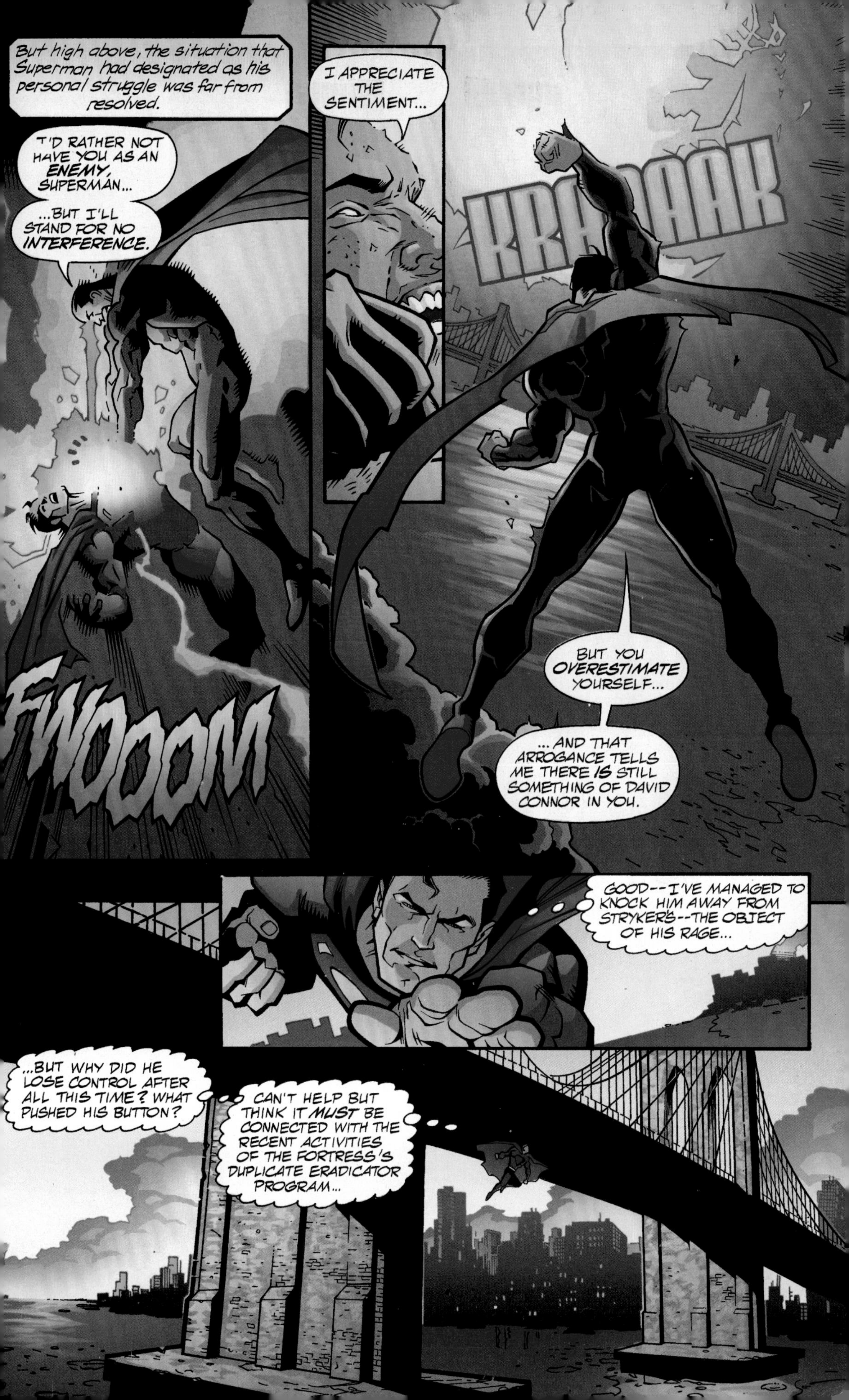

But high above, the situation that Superman had designated as his personal struggle was far from resolved.
I'D RATHER NOT HAVE YOU AS AN ENEMY, SUPERMAN...
...BUT I'LL STAND FOR NO INTERFERENCE.
FWOOOM
I APPRECIATE THE SENTIMENT...
KRAAAAK
BUT YOU OVERESTIMATE YOURSELF...
... AND THAT ARROGANCE TELLS ME THERE IS STILL SOMETHING OF DAVID CONNOR IN YOU.
GOOD--I'VE MANAGED TO KNOCK HIM AWAY FROM STRYKER'S--THE OBJECT OF HIS RAGE...
...BUT WHY DID HE LOSE CONTROL AFTER ALL THIS TIME? WHAT PUSHED HIS BUTTON?
CAN'T HELP BUT THINK IT MUST BE CONNECTED WITH THE RECENT ACTIVITIES OF THE FORTRESS'S DUPLICATE ERADICATOR PROGRAM...

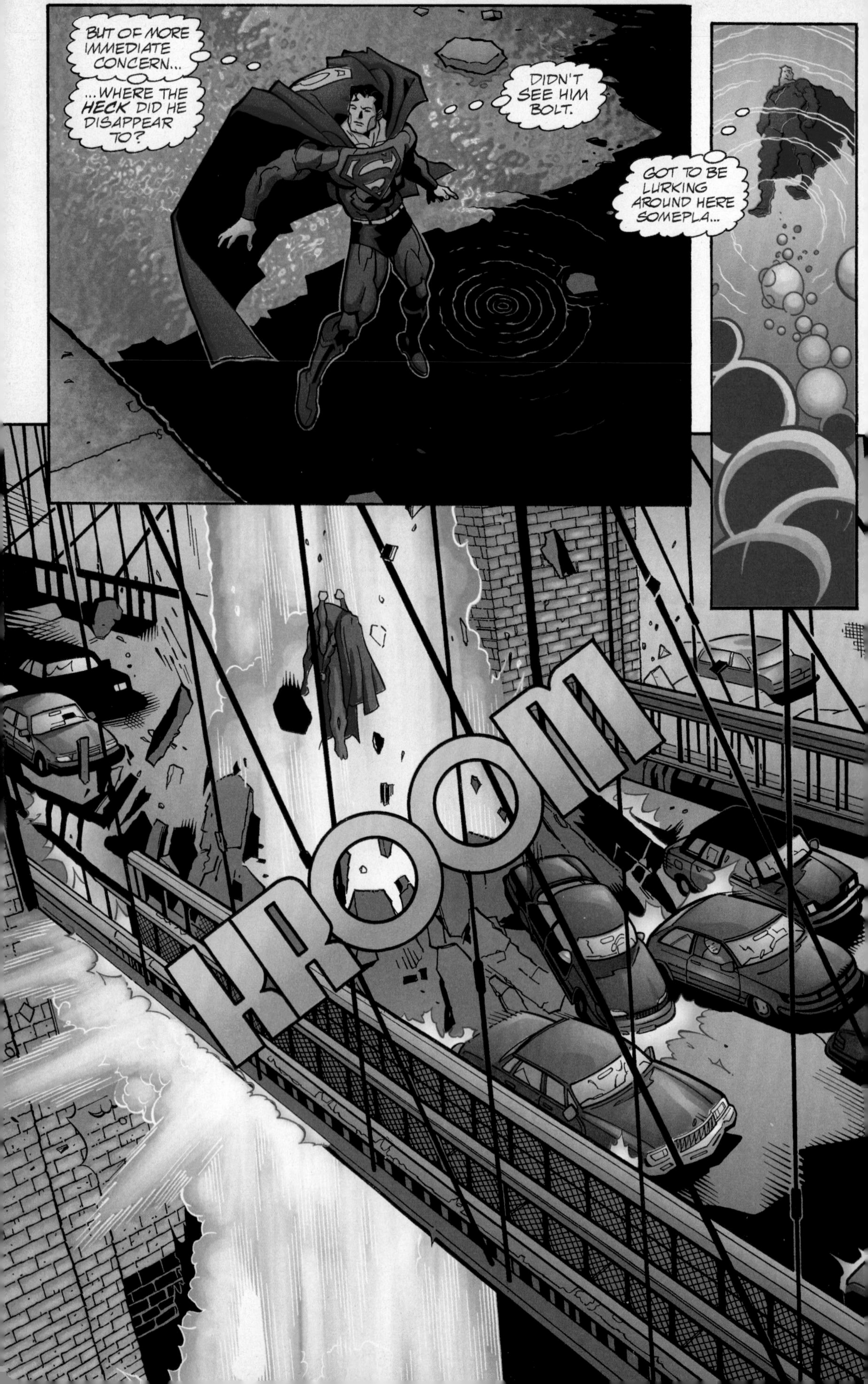
BUT OF MORE IMMEDIATE CONCERN...
...WHERE THE HECK DID HE DISAPPEAR TO?
DIDN'T SEE HIM BOLT.
GOT TO BE LURKING AROUND HERE SOMEPLA...
KROOM

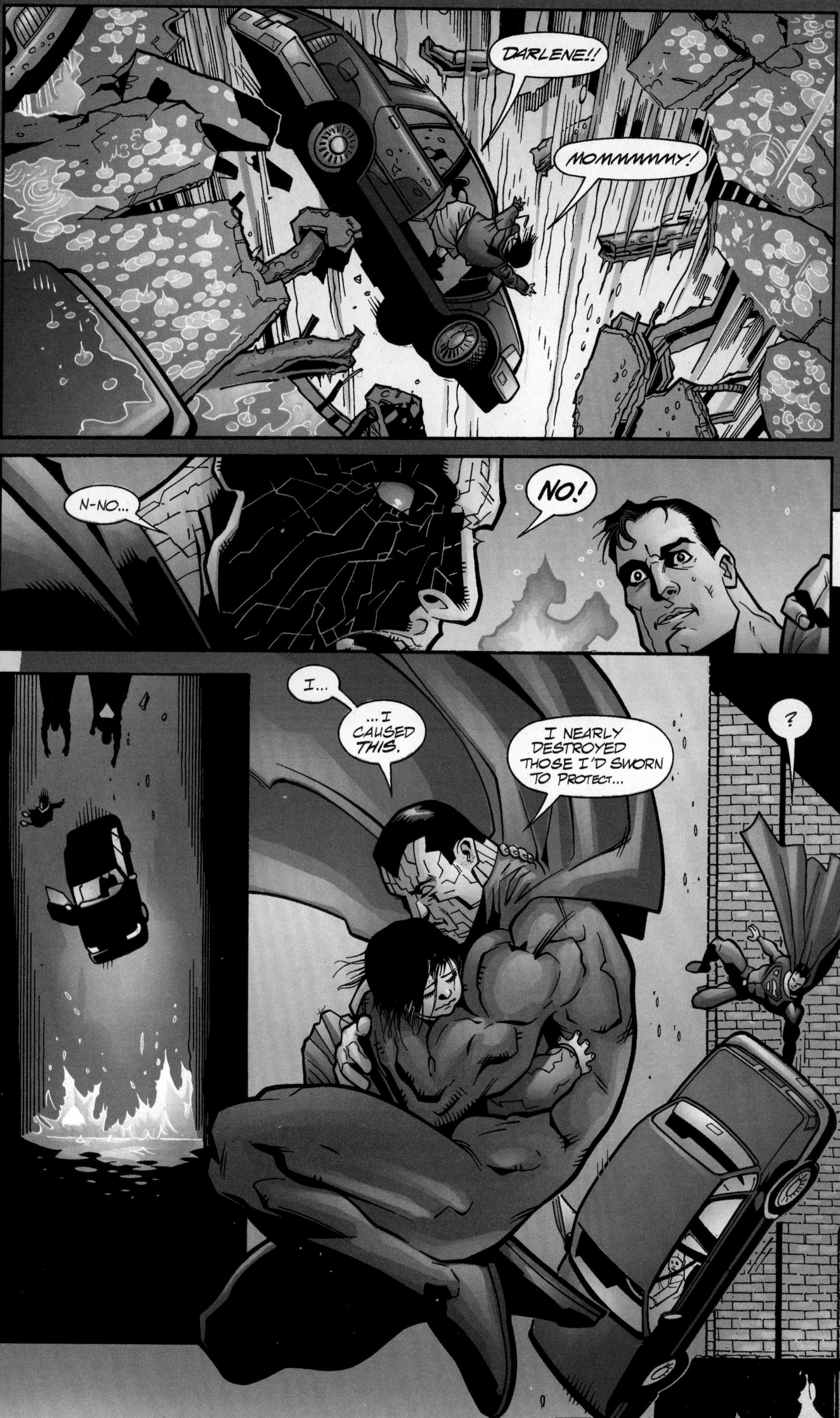
DARLENE!!
MOMMMMMY!
N-NO...
NO!
I...
...I CAUSED THIS.
I NEARLY DESTROYED THOSE I'D SWORN TO PROTECT...
?

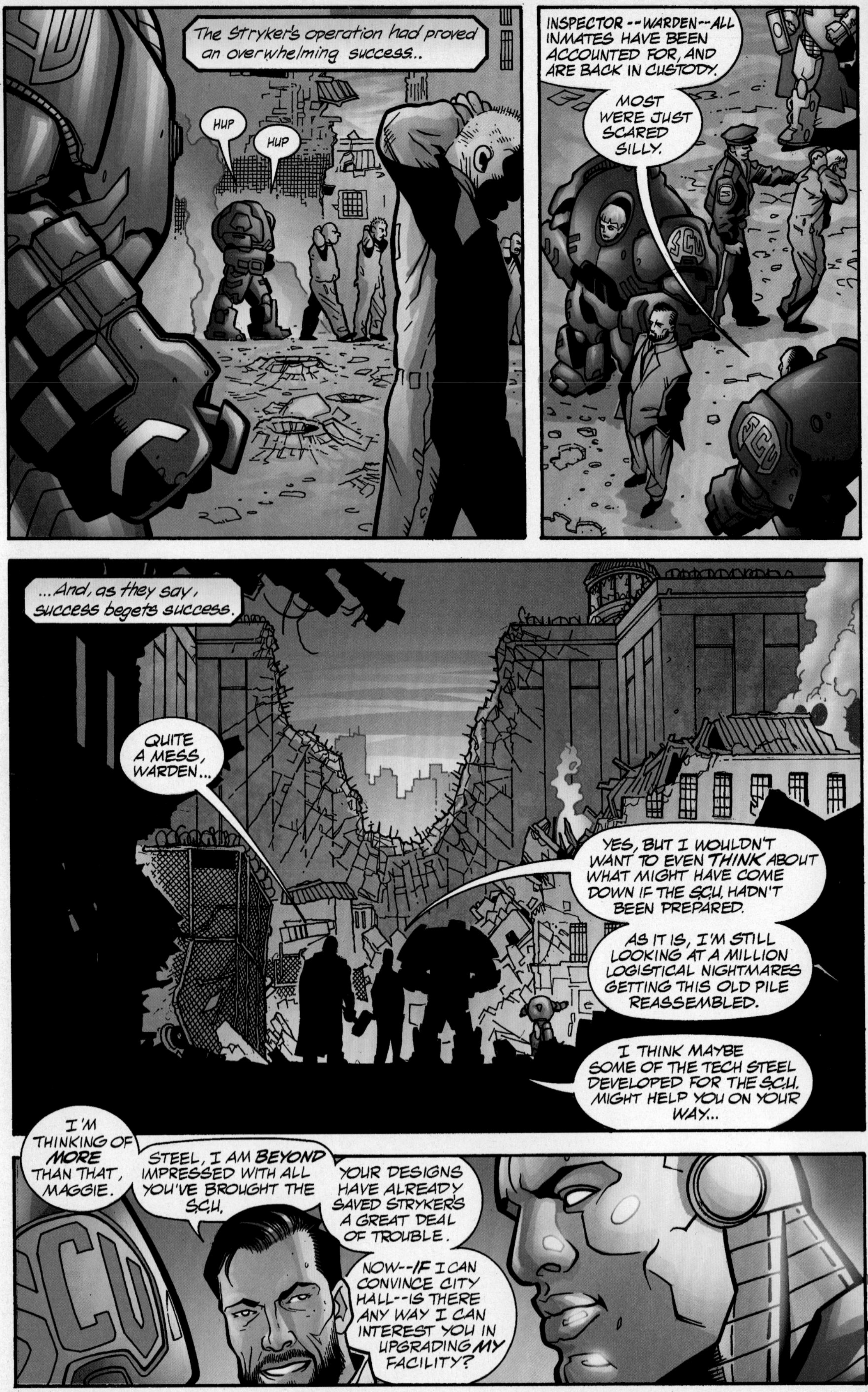

The Stryker's operation had proved an overwhelming success..
HUP
HUP
INSPECTOR --WARDEN--ALL INMATES HAVE BEEN ACCOUNTED FOR, AND ARE BACK IN CUSTODY.
MOST WERE JUST SCARED SILLY.
...And, as they say, success begets success.
QUITE A MESS, WARDEN...
YES, BUT I WOULDN'T WANT TO EVEN THINK ABOUT WHAT MIGHT HAVE COME DOWN IF THE S.C.U. HADN'T BEEN PREPARED.
AS IT IS, I'M STILL LOOKING AT A MILLION LOGISTICAL NIGHTMARES GETTING THIS OLD PILE REASSEMBLED.
I THINK MAYBE SOME OF THE TECH STEEL DEVELOPED FOR THE S.C.U. MIGHT HELP YOU ON YOUR WAY...
I'M THINKING OF MORE THAN THAT, MAGGIE.
STEEL, I AM BEYOND IMPRESSED WITH ALL YOU'VE BROUGHT THE S.C.U.
YOUR DESIGNS HAVE ALREADY SAVED STRYKER'S A GREAT DEAL OF TROUBLE.
NOW--IF I CAN CONVINCE CITY HALL--IS THERE ANY WAY I CAN INTEREST YOU IN UPGRADING MY FACILITY?

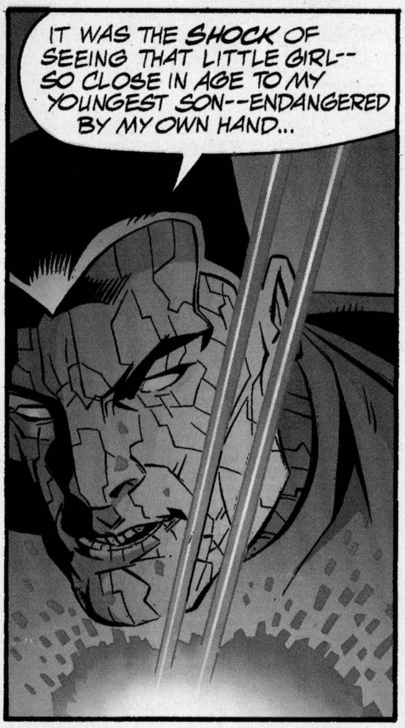
IT WAS THE SHOCK OF SEEING THAT LITTLE GIRL-- SO CLOSE IN AGE TO MY YOUNGEST SON--ENDANGERED BY MY OWN HAND...

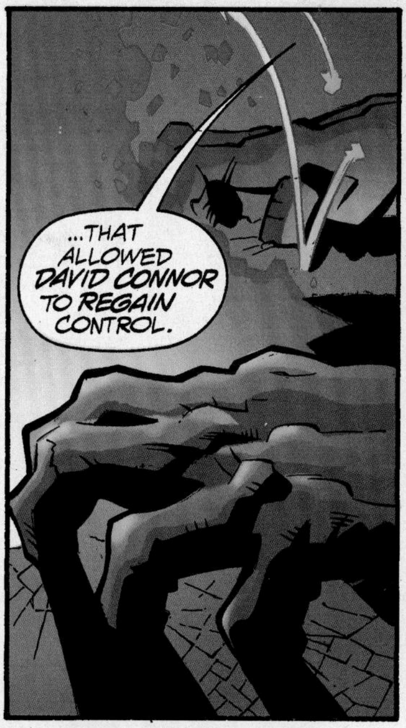
...THAT ALLOWED DAVID CONNOR TO REGAIN CONTROL.

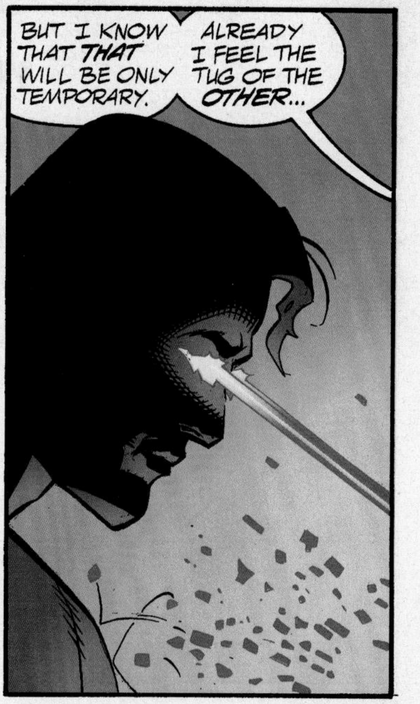
BUT I KNOW THAT THAT WILL BE ONLY TEMPORARY.
ALREADY I FEEL THE TUG OF THE OTHER...

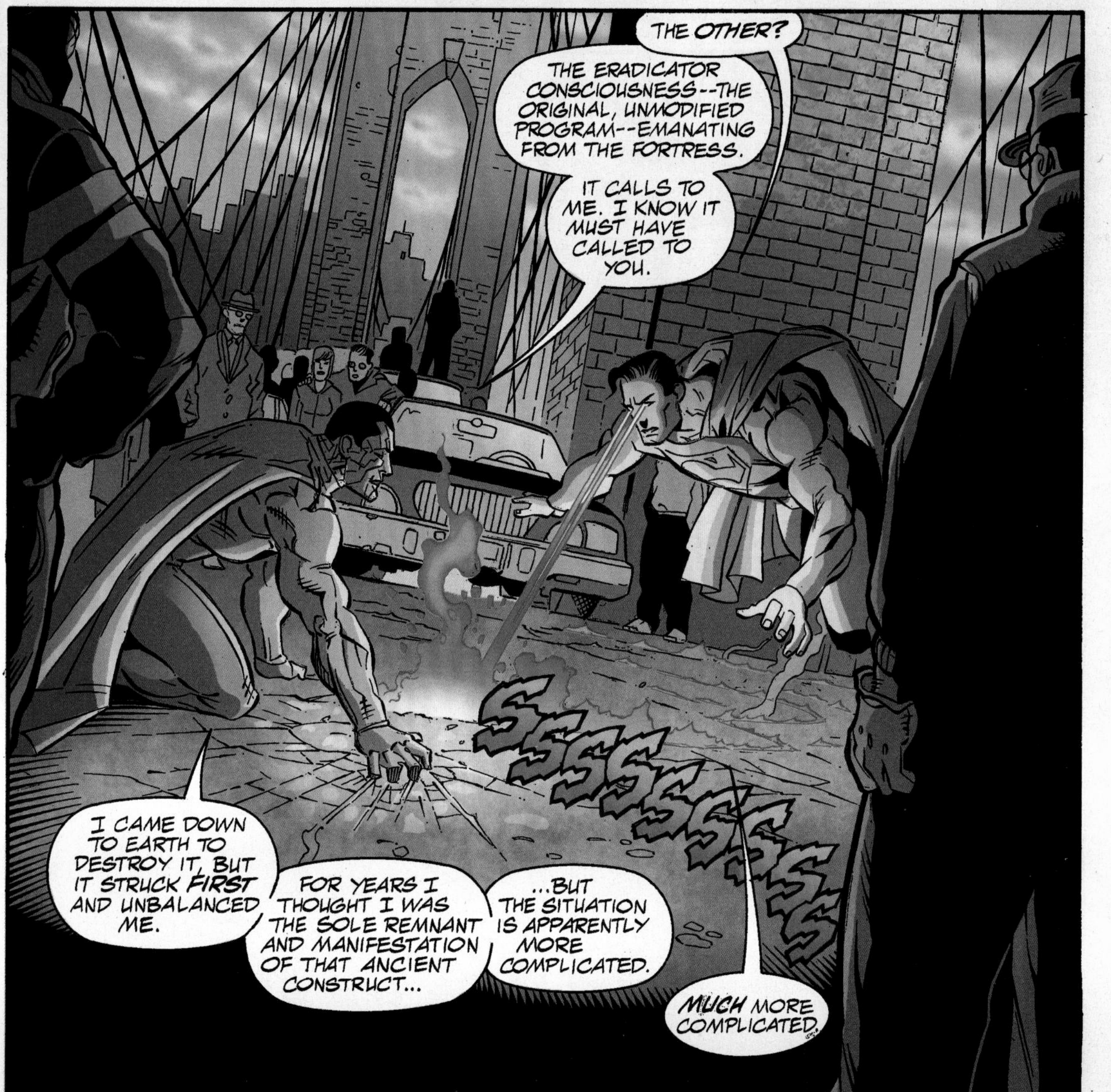
THE OTHER?
THE ERADICATOR CONSCIOUSNESS--THE ORIGINAL, UNMODIFIED PROGRAM--EMANATING FROM THE FORTRESS.
IT CALLS TO ME. I KNOW IT MUST HAVE CALLED TO YOU.
SSSSSSSSSSS
I CAME DOWN TO EARTH TO DESTROY IT, BUT IT STRUCK FIRST AND UNBALANCED ME.
FOR YEARS I THOUGHT I WAS THE SOLE REMNANT AND MANIFESTATION OF THAT ANCIENT CONSTRUCT...
...BUT THE SITUATION IS APPARENTLY MORE COMPLICATED.
MUCH MORE COMPLICATED.

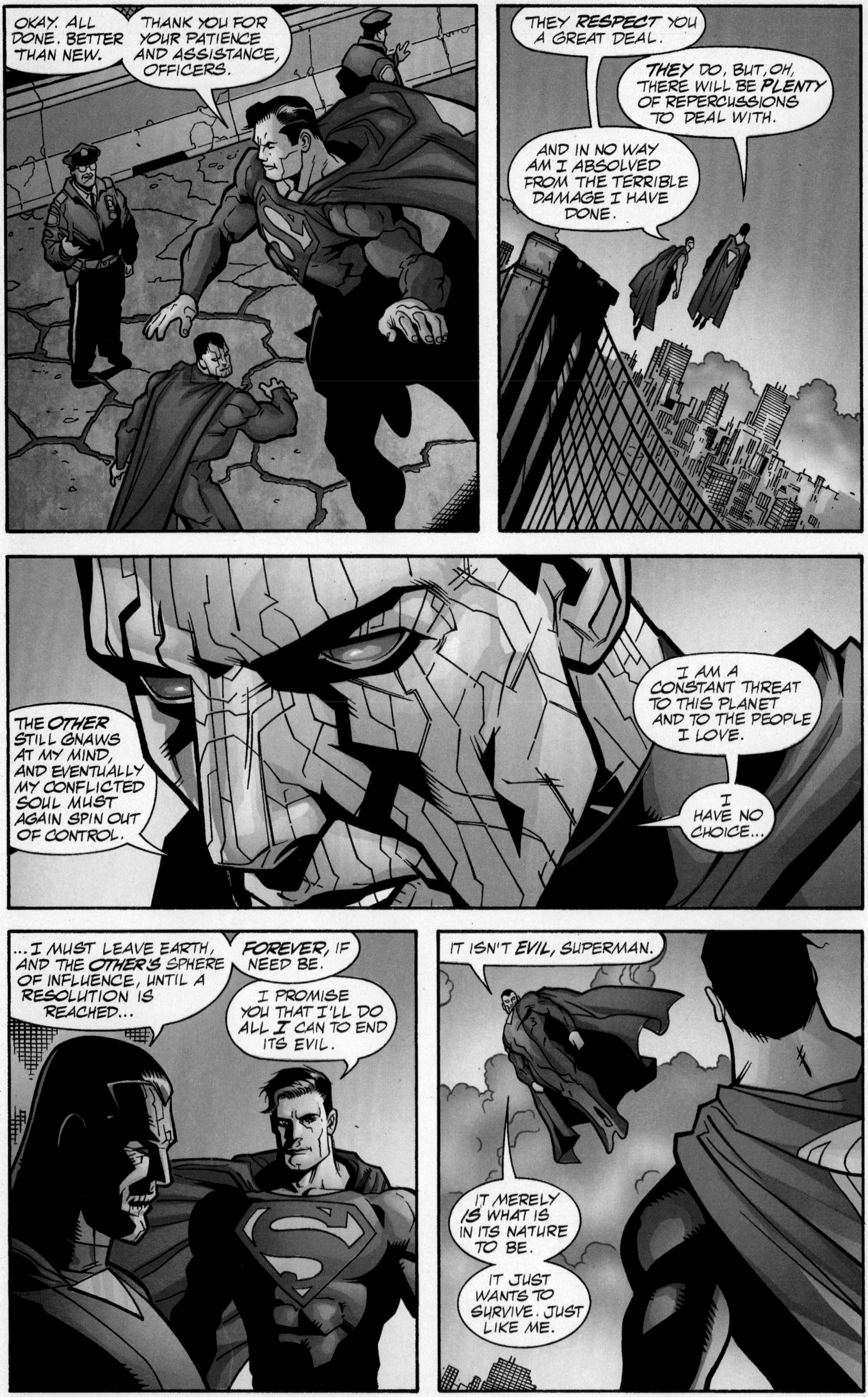

OKAY. ALL DONE. BETTER THAN NEW.
THANK YOU FOR YOUR PATIENCE AND ASSISTANCE, OFFICERS.
THEY RESPECT YOU A GREAT DEAL.
THEY DO, BUT, OH, THERE WILL BE PLENTY OF REPERCUSSIONS TO DEAL WITH.
AND IN NO WAY AM I ABSOLVED FROM THE TERRIBLE DAMAGE I HAVE DONE.
THE OTHER STILL GNAWS AT MY MIND, AND EVENTUALLY MY CONFLICTED SOUL MUST AGAIN SPIN OUT OF CONTROL.
I AM A CONSTANT THREAT TO THIS PLANET AND TO THE PEOPLE I LOVE.
I HAVE NO CHOICE...
...I MUST LEAVE EARTH, AND THE OTHER'S SPHERE OF INFLUENCE, UNTIL A RESOLUTION IS REACHED...
FOREVER, IF NEED BE.
I PROMISE YOU THAT I'LL DO ALL I CAN TO END ITS EVIL.
IT ISN'T EVIL, SUPERMAN.
IT MERELY IS WHAT IS IN ITS NATURE TO BE.
IT JUST WANTS TO SURVIVE. JUST LIKE ME.

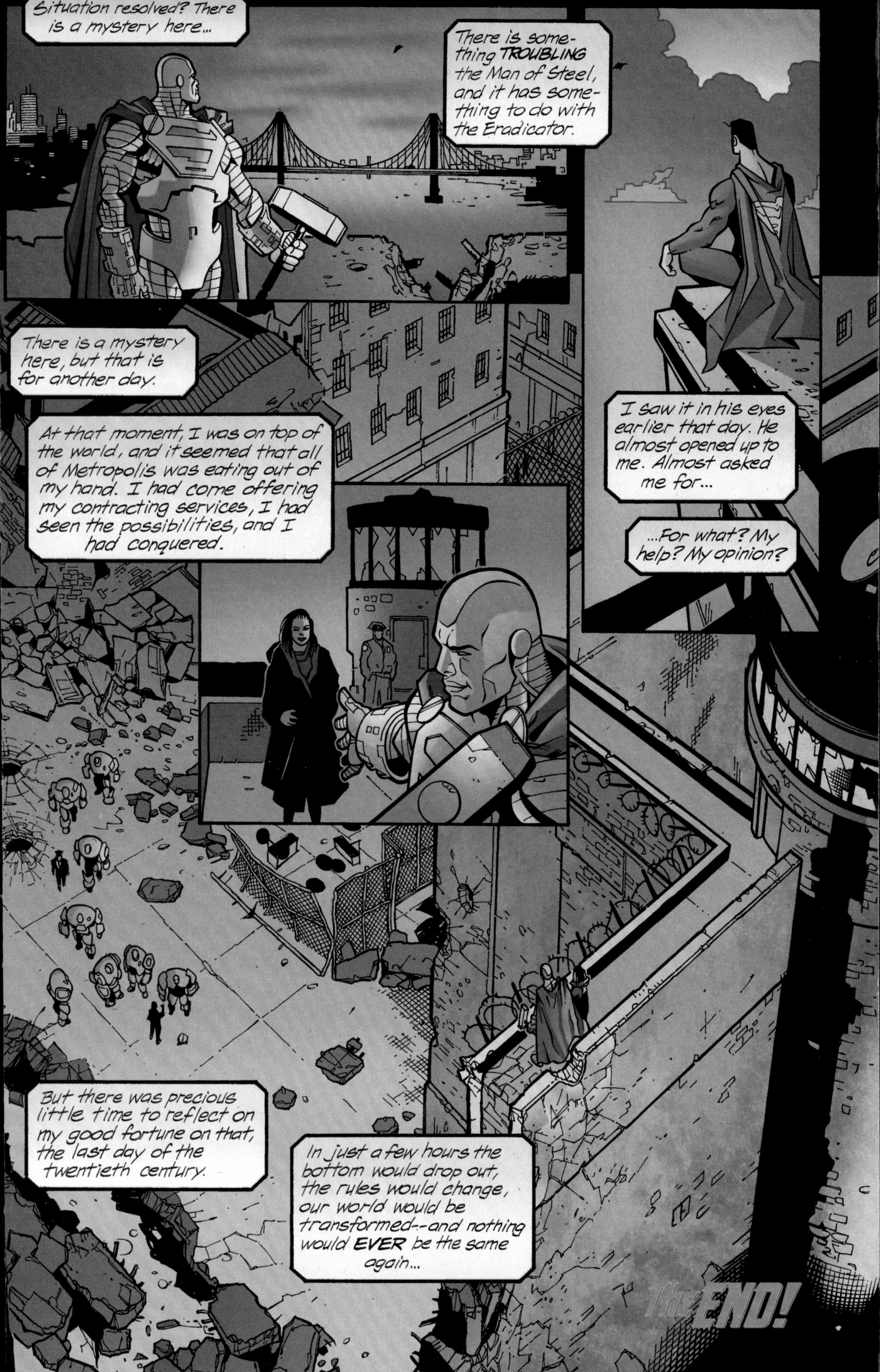
Situation resolved? There is a mystery here...
There is something TROUBLING the Man of Steel, and it has something to do with the Eradicator.
There is a mystery here, but that is for another day.
At that moment, I was on top of the world, and it seemed that all of Metropolis was eating out of my hand. I had come offering my contracting services, I had seen the possibilities, and I had conquered.
I saw it in his eyes earlier that day. He almost opened up to me. Almost asked me for...
...For what? My help? My opinion?
But there was precious little time to reflect on my good fortune on that, the last day of the twentieth century.
In just a few hours the bottom would drop out, the rules would change, our world would be transformed--and nothing would EVER be the same again...
The END!

RALPH DIBNY (formerly the Elongated Man)

DETECTIVE COMICS #350

Ralph (The Elongated Man) Dibny and his love for his wife Sue were one of the emotional cornerstones of 52. By the time we picked up on Ralph, it was about a year after his wife's tragic murder. This story recalls Ralph and Sue at their best and is a reminder of why we cared about what eventually became of them.

On a less somber note, I should point out that this story is noteworthy because it shows Elongated Man abandoning his original purple costume for what I still, forty years later, refer to as "his new one." —**MW**

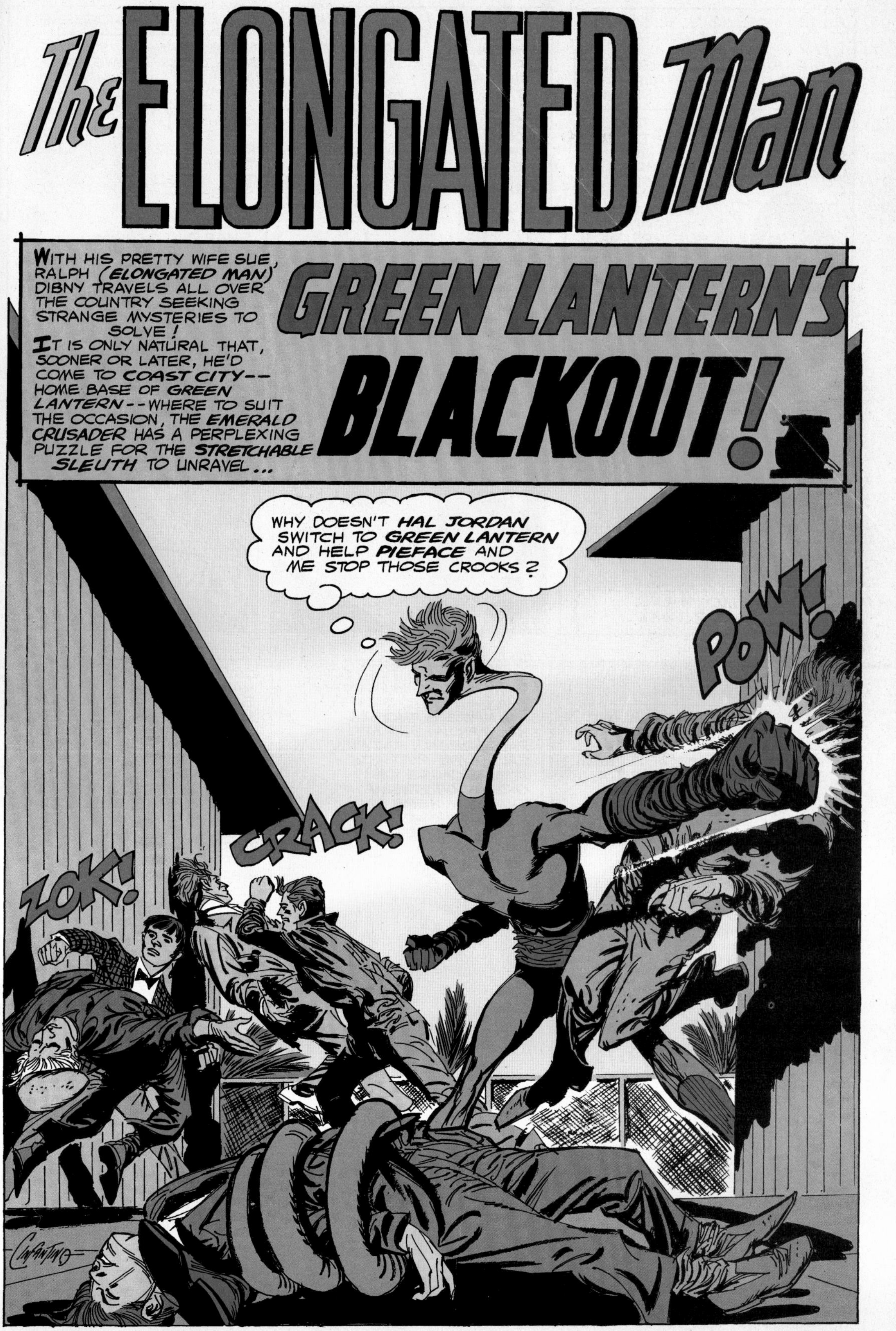
The ELONGATED Man
WITH HIS PRETTY WIFE SUE, RALPH (ELONGATED MAN) DIBNY TRAVELS ALL OVER THE COUNTRY SEEKING STRANGE MYSTERIES TO SOLVE! IT IS ONLY NATURAL THAT, SOONER OR LATER, HE'D COME TO COAST CITY-- HOME BASE OF GREEN LANTERN--WHERE TO SUIT THE OCCASION, THE EMERALD CRUSADER HAS A PERPLEXING PUZZLE FOR THE STRETCHABLE SLEUTH TO UNRAVEL...
GREEN LANTERN'S BLACKOUT!
WHY DOESN'T HAL JORDAN SWITCH TO GREEN LANTERN AND HELP PIEFACE AND ME STOP THOSE CROOKS?
POW!
CRACK!
ZOK!
CINFANTINO

WRITER: Gardner Fox

ARTIST: Carmine Infantino

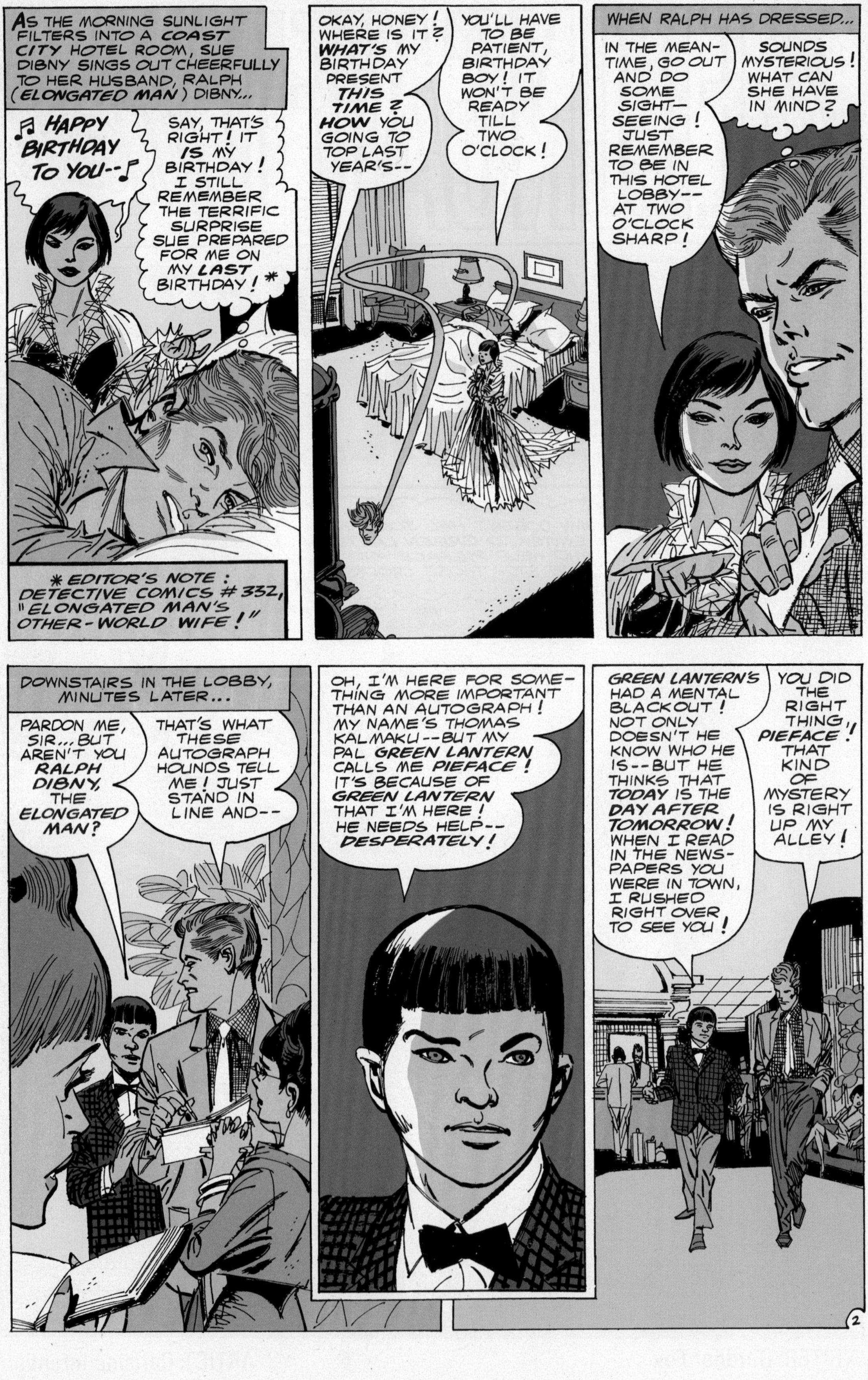
AS THE MORNING SUNLIGHT FILTERS INTO A COAST CITY HOTEL ROOM, SUE DIBNY SINGS OUT CHEERFULLY TO HER HUSBAND, RALPH (ELONGATED MAN) DIBNY...
♫ HAPPY BIRTHDAY TO YOU-- ♪
SAY, THAT'S RIGHT! IT IS MY BIRTHDAY! I STILL REMEMBER THE TERRIFIC SURPRISE SUE PREPARED FOR ME ON MY LAST BIRTHDAY! *
* EDITOR'S NOTE: DETECTIVE COMICS #332, "ELONGATED MAN'S OTHER-WORLD WIFE!"
OKAY, HONEY! WHERE IS IT? WHAT'S MY BIRTHDAY PRESENT THIS TIME? HOW YOU GOING TO TOP LAST YEAR'S--
YOU'LL HAVE TO BE PATIENT, BIRTHDAY BOY! IT WON'T BE READY TILL TWO O'CLOCK!
WHEN RALPH HAS DRESSED...
IN THE MEAN-TIME, GO OUT AND DO SOME SIGHT-SEEING! JUST REMEMBER TO BE IN THIS HOTEL LOBBY--AT TWO O'CLOCK SHARP!
SOUNDS MYSTERIOUS! WHAT CAN SHE HAVE IN MIND?
DOWNSTAIRS IN THE LOBBY, MINUTES LATER...
PARDON ME, SIR... BUT AREN'T YOU RALPH DIBNY, THE ELONGATED MAN?
THAT'S WHAT THESE AUTOGRAPH HOUNDS TELL ME! JUST STAND IN LINE AND--
OH, I'M HERE FOR SOMETHING MORE IMPORTANT THAN AN AUTOGRAPH! MY NAME'S THOMAS KALMAKU--BUT MY PAL GREEN LANTERN CALLS ME PIEFACE! IT'S BECAUSE OF GREEN LANTERN THAT I'M HERE! HE NEEDS HELP--DESPERATELY!
GREEN LANTERN'S HAD A MENTAL BLACKOUT! NOT ONLY DOESN'T HE KNOW WHO HE IS--BUT HE THINKS THAT TODAY IS THE DAY AFTER TOMORROW! WHEN I READ IN THE NEWSPAPERS YOU WERE IN TOWN, I RUSHED RIGHT OVER TO SEE YOU!
YOU DID THE RIGHT THING, PIEFACE! THAT KIND OF MYSTERY IS RIGHT UP MY ALLEY!
2

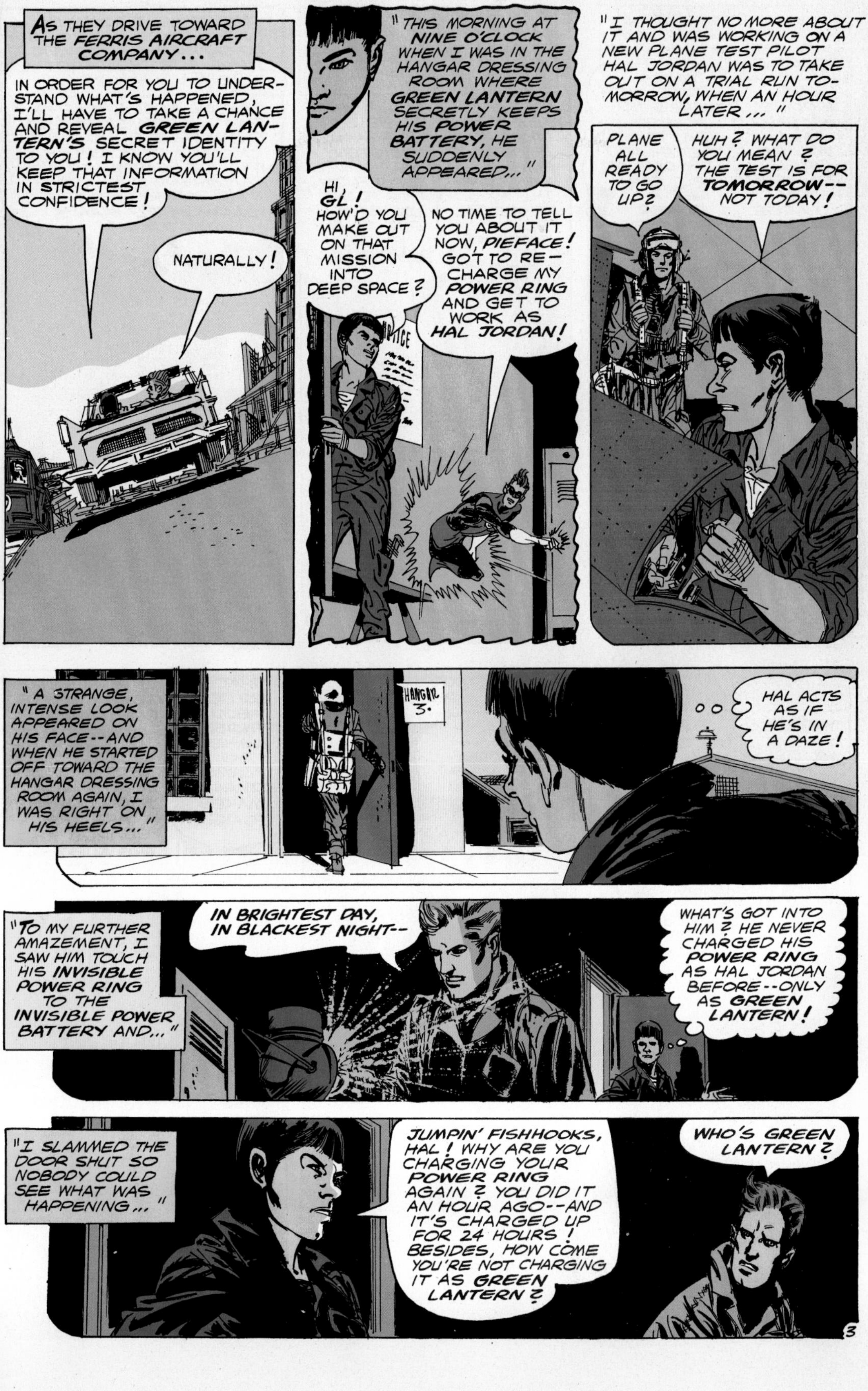
AS THEY DRIVE TOWARD THE FERRIS AIRCRAFT COMPANY...
IN ORDER FOR YOU TO UNDERSTAND WHAT'S HAPPENED, I'LL HAVE TO TAKE A CHANCE AND REVEAL GREEN LANTERN'S SECRET IDENTITY TO YOU! I KNOW YOU'LL KEEP THAT INFORMATION IN STRICTEST CONFIDENCE!
NATURALLY!
"THIS MORNING AT NINE O'CLOCK WHEN I WAS IN THE HANGAR DRESSING ROOM WHERE GREEN LANTERN SECRETLY KEEPS HIS POWER BATTERY, HE SUDDENLY APPEARED..."
HI, GL! HOW'D YOU MAKE OUT ON THAT MISSION INTO DEEP SPACE?
NO TIME TO TELL YOU ABOUT IT NOW, PIEFACE! GOT TO RE-CHARGE MY POWER RING AND GET TO WORK AS HAL JORDAN!
"I THOUGHT NO MORE ABOUT IT AND WAS WORKING ON A NEW PLANE TEST PILOT HAL JORDAN WAS TO TAKE OUT ON A TRIAL RUN TOMORROW, WHEN AN HOUR LATER..."
PLANE ALL READY TO GO UP?
HUH? WHAT DO YOU MEAN? THE TEST IS FOR TOMORROW-- NOT TODAY!
"A STRANGE, INTENSE LOOK APPEARED ON HIS FACE--AND WHEN HE STARTED OFF TOWARD THE HANGAR DRESSING ROOM AGAIN, I WAS RIGHT ON HIS HEELS..."
HANGAR 3.
HAL ACTS AS IF HE'S IN A DAZE!
"TO MY FURTHER AMAZEMENT, I SAW HIM TOUCH HIS INVISIBLE POWER RING TO THE INVISIBLE POWER BATTERY AND..."
IN BRIGHTEST DAY, IN BLACKEST NIGHT--
WHAT'S GOT INTO HIM? HE NEVER CHARGED HIS POWER RING AS HAL JORDAN BEFORE--ONLY AS GREEN LANTERN!
"I SLAMMED THE DOOR SHUT SO NOBODY COULD SEE WHAT WAS HAPPENING..."
JUMPIN' FISHHOOKS, HAL! WHY ARE YOU CHARGING YOUR POWER RING AGAIN? YOU DID IT AN HOUR AGO--AND IT'S CHARGED UP FOR 24 HOURS! BESIDES, HOW COME YOU'RE NOT CHARGING IT AS GREEN LANTERN?
WHO'S GREEN LANTERN?
3

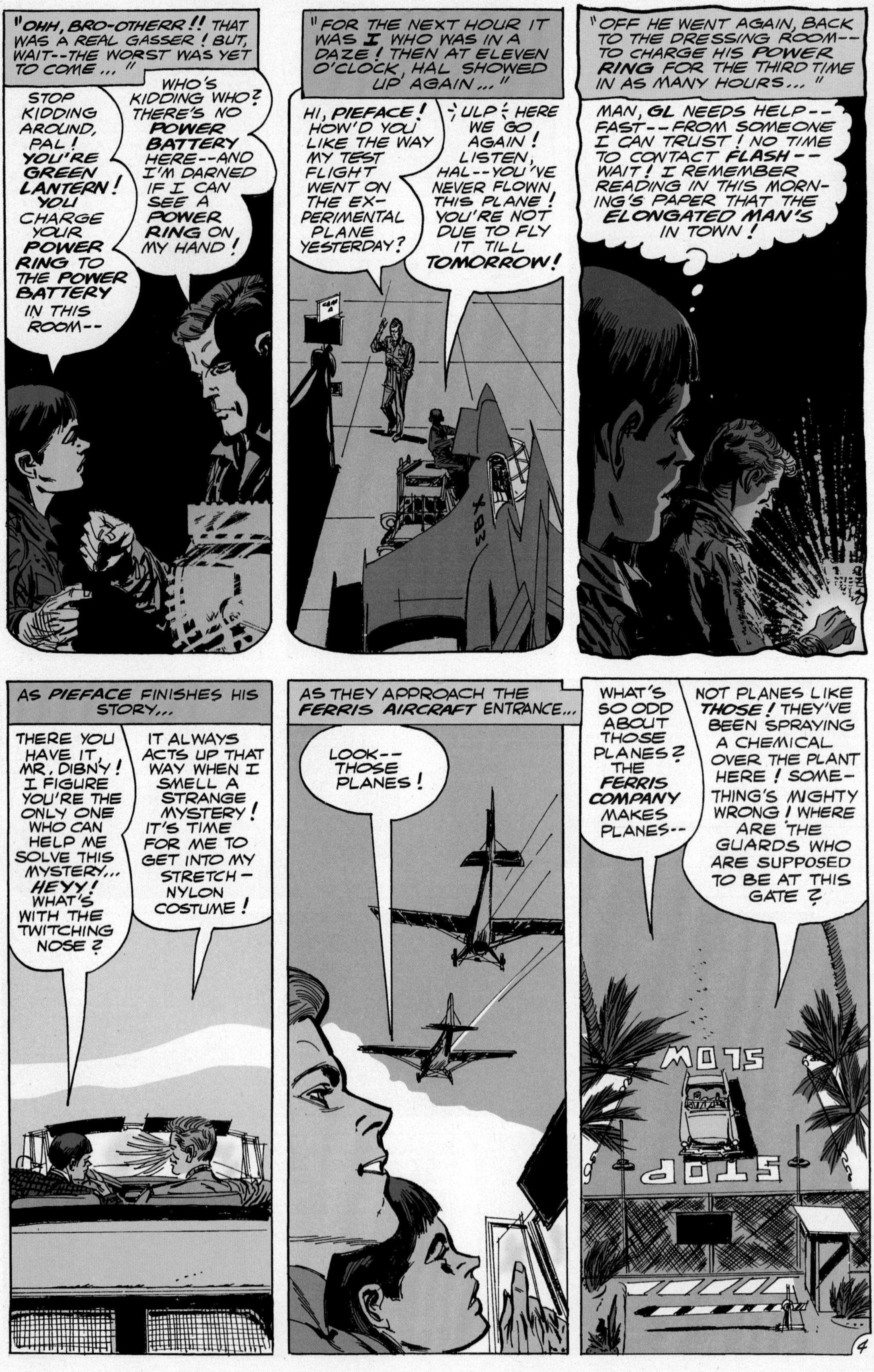
"OHH, BRO-OTHERR!! THAT WAS A REAL GASSER! BUT, WAIT--THE WORST WAS YET TO COME..."
STOP KIDDING AROUND, PAL! YOU'RE GREEN LANTERN! YOU CHARGE YOUR POWER RING TO THE POWER BATTERY IN THIS ROOM--
WHO'S KIDDING WHO? THERE'S NO POWER BATTERY HERE--AND I'M DARNED IF I CAN SEE A POWER RING ON MY HAND!
"FOR THE NEXT HOUR IT WAS I, WHO WAS IN A DAZE! THEN AT ELEVEN O'CLOCK, HAL SHOWED UP AGAIN..."
HI, PIEFACE! HOW'D YOU LIKE THE WAY MY TEST FLIGHT WENT ON THE EX-PERIMENTAL PLANE YESTERDAY?
-ULP- HERE WE GO AGAIN! LISTEN, HAL--YOU'VE NEVER FLOWN THIS PLANE! YOU'RE NOT DUE TO FLY IT TILL TOMORROW!
X-83
"OFF HE WENT AGAIN, BACK TO THE DRESSING ROOM--TO CHARGE HIS POWER RING FOR THE THIRD TIME IN AS MANY HOURS..."
MAN, GL NEEDS HELP--FAST--FROM SOMEONE I CAN TRUST! NO TIME TO CONTACT FLASH--WAIT! I REMEMBER READING IN THIS MORNING'S PAPER THAT THE ELONGATED MAN'S IN TOWN!
AS PIEFACE FINISHES HIS STORY...
THERE YOU HAVE IT, MR. DIBNY! I FIGURE YOU'RE THE ONLY ONE WHO CAN HELP ME SOLVE THIS MYSTERY... HEYY! WHAT'S WITH THE TWITCHING NOSE?
IT ALWAYS ACTS UP THAT WAY WHEN I SMELL A STRANGE MYSTERY! IT'S TIME FOR ME TO GET INTO MY STRETCH-NYLON COSTUME!
AS THEY APPROACH THE FERRIS AIRCRAFT ENTRANCE...
LOOK--THOSE PLANES!
WHAT'S SO ODD ABOUT THOSE PLANES? THE FERRIS COMPANY MAKES PLANES--
NOT PLANES LIKE THOSE! THEY'VE BEEN SPRAYING A CHEMICAL OVER THE PLANT HERE! SOME-THING'S MIGHTY WRONG! WHERE ARE THE GUARDS WHO ARE SUPPOSED TO BE AT THIS GATE?
SLOW
STOP
4

As THEY DRIVE THROUGH THE GATE...

THERE THEY ARE-- SLUMPED OVER--AS IF ASLEEP!

AND SEE THERE! THOSE MEN RUNNING FROM THE OFFICE! LOOKS LIKE THEY'VE JUST PULLED A JOB!

THERE'S NOT MUCH CASH HERE! THEY MUST'VE SWIPED OUR TOP-SECRET PLANS--

ONE OF THEM HAS A HAND SPRAYER-- PROBABLY FILLED WITH THE SAME GAS THAT PUT EVERY-ONE HERE INTO A DEEP SLEEP! HE'S SPOTTED US--GONNA GIVE US THE SAME TREAT-MENT!

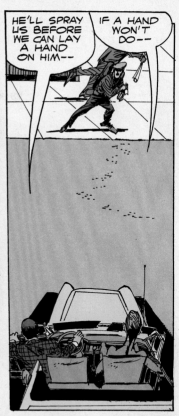

HE'LL SPRAY US BEFORE WE CAN LAY A HAND ON HIM--

IF A HAND WON'T DO--

--HOW ABOUT A FOOT?

A FOOT BEATS A HAND BY A MILE! NOW LET'S GET THOSE PLANS BACK!

WOWW! HE COULD FIGHT OFF THOSE GUYS JUST BY STAYING WHERE HE IS!

NO ADMITTANCE

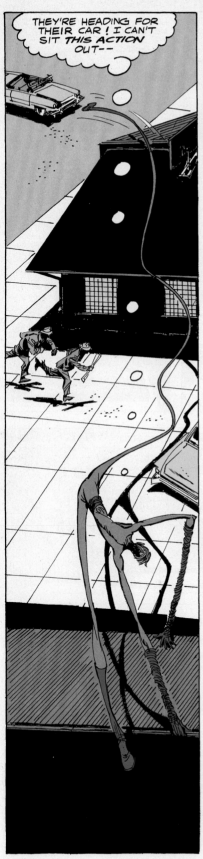

THEY'RE HEADING FOR THEIR CAR! I CAN'T SIT *THIS ACTION* OUT--

As HE STEPS ONTO A ROOF, HE TRAILS ONE LEG BEHIND HIM, SO THAT...

WATCH OUT!

THAT *ELONGATED MAN* IS PLAYING *FOOTSIE* WITH US!

BRACE YOUR-SELVES, MEN! YOU'RE GOING ON A FREE AIR-RIDE--

SORRRYY! IT ENDED IN A *CRASH-LANDING!*

BONK! THUDD!

PIEFACE IS SO ABSORBED IN WATCHING THE *DUCTILE DETECTIVE* THAT HE DOES NOT SEE A FIST COMING...

NOW I KNOW HOW HE GOT SUCH A *REPUTATION!* HE FIGHTS IN ALL DIRECTIONS!

6

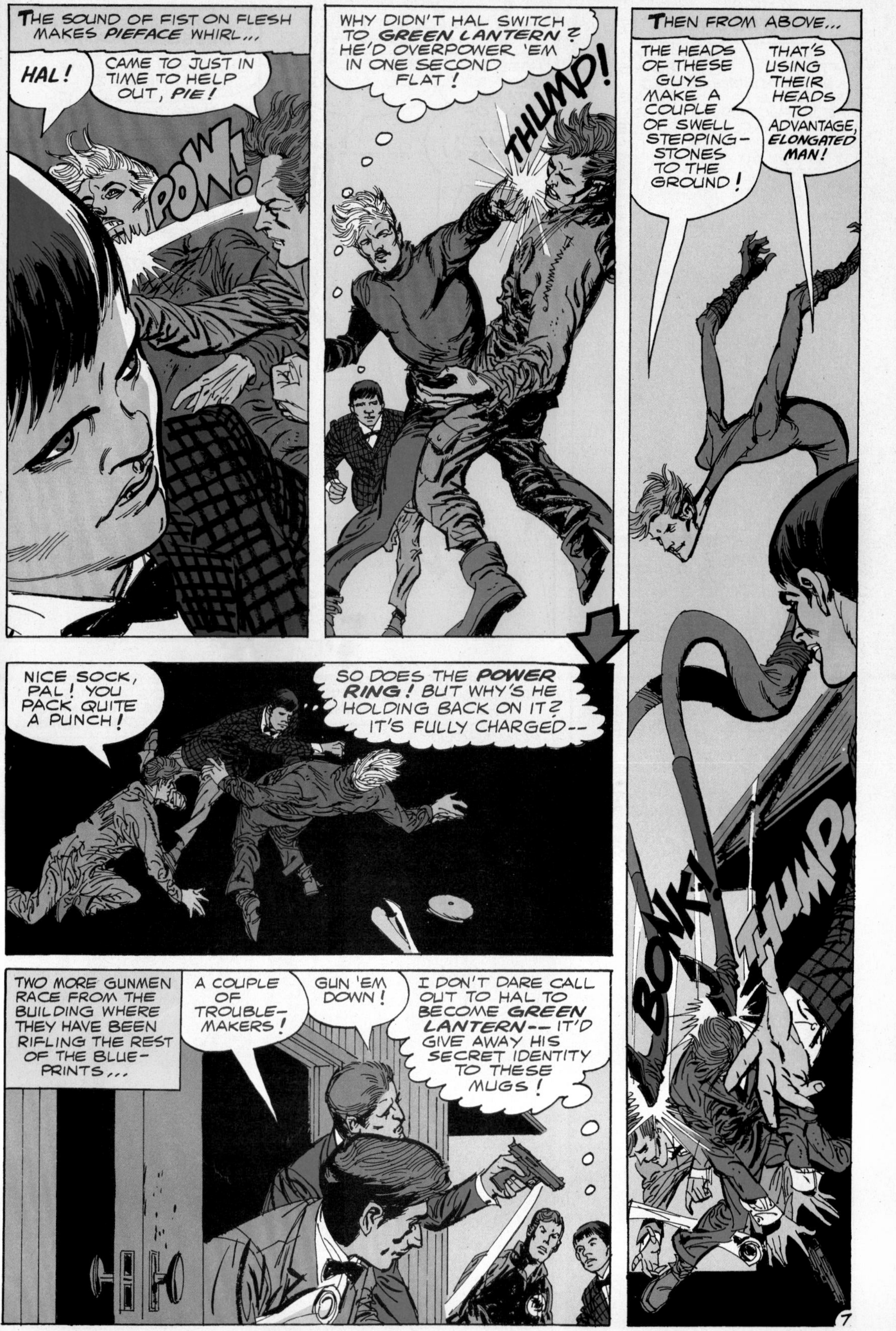

THE SOUND OF FIST ON FLESH MAKES PIEFACE WHIRL...
HAL!
CAME TO JUST IN TIME TO HELP OUT, PIE!
POW!
WHY DIDN'T HAL SWITCH TO GREEN LANTERN? HE'D OVERPOWER 'EM IN ONE SECOND FLAT!
THUMP!
THEN FROM ABOVE...
THE HEADS OF THESE GUYS MAKE A COUPLE OF SWELL STEPPING-STONES TO THE GROUND!
THAT'S USING THEIR HEADS TO ADVANTAGE, ELONGATED MAN!
BONK!
NICE SOCK, PAL! YOU PACK QUITE A PUNCH!
SO DOES THE POWER RING! BUT WHY'S HE HOLDING BACK ON IT? IT'S FULLY CHARGED--
TWO MORE GUNMEN RACE FROM THE BUILDING WHERE THEY HAVE BEEN RIFLING THE REST OF THE BLUE-PRINTS...
A COUPLE OF TROUBLE-MAKERS!
GUN 'EM DOWN!
I DON'T DARE CALL OUT TO HAL TO BECOME GREEN LANTERN-- IT'D GIVE AWAY HIS SECRET IDENTITY TO THESE MUGS!
7

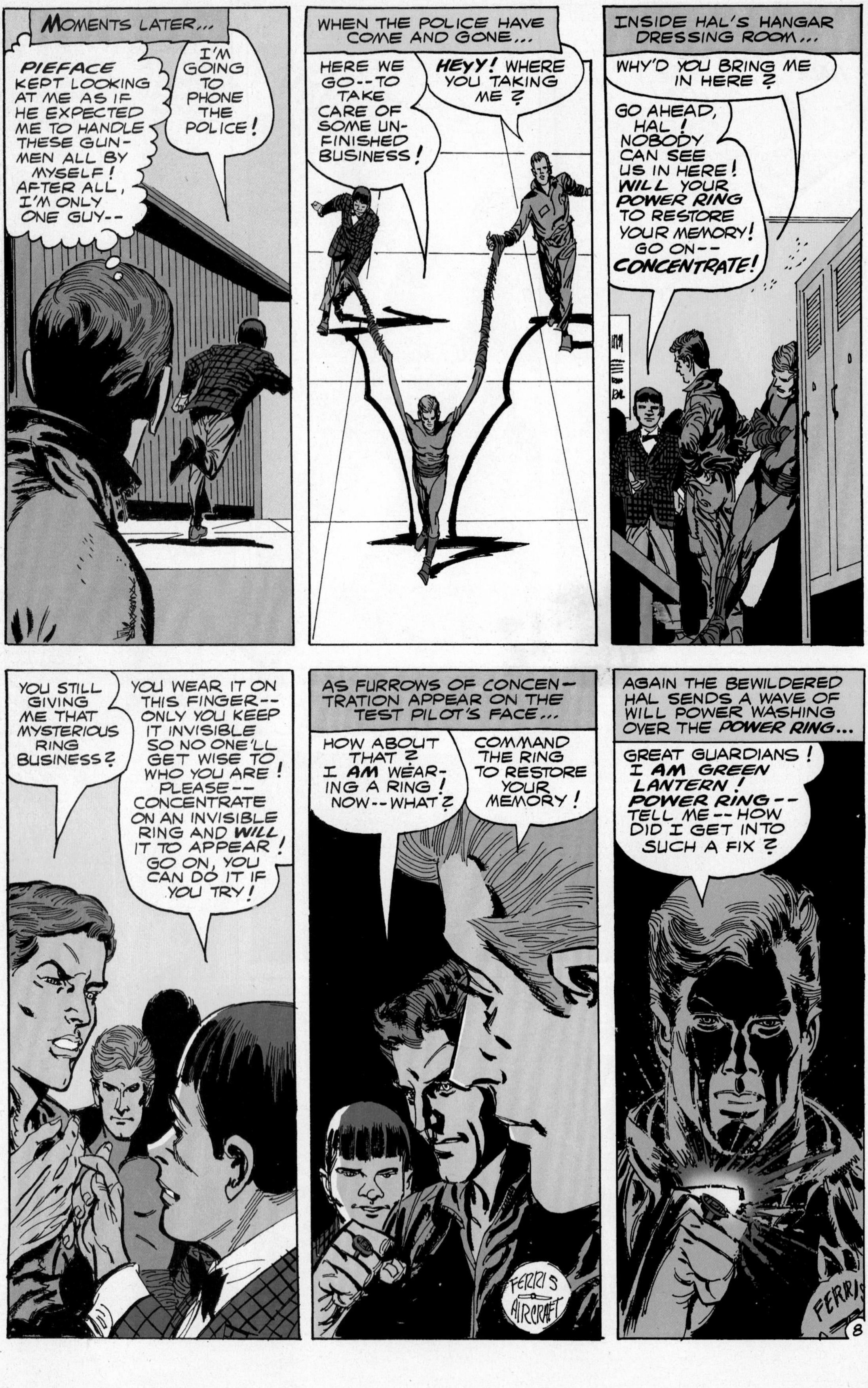
MOMENTS LATER...
PIEFACE KEPT LOOKING AT ME AS IF HE EXPECTED ME TO HANDLE THESE GUNMEN ALL BY MYSELF! AFTER ALL, I'M ONLY ONE GUY--
I'M GOING TO PHONE THE POLICE!
WHEN THE POLICE HAVE COME AND GONE...
HERE WE GO--TO TAKE CARE OF SOME UNFINISHED BUSINESS!
HEYY! WHERE YOU TAKING ME?
INSIDE HAL'S HANGAR DRESSING ROOM...
WHY'D YOU BRING ME IN HERE?
GO AHEAD, HAL! NOBODY CAN SEE US IN HERE! WILL YOUR POWER RING TO RESTORE YOUR MEMORY! GO ON-- CONCENTRATE!
YOU STILL GIVING ME THAT MYSTERIOUS RING BUSINESS?
YOU WEAR IT ON THIS FINGER-- ONLY YOU KEEP IT INVISIBLE SO NO ONE'LL GET WISE TO WHO YOU ARE! PLEASE-- CONCENTRATE ON AN INVISIBLE RING AND WILL IT TO APPEAR! GO ON, YOU CAN DO IT IF YOU TRY!
AS FURROWS OF CONCENTRATION APPEAR ON THE TEST PILOT'S FACE...
HOW ABOUT THAT? I AM WEARING A RING! NOW--WHAT?
COMMAND THE RING TO RESTORE YOUR MEMORY!
FERRIS AIRCRAFT
AGAIN THE BEWILDERED HAL SENDS A WAVE OF WILL POWER WASHING OVER THE POWER RING...
GREAT GUARDIANS! I AM GREEN LANTERN! POWER RING-- TELL ME--HOW DID I GET INTO SUCH A FIX?
FERRIS
8

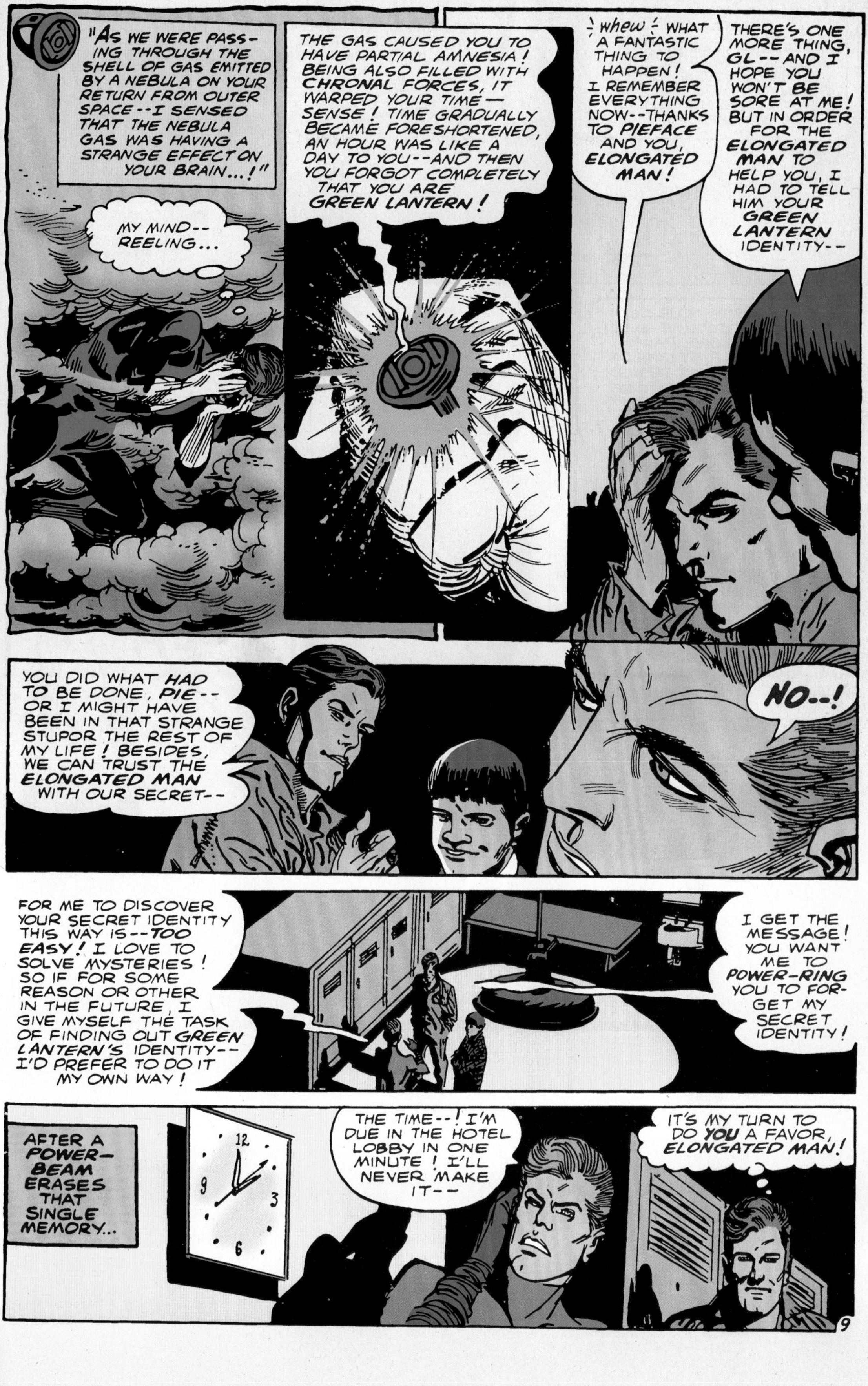
"AS WE WERE PASSING THROUGH THE SHELL OF GAS EMITTED BY A NEBULA ON YOUR RETURN FROM OUTER SPACE--I SENSED THAT THE NEBULA GAS WAS HAVING A STRANGE EFFECT ON YOUR BRAIN...!"
MY MIND--REELING...
THE GAS CAUSED YOU TO HAVE PARTIAL AMNESIA! BEING ALSO FILLED WITH CHRONAL FORCES, IT WARPED YOUR TIME—SENSE! TIME GRADUALLY BECAME FORESHORTENED, AN HOUR WAS LIKE A DAY TO YOU--AND THEN YOU FORGOT COMPLETELY THAT YOU ARE GREEN LANTERN!
-WHEW- WHAT A FANTASTIC THING TO HAPPEN! I REMEMBER EVERYTHING NOW--THANKS TO PIEFACE AND YOU, ELONGATED MAN!
THERE'S ONE MORE THING, GL--AND I HOPE YOU WON'T BE SORE AT ME! BUT IN ORDER FOR THE ELONGATED MAN TO HELP YOU, I HAD TO TELL HIM YOUR GREEN LANTERN IDENTITY--
YOU DID WHAT HAD TO BE DONE, PIE--OR I MIGHT HAVE BEEN IN THAT STRANGE STUPOR THE REST OF MY LIFE! BESIDES, WE CAN TRUST THE ELONGATED MAN WITH OUR SECRET--
NO--!
FOR ME TO DISCOVER YOUR SECRET IDENTITY THIS WAY IS--TOO EASY! I LOVE TO SOLVE MYSTERIES! SO IF FOR SOME REASON OR OTHER IN THE FUTURE, I GIVE MYSELF THE TASK OF FINDING OUT GREEN LANTERN'S IDENTITY--I'D PREFER TO DO IT MY OWN WAY!
I GET THE MESSAGE! YOU WANT ME TO POWER-RING YOU TO FORGET MY SECRET IDENTITY!
AFTER A POWER-BEAM ERASES THAT SINGLE MEMORY...
THE TIME--! I'M DUE IN THE HOTEL LOBBY IN ONE MINUTE! I'LL NEVER MAKE IT--
IT'S MY TURN TO DO YOU A FAVOR, ELONGATED MAN!
9

A BLAZE OF EMERALD ENERGY-- AND THE *STRETCHABLE SLEUTH* FINDS HIM-SELF IN THE HOTEL LOBBY WHERE...

TV CAMERAS--REPORTERS-- MY ADMIRING PUBLIC-- ALL GATHERED HERE!

RALPH, YOU GOT HERE JUST IN TIME! HERE'S YOUR BIRTHDAY PRESENT!

WHY-- IT'S A NEW COSTUME!

YES, YOUR OLD COSTUME IS SO *DRAB*, RALPH! I JUST COULDN'T RESIST DESIGN-ING A NEW ONE AND GIVING IT TO YOU FOR YOUR BIRTHDAY!

NATURALLY, I ARRANGED FOR SUITABLE PUBLICITY TO LET THE WHOLE WORLD KNOW ABOUT THE *ELONGATED MAN'S* "NEW LOOK"! NOW PUT ON YOUR COSTUME--AND SHOW YOURSELF OFF!

HAPPY BIRTHDAY, *ELONGATED MAN!*

CLAP! CLAP!

CLAP!

The End

10

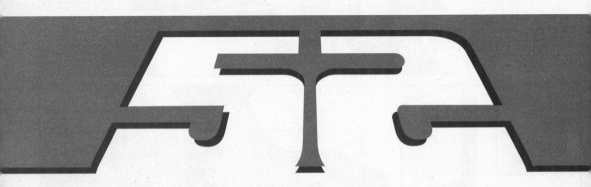

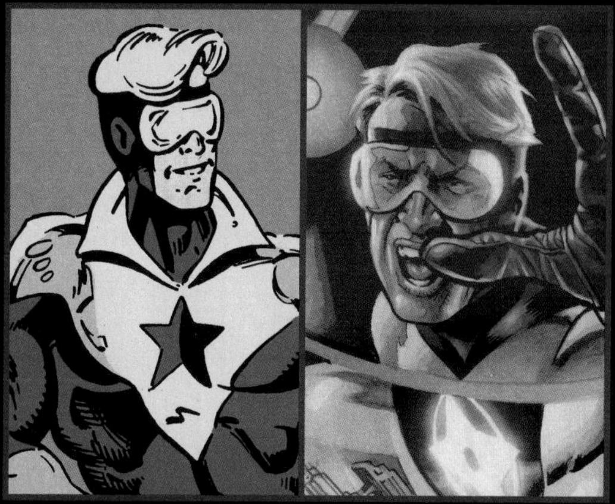

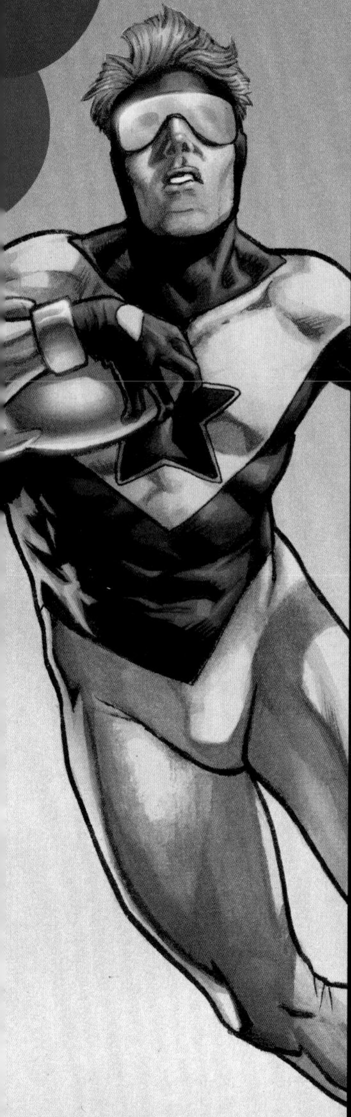

SECRET ORIGINS #35

Booster Gold came to our era from the future — with a Legion of Super-Heroes flight ring, a whackload of 25th century technology, and a simple plan: to turn super-heroics into a path to riches and fame. This stew of science fiction ideas and unashamed Reagan-era greed seemed to say "The future is coming and it wants your money." (This prediction has since come true, of course, as a glance at your Byzantine cell phone plan will confirm.)

Still, Booster's constant struggle to keep things together — he was making it up as he went along, just like you and me — made cartoonist Dan Jurgens's eccentric creation seem awfully lovable. Eventually, his ethics began to override his ego (most of the time, at least) and by the time the 52 writers got hold of him, Booster was the perfect prism through which to view the concept of celebrity in the DC Universe.

—**MW**

BOOSTER GOLD

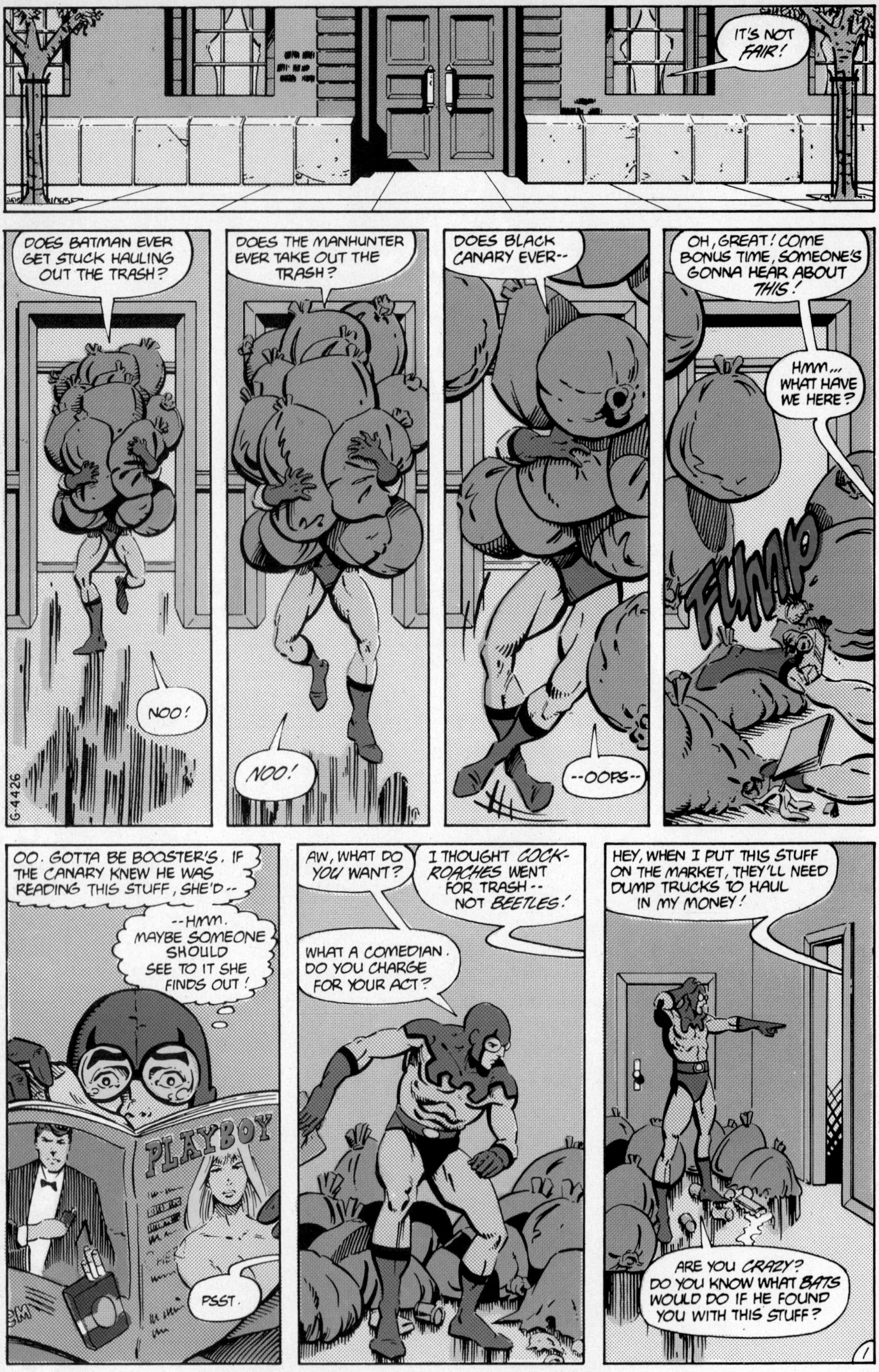
IT'S NOT FAIR!
DOES BATMAN EVER GET STUCK HAULING OUT THE TRASH?
NOO!
DOES THE MANHUNTER EVER TAKE OUT THE TRASH?
NOO!
DOES BLACK CANARY EVER--
--OOPS--
OH, GREAT! COME BONUS TIME, SOMEONE'S GONNA HEAR ABOUT THIS!
HMM... WHAT HAVE WE HERE?
FUMP
OO. GOTTA BE BOOSTER'S. IF THE CANARY KNEW HE WAS READING THIS STUFF, SHE'D--
--HMM. MAYBE SOMEONE SHOULD SEE TO IT SHE FINDS OUT!
PLAYBOY
PSST.
AW, WHAT DO YOU WANT?
I THOUGHT COCKROACHES WENT FOR TRASH -- NOT BEETLES!
WHAT A COMEDIAN. DO YOU CHARGE FOR YOUR ACT?
HEY, WHEN I PUT THIS STUFF ON THE MARKET, THEY'LL NEED DUMP TRUCKS TO HAUL IN MY MONEY!
ARE YOU CRAZY? DO YOU KNOW WHAT BATS WOULD DO IF HE FOUND YOU WITH THIS STUFF?
G-4426
1

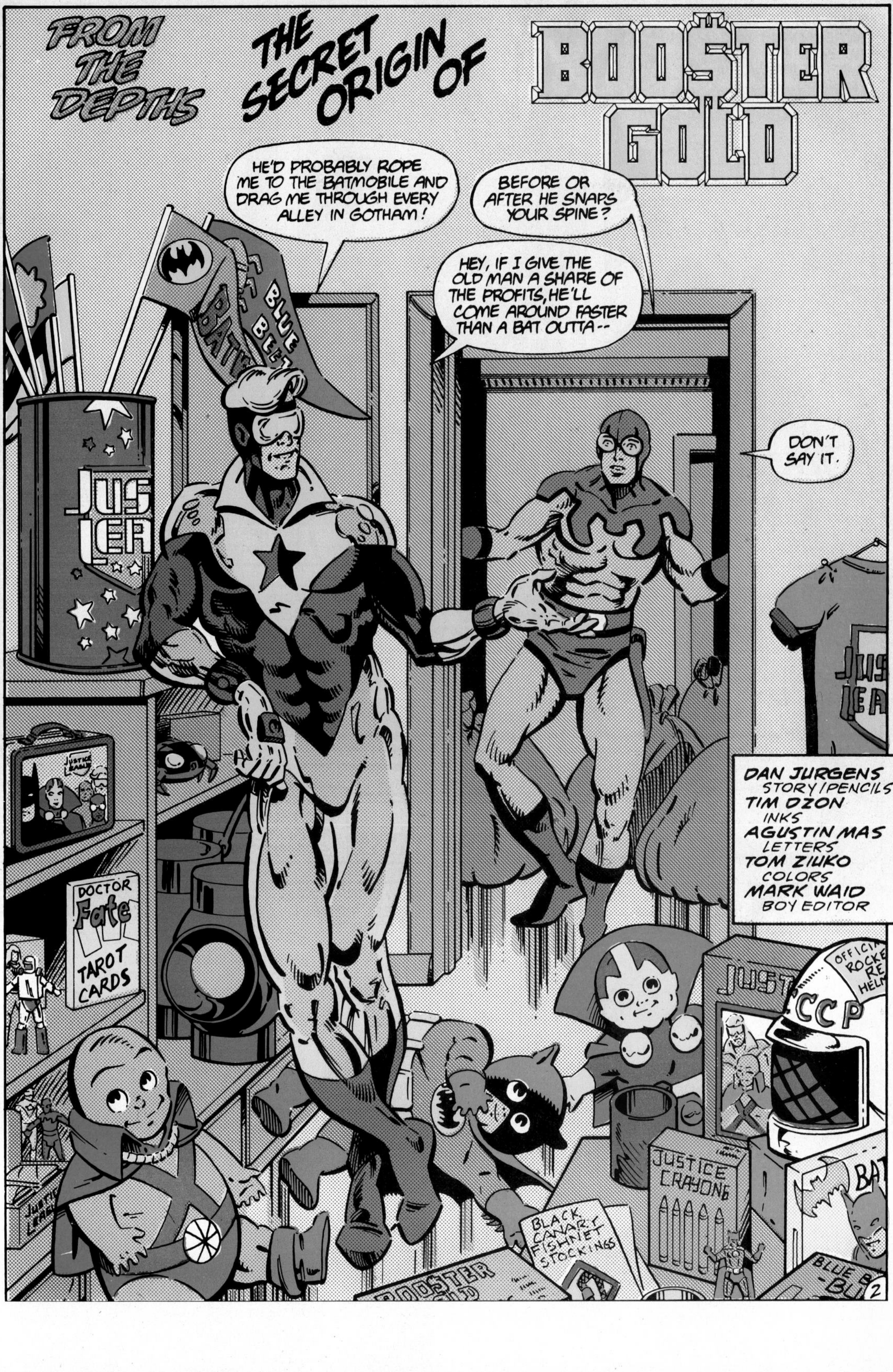
FROM THE DEPTHS
THE SECRET ORIGIN OF
BOO$TER GOLD
HE'D PROBABLY ROPE ME TO THE BATMOBILE AND DRAG ME THROUGH EVERY ALLEY IN GOTHAM!
BEFORE OR AFTER HE SNAPS YOUR SPINE?
HEY, IF I GIVE THE OLD MAN A SHARE OF THE PROFITS, HE'LL COME AROUND FASTER THAN A BAT OUTTA--
DON'T SAY IT.
DAN JURGENS STORY/PENCILS
TIM DZON INKS
AGUSTIN MAS LETTERS
TOM ZIUKO COLORS
MARK WAID BOY EDITOR
DOCTOR Fate TAROT CARDS
JUSTICE CRAYONS
BLACK CANARY FISHNET STOCKINGS
2

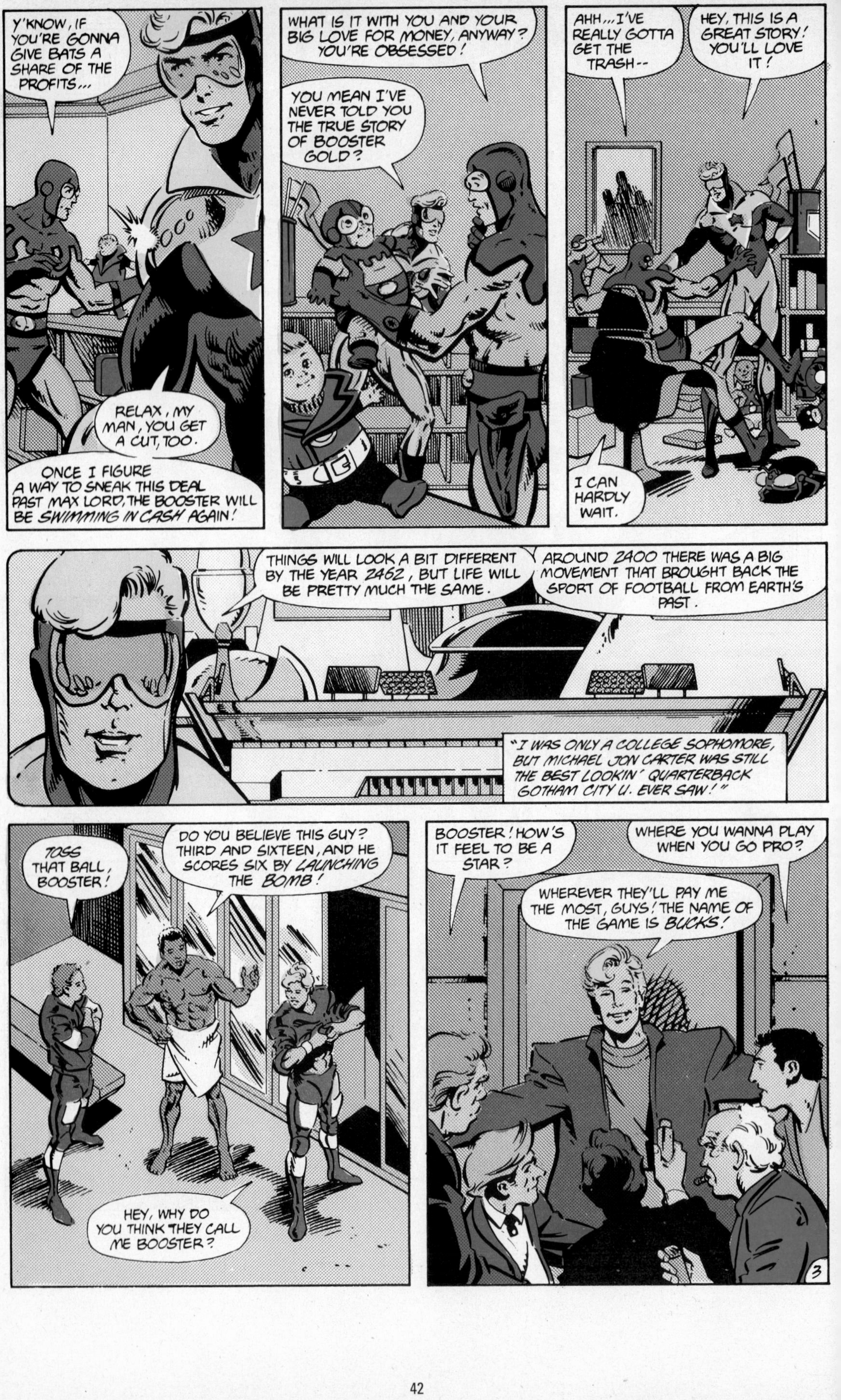
Y'KNOW, IF YOU'RE GONNA GIVE BATS A SHARE OF THE PROFITS...
RELAX, MY MAN, YOU GET A CUT, TOO.
ONCE I FIGURE A WAY TO SNEAK THIS DEAL PAST MAX LORD, THE BOOSTER WILL BE SWIMMING IN CASH AGAIN!
WHAT IS IT WITH YOU AND YOUR BIG LOVE FOR MONEY, ANYWAY? YOU'RE OBSESSED!
YOU MEAN I'VE NEVER TOLD YOU THE TRUE STORY OF BOOSTER GOLD?
AHH... I'VE REALLY GOTTA GET THE TRASH--
HEY, THIS IS A GREAT STORY! YOU'LL LOVE IT!
I CAN HARDLY WAIT.
THINGS WILL LOOK A BIT DIFFERENT BY THE YEAR 2462, BUT LIFE WILL BE PRETTY MUCH THE SAME.
AROUND 2400 THERE WAS A BIG MOVEMENT THAT BROUGHT BACK THE SPORT OF FOOTBALL FROM EARTH'S PAST.
"I WAS ONLY A COLLEGE SOPHOMORE, BUT MICHAEL JON CARTER WAS STILL THE BEST LOOKIN' QUARTERBACK GOTHAM CITY U. EVER SAW!"
TOSS THAT BALL, BOOSTER!
DO YOU BELIEVE THIS GUY? THIRD AND SIXTEEN, AND HE SCORES SIX BY LAUNCHING THE BOMB!
HEY, WHY DO YOU THINK THEY CALL ME BOOSTER?
BOOSTER! HOW'S IT FEEL TO BE A STAR?
WHERE YOU WANNA PLAY WHEN YOU GO PRO?
WHEREVER THEY'LL PAY ME THE MOST, GUYS! THE NAME OF THE GAME IS BUCKS!
3

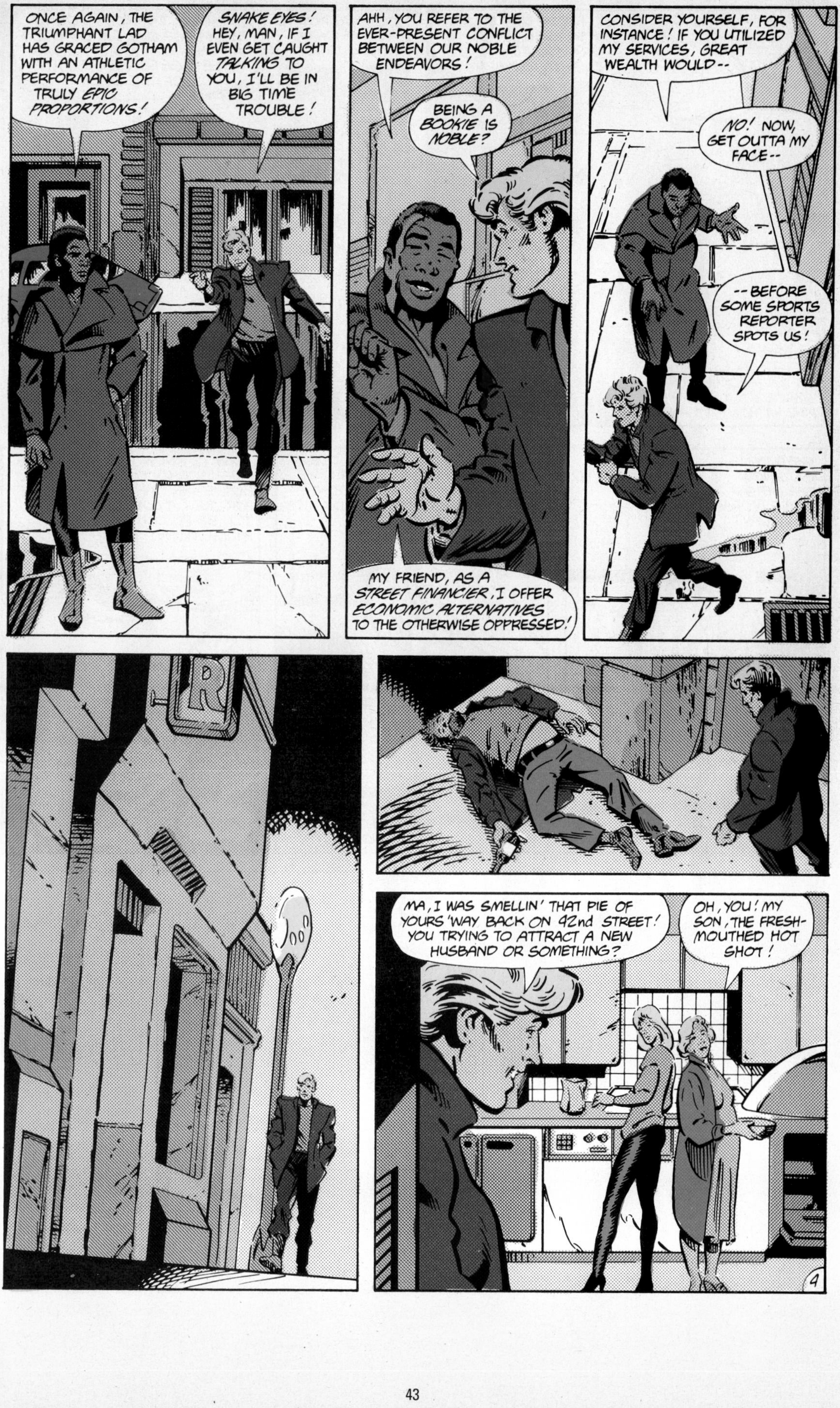
ONCE AGAIN, THE TRIUMPHANT LAD HAS GRACED GOTHAM WITH AN ATHLETIC PERFORMANCE OF TRULY EPIC PROPORTIONS!
SNAKE EYES! HEY, MAN, IF I EVEN GET CAUGHT TALKING TO YOU, I'LL BE IN BIG TIME TROUBLE!
AHH, YOU REFER TO THE EVER-PRESENT CONFLICT BETWEEN OUR NOBLE ENDEAVORS!
BEING A BOOKIE IS NOBLE?
MY FRIEND, AS A STREET FINANCIER, I OFFER ECONOMIC ALTERNATIVES TO THE OTHERWISE OPPRESSED!
CONSIDER YOURSELF, FOR INSTANCE! IF YOU UTILIZED MY SERVICES, GREAT WEALTH WOULD--
NO! NOW, GET OUTTA MY FACE--
--BEFORE SOME SPORTS REPORTER SPOTS US!
R
MA, I WAS SMELLIN' THAT PIE OF YOURS 'WAY BACK ON 42nd STREET! YOU TRYING TO ATTRACT A NEW HUSBAND OR SOMETHING?
OH, YOU! MY SON, THE FRESH-MOUTHED HOT SHOT!
4

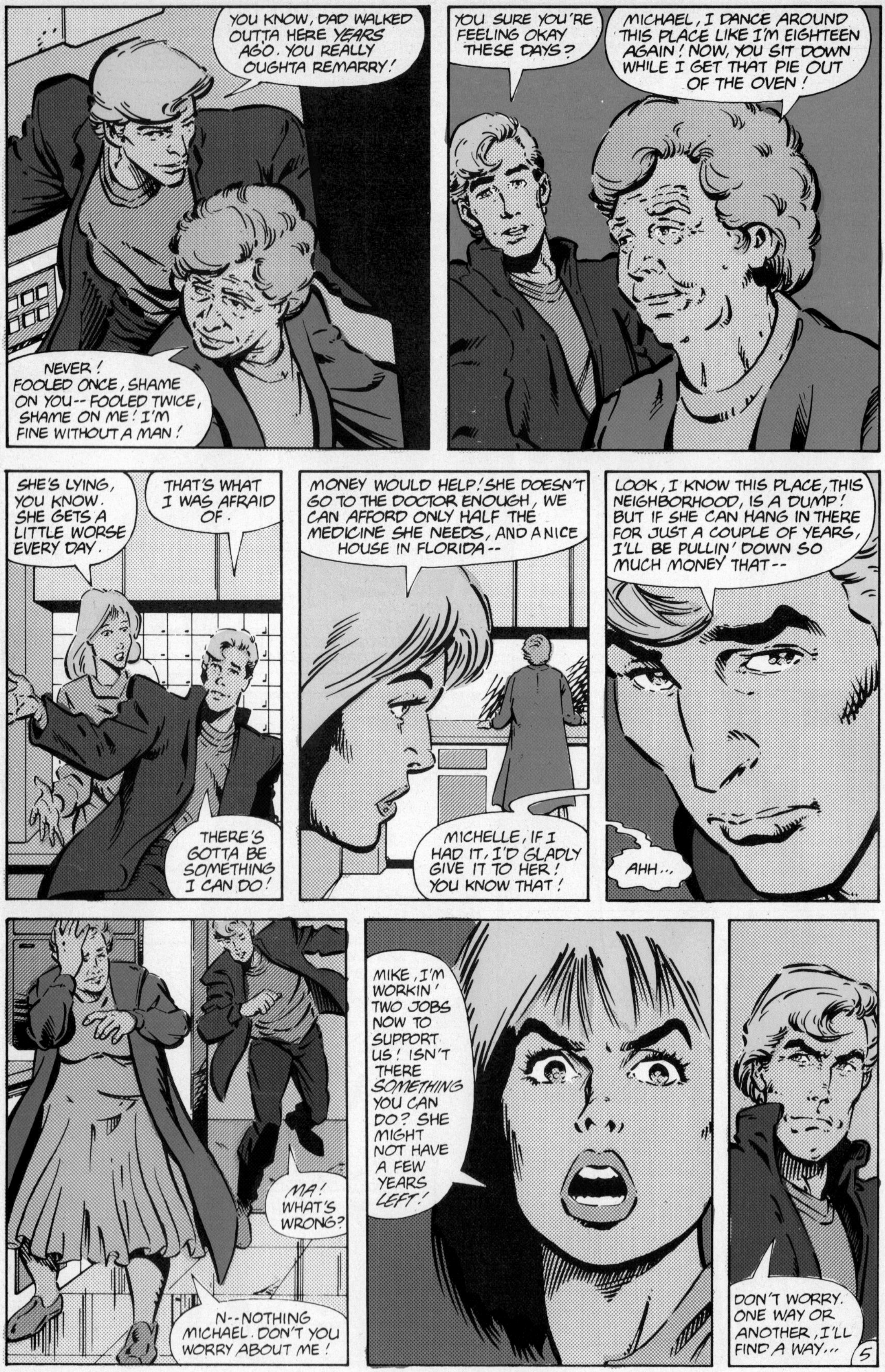

YOU KNOW, DAD WALKED OUTTA HERE YEARS AGO. YOU REALLY OUGHTA REMARRY!
NEVER! FOOLED ONCE, SHAME ON YOU--FOOLED TWICE, SHAME ON ME! I'M FINE WITHOUT A MAN!
YOU SURE YOU'RE FEELING OKAY THESE DAYS?
MICHAEL, I DANCE AROUND THIS PLACE LIKE I'M EIGHTEEN AGAIN! NOW, YOU SIT DOWN WHILE I GET THAT PIE OUT OF THE OVEN!
SHE'S LYING, YOU KNOW. SHE GETS A LITTLE WORSE EVERY DAY.
THAT'S WHAT I WAS AFRAID OF.
THERE'S GOTTA BE SOMETHING I CAN DO!
MONEY WOULD HELP! SHE DOESN'T GO TO THE DOCTOR ENOUGH, WE CAN AFFORD ONLY HALF THE MEDICINE SHE NEEDS, AND A NICE HOUSE IN FLORIDA--
MICHELLE, IF I HAD IT, I'D GLADLY GIVE IT TO HER! YOU KNOW THAT!
LOOK, I KNOW THIS PLACE, THIS NEIGHBORHOOD, IS A DUMP! BUT IF SHE CAN HANG IN THERE FOR JUST A COUPLE OF YEARS, I'LL BE PULLIN' DOWN SO MUCH MONEY THAT--
AHH...
MA! WHAT'S WRONG?
N--NOTHING MICHAEL. DON'T YOU WORRY ABOUT ME!
MIKE, I'M WORKIN' TWO JOBS NOW TO SUPPORT US! ISN'T THERE SOMETHING YOU CAN DO? SHE MIGHT NOT HAVE A FEW YEARS LEFT!
DON'T WORRY. ONE WAY OR ANOTHER, I'LL FIND A WAY...
5

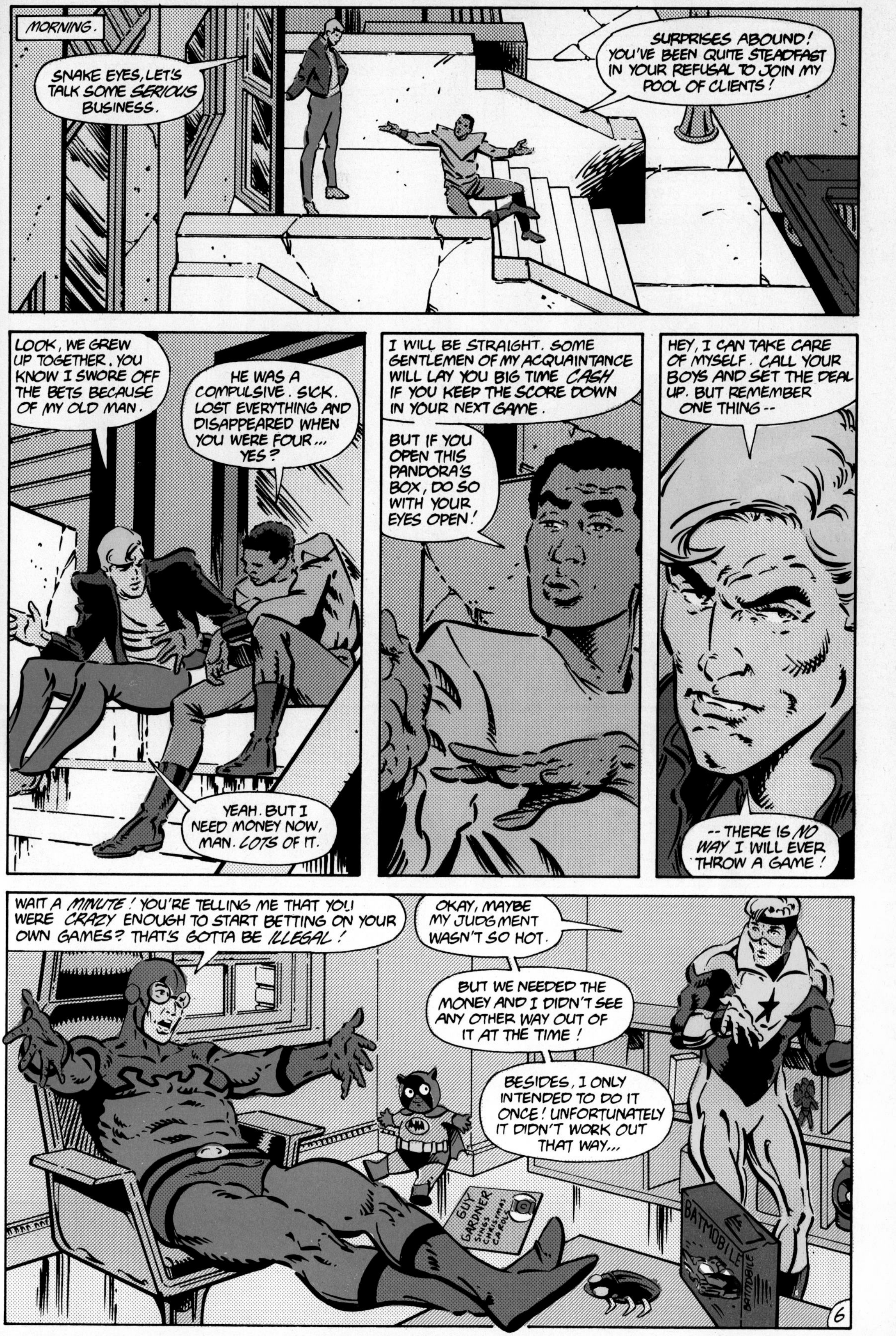
MORNING.
SNAKE EYES, LET'S TALK SOME SERIOUS BUSINESS.
SURPRISES ABOUND! YOU'VE BEEN QUITE STEADFAST IN YOUR REFUSAL TO JOIN MY POOL OF CLIENTS!
LOOK, WE GREW UP TOGETHER. YOU KNOW I SWORE OFF THE BETS BECAUSE OF MY OLD MAN.
HE WAS A COMPULSIVE. SICK. LOST EVERYTHING AND DISAPPEARED WHEN YOU WERE FOUR... YES?
YEAH. BUT I NEED MONEY NOW, MAN. LOTS OF IT.
I WILL BE STRAIGHT. SOME GENTLEMEN OF MY ACQUAINTANCE WILL LAY YOU BIG TIME CASH IF YOU KEEP THE SCORE DOWN IN YOUR NEXT GAME.
BUT IF YOU OPEN THIS PANDORA'S BOX, DO SO WITH YOUR EYES OPEN!
HEY, I CAN TAKE CARE OF MYSELF. CALL YOUR BOYS AND SET THE DEAL UP. BUT REMEMBER ONE THING--
--THERE IS NO WAY I WILL EVER THROW A GAME!
WAIT A MINUTE! YOU'RE TELLING ME THAT YOU WERE CRAZY ENOUGH TO START BETTING ON YOUR OWN GAMES? THAT'S GOTTA BE ILLEGAL!
OKAY, MAYBE MY JUDGMENT WASN'T SO HOT.
BUT WE NEEDED THE MONEY AND I DIDN'T SEE ANY OTHER WAY OUT OF IT AT THE TIME!
BESIDES, I ONLY INTENDED TO DO IT ONCE! UNFORTUNATELY IT DIDN'T WORK OUT THAT WAY...
GUY GARDNER SINGS CHRISTMAS CAROLS
BATMOBILE
6

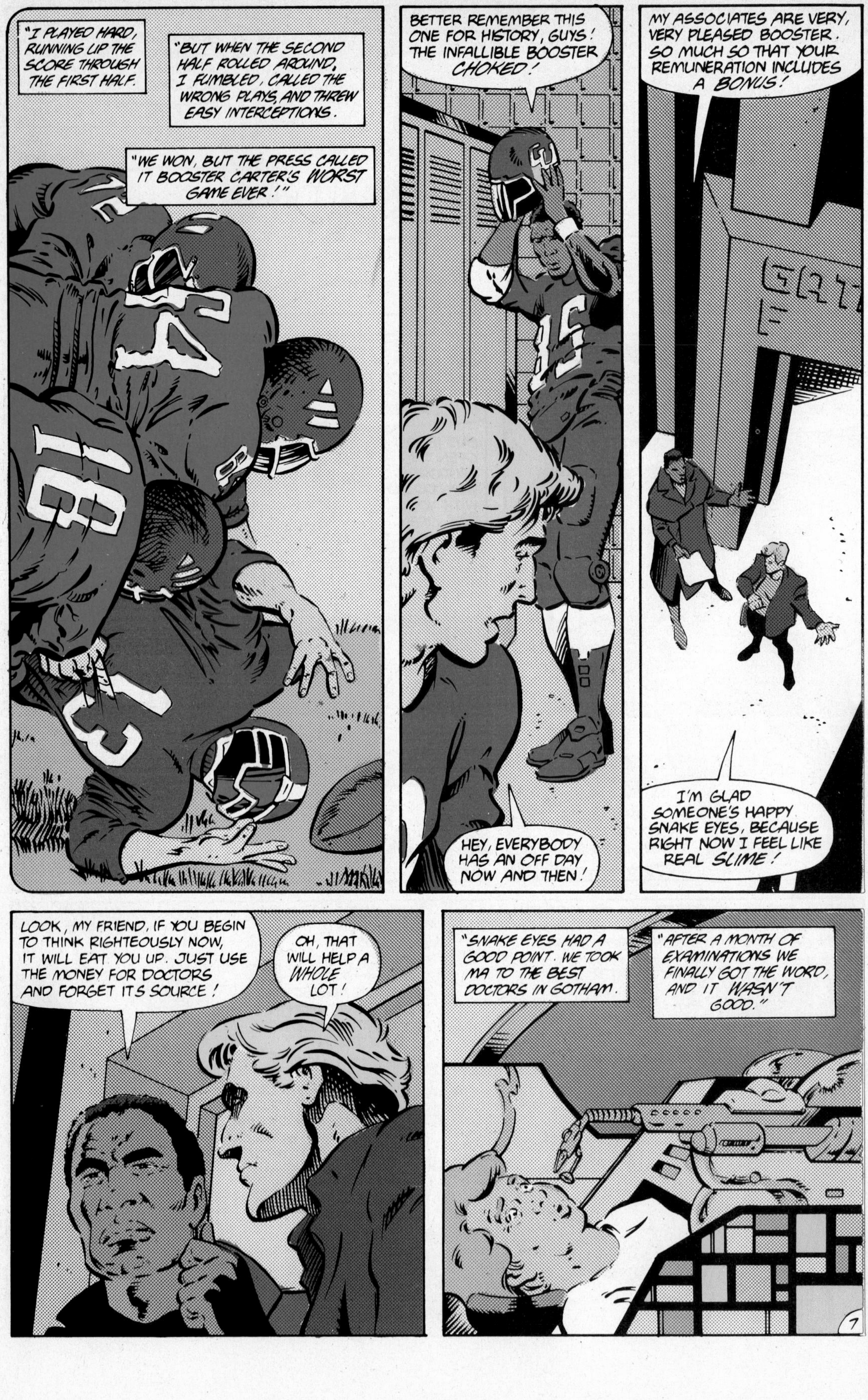

"I PLAYED HARD, RUNNING UP THE SCORE THROUGH THE FIRST HALF.
"BUT WHEN THE SECOND HALF ROLLED AROUND, I FUMBLED, CALLED THE WRONG PLAYS, AND THREW EASY INTERCEPTIONS.
"WE WON, BUT THE PRESS CALLED IT BOOSTER CARTER'S WORST GAME EVER!"
BETTER REMEMBER THIS ONE FOR HISTORY, GUYS! THE INFALLIBLE BOOSTER CHOKED!
HEY, EVERYBODY HAS AN OFF DAY NOW AND THEN!
MY ASSOCIATES ARE VERY, VERY PLEASED BOOSTER. SO MUCH SO THAT YOUR REMUNERATION INCLUDES A BONUS!
I'M GLAD SOMEONE'S HAPPY SNAKE EYES, BECAUSE RIGHT NOW I FEEL LIKE REAL SLIME!
LOOK, MY FRIEND, IF YOU BEGIN TO THINK RIGHTEOUSLY NOW, IT WILL EAT YOU UP. JUST USE THE MONEY FOR DOCTORS AND FORGET ITS SOURCE!
OH, THAT WILL HELP A WHOLE LOT!
"SNAKE EYES HAD A GOOD POINT. WE TOOK MA TO THE BEST DOCTORS IN GOTHAM.
"AFTER A MONTH OF EXAMINATIONS WE FINALLY GOT THE WORD, AND IT WASN'T GOOD."
7

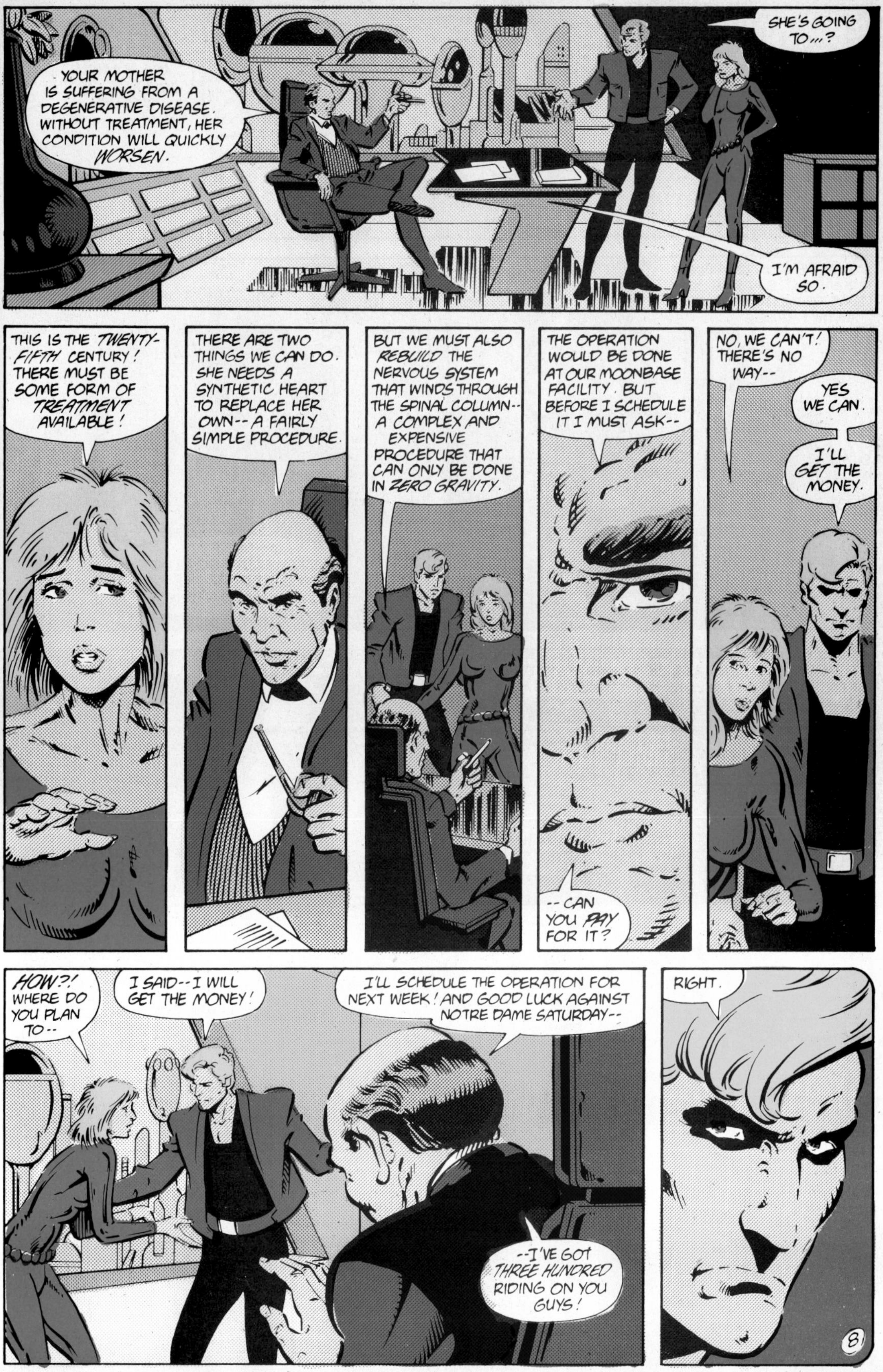

...YOUR MOTHER IS SUFFERING FROM A DEGENERATIVE DISEASE. WITHOUT TREATMENT, HER CONDITION WILL QUICKLY WORSEN.
SHE'S GOING TO...?
I'M AFRAID SO.
THIS IS THE TWENTY-FIFTH CENTURY! THERE MUST BE SOME FORM OF TREATMENT AVAILABLE!
THERE ARE TWO THINGS WE CAN DO. SHE NEEDS A SYNTHETIC HEART TO REPLACE HER OWN-- A FAIRLY SIMPLE PROCEDURE.
BUT WE MUST ALSO REBUILD THE NERVOUS SYSTEM THAT WINDS THROUGH THE SPINAL COLUMN-- A COMPLEX AND EXPENSIVE PROCEDURE THAT CAN ONLY BE DONE IN ZERO GRAVITY.
THE OPERATION WOULD BE DONE AT OUR MOONBASE FACILITY. BUT BEFORE I SCHEDULE IT I MUST ASK--
--CAN YOU PAY FOR IT?
NO, WE CAN'T! THERE'S NO WAY--
YES WE CAN.
I'LL GET THE MONEY.
HOW?! WHERE DO YOU PLAN TO--
I SAID--I WILL GET THE MONEY!
I'LL SCHEDULE THE OPERATION FOR NEXT WEEK! AND GOOD LUCK AGAINST NOTRE DAME SATURDAY--
--I'VE GOT THREE HUNDRED RIDING ON YOU GUYS!
RIGHT.
8

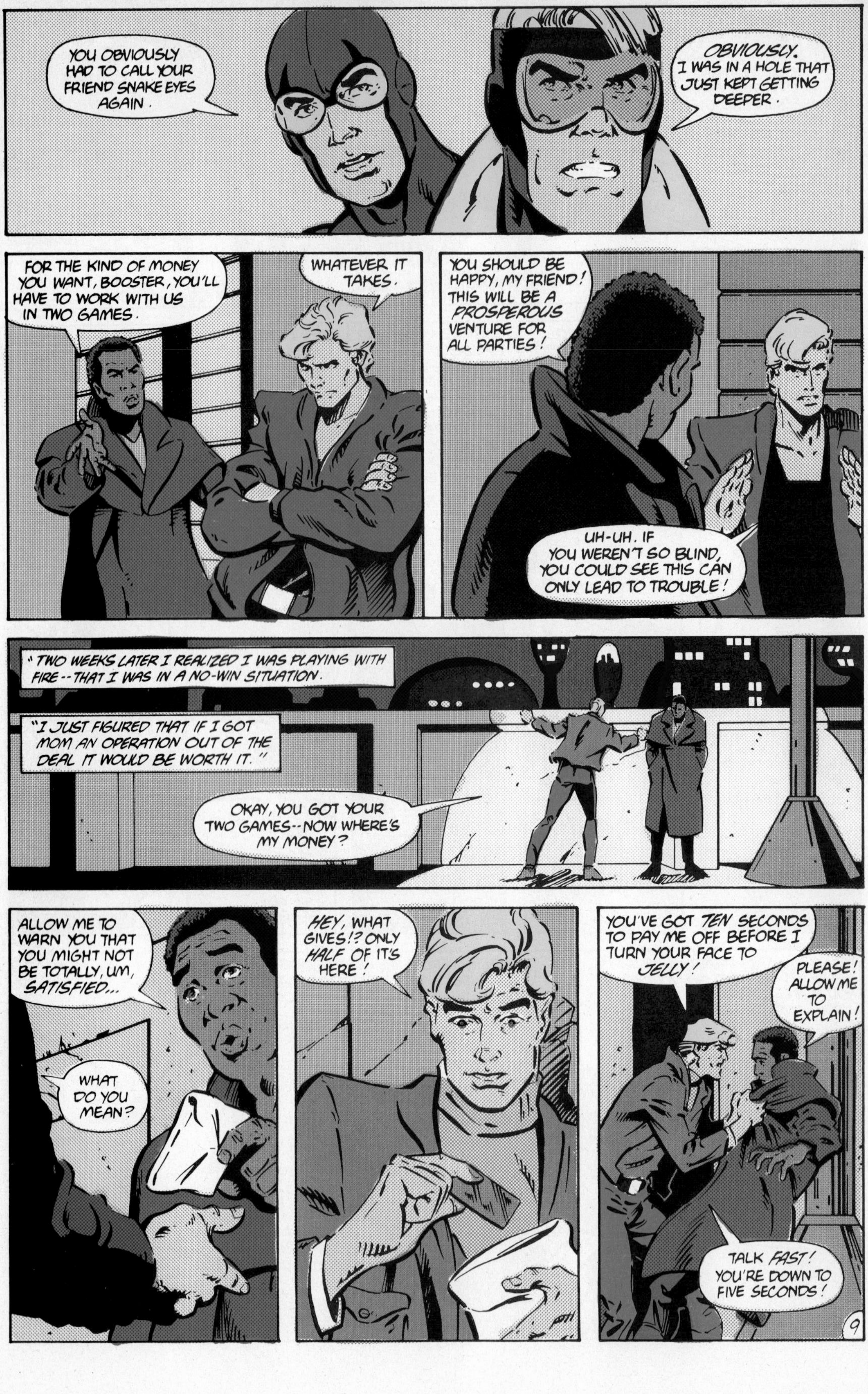
YOU OBVIOUSLY HAD TO CALL YOUR FRIEND SNAKE EYES AGAIN.
OBVIOUSLY. I WAS IN A HOLE THAT JUST KEPT GETTING DEEPER.
FOR THE KIND OF MONEY YOU WANT, BOOSTER, YOU'LL HAVE TO WORK WITH US IN TWO GAMES.
WHATEVER IT TAKES.
YOU SHOULD BE HAPPY, MY FRIEND! THIS WILL BE A PROSPEROUS VENTURE FOR ALL PARTIES!
UH-UH. IF YOU WEREN'T SO BLIND, YOU COULD SEE THIS CAN ONLY LEAD TO TROUBLE!
"TWO WEEKS LATER I REALIZED I WAS PLAYING WITH FIRE--THAT I WAS IN A NO-WIN SITUATION.
"I JUST FIGURED THAT IF I GOT MOM AN OPERATION OUT OF THE DEAL IT WOULD BE WORTH IT."
OKAY, YOU GOT YOUR TWO GAMES--NOW WHERE'S MY MONEY?
ALLOW ME TO WARN YOU THAT YOU MIGHT NOT BE TOTALLY, UM, SATISFIED...
WHAT DO YOU MEAN?
HEY, WHAT GIVES!? ONLY HALF OF IT'S HERE!
YOU'VE GOT TEN SECONDS TO PAY ME OFF BEFORE I TURN YOUR FACE TO JELLY!
PLEASE! ALLOW ME TO EXPLAIN!
TALK FAST! YOU'RE DOWN TO FIVE SECONDS!
9

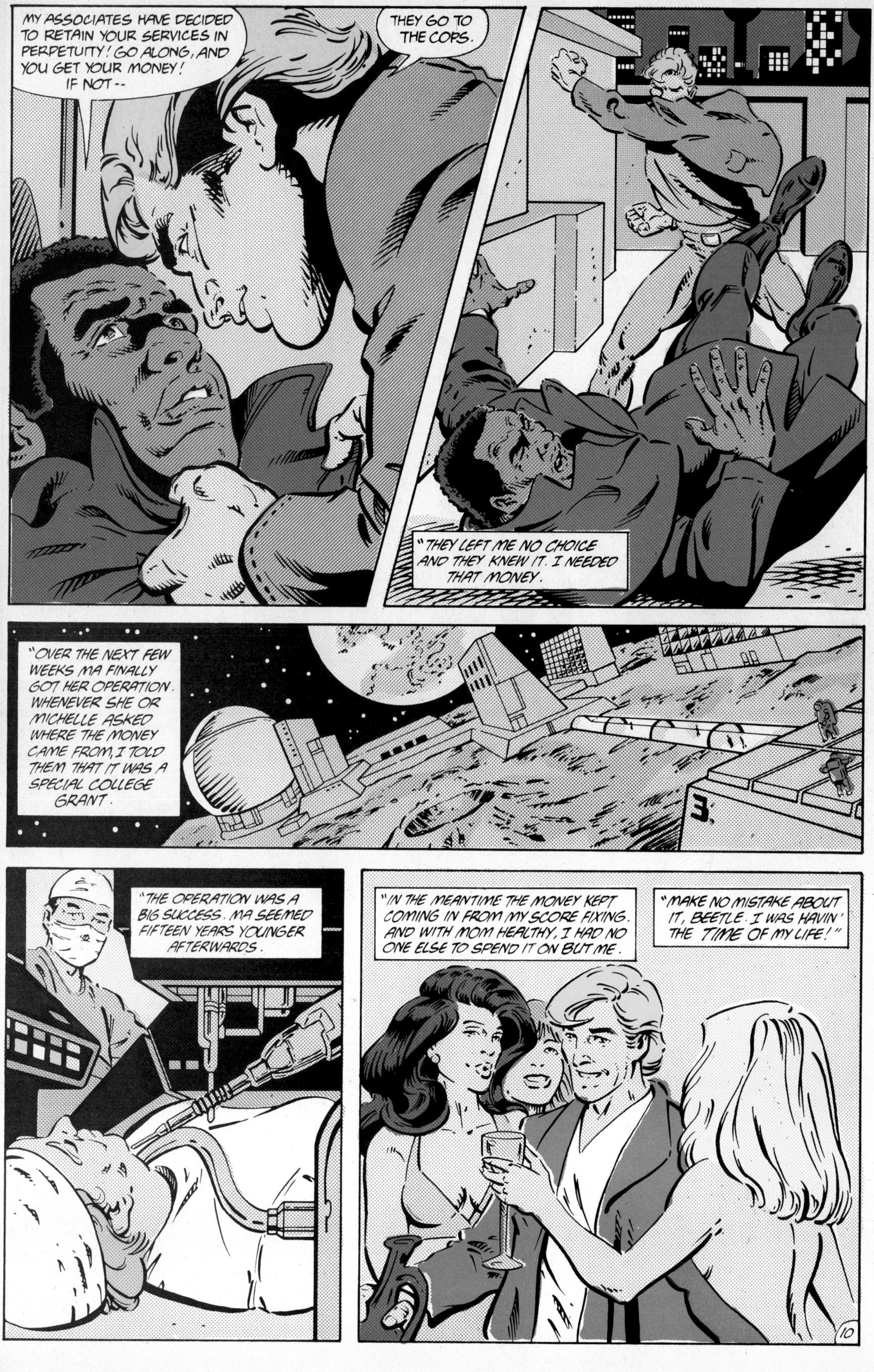
MY ASSOCIATES HAVE DECIDED TO RETAIN YOUR SERVICES IN PERPETUITY! GO ALONG, AND YOU GET YOUR MONEY! IF NOT --
THEY GO TO THE COPS.
"THEY LEFT ME NO CHOICE AND THEY KNEW IT. I NEEDED THAT MONEY.
"OVER THE NEXT FEW WEEKS MA FINALLY GOT HER OPERATION. WHENEVER SHE OR MICHELLE ASKED WHERE THE MONEY CAME FROM, I TOLD THEM THAT IT WAS A SPECIAL COLLEGE GRANT.
3
"THE OPERATION WAS A BIG SUCCESS. MA SEEMED FIFTEEN YEARS YOUNGER AFTERWARDS.
"IN THE MEANTIME THE MONEY KEPT COMING IN FROM MY SCORE FIXING. AND WITH MOM HEALTHY, I HAD NO ONE ELSE TO SPEND IT ON BUT ME.
"MAKE NO MISTAKE ABOUT IT, BEETLE. I WAS HAVIN' THE TIME OF MY LIFE!"
10

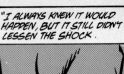

"BEFORE LONG I WAS BETTING ON OTHER GAMES AS WELL. ALL IN THE PURSUIT OF *MONEY*.

"I FIGURED I COULD BUY MYSELF OUT OF THE GHETTO. AND IT DIDN'T MATTER HOW I DID IT."

MICHAEL, THESE ARE FAR TOO EXTRAVAGANT FOR ME!

BzZZ

OH, SOMEONE'S AT THE DOOR!

YEAH, WHAT CAN I DO FOR YOU GUYS?

GOTHAM VICE, CARTER. WE REGRET TO INFORM YOU THAT YOU ARE UNDER ARREST FOR CONSPIRACY TO FIX COLLEGE FOOTBALL GAMES.

"I ALWAYS KNEW IT WOULD HAPPEN, BUT IT STILL DIDN'T LESSEN THE SHOCK.

"AS FOR MA... MY SISTER... THERE WAS NO EXPLAINING IT. GAMBLING DESTROYED OUR FAMILY YEARS EARLIER ...

"... AND IT WAS DOING SO AGAIN. IF I WERE A MURDERER I COULDN'T HAVE HURT THEM MORE DEEPLY."

HOW COULD YOU DO THIS TO ME? YOUR FATHER DESERTED US YEARS AGO! WE BARELY SURVIVED!

BETTER I *DIE* THAN TO HAVE YOU BRING THIS SHAME INTO MY HOME AGAIN!

GAMBLING DESTROYED YOUR FATHER AND NOW IT EATS AT YOU! WELL, I WON'T WATCH THE SICKNESS RUIN ANOTHER!

WHATEVER YOU DO WITH THE REST OF YOUR LIFE, YOU WILL *NEVER* MAKE UP FOR WHAT YOU'VE DONE NOW!

FROM THIS MOMENT ON, I HAVE NO SON!

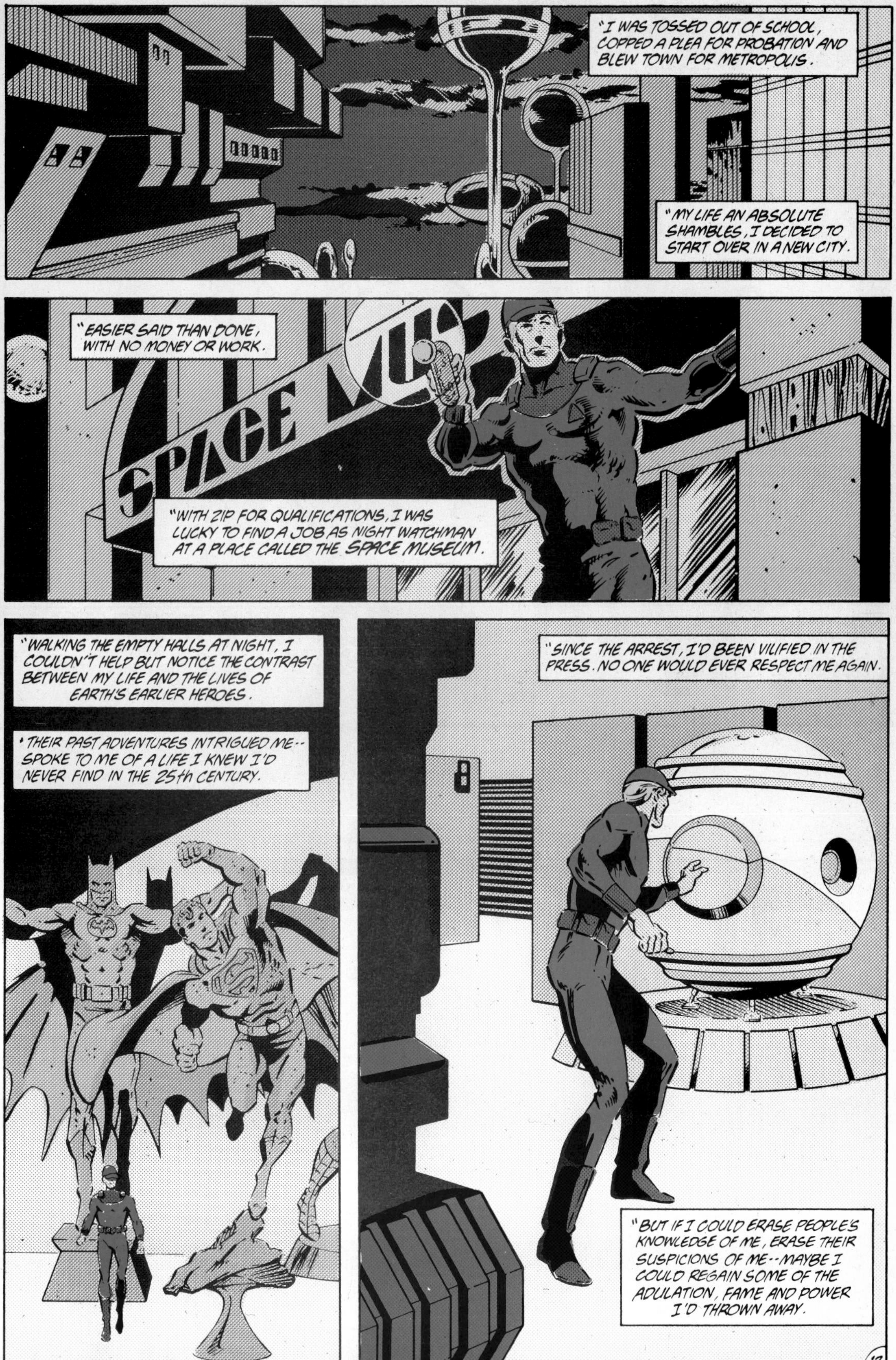
"I WAS TOSSED OUT OF SCHOOL, COPPED A PLEA FOR PROBATION AND BLEW TOWN FOR METROPOLIS.
"MY LIFE AN ABSOLUTE SHAMBLES, I DECIDED TO START OVER IN A NEW CITY.
"EASIER SAID THAN DONE, WITH NO MONEY OR WORK.
"WITH ZIP FOR QUALIFICATIONS, I WAS LUCKY TO FIND A JOB AS NIGHT WATCHMAN AT A PLACE CALLED THE SPACE MUSEUM.
"WALKING THE EMPTY HALLS AT NIGHT, I COULDN'T HELP BUT NOTICE THE CONTRAST BETWEEN MY LIFE AND THE LIVES OF EARTH'S EARLIER HEROES.
"THEIR PAST ADVENTURES INTRIGUED ME--SPOKE TO ME OF A LIFE I KNEW I'D NEVER FIND IN THE 25th CENTURY.
"SINCE THE ARREST, I'D BEEN VILIFIED IN THE PRESS. NO ONE WOULD EVER RESPECT ME AGAIN.
"BUT IF I COULD ERASE PEOPLE'S KNOWLEDGE OF ME, ERASE THEIR SUSPICIONS OF ME--MAYBE I COULD REGAIN SOME OF THE ADULATION, FAME AND POWER I'D THROWN AWAY.
12

"THE CHOICE WAS CLEAR! I WAS GONNA START OVER LIKE NO MAN HAD EVER DONE BEFORE!"

"RIP HUNTER'S ANCIENT TIME MACHINE WOULD BE MY TICKET TO SUCCESS IN THE PAST!"

MICHAEL, YOU ARE IN A RESTRICTED AREA! PLEASE LEAVE, OR I WILL BE FORCED TO MAKE YOU LEAVE!

LISTEN, SKEETS, I'VE LOST EVERYTHING! SWIPING A TIME MACHINE AND HEADING FOR THE 20th CENTURY IS THE PERFECT CURE!

YOU WOULD BE FOOLISH TO JOURNEY INTO THE PAST. OUR HISTORICAL RECORDS OF THAT ERA ARE TERRIBLY INCOMPLETE!

YOU THINK I CARE? ANYTHING'S BETTER THAN THIS!

ONCE I GET THERE, I'M GONNA A BE A RICH, FAMOUS SUPER-HERO! AND SINCE I'LL NEED A LITTLE LOGISTICAL HELP...

CHK

...I'LL BRING YOU WITH ME!

PLEASE! DON'T SHUT ME-- DOWNNN...

CLANG

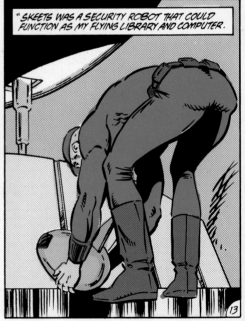

"SKEETS WAS A SECURITY ROBOT THAT COULD FUNCTION AS MY FLYING LIBRARY AND COMPUTER.

13

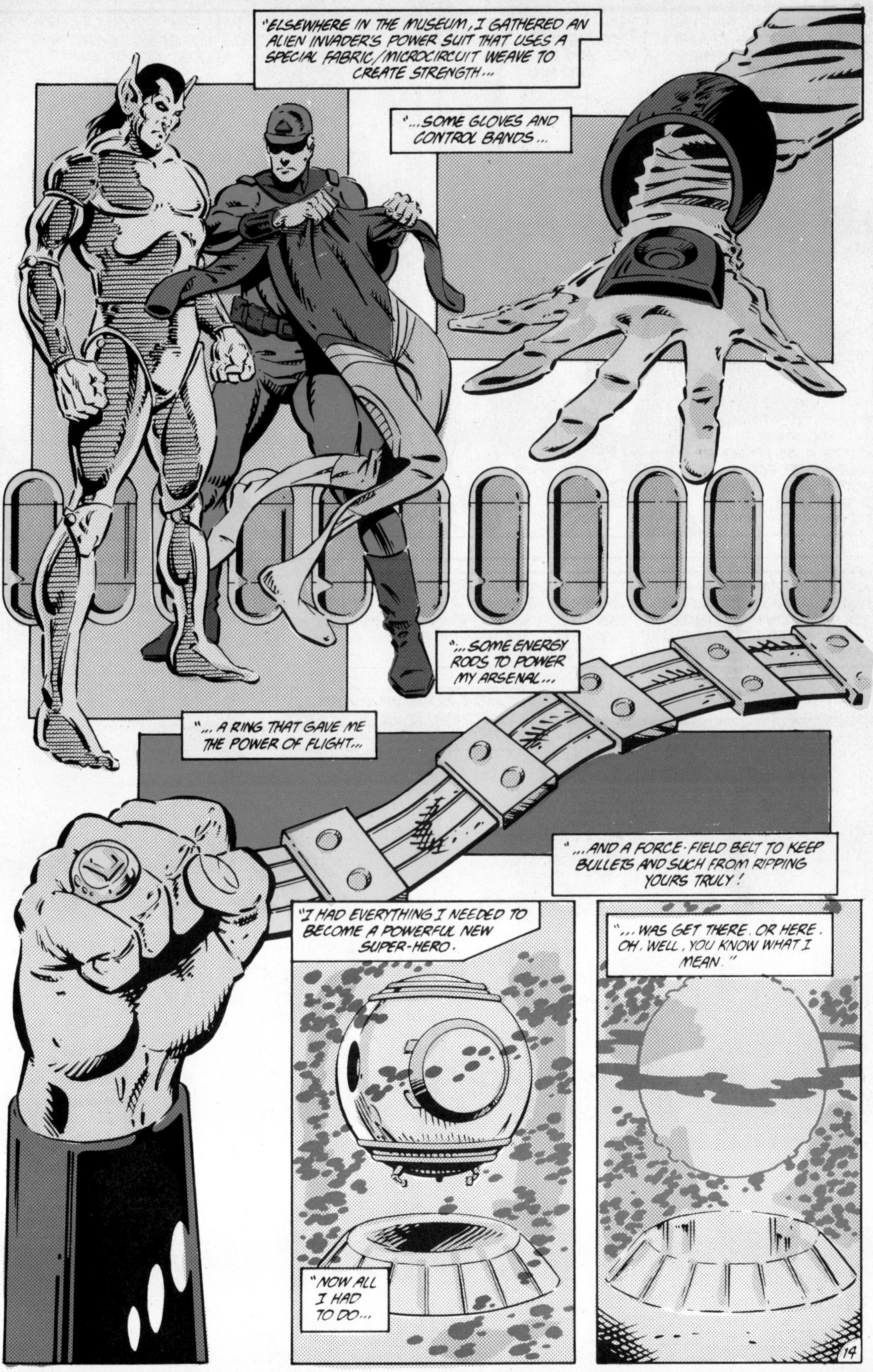
"ELSEWHERE IN THE MUSEUM, I GATHERED AN ALIEN INVADER'S POWER SUIT THAT USES A SPECIAL FABRIC/MICROCIRCUIT WEAVE TO CREATE STRENGTH...
"...SOME GLOVES AND CONTROL BANDS...
"...SOME ENERGY RODS TO POWER MY ARSENAL...
"... A RING THAT GAVE ME THE POWER OF FLIGHT...
"...AND A FORCE-FIELD BELT TO KEEP BULLETS AND SUCH FROM RIPPING YOURS TRULY!
"I HAD EVERYTHING I NEEDED TO BECOME A POWERFUL NEW SUPER-HERO.
"NOW ALL I HAD TO DO...
"...WAS GET THERE. OR HERE. OH, WELL, YOU KNOW WHAT I MEAN."
14

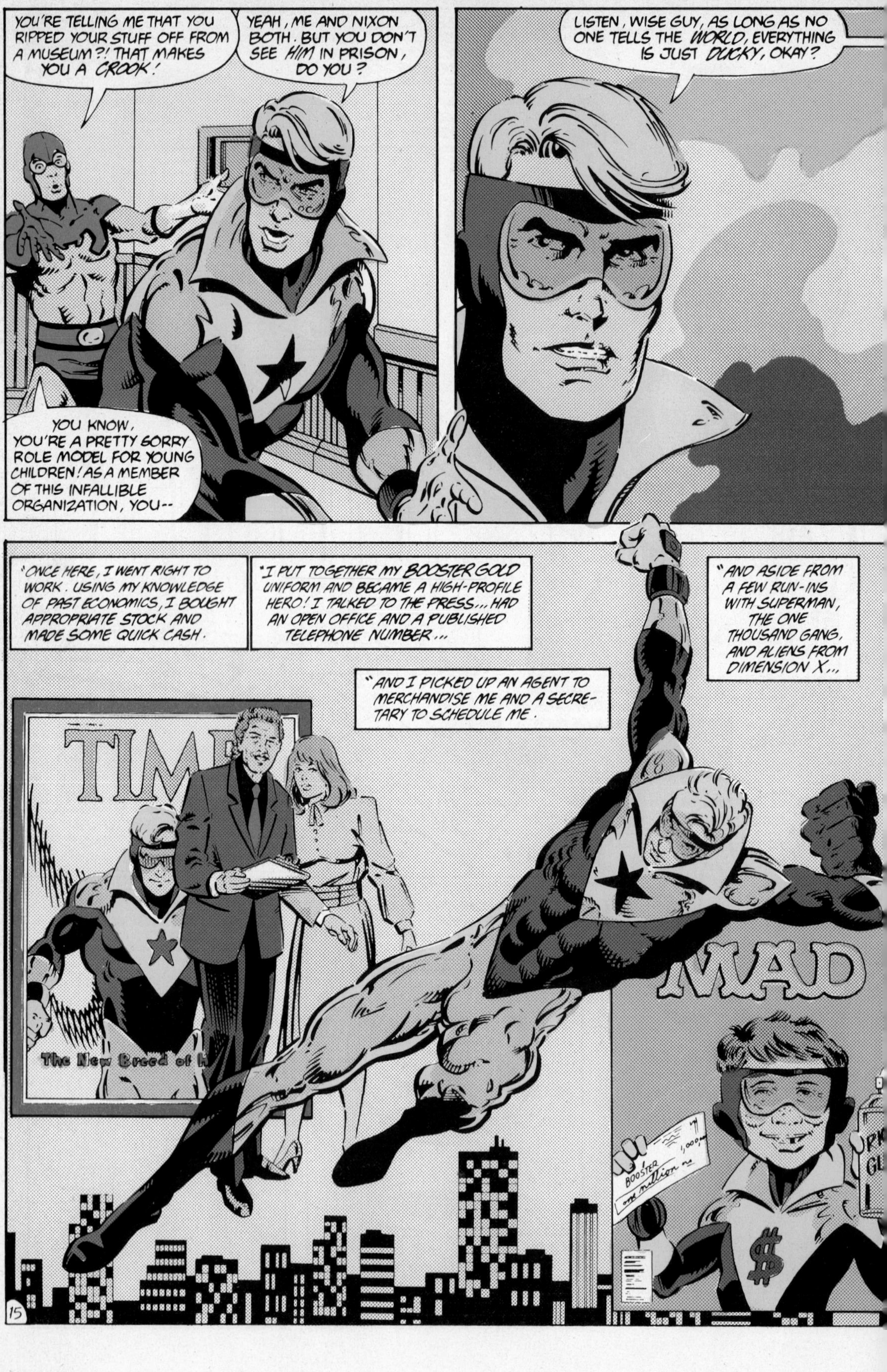
YOU'RE TELLING ME THAT YOU RIPPED YOUR STUFF OFF FROM A MUSEUM?! THAT MAKES YOU A CROOK!
YEAH, ME AND NIXON BOTH. BUT YOU DON'T SEE HIM IN PRISON, DO YOU?
YOU KNOW, YOU'RE A PRETTY SORRY ROLE MODEL FOR YOUNG CHILDREN! AS A MEMBER OF THIS INFALLIBLE ORGANIZATION, YOU--
LISTEN, WISE GUY, AS LONG AS NO ONE TELLS THE WORLD, EVERYTHING IS JUST DUCKY, OKAY?
"ONCE HERE, I WENT RIGHT TO WORK. USING MY KNOWLEDGE OF PAST ECONOMICS, I BOUGHT APPROPRIATE STOCK AND MADE SOME QUICK CASH.
"I PUT TOGETHER MY BOOSTER GOLD UNIFORM AND BECAME A HIGH-PROFILE HERO! I TALKED TO THE PRESS... HAD AN OPEN OFFICE AND A PUBLISHED TELEPHONE NUMBER...
"AND ASIDE FROM A FEW RUN-INS WITH SUPERMAN, THE ONE THOUSAND GANG, AND ALIENS FROM DIMENSION X...
"AND I PICKED UP AN AGENT TO MERCHANDISE ME AND A SECRETARY TO SCHEDULE ME.
TIME
The New Breed of H
MAD
BOOSTER
15

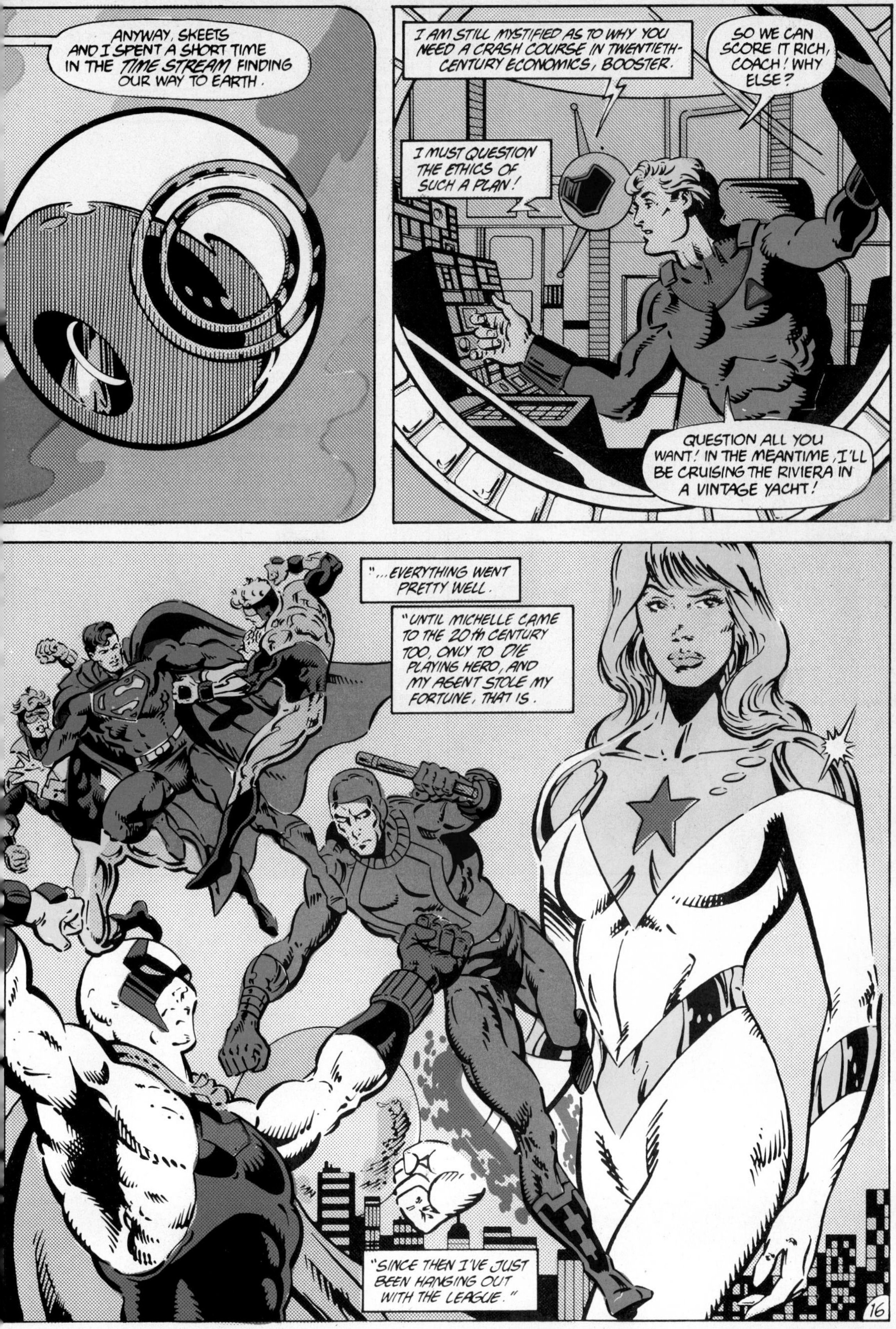
ANYWAY, SKEETS AND I SPENT A SHORT TIME IN THE TIME STREAM FINDING OUR WAY TO EARTH.
I AM STILL MYSTIFIED AS TO WHY YOU NEED A CRASH COURSE IN TWENTIETH-CENTURY ECONOMICS, BOOSTER.
SO WE CAN SCORE IT RICH, COACH! WHY ELSE?
I MUST QUESTION THE ETHICS OF SUCH A PLAN!
QUESTION ALL YOU WANT! IN THE MEANTIME, I'LL BE CRUISING THE RIVIERA IN A VINTAGE YACHT!
"...EVERYTHING WENT PRETTY WELL.
"UNTIL MICHELLE CAME TO THE 20th CENTURY TOO, ONLY TO DIE PLAYING HERO, AND MY AGENT STOLE MY FORTUNE, THAT IS.
"SINCE THEN I'VE JUST BEEN HANGING OUT WITH THE LEAGUE."
16

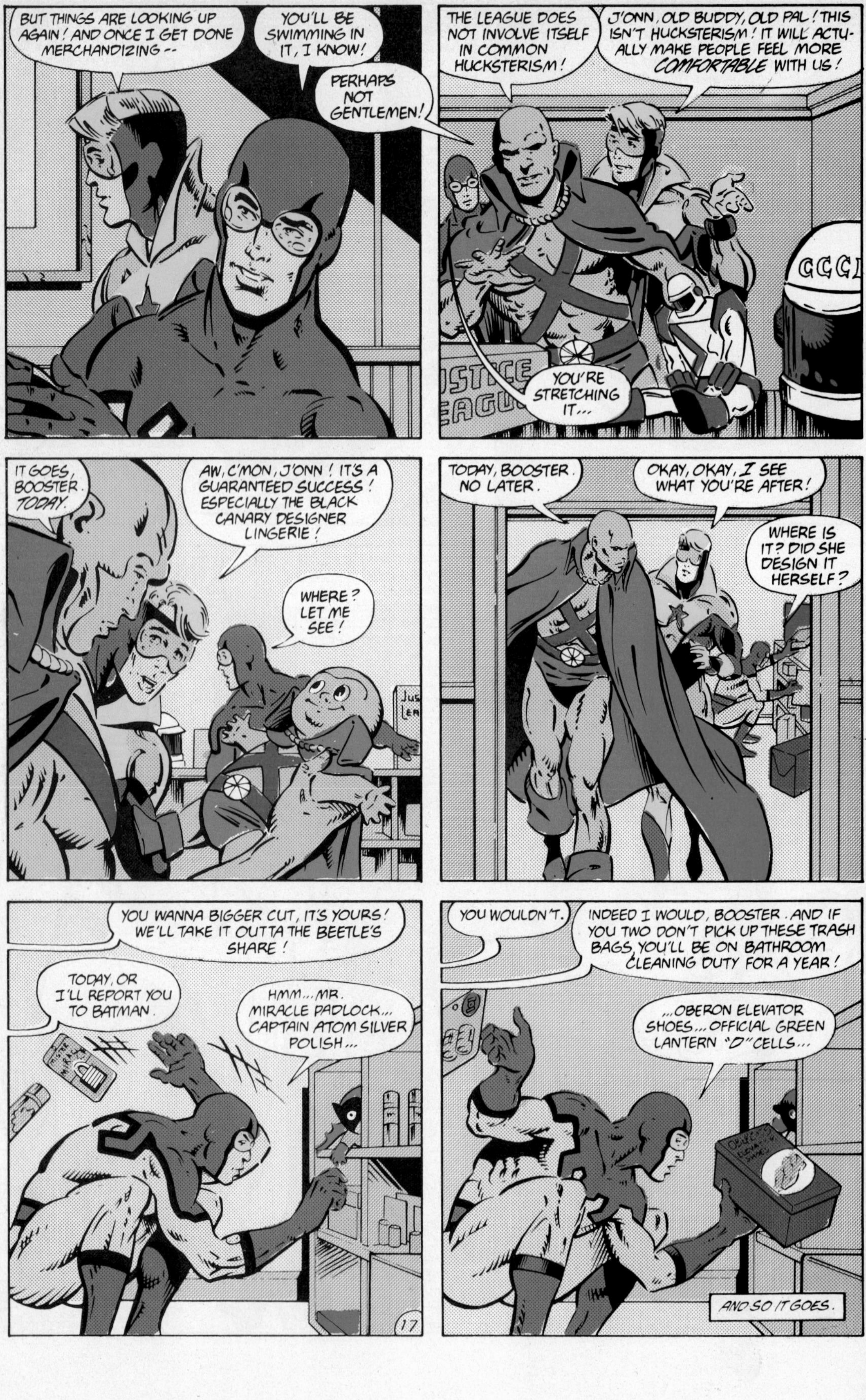
BUT THINGS ARE LOOKING UP AGAIN! AND ONCE I GET DONE MERCHANDIZING --
YOU'LL BE SWIMMING IN IT, I KNOW!
PERHAPS NOT GENTLEMEN!
THE LEAGUE DOES NOT INVOLVE ITSELF IN COMMON HUCKSTERISM!
J'ONN, OLD BUDDY, OLD PAL! THIS ISN'T HUCKSTERISM! IT WILL ACTUALLY MAKE PEOPLE FEEL MORE COMFORTABLE WITH US!
YOU'RE STRETCHING IT...
IT GOES, BOOSTER. TODAY.
AW, C'MON, J'ONN! IT'S A GUARANTEED SUCCESS! ESPECIALLY THE BLACK CANARY DESIGNER LINGERIE!
WHERE? LET ME SEE!
TODAY, BOOSTER. NO LATER.
OKAY, OKAY, I SEE WHAT YOU'RE AFTER!
WHERE IS IT? DID SHE DESIGN IT HERSELF?
YOU WANNA BIGGER CUT, IT'S YOURS! WE'LL TAKE IT OUTTA THE BEETLE'S SHARE!
TODAY, OR I'LL REPORT YOU TO BATMAN.
HMM... MR. MIRACLE PADLOCK... CAPTAIN ATOM SILVER POLISH...
17
YOU WOULDN'T.
INDEED I WOULD, BOOSTER. AND IF YOU TWO DON'T PICK UP THESE TRASH BAGS, YOU'LL BE ON BATHROOM CLEANING DUTY FOR A YEAR!
...OBERON ELEVATOR SHOES... OFFICIAL GREEN LANTERN "D" CELLS...
AND SO IT GOES.

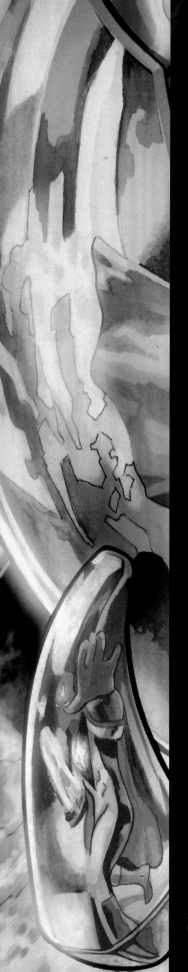

RIP HUNTER: TIME MASTER #6

Until I read the adventures of Rip Hunter, I never knew how many historical events were secretly influenced by alien invaders. I also never wanted my own bathysphere. But now I have one, and I'm sitting in it as I write this. And the water is rising. And the shower door is stuck.

For those of you who grew up familiar with a "DC Universe" where characters meet one another on a regular basis, this will seem bizarre — but DC Comics during the 1960s was a collection of editorial fiefdoms that interacted as little as possible. The idea that Rip, the star of a peripheral book from an even more peripheral fiefdom, would become a core player in a linewide event like 52 and be responsible for the fates of, say, Superman and the Flash was not one-one-millionth as likely or as natural-seeming as it is today. This might make Rip the greatest comeback character of all time.

This rare treat of a story is one of two Rip adventures that were drawn by the legendary Alex Toth, and the only one he completely inked. **—MW**

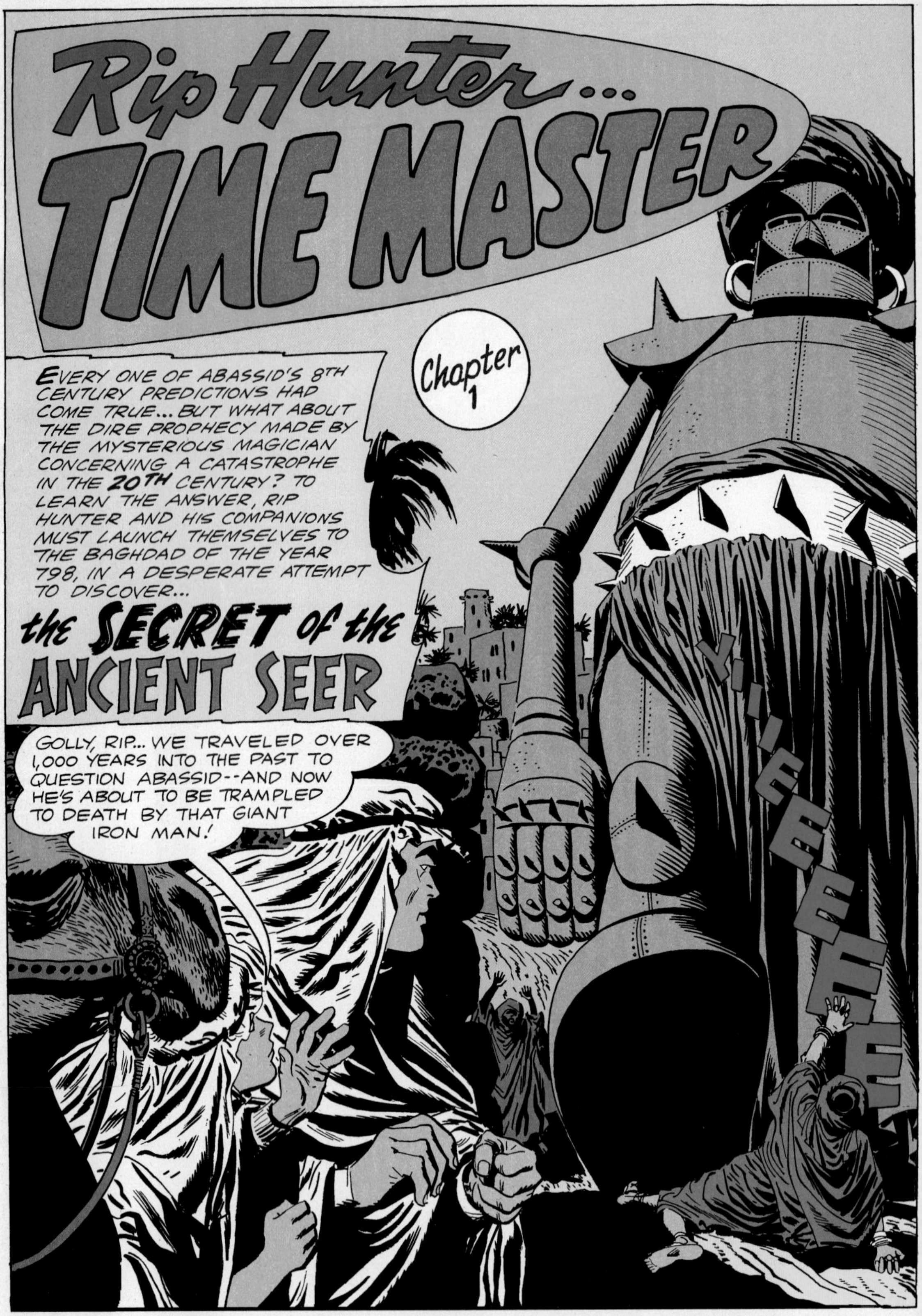
Rip Hunter...
TIME MASTER
Chapter 1
EVERY ONE OF ABASSID'S 8TH CENTURY PREDICTIONS HAD COME TRUE... BUT WHAT ABOUT THE DIRE PROPHECY MADE BY THE MYSTERIOUS MAGICIAN CONCERNING A CATASTROPHE IN THE 20TH CENTURY? TO LEARN THE ANSWER, RIP HUNTER AND HIS COMPANIONS MUST LAUNCH THEMSELVES TO THE BAGHDAD OF THE YEAR 798, IN A DESPERATE ATTEMPT TO DISCOVER...
the SECRET of the ANCIENT SEER
GOLLY, RIP... WE TRAVELED OVER 1,000 YEARS INTO THE PAST TO QUESTION ABASSID--AND NOW HE'S ABOUT TO BE TRAMPLED TO DEATH BY THAT GIANT IRON MAN!
YIIEEEEEEE

WRITER: Jack Miller

ARTIST: Alex Toth

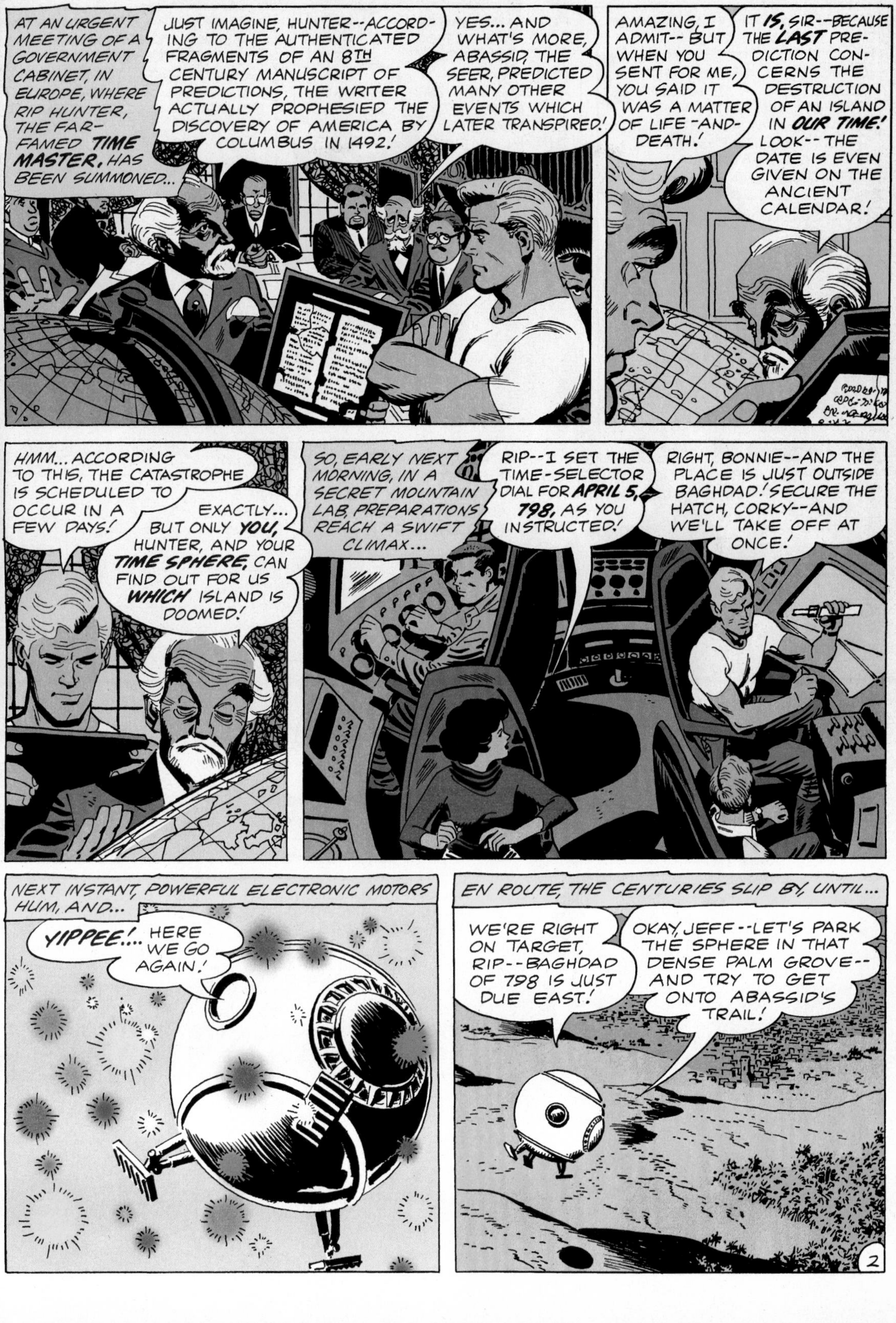
AT AN URGENT MEETING OF A GOVERNMENT CABINET, IN EUROPE, WHERE RIP HUNTER, THE FAR-FAMED TIME MASTER, HAS BEEN SUMMONED...
JUST IMAGINE, HUNTER--ACCORDING TO THE AUTHENTICATED FRAGMENTS OF AN 8TH CENTURY MANUSCRIPT OF PREDICTIONS, THE WRITER ACTUALLY PROPHESIED THE DISCOVERY OF AMERICA BY COLUMBUS IN 1492!
YES... AND WHAT'S MORE, ABASSID, THE SEER, PREDICTED MANY OTHER EVENTS WHICH LATER TRANSPIRED!
AMAZING, I ADMIT-- BUT WHEN YOU SENT FOR ME, YOU SAID IT WAS A MATTER OF LIFE-AND-DEATH!
IT IS, SIR--BECAUSE THE LAST PREDICTION CONCERNS THE DESTRUCTION OF AN ISLAND IN OUR TIME! LOOK-- THE DATE IS EVEN GIVEN ON THE ANCIENT CALENDAR!
HMM... ACCORDING TO THIS, THE CATASTROPHE IS SCHEDULED TO OCCUR IN A FEW DAYS!
EXACTLY... BUT ONLY YOU, HUNTER, AND YOUR TIME SPHERE, CAN FIND OUT FOR US WHICH ISLAND IS DOOMED!
SO, EARLY NEXT MORNING, IN A SECRET MOUNTAIN LAB, PREPARATIONS REACH A SWIFT CLIMAX...
RIP--I SET THE TIME-SELECTOR DIAL FOR APRIL 5, 798, AS YOU INSTRUCTED!
RIGHT, BONNIE--AND THE PLACE IS JUST OUTSIDE BAGHDAD! SECURE THE HATCH, CORKY--AND WE'LL TAKE OFF AT ONCE!
NEXT INSTANT, POWERFUL ELECTRONIC MOTORS HUM, AND...
YIPPEE!... HERE WE GO AGAIN!
EN ROUTE, THE CENTURIES SLIP BY, UNTIL...
WE'RE RIGHT ON TARGET, RIP--BAGHDAD OF 798 IS JUST DUE EAST!
OKAY, JEFF--LET'S PARK THE SPHERE IN THAT DENSE PALM GROVE--AND TRY TO GET ONTO ABASSID'S TRAIL!
2

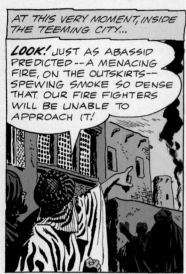

AT THIS VERY MOMENT, INSIDE THE TEEMING CITY...

LOOK! JUST AS ABASSID PREDICTED--A MENACING FIRE, ON THE OUTSKIRTS--SPEWING SMOKE SO DENSE THAT OUR FIRE FIGHTERS WILL BE UNABLE TO APPROACH IT!

FEAR NOT...ABASSID ALSO PREDICTED THAT A GIANT IRON MAN WOULD APPEAR OUT OF THE NORTH, TO EXTINGUISH THE FLAMES!

A--A GIANT IRON MAN? CAN SUCH A THING REALLY BE?

NOT FAR AWAY, THE QUESTION IS ABOUT TO BE ANSWERED...

GOLLY! WHAT KIND OF A--A BEING IS THAT, RIP?

DON'T KNOW, CORKY--BUT I INTEND TO FIND OUT...

AS THEY APPROACH THE LUMBERING IRON GIANT, HOWEVER...

AFTER THE STRANGERS! THEY HAVE NOT HEEDED THE WARNING TO STAY AWAY FROM THE IRON MAN WHO COMES TO RESCUE US!

OH, OH... I'LL NEED MY KNIFE TO HANDLE THIS!

THE TIME MASTER HURLS HIS KNIFE WITH UNERRING AIM, SO THAT...

SNAP

NICE WORK, RIP! YOU CUT LOOSE THOSE CAMELS--AND THEY'RE BLOCKING OUR PURSUERS!

YES--BUT OUR PATH BACK TO THE TIME SPHERE IS CUT OFF, TOO! HEAD FOR THE CITY!

3

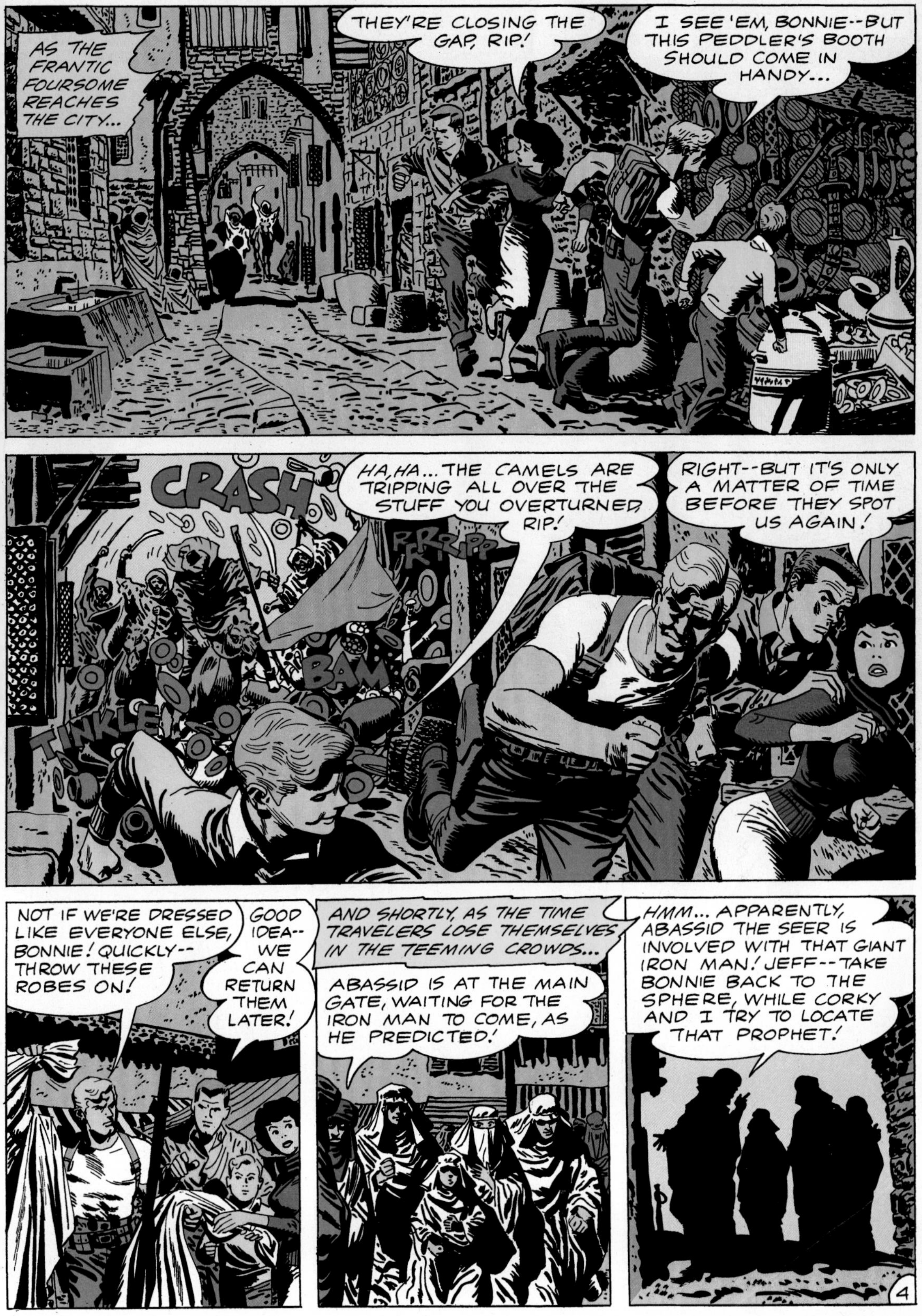
AS THE FRANTIC FOURSOME REACHES THE CITY...
THEY'RE CLOSING THE GAP, RIP!
I SEE 'EM, BONNIE--BUT THIS PEDDLER'S BOOTH SHOULD COME IN HANDY...
CRASH
HA,HA... THE CAMELS ARE TRIPPING ALL OVER THE STUFF YOU OVERTURNED, RIP!
RIGHT--BUT IT'S ONLY A MATTER OF TIME BEFORE THEY SPOT US AGAIN!
RRRRIPP
BAM
TINKLE
NOT IF WE'RE DRESSED LIKE EVERYONE ELSE, BONNIE! QUICKLY-- THROW THESE ROBES ON!
GOOD IDEA-- WE CAN RETURN THEM LATER!
AND SHORTLY, AS THE TIME TRAVELERS LOSE THEMSELVES IN THE TEEMING CROWDS...
ABASSID IS AT THE MAIN GATE, WAITING FOR THE IRON MAN TO COME, AS HE PREDICTED!
HMM... APPARENTLY, ABASSID THE SEER IS INVOLVED WITH THAT GIANT IRON MAN! JEFF--TAKE BONNIE BACK TO THE SPHERE, WHILE CORKY AND I TRY TO LOCATE THAT PROPHET!
4

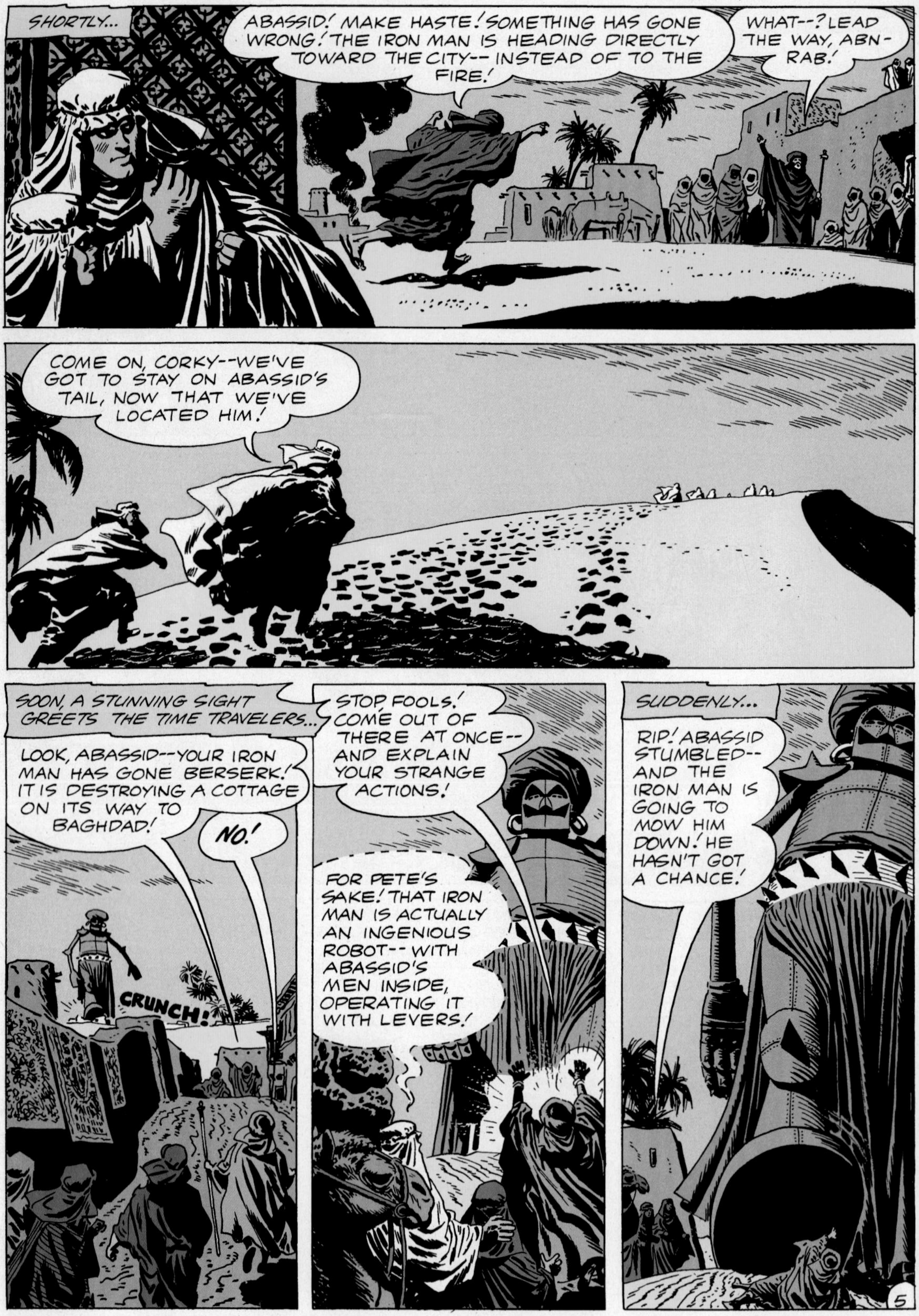
SHORTLY...
ABASSID! MAKE HASTE! SOMETHING HAS GONE WRONG! THE IRON MAN IS HEADING DIRECTLY TOWARD THE CITY-- INSTEAD OF TO THE FIRE!
WHAT--? LEAD THE WAY, ABN-RAB!
COME ON, CORKY--WE'VE GOT TO STAY ON ABASSID'S TAIL, NOW THAT WE'VE LOCATED HIM!
SOON, A STUNNING SIGHT GREETS THE TIME TRAVELERS...
LOOK, ABASSID--YOUR IRON MAN HAS GONE BERSERK! IT IS DESTROYING A COTTAGE ON ITS WAY TO BAGHDAD!
NO!
CRUNCH!
STOP, FOOLS! COME OUT OF THERE AT ONCE-- AND EXPLAIN YOUR STRANGE ACTIONS!
FOR PETE'S SAKE! THAT IRON MAN IS ACTUALLY AN INGENIOUS ROBOT-- WITH ABASSID'S MEN INSIDE, OPERATING IT WITH LEVERS!
SUDDENLY...
RIP! ABASSID STUMBLED-- AND THE IRON MAN IS GOING TO MOW HIM DOWN! HE HASN'T GOT A CHANCE!
5

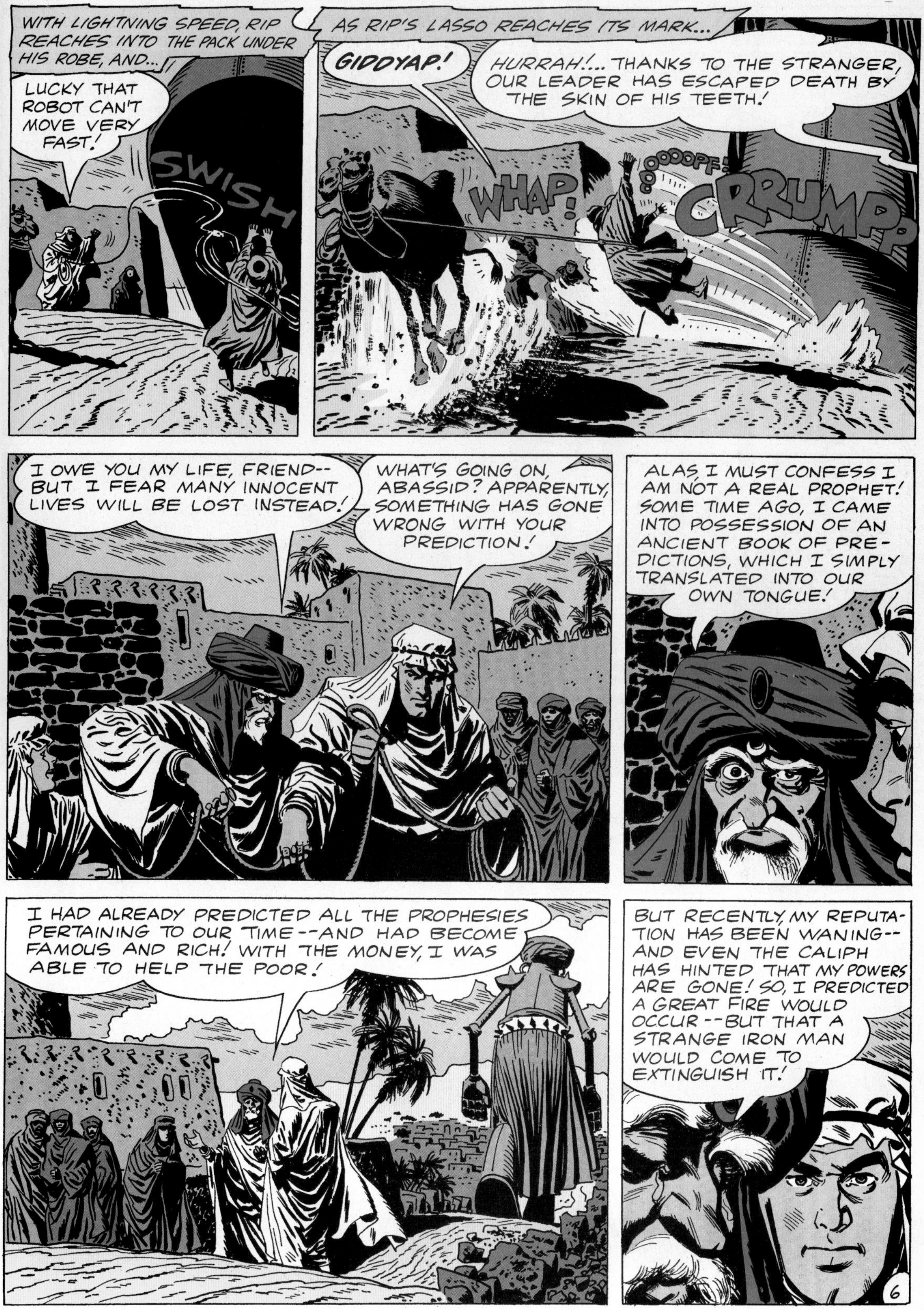
WITH LIGHTNING SPEED, RIP REACHES INTO THE PACK UNDER HIS ROBE, AND...
LUCKY THAT ROBOT CAN'T MOVE VERY FAST!
SWISH
AS RIP'S LASSO REACHES ITS MARK...
GIDDYAP!
HURRAH!... THANKS TO THE STRANGER, OUR LEADER HAS ESCAPED DEATH BY THE SKIN OF HIS TEETH!
WHAP!
OOOOOPF!
CRRUMP!
I OWE YOU MY LIFE, FRIEND-- BUT I FEAR MANY INNOCENT LIVES WILL BE LOST INSTEAD!
WHAT'S GOING ON, ABASSID? APPARENTLY, SOMETHING HAS GONE WRONG WITH YOUR PREDICTION!
ALAS, I MUST CONFESS I AM NOT A REAL PROPHET! SOME TIME AGO, I CAME INTO POSSESSION OF AN ANCIENT BOOK OF PREDICTIONS, WHICH I SIMPLY TRANSLATED INTO OUR OWN TONGUE!
I HAD ALREADY PREDICTED ALL THE PROPHESIES PERTAINING TO OUR TIME--AND HAD BECOME FAMOUS AND RICH! WITH THE MONEY, I WAS ABLE TO HELP THE POOR!
BUT RECENTLY, MY REPUTATION HAS BEEN WANING-- AND EVEN THE CALIPH HAS HINTED THAT MY POWERS ARE GONE! SO, I PREDICTED A GREAT FIRE WOULD OCCUR--BUT THAT A STRANGE IRON MAN WOULD COME TO EXTINGUISH IT!
6

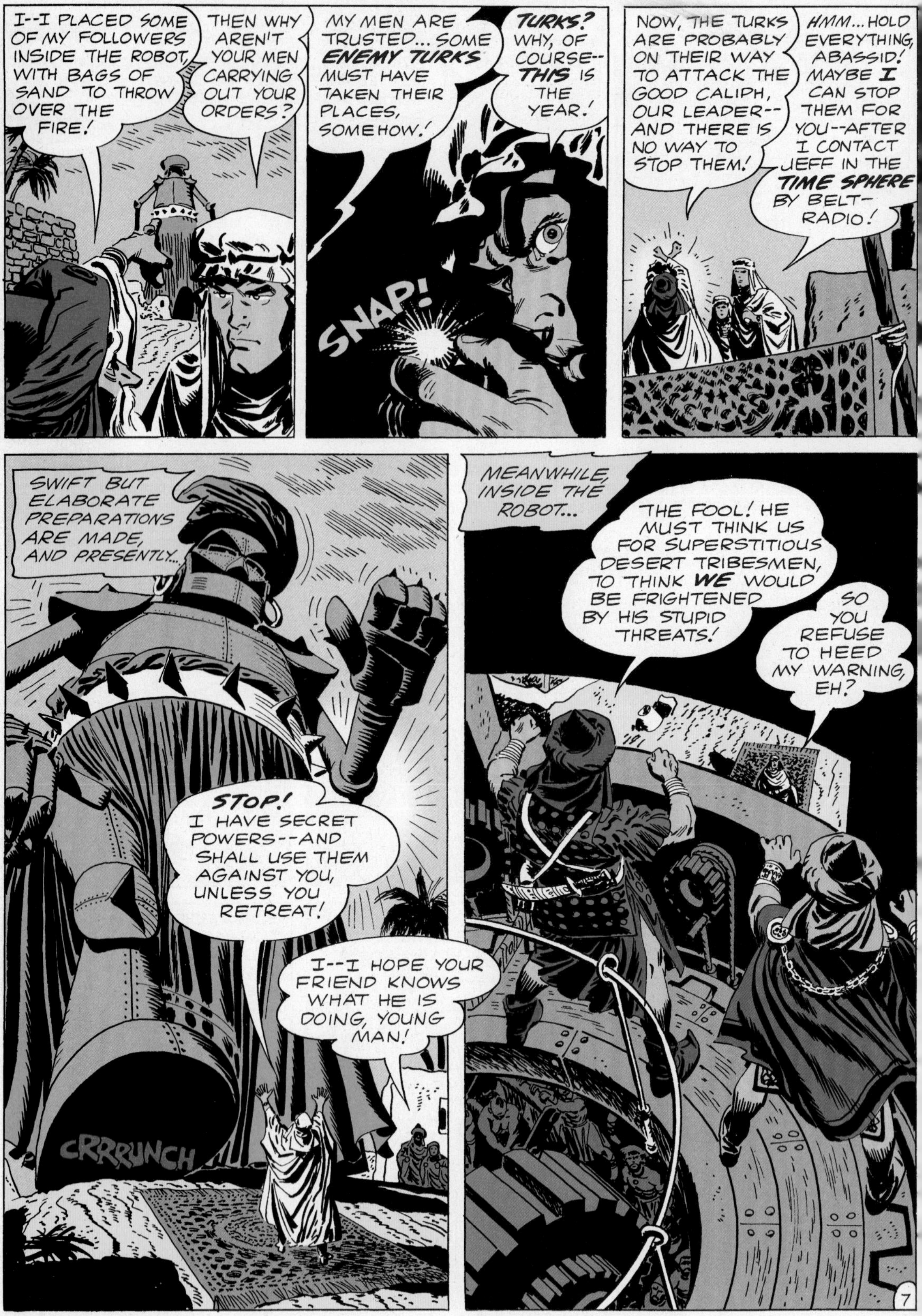
I--I PLACED SOME OF MY FOLLOWERS INSIDE THE ROBOT, WITH BAGS OF SAND TO THROW OVER THE FIRE!
THEN WHY AREN'T YOUR MEN CARRYING OUT YOUR ORDERS?
MY MEN ARE TRUSTED... SOME ENEMY TURKS MUST HAVE TAKEN THEIR PLACES, SOMEHOW!
TURKS? WHY, OF COURSE-- THIS IS THE YEAR!
SNAP!
NOW, THE TURKS ARE PROBABLY ON THEIR WAY TO ATTACK THE GOOD CALIPH, OUR LEADER-- AND THERE IS NO WAY TO STOP THEM!
HMM... HOLD EVERYTHING, ABASSID! MAYBE I CAN STOP THEM FOR YOU--AFTER I CONTACT JEFF IN THE TIME SPHERE BY BELT-RADIO!
SWIFT BUT ELABORATE PREPARATIONS ARE MADE, AND PRESENTLY...
STOP! I HAVE SECRET POWERS--AND SHALL USE THEM AGAINST YOU, UNLESS YOU RETREAT!
I--I HOPE YOUR FRIEND KNOWS WHAT HE IS DOING, YOUNG MAN!
CRRRUNCH
MEANWHILE, INSIDE THE ROBOT...
THE FOOL! HE MUST THINK US FOR SUPERSTITIOUS DESERT TRIBESMEN, TO THINK WE WOULD BE FRIGHTENED BY HIS STUPID THREATS!
SO YOU REFUSE TO HEED MY WARNING, EH?
7

IN THE NEXT AWESOME MOMENT...

GREAT GODS OF AVAR-- HE *IS* A MAN OF MYSTERIOUS POWERS! SEE?... HE FLIES ON A *MAGIC CARPET!*

FLEE! FLEE!

HA, HA! CLEVER OF RIP, ATTACHING THIN WIRES TO THE *TIME SPHERE,* WHICH JEFF IS MANEUVERING IN THOSE DENSE CLOUDS -- TURNING THE "MAGIC CARPET" INTO A GLIDER!

SHORTLY AFTER...

ABASSID! GOOD NEWS! OUR OWN MEN, WHOSE PLACES THE TURKS TOOK, WERE DISCOVERED BOUND AND GAGGED-- BUT WELL!

YES-- BUT THE FIRE IS NOW OUT OF CONTROL, AND THERE IS NOT ENOUGH SAND INSIDE THE IRON MAN TO STOP THE BLAZE FROM SPREADING INTO THE CITY!

MAYBE I CAN HELP THE REST OF YOUR PREDICTION COME TRUE, TOO, ABASSID! JEFF--HOP ON THAT CAMEL, AND RACE BACK TO THE SPHERE! THIS IS WHAT I PLAN...

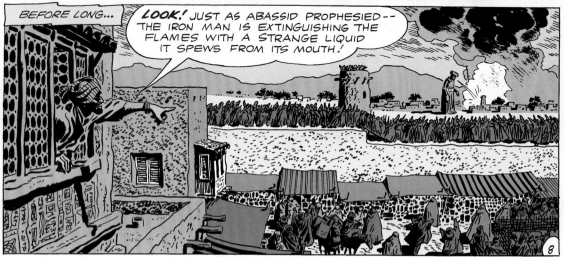

BEFORE LONG...

LOOK! JUST AS ABASSID PROPHESIED-- THE IRON MAN IS EXTINGUISHING THE FLAMES WITH A STRANGE LIQUID IT SPEWS FROM ITS MOUTH!

8

I WONDER WHAT THEY'D THINK IF THEY KNEW THE FIRE WAS BEING SNUFFED OUT WITH A COUPLE OF *20TH CENTURY FIRE EXTINGUISHERS*, RIP!

YOU SAID IT, CORKY! AFTER WE LEAVE, WE'LL HAVE TO GET RID OF THIS ROBOT FOR ABASSID!

LATER...

HOW CAN I THANK YOU FOR WHAT YOU HAVE DONE, MY FRIENDS?

EASY, ABASSID -- LET ME TAKE A CLOSE LOOK AT THE BOOK OF PREDICTIONS RELATING TO THE CATASTROPHE IN MY OWN TIME!

B-BUT... THE PAGES I RECEIVED DID NOT CONTAIN ANY PREDICTIONS ABOUT THE 20TH CENTURY!

OH, NO! WE'RE RIGHT BACK WHERE WE STARTED FROM!

9

CONTINUED IN CHAPTER 2

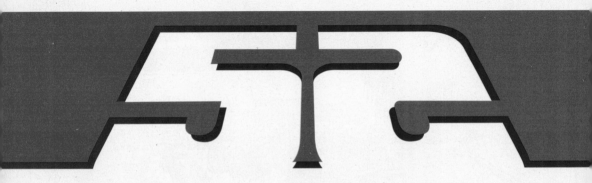

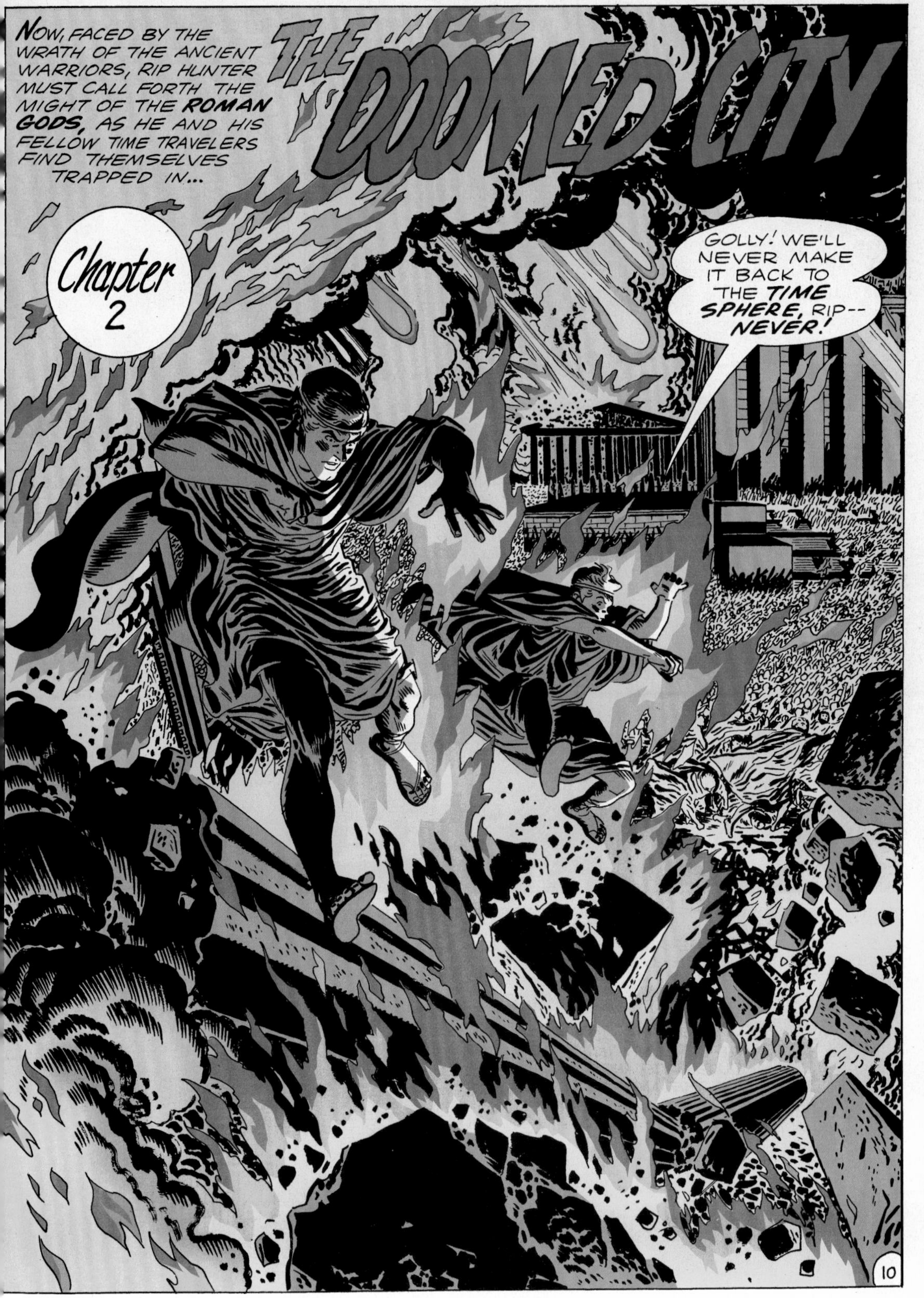
NOW, FACED BY THE WRATH OF THE ANCIENT WARRIORS, RIP HUNTER MUST CALL FORTH THE MIGHT OF THE **ROMAN GODS**, AS HE AND HIS FELLOW TIME TRAVELERS FIND THEMSELVES TRAPPED IN...
THE DOOMED CITY
Chapter 2
GOLLY! WE'LL NEVER MAKE IT BACK TO THE **TIME SPHERE**, RIP-- **NEVER!**
10

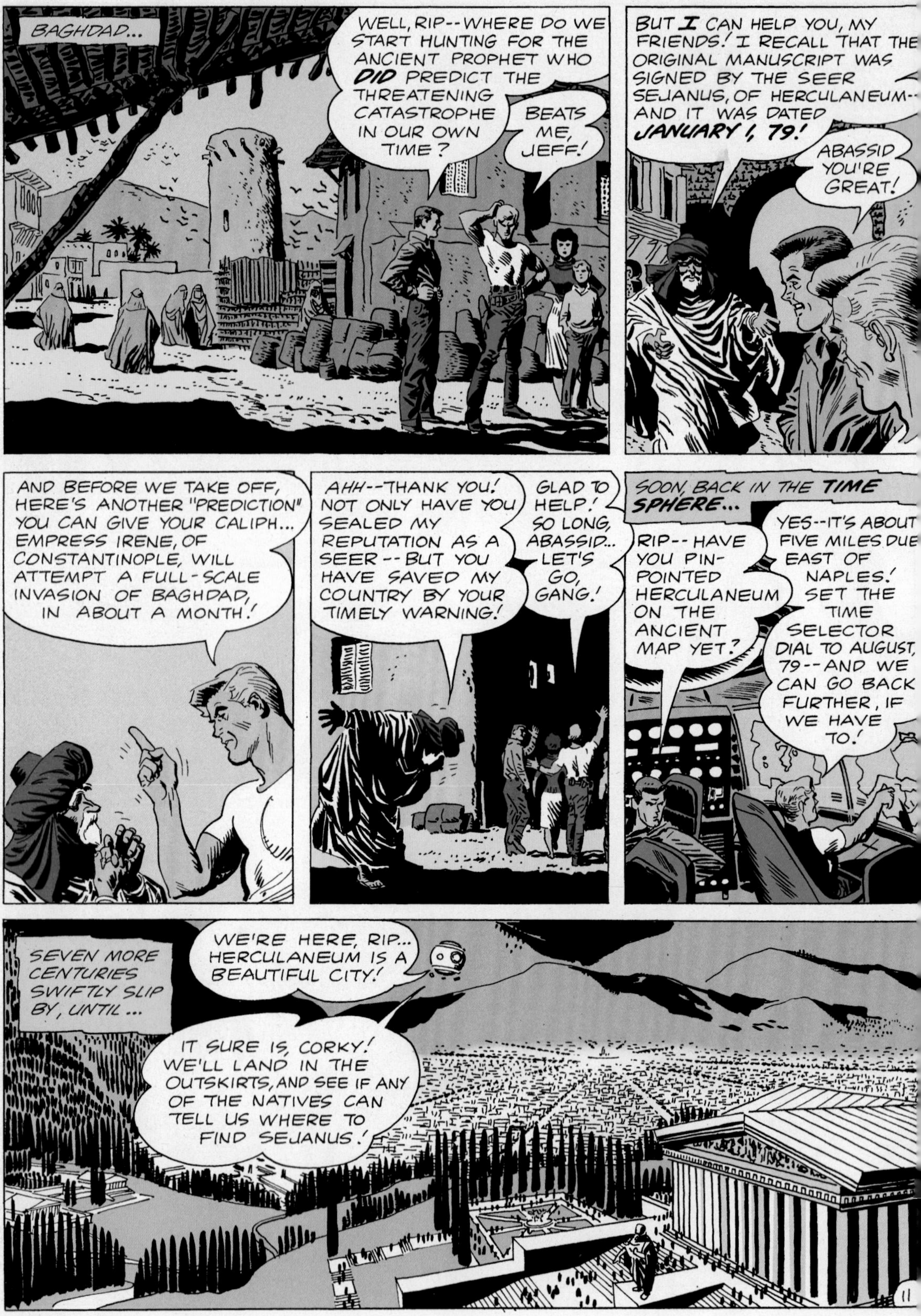
BAGHDAD...
WELL, RIP--WHERE DO WE START HUNTING FOR THE ANCIENT PROPHET WHO DID PREDICT THE THREATENING CATASTROPHE IN OUR OWN TIME?
BEATS ME, JEFF!
BUT I CAN HELP YOU, MY FRIENDS! I RECALL THAT THE ORIGINAL MANUSCRIPT WAS SIGNED BY THE SEER SEJANUS, OF HERCULANEUM--AND IT WAS DATED JANUARY 1, 79!
ABASSID YOU'RE GREAT!
AND BEFORE WE TAKE OFF, HERE'S ANOTHER "PREDICTION" YOU CAN GIVE YOUR CALIPH... EMPRESS IRENE, OF CONSTANTINOPLE, WILL ATTEMPT A FULL-SCALE INVASION OF BAGHDAD, IN ABOUT A MONTH!
AHH--THANK YOU! NOT ONLY HAVE YOU SEALED MY REPUTATION AS A SEER--BUT YOU HAVE SAVED MY COUNTRY BY YOUR TIMELY WARNING!
GLAD TO HELP! SO LONG, ABASSID... LET'S GO, GANG!
SOON, BACK IN THE TIME SPHERE...
RIP--HAVE YOU PIN-POINTED HERCULANEUM ON THE ANCIENT MAP YET?
YES--IT'S ABOUT FIVE MILES DUE EAST OF NAPLES! SET THE TIME SELECTOR DIAL TO AUGUST, 79--AND WE CAN GO BACK FURTHER, IF WE HAVE TO!
SEVEN MORE CENTURIES SWIFTLY SLIP BY, UNTIL...
WE'RE HERE, RIP... HERCULANEUM IS A BEAUTIFUL CITY!
IT SURE IS, CORKY! WE'LL LAND IN THE OUTSKIRTS, AND SEE IF ANY OF THE NATIVES CAN TELL US WHERE TO FIND SEJANUS!
11

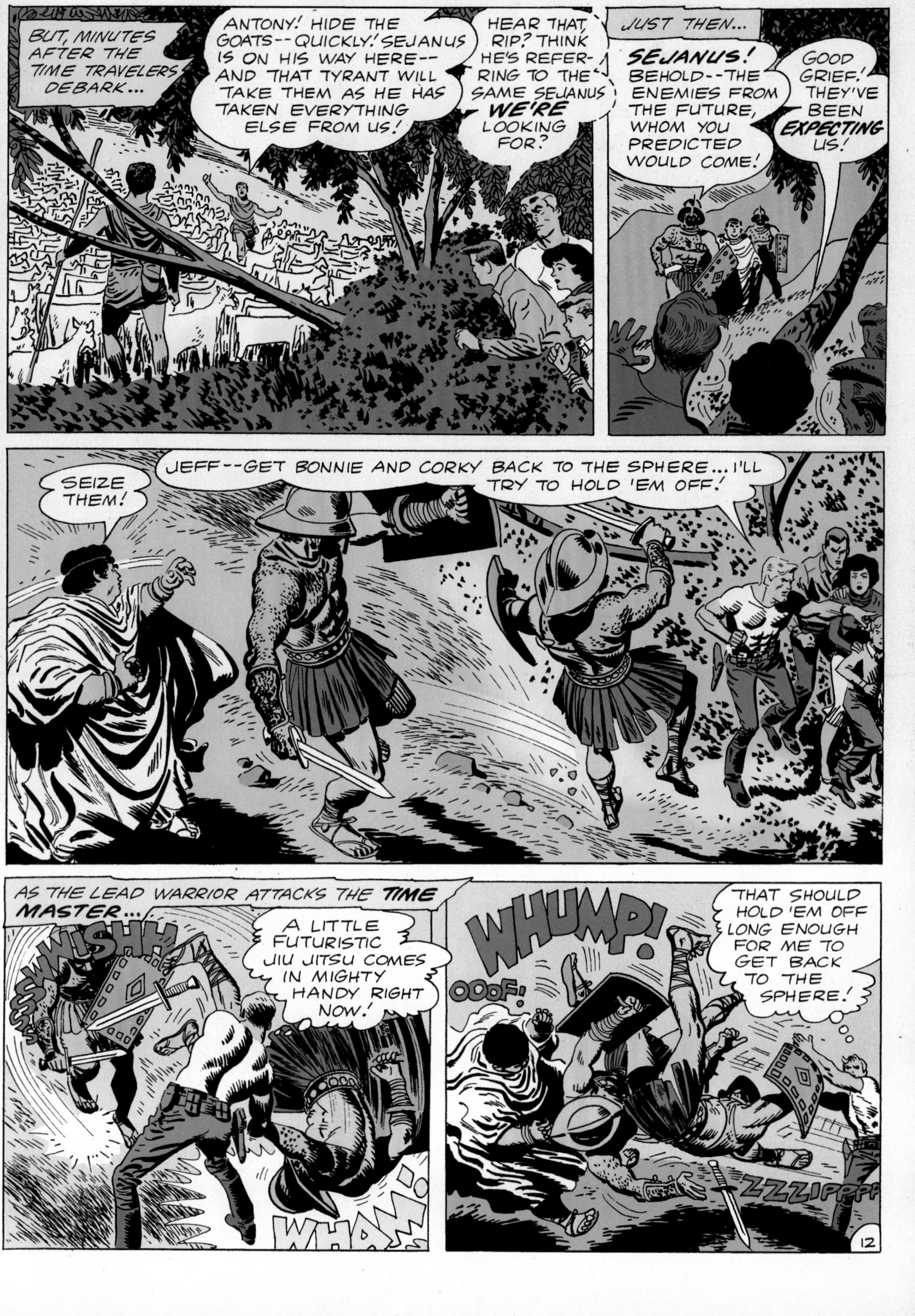
BUT, MINUTES AFTER THE TIME TRAVELERS DEBARK...
ANTONY! HIDE THE GOATS--QUICKLY! SEJANUS IS ON HIS WAY HERE--AND THAT TYRANT WILL TAKE THEM AS HE HAS TAKEN EVERYTHING ELSE FROM US!
HEAR THAT, RIP? THINK HE'S REFERRING TO THE SAME SEJANUS **WE'RE** LOOKING FOR?
JUST THEN...
SEJANUS! BEHOLD--THE ENEMIES FROM THE FUTURE, WHOM YOU PREDICTED WOULD COME!
GOOD GRIEF! THEY'VE BEEN **EXPECTING** US!
SEIZE THEM!
JEFF--GET BONNIE AND CORKY BACK TO THE SPHERE... I'LL TRY TO HOLD 'EM OFF!
AS THE LEAD WARRIOR ATTACKS THE **TIME MASTER**...
A LITTLE FUTURISTIC JIU JITSU COMES IN MIGHTY HANDY RIGHT NOW!
WHUMP!
OOOF!
THAT SHOULD HOLD 'EM OFF LONG ENOUGH FOR ME TO GET BACK TO THE SPHERE!
12

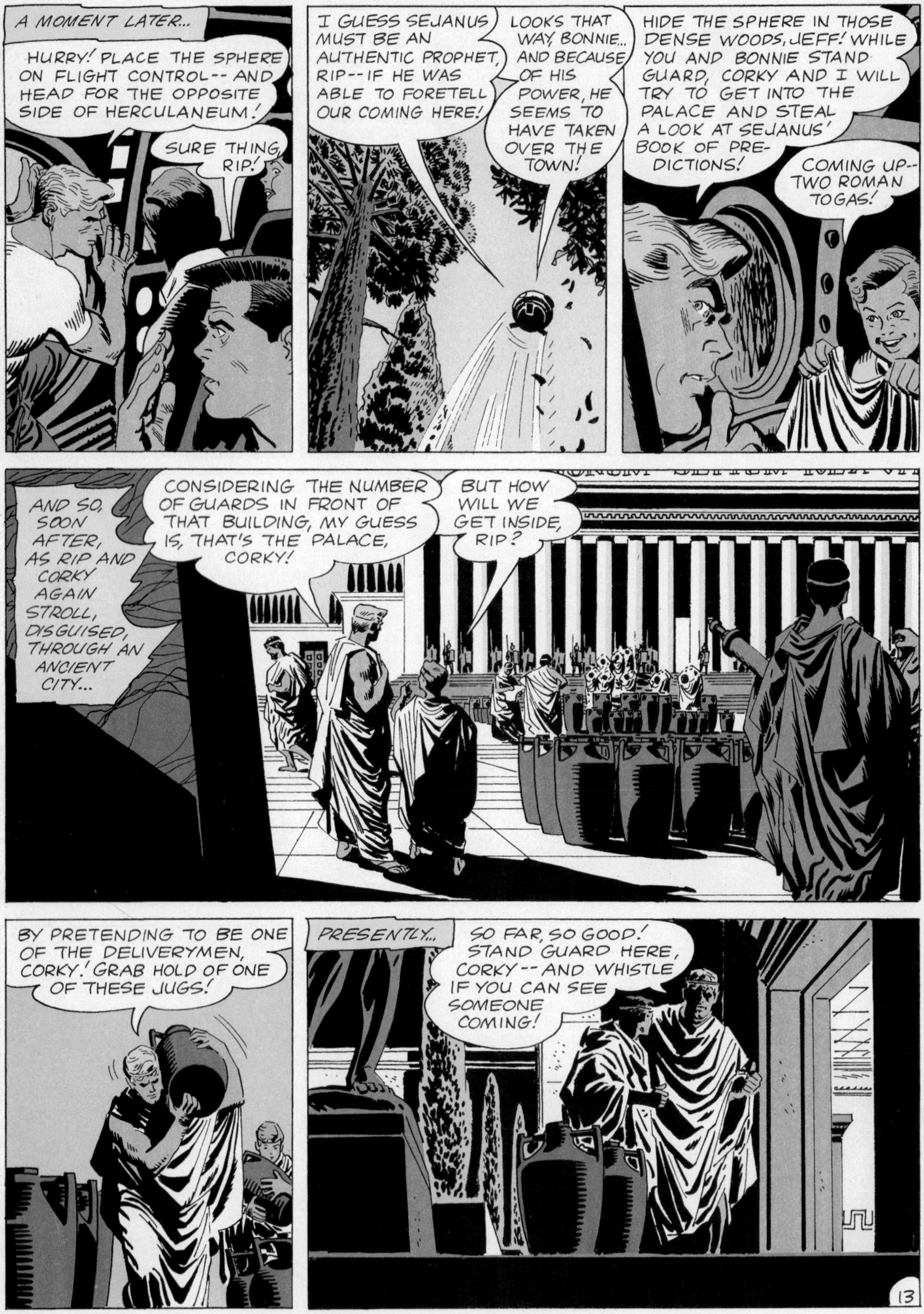
A MOMENT LATER...
HURRY! PLACE THE SPHERE ON FLIGHT CONTROL-- AND HEAD FOR THE OPPOSITE SIDE OF HERCULANEUM!
SURE THING, RIP!
I GUESS SEJANUS MUST BE AN AUTHENTIC PROPHET, RIP--IF HE WAS ABLE TO FORETELL OUR COMING HERE!
LOOKS THAT WAY, BONNIE... AND BECAUSE OF HIS POWER, HE SEEMS TO HAVE TAKEN OVER THE TOWN!
HIDE THE SPHERE IN THOSE DENSE WOODS, JEFF! WHILE YOU AND BONNIE STAND GUARD, CORKY AND I WILL TRY TO GET INTO THE PALACE AND STEAL A LOOK AT SEJANUS' BOOK OF PREDICTIONS!
COMING UP-- TWO ROMAN TOGAS!
AND SO, SOON AFTER, AS RIP AND CORKY AGAIN STROLL, DISGUISED, THROUGH AN ANCIENT CITY...
CONSIDERING THE NUMBER OF GUARDS IN FRONT OF THAT BUILDING, MY GUESS IS, THAT'S THE PALACE, CORKY!
BUT HOW WILL WE GET INSIDE, RIP?
BY PRETENDING TO BE ONE OF THE DELIVERYMEN, CORKY! GRAB HOLD OF ONE OF THESE JUGS!
PRESENTLY...
SO FAR, SO GOOD! STAND GUARD HERE, CORKY -- AND WHISTLE IF YOU CAN SEE SOMEONE COMING!
13

INSIDE, RIP SOON STRIKES PAYDIRT...

HERE IT IS--THE BOOK OF PREDICTIONS... AND HERE'S AN ACCOUNT OF THE CATASTROPHE THAT'S SCHEDULED TO OCCUR IN *OUR* TIME!

SPELLBOUND, HE SCANS THE ANCIENT LINES, UNTIL...

GREAT THUNDER! HIDDEN BETWEEN THE PAGES, A--A COIN DATED *2025!* H-HOW DID *THIS* GET HERE?

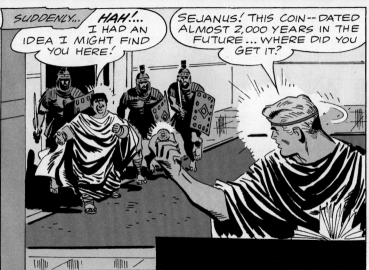

SUDDENLY... *HAH!*... I HAD AN IDEA I MIGHT FIND YOU HERE!

SEJANUS! THIS COIN--DATED ALMOST 2,000 YEARS IN THE FUTURE... WHERE DID YOU GET IT?

SINCE YOU WILL NOT BE ALIVE TO EXPOSE ME, I DON'T MIND REVEALING THE SECRET OF THE PROPHESIES! YOU SEE, YOU ARE NOT THE *ONLY* MAN FROM THE FUTURE TO VISIT HERCULANEUM!

"IN THE FIRST MONTH OF THE YEAR, MY MEN BROUGHT TO ME A STRANGE PRISONER THEY HAD CAPTURED..."

SEJANUS--HE EMERGED FROM A FANTASTIC SPHERE THAT MATERIAL-IZED OUT OF NOWHERE!

YOU DO NOT UNDER-STAND! I AM FROM THE FUTURE-- FROM THE YEAR *2025!*

"I FORCED THE PRISONER TO EMPTY HIS POCKETS, AND..."

HMM... HE IS TELLING THE TRUTH! THIS COIN BEARS THE DATE 2025!

SHALL WE RELEASE HIM THEN, SEJANUS?

14

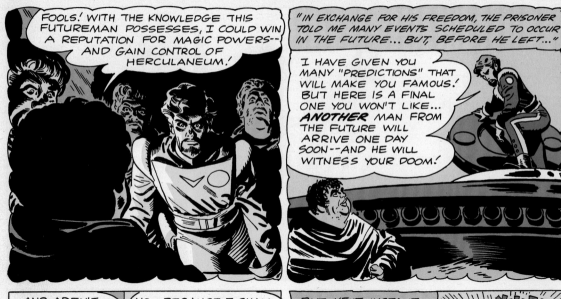

FOOLS! WITH THE KNOWLEDGE THIS FUTUREMAN POSSESSES, I COULD WIN A REPUTATION FOR MAGIC POWERS-- AND GAIN CONTROL OF HERCULANEUM!

"IN EXCHANGE FOR HIS FREEDOM, THE PRISONER TOLD ME MANY EVENTS SCHEDULED TO OCCUR IN THE FUTURE... BUT, BEFORE HE LEFT..."

I HAVE GIVEN YOU MANY "PREDICTIONS" THAT WILL MAKE YOU FAMOUS! BUT HERE IS A FINAL ONE YOU WON'T LIKE... *ANOTHER* MAN FROM THE FUTURE WILL ARRIVE ONE DAY SOON--AND HE WILL WITNESS YOUR DOOM!

AND AREN'T YOU WORRIED ABOUT THAT FINAL "PRE-DICTION", SEJANUS?

NO--BECAUSE I SHALL DESTROY YOU BEFORE ANYTHING CAN HAPPEN TO ME! SEIZE HIM!

BUT, NEXT INSTANT...

MAKE A BREAK FOR IT, RIP!

GOOD WORK, CORKY!

YIIEEE!

KAWAP!

ON THE DOUBLE -- BACK TO THE SPHERE!

15

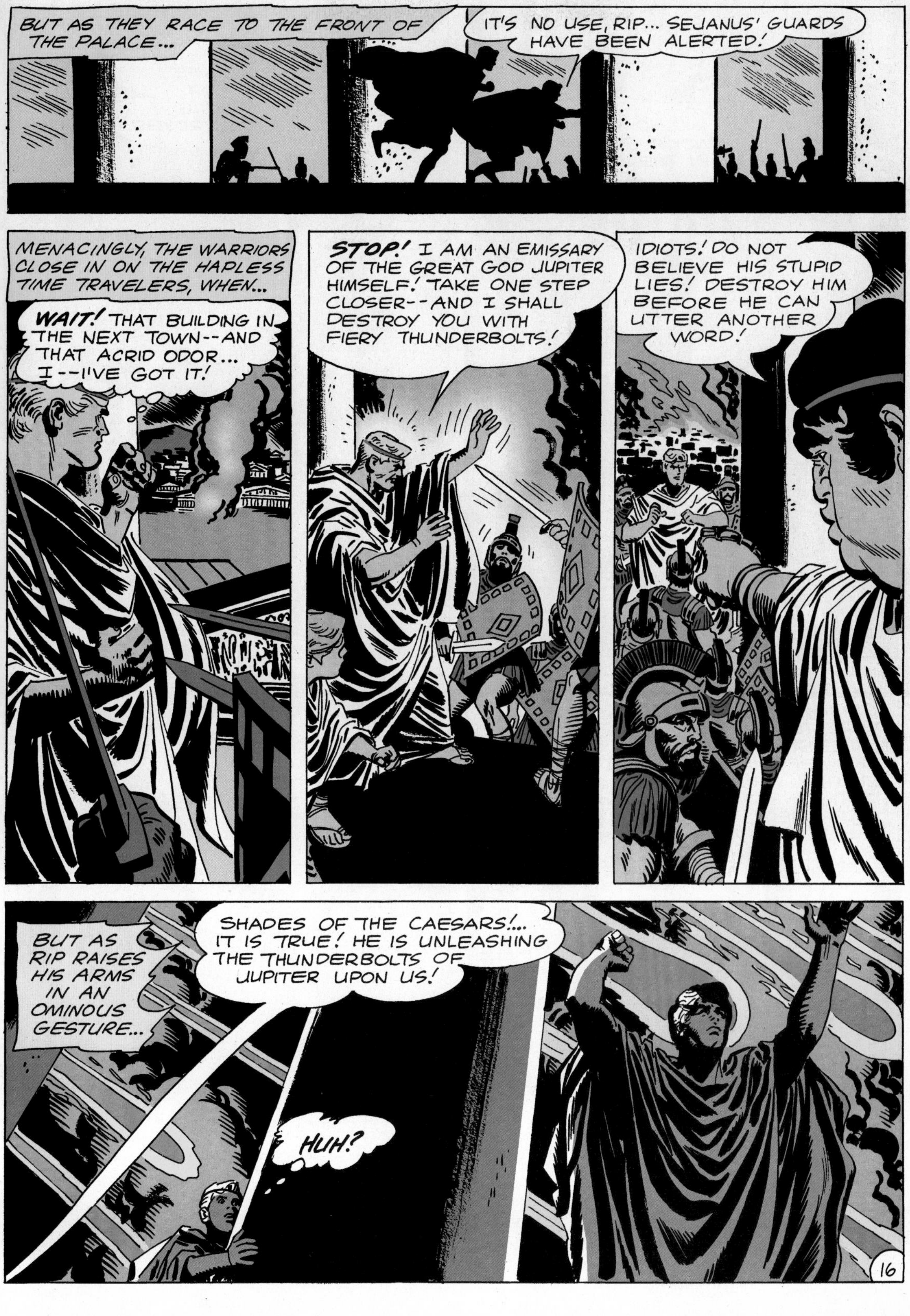
BUT AS THEY RACE TO THE FRONT OF THE PALACE...
IT'S NO USE, RIP... SEJANUS' GUARDS HAVE BEEN ALERTED!
MENACINGLY, THE WARRIORS CLOSE IN ON THE HAPLESS TIME TRAVELERS, WHEN...
WAIT! THAT BUILDING IN THE NEXT TOWN--AND THAT ACRID ODOR... I--I'VE GOT IT!
STOP! I AM AN EMISSARY OF THE GREAT GOD JUPITER HIMSELF! TAKE ONE STEP CLOSER--AND I SHALL DESTROY YOU WITH FIERY THUNDERBOLTS!
IDIOTS! DO NOT BELIEVE HIS STUPID LIES! DESTROY HIM BEFORE HE CAN UTTER ANOTHER WORD!
BUT AS RIP RAISES HIS ARMS IN AN OMINOUS GESTURE...
SHADES OF THE CAESARS!... IT IS TRUE! HE IS UNLEASHING THE THUNDERBOLTS OF JUPITER UPON US!
HUH?
16

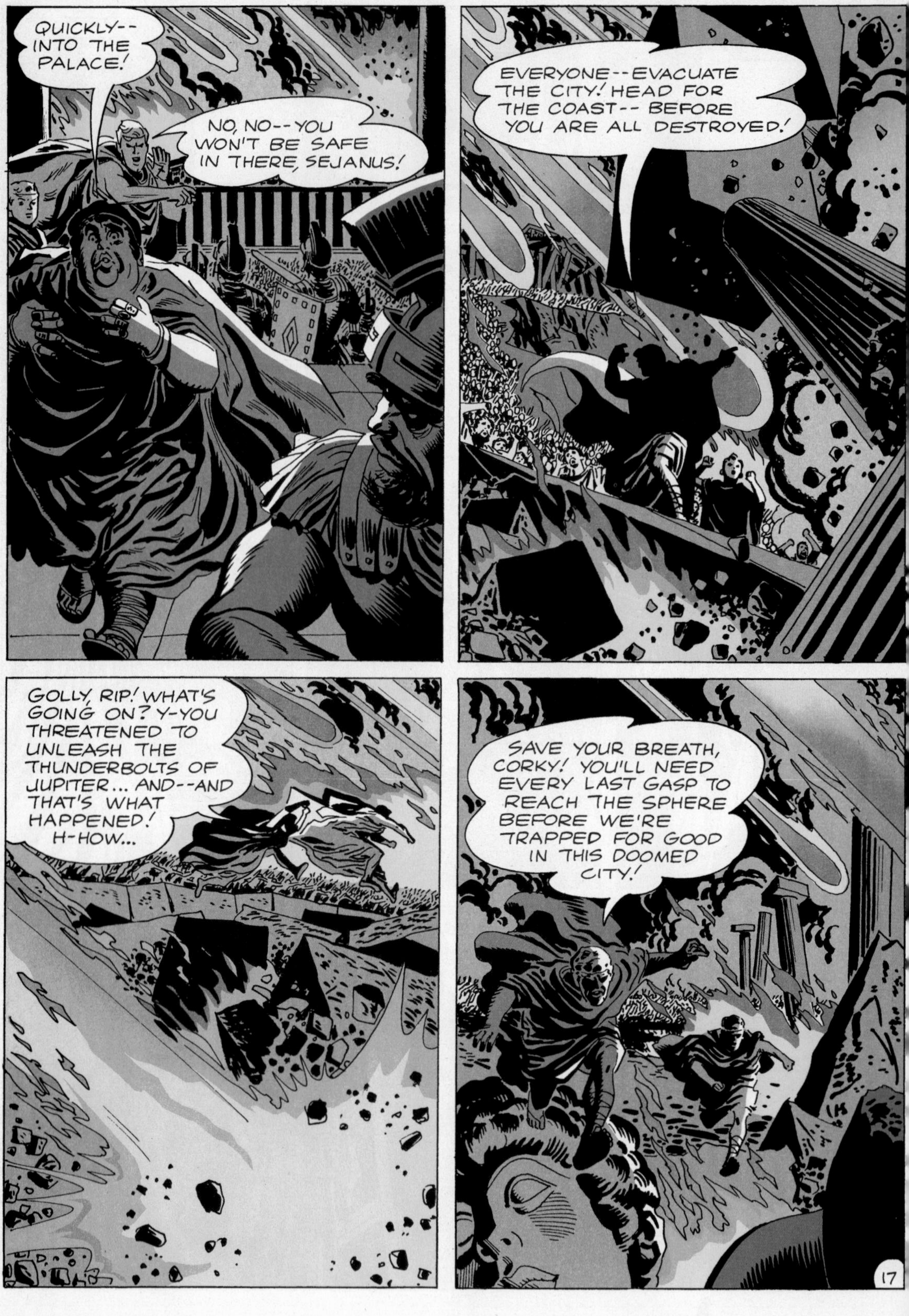
QUICKLY-- INTO THE PALACE!
NO, NO--YOU WON'T BE SAFE IN THERE, SEJANUS!
EVERYONE--EVACUATE THE CITY! HEAD FOR THE COAST-- BEFORE YOU ARE ALL DESTROYED!
GOLLY, RIP! WHAT'S GOING ON? Y-YOU THREATENED TO UNLEASH THE THUNDERBOLTS OF JUPITER... AND--AND THAT'S WHAT HAPPENED! H-HOW...
SAVE YOUR BREATH, CORKY! YOU'LL NEED EVERY LAST GASP TO REACH THE SPHERE BEFORE WE'RE TRAPPED FOR GOOD IN THIS DOOMED CITY!
17

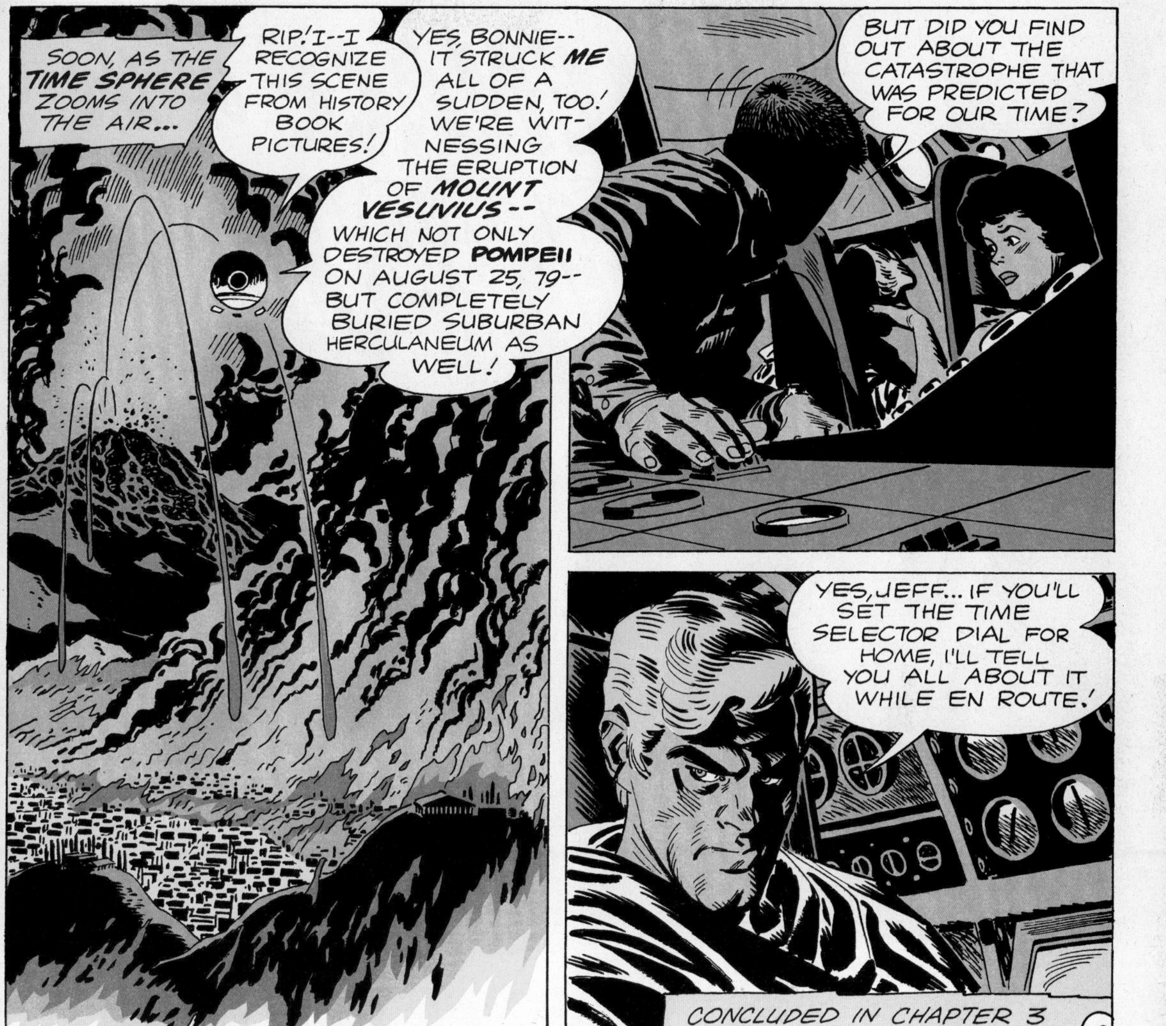
SOON, AS THE TIME SPHERE ZOOMS INTO THE AIR...
RIP! I--I RECOGNIZE THIS SCENE FROM HISTORY BOOK PICTURES!
YES, BONNIE-- IT STRUCK ME ALL OF A SUDDEN, TOO! WE'RE WITNESSING THE ERUPTION OF MOUNT VESUVIUS -- WHICH NOT ONLY DESTROYED POMPEII ON AUGUST 25, 79-- BUT COMPLETELY BURIED SUBURBAN HERCULANEUM AS WELL!
BUT DID YOU FIND OUT ABOUT THE CATASTROPHE THAT WAS PREDICTED FOR OUR TIME?
YES, JEFF... IF YOU'LL SET THE TIME SELECTOR DIAL FOR HOME, I'LL TELL YOU ALL ABOUT IT WHILE EN ROUTE!
CONCLUDED IN CHAPTER 3
18

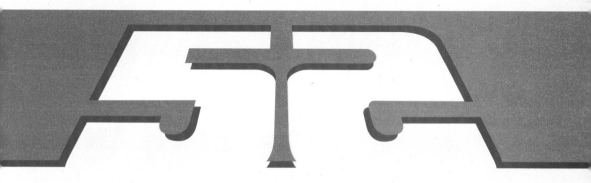

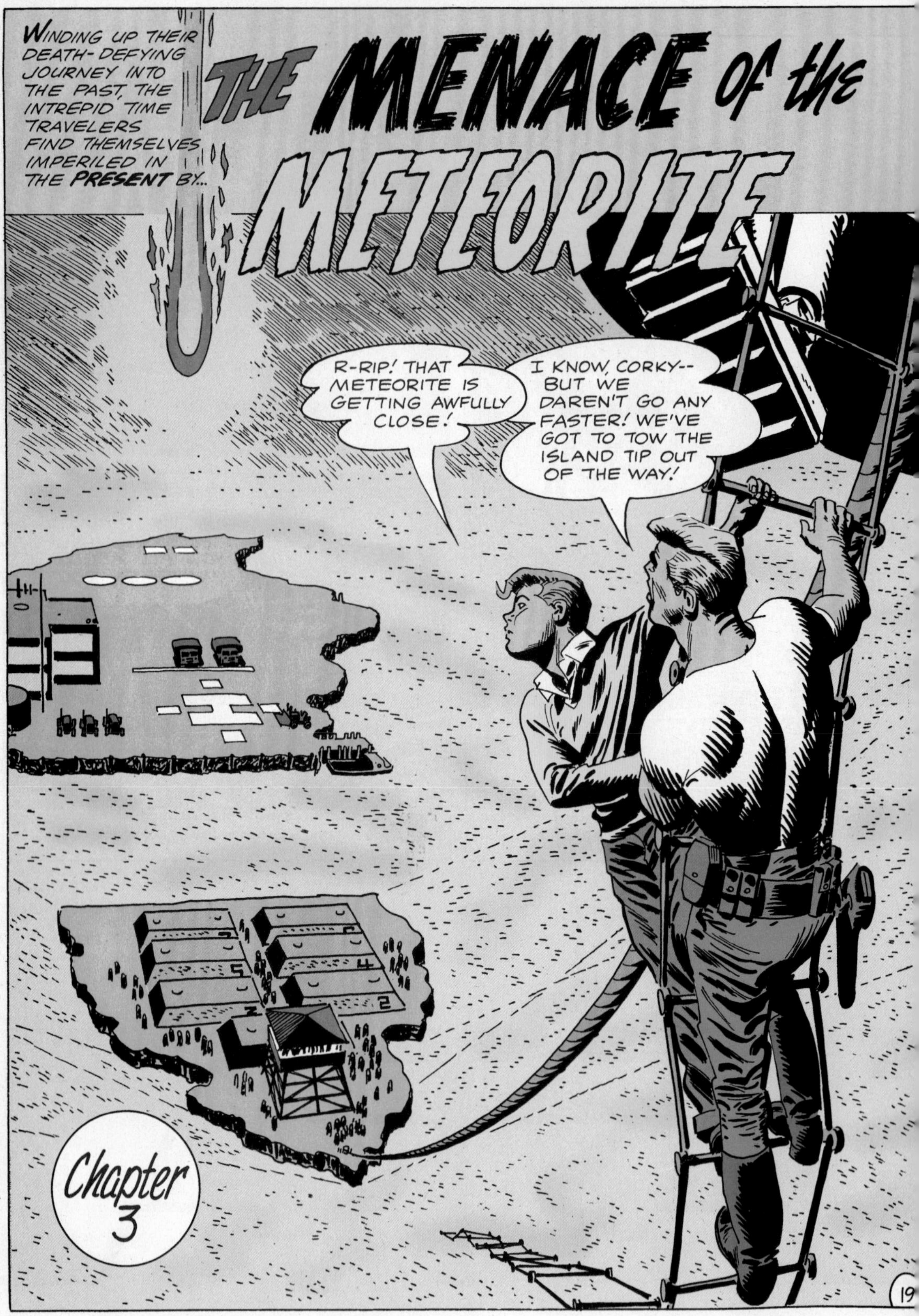
WINDING UP THEIR DEATH-DEFYING JOURNEY INTO THE PAST, THE INTREPID TIME TRAVELERS FIND THEMSELVES IMPERILED IN THE PRESENT BY...
THE MENACE OF THE METEORITE
R-RIP! THAT METEORITE IS GETTING AWFULLY CLOSE!
I KNOW, CORKY-- BUT WE DAREN'T GO ANY FASTER! WE'VE GOT TO TOW THE ISLAND TIP OUT OF THE WAY!
Chapter 3
19

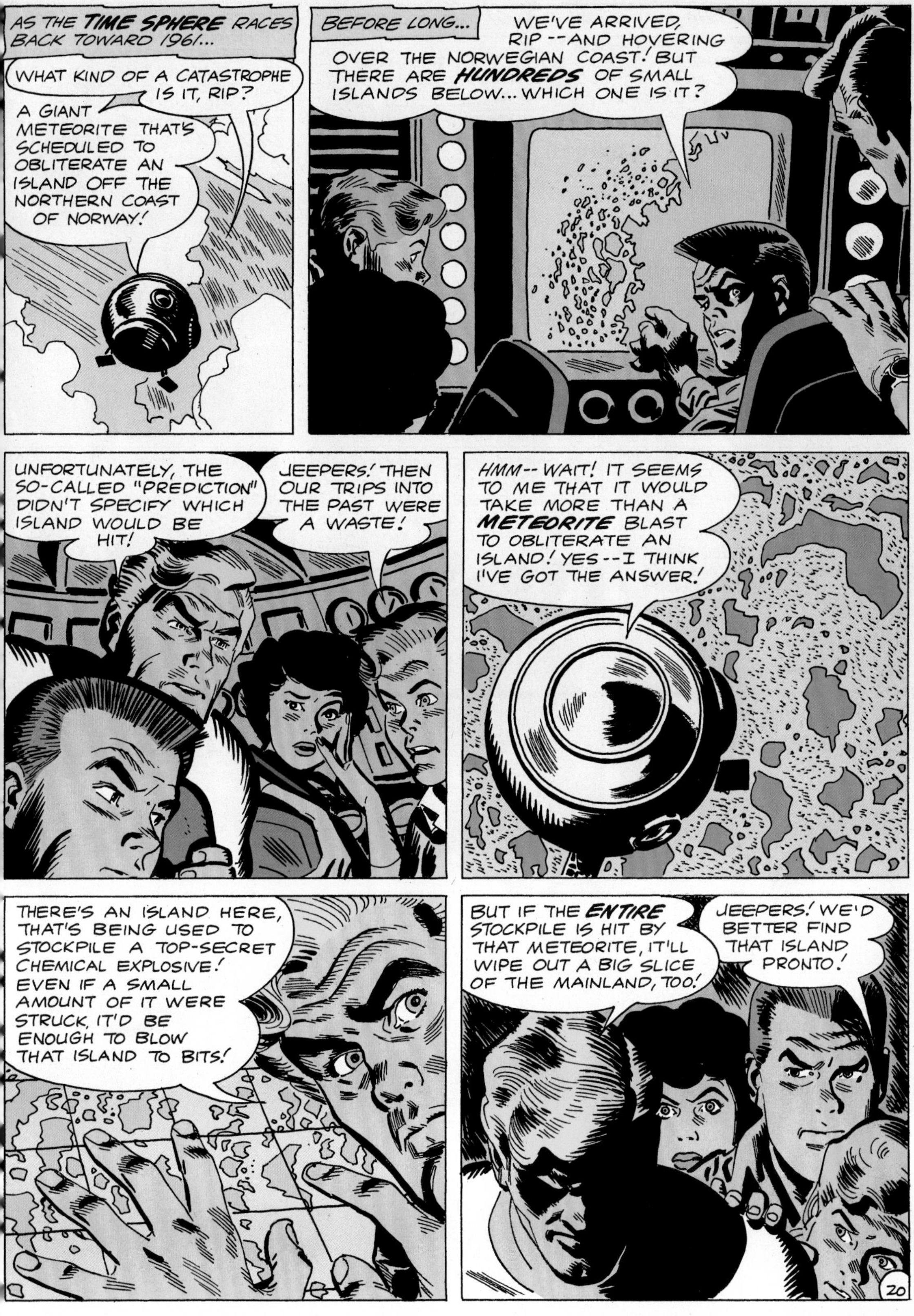
AS THE TIME SPHERE RACES BACK TOWARD 1961...
WHAT KIND OF A CATASTROPHE IS IT, RIP?
A GIANT METEORITE THAT'S SCHEDULED TO OBLITERATE AN ISLAND OFF THE NORTHERN COAST OF NORWAY!
BEFORE LONG...
WE'VE ARRIVED, RIP--AND HOVERING OVER THE NORWEGIAN COAST! BUT THERE ARE HUNDREDS OF SMALL ISLANDS BELOW... WHICH ONE IS IT?
UNFORTUNATELY, THE SO-CALLED "PREDICTION" DIDN'T SPECIFY WHICH ISLAND WOULD BE HIT!
JEEPERS! THEN OUR TRIPS INTO THE PAST WERE A WASTE!
HMM--WAIT! IT SEEMS TO ME THAT IT WOULD TAKE MORE THAN A METEORITE BLAST TO OBLITERATE AN ISLAND! YES--I THINK I'VE GOT THE ANSWER!
THERE'S AN ISLAND HERE, THAT'S BEING USED TO STOCKPILE A TOP-SECRET CHEMICAL EXPLOSIVE! EVEN IF A SMALL AMOUNT OF IT WERE STRUCK, IT'D BE ENOUGH TO BLOW THAT ISLAND TO BITS!
BUT IF THE ENTIRE STOCKPILE IS HIT BY THAT METEORITE, IT'LL WIPE OUT A BIG SLICE OF THE MAINLAND, TOO!
JEEPERS! WE'D BETTER FIND THAT ISLAND PRONTO!
20

BUT WHEN THE TIME TRAVELERS REACH THE DOOMED ISLAND...

COLONEL-- YOU'LL HAVE TO CART EVERY CASE OF CHEMICAL "X" OFF THIS PLACE AT ONCE! A METEORITE IS SCHEDULED TO BLAST IT WITHIN AN HOUR!

WHAT? BUT THAT'S IMPOSSIBLE!

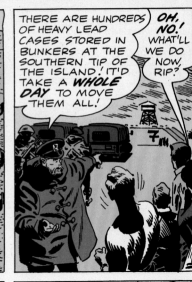

THERE ARE HUNDREDS OF HEAVY LEAD CASES STORED IN BUNKERS AT THE SOUTHERN TIP OF THE ISLAND! IT'D TAKE A WHOLE DAY TO MOVE THEM ALL!

OH, NO! WHAT'LL WE DO NOW, RIP?

SEARCH ME! THERE ISN'T EVEN TIME TO ALERT THE PEOPLE ON THE MAINLAND TO EVACUATE THE COASTAL AREAS!

THOUSANDS WILL BE KILLED!

HOLD IT! I JUST NOTICED-- THAT FLOATING LOG... IT SEEMS TO BE GOING UNDERNEATH THIS ISLAND!

WHAT'RE YOU GETTING AT, RIP?

NO TIME TO EXPLAIN! QUICK, JEFF--GET OUR SKIN-DIVING GEAR OUT OF THE SPHERE!

CORKY AND I ARE GOING ALONG, TOO, RIP!

PRESENTLY, AS THE FEARLESS FOURSOME PLUNGES INTO THE COLD WATERS...

WHAT'RE WE SUPPOSED TO BE LOOKING FOR, RIP?

I HOPE TO BE ABLE TO SHOW IT TO YOU SOON!

21

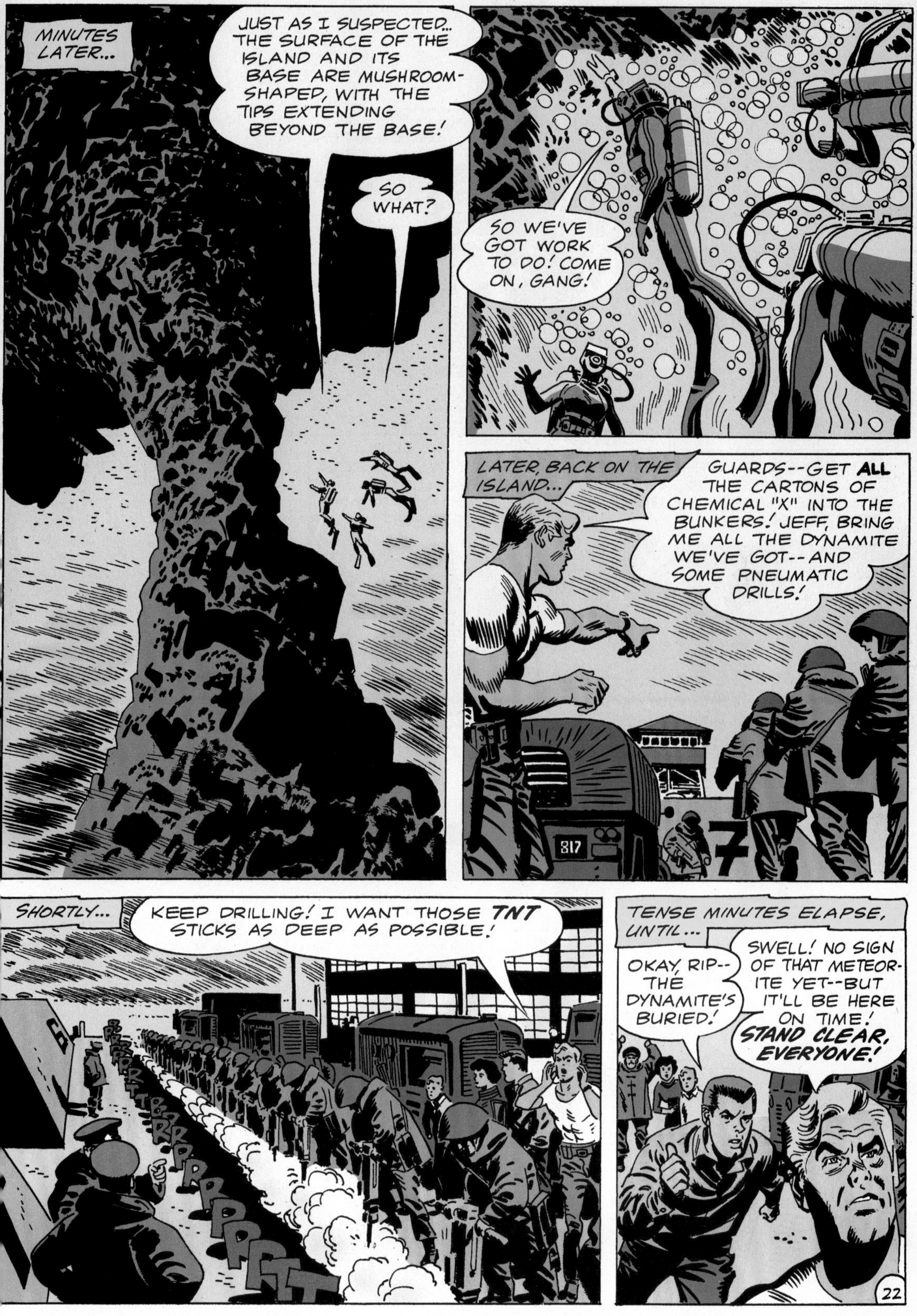
MINUTES LATER...
JUST AS I SUSPECTED... THE SURFACE OF THE ISLAND AND ITS BASE ARE MUSHROOM-SHAPED, WITH THE TIPS EXTENDING BEYOND THE BASE!
SO WHAT?
SO WE'VE GOT WORK TO DO! COME ON, GANG!
LATER, BACK ON THE ISLAND...
GUARDS--GET ALL THE CARTONS OF CHEMICAL "X" INTO THE BUNKERS! JEFF, BRING ME ALL THE DYNAMITE WE'VE GOT--AND SOME PNEUMATIC DRILLS!
817
SHORTLY...
KEEP DRILLING! I WANT THOSE TNT STICKS AS DEEP AS POSSIBLE!
TENSE MINUTES ELAPSE, UNTIL...
OKAY, RIP--THE DYNAMITE'S BURIED!
SWELL! NO SIGN OF THAT METEORITE YET--BUT IT'LL BE HERE ON TIME! STAND CLEAR, EVERYONE!
22

A QUICK COMMAND GOES OUT, AND...

VARRROOMM

IT WORKED, RIP! THE SOUTHERN TIP, WITH THE BUNKERS ON IT, IS LOOSE FROM THE REST OF THE ISLAND!

RIGHT... NOW, LOWER A LINE FROM THE SPHERE--AND START TOWING, JEFF!

JUST THEN...

RIP! THAT SPECK UP THERE--IT MUST BE THE METEORITE!

I THINK YOU'RE RIGHT, BONNIE! ON THE DOUBLE WITH THAT SPHERE!

BUT NEXT MOMENT...

HUNTER! WE OVERLOOKED A COUPLE OF CASES OF CHEMICAL "X" ON THIS NORTH END!

WHAT--?

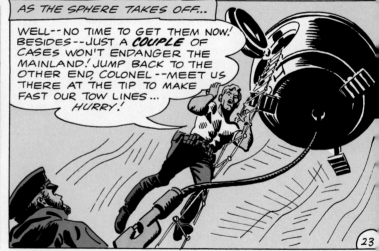

AS THE SPHERE TAKES OFF...

WELL--NO TIME TO GET THEM NOW! BESIDES--JUST A *COUPLE* OF CASES WON'T ENDANGER THE MAINLAND! JUMP BACK TO THE OTHER END, COLONEL--MEET US THERE AT THE TIP TO MAKE FAST OUR TOW LINES... HURRY!

23

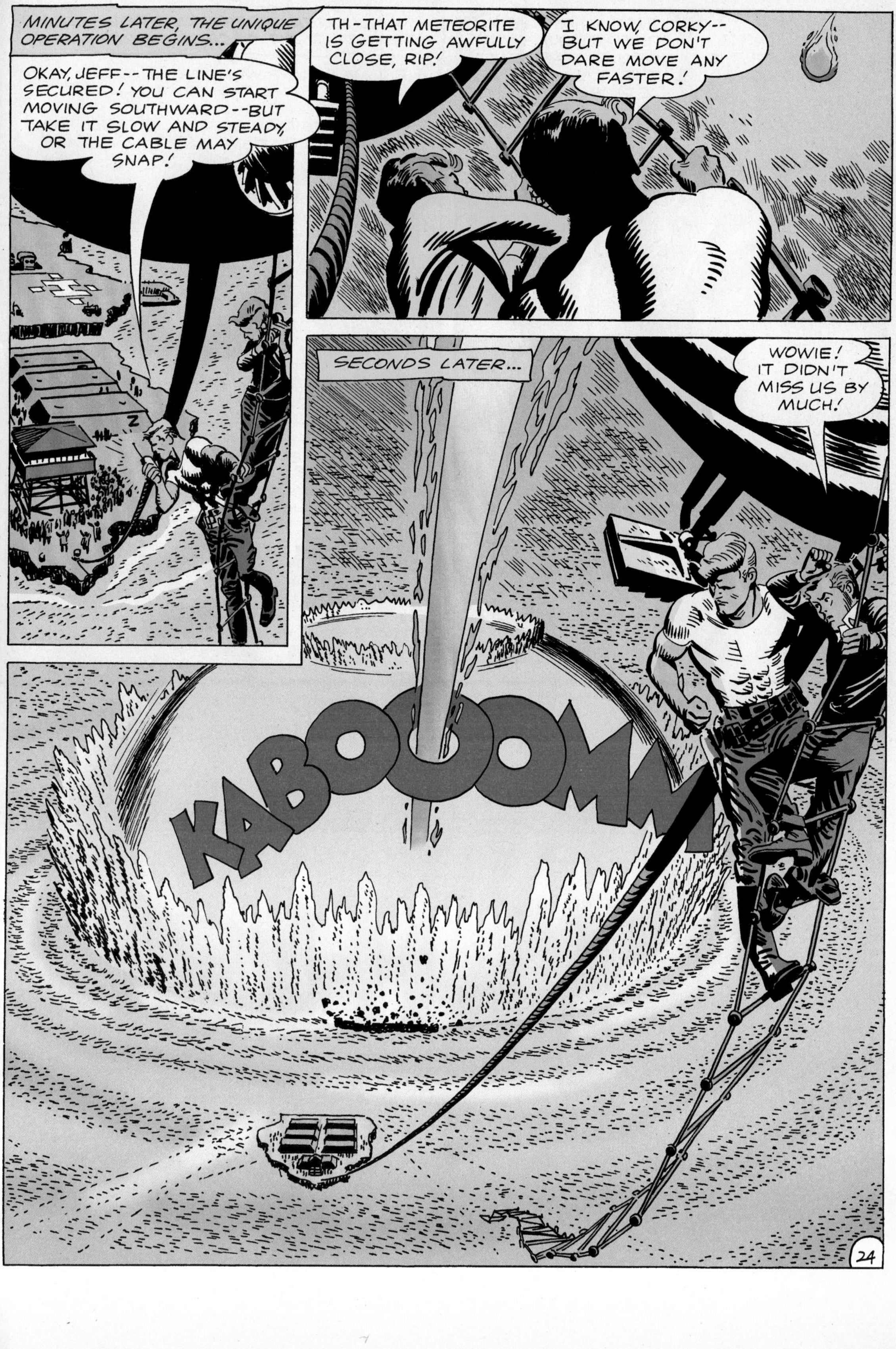

MINUTES LATER, THE UNIQUE OPERATION BEGINS...
OKAY, JEFF--THE LINE'S SECURED! YOU CAN START MOVING SOUTHWARD--BUT TAKE IT SLOW AND STEADY, OR THE CABLE MAY SNAP!
TH-THAT METEORITE IS GETTING AWFULLY CLOSE, RIP!
I KNOW, CORKY--BUT WE DON'T DARE MOVE ANY FASTER!
SECONDS LATER...
WOWIE! IT DIDN'T MISS US BY MUCH!
KABOOOMM
24

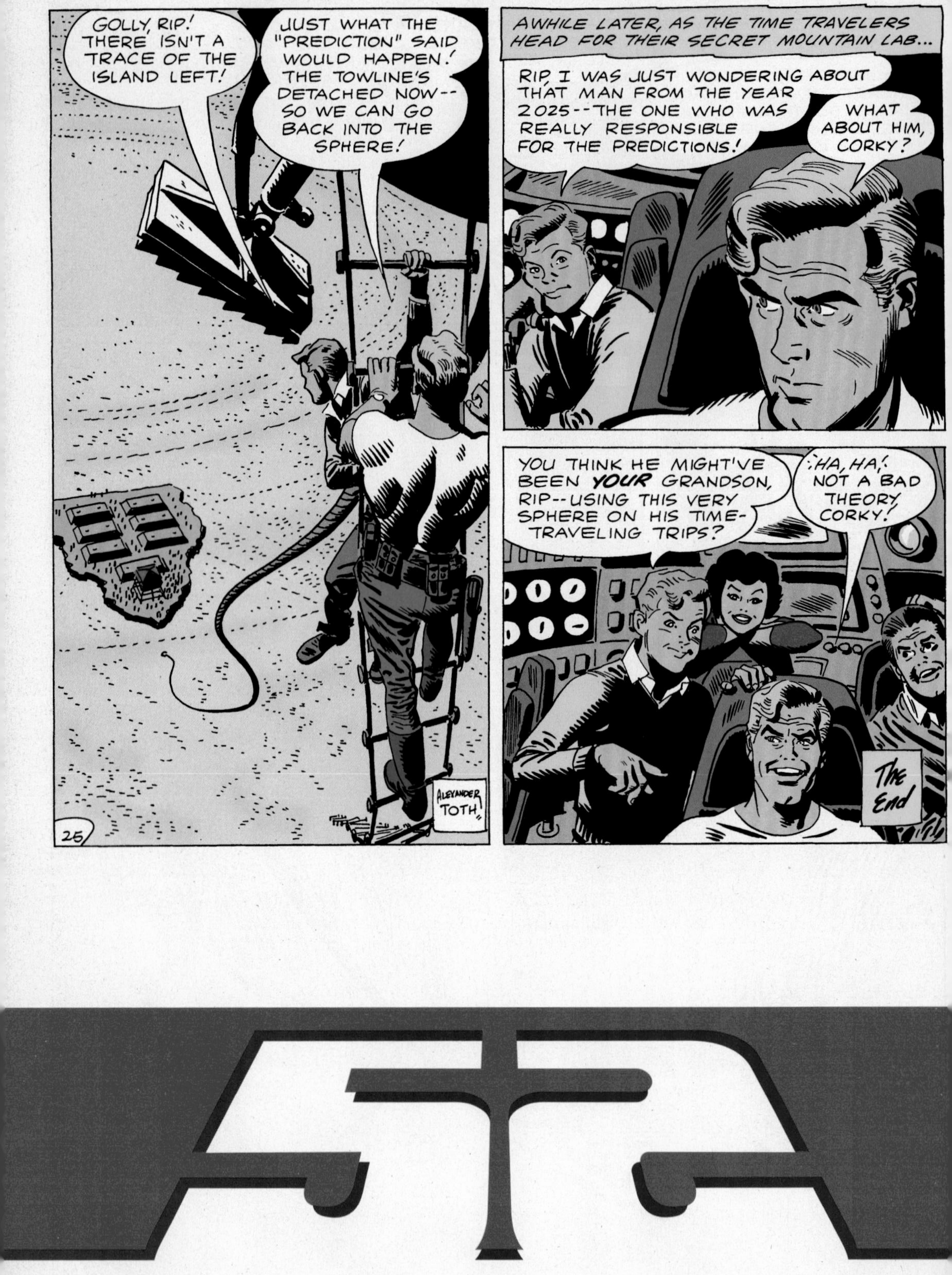
GOLLY, RIP! THERE ISN'T A TRACE OF THE ISLAND LEFT!
JUST WHAT THE "PREDICTION" SAID WOULD HAPPEN! THE TOWLINE'S DETACHED NOW--SO WE CAN GO BACK INTO THE SPHERE!
ALEXANDER TOTH
25
AWHILE LATER, AS THE TIME TRAVELERS HEAD FOR THEIR SECRET MOUNTAIN LAB...
RIP, I WAS JUST WONDERING ABOUT THAT MAN FROM THE YEAR 2025--THE ONE WHO WAS REALLY RESPONSIBLE FOR THE PREDICTIONS!
WHAT ABOUT HIM, CORKY?
YOU THINK HE MIGHT'VE BEEN *YOUR* GRANDSON, RIP--USING THIS VERY SPHERE ON HIS TIME-TRAVELING TRIPS?
HA, HA! NOT A BAD THEORY, CORKY!
The End

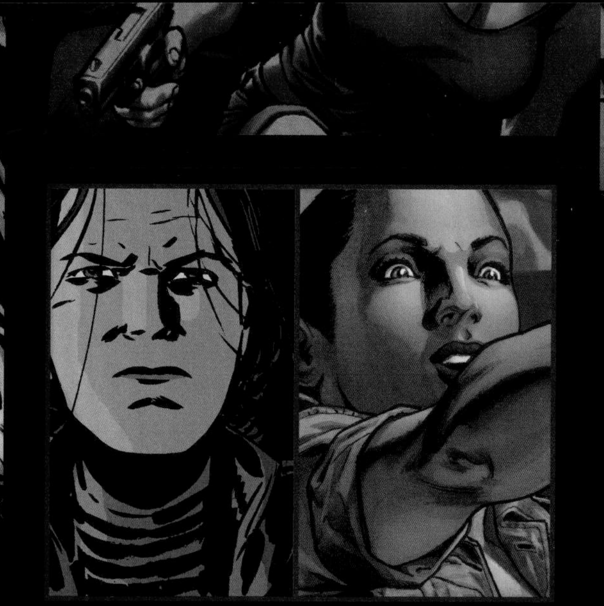

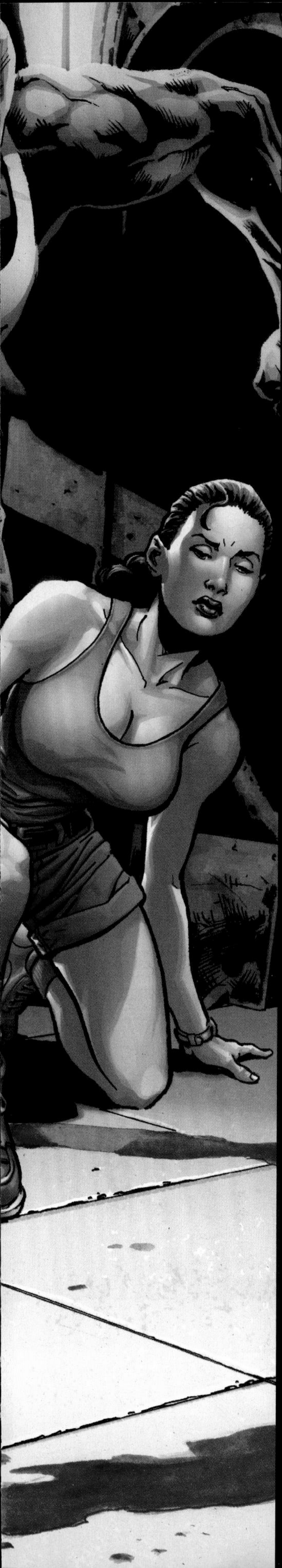

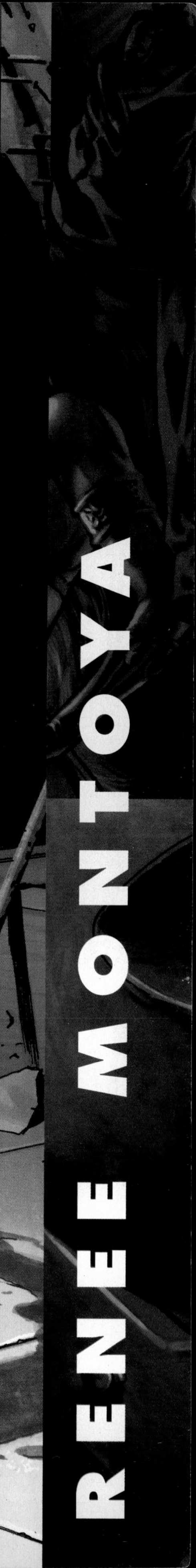

RENEE MONTOYA

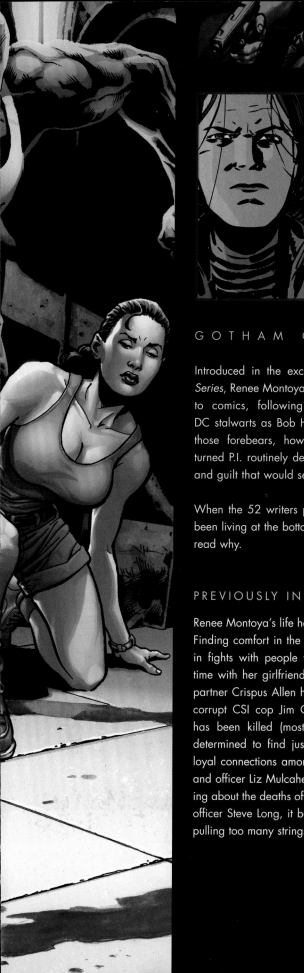

GOTHAM CENTRAL #40

Introduced in the excellent *Batman: The Animated Series*, Renee Montoya made the leap from television to comics, following the path of such bygone DC stalwarts as Bob Hope and Dobie Gillis. Unlike those forebears, however, this Gotham City cop turned P.I. routinely deals with intensities of revenge and guilt that would send Elvis Costello into hiding.

When the 52 writers picked up on her story, she'd been living at the bottom of a bottle. You're about to read why.

—**MW**

PREVIOUSLY IN GOTHAM CENTRAL:

Renee Montoya's life has been spiraling downwards. Finding comfort in the bottle, Renee continues to get in fights with people while spending less and less time with her girlfriend Daria. When she learns her partner Crispus Allen has been secretly investigating corrupt CSI cop Jim Corrigan, only to learn Allen has been killed (most likely by Corrigan), she is determined to find justice. But Corrigan has many loyal connections among his peers — and when he and officer Liz Mulcahey are brought in for questioning about the deaths of Allen and Mulcahey's partner officer Steve Long, it becomes clear that Corrigan is pulling too many strings within the Department.

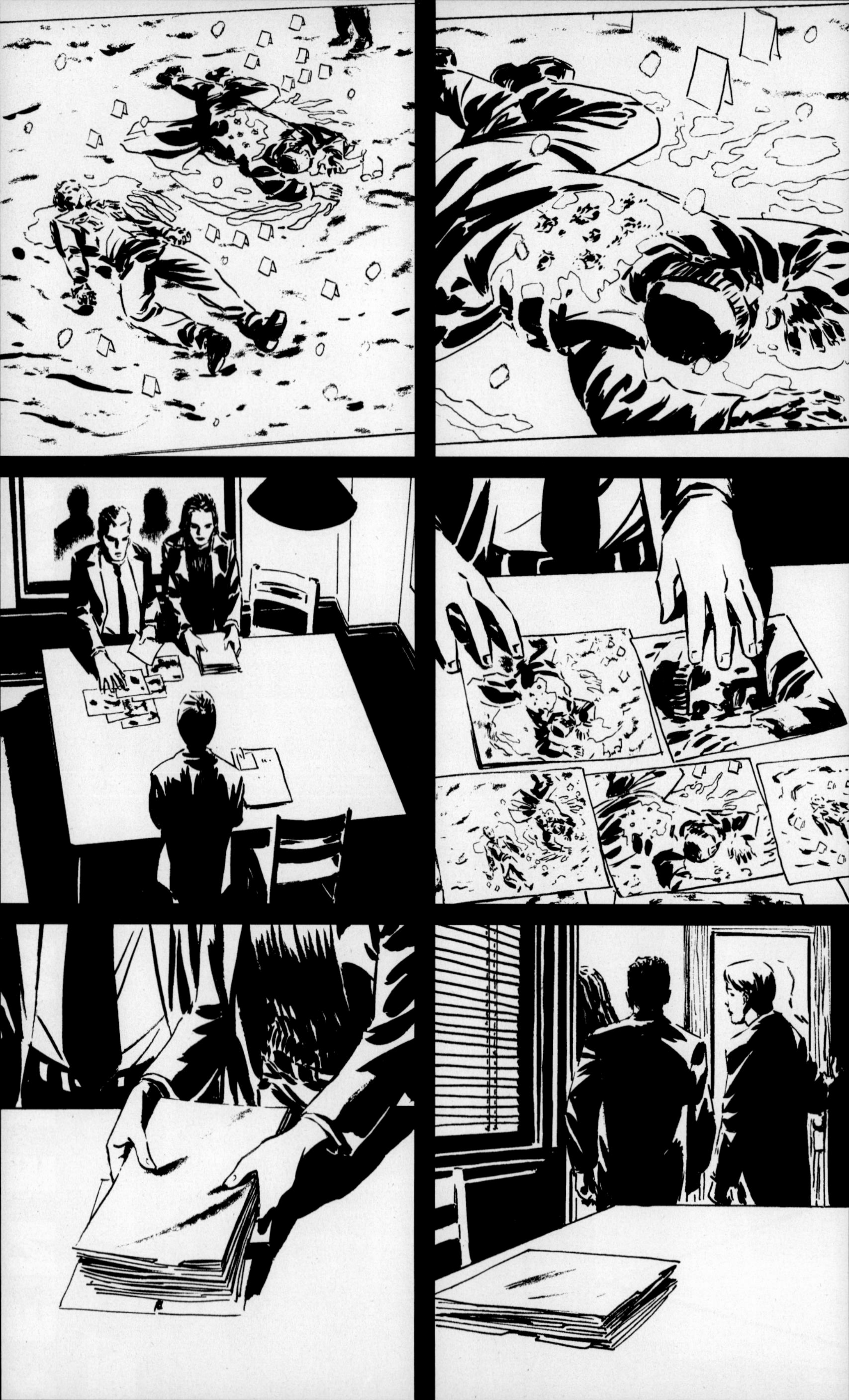

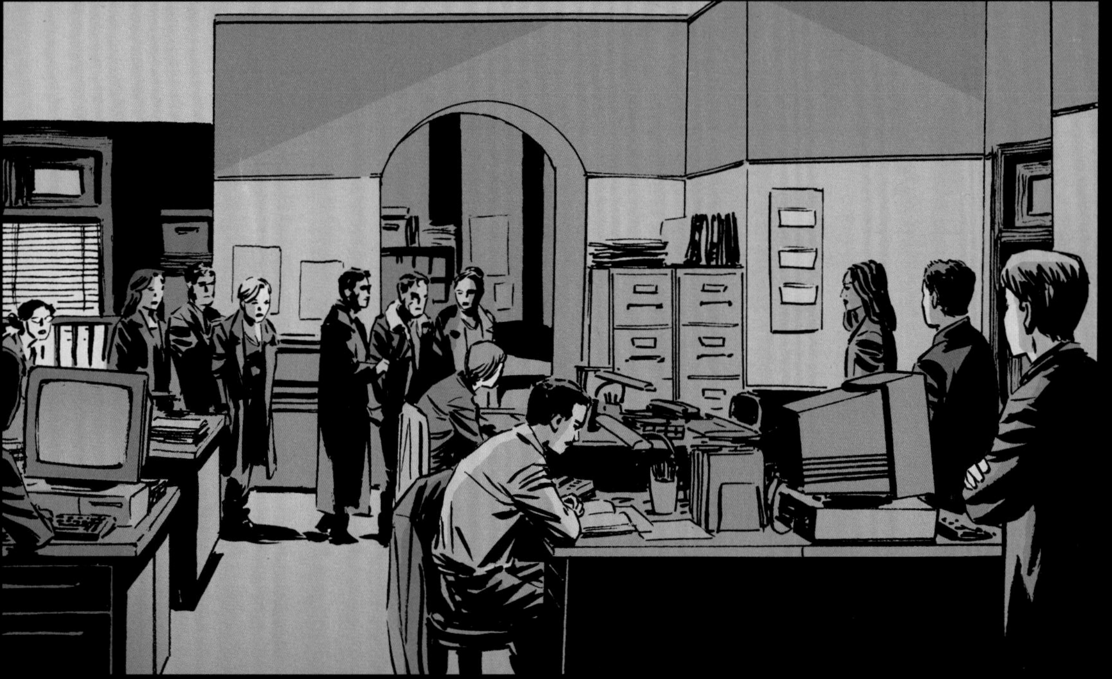

CORRIGAN II

WRITER GREG RUCKA — KANO & STEFANO GAUDIANO ARTISTS

CLEM ROBINS letterer LEE LOUGHRIDGE colorist NACHIE CASTRO associate editor MATT IDELSON editor

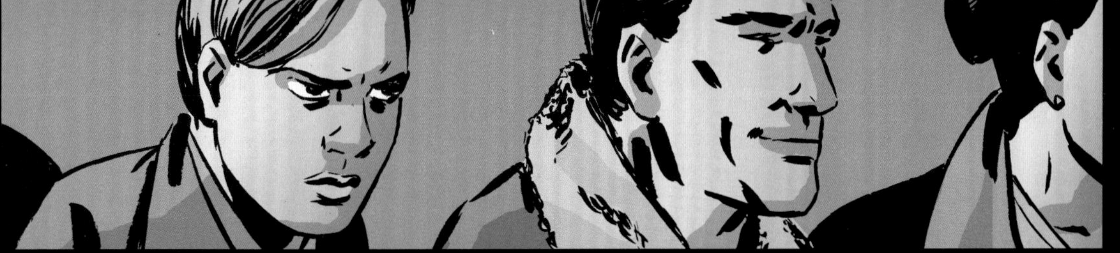

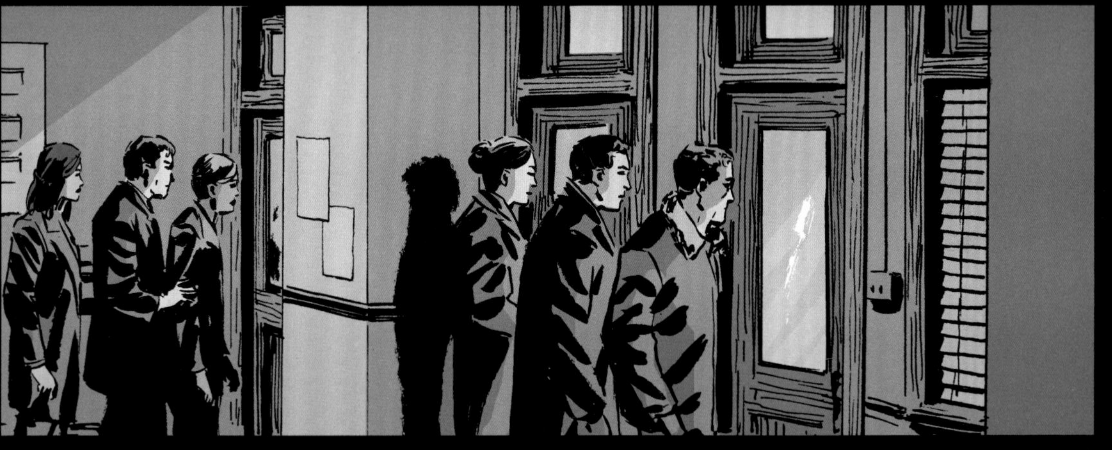

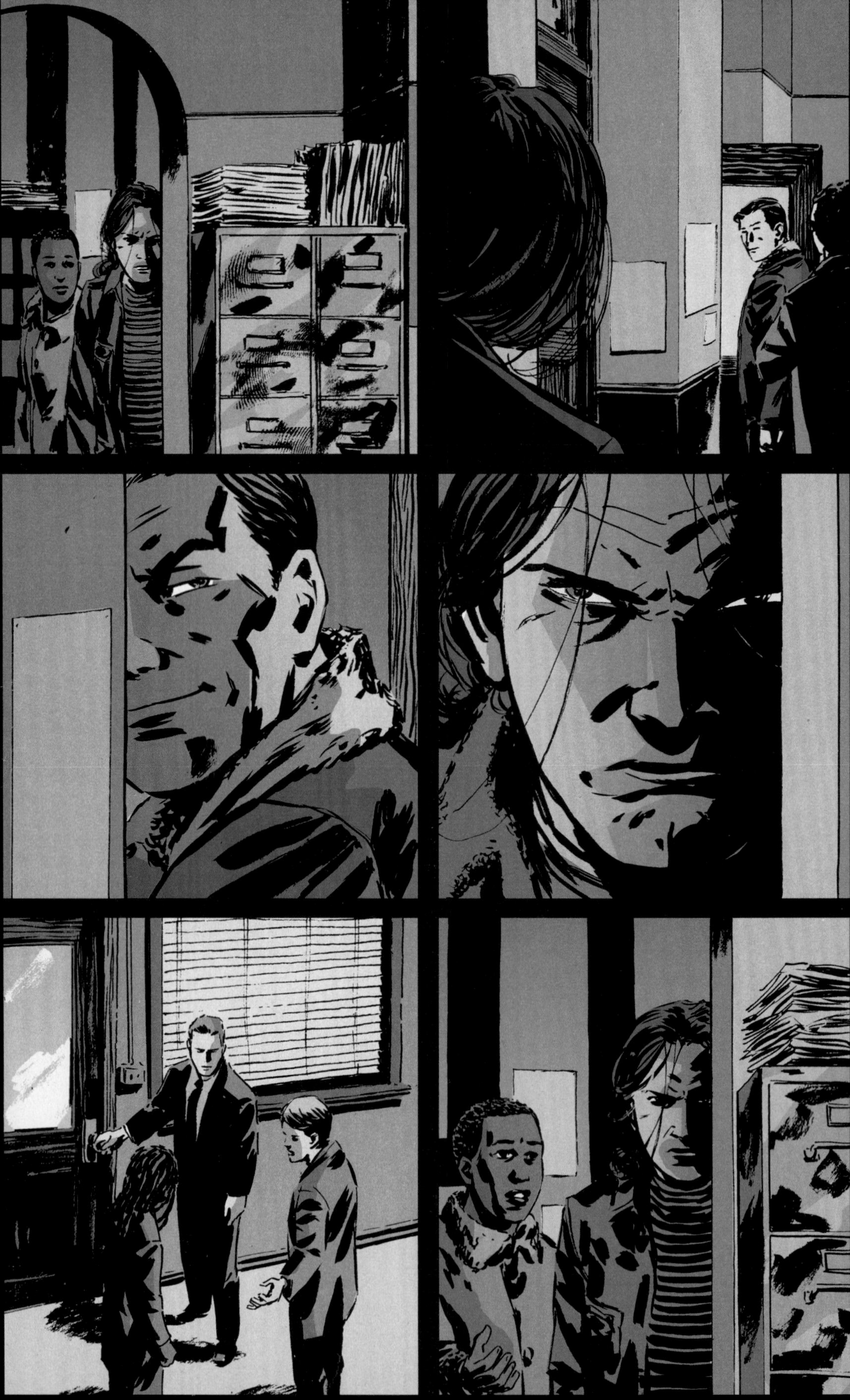

SORRY TO HEAR ABOUT YOUR PARTNER.

YEAH. YEAH, IT PRETTY MUCH **SUCKS.**

YOU AND LONG HAD BEEN **PARTNERED** FOR, WHAT, THREE YEARS?

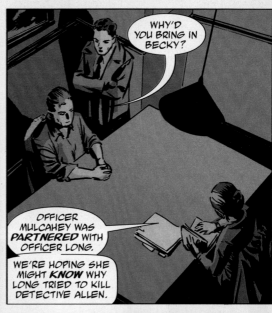

WHY'D YOU BRING IN BECKY?

OFFICER MULCAHEY WAS **PARTNERED** WITH OFFICER LONG.

WE'RE HOPING SHE MIGHT **KNOW** WHY LONG TRIED TO KILL DETECTIVE ALLEN.

HEY, HE WAS MY **PARTNER,** NOT MY **LOVER.**

JUST BECAUSE WE **RODE** TOGETHER DOESN'T MEAN I KNOW WHAT HE WAS **INTO.**

DID HE **KNOW** DETECTIVE KENZIE IN NARCOTICS?

YOU THINK LONG KILLED KENZIE, THEN TRIED TO KILL ALLEN?

DON'T YOU?

C'MON, DETECTIVE PROCJNOW, MY JOB IS TO **COLLECT** THE EVIDENCE, **NOT** TO **INTERPRET** IT.

NO, I WAS OUT WITH **JIMMY,** AS I'M SURE YOU ALREADY **KNOW,** DETECTIVE DEL ARRAZIO.

DOING WHAT?

WE WENT **SHOOTING.**

NO, NOT AT THE RANGE, WE WENT OUT TO BRENTWOOD.

TO THE WOODS.

DID ANYONE **SEE** YOU?

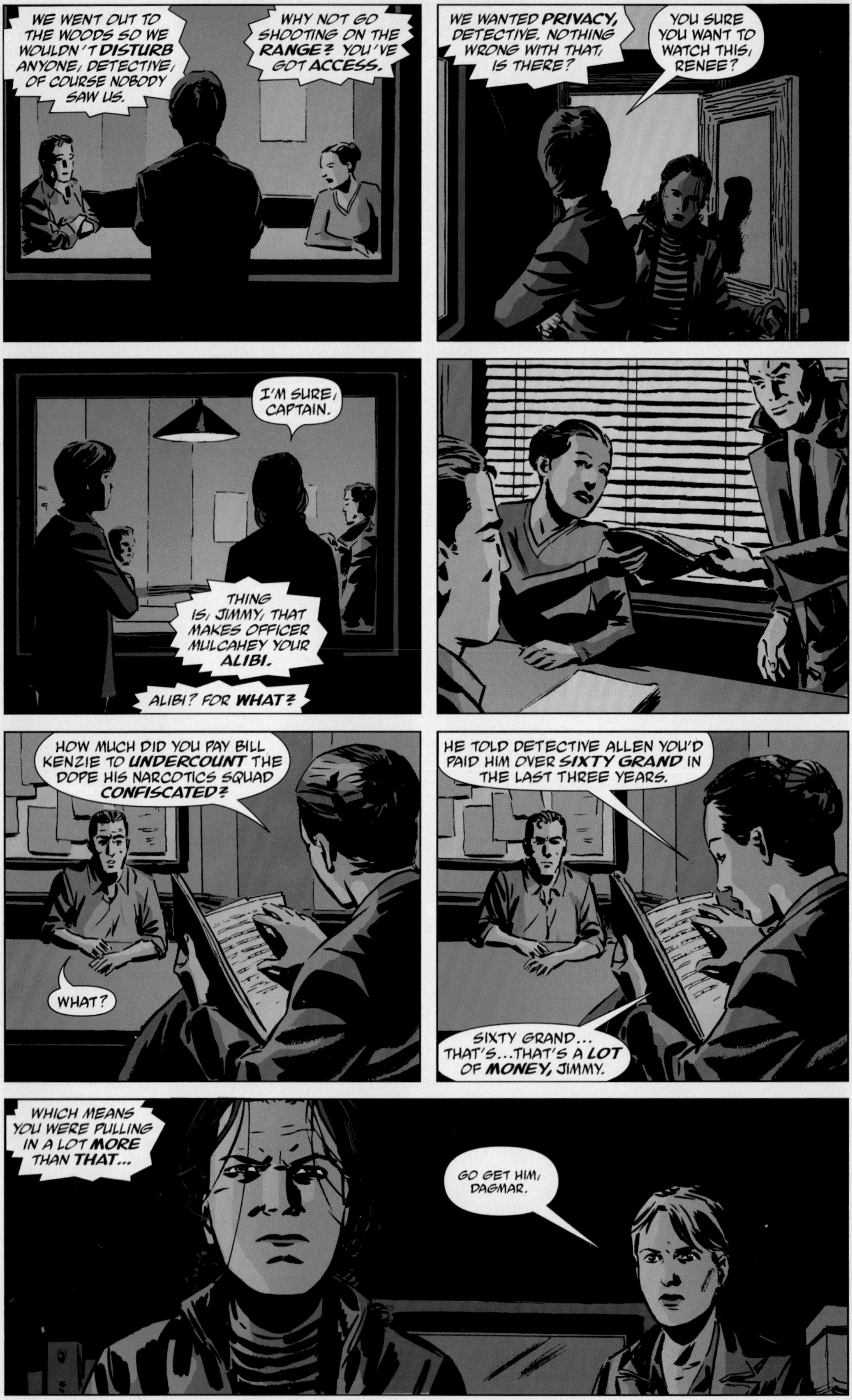
WE WENT OUT TO THE WOODS SO WE WOULDN'T DISTURB ANYONE, DETECTIVE, OF COURSE NOBODY SAW US.
WHY NOT GO SHOOTING ON THE RANGE? YOU'VE GOT ACCESS.
WE WANTED PRIVACY, DETECTIVE. NOTHING WRONG WITH THAT, IS THERE?
YOU SURE YOU WANT TO WATCH THIS, RENEE?
I'M SURE, CAPTAIN.
THING IS, JIMMY, THAT MAKES OFFICER MULCAHEY YOUR ALIBI.
ALIBI? FOR WHAT?
HOW MUCH DID YOU PAY BILL KENZIE TO UNDERCOUNT THE DOPE HIS NARCOTICS SQUAD CONFISCATED?
WHAT?
HE TOLD DETECTIVE ALLEN YOU'D PAID HIM OVER SIXTY GRAND IN THE LAST THREE YEARS.
SIXTY GRAND... THAT'S...THAT'S A LOT OF MONEY, JIMMY.
WHICH MEANS YOU WERE PULLING IN A LOT MORE THAN THAT...
GO GET HIM, DAGMAR.

I DON'T KNOW ANY-THING ABOUT THAT.

I ALREADY TOLD YOU, JIMMY AND I WENT SHOOTING.

ALL RIGHT, LET'S TALK ABOUT THAT, THEN.

WHAT'S UP WITH THAT? WHY WEREN'T YOU AT THE RANGE?

WE WANTED PRIVACY.

WHAT CAN I TELL YOU, SARGE? GUNS GET ME HOT.

YOU AND ME BOTH.

JUST GOT A TITANIUM SLIDE P99 FOR MY COLLECTION, YOU WOULDN'T BELIEVE HOW SWEET THIS PISTOL IS.

YOU GET THAT IN NINE?

S&W FORTY, WITH THE LAW-ENFORCEMENT MAGAZINES.

OH, DAMN, THAT'S SWEET.

YOU GOTTA GO WITH THE FORTY, I JUST GOT AN HK P2000 IN FORTY.

WHAT ABOUT TWO-TWO-FOUR?

THAT'S A RIFLE ROUND, SARGE, NOT A PISTOL ROUND.

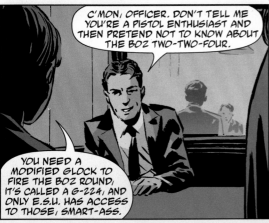

C'MON, OFFICER. DON'T TELL ME YOU'RE A PISTOL ENTHUSIAST AND THEN PRETEND NOT TO KNOW ABOUT THE BOZ TWO-TWO-FOUR.

YOU NEED A MODIFIED GLOCK TO FIRE THE BOZ ROUND, IT'S CALLED A G-224, AND ONLY E.S.U. HAS ACCESS TO THOSE, SMART-ASS.

THEN WHAT WAS CORRIGAN DOING WITH ONE LAST NIGHT?

--HIM TWO HUNDRED BUCKS TO **LOAN** ME ONE, THAT'S ALL! THERE ARE SIX OF THEM, JUST SITTING IN INVENTORY!

I BROUGHT IT BACK THIS MORNING, NO HARM, NO FOUL!

SO YOU'RE ADMITTING YOU TOOK ONE OF THE G-224'S FROM E.S.U. INVENTORY?

YOU TOOK A GUN MADE TO BLOW THROUGH BODY ARMOR FROM E.S.U. INVENTORY YESTERDAY, THAT'S WHAT YOU'RE SAYING?

BECKY WANTED TO TAKE ONE SHOOTING, THAT'S--

INTERESTING. WE'VE GOT **THREE** BODIES...

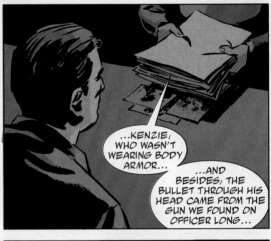

...KENZIE, WHO WASN'T WEARING BODY ARMOR...

...AND BESIDES, THE BULLET THROUGH HIS HEAD CAME FROM THE GUN WE FOUND ON OFFICER LONG...

...AND NO VEST ON OFFICER LONG HIMSELF, OR ELSE ALLEN'S SHOTS WOULDN'T HAVE **KILLED** HIM...

CAPTAIN?

...BUT HERE'S DETECTIVE ALLEN, **WEARING** HIS KEVLAR...

WE'VE GOT A PROBLEM WITH THE BALLISTICS REPORT.

...AND YOU JUST PUT THE GUN THAT **KILLED** HIM IN **YOUR** HAND.

PROVE IT.

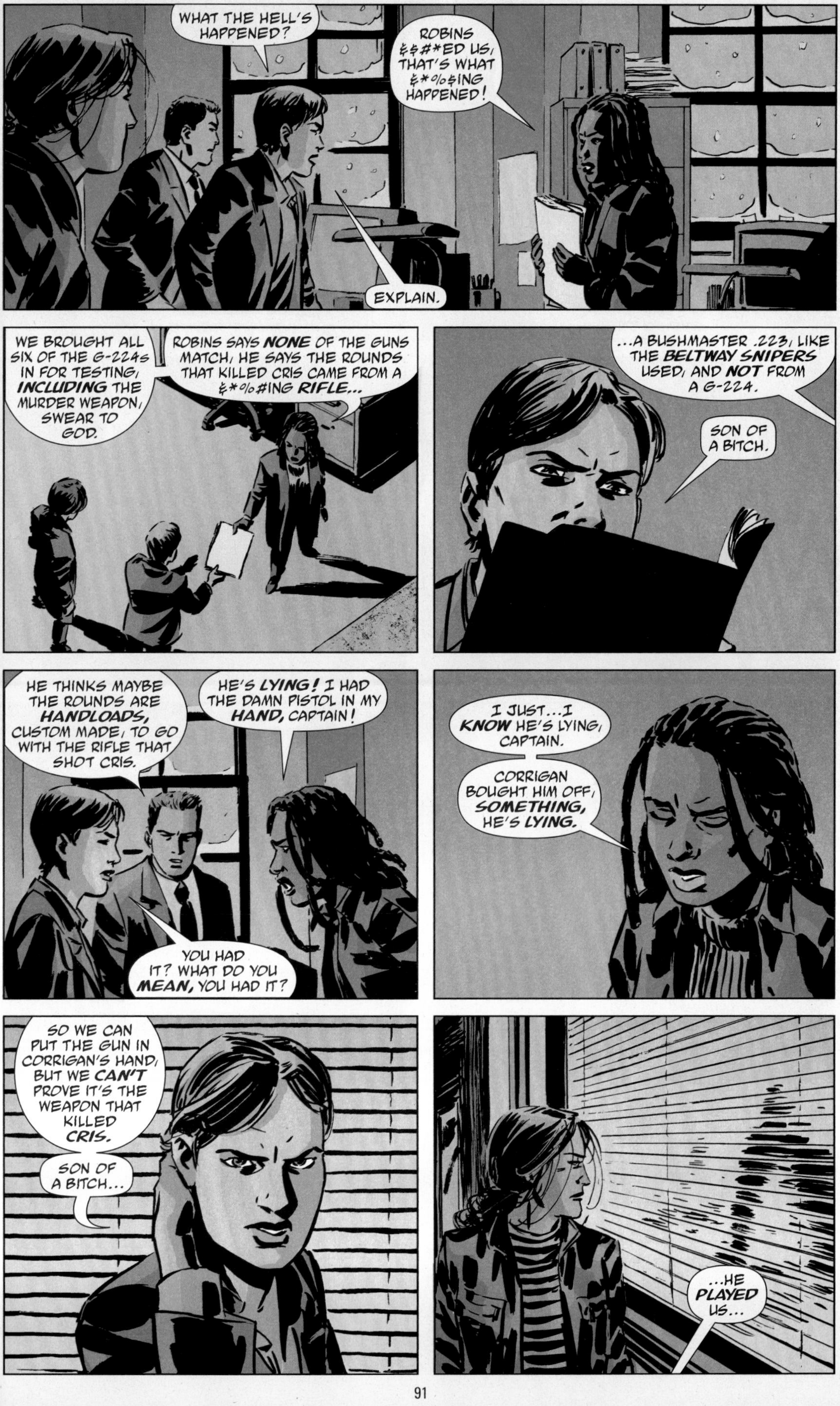
WHAT THE HELL'S HAPPENED?
ROBINS &$#*ED US, THAT'S WHAT &*%$ING HAPPENED!
EXPLAIN.
WE BROUGHT ALL SIX OF THE G-224s IN FOR TESTING, **INCLUDING** THE MURDER WEAPON, SWEAR TO GOD.
ROBINS SAYS **NONE** OF THE GUNS MATCH, HE SAYS THE ROUNDS THAT KILLED CRIS CAME FROM A &*%#ING **RIFLE...**
...A BUSHMASTER .223, LIKE THE **BELTWAY SNIPERS** USED, AND **NOT** FROM A G-224.
SON OF A BITCH.
HE THINKS MAYBE THE ROUNDS ARE **HANDLOADS,** CUSTOM MADE, TO GO WITH THE RIFLE THAT SHOT CRIS.
HE'S **LYING!** I HAD THE DAMN PISTOL IN MY **HAND,** CAPTAIN!
YOU HAD IT? WHAT DO YOU **MEAN,** YOU HAD IT?
I JUST...I **KNOW** HE'S LYING, CAPTAIN.
CORRIGAN BOUGHT HIM OFF, **SOMETHING,** HE'S **LYING.**
SO WE CAN PUT THE GUN IN CORRIGAN'S HAND, BUT WE **CAN'T** PROVE IT'S THE WEAPON THAT KILLED **CRIS.**
SON OF A BITCH...
...HE **PLAYED** US...

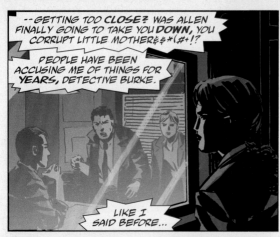

--GETTING TOO **CLOSE**? WAS ALLEN FINALLY GOING TO TAKE YOU **DOWN**, YOU CORRUPT LITTLE MOTHER$$*(#+!?

PEOPLE HAVE BEEN ACCUSING ME OF THINGS FOR **YEARS**, DETECTIVE BURKE.

LIKE I SAID BEFORE...

...**PROVE** IT, DETECTIVES.

A MOMENT, PLEASE.

GET OUT OF HERE.

I'M SORRY?

YOU HEARD ME.

YOU KNOW WHERE TO FIND ME IF YOU WANT TO TRY AGAIN.

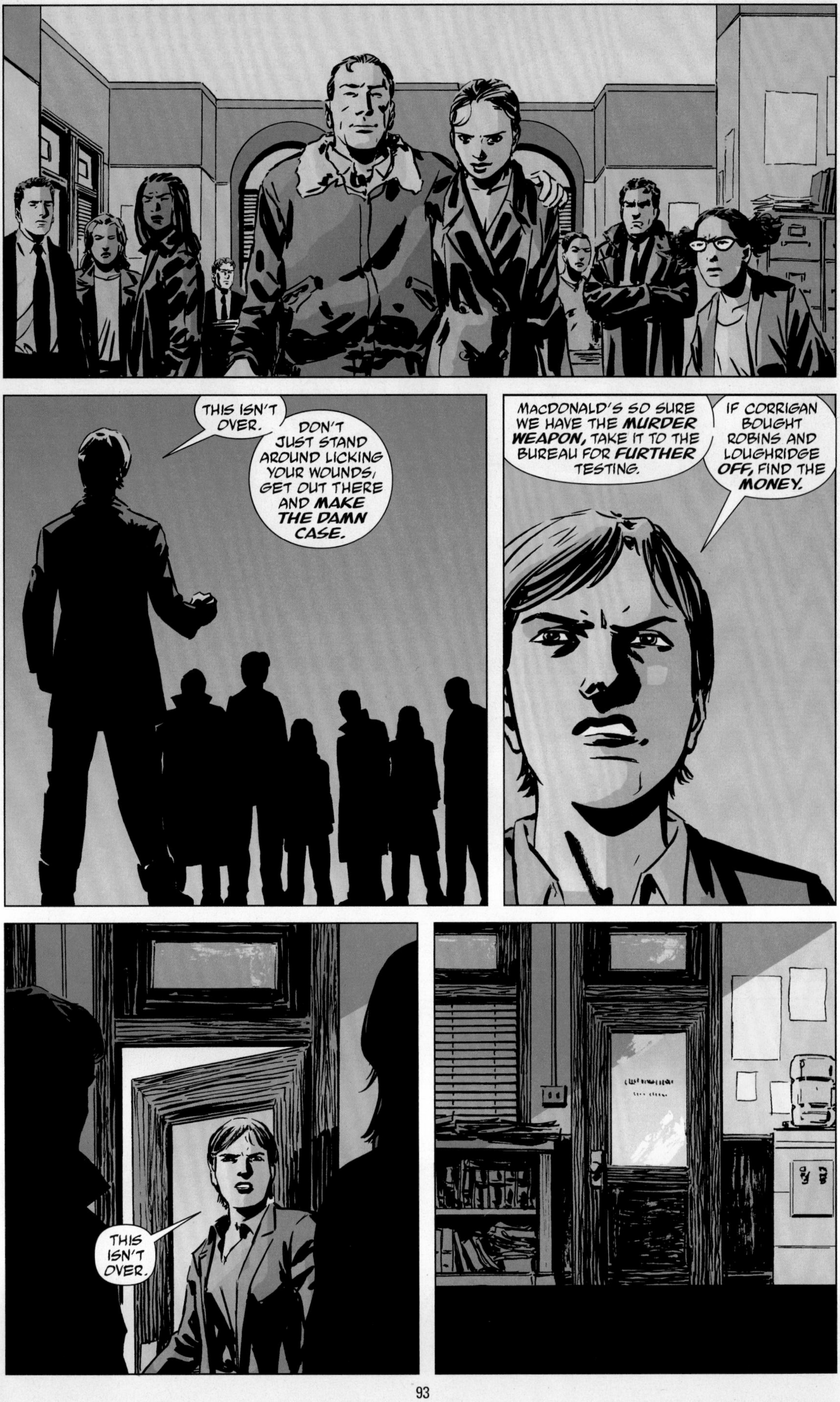
THIS ISN'T OVER.
DON'T JUST STAND AROUND LICKING YOUR WOUNDS, GET OUT THERE AND MAKE THE DAMN CASE.
MACDONALD'S SO SURE WE HAVE THE MURDER WEAPON, TAKE IT TO THE BUREAU FOR FURTHER TESTING.
IF CORRIGAN BOUGHT ROBINS AND LOUGHRIDGE OFF, FIND THE MONEY.
THIS ISN'T OVER.

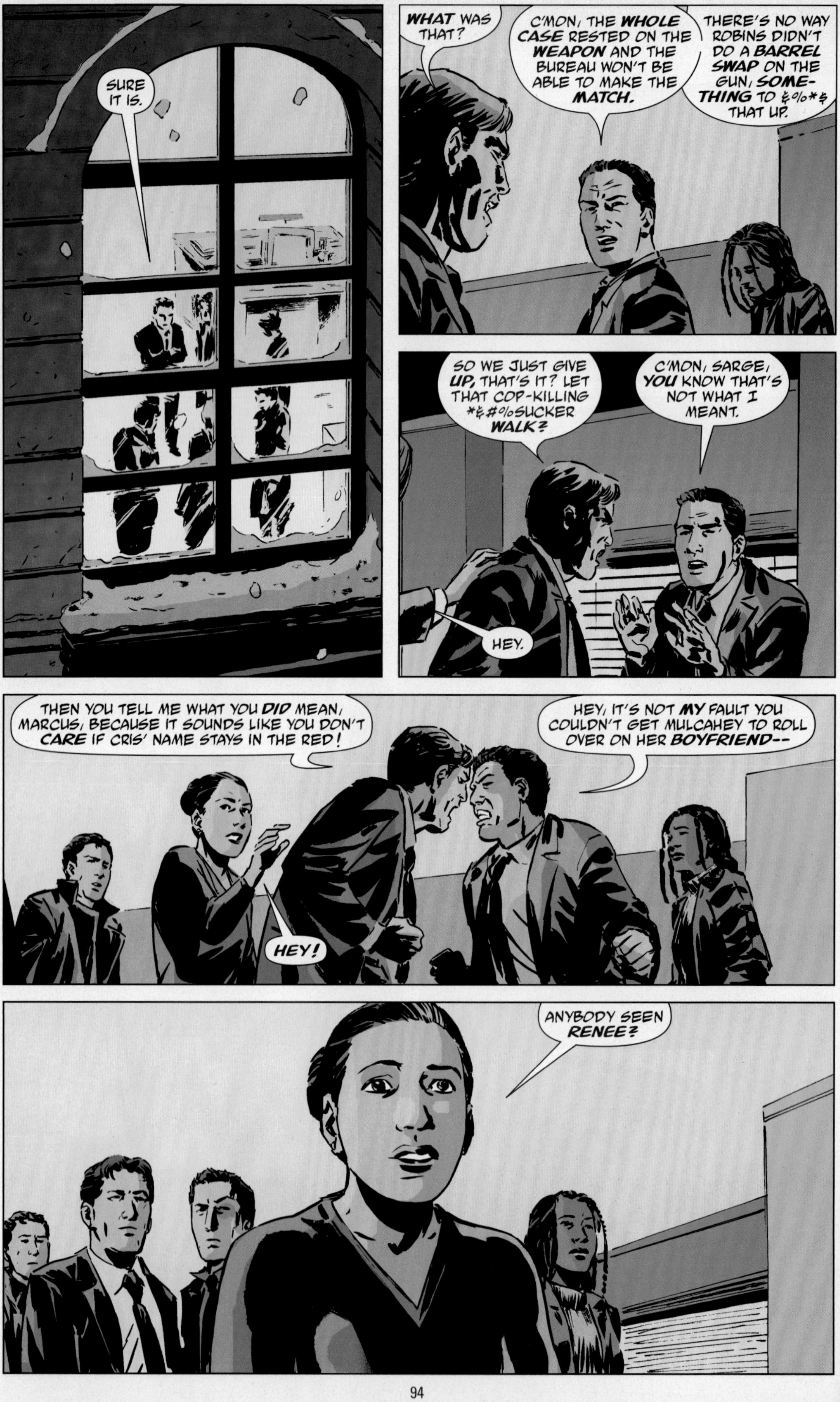

SURE IT IS.
WHAT WAS THAT?
C'MON, THE WHOLE CASE RESTED ON THE WEAPON AND THE BUREAU WON'T BE ABLE TO MAKE THE MATCH.
THERE'S NO WAY ROBINS DIDN'T DO A BARREL SWAP ON THE GUN, SOMETHING TO &%*$ THAT UP.
SO WE JUST GIVE UP, THAT'S IT? LET THAT COP-KILLING *&#%SUCKER WALK?
C'MON, SARGE, YOU KNOW THAT'S NOT WHAT I MEANT.
HEY.
THEN YOU TELL ME WHAT YOU DID MEAN, MARCUS, BECAUSE IT SOUNDS LIKE YOU DON'T CARE IF CRIS' NAME STAYS IN THE RED!
HEY, IT'S NOT MY FAULT YOU COULDN'T GET MULCAHEY TO ROLL OVER ON HER BOYFRIEND--
HEY!
ANYBODY SEEN RENEE?

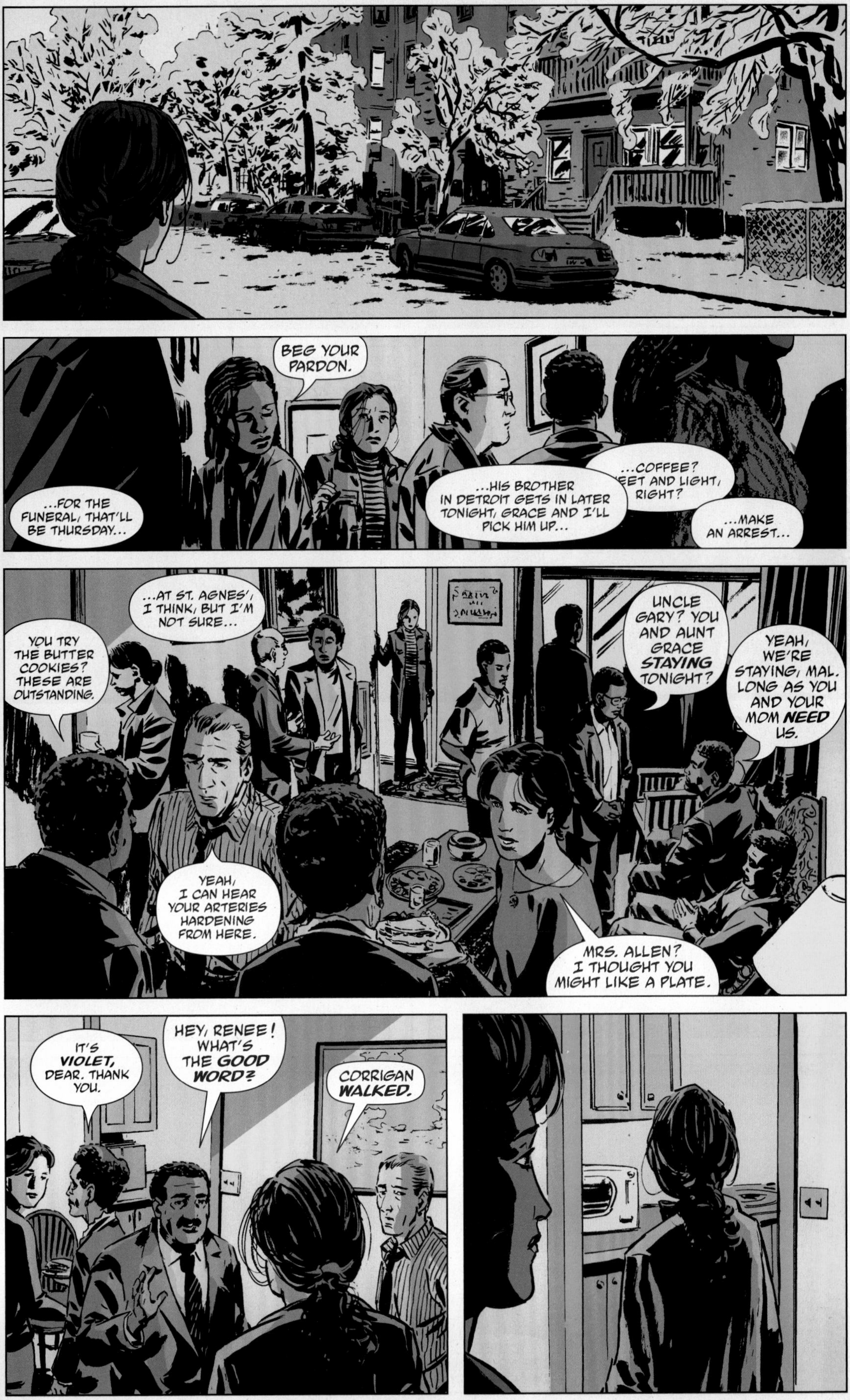
BEG YOUR PARDON.
...FOR THE FUNERAL, THAT'LL BE THURSDAY...
...HIS BROTHER IN DETROIT GETS IN LATER TONIGHT, GRACE AND I'LL PICK HIM UP...
...COFFEE? EET AND LIGHT, RIGHT?
...MAKE AN ARREST...
YOU TRY THE BUTTER COOKIES? THESE ARE OUTSTANDING.
...AT ST. AGNES', I THINK, BUT I'M NOT SURE...
YEAH, I CAN HEAR YOUR ARTERIES HARDENING FROM HERE.
UNCLE GARY? YOU AND AUNT GRACE **STAYING** TONIGHT?
YEAH, WE'RE STAYING, MAL. LONG AS YOU AND YOUR MOM **NEED** US.
MRS. ALLEN? I THOUGHT YOU MIGHT LIKE A PLATE.
IT'S **VIOLET,** DEAR. THANK YOU.
HEY, RENEE! WHAT'S THE **GOOD WORD?**
CORRIGAN **WALKED.**

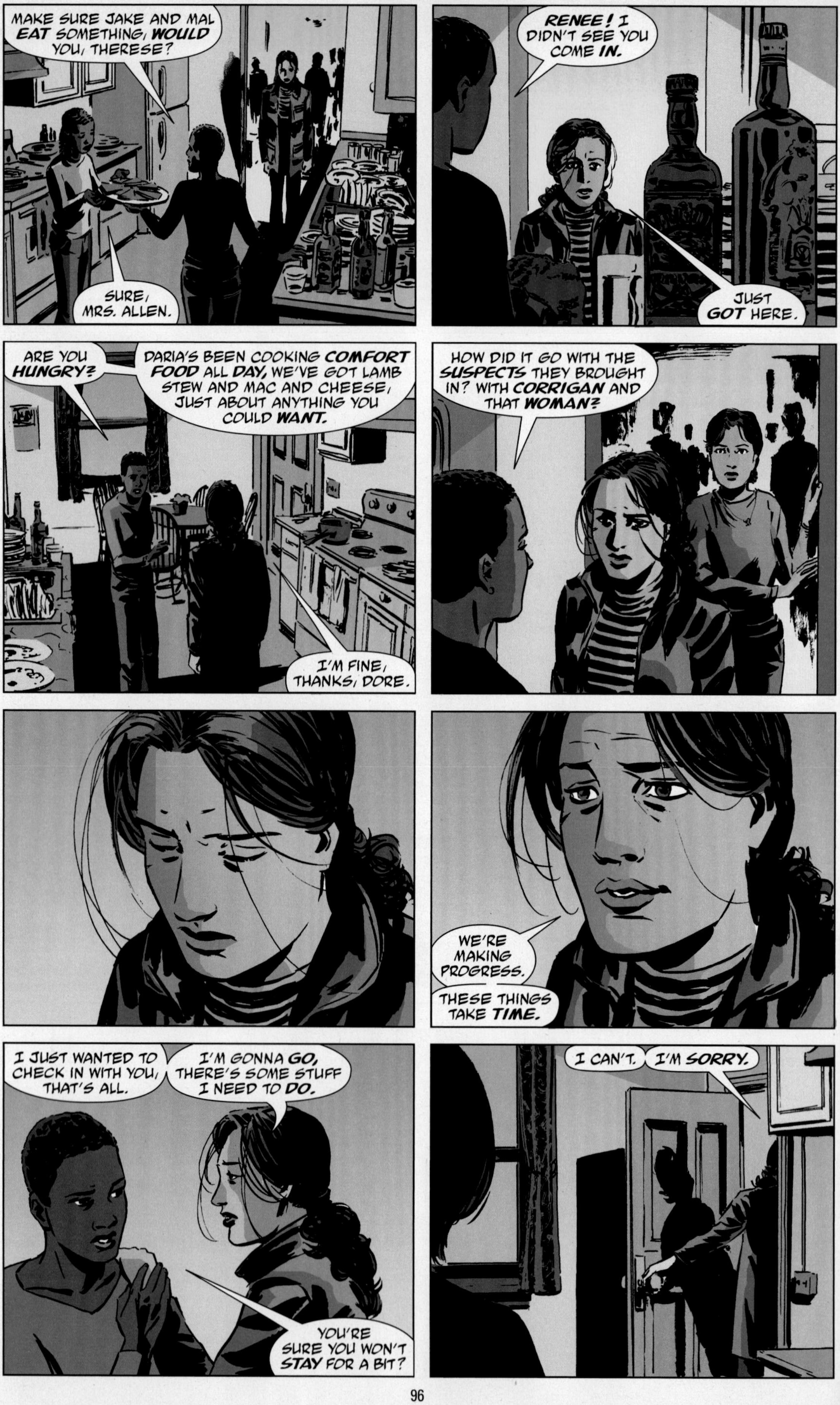

MAKE SURE JAKE AND MAL EAT SOMETHING, WOULD YOU, THERESE?
SURE, MRS. ALLEN.
RENEE! I DIDN'T SEE YOU COME IN.
JUST GOT HERE.
ARE YOU HUNGRY?
DARIA'S BEEN COOKING COMFORT FOOD ALL DAY, WE'VE GOT LAMB STEW AND MAC AND CHEESE, JUST ABOUT ANYTHING YOU COULD WANT.
I'M FINE, THANKS, DORE.
HOW DID IT GO WITH THE SUSPECTS THEY BROUGHT IN? WITH CORRIGAN AND THAT WOMAN?
WE'RE MAKING PROGRESS.
THESE THINGS TAKE TIME.
I JUST WANTED TO CHECK IN WITH YOU, THAT'S ALL.
I'M GONNA GO, THERE'S SOME STUFF I NEED TO DO.
YOU'RE SURE YOU WON'T STAY FOR A BIT?
I CAN'T.
I'M SORRY.

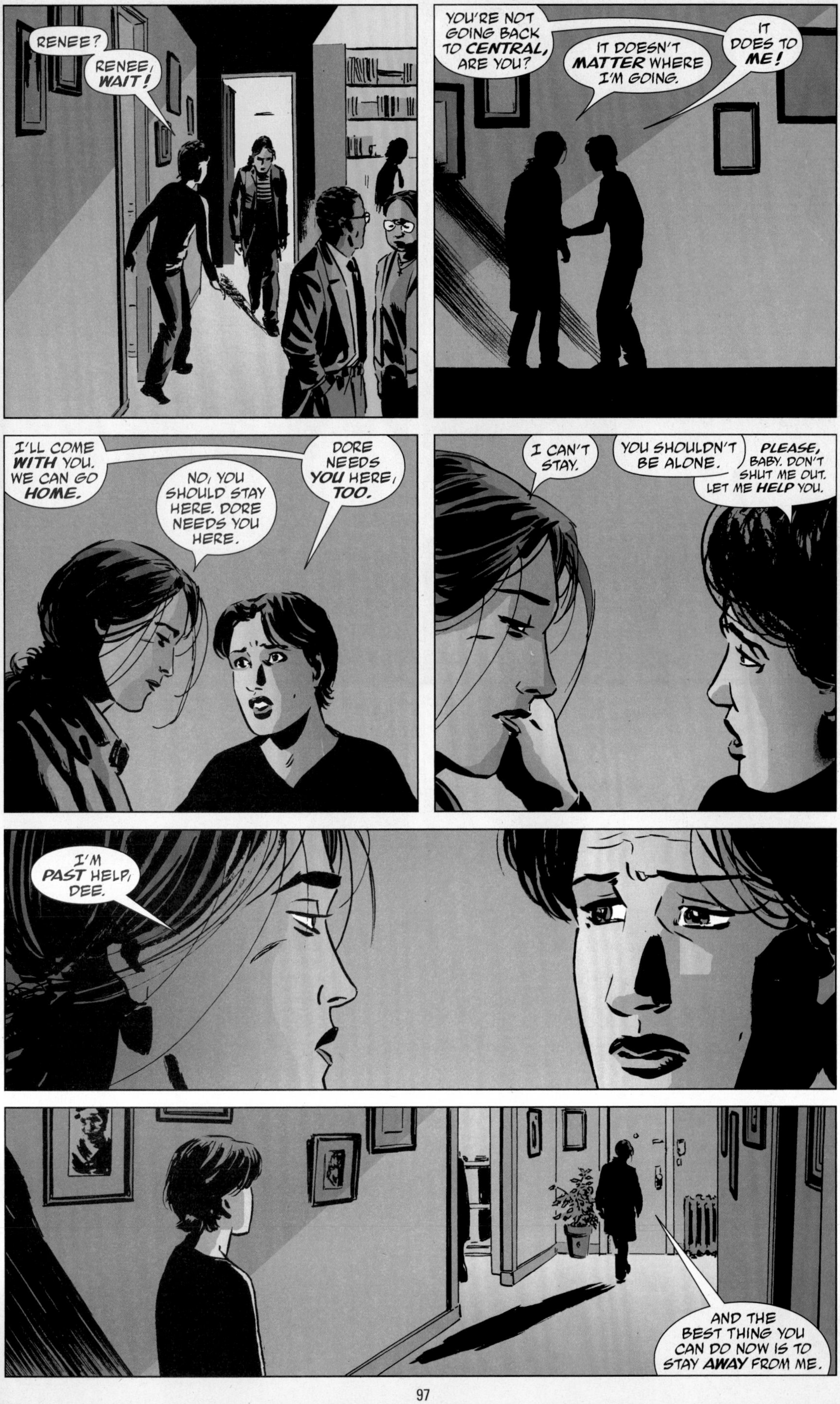
RENEE?
RENEE, WAIT!
YOU'RE NOT GOING BACK TO CENTRAL, ARE YOU?
IT DOESN'T MATTER WHERE I'M GOING.
IT DOES TO ME!
I'LL COME WITH YOU. WE CAN GO HOME.
NO, YOU SHOULD STAY HERE. DORE NEEDS YOU HERE.
DORE NEEDS YOU HERE, TOO.
I CAN'T STAY.
YOU SHOULDN'T BE ALONE.
PLEASE, BABY. DON'T SHUT ME OUT. LET ME HELP YOU.
I'M PAST HELP, DEE.
AND THE BEST THING YOU CAN DO NOW IS TO STAY AWAY FROM ME.

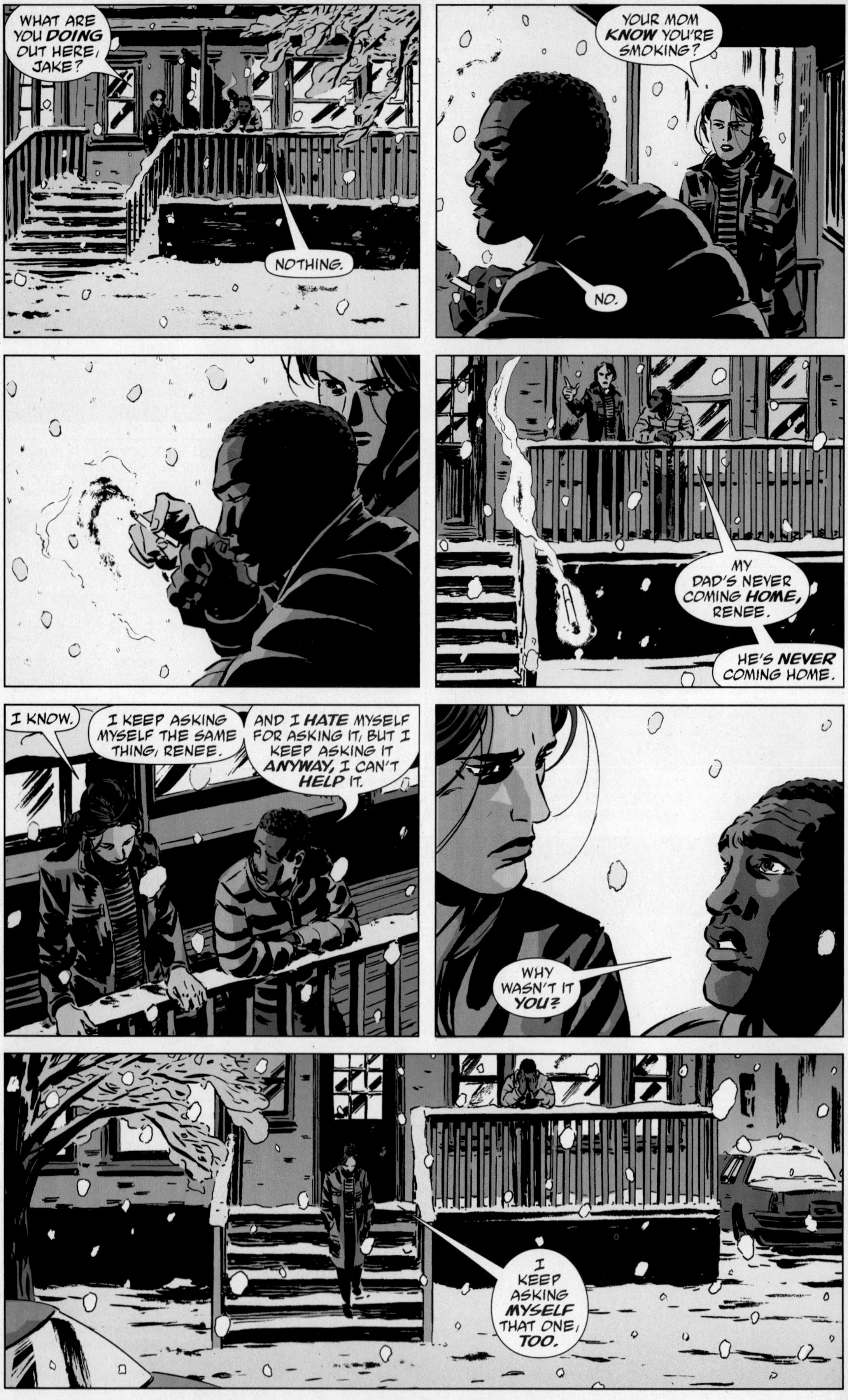
WHAT ARE YOU DOING OUT HERE, JAKE?
NOTHING.
YOUR MOM KNOW YOU'RE SMOKING?
NO.
MY DAD'S NEVER COMING HOME, RENEE.
HE'S NEVER COMING HOME.
I KNOW.
I KEEP ASKING MYSELF THE SAME THING, RENEE.
AND I HATE MYSELF FOR ASKING IT, BUT I KEEP ASKING IT ANYWAY, I CAN'T HELP IT.
WHY WASN'T IT YOU?
I KEEP ASKING MYSELF THAT ONE, TOO.

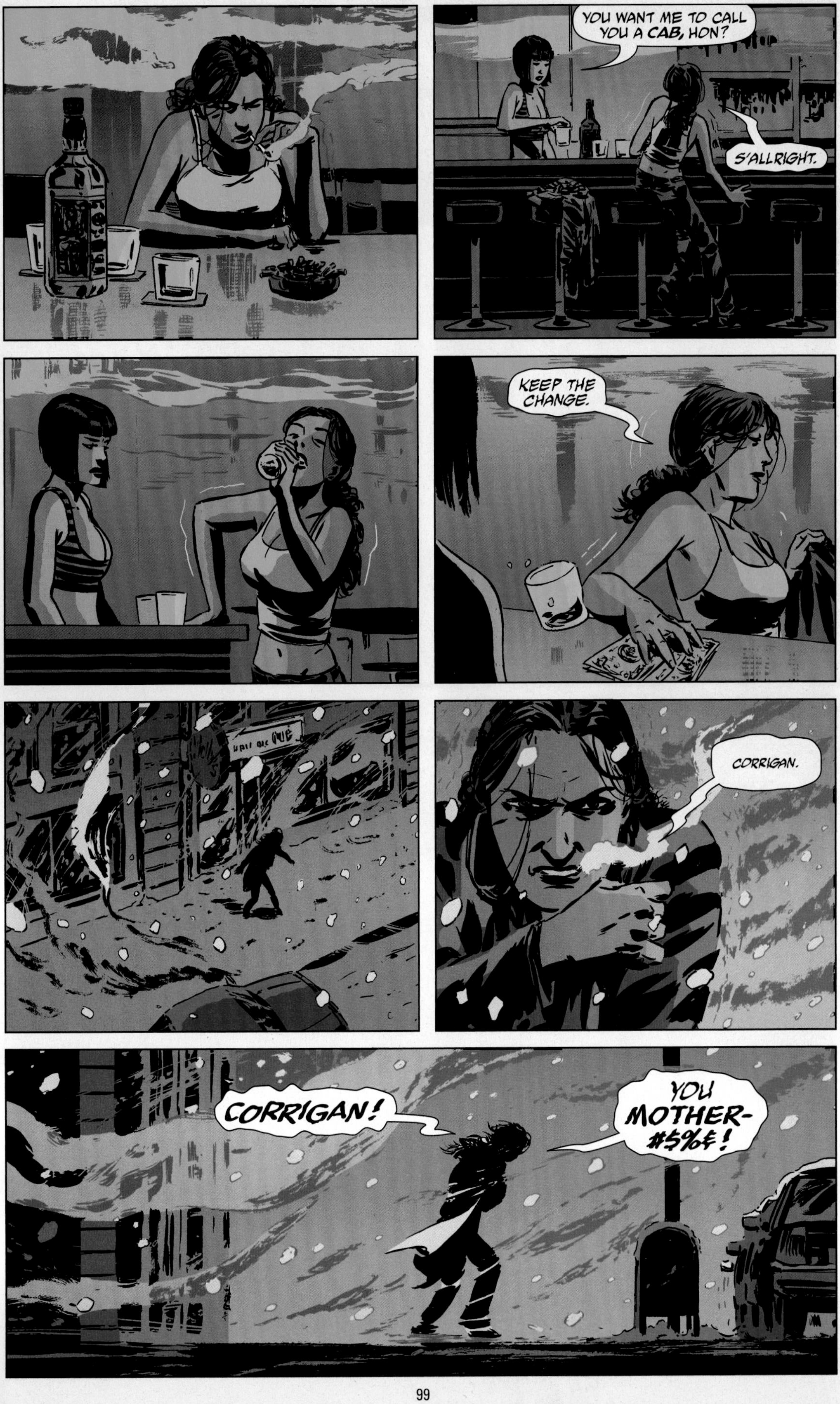
YOU WANT ME TO CALL YOU A CAB, HON?
S'ALLRIGHT.
KEEP THE CHANGE.
CORRIGAN.
CORRIGAN!
YOU MOTHER- #$%€!

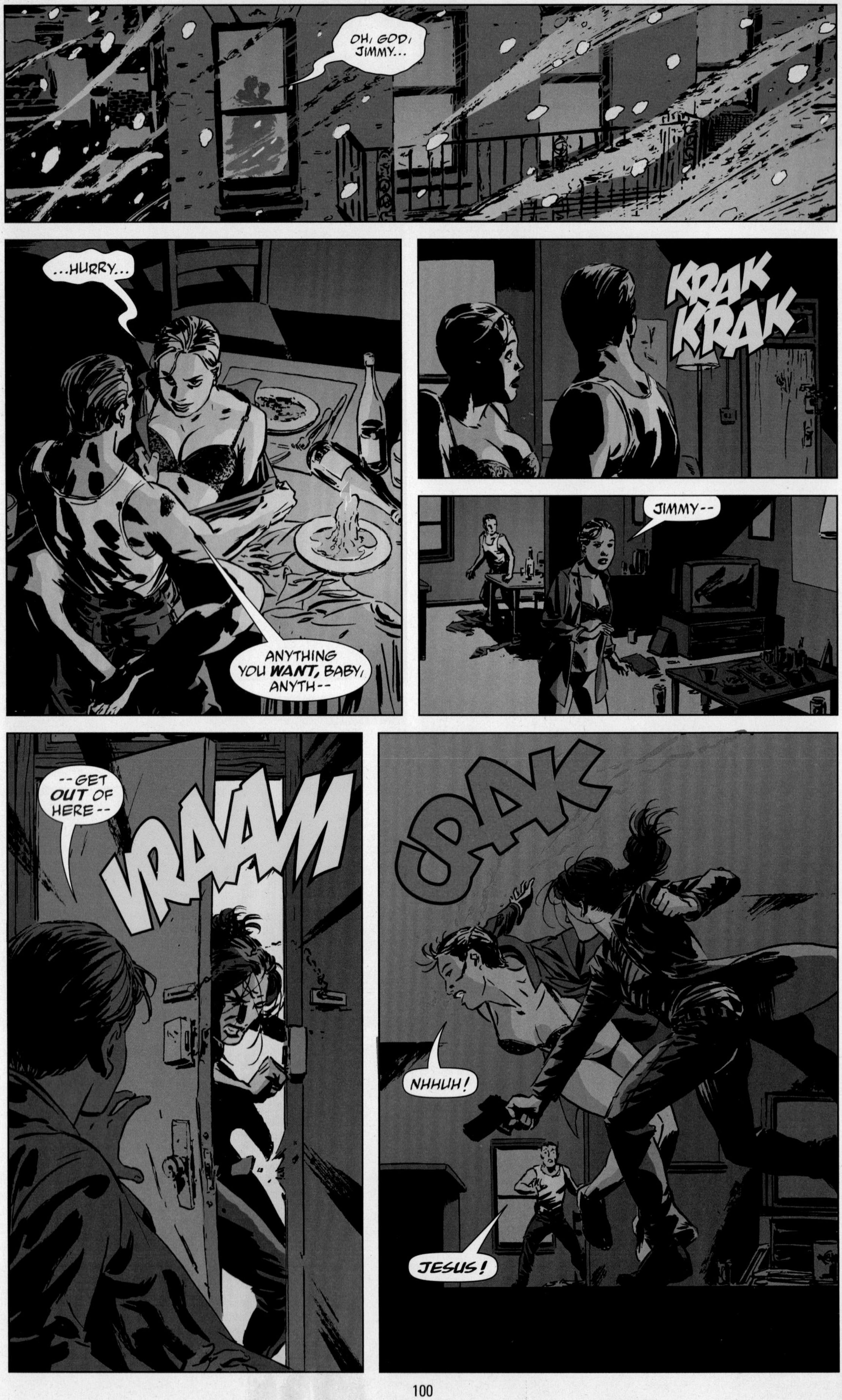

OH, GOD, JIMMY...
...HURRY...
ANYTHING YOU WANT, BABY, ANYTH--
KRAK KRAK
JIMMY--
--GET OUT OF HERE--
VRAAM
CRAK
NHHUH!
JESUS!

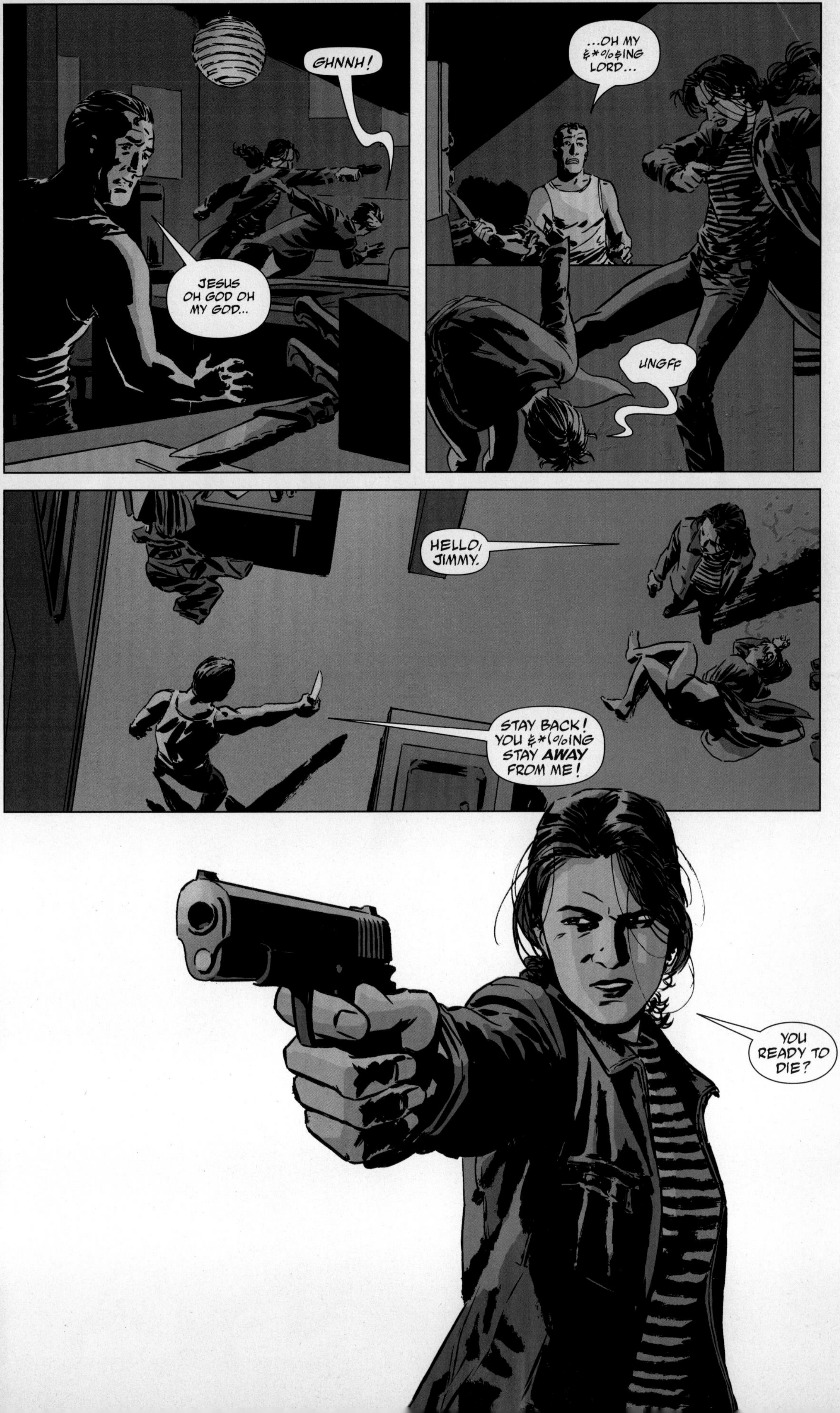
GHNNH!
JESUS OH GOD OH MY GOD...
...OH MY &*%$ING LORD...
UNGFF
HELLO, JIMMY.
STAY BACK! YOU &*(%ING STAY AWAY FROM ME!
YOU READY TO DIE?

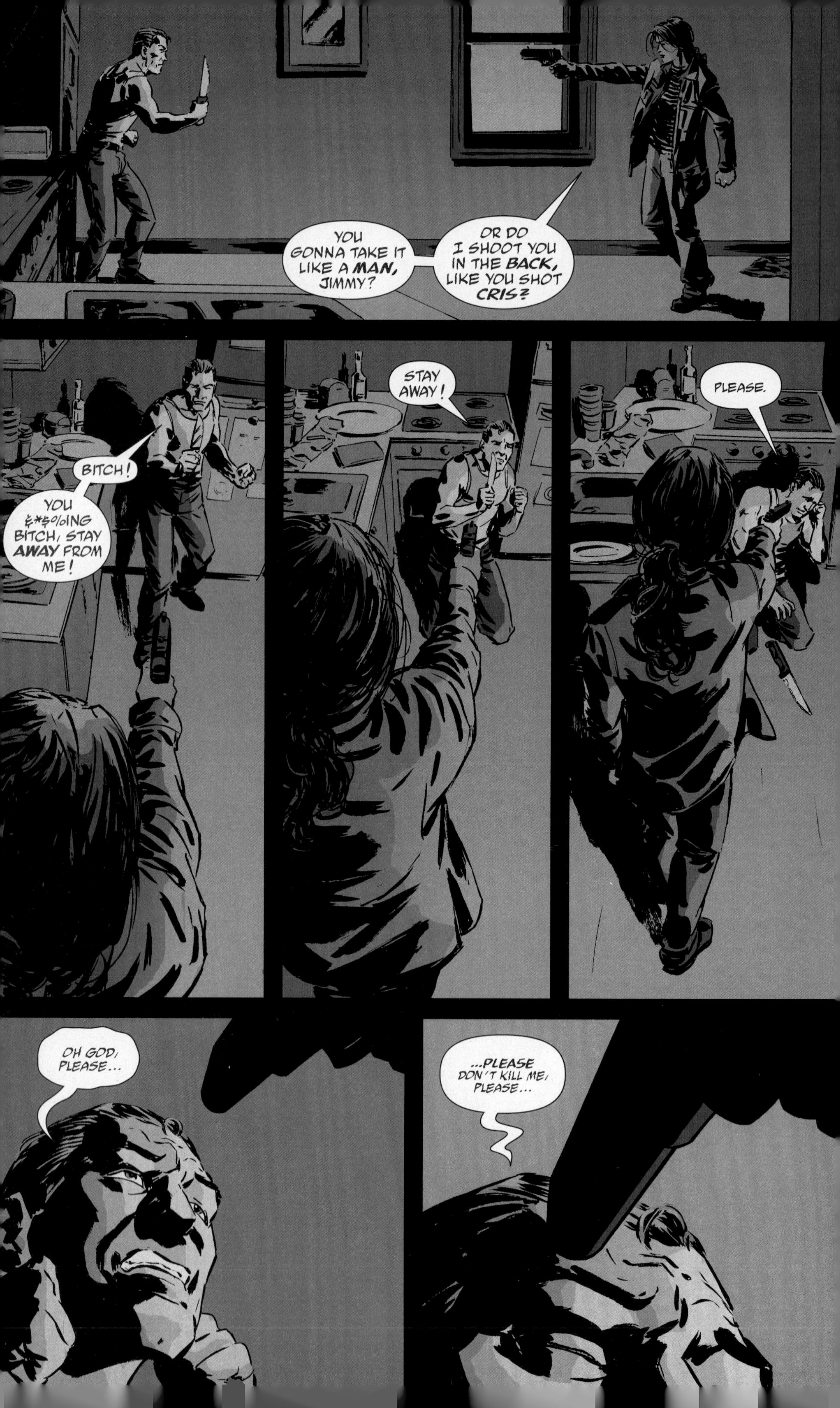
YOU GONNA TAKE IT LIKE A MAN, JIMMY?
OR DO I SHOOT YOU IN THE BACK, LIKE YOU SHOT CRIS?
BITCH!
YOU &*$%ING BITCH, STAY AWAY FROM ME!
STAY AWAY!
PLEASE.
OH GOD, PLEASE...
...PLEASE DON'T KILL ME, PLEASE...

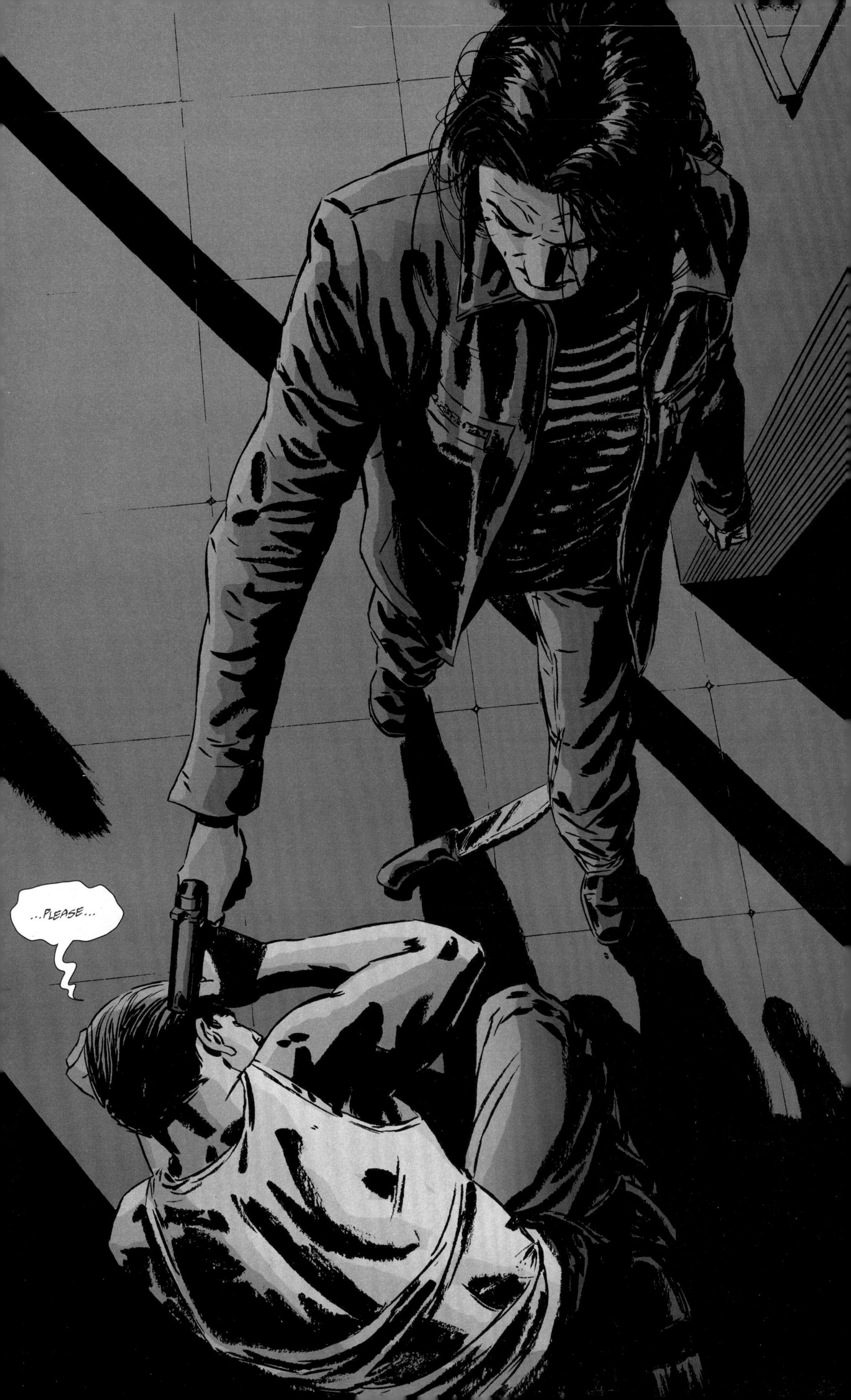
...PLEASE...

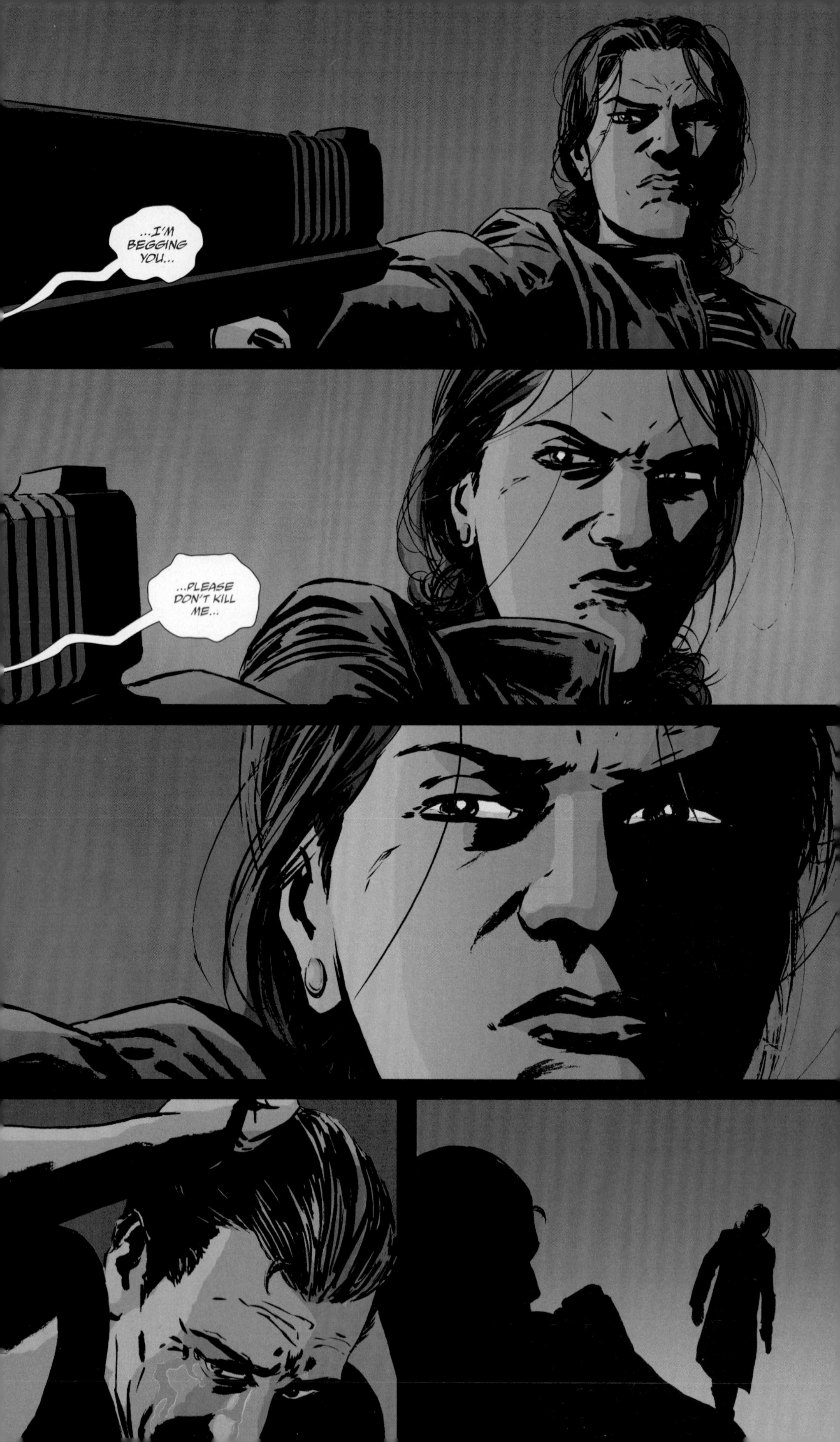
...I'M BEGGING YOU...
...PLEASE DON'T KILL ME...

...GONNA HAVE THE FUNERAL?

TOMORROW AFTERNOON.

COMMISSIONER AKINS SAYS IT'S FULL-DRESS...

RENEE...

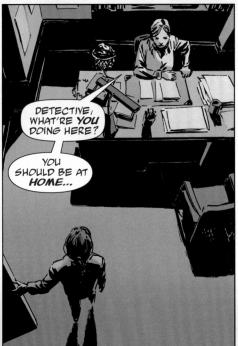

DETECTIVE, WHAT'RE *YOU* DOING HERE?

YOU SHOULD BE AT *HOME*...

...YOU NEED SOME *TIME*--

MORE THAN YOU KNOW.

I CAN'T *DO* IT ANYMORE, CAPTAIN.

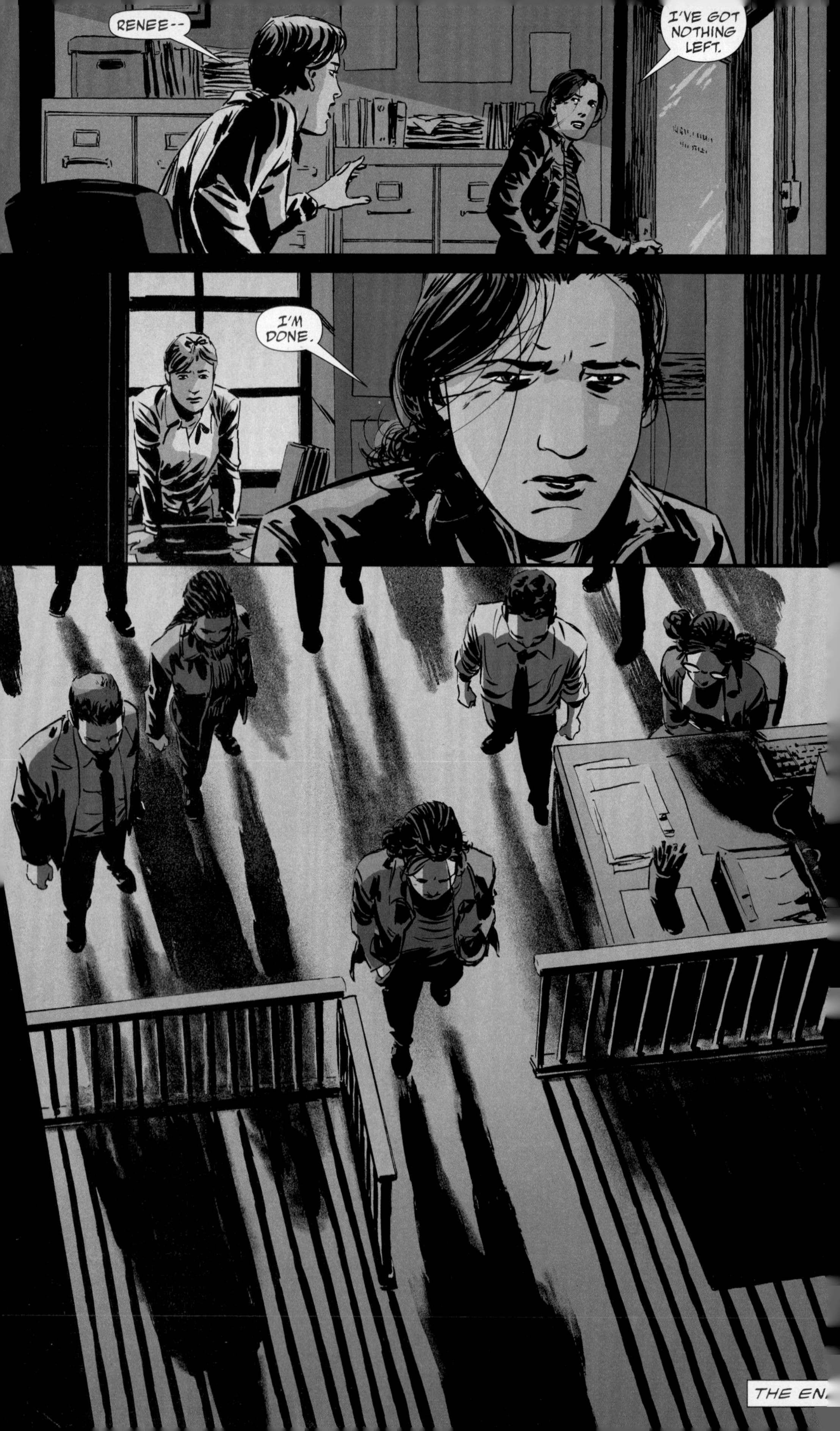
RENEE--
I'VE GOT NOTHING LEFT.
I'M DONE.
THE EN

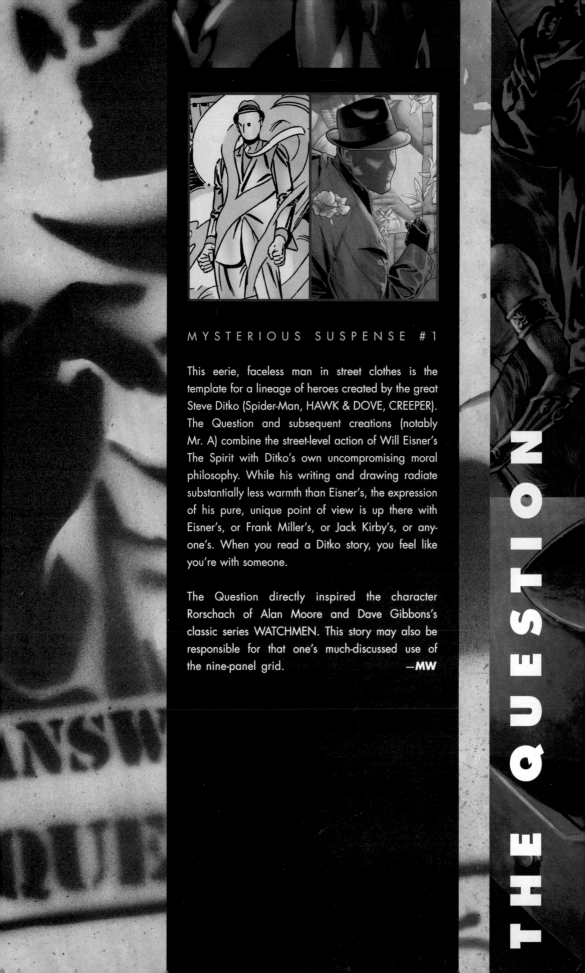

MYSTERIOUS SUSPENSE #1

This eerie, faceless man in street clothes is the template for a lineage of heroes created by the great Steve Ditko (Spider-Man, HAWK & DOVE, CREEPER). The Question and subsequent creations (notably Mr. A) combine the street-level action of Will Eisner's The Spirit with Ditko's own uncompromising moral philosophy. While his writing and drawing radiate substantially less warmth than Eisner's, the expression of his pure, unique point of view is up there with Eisner's, or Frank Miller's, or Jack Kirby's, or anyone's. When you read a Ditko story, you feel like you're with someone.

The Question directly inspired the character Rorschach of Alan Moore and Dave Gibbons's classic series WATCHMEN. This story may also be responsible for that one's much-discussed use of the nine-panel grid. —MW

THE QUESTION

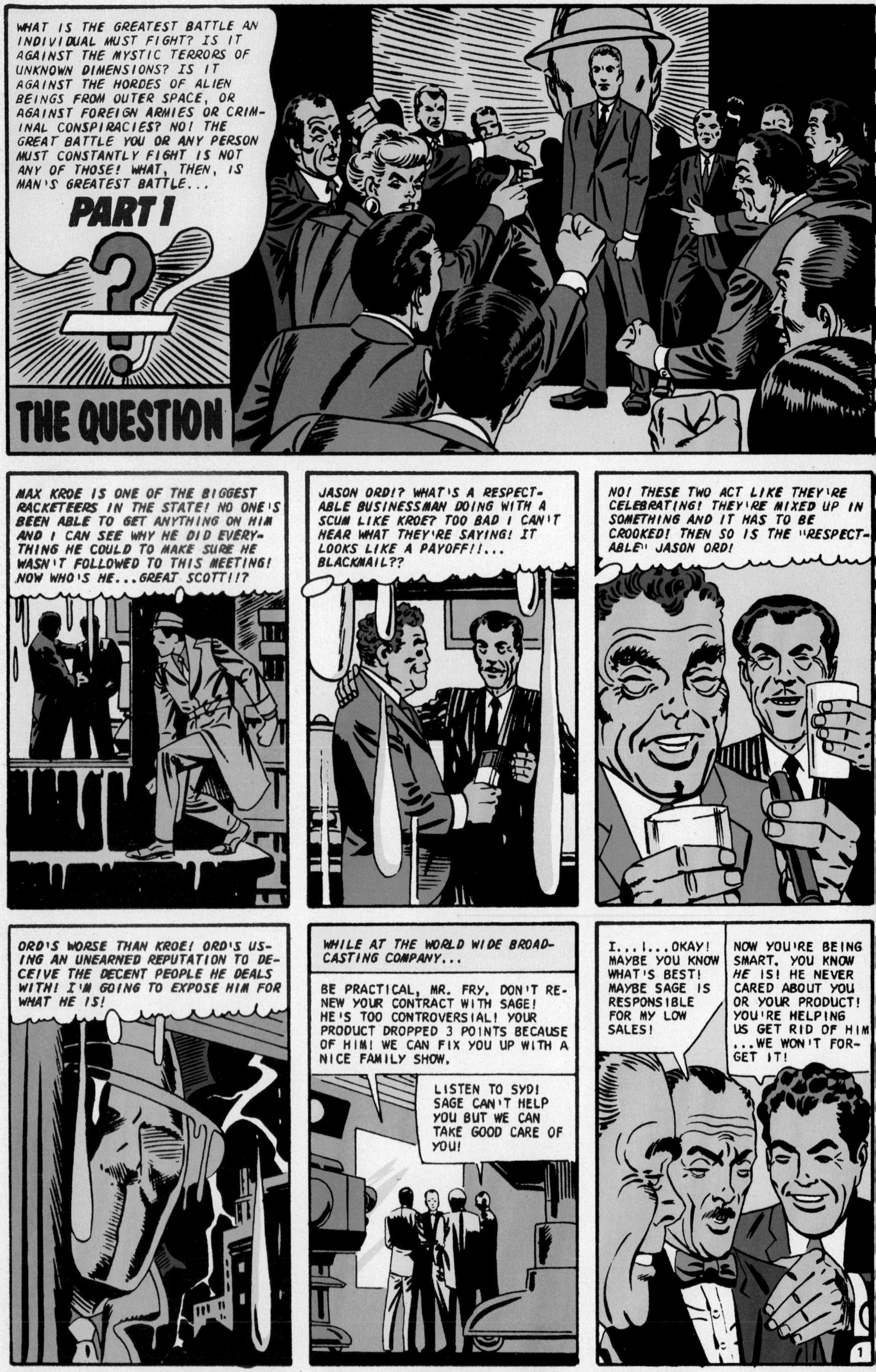
WHAT IS THE GREATEST BATTLE AN INDIVIDUAL MUST FIGHT? IS IT AGAINST THE MYSTIC TERRORS OF UNKNOWN DIMENSIONS? IS IT AGAINST THE HORDES OF ALIEN BEINGS FROM OUTER SPACE, OR AGAINST FOREIGN ARMIES OR CRIMINAL CONSPIRACIES? NO! THE GREAT BATTLE YOU OR ANY PERSON MUST CONSTANTLY FIGHT IS NOT ANY OF THOSE! WHAT, THEN, IS MAN'S GREATEST BATTLE...
PART I
THE QUESTION
MAX KROE IS ONE OF THE BIGGEST RACKETEERS IN THE STATE! NO ONE'S BEEN ABLE TO GET ANYTHING ON HIM AND I CAN SEE WHY HE DID EVERYTHING HE COULD TO MAKE SURE HE WASN'T FOLLOWED TO THIS MEETING! NOW WHO'S HE...GREAT SCOTT!!?
JASON ORD!? WHAT'S A RESPECTABLE BUSINESSMAN DOING WITH A SCUM LIKE KROE? TOO BAD I CAN'T HEAR WHAT THEY'RE SAYING! IT LOOKS LIKE A PAYOFF!!... BLACKMAIL??
NO! THESE TWO ACT LIKE THEY'RE CELEBRATING! THEY'RE MIXED UP IN SOMETHING AND IT HAS TO BE CROOKED! THEN SO IS THE "RESPECTABLE" JASON ORD!
ORD'S WORSE THAN KROE! ORD'S USING AN UNEARNED REPUTATION TO DECEIVE THE DECENT PEOPLE HE DEALS WITH! I'M GOING TO EXPOSE HIM FOR WHAT HE IS!
WHILE AT THE WORLD WIDE BROADCASTING COMPANY...
BE PRACTICAL, MR. FRY. DON'T RENEW YOUR CONTRACT WITH SAGE! HE'S TOO CONTROVERSIAL! YOUR PRODUCT DROPPED 3 POINTS BECAUSE OF HIM! WE CAN FIX YOU UP WITH A NICE FAMILY SHOW.
LISTEN TO SYD! SAGE CAN'T HELP YOU BUT WE CAN TAKE GOOD CARE OF YOU!
I...I...OKAY! MAYBE YOU KNOW WHAT'S BEST! MAYBE SAGE IS RESPONSIBLE FOR MY LOW SALES!
NOW YOU'RE BEING SMART. YOU KNOW HE IS! HE NEVER CARED ABOUT YOU OR YOUR PRODUCT! YOU'RE HELPING US GET RID OF HIM ...WE WON'T FORGET IT!
1

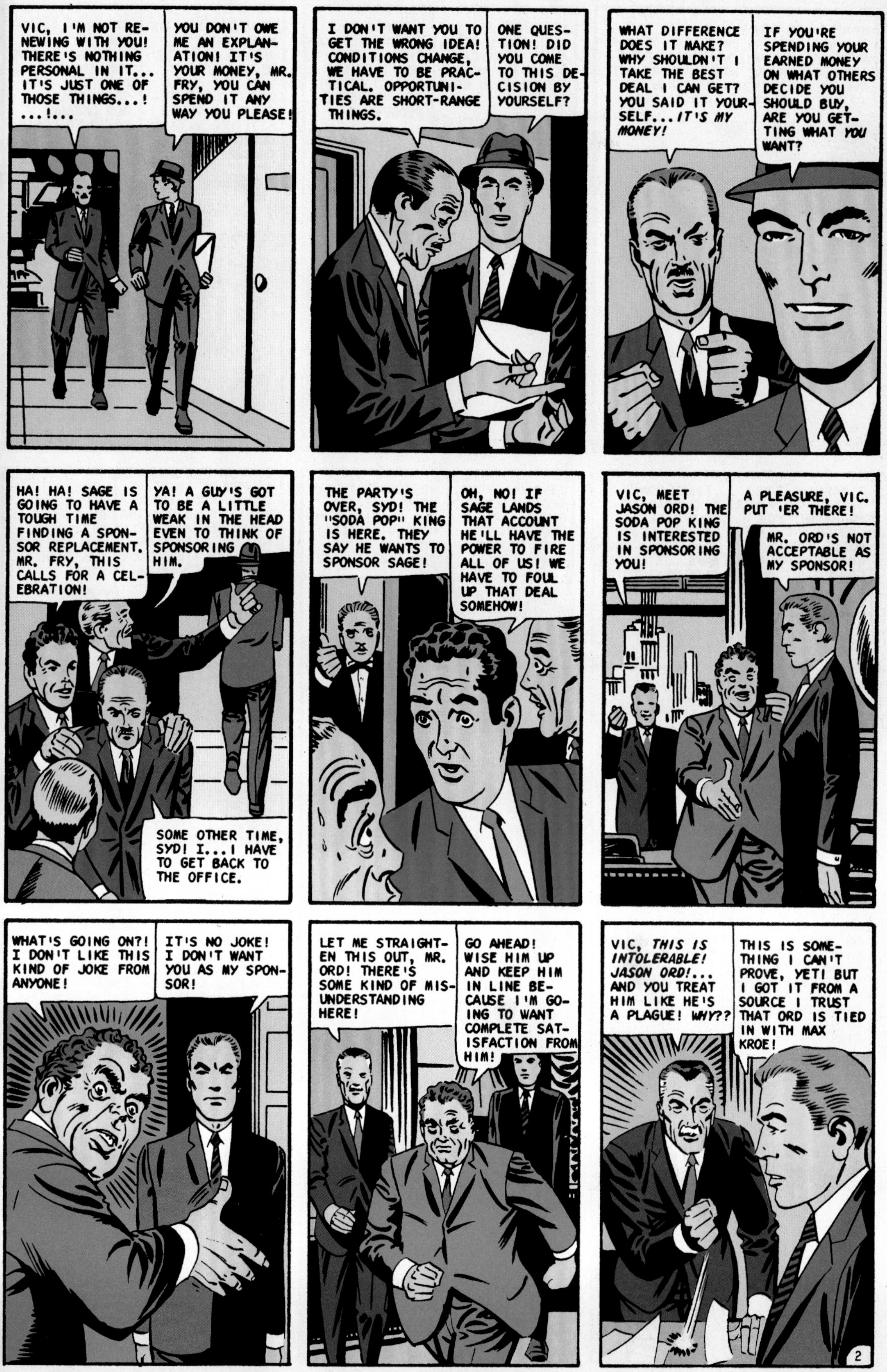
VIC, I'M NOT RENEWING WITH YOU! THERE'S NOTHING PERSONAL IN IT... IT'S JUST ONE OF THOSE THINGS...! ...!...
YOU DON'T OWE ME AN EXPLANATION! IT'S YOUR MONEY, MR. FRY, YOU CAN SPEND IT ANY WAY YOU PLEASE!
I DON'T WANT YOU TO GET THE WRONG IDEA! CONDITIONS CHANGE, WE HAVE TO BE PRACTICAL. OPPORTUNITIES ARE SHORT-RANGE THINGS.
ONE QUESTION! DID YOU COME TO THIS DECISION BY YOURSELF?
WHAT DIFFERENCE DOES IT MAKE? WHY SHOULDN'T I TAKE THE BEST DEAL I CAN GET? YOU SAID IT YOURSELF... IT'S MY MONEY!
IF YOU'RE SPENDING YOUR EARNED MONEY ON WHAT OTHERS DECIDE YOU SHOULD BUY, ARE YOU GETTING WHAT YOU WANT?
HA! HA! SAGE IS GOING TO HAVE A TOUGH TIME FINDING A SPONSOR REPLACEMENT. MR. FRY, THIS CALLS FOR A CELEBRATION!
YA! A GUY'S GOT TO BE A LITTLE WEAK IN THE HEAD EVEN TO THINK OF SPONSORING HIM.
SOME OTHER TIME, SYD! I...I HAVE TO GET BACK TO THE OFFICE.
THE PARTY'S OVER, SYD! THE "SODA POP" KING IS HERE. THEY SAY HE WANTS TO SPONSOR SAGE!
OH, NO! IF SAGE LANDS THAT ACCOUNT HE'LL HAVE THE POWER TO FIRE ALL OF US! WE HAVE TO FOUL UP THAT DEAL SOMEHOW!
VIC, MEET JASON ORD! THE SODA POP KING IS INTERESTED IN SPONSORING YOU!
A PLEASURE, VIC. PUT 'ER THERE!
MR. ORD'S NOT ACCEPTABLE AS MY SPONSOR!
WHAT'S GOING ON?! I DON'T LIKE THIS KIND OF JOKE FROM ANYONE!
IT'S NO JOKE! I DON'T WANT YOU AS MY SPONSOR!
LET ME STRAIGHTEN THIS OUT, MR. ORD! THERE'S SOME KIND OF MISUNDERSTANDING HERE!
GO AHEAD! WISE HIM UP AND KEEP HIM IN LINE BECAUSE I'M GOING TO WANT COMPLETE SATISFACTION FROM HIM!
VIC, THIS IS INTOLERABLE! JASON ORD!... AND YOU TREAT HIM LIKE HE'S A PLAGUE! WHY??
THIS IS SOMETHING I CAN'T PROVE, YET! BUT I GOT IT FROM A SOURCE I TRUST THAT ORD IS TIED IN WITH MAX KROE!
2

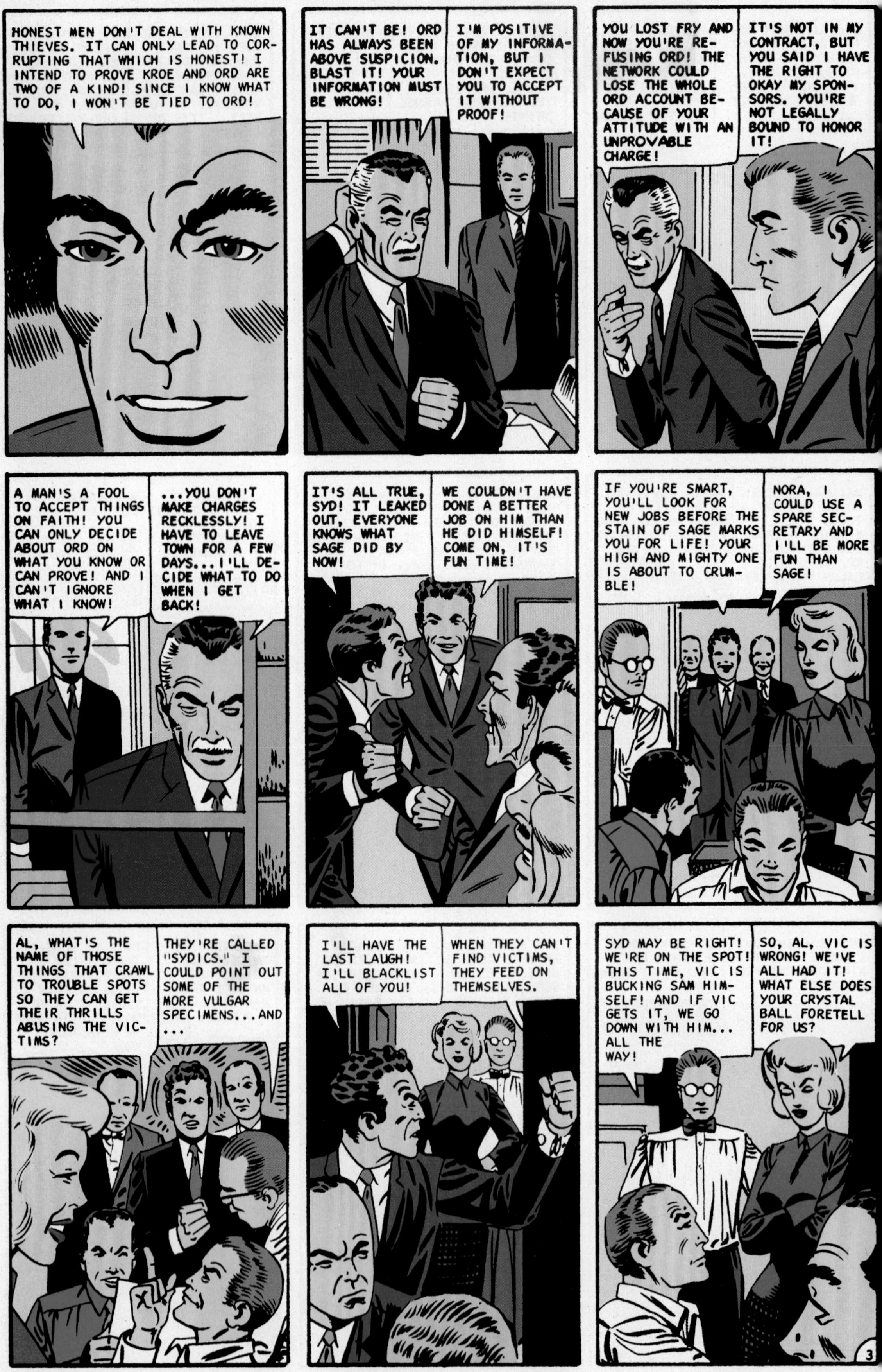
HONEST MEN DON'T DEAL WITH KNOWN THIEVES. IT CAN ONLY LEAD TO CORRUPTING THAT WHICH IS HONEST! I INTEND TO PROVE KROE AND ORD ARE TWO OF A KIND! SINCE I KNOW WHAT TO DO, I WON'T BE TIED TO ORD!
IT CAN'T BE! ORD HAS ALWAYS BEEN ABOVE SUSPICION. BLAST IT! YOUR INFORMATION MUST BE WRONG!
I'M POSITIVE OF MY INFORMATION, BUT I DON'T EXPECT YOU TO ACCEPT IT WITHOUT PROOF!
YOU LOST FRY AND NOW YOU'RE REFUSING ORD! THE NETWORK COULD LOSE THE WHOLE ORD ACCOUNT BECAUSE OF YOUR ATTITUDE WITH AN UNPROVABLE CHARGE!
IT'S NOT IN MY CONTRACT, BUT YOU SAID I HAVE THE RIGHT TO OKAY MY SPONSORS. YOU'RE NOT LEGALLY BOUND TO HONOR IT!
A MAN'S A FOOL TO ACCEPT THINGS ON FAITH! YOU CAN ONLY DECIDE ABOUT ORD ON WHAT YOU KNOW OR CAN PROVE! AND I CAN'T IGNORE WHAT I KNOW!
...YOU DON'T MAKE CHARGES RECKLESSLY! I HAVE TO LEAVE TOWN FOR A FEW DAYS... I'LL DECIDE WHAT TO DO WHEN I GET BACK!
IT'S ALL TRUE, SYD! IT LEAKED OUT, EVERYONE KNOWS WHAT SAGE DID BY NOW!
WE COULDN'T HAVE DONE A BETTER JOB ON HIM THAN HE DID HIMSELF! COME ON, IT'S FUN TIME!
IF YOU'RE SMART, YOU'LL LOOK FOR NEW JOBS BEFORE THE STAIN OF SAGE MARKS YOU FOR LIFE! YOUR HIGH AND MIGHTY ONE IS ABOUT TO CRUMBLE!
NORA, I COULD USE A SPARE SECRETARY AND I'LL BE MORE FUN THAN SAGE!
AL, WHAT'S THE NAME OF THOSE THINGS THAT CRAWL TO TROUBLE SPOTS SO THEY CAN GET THEIR THRILLS ABUSING THE VICTIMS?
THEY'RE CALLED "SYDICS." I COULD POINT OUT SOME OF THE MORE VULGAR SPECIMENS...AND ...
I'LL HAVE THE LAST LAUGH! I'LL BLACKLIST ALL OF YOU!
WHEN THEY CAN'T FIND VICTIMS, THEY FEED ON THEMSELVES.
SYD MAY BE RIGHT! WE'RE ON THE SPOT! THIS TIME, VIC IS BUCKING SAM HIMSELF! AND IF VIC GETS IT, WE GO DOWN WITH HIM... ALL THE WAY!
SO, AL, VIC IS WRONG! WE'VE ALL HAD IT! WHAT ELSE DOES YOUR CRYSTAL BALL FORETELL FOR US?
3

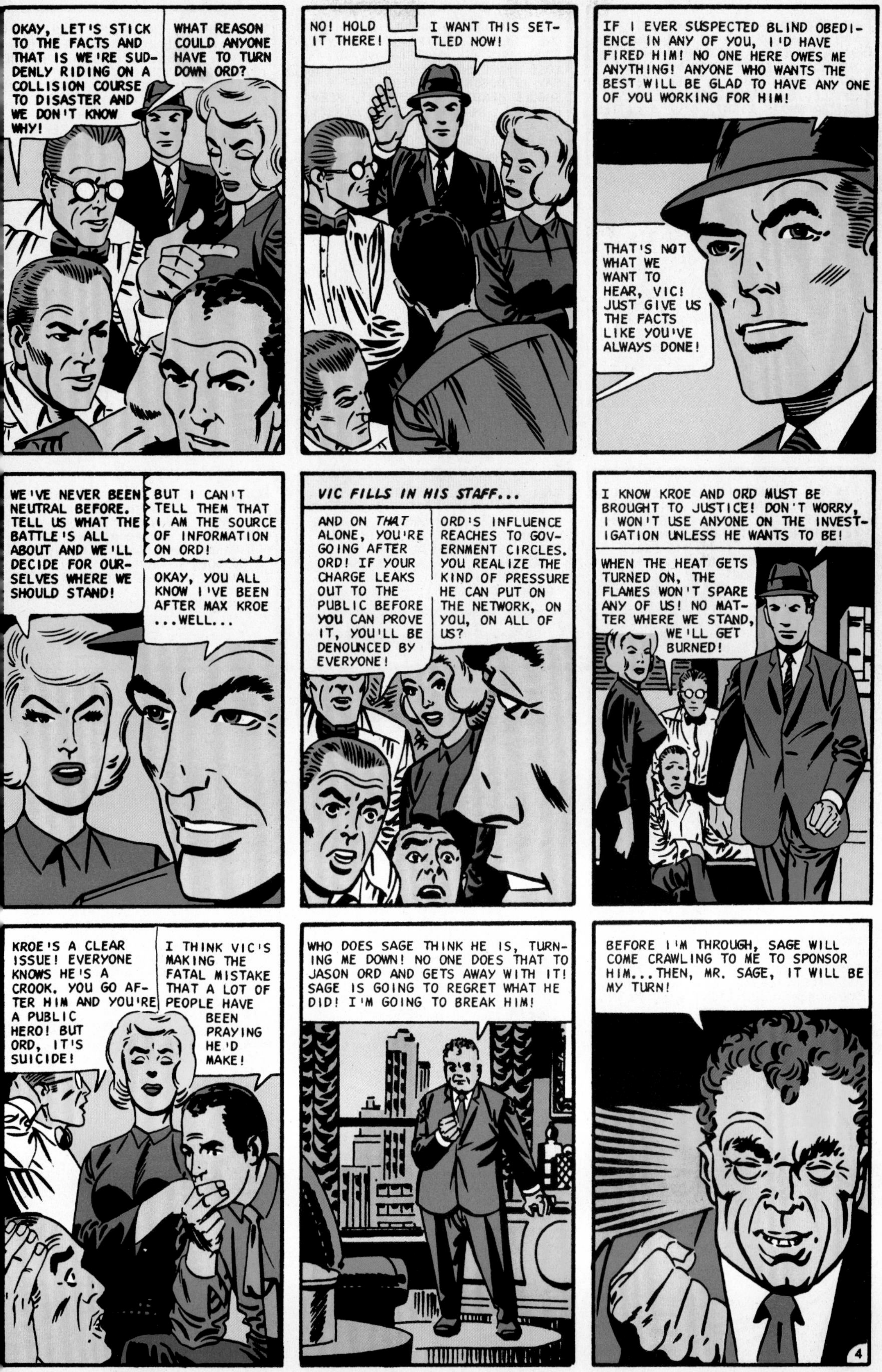
OKAY, LET'S STICK TO THE FACTS AND THAT IS WE'RE SUDDENLY RIDING ON A COLLISION COURSE TO DISASTER AND WE DON'T KNOW WHY!
WHAT REASON COULD ANYONE HAVE TO TURN DOWN ORD?
NO! HOLD IT THERE!
I WANT THIS SETTLED NOW!
IF I EVER SUSPECTED BLIND OBEDIENCE IN ANY OF YOU, I'D HAVE FIRED HIM! NO ONE HERE OWES ME ANYTHING! ANYONE WHO WANTS THE BEST WILL BE GLAD TO HAVE ANY ONE OF YOU WORKING FOR HIM!
THAT'S NOT WHAT WE WANT TO HEAR, VIC! JUST GIVE US THE FACTS LIKE YOU'VE ALWAYS DONE!
WE'VE NEVER BEEN NEUTRAL BEFORE. TELL US WHAT THE BATTLE'S ALL ABOUT AND WE'LL DECIDE FOR OURSELVES WHERE WE SHOULD STAND!
BUT I CAN'T TELL THEM THAT I AM THE SOURCE OF INFORMATION ON ORD!
OKAY, YOU ALL KNOW I'VE BEEN AFTER MAX KROE ...WELL...
VIC FILLS IN HIS STAFF...
AND ON THAT ALONE, YOU'RE GOING AFTER ORD! IF YOUR CHARGE LEAKS OUT TO THE PUBLIC BEFORE YOU CAN PROVE IT, YOU'LL BE DENOUNCED BY EVERYONE!
ORD'S INFLUENCE REACHES TO GOVERNMENT CIRCLES. YOU REALIZE THE KIND OF PRESSURE HE CAN PUT ON THE NETWORK, ON YOU, ON ALL OF US?
I KNOW KROE AND ORD MUST BE BROUGHT TO JUSTICE! DON'T WORRY, I WON'T USE ANYONE ON THE INVESTIGATION UNLESS HE WANTS TO BE!
WHEN THE HEAT GETS TURNED ON, THE FLAMES WON'T SPARE ANY OF US! NO MATTER WHERE WE STAND, WE'LL GET BURNED!
KROE'S A CLEAR ISSUE! EVERYONE KNOWS HE'S A CROOK. YOU GO AFTER HIM AND YOU'RE A PUBLIC HERO! BUT ORD, IT'S SUICIDE!
I THINK VIC'S MAKING THE FATAL MISTAKE THAT A LOT OF PEOPLE HAVE BEEN PRAYING HE'D MAKE!
WHO DOES SAGE THINK HE IS, TURNING ME DOWN! NO ONE DOES THAT TO JASON ORD AND GETS AWAY WITH IT! SAGE IS GOING TO REGRET WHAT HE DID! I'M GOING TO BREAK HIM!
BEFORE I'M THROUGH, SAGE WILL COME CRAWLING TO ME TO SPONSOR HIM...THEN, MR. SAGE, IT WILL BE MY TURN!
4

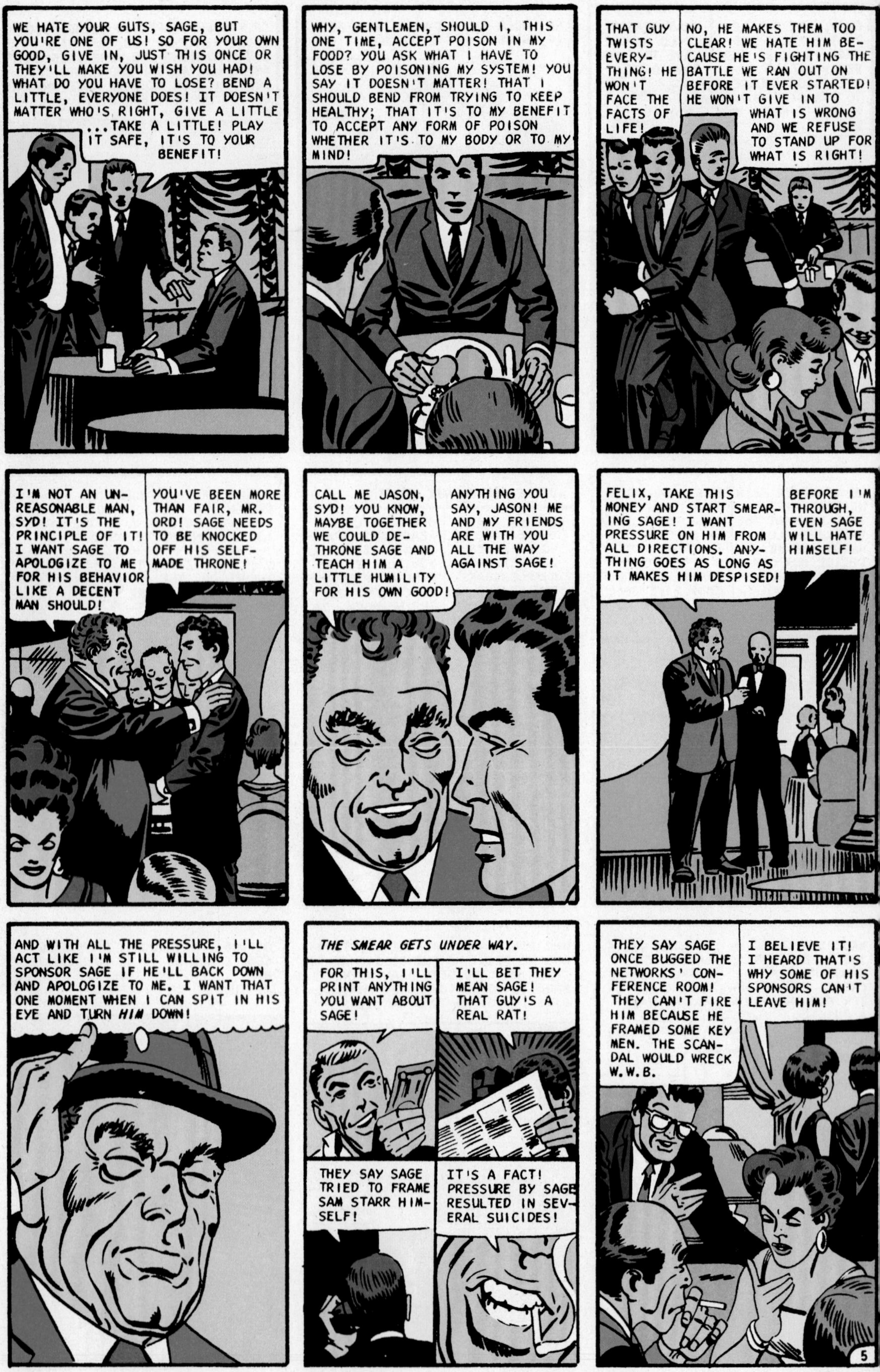
WE HATE YOUR GUTS, SAGE, BUT YOU'RE ONE OF US! SO FOR YOUR OWN GOOD, GIVE IN, JUST THIS ONCE OR THEY'LL MAKE YOU WISH YOU HAD! WHAT DO YOU HAVE TO LOSE? BEND A LITTLE, EVERYONE DOES! IT DOESN'T MATTER WHO'S RIGHT, GIVE A LITTLE ...TAKE A LITTLE! PLAY IT SAFE, IT'S TO YOUR BENEFIT!
WHY, GENTLEMEN, SHOULD I, THIS ONE TIME, ACCEPT POISON IN MY FOOD? YOU ASK WHAT I HAVE TO LOSE BY POISONING MY SYSTEM! YOU SAY IT DOESN'T MATTER! THAT I SHOULD BEND FROM TRYING TO KEEP HEALTHY; THAT IT'S TO MY BENEFIT TO ACCEPT ANY FORM OF POISON WHETHER IT'S TO MY BODY OR TO MY MIND!
THAT GUY TWISTS EVERYTHING! HE WON'T FACE THE FACTS OF LIFE!
NO, HE MAKES THEM TOO CLEAR! WE HATE HIM BECAUSE HE'S FIGHTING THE BATTLE WE RAN OUT ON BEFORE IT EVER STARTED! HE WON'T GIVE IN TO WHAT IS WRONG AND WE REFUSE TO STAND UP FOR WHAT IS RIGHT!
I'M NOT AN UNREASONABLE MAN, SYD! IT'S THE PRINCIPLE OF IT! I WANT SAGE TO APOLOGIZE TO ME FOR HIS BEHAVIOR LIKE A DECENT MAN SHOULD!
YOU'VE BEEN MORE THAN FAIR, MR. ORD! SAGE NEEDS TO BE KNOCKED OFF HIS SELF-MADE THRONE!
CALL ME JASON, SYD! YOU KNOW, MAYBE TOGETHER WE COULD DETHRONE SAGE AND TEACH HIM A LITTLE HUMILITY FOR HIS OWN GOOD!
ANYTHING YOU SAY, JASON! ME AND MY FRIENDS ARE WITH YOU ALL THE WAY AGAINST SAGE!
FELIX, TAKE THIS MONEY AND START SMEARING SAGE! I WANT PRESSURE ON HIM FROM ALL DIRECTIONS. ANYTHING GOES AS LONG AS IT MAKES HIM DESPISED!
BEFORE I'M THROUGH, EVEN SAGE WILL HATE HIMSELF!
AND WITH ALL THE PRESSURE, I'LL ACT LIKE I'M STILL WILLING TO SPONSOR SAGE IF HE'LL BACK DOWN AND APOLOGIZE TO ME. I WANT THAT ONE MOMENT WHEN I CAN SPIT IN HIS EYE AND TURN HIM DOWN!
THE SMEAR GETS UNDER WAY.
FOR THIS, I'LL PRINT ANYTHING YOU WANT ABOUT SAGE!
I'LL BET THEY MEAN SAGE! THAT GUY'S A REAL RAT!
THEY SAY SAGE TRIED TO FRAME SAM STARR HIMSELF!
IT'S A FACT! PRESSURE BY SAGE RESULTED IN SEVERAL SUICIDES!
THEY SAY SAGE ONCE BUGGED THE NETWORKS' CONFERENCE ROOM! THEY CAN'T FIRE HIM BECAUSE HE FRAMED SOME KEY MEN. THE SCANDAL WOULD WRECK W.W.B.
I BELIEVE IT! I HEARD THAT'S WHY SOME OF HIS SPONSORS CAN'T LEAVE HIM!
5

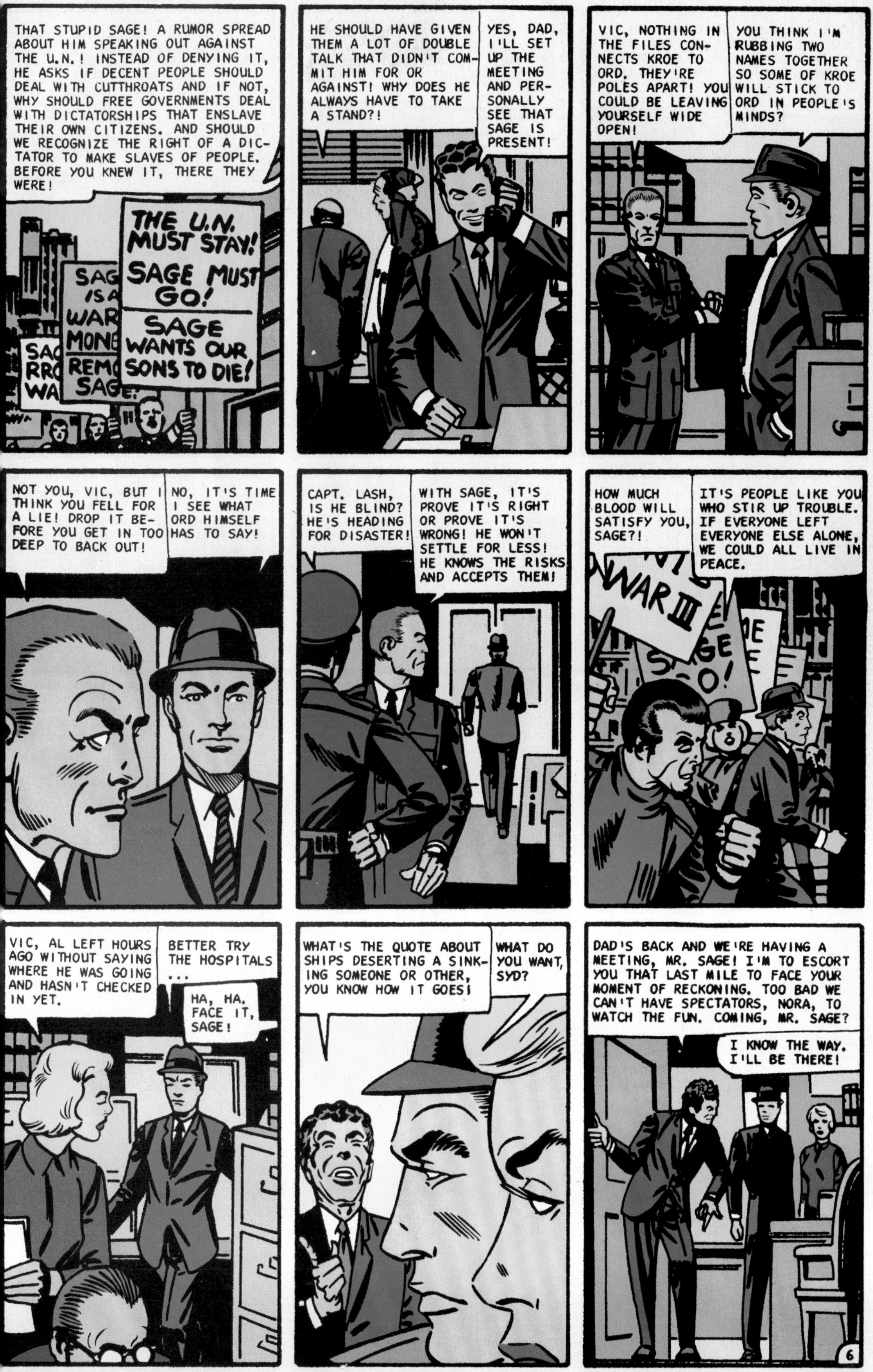
THAT STUPID SAGE! A RUMOR SPREAD ABOUT HIM SPEAKING OUT AGAINST THE U.N.! INSTEAD OF DENYING IT, HE ASKS IF DECENT PEOPLE SHOULD DEAL WITH CUTTHROATS AND IF NOT, WHY SHOULD FREE GOVERNMENTS DEAL WITH DICTATORSHIPS THAT ENSLAVE THEIR OWN CITIZENS. AND SHOULD WE RECOGNIZE THE RIGHT OF A DICTATOR TO MAKE SLAVES OF PEOPLE. BEFORE YOU KNEW IT, THERE THEY WERE!
THE U.N. MUST STAY!
SAGE MUST GO!
SAGE WANTS OUR SONS TO DIE!
HE SHOULD HAVE GIVEN THEM A LOT OF DOUBLE TALK THAT DIDN'T COMMIT HIM FOR OR AGAINST! WHY DOES HE ALWAYS HAVE TO TAKE A STAND?!
YES, DAD, I'LL SET UP THE MEETING AND PERSONALLY SEE THAT SAGE IS PRESENT!
VIC, NOTHING IN THE FILES CONNECTS KROE TO ORD. THEY'RE POLES APART! YOU COULD BE LEAVING YOURSELF WIDE OPEN!
YOU THINK I'M RUBBING TWO NAMES TOGETHER SO SOME OF KROE WILL STICK TO ORD IN PEOPLE'S MINDS?
NOT YOU, VIC, BUT I THINK YOU FELL FOR A LIE! DROP IT BEFORE YOU GET IN TOO DEEP TO BACK OUT!
NO, IT'S TIME I SEE WHAT ORD HIMSELF HAS TO SAY!
CAPT. LASH, IS HE BLIND? HE'S HEADING FOR DISASTER!
WITH SAGE, IT'S PROVE IT'S RIGHT OR PROVE IT'S WRONG! HE WON'T SETTLE FOR LESS! HE KNOWS THE RISKS AND ACCEPTS THEM!
HOW MUCH BLOOD WILL SATISFY YOU, SAGE?!
IT'S PEOPLE LIKE YOU WHO STIR UP TROUBLE. IF EVERYONE LEFT EVERYONE ELSE ALONE, WE COULD ALL LIVE IN PEACE.
WAR III
VIC, AL LEFT HOURS AGO WITHOUT SAYING WHERE HE WAS GOING AND HASN'T CHECKED IN YET.
BETTER TRY THE HOSPITALS ...
HA, HA, FACE IT, SAGE!
WHAT'S THE QUOTE ABOUT SHIPS DESERTING A SINKING SOMEONE OR OTHER, YOU KNOW HOW IT GOES!
WHAT DO YOU WANT, SYD?
DAD'S BACK AND WE'RE HAVING A MEETING, MR. SAGE! I'M TO ESCORT YOU THAT LAST MILE TO FACE YOUR MOMENT OF RECKONING. TOO BAD WE CAN'T HAVE SPECTATORS, NORA, TO WATCH THE FUN. COMING, MR. SAGE?
I KNOW THE WAY. I'LL BE THERE!
6

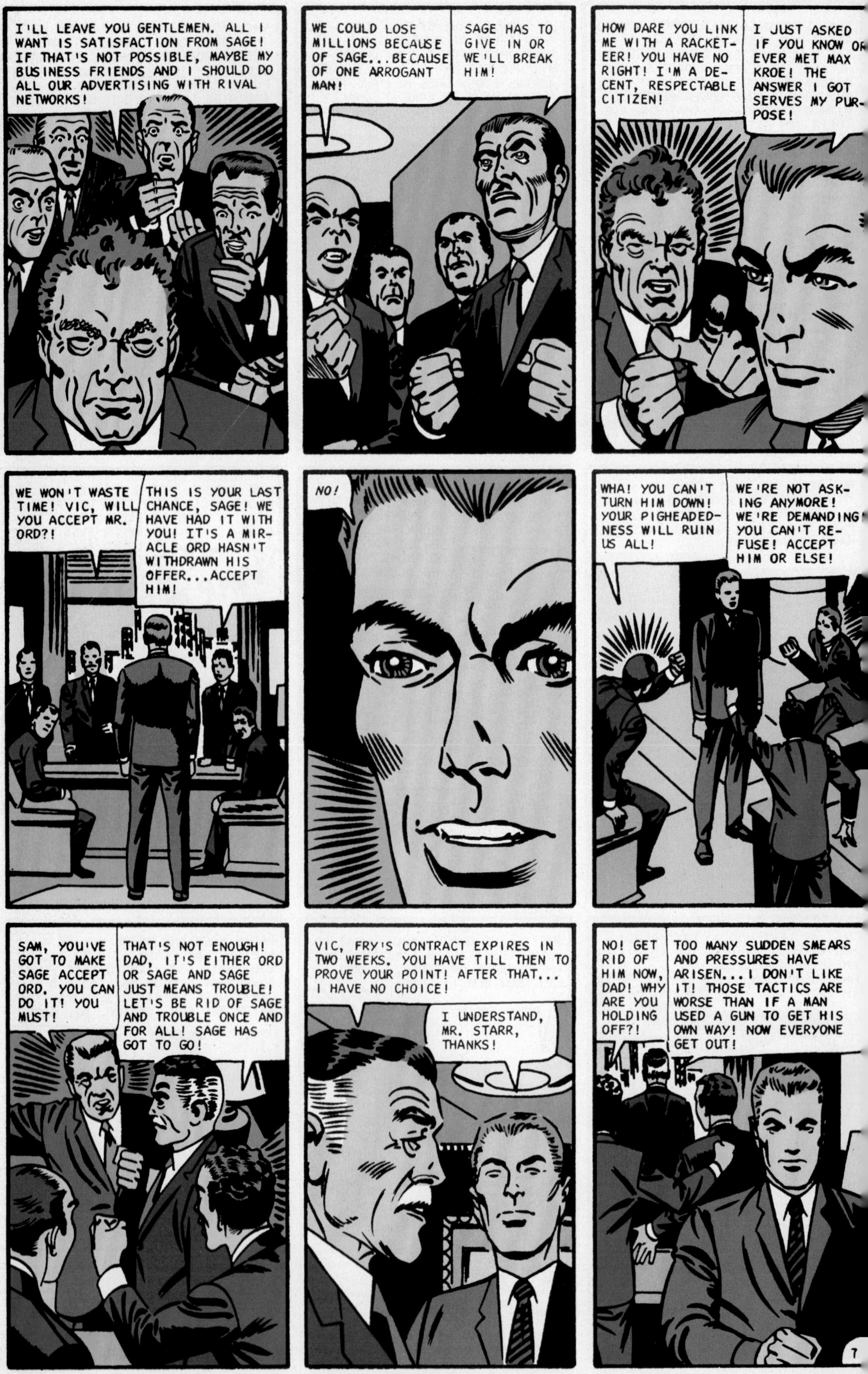
I'LL LEAVE YOU GENTLEMEN. ALL I WANT IS SATISFACTION FROM SAGE! IF THAT'S NOT POSSIBLE, MAYBE MY BUSINESS FRIENDS AND I SHOULD DO ALL OUR ADVERTISING WITH RIVAL NETWORKS!
WE COULD LOSE MILLIONS BECAUSE OF SAGE...BECAUSE OF ONE ARROGANT MAN!
SAGE HAS TO GIVE IN OR WE'LL BREAK HIM!
HOW DARE YOU LINK ME WITH A RACKETEER! YOU HAVE NO RIGHT! I'M A DECENT, RESPECTABLE CITIZEN!
I JUST ASKED IF YOU KNOW OR EVER MET MAX KROE! THE ANSWER I GOT SERVES MY PURPOSE!
WE WON'T WASTE TIME! VIC, WILL YOU ACCEPT MR. ORD?!
THIS IS YOUR LAST CHANCE, SAGE! WE HAVE HAD IT WITH YOU! IT'S A MIRACLE ORD HASN'T WITHDRAWN HIS OFFER...ACCEPT HIM!
NO!
WHA! YOU CAN'T TURN HIM DOWN! YOUR PIGHEADEDNESS WILL RUIN US ALL!
WE'RE NOT ASKING ANYMORE! WE'RE DEMANDING! YOU CAN'T REFUSE! ACCEPT HIM OR ELSE!
SAM, YOU'VE GOT TO MAKE SAGE ACCEPT ORD. YOU CAN DO IT! YOU MUST!
THAT'S NOT ENOUGH! DAD, IT'S EITHER ORD OR SAGE AND SAGE JUST MEANS TROUBLE! LET'S BE RID OF SAGE AND TROUBLE ONCE AND FOR ALL! SAGE HAS GOT TO GO!
VIC, FRY'S CONTRACT EXPIRES IN TWO WEEKS. YOU HAVE TILL THEN TO PROVE YOUR POINT! AFTER THAT... I HAVE NO CHOICE!
I UNDERSTAND, MR. STARR, THANKS!
NO! GET RID OF HIM NOW, DAD! WHY ARE YOU HOLDING OFF?!
TOO MANY SUDDEN SMEARS AND PRESSURES HAVE ARISEN... I DON'T LIKE IT! THOSE TACTICS ARE WORSE THAN IF A MAN USED A GUN TO GET HIS OWN WAY! NOW EVERYONE GET OUT!
7

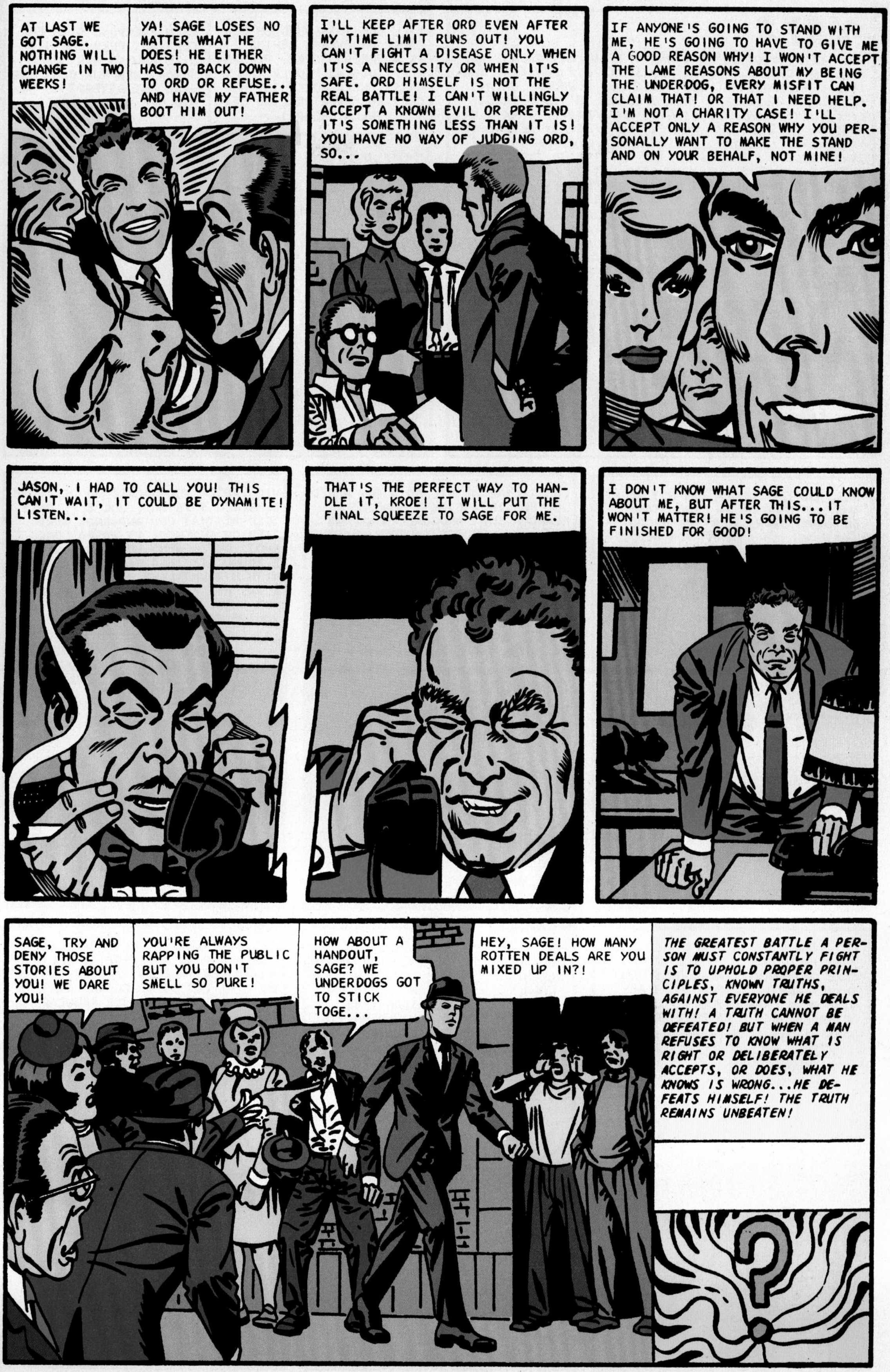
AT LAST WE GOT SAGE. NOTHING WILL CHANGE IN TWO WEEKS!
YA! SAGE LOSES NO MATTER WHAT HE DOES! HE EITHER HAS TO BACK DOWN TO ORD OR REFUSE... AND HAVE MY FATHER BOOT HIM OUT!
I'LL KEEP AFTER ORD EVEN AFTER MY TIME LIMIT RUNS OUT! YOU CAN'T FIGHT A DISEASE ONLY WHEN IT'S A NECESSITY OR WHEN IT'S SAFE. ORD HIMSELF IS NOT THE REAL BATTLE! I CAN'T WILLINGLY ACCEPT A KNOWN EVIL OR PRETEND IT'S SOMETHING LESS THAN IT IS! YOU HAVE NO WAY OF JUDGING ORD, SO...
IF ANYONE'S GOING TO STAND WITH ME, HE'S GOING TO HAVE TO GIVE ME A GOOD REASON WHY! I WON'T ACCEPT THE LAME REASONS ABOUT MY BEING THE UNDERDOG, EVERY MISFIT CAN CLAIM THAT! OR THAT I NEED HELP. I'M NOT A CHARITY CASE! I'LL ACCEPT ONLY A REASON WHY YOU PERSONALLY WANT TO MAKE THE STAND AND ON YOUR BEHALF, NOT MINE!
JASON, I HAD TO CALL YOU! THIS CAN'T WAIT, IT COULD BE DYNAMITE! LISTEN...
THAT'S THE PERFECT WAY TO HANDLE IT, KROE! IT WILL PUT THE FINAL SQUEEZE TO SAGE FOR ME.
I DON'T KNOW WHAT SAGE COULD KNOW ABOUT ME, BUT AFTER THIS... IT WON'T MATTER! HE'S GOING TO BE FINISHED FOR GOOD!
SAGE, TRY AND DENY THOSE STORIES ABOUT YOU! WE DARE YOU!
YOU'RE ALWAYS RAPPING THE PUBLIC BUT YOU DON'T SMELL SO PURE!
HOW ABOUT A HANDOUT, SAGE? WE UNDERDOGS GOT TO STICK TOGE...
HEY, SAGE! HOW MANY ROTTEN DEALS ARE YOU MIXED UP IN?!
THE GREATEST BATTLE A PERSON MUST CONSTANTLY FIGHT IS TO UPHOLD PROPER PRINCIPLES, KNOWN TRUTHS, AGAINST EVERYONE HE DEALS WITH! A TRUTH CANNOT BE DEFEATED! BUT WHEN A MAN REFUSES TO KNOW WHAT IS RIGHT OR DELIBERATELY ACCEPTS, OR DOES, WHAT HE KNOWS IS WRONG...HE DEFEATS HIMSELF! THE TRUTH REMAINS UNBEATEN!

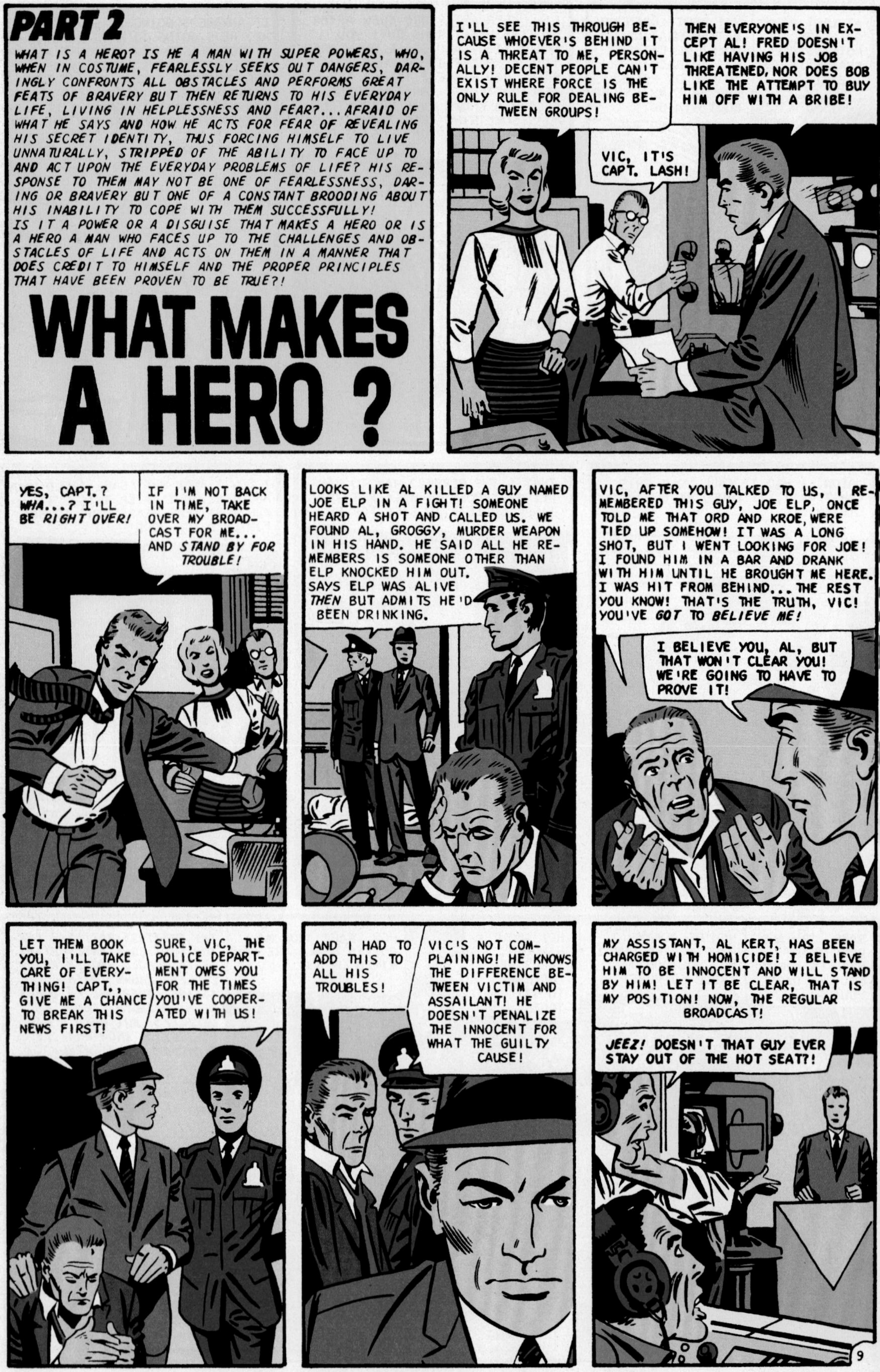
PART 2
WHAT IS A HERO? IS HE A MAN WITH SUPER POWERS, WHO, WHEN IN COSTUME, FEARLESSLY SEEKS OUT DANGERS, DARINGLY CONFRONTS ALL OBSTACLES AND PERFORMS GREAT FEATS OF BRAVERY BUT THEN RETURNS TO HIS EVERYDAY LIFE, LIVING IN HELPLESSNESS AND FEAR?...AFRAID OF WHAT HE SAYS AND HOW HE ACTS FOR FEAR OF REVEALING HIS SECRET IDENTITY, THUS FORCING HIMSELF TO LIVE UNNATURALLY, STRIPPED OF THE ABILITY TO FACE UP TO AND ACT UPON THE EVERYDAY PROBLEMS OF LIFE? HIS RESPONSE TO THEM MAY NOT BE ONE OF FEARLESSNESS, DARING OR BRAVERY BUT ONE OF A CONSTANT BROODING ABOUT HIS INABILITY TO COPE WITH THEM SUCCESSFULLY!
IS IT A POWER OR A DISGUISE THAT MAKES A HERO OR IS A HERO A MAN WHO FACES UP TO THE CHALLENGES AND OBSTACLES OF LIFE AND ACTS ON THEM IN A MANNER THAT DOES CREDIT TO HIMSELF AND THE PROPER PRINCIPLES THAT HAVE BEEN PROVEN TO BE TRUE?!
WHAT MAKES A HERO ?
I'LL SEE THIS THROUGH BECAUSE WHOEVER'S BEHIND IT IS A THREAT TO ME, PERSONALLY! DECENT PEOPLE CAN'T EXIST WHERE FORCE IS THE ONLY RULE FOR DEALING BETWEEN GROUPS!
THEN EVERYONE'S IN EXCEPT AL! FRED DOESN'T LIKE HAVING HIS JOB THREATENED, NOR DOES BOB LIKE THE ATTEMPT TO BUY HIM OFF WITH A BRIBE!
VIC, IT'S CAPT. LASH!
YES, CAPT.? WHA...? I'LL BE RIGHT OVER!
IF I'M NOT BACK IN TIME, TAKE OVER MY BROADCAST FOR ME... AND STAND BY FOR TROUBLE!
LOOKS LIKE AL KILLED A GUY NAMED JOE ELP IN A FIGHT! SOMEONE HEARD A SHOT AND CALLED US. WE FOUND AL, GROGGY, MURDER WEAPON IN HIS HAND. HE SAID ALL HE REMEMBERS IS SOMEONE OTHER THAN ELP KNOCKED HIM OUT. SAYS ELP WAS ALIVE THEN BUT ADMITS HE'D BEEN DRINKING.
VIC, AFTER YOU TALKED TO US, I REMEMBERED THIS GUY, JOE ELP, ONCE TOLD ME THAT ORD AND KROE, WERE TIED UP SOMEHOW! IT WAS A LONG SHOT, BUT I WENT LOOKING FOR JOE! I FOUND HIM IN A BAR AND DRANK WITH HIM UNTIL HE BROUGHT ME HERE. I WAS HIT FROM BEHIND... THE REST YOU KNOW! THAT'S THE TRUTH, VIC! YOU'VE GOT TO BELIEVE ME!
I BELIEVE YOU, AL, BUT THAT WON'T CLEAR YOU! WE'RE GOING TO HAVE TO PROVE IT!
LET THEM BOOK YOU, I'LL TAKE CARE OF EVERYTHING! CAPT., GIVE ME A CHANCE TO BREAK THIS NEWS FIRST!
SURE, VIC, THE POLICE DEPARTMENT OWES YOU FOR THE TIMES YOU'VE COOPERATED WITH US!
AND I HAD TO ADD THIS TO ALL HIS TROUBLES!
VIC'S NOT COMPLAINING! HE KNOWS THE DIFFERENCE BETWEEN VICTIM AND ASSAILANT! HE DOESN'T PENALIZE THE INNOCENT FOR WHAT THE GUILTY CAUSE!
MY ASSISTANT, AL KERT, HAS BEEN CHARGED WITH HOMICIDE! I BELIEVE HIM TO BE INNOCENT AND WILL STAND BY HIM! LET IT BE CLEAR, THAT IS MY POSITION! NOW, THE REGULAR BROADCAST!
JEEZ! DOESN'T THAT GUY EVER STAY OUT OF THE HOT SEAT?!
9

WHA!...AL KILLED SOMEONE! NO! IT CAN'T BE! VIC WOULDN'T...

YOU KNOW VIC BETTER THAN THAT!... HE'S SPEAKING FOR ALL OF US! HE AND AL AREN'T STANDING ALONE!

WHERE WILL IT END? SAGE WILL HAVE THE ENTIRE NETWORK CRUMBLE BEFORE WE CAN DUMP HIM! DAD, THE PUBLIC WOULD CHEER US IF WE GOT RID OF VIC NOW!

I SAID WE WON'T DISCUSS VIC UNTIL HIS TIME LIMIT IS UP AND I MEANT JUST THAT!

BUT, DAD! THIS IS A PERFECT OUT FOR US!

WE'RE JAMMED WITH CALLS DENOUNCING SAGE! IT'S YOUR TURN TO TELL SYDI HE ALMOST HAD A STROKE WHEN I SHOWED HIM THE ANTI-SAGE MAIL! WHAT'S THE BRASS WAITING FOR? THIS MANY "HATE SAGE" GROUPS CAN'T BE WRONG...THEY MUST FIRE SAGE!

BEAUTIFUL JOB, KROE! SAGE IS BOXED IN TIGHT AND I'M GOING TO SEAL HIM UP FOR GOOD!

HAVE FUN, JASON ...BUT DON'T FORGET YOU OWE A FAVOR FOR WHAT I DID!

YOU'RE ALWAYS KNOCKING EVERYONE AND NOW YOU'RE STANDING UP FOR A KILLER! YOU PUT HIM UP TO IT, SAGE!

HE'S INNOCENT BECAUSE YOU SAY HE IS, HUH, SAGE! YOU'RE A PHONY...A HYPOCRITE!

THANKS FOR STANDING BAIL, VIC, BUT I CAN'T GO BACK WITH YOU! I'VE CAUSED YOU ENOUGH TROUBLE! IT'LL BE BETTER FOR YOU IF I KEEP OUT OF THE WAY!

LET'S GET ONE THING STRAIGHT, AL! WHATEVER YOU DO, YOU'RE NOT DOING FOR MY SAKE!

IF YOU WANT TO CRAWL IN A HOLE EVEN THOUGH YOU'RE INNOCENT...GO AHEAD! IF YOU'RE ASHAMED TO BE SEEN WITH YOUR FRIENDS...RUN AWAY! IF YOU CAN'T STAND THE STARES AND TONGUES OF PUBLIC IDIOTS...GO HIDE! BUT DON'T TELL ME I'M RESPONSIBLE FOR WHAT YOU DECIDE...THAT IT'S FOR MY BENEFIT! YOU OWE ME NOTHING!

DO WHAT YOU WANT! I'LL STILL TRY TO CLEAR YOU BUT NOT BECAUSE YOU WORK FOR ME! THE INNOCENT SHOULD NOT PAY FOR THE CRIMES OF THE GUILTY! HIDE, IF YOU WANT, BUT DON'T MAKE ME THE FALL GUY FOR YOUR DECISION!

SORRY, VIC, I...I STARTED TO GIVE UP BECAUSE I BEGAN FEELING SORRY FOR MYSELF!

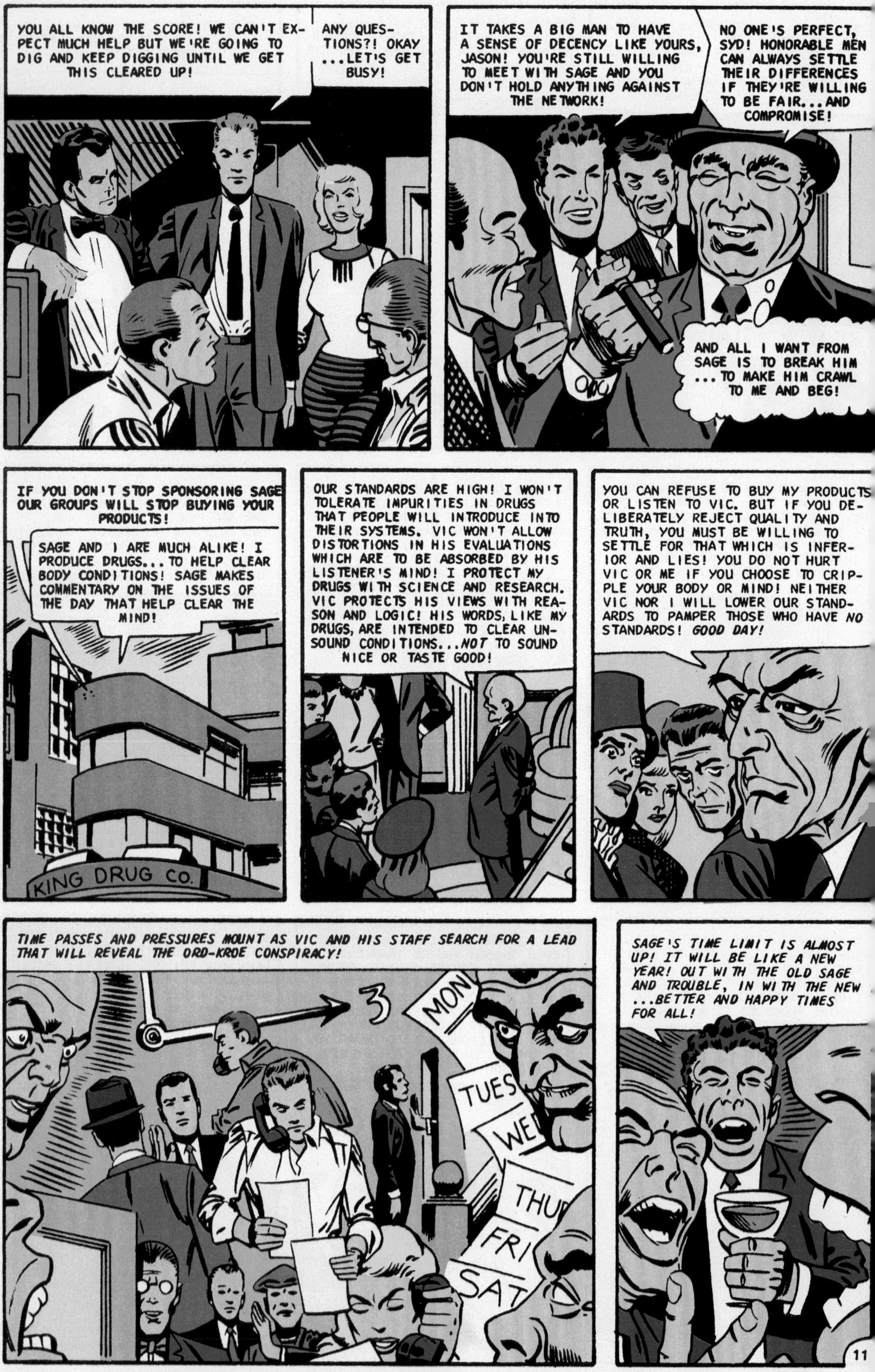

YOU ALL KNOW THE SCORE! WE CAN'T EXPECT MUCH HELP BUT WE'RE GOING TO DIG AND KEEP DIGGING UNTIL WE GET THIS CLEARED UP!
ANY QUESTIONS?! OKAY ...LET'S GET BUSY!
IT TAKES A BIG MAN TO HAVE A SENSE OF DECENCY LIKE YOURS, JASON! YOU'RE STILL WILLING TO MEET WITH SAGE AND YOU DON'T HOLD ANYTHING AGAINST THE NETWORK!
NO ONE'S PERFECT, SYD! HONORABLE MEN CAN ALWAYS SETTLE THEIR DIFFERENCES IF THEY'RE WILLING TO BE FAIR...AND COMPROMISE!
AND ALL I WANT FROM SAGE IS TO BREAK HIM ...TO MAKE HIM CRAWL TO ME AND BEG!
IF YOU DON'T STOP SPONSORING SAGE OUR GROUPS WILL STOP BUYING YOUR PRODUCTS!
SAGE AND I ARE MUCH ALIKE! I PRODUCE DRUGS...TO HELP CLEAR BODY CONDITIONS! SAGE MAKES COMMENTARY ON THE ISSUES OF THE DAY THAT HELP CLEAR THE MIND!
KING DRUG CO.
OUR STANDARDS ARE HIGH! I WON'T TOLERATE IMPURITIES IN DRUGS THAT PEOPLE WILL INTRODUCE INTO THEIR SYSTEMS. VIC WON'T ALLOW DISTORTIONS IN HIS EVALUATIONS WHICH ARE TO BE ABSORBED BY HIS LISTENER'S MIND! I PROTECT MY DRUGS WITH SCIENCE AND RESEARCH. VIC PROTECTS HIS VIEWS WITH REASON AND LOGIC! HIS WORDS, LIKE MY DRUGS, ARE INTENDED TO CLEAR UNSOUND CONDITIONS...*NOT* TO SOUND NICE OR TASTE GOOD!
YOU CAN REFUSE TO BUY MY PRODUCTS OR LISTEN TO VIC. BUT IF YOU DELIBERATELY REJECT QUALITY AND TRUTH, YOU MUST BE WILLING TO SETTLE FOR THAT WHICH IS INFERIOR AND LIES! YOU DO NOT HURT VIC OR ME IF YOU CHOOSE TO CRIPPLE YOUR BODY OR MIND! NEITHER VIC NOR I WILL LOWER OUR STANDARDS TO PAMPER THOSE WHO HAVE *NO* STANDARDS! *GOOD DAY!*
TIME PASSES AND PRESSURES MOUNT AS VIC AND HIS STAFF SEARCH FOR A LEAD THAT WILL REVEAL THE ORD-KROE CONSPIRACY!
3
MON
TUES
WE
THU
FRI
SAT
SAGE'S TIME LIMIT IS ALMOST UP! IT WILL BE LIKE A NEW YEAR! OUT WITH THE OLD SAGE AND TROUBLE, IN WITH THE NEW ...BETTER AND HAPPY TIMES FOR ALL!
11

YOU'RE NOT INTERESTED IN SPONSORING SAGE, JASON. YOU COULD STOP THIS BARBARIC SPECTACLE! WHY DON'T YOU?

IT'S BECOME A MATTER OF PRINCIPLE! SAGE STARTED IT... LET HIM END IT!

SAGE, APOLOGIZE TO JASON AND WE MIGHT FIND SOMETHING FOR YOU TO DO... SAGE, ANSWER ME!

WHEN YOU HAVE SOMETHING WORTH DISCUSSING... I'LL OBLIGE YOU!

THAT ARROGANT... I WANT TO SEE HIM BROUGHT DOWN HARD!

YOU WILL, SYD! AND WE WON'T LET UP ON HIM TILL HIS LAST BREATH!

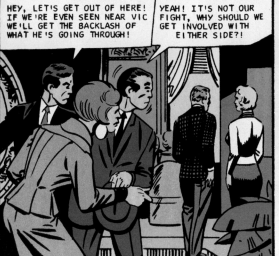

HEY, LET'S GET OUT OF HERE! IF WE'RE EVEN SEEN NEAR VIC WE'LL GET THE BACKLASH OF WHAT HE'S GOING THROUGH!

YEAH! IT'S NOT OUR FIGHT, WHY SHOULD WE GET INVOLVED WITH EITHER SIDE?!

SAY, CHUCK, DO YOU KNOW A...

SORRY, VIC. I'VE GOT AN IMPORTANT CLIENT WAITING! GOTTA HURRY!

HE DID US A FEW FAVORS AND NOW HE WANTS TO RUIN US!

SAGE, I GOT SOME BLUSHING INFO ON SYD'S CROWD... IT WOULD EVEN THINGS UP... INTERESTED?

GET LOST, SCUM!

I DON'T THINK AL DID IT BUT WE HAVEN'T TURNED UP ANYTHING TO CLEAR HIM! THAT STOOLIE, LIPPY, SHOULD KNOW IF ANYONE ELSE DID THE JOB ON ELP BUT HE'S NOT TALKING!

OKAY! THANKS, CAPT.!

IF LIPPY WON'T TALK FOR THE POLICE, HE WON'T TALK TO VIC SAGE! BUT ONCE HE GETS TO WHERE HE'S GOING HE'LL MEET SOMEONE HE'LL HAVE TO TALK TO!

12

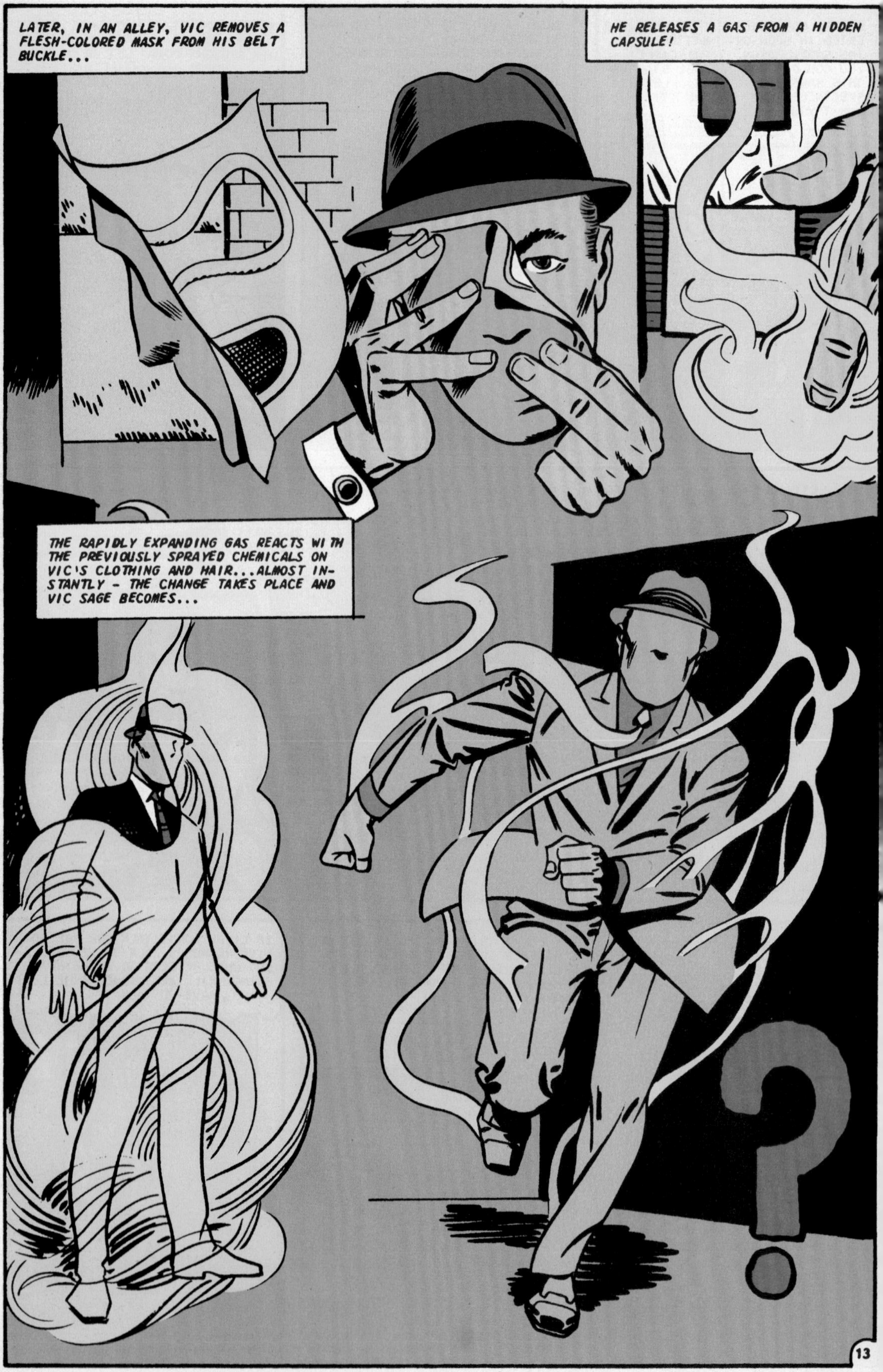
LATER, IN AN ALLEY, VIC REMOVES A FLESH-COLORED MASK FROM HIS BELT BUCKLE...
HE RELEASES A GAS FROM A HIDDEN CAPSULE!
THE RAPIDLY EXPANDING GAS REACTS WITH THE PREVIOUSLY SPRAYED CHEMICALS ON VIC'S CLOTHING AND HAIR...ALMOST IN-STANTLY - THE CHANGE TAKES PLACE AND VIC SAGE BECOMES...
13

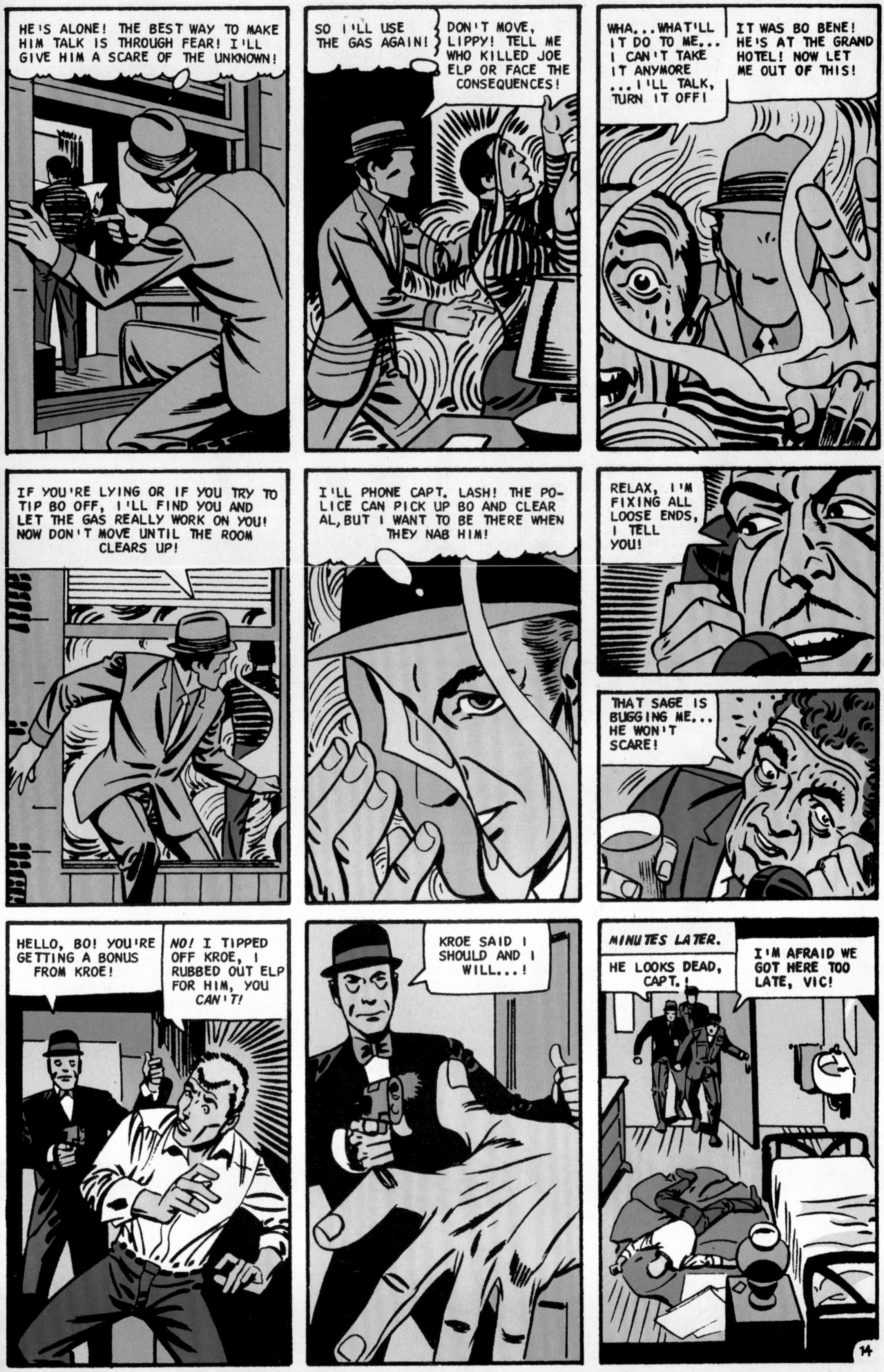
HE'S ALONE! THE BEST WAY TO MAKE HIM TALK IS THROUGH FEAR! I'LL GIVE HIM A SCARE OF THE UNKNOWN!
SO I'LL USE THE GAS AGAIN!
DON'T MOVE, LIPPY! TELL ME WHO KILLED JOE ELP OR FACE THE CONSEQUENCES!
WHA...WHAT'LL IT DO TO ME... I CAN'T TAKE IT ANYMORE ...I'LL TALK, TURN IT OFF!
IT WAS BO BENE! HE'S AT THE GRAND HOTEL! NOW LET ME OUT OF THIS!
IF YOU'RE LYING OR IF YOU TRY TO TIP BO OFF, I'LL FIND YOU AND LET THE GAS REALLY WORK ON YOU! NOW DON'T MOVE UNTIL THE ROOM CLEARS UP!
I'LL PHONE CAPT. LASH! THE POLICE CAN PICK UP BO AND CLEAR AL, BUT I WANT TO BE THERE WHEN THEY NAB HIM!
RELAX, I'M FIXING ALL LOOSE ENDS, I TELL YOU!
THAT SAGE IS BUGGING ME... HE WON'T SCARE!
HELLO, BO! YOU'RE GETTING A BONUS FROM KROE!
NO! I TIPPED OFF KROE, I RUBBED OUT ELP FOR HIM, YOU CAN'T!
KROE SAID I SHOULD AND I WILL...!
MINUTES LATER.
HE LOOKS DEAD, CAPT.!
I'M AFRAID WE GOT HERE TOO LATE, VIC!
14

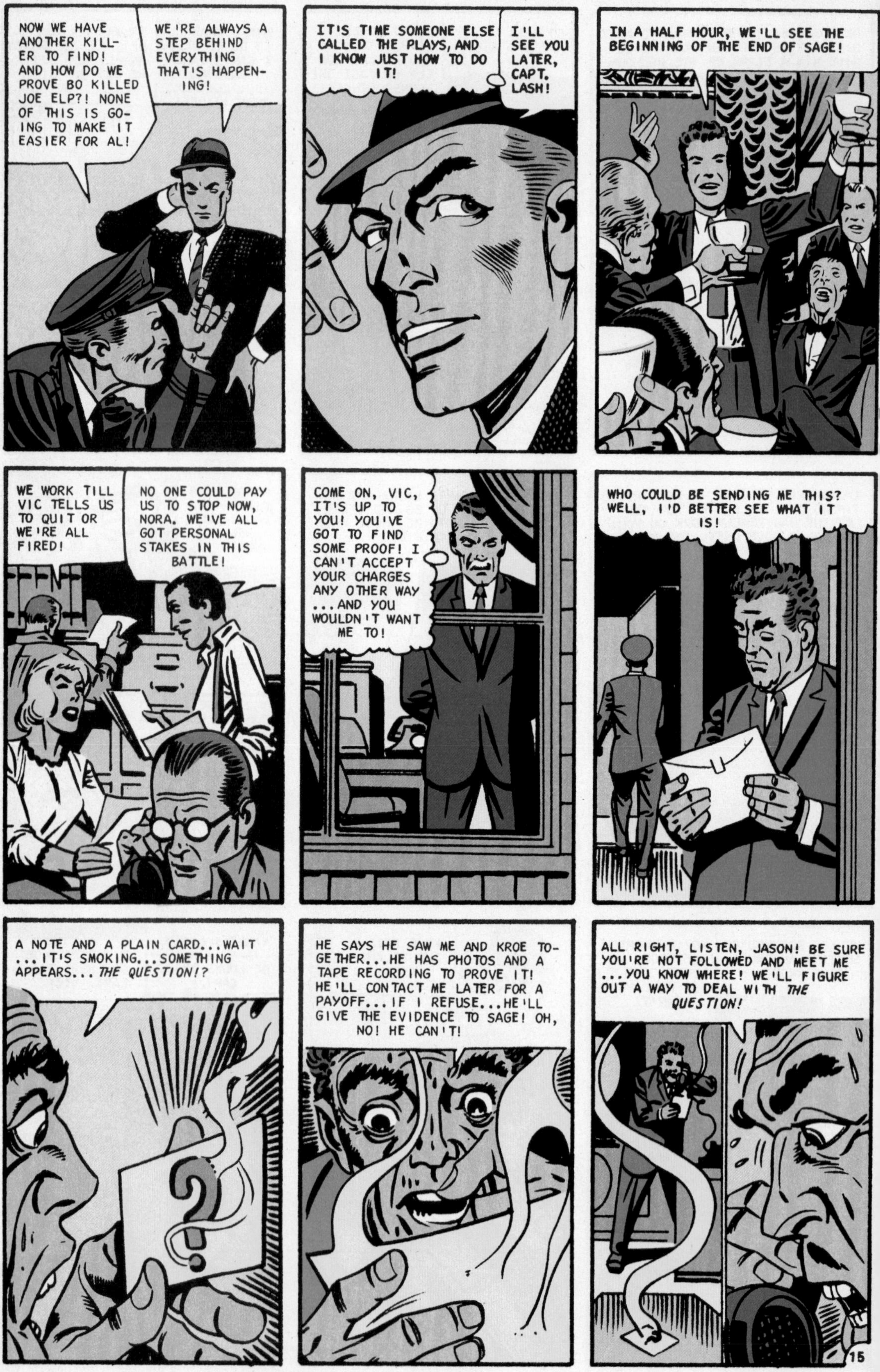
NOW WE HAVE ANOTHER KILLER TO FIND! AND HOW DO WE PROVE BO KILLED JOE ELP?! NONE OF THIS IS GOING TO MAKE IT EASIER FOR AL!
WE'RE ALWAYS A STEP BEHIND EVERYTHING THAT'S HAPPENING!
IT'S TIME SOMEONE ELSE CALLED THE PLAYS, AND I KNOW JUST HOW TO DO IT!
I'LL SEE YOU LATER, CAPT. LASH!
IN A HALF HOUR, WE'LL SEE THE BEGINNING OF THE END OF SAGE!
WE WORK TILL VIC TELLS US TO QUIT OR WE'RE ALL FIRED!
NO ONE COULD PAY US TO STOP NOW, NORA. WE'VE ALL GOT PERSONAL STAKES IN THIS BATTLE!
COME ON, VIC, IT'S UP TO YOU! YOU'VE GOT TO FIND SOME PROOF! I CAN'T ACCEPT YOUR CHARGES ANY OTHER WAY ...AND YOU WOULDN'T WANT ME TO!
WHO COULD BE SENDING ME THIS? WELL, I'D BETTER SEE WHAT IT IS!
A NOTE AND A PLAIN CARD...WAIT ...IT'S SMOKING...SOMETHING APPEARS... *THE QUESTION!?*
HE SAYS HE SAW ME AND KROE TOGETHER...HE HAS PHOTOS AND A TAPE RECORDING TO PROVE IT! HE'LL CONTACT ME LATER FOR A PAYOFF...IF I REFUSE...HE'LL GIVE THE EVIDENCE TO SAGE! OH, NO! HE CAN'T!
ALL RIGHT, LISTEN, JASON! BE SURE YOU'RE NOT FOLLOWED AND MEET ME ...YOU KNOW WHERE! WE'LL FIGURE OUT A WAY TO DEAL WITH *THE QUESTION!*
15

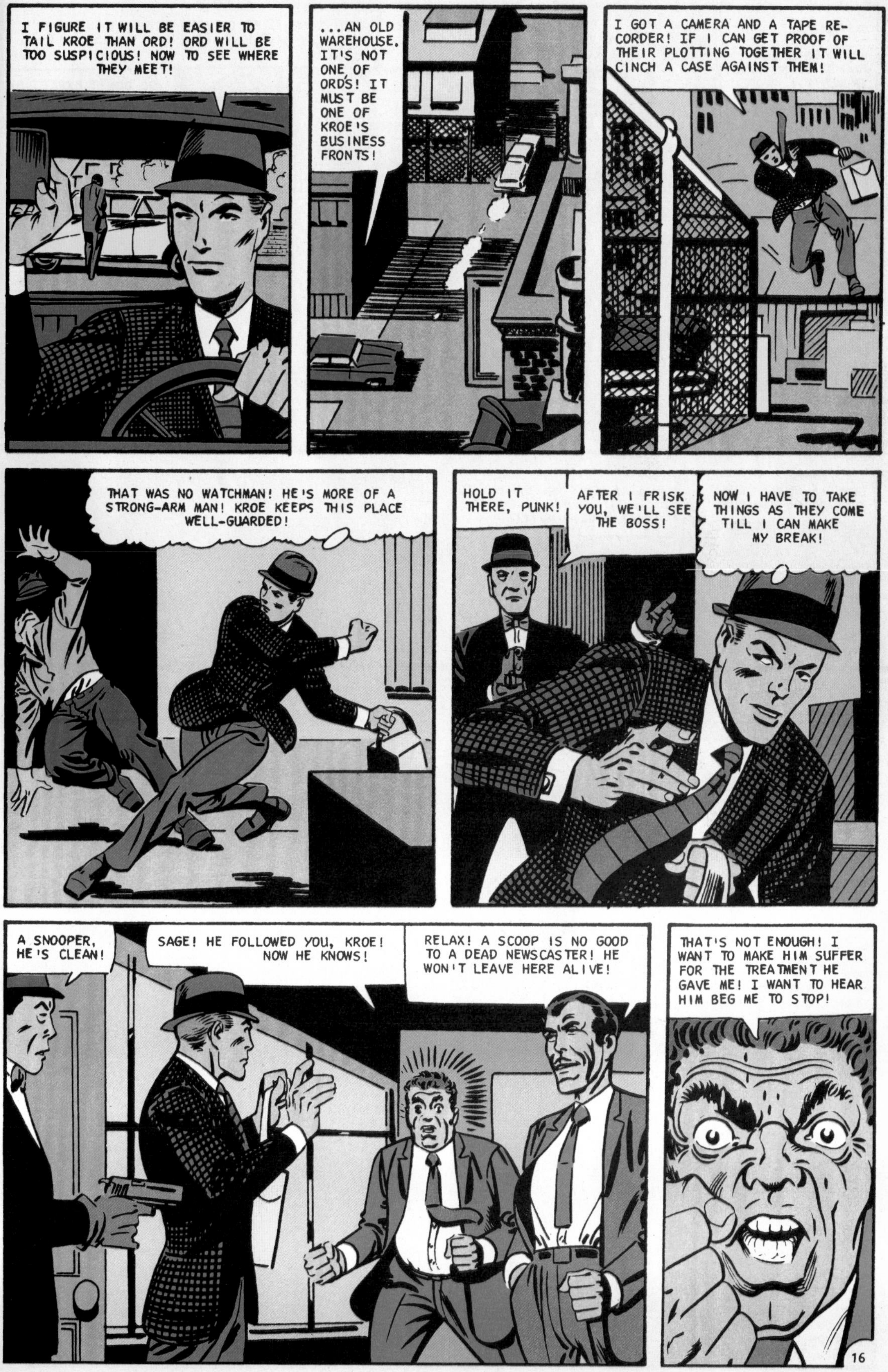
I FIGURE IT WILL BE EASIER TO TAIL KROE THAN ORD! ORD WILL BE TOO SUSPICIOUS! NOW TO SEE WHERE THEY MEET!
...AN OLD WAREHOUSE. IT'S NOT ONE OF ORD'S! IT MUST BE ONE OF KROE'S BUSINESS FRONTS!
I GOT A CAMERA AND A TAPE RECORDER! IF I CAN GET PROOF OF THEIR PLOTTING TOGETHER IT WILL CINCH A CASE AGAINST THEM!
THAT WAS NO WATCHMAN! HE'S MORE OF A STRONG-ARM MAN! KROE KEEPS THIS PLACE WELL-GUARDED!
HOLD IT THERE, PUNK!
AFTER I FRISK YOU, WE'LL SEE THE BOSS!
NOW I HAVE TO TAKE THINGS AS THEY COME TILL I CAN MAKE MY BREAK!
A SNOOPER, HE'S CLEAN!
SAGE! HE FOLLOWED YOU, KROE! NOW HE KNOWS!
RELAX! A SCOOP IS NO GOOD TO A DEAD NEWSCASTER! HE WON'T LEAVE HERE ALIVE!
THAT'S NOT ENOUGH! I WANT TO MAKE HIM SUFFER FOR THE TREATMENT HE GAVE ME! I WANT TO HEAR HIM BEG ME TO STOP!
16

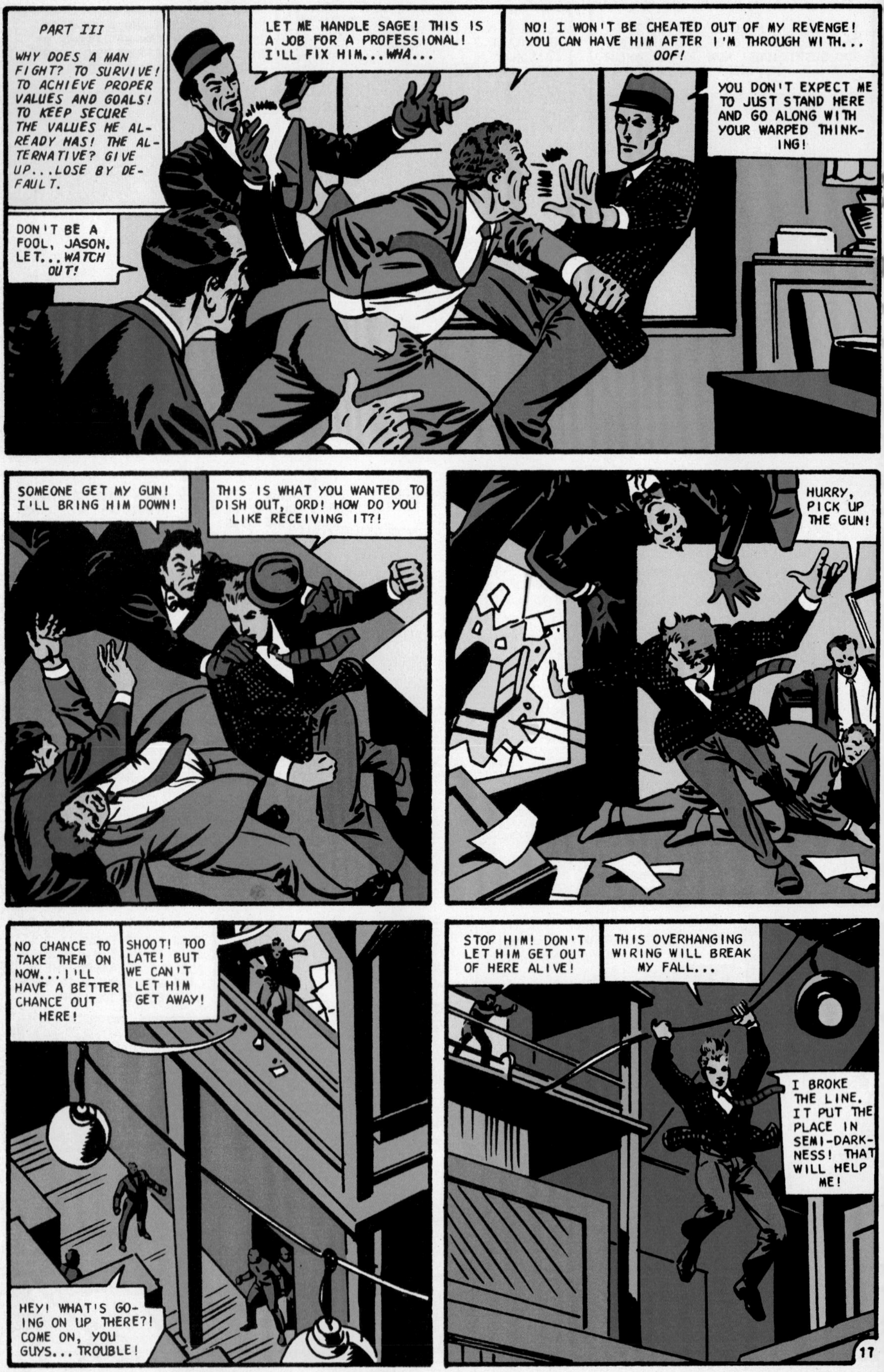
PART III
WHY DOES A MAN FIGHT? TO SURVIVE! TO ACHIEVE PROPER VALUES AND GOALS! TO KEEP SECURE THE VALUES HE ALREADY HAS! THE ALTERNATIVE? GIVE UP...LOSE BY DEFAULT.
LET ME HANDLE SAGE! THIS IS A JOB FOR A PROFESSIONAL! I'LL FIX HIM...WHA...
NO! I WON'T BE CHEATED OUT OF MY REVENGE! YOU CAN HAVE HIM AFTER I'M THROUGH WITH... OOF!
YOU DON'T EXPECT ME TO JUST STAND HERE AND GO ALONG WITH YOUR WARPED THINKING!
DON'T BE A FOOL, JASON. LET... WATCH OUT!
SOMEONE GET MY GUN! I'LL BRING HIM DOWN!
THIS IS WHAT YOU WANTED TO DISH OUT, ORD! HOW DO YOU LIKE RECEIVING IT?!
HURRY, PICK UP THE GUN!
NO CHANCE TO TAKE THEM ON NOW...I'LL HAVE A BETTER CHANCE OUT HERE!
SHOOT! TOO LATE! BUT WE CAN'T LET HIM GET AWAY!
HEY! WHAT'S GOING ON UP THERE?! COME ON, YOU GUYS... TROUBLE!
STOP HIM! DON'T LET HIM GET OUT OF HERE ALIVE!
THIS OVERHANGING WIRING WILL BREAK MY FALL...
I BROKE THE LINE. IT PUT THE PLACE IN SEMI-DARKNESS! THAT WILL HELP ME!
17

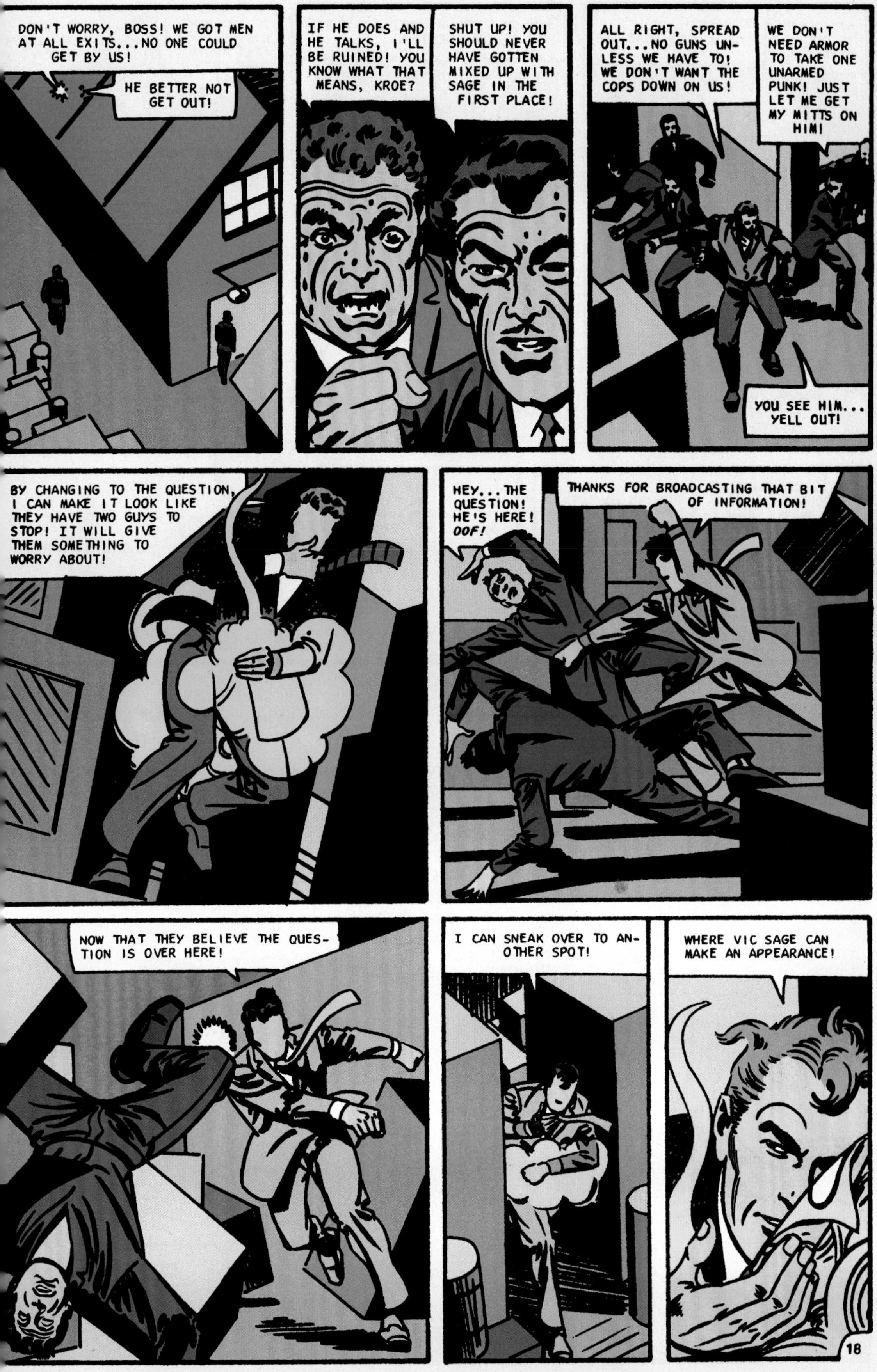

DON'T WORRY, BOSS! WE GOT MEN AT ALL EXITS...NO ONE COULD GET BY US!
HE BETTER NOT GET OUT!
IF HE DOES AND HE TALKS, I'LL BE RUINED! YOU KNOW WHAT THAT MEANS, KROE?
SHUT UP! YOU SHOULD NEVER HAVE GOTTEN MIXED UP WITH SAGE IN THE FIRST PLACE!
ALL RIGHT, SPREAD OUT...NO GUNS UNLESS WE HAVE TO! WE DON'T WANT THE COPS DOWN ON US!
WE DON'T NEED ARMOR TO TAKE ONE UNARMED PUNK! JUST LET ME GET MY MITTS ON HIM!
YOU SEE HIM... YELL OUT!
BY CHANGING TO THE QUESTION, I CAN MAKE IT LOOK LIKE THEY HAVE TWO GUYS TO STOP! IT WILL GIVE THEM SOMETHING TO WORRY ABOUT!
HEY...THE QUESTION! HE'S HERE! OOF!
THANKS FOR BROADCASTING THAT BIT OF INFORMATION!
NOW THAT THEY BELIEVE THE QUESTION IS OVER HERE!
I CAN SNEAK OVER TO ANOTHER SPOT!
WHERE VIC SAGE CAN MAKE AN APPEARANCE!
18

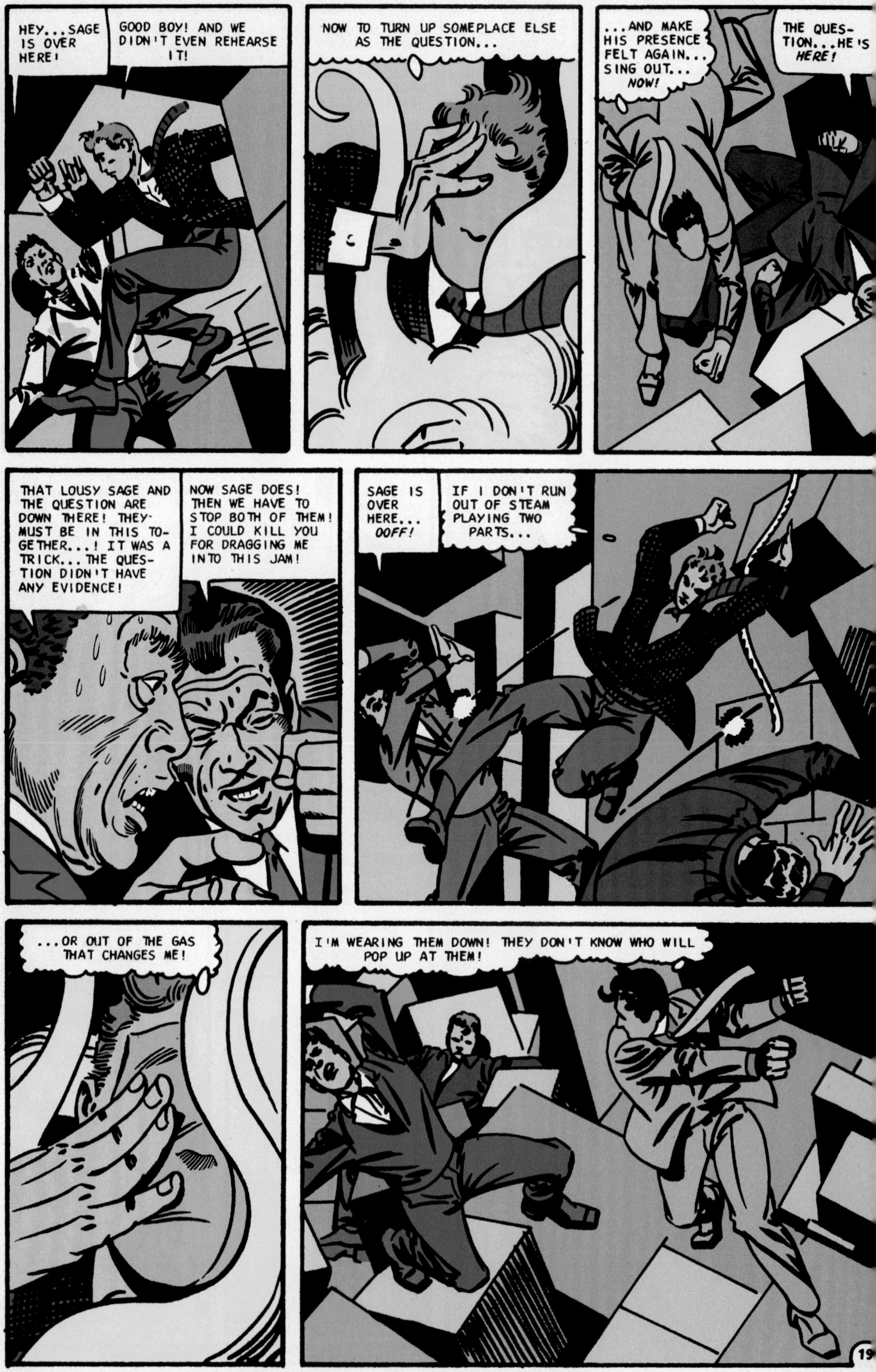
HEY...SAGE IS OVER HERE!
GOOD BOY! AND WE DIDN'T EVEN REHEARSE IT!
NOW TO TURN UP SOMEPLACE ELSE AS THE QUESTION...
...AND MAKE HIS PRESENCE FELT AGAIN... SING OUT... NOW!
THE QUES-TION...HE'S HERE!
THAT LOUSY SAGE AND THE QUESTION ARE DOWN THERE! THEY MUST BE IN THIS TOGETHER...! IT WAS A TRICK... THE QUESTION DIDN'T HAVE ANY EVIDENCE!
NOW SAGE DOES! THEN WE HAVE TO STOP BOTH OF THEM! I COULD KILL YOU FOR DRAGGING ME INTO THIS JAM!
SAGE IS OVER HERE... OOFF!
IF I DON'T RUN OUT OF STEAM PLAYING TWO PARTS...
...OR OUT OF THE GAS THAT CHANGES ME!
I'M WEARING THEM DOWN! THEY DON'T KNOW WHO WILL POP UP AT THEM!
19

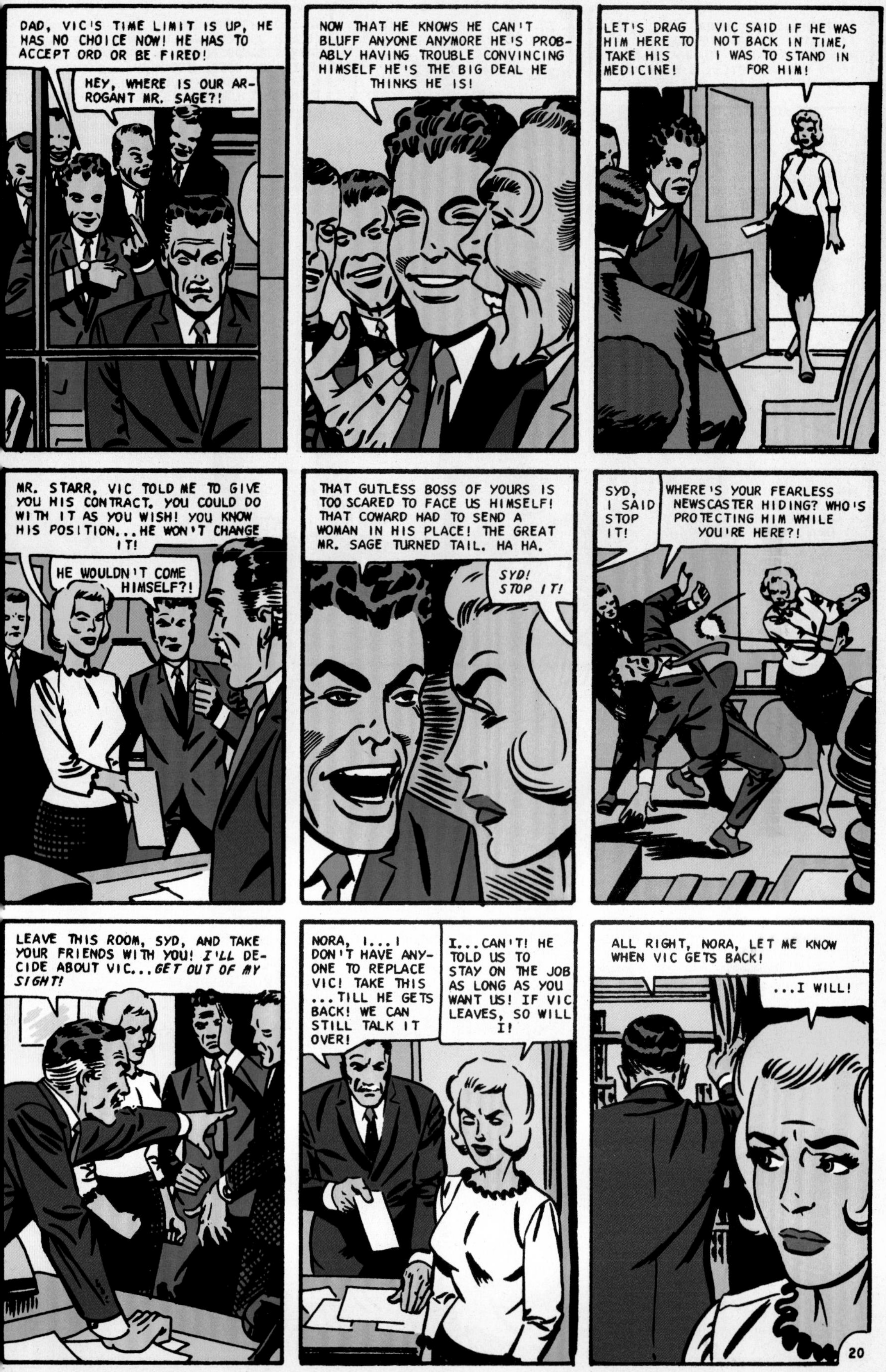

DAD, VIC'S TIME LIMIT IS UP, HE HAS NO CHOICE NOW! HE HAS TO ACCEPT ORD OR BE FIRED!
HEY, WHERE IS OUR ARROGANT MR. SAGE?!
NOW THAT HE KNOWS HE CAN'T BLUFF ANYONE ANYMORE HE'S PROBABLY HAVING TROUBLE CONVINCING HIMSELF HE'S THE BIG DEAL HE THINKS HE IS!
LET'S DRAG HIM HERE TO TAKE HIS MEDICINE!
VIC SAID IF HE WAS NOT BACK IN TIME, I WAS TO STAND IN FOR HIM!
MR. STARR, VIC TOLD ME TO GIVE YOU HIS CONTRACT. YOU COULD DO WITH IT AS YOU WISH! YOU KNOW HIS POSITION...HE WON'T CHANGE IT!
HE WOULDN'T COME HIMSELF?!
THAT GUTLESS BOSS OF YOURS IS TOO SCARED TO FACE US HIMSELF! THAT COWARD HAD TO SEND A WOMAN IN HIS PLACE! THE GREAT MR. SAGE TURNED TAIL. HA HA.
SYD! STOP IT!
SYD, I SAID STOP IT!
WHERE'S YOUR FEARLESS NEWSCASTER HIDING? WHO'S PROTECTING HIM WHILE YOU'RE HERE?!
LEAVE THIS ROOM, SYD, AND TAKE YOUR FRIENDS WITH YOU! I'LL DECIDE ABOUT VIC...GET OUT OF MY SIGHT!
NORA, I...I DON'T HAVE ANYONE TO REPLACE VIC! TAKE THIS ...TILL HE GETS BACK! WE CAN STILL TALK IT OVER!
I...CAN'T! HE TOLD US TO STAY ON THE JOB AS LONG AS YOU WANT US! IF VIC LEAVES, SO WILL I!
ALL RIGHT, NORA, LET ME KNOW WHEN VIC GETS BACK!
...I WILL!
20

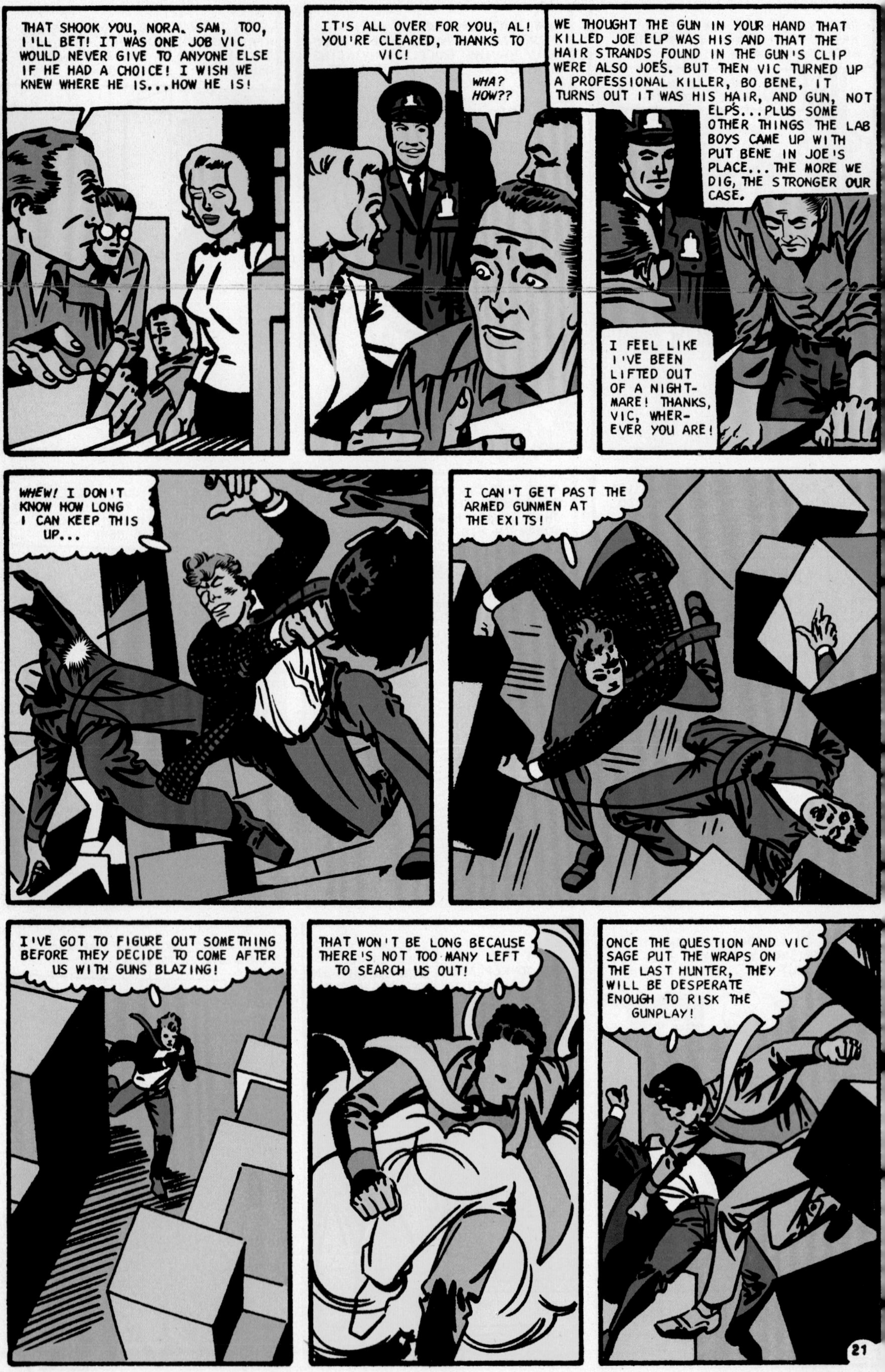
THAT SHOOK YOU, NORA. SAM, TOO, I'LL BET! IT WAS ONE JOB VIC WOULD NEVER GIVE TO ANYONE ELSE IF HE HAD A CHOICE! I WISH WE KNEW WHERE HE IS...HOW HE IS!
IT'S ALL OVER FOR YOU, AL! YOU'RE CLEARED, THANKS TO VIC!
WHA? HOW??
WE THOUGHT THE GUN IN YOUR HAND THAT KILLED JOE ELP WAS HIS AND THAT THE HAIR STRANDS FOUND IN THE GUN'S CLIP WERE ALSO JOE'S. BUT THEN VIC TURNED UP A PROFESSIONAL KILLER, BO BENE, IT TURNS OUT IT WAS HIS HAIR, AND GUN, NOT ELP'S...PLUS SOME OTHER THINGS THE LAB BOYS CAME UP WITH PUT BENE IN JOE'S PLACE... THE MORE WE DIG, THE STRONGER OUR CASE.
I FEEL LIKE I'VE BEEN LIFTED OUT OF A NIGHTMARE! THANKS, VIC, WHEREVER YOU ARE!
WHEW! I DON'T KNOW HOW LONG I CAN KEEP THIS UP...
I CAN'T GET PAST THE ARMED GUNMEN AT THE EXITS!
I'VE GOT TO FIGURE OUT SOMETHING BEFORE THEY DECIDE TO COME AFTER US WITH GUNS BLAZING!
THAT WON'T BE LONG BECAUSE THERE'S NOT TOO MANY LEFT TO SEARCH US OUT!
ONCE THE QUESTION AND VIC SAGE PUT THE WRAPS ON THE LAST HUNTER, THEY WILL BE DESPERATE ENOUGH TO RISK THE GUNPLAY!
21

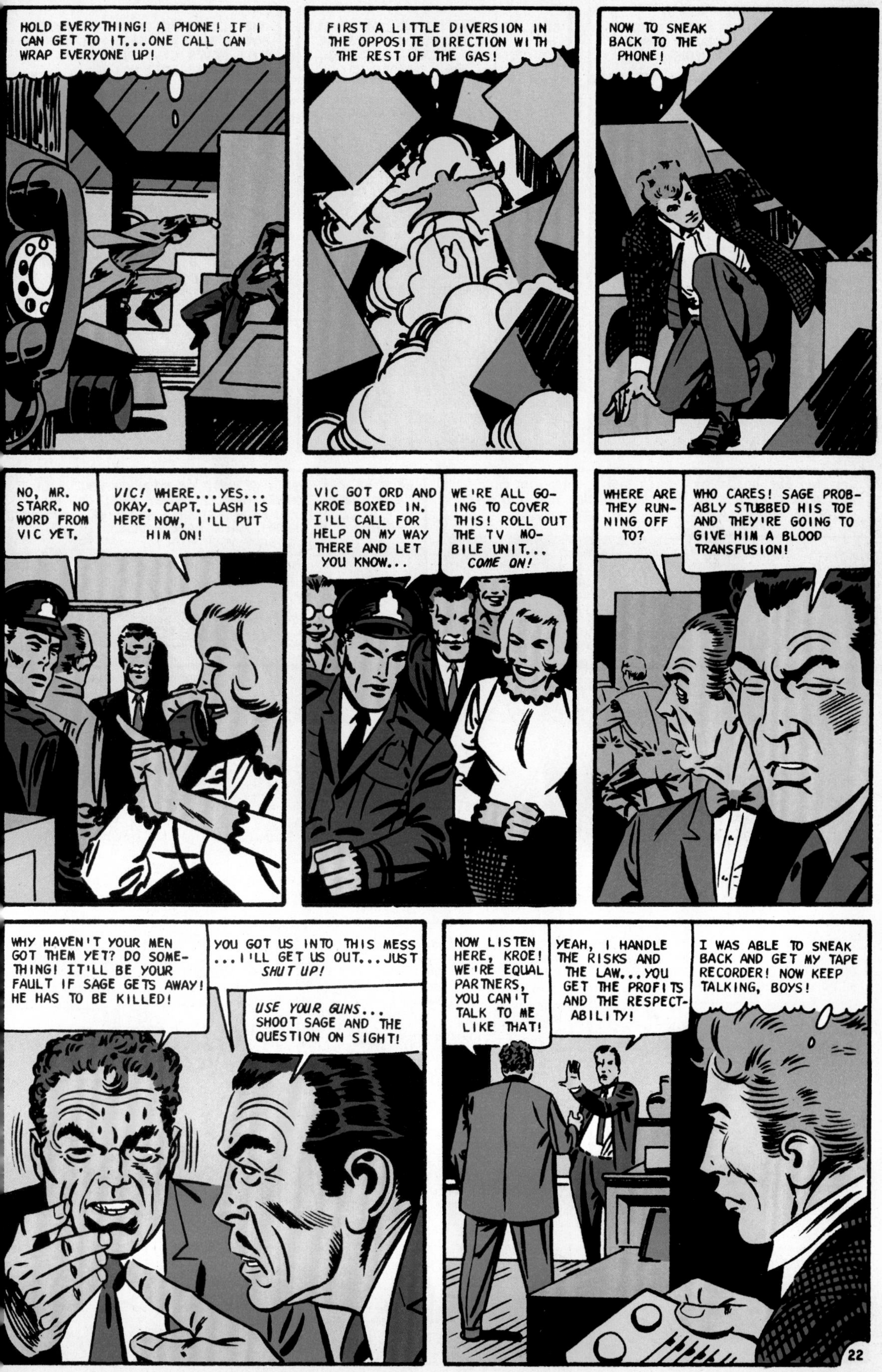
HOLD EVERYTHING! A PHONE! IF I CAN GET TO IT...ONE CALL CAN WRAP EVERYONE UP!
FIRST A LITTLE DIVERSION IN THE OPPOSITE DIRECTION WITH THE REST OF THE GAS!
NOW TO SNEAK BACK TO THE PHONE!
NO, MR. STARR. NO WORD FROM VIC YET.
VIC! WHERE...YES... OKAY. CAPT. LASH IS HERE NOW, I'LL PUT HIM ON!
VIC GOT ORD AND KROE BOXED IN. I'LL CALL FOR HELP ON MY WAY THERE AND LET YOU KNOW...
WE'RE ALL GO-ING TO COVER THIS! ROLL OUT THE TV MO-BILE UNIT... COME ON!
WHERE ARE THEY RUN-NING OFF TO?
WHO CARES! SAGE PROB-ABLY STUBBED HIS TOE AND THEY'RE GOING TO GIVE HIM A BLOOD TRANSFUSION!
WHY HAVEN'T YOUR MEN GOT THEM YET? DO SOME-THING! IT'LL BE YOUR FAULT IF SAGE GETS AWAY! HE HAS TO BE KILLED!
YOU GOT US INTO THIS MESS ...I'LL GET US OUT...JUST SHUT UP!
USE YOUR GUNS... SHOOT SAGE AND THE QUESTION ON SIGHT!
NOW LISTEN HERE, KROE! WE'RE EQUAL PARTNERS, YOU CAN'T TALK TO ME LIKE THAT!
YEAH, I HANDLE THE RISKS AND THE LAW...YOU GET THE PROFITS AND THE RESPECT-ABILITY!
I WAS ABLE TO SNEAK BACK AND GET MY TAPE RECORDER! NOW KEEP TALKING, BOYS!
22

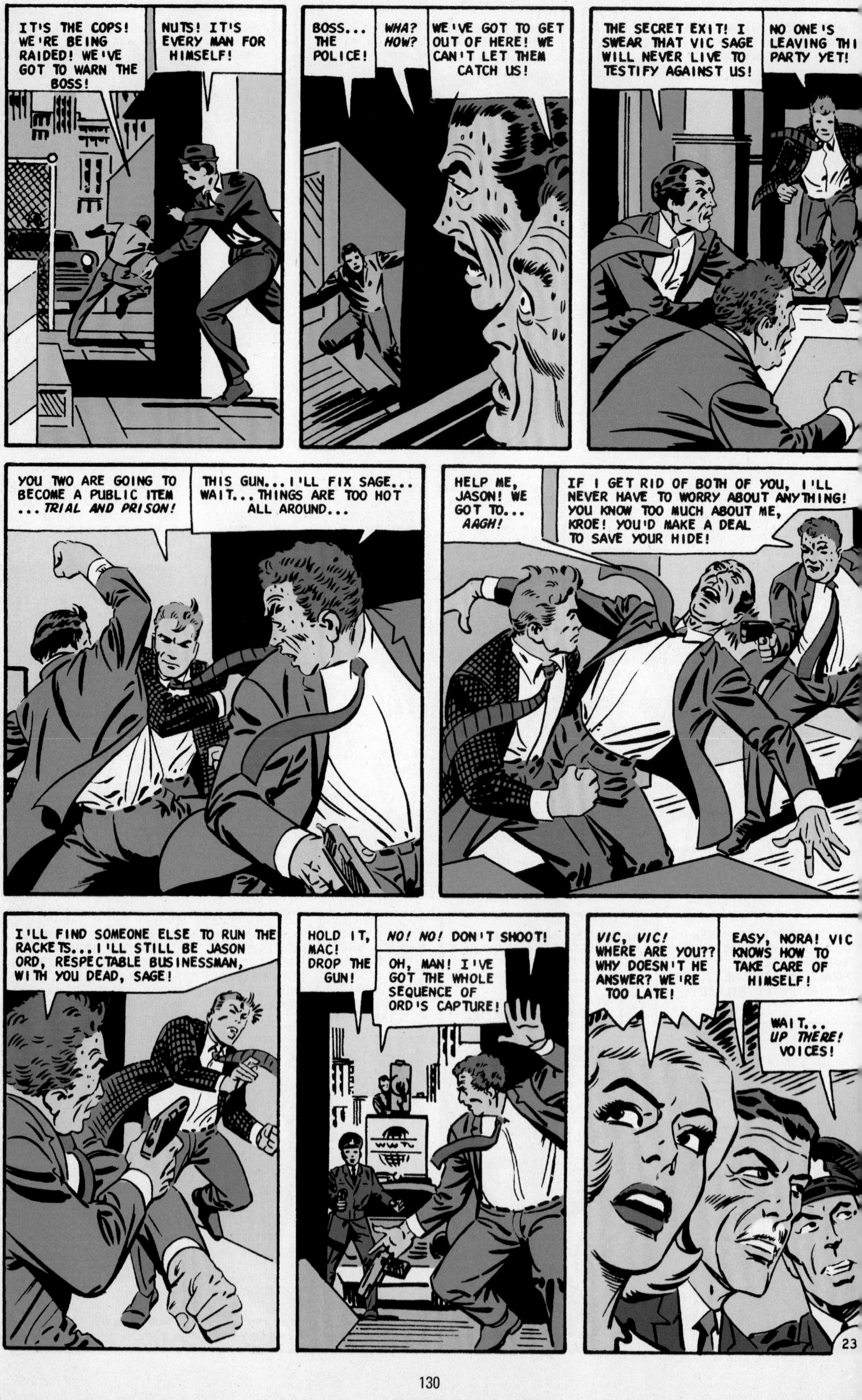
IT'S THE COPS! WE'RE BEING RAIDED! WE'VE GOT TO WARN THE BOSS!
NUTS! IT'S EVERY MAN FOR HIMSELF!
BOSS... THE POLICE!
WHA? HOW?
WE'VE GOT TO GET OUT OF HERE! WE CAN'T LET THEM CATCH US!
THE SECRET EXIT! I SWEAR THAT VIC SAGE WILL NEVER LIVE TO TESTIFY AGAINST US!
NO ONE'S LEAVING THI PARTY YET!
YOU TWO ARE GOING TO BECOME A PUBLIC ITEM ...TRIAL AND PRISON!
THIS GUN...I'LL FIX SAGE... WAIT...THINGS ARE TOO HOT ALL AROUND...
HELP ME, JASON! WE GOT TO... AAGH!
IF I GET RID OF BOTH OF YOU, I'LL NEVER HAVE TO WORRY ABOUT ANYTHING! YOU KNOW TOO MUCH ABOUT ME, KROE! YOU'D MAKE A DEAL TO SAVE YOUR HIDE!
I'LL FIND SOMEONE ELSE TO RUN THE RACKETS...I'LL STILL BE JASON ORD, RESPECTABLE BUSINESSMAN, WITH YOU DEAD, SAGE!
HOLD IT, MAC! DROP THE GUN!
NO! NO! DON'T SHOOT!
OH, MAN! I'VE GOT THE WHOLE SEQUENCE OF ORD'S CAPTURE!
VIC, VIC! WHERE ARE YOU?? WHY DOESN'T HE ANSWER? WE'RE TOO LATE!
EASY, NORA! VIC KNOWS HOW TO TAKE CARE OF HIMSELF!
WAIT... UP THERE! VOICES!
23

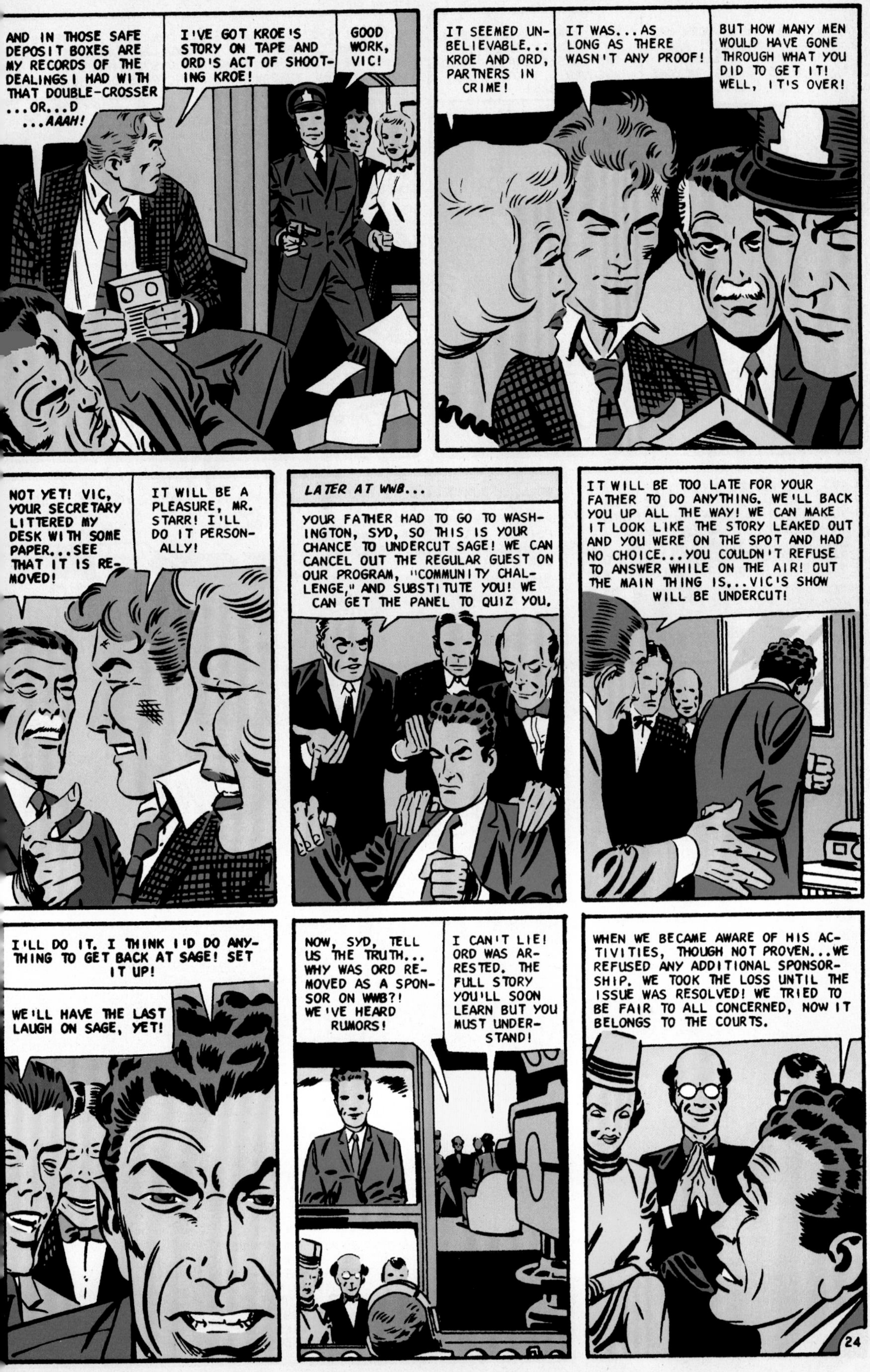
AND IN THOSE SAFE DEPOSIT BOXES ARE MY RECORDS OF THE DEALINGS I HAD WITH THAT DOUBLE-CROSSER ...OR...D ...AAAH!
I'VE GOT KROE'S STORY ON TAPE AND ORD'S ACT OF SHOOTING KROE!
GOOD WORK, VIC!
IT SEEMED UNBELIEVABLE... KROE AND ORD, PARTNERS IN CRIME!
IT WAS...AS LONG AS THERE WASN'T ANY PROOF!
BUT HOW MANY MEN WOULD HAVE GONE THROUGH WHAT YOU DID TO GET IT! WELL, IT'S OVER!
NOT YET! VIC, YOUR SECRETARY LITTERED MY DESK WITH SOME PAPER...SEE THAT IT IS REMOVED!
IT WILL BE A PLEASURE, MR. STARR! I'LL DO IT PERSONALLY!
LATER AT WWB...
YOUR FATHER HAD TO GO TO WASHINGTON, SYD, SO THIS IS YOUR CHANCE TO UNDERCUT SAGE! WE CAN CANCEL OUT THE REGULAR GUEST ON OUR PROGRAM, "COMMUNITY CHALLENGE," AND SUBSTITUTE YOU! WE CAN GET THE PANEL TO QUIZ YOU.
IT WILL BE TOO LATE FOR YOUR FATHER TO DO ANYTHING. WE'LL BACK YOU UP ALL THE WAY! WE CAN MAKE IT LOOK LIKE THE STORY LEAKED OUT AND YOU WERE ON THE SPOT AND HAD NO CHOICE...YOU COULDN'T REFUSE TO ANSWER WHILE ON THE AIR! OUT THE MAIN THING IS...VIC'S SHOW WILL BE UNDERCUT!
I'LL DO IT. I THINK I'D DO ANYTHING TO GET BACK AT SAGE! SET IT UP!
WE'LL HAVE THE LAST LAUGH ON SAGE, YET!
NOW, SYD, TELL US THE TRUTH... WHY WAS ORD REMOVED AS A SPONSOR ON WWB?! WE'VE HEARD RUMORS!
I CAN'T LIE! ORD WAS ARRESTED. THE FULL STORY YOU'LL SOON LEARN BUT YOU MUST UNDERSTAND!
WHEN WE BECAME AWARE OF HIS ACTIVITIES, THOUGH NOT PROVEN...WE REFUSED ANY ADDITIONAL SPONSORSHIP. WE TOOK THE LOSS UNTIL THE ISSUE WAS RESOLVED! WE TRIED TO BE FAIR TO ALL CONCERNED, NOW IT BELONGS TO THE COURTS.
24

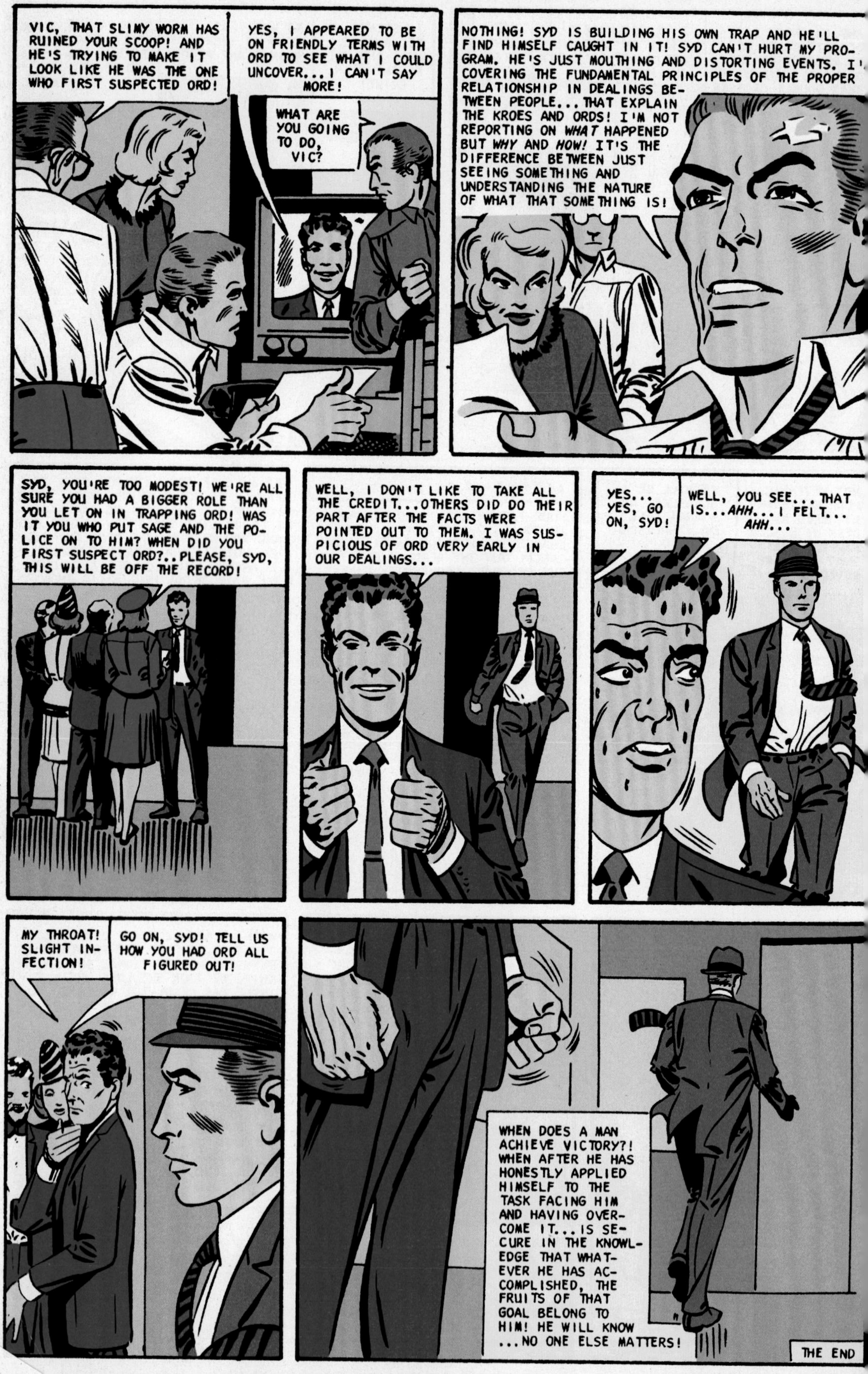

VIC, THAT SLIMY WORM HAS RUINED YOUR SCOOP! AND HE'S TRYING TO MAKE IT LOOK LIKE HE WAS THE ONE WHO FIRST SUSPECTED ORD!
YES, I APPEARED TO BE ON FRIENDLY TERMS WITH ORD TO SEE WHAT I COULD UNCOVER... I CAN'T SAY MORE!
WHAT ARE YOU GOING TO DO, VIC?
NOTHING! SYD IS BUILDING HIS OWN TRAP AND HE'LL FIND HIMSELF CAUGHT IN IT! SYD CAN'T HURT MY PROGRAM. HE'S JUST MOUTHING AND DISTORTING EVENTS. I'M COVERING THE FUNDAMENTAL PRINCIPLES OF THE PROPER RELATIONSHIP IN DEALINGS BETWEEN PEOPLE... THAT EXPLAIN THE KROES AND ORDS! I'M NOT REPORTING ON WHAT HAPPENED BUT WHY AND HOW! IT'S THE DIFFERENCE BETWEEN JUST SEEING SOMETHING AND UNDERSTANDING THE NATURE OF WHAT THAT SOMETHING IS!
SYD, YOU'RE TOO MODEST! WE'RE ALL SURE YOU HAD A BIGGER ROLE THAN YOU LET ON IN TRAPPING ORD! WAS IT YOU WHO PUT SAGE AND THE POLICE ON TO HIM? WHEN DID YOU FIRST SUSPECT ORD?.. PLEASE, SYD, THIS WILL BE OFF THE RECORD!
WELL, I DON'T LIKE TO TAKE ALL THE CREDIT...OTHERS DID DO THEIR PART AFTER THE FACTS WERE POINTED OUT TO THEM. I WAS SUSPICIOUS OF ORD VERY EARLY IN OUR DEALINGS...
YES... YES, GO ON, SYD!
WELL, YOU SEE... THAT IS...AHH...I FELT... AHH...
MY THROAT! SLIGHT INFECTION!
GO ON, SYD! TELL US HOW YOU HAD ORD ALL FIGURED OUT!
WHEN DOES A MAN ACHIEVE VICTORY?! WHEN AFTER HE HAS HONESTLY APPLIED HIMSELF TO THE TASK FACING HIM AND HAVING OVERCOME IT... IS SECURE IN THE KNOWLEDGE THAT WHATEVER HE HAS ACCOMPLISHED, THE FRUITS OF THAT GOAL BELONG TO HIM! HE WILL KNOW ...NO ONE ELSE MATTERS!
THE END

ANIMAL MAN #16

Animal Man is the only DC hero to make the leap from late-'60s also-ran to star of an acknowledged masterpiece. Twenty years after his debut, Grant Morrison, with artist Chas Truog, spun a series that made the DC Universe feel like the idea-filled playground it is at its best. It played honestly, even transgressively, with Animal Man's relationship to the real world and his readers. Grant's series climaxed when, in a moment of expanded consciousness, Animal Man looked out of the frame and saw us reading his comic. My eyes actually met Animal Man's, and it gave me a shiver.

I chose this story from Grant's run because it stands alone nicely — and because it features the Time Commander and Elongated Man, two characters who also had roles to play in 52.   —MW

ANIMAL MAN

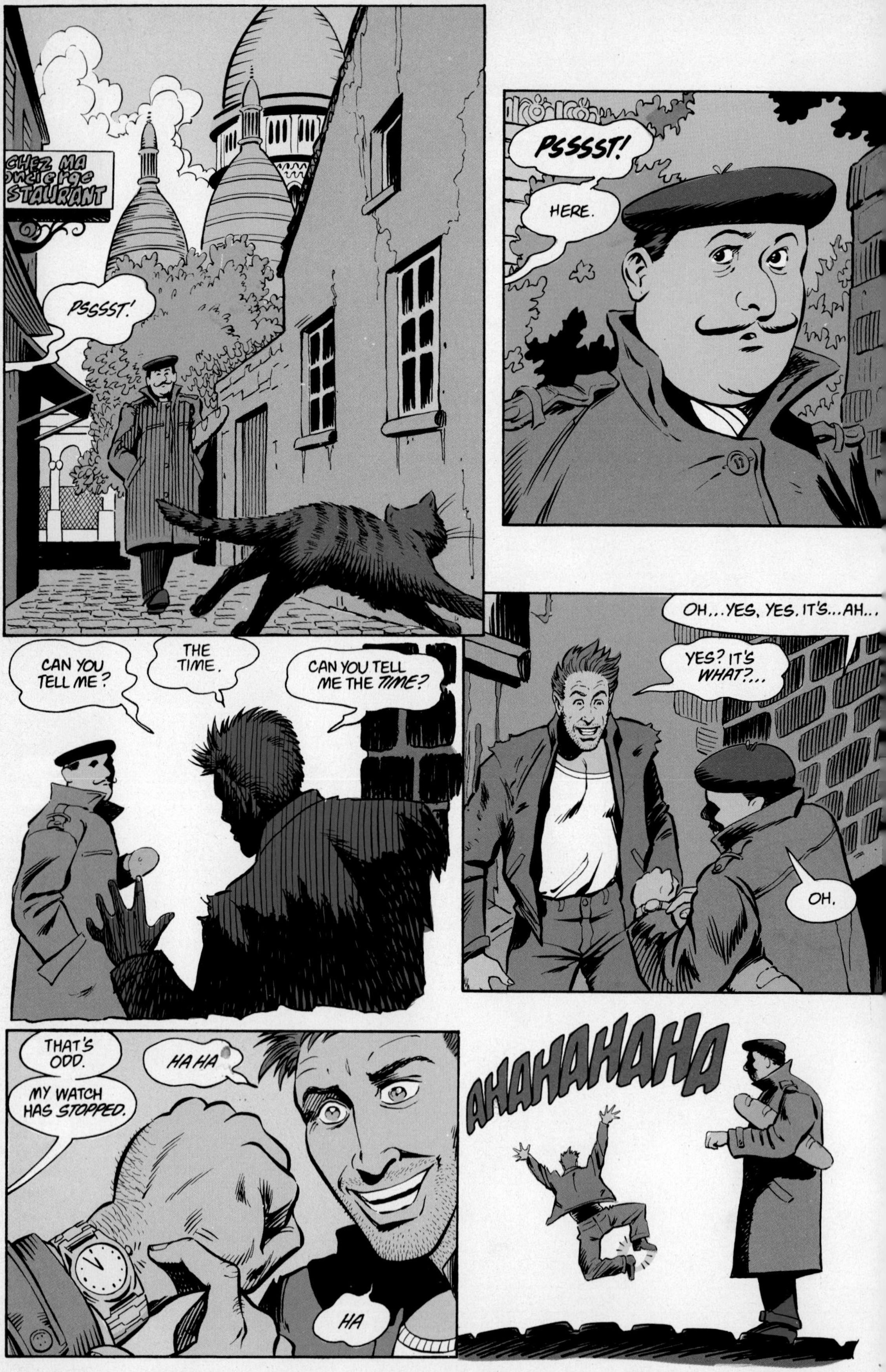
CHEZ MA
PSSSST!
PSSSST!
HERE.
CAN YOU TELL ME?
THE TIME.
CAN YOU TELL ME THE *TIME?*
OH... YES, YES. IT'S...AH...
YES? IT'S *WHAT?...*
OH.
THAT'S ODD.
MY WATCH HAS *STOPPED.*
HA HA
HA
AHAHAHAHAHA

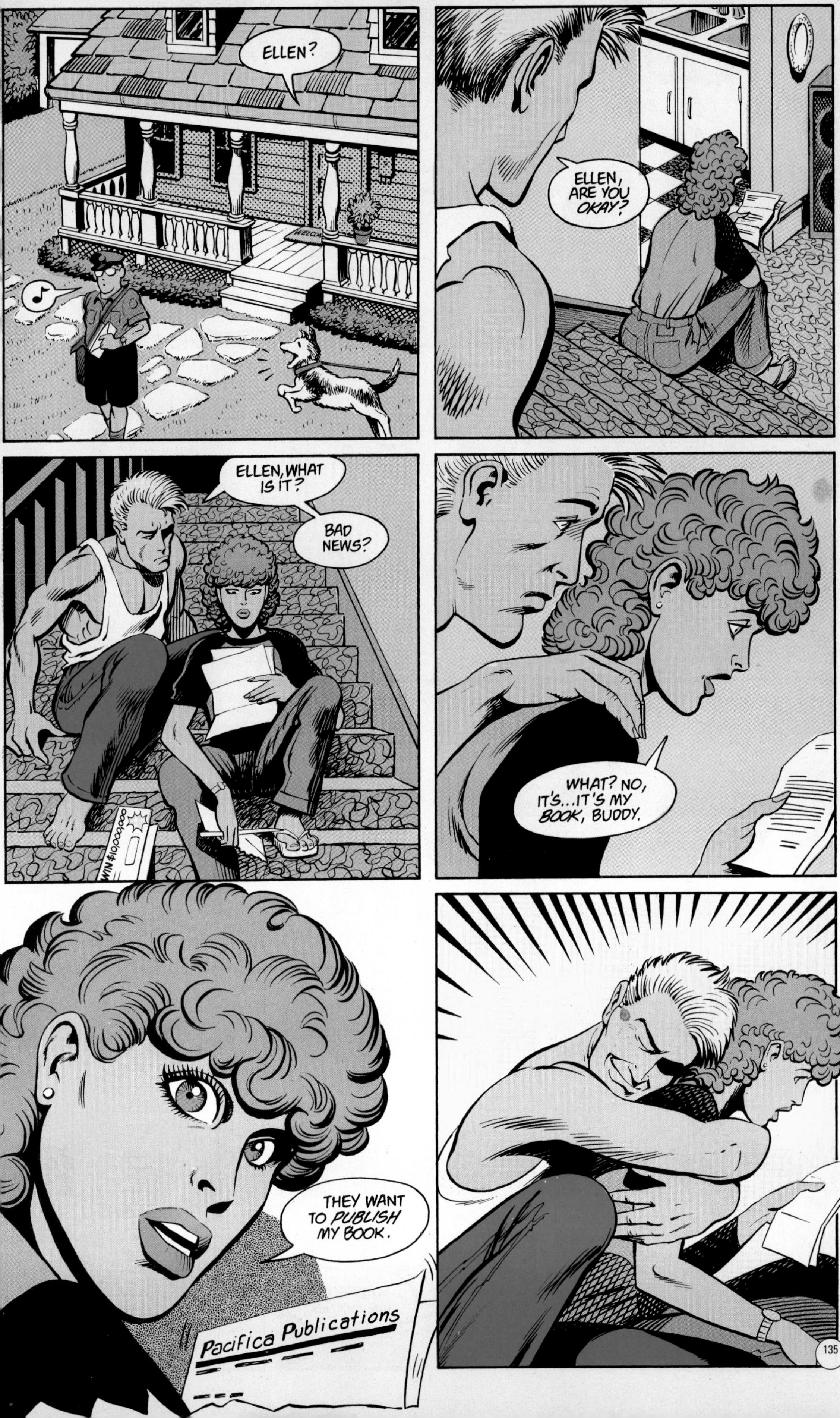
ELLEN?
ELLEN, ARE YOU *OKAY*?
ELLEN, WHAT IS IT?
BAD NEWS?
WHAT? NO, IT'S...IT'S MY *BOOK*, BUDDY.
THEY WANT TO *PUBLISH* MY BOOK.
Pacifica Publications

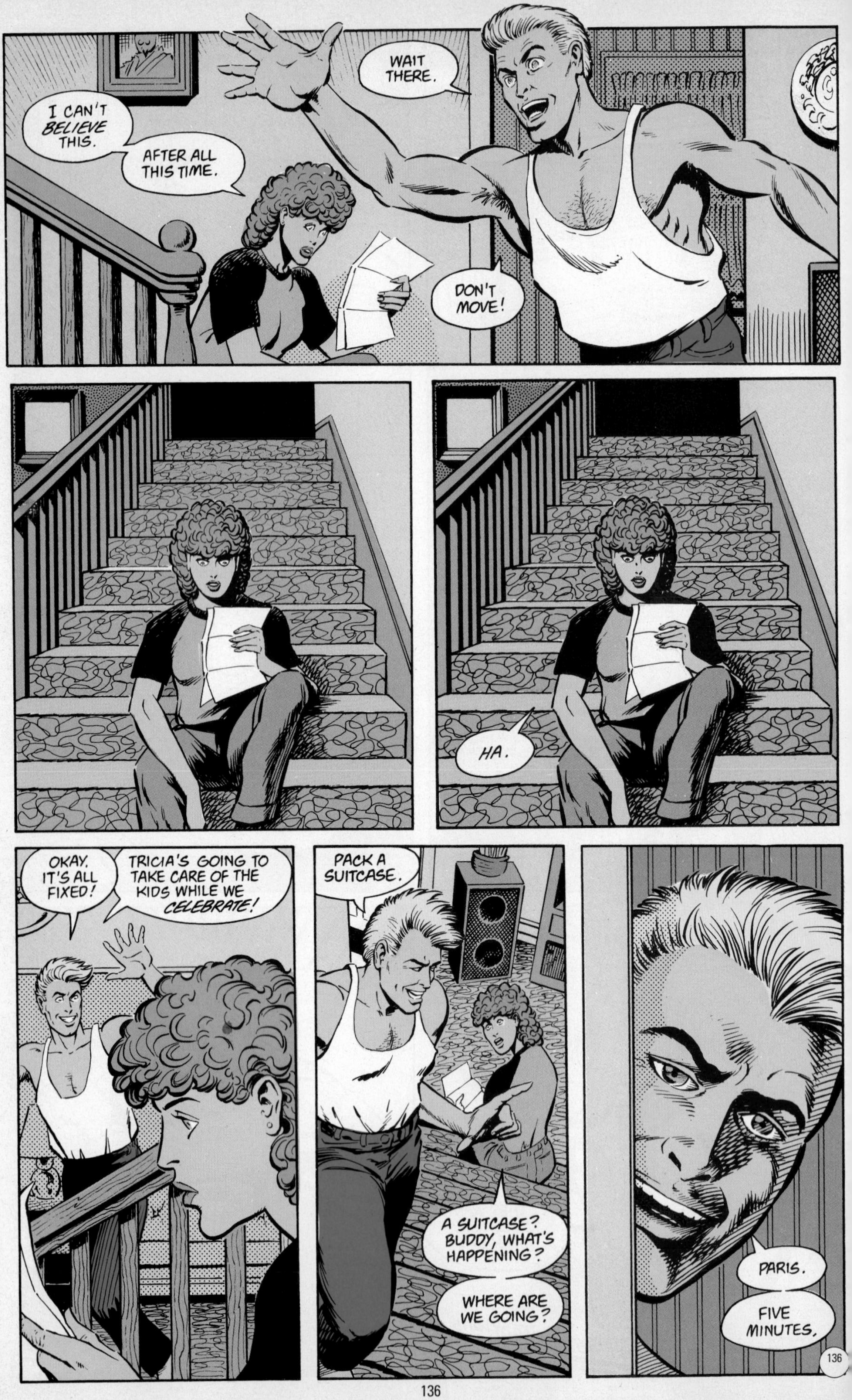
I CAN'T *BELIEVE* THIS.
AFTER ALL THIS TIME.
WAIT THERE.
DON'T MOVE!
HA.
OKAY. IT'S ALL FIXED!
TRICIA'S GOING TO TAKE CARE OF THE KIDS WHILE WE *CELEBRATE!*
PACK A SUITCASE.
A SUITCASE? BUDDY, WHAT'S HAPPENING?
WHERE ARE WE GOING?
PARIS.
FIVE MINUTES.
136

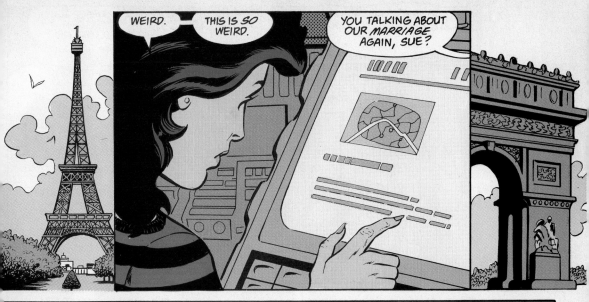

WEIRD. THIS IS *SO* WEIRD.

YOU TALKING ABOUT OUR *MARRIAGE* AGAIN, SUE?

PROBABLY.

WHAT ARE *YOU* DOING HERE? I THOUGHT YOU WERE IN THE MEN'S ROOM.

I *AM* IN THE MEN'S ROOM.

RALPH, THAT IS *GROSS.*

BUT YOU LOVE ME REALLY.

SO WHAT'S SO WEIRD? APART FROM *ME?*

SEE FOR YOURSELF. ACCORDING TO THIS, EVERY CLOCK IN *PARIS* HAS STOPPED AT *11:55.*

WHAT?

I TOLD YOU IT WAS WEIRD.

IS THERE ANYONE ON *TRANSPORTER* DUTY? SOME-ONE'S JUST BEAMED IN.

YEAH, *METAMORPHO'S* DOWN THERE. WHO CARES?

THIS CLOCK THING'S *TERRIFIC,* SUE! MY *MYSTERY-LOVING* NOSE IS TWITCHING ALREADY AND YOU KNOW WHAT *THAT* MEANS.

YEAH.

DIVORCE PROCEEDINGS.

137

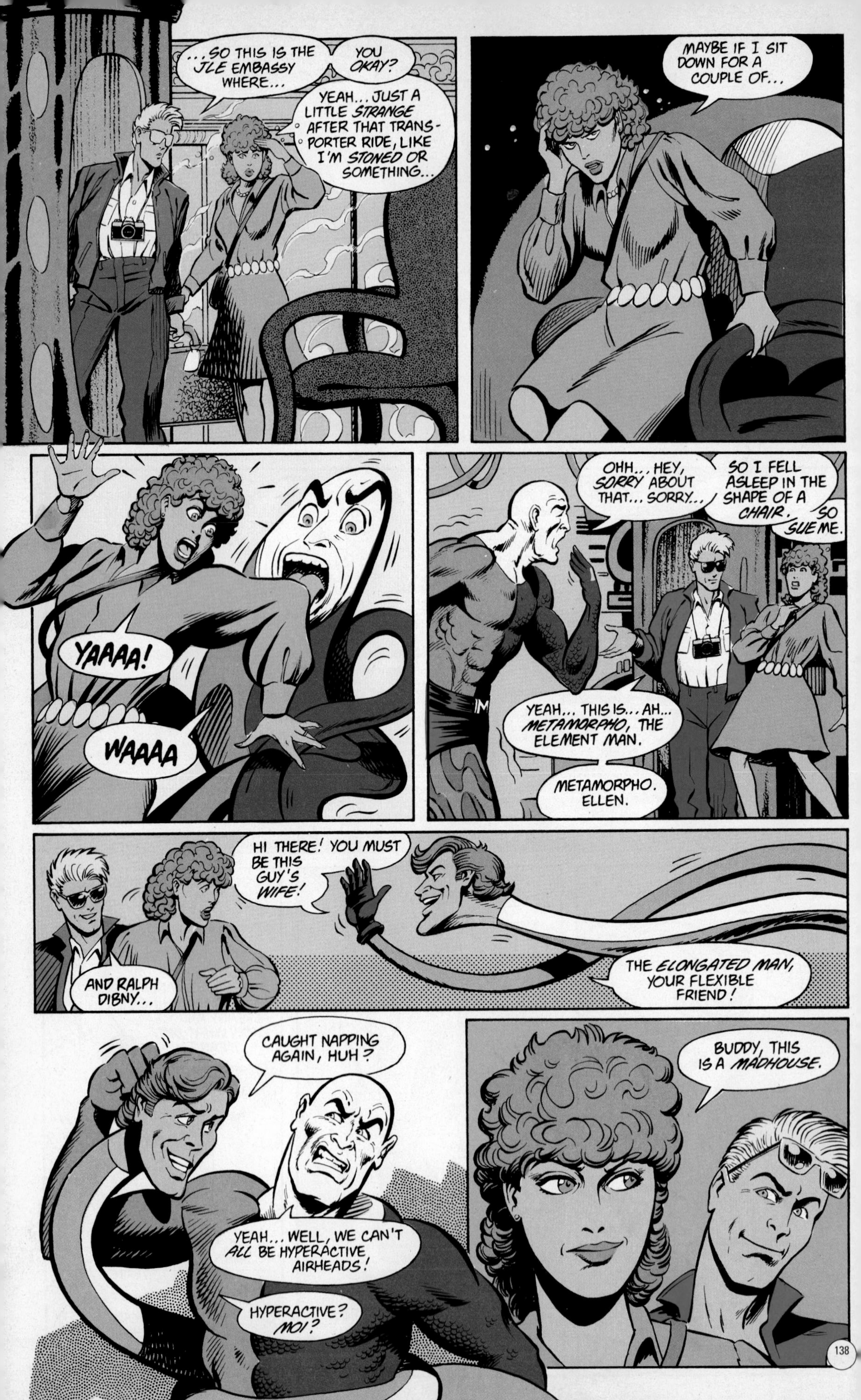
...SO THIS IS THE JLE EMBASSY WHERE...
YOU OKAY?
YEAH... JUST A LITTLE STRANGE AFTER THAT TRANS-PORTER RIDE, LIKE I'M STONED OR SOMETHING...
MAYBE IF I SIT DOWN FOR A COUPLE OF...
YAAAA!
WAAAA
OHH... HEY, SORRY ABOUT THAT... SORRY...
SO I FELL ASLEEP IN THE SHAPE OF A CHAIR.
SO SUE ME.
YEAH... THIS IS... AH... METAMORPHO, THE ELEMENT MAN.
METAMORPHO. ELLEN.
HI THERE! YOU MUST BE THIS GUY'S WIFE!
AND RALPH DIBNY...
THE ELONGATED MAN, YOUR FLEXIBLE FRIEND!
CAUGHT NAPPING AGAIN, HUH?
YEAH... WELL, WE CAN'T ALL BE HYPERACTIVE AIRHEADS!
HYPERACTIVE? MOI?
BUDDY, THIS IS A MADHOUSE.

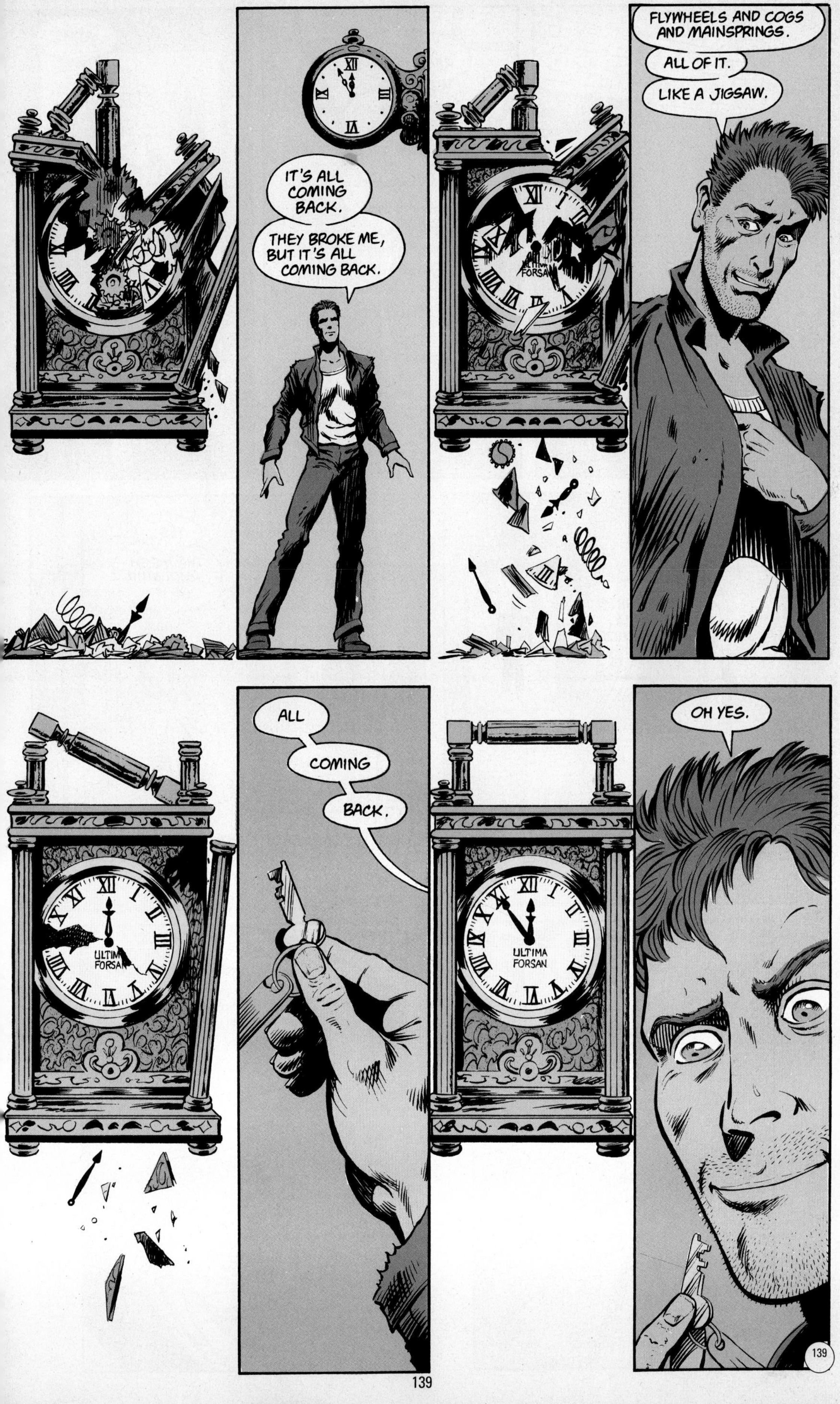
IT'S ALL COMING BACK.
THEY BROKE ME, BUT IT'S ALL COMING BACK.
ULTIMA FORSAN
FLYWHEELS AND COGS AND MAINSPRINGS.
ALL OF IT.
LIKE A JIGSAW.
ULTIMA FORSAN
ALL
COMING
BACK.
ULTIMA FORSAN
OH YES.

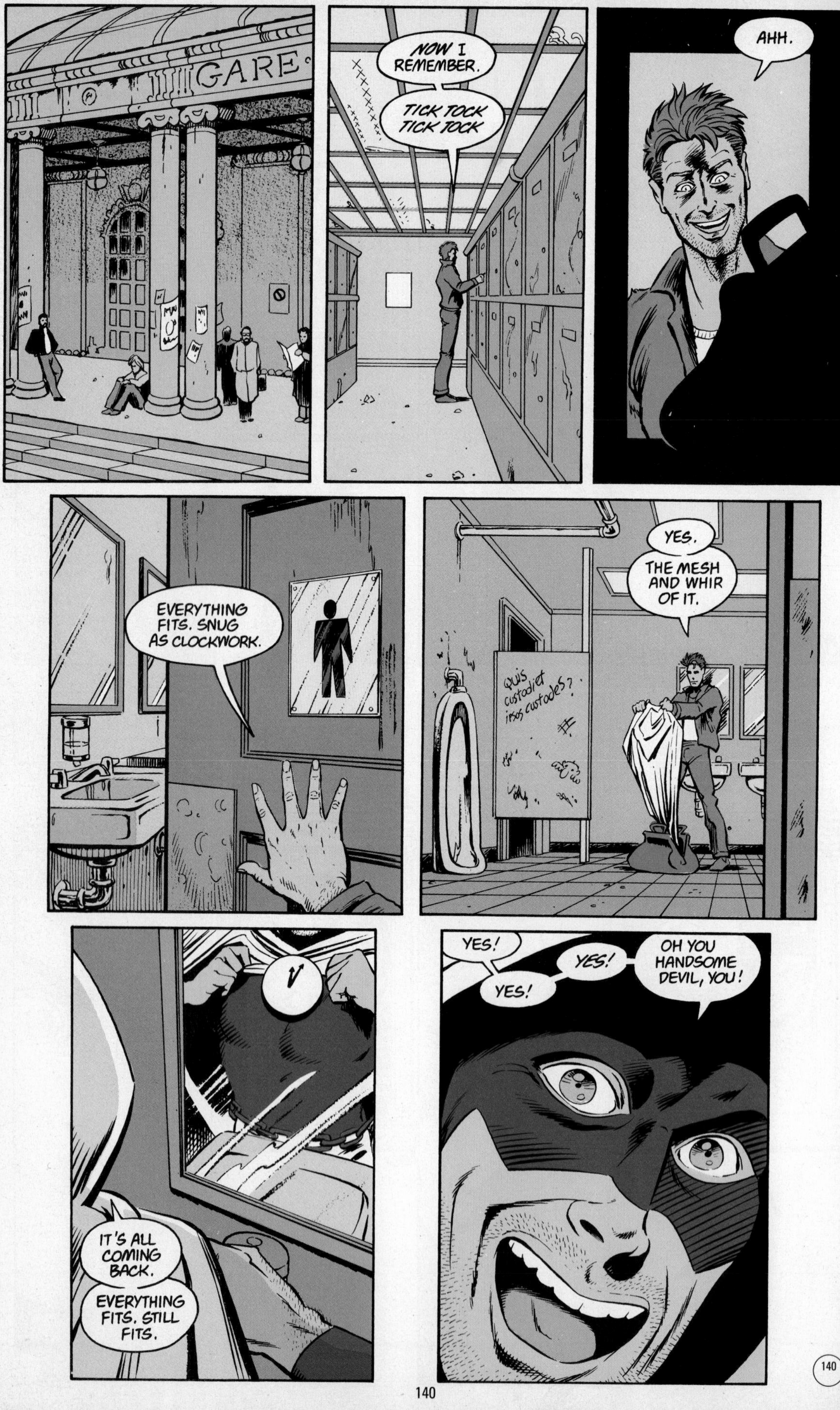
GARE
NOW I REMEMBER.
TICK TOCK TICK TOCK
AHH.
EVERYTHING FITS. SNUG AS CLOCKWORK.
YES.
THE MESH AND WHIR OF IT.
Quis custodiet ipsos custodes?
IT'S ALL COMING BACK.
EVERYTHING FITS. STILL FITS.
YES!
YES!
YES!
OH YOU HANDSOME DEVIL, YOU!
140

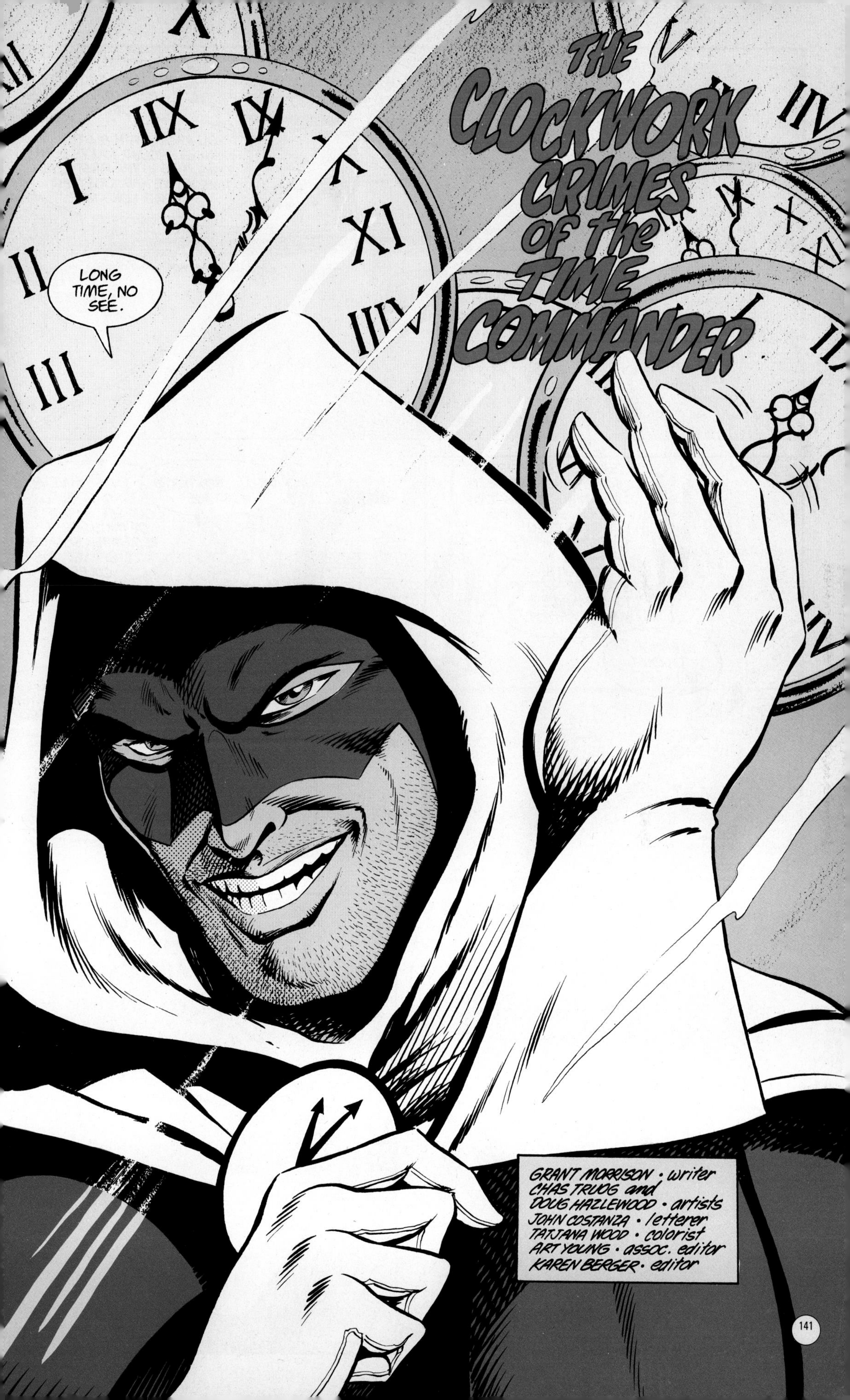
THE CLOCKWORK CRIMES OF THE TIME COMMANDER
LONG TIME, NO SEE.
GRANT MORRISON • writer
CHAS TRUOG and DOUG HAZLEWOOD • artists
JOHN COSTANZA • letterer
TATJANA WOOD • colorist
ART YOUNG • assoc. editor
KAREN BERGER • editor

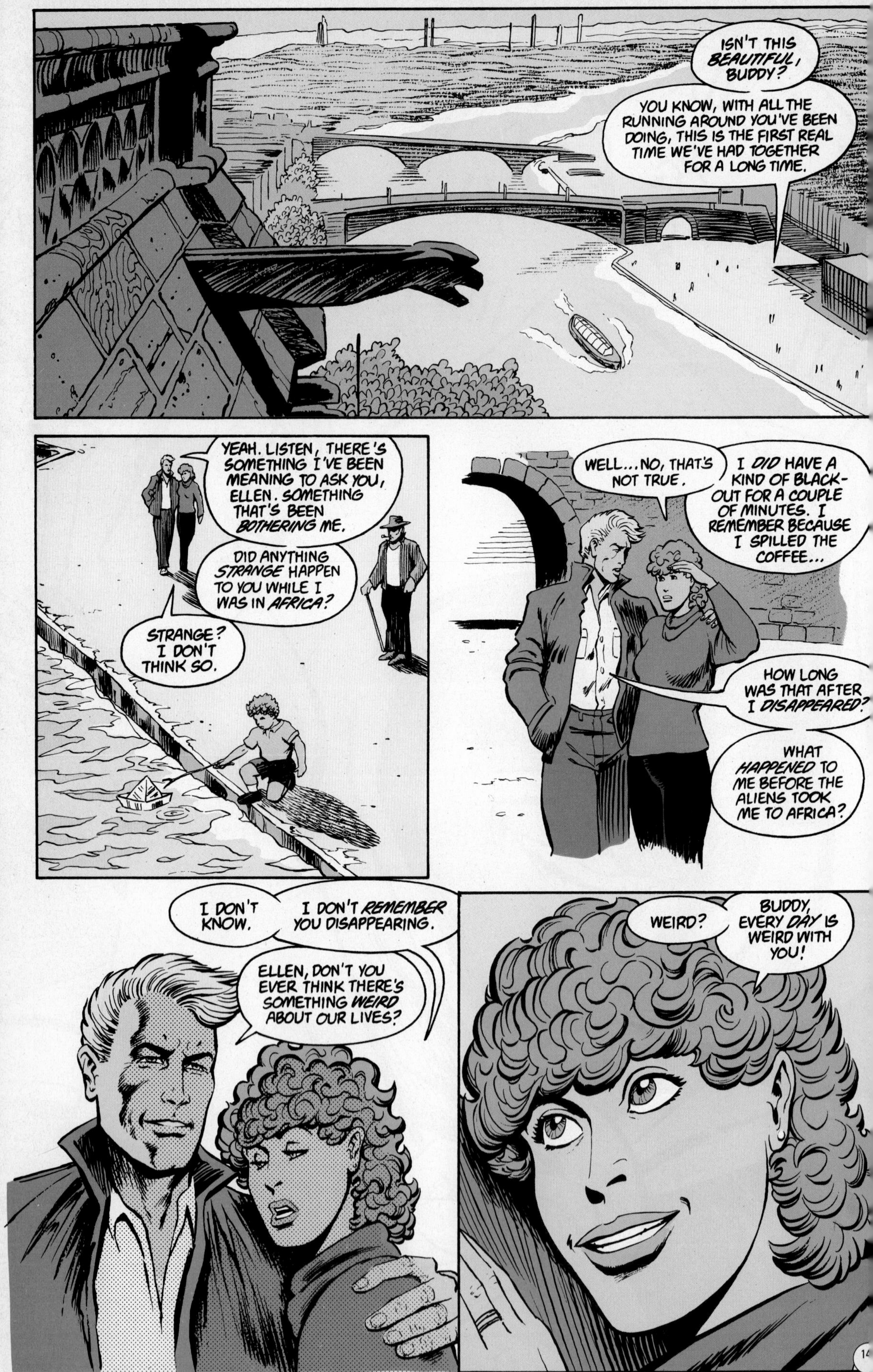
ISN'T THIS BEAUTIFUL, BUDDY?
YOU KNOW, WITH ALL THE RUNNING AROUND YOU'VE BEEN DOING, THIS IS THE FIRST REAL TIME WE'VE HAD TOGETHER FOR A LONG TIME.
YEAH. LISTEN, THERE'S SOMETHING I'VE BEEN MEANING TO ASK YOU, ELLEN. SOMETHING THAT'S BEEN BOTHERING ME.
DID ANYTHING STRANGE HAPPEN TO YOU WHILE I WAS IN AFRICA?
STRANGE? I DON'T THINK SO.
WELL... NO, THAT'S NOT TRUE.
I DID HAVE A KIND OF BLACK-OUT FOR A COUPLE OF MINUTES. I REMEMBER BECAUSE I SPILLED THE COFFEE...
HOW LONG WAS THAT AFTER I DISAPPEARED?
WHAT HAPPENED TO ME BEFORE THE ALIENS TOOK ME TO AFRICA?
I DON'T KNOW.
I DON'T REMEMBER YOU DISAPPEARING.
ELLEN, DON'T YOU EVER THINK THERE'S SOMETHING WEIRD ABOUT OUR LIVES?
WEIRD?
BUDDY, EVERY DAY IS WEIRD WITH YOU!

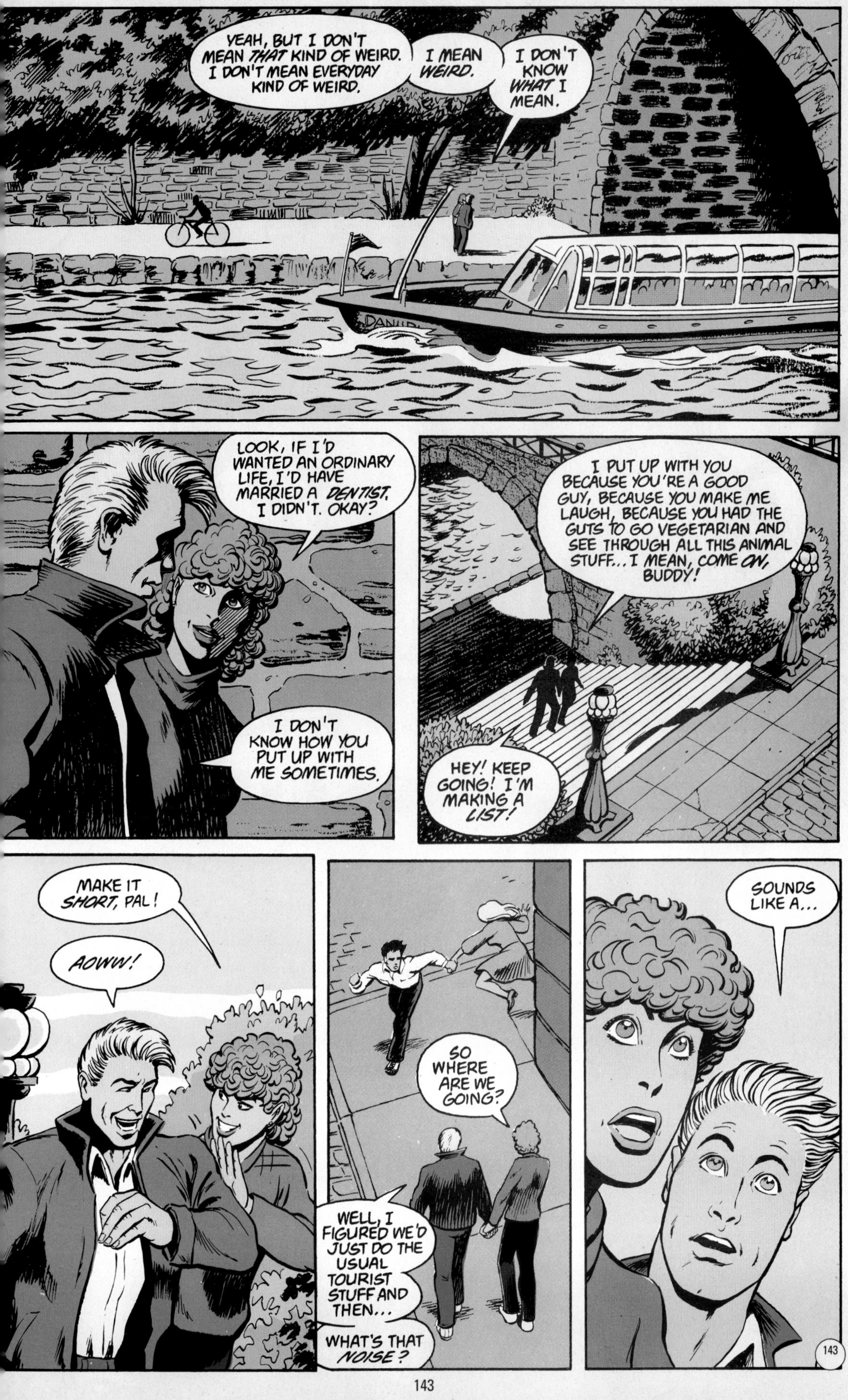
YEAH, BUT I DON'T MEAN THAT KIND OF WEIRD. I DON'T MEAN EVERYDAY KIND OF WEIRD.
I MEAN WEIRD.
I DON'T KNOW WHAT I MEAN.
LOOK, IF I'D WANTED AN ORDINARY LIFE, I'D HAVE MARRIED A DENTIST. I DIDN'T. OKAY?
I DON'T KNOW HOW YOU PUT UP WITH ME SOMETIMES.
I PUT UP WITH YOU BECAUSE YOU'RE A GOOD GUY, BECAUSE YOU MAKE ME LAUGH, BECAUSE YOU HAD THE GUTS TO GO VEGETARIAN AND SEE THROUGH ALL THIS ANIMAL STUFF... I MEAN, COME ON, BUDDY!
HEY! KEEP GOING! I'M MAKING A LIST!
MAKE IT SHORT, PAL!
AOWW!
SO WHERE ARE WE GOING?
WELL, I FIGURED WE'D JUST DO THE USUAL TOURIST STUFF AND THEN...
WHAT'S THAT NOISE?
SOUNDS LIKE A...
143

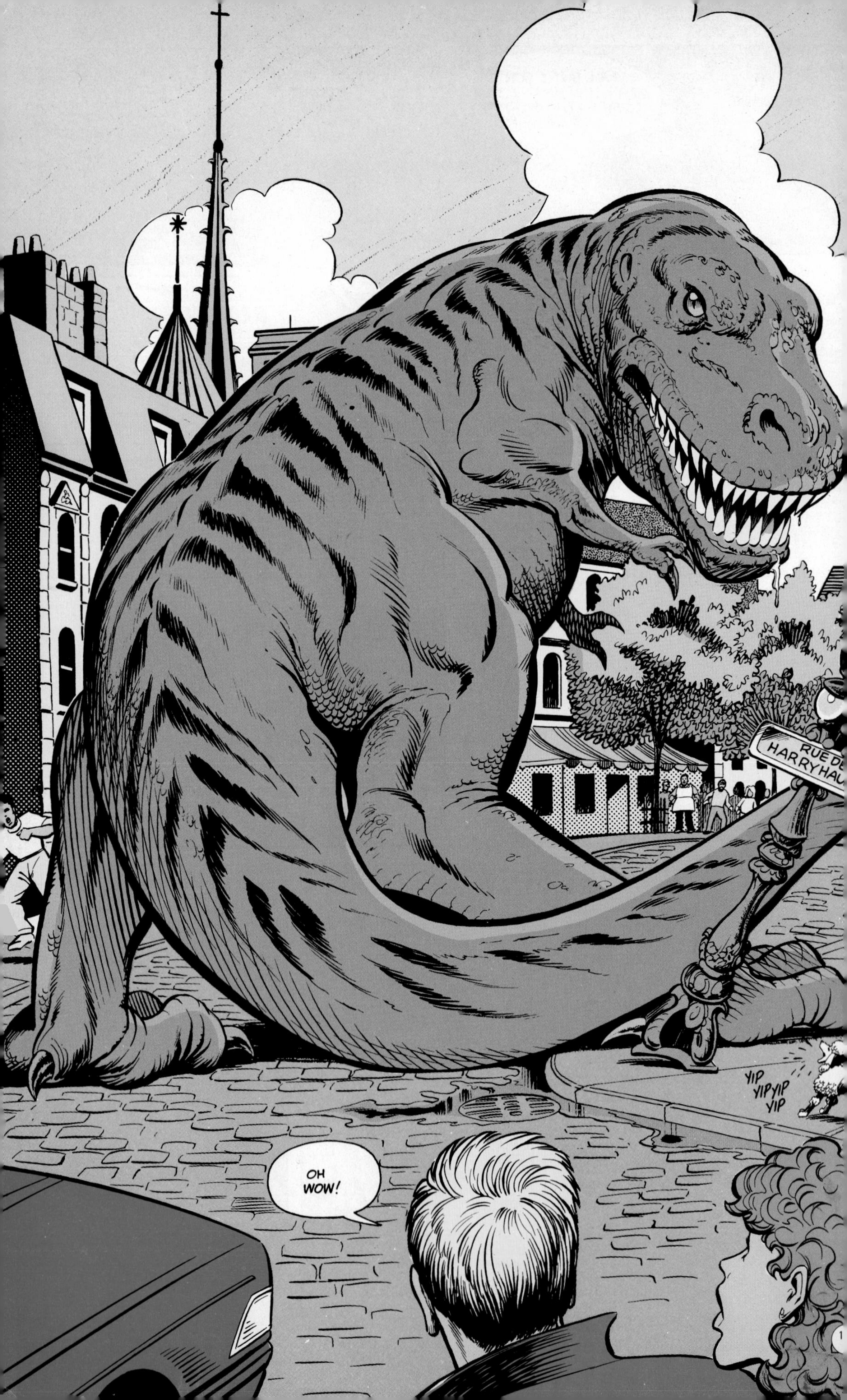
YIP
YIPYIP
YIP
OH
WOW!

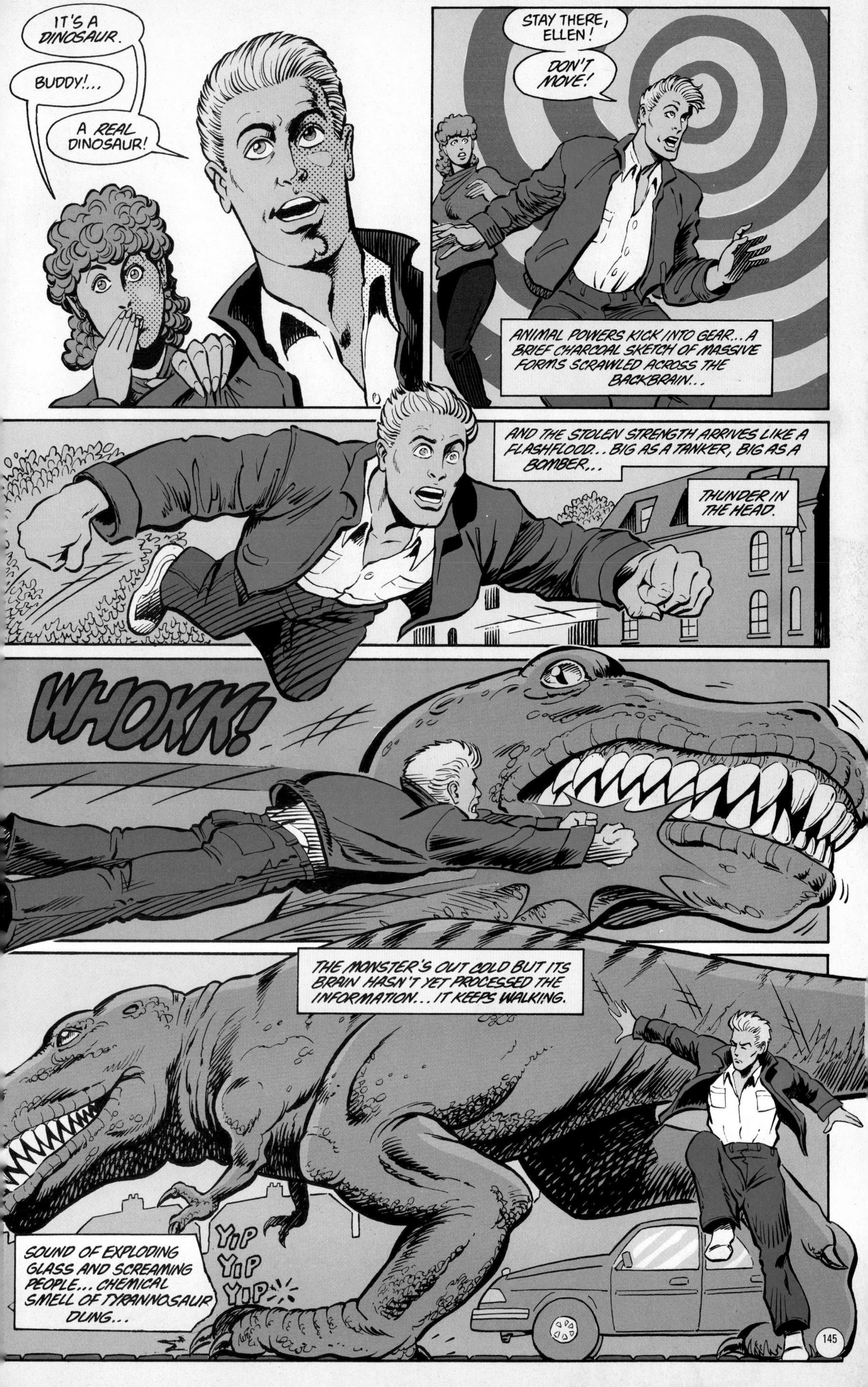
IT'S A DINOSAUR.
BUDDY!...
A REAL DINOSAUR!
STAY THERE, ELLEN!
DON'T MOVE!
ANIMAL POWERS KICK INTO GEAR... A BRIEF CHARCOAL SKETCH OF MASSIVE FORMS SCRAWLED ACROSS THE BACKBRAIN...
AND THE STOLEN STRENGTH ARRIVES LIKE A FLASHFLOOD... BIG AS A TANKER, BIG AS A BOMBER...
THUNDER IN THE HEAD.
WHOKK!
THE MONSTER'S OUT COLD BUT ITS BRAIN HASN'T YET PROCESSED THE INFORMATION... IT KEEPS WALKING.
SOUND OF EXPLODING GLASS AND SCREAMING PEOPLE... CHEMICAL SMELL OF TYRANNOSAUR DUNG...
YIP
YIP
YIP

NNNGH!!

BUDDY!

BUDDY, ARE YOU OKAY?

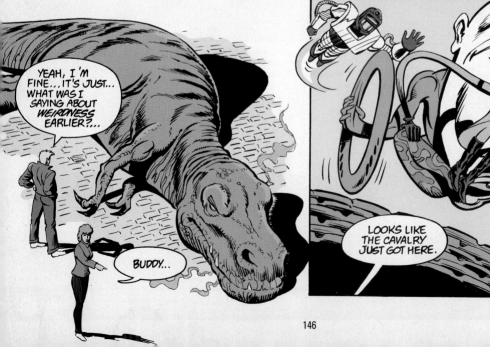

YEAH, I'M FINE... IT'S JUST... WHAT WAS I SAYING ABOUT WEIRDNESS EARLIER?...

BUDDY...

LOOKS LIKE THE CAVALRY JUST GOT HERE.

146

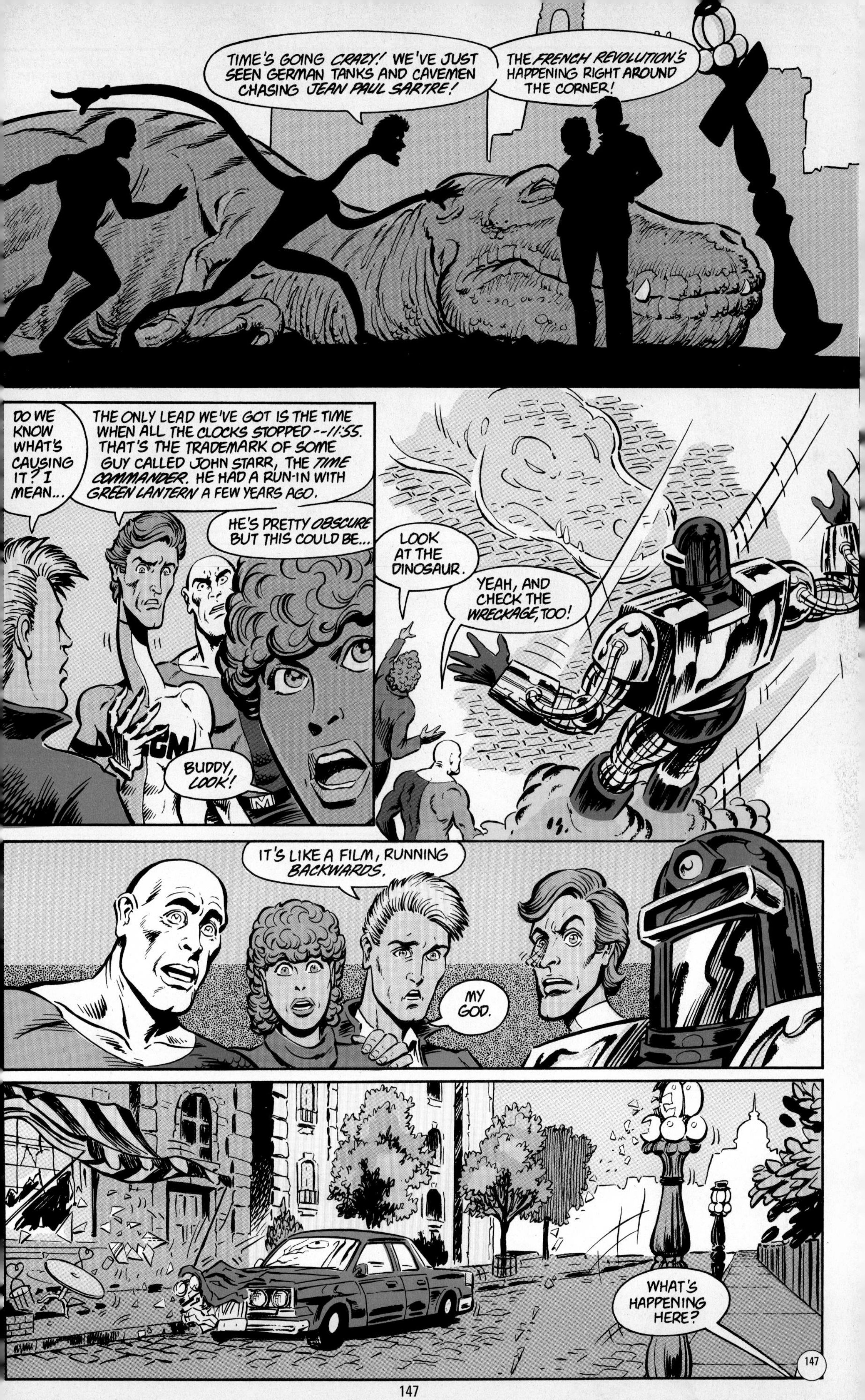
TIME'S GOING CRAZY! WE'VE JUST SEEN GERMAN TANKS AND CAVEMEN CHASING JEAN PAUL SARTRE!
THE FRENCH REVOLUTION'S HAPPENING RIGHT AROUND THE CORNER!
DO WE KNOW WHAT'S CAUSING IT? I MEAN...
THE ONLY LEAD WE'VE GOT IS THE TIME WHEN ALL THE CLOCKS STOPPED--11:55. THAT'S THE TRADEMARK OF SOME GUY CALLED JOHN STARR, THE TIME COMMANDER. HE HAD A RUN-IN WITH GREEN LANTERN A FEW YEARS AGO.
HE'S PRETTY OBSCURE BUT THIS COULD BE...
BUDDY, LOOK!
LOOK AT THE DINOSAUR.
YEAH, AND CHECK THE WRECKAGE, TOO!
IT'S LIKE A FILM, RUNNING BACKWARDS.
MY GOD.
WHAT'S HAPPENING HERE?
147

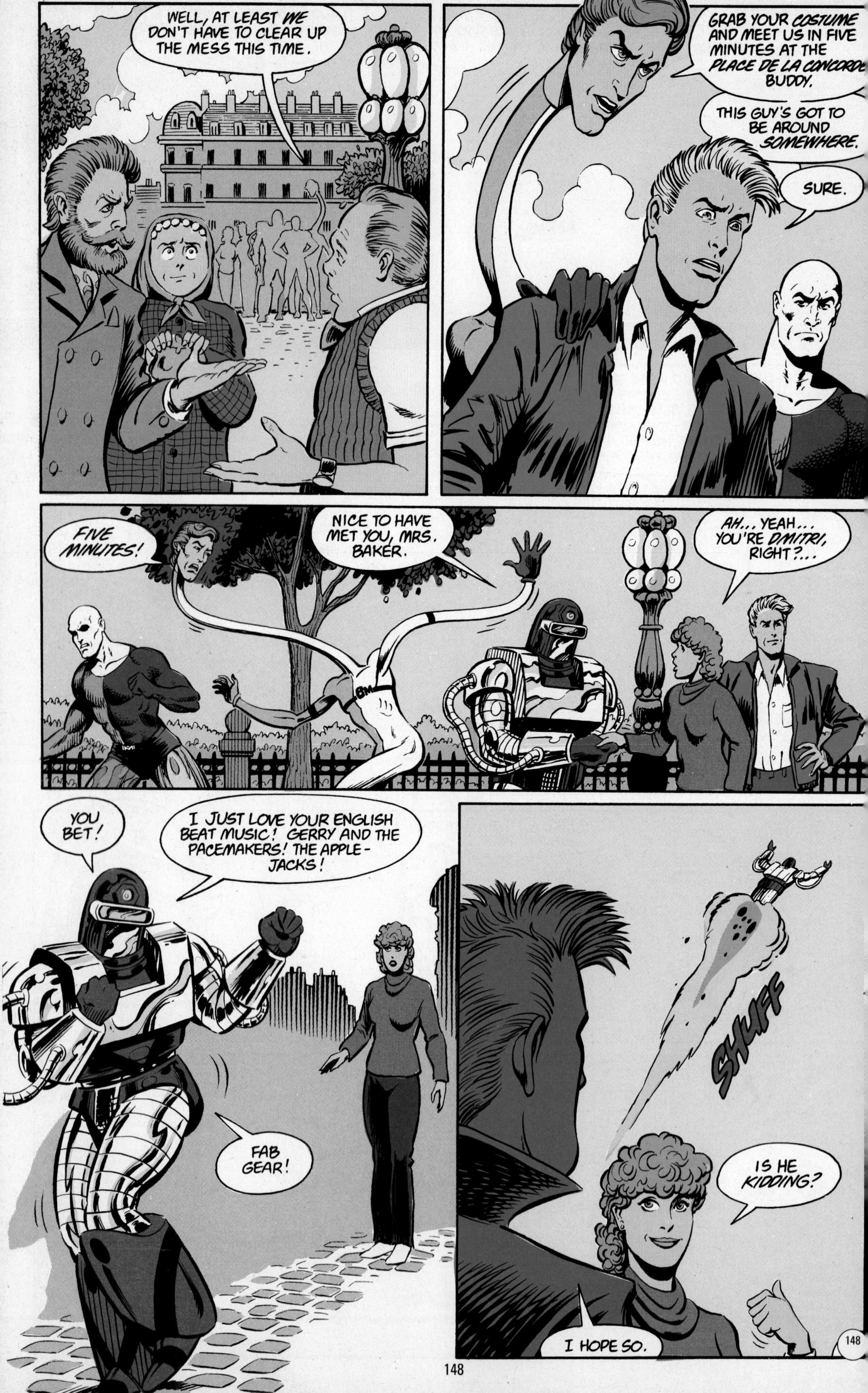
WELL, AT LEAST WE DON'T HAVE TO CLEAR UP THE MESS THIS TIME.
GRAB YOUR COSTUME AND MEET US IN FIVE MINUTES AT THE PLACE DE LA CONCORDE, BUDDY.
THIS GUY'S GOT TO BE AROUND SOMEWHERE.
SURE.
FIVE MINUTES!
NICE TO HAVE MET YOU, MRS. BAKER.
AH... YEAH... YOU'RE DMITRI, RIGHT?...
YOU BET!
I JUST LOVE YOUR ENGLISH BEAT MUSIC! GERRY AND THE PACEMAKERS! THE APPLE-JACKS!
FAB GEAR!
SHUFF
IS HE KIDDING?
I HOPE SO.
148

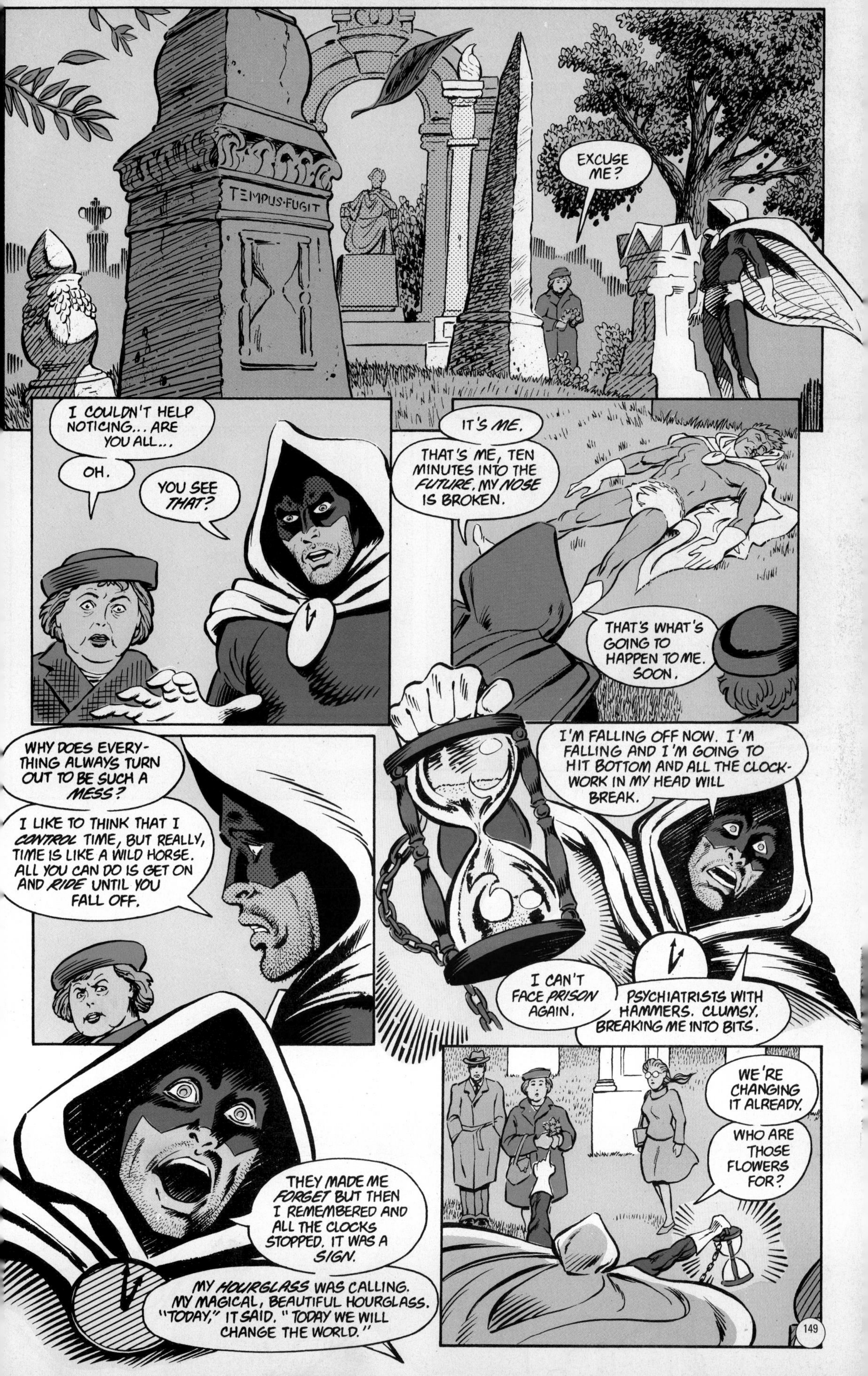
TEMPUS·FUGIT
EXCUSE ME?
I COULDN'T HELP NOTICING... ARE YOU ALL...
OH.
YOU SEE THAT?
IT'S ME.
THAT'S ME, TEN MINUTES INTO THE FUTURE. MY NOSE IS BROKEN.
THAT'S WHAT'S GOING TO HAPPEN TO ME. SOON.
WHY DOES EVERYTHING ALWAYS TURN OUT TO BE SUCH A MESS?
I LIKE TO THINK THAT I CONTROL TIME, BUT REALLY, TIME IS LIKE A WILD HORSE. ALL YOU CAN DO IS GET ON AND RIDE UNTIL YOU FALL OFF.
I'M FALLING OFF NOW. I'M FALLING AND I'M GOING TO HIT BOTTOM AND ALL THE CLOCKWORK IN MY HEAD WILL BREAK.
I CAN'T FACE PRISON AGAIN.
PSYCHIATRISTS WITH HAMMERS. CLUMSY. BREAKING ME INTO BITS.
THEY MADE ME FORGET BUT THEN I REMEMBERED AND ALL THE CLOCKS STOPPED. IT WAS A SIGN.
MY HOURGLASS WAS CALLING. MY MAGICAL, BEAUTIFUL HOURGLASS. "TODAY," IT SAID. "TODAY WE WILL CHANGE THE WORLD."
WE'RE CHANGING IT ALREADY.
WHO ARE THOSE FLOWERS FOR?

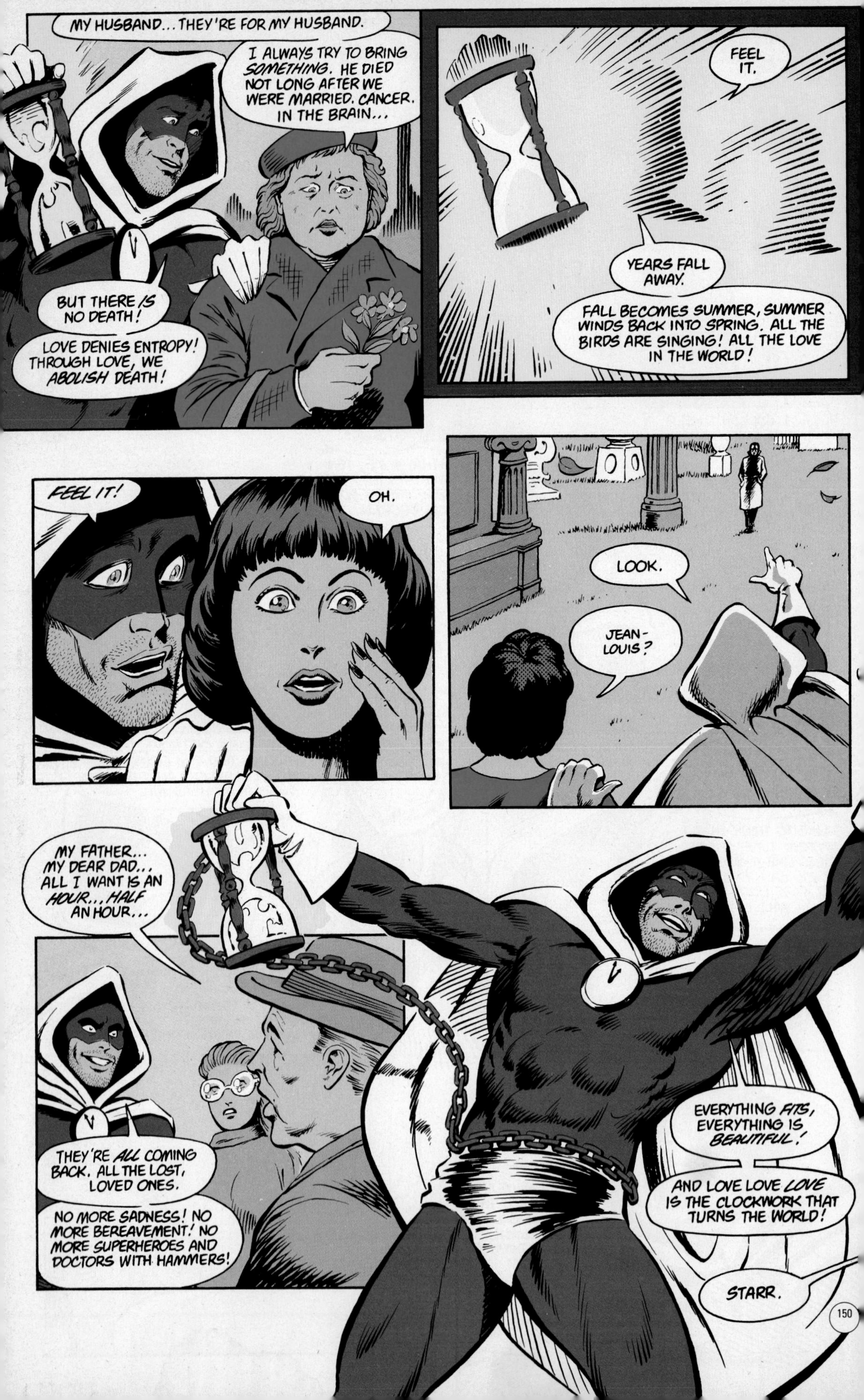
MY HUSBAND... THEY'RE FOR MY HUSBAND.
I ALWAYS TRY TO BRING *SOMETHING*. HE DIED NOT LONG AFTER WE WERE MARRIED. CANCER. IN THE BRAIN...
BUT THERE *IS* NO DEATH!
LOVE DENIES ENTROPY! THROUGH LOVE, WE *ABOLISH* DEATH!
FEEL IT.
YEARS FALL AWAY.
FALL BECOMES SUMMER, SUMMER WINDS BACK INTO SPRING. ALL THE BIRDS ARE SINGING! ALL THE LOVE IN THE WORLD!
FEEL IT!
OH.
LOOK.
JEAN-LOUIS?
MY FATHER... MY DEAR DAD... ALL I WANT IS AN *HOUR*... *HALF* AN HOUR...
THEY'RE *ALL* COMING BACK. ALL THE LOST, LOVED ONES.
NO MORE SADNESS! NO MORE BEREAVEMENT! NO MORE SUPERHEROES AND DOCTORS WITH HAMMERS!
EVERYTHING *FITS*, EVERYTHING IS *BEAUTIFUL*!
AND LOVE LOVE *LOVE* IS THE CLOCKWORK THAT TURNS THE WORLD!
STARR.

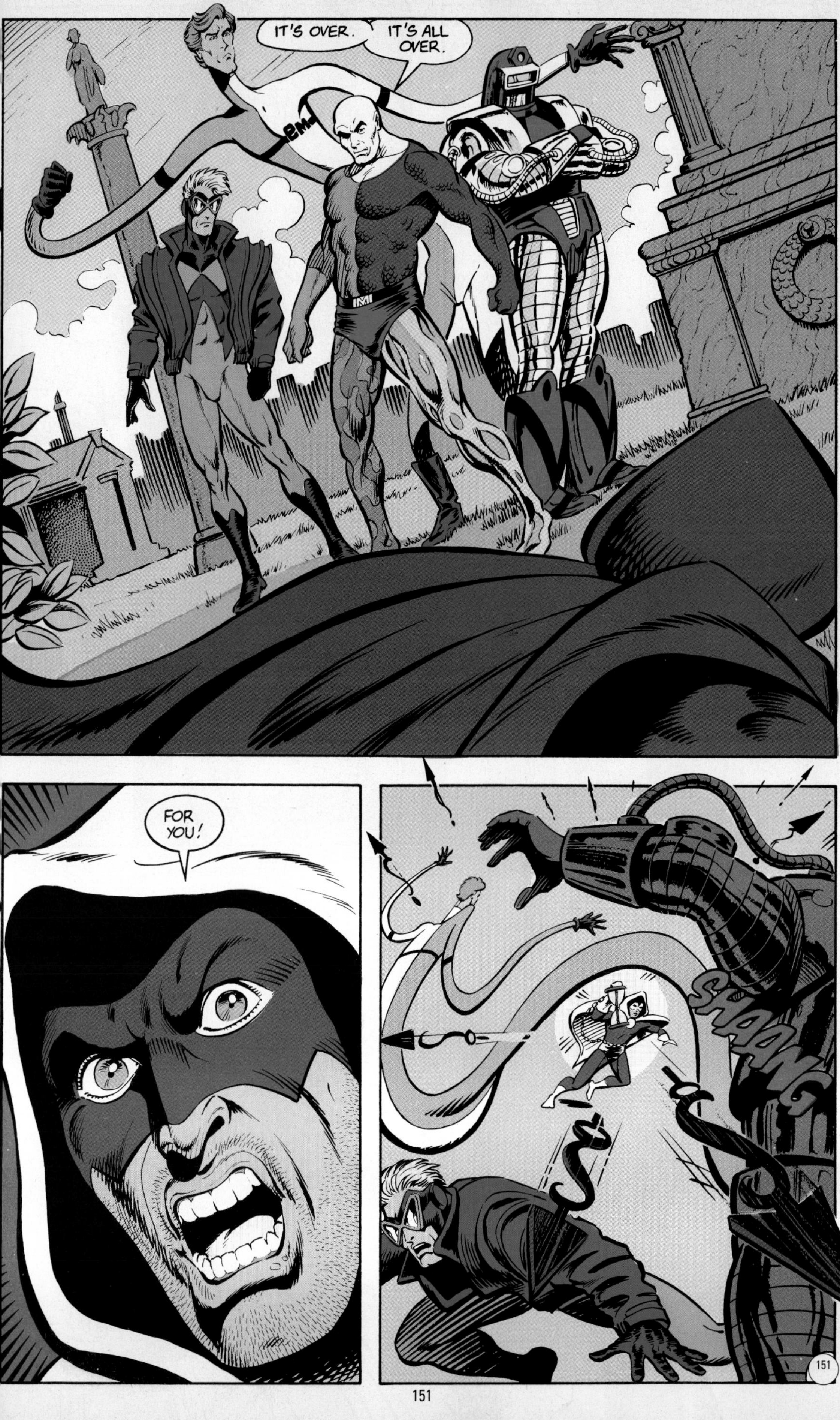
IT'S OVER.
IT'S ALL OVER.
FOR YOU!
SHAANG

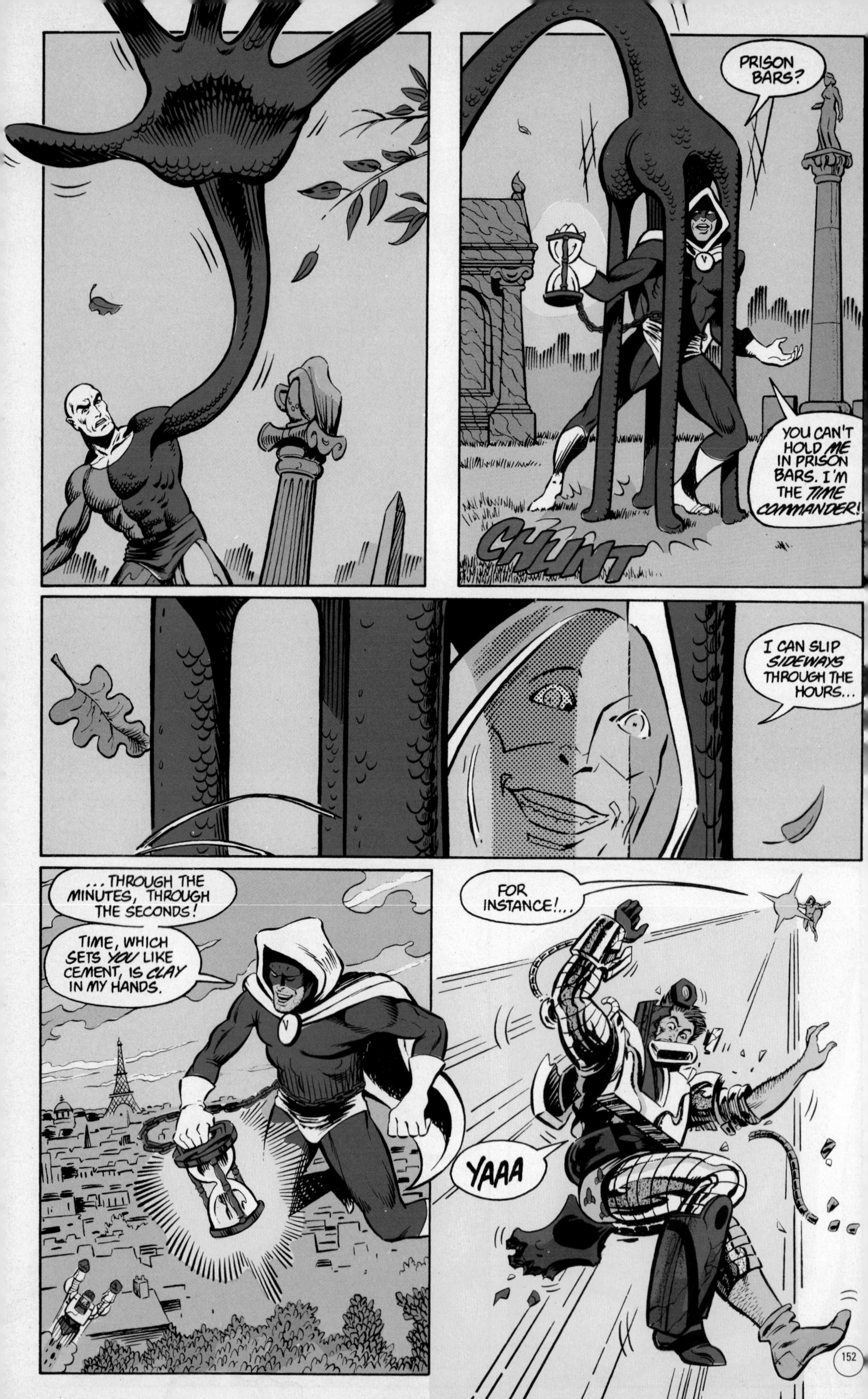
PRISON BARS?
CHUNT
YOU CAN'T HOLD ME IN PRISON BARS. I'M THE TIME COMMANDER!
I CAN SLIP SIDEWAYS THROUGH THE HOURS...
...THROUGH THE MINUTES, THROUGH THE SECONDS!
TIME, WHICH SETS YOU LIKE CEMENT, IS CLAY IN MY HANDS.
FOR INSTANCE!...
YAAA

AAAAAA

WUFF!

FROM SOME FAR-AWAY STREET COMES THE LONG CRY OF A SABRE-TOOTH...A GUILLOTINE BLADE RINGS DOWN...

BIPLANES BUZZ ACROSS BLUE, BLUE SKIES... THE DEAD AND THE LIVING ARE REUNITED...

AND TIME IS SET FREE.

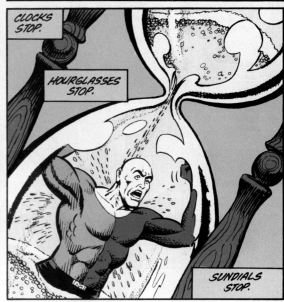

CLOCKS STOP.

HOURGLASSES STOP.

SUNDIALS STOP.

THE YEARS AND THE SEASONS ARE SHUFFLED LIKE PLAYING CARDS.

BLOSSOM SHOWERS OUT OF THE TREES...PERFUMED CONFETTI FOR THE ALCHEMICAL WEDDING OF TIME TO TIME... THERE IS NO MORE DEATH, NOR ANY SORROW...

THE PAST IS NO LONGER ANOTHER COUNTRY.

SO, DO YOU WANT TO FIGHT ME, TOO?

DO YOU WANT TO TRY TO HIT ME?

153

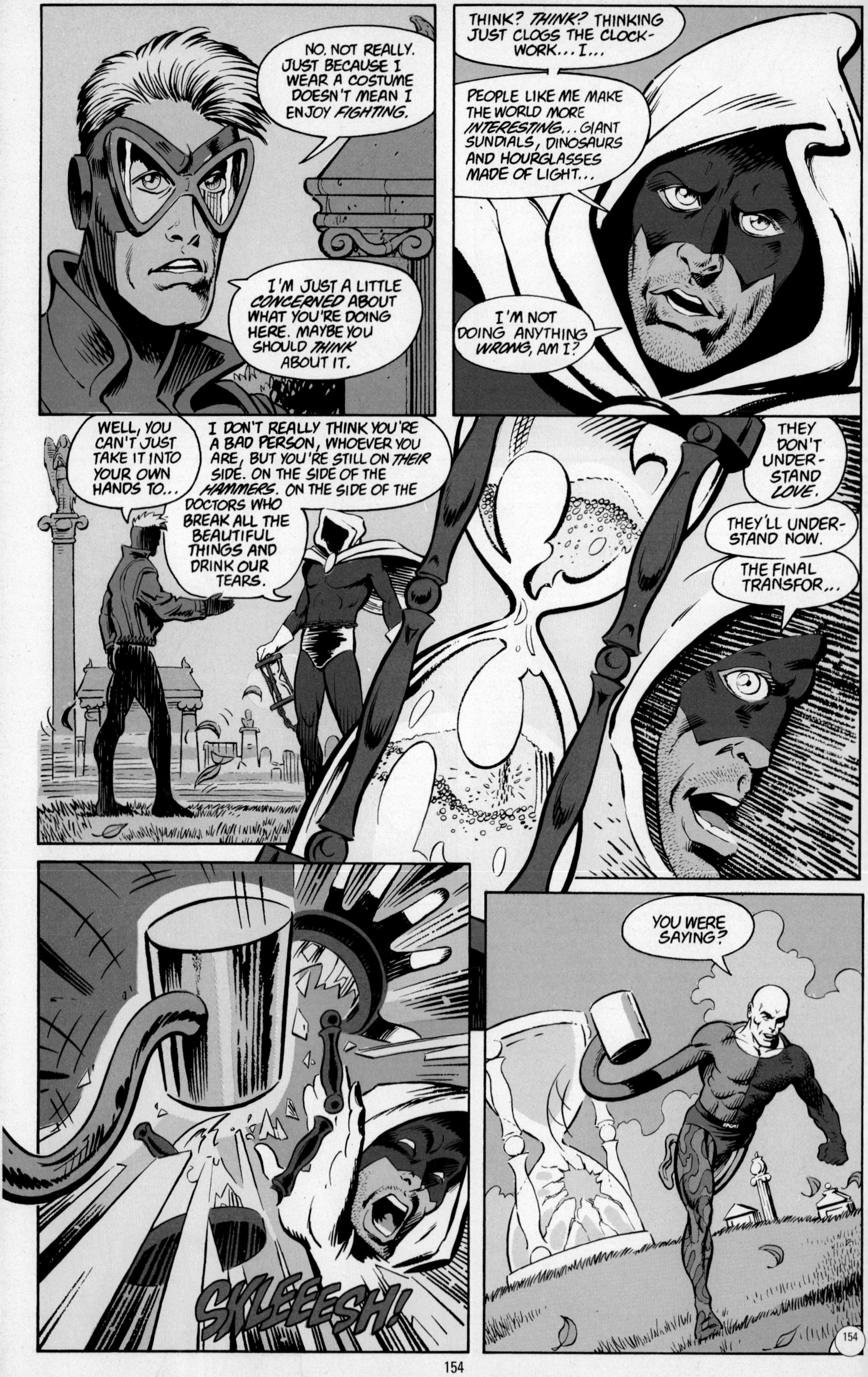
NO. NOT REALLY. JUST BECAUSE I WEAR A COSTUME DOESN'T MEAN I ENJOY FIGHTING.
I'M JUST A LITTLE CONCERNED ABOUT WHAT YOU'RE DOING HERE. MAYBE YOU SHOULD THINK ABOUT IT.
THINK? THINK? THINKING JUST CLOGS THE CLOCK-WORK... I...
PEOPLE LIKE ME MAKE THE WORLD MORE INTERESTING... GIANT SUNDIALS, DINOSAURS AND HOURGLASSES MADE OF LIGHT...
I'M NOT DOING ANYTHING WRONG, AM I?
WELL, YOU CAN'T JUST TAKE IT INTO YOUR OWN HANDS TO...
I DON'T REALLY THINK YOU'RE A BAD PERSON, WHOEVER YOU ARE, BUT YOU'RE STILL ON THEIR SIDE. ON THE SIDE OF THE HAMMERS. ON THE SIDE OF THE DOCTORS WHO BREAK ALL THE BEAUTIFUL THINGS AND DRINK OUR TEARS.
THEY DON'T UNDER-STAND LOVE.
THEY'LL UNDER-STAND NOW.
THE FINAL TRANSFOR...
SKLEEESH!
YOU WERE SAYING?
154

NO... I COULD HAVE TURNED IT ALL BACK... I COULD HAVE TAKEN US ALL BACK TO THE GARDEN.

TO THE GARDEN OF *EDEN*...

ULTIMA FORSAN

METAMORPHO... METAMORPHO, WAIT!

DON'T HIT HIM...

ULTIMA FORSAN

TICK TOCK TICK... NO NO *NO!*

STOP THE SIREN! THE HAMMERS SMASHING!

STOP IT!

ULTIMA FORSAN

STOP! OH GOD, STOP THEM *BREAKING.*

BREAKING IT ALL.

CRASH CRASH CRASH!

...DON'T...

155

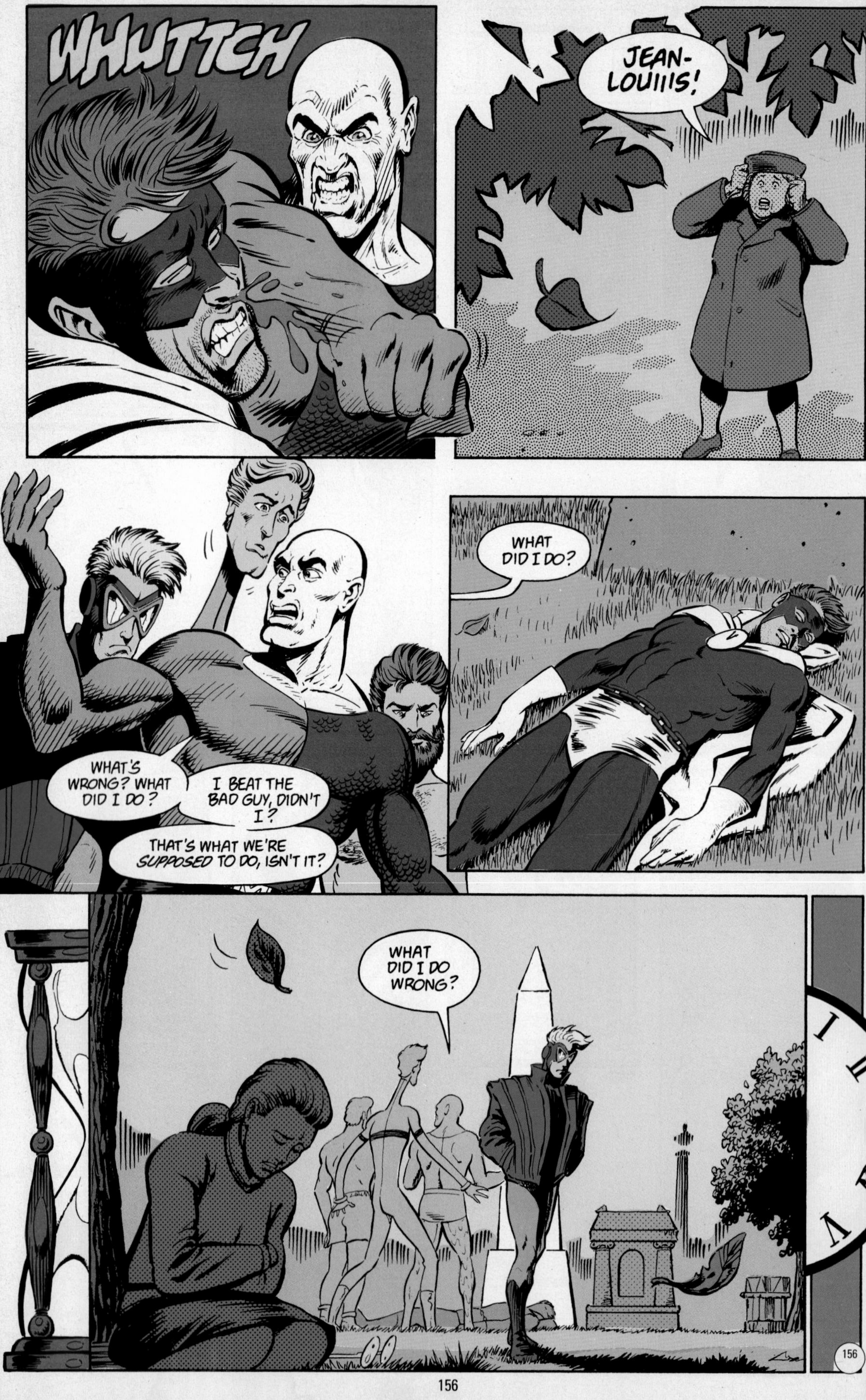
WHUTTCH
JEAN-LOUIIIS!
WHAT'S WRONG? WHAT DID I DO?
I BEAT THE BAD GUY, DIDN'T I?
THAT'S WHAT WE'RE *SUPPOSED* TO DO, ISN'T IT?
WHAT DID I DO?
WHAT DID I DO WRONG?
156

BUDDY, I'M *IMPRESSED!*

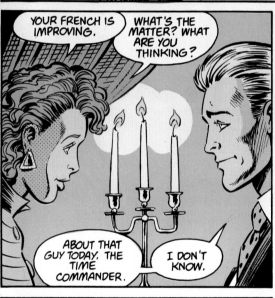

YOUR FRENCH IS IMPROVING.

WHAT'S THE MATTER? WHAT ARE YOU THINKING?

ABOUT THAT GUY TODAY, THE TIME COMMANDER.

I DON'T KNOW.

YOU CAN'T *ALWAYS* DO THE RIGHT THING...

YEAH.

LET'S NOT TALK ABOUT IT. THIS IS *YOUR* NIGHT, ELLEN.

I MEAN, YOU'VE SOLD YOUR BOOK, IT'S GOING TO BE A MILLION SELLER, YOUR HUSBAND'S IN THE JUSTICE LEAGUE, THE KIDS ARE DOING FINE...

I KNOW. IT'S ALL WORKING OUT, ISN'T IT?

EVERYTHING'S WORKING OUT.

EVERYTHING'S GOING TO BE ALL RIGHT.

STRANGE ADVENTURES #226

As expatriate Earthman Adam Strange defended his adopted planet Rann from a steady supply of fantastic menaces, he stood out from the pack of second-string heroes for one reason: he always won with his wits. He wasn't above throwing a punch or shooting a ray-gun, but every story delivered a dire situation he'd think his way through. Evil aliens had the superior technology, but Earthlings had the brains.

He had a heart, too. Adam fell in love with the beautiful science princess Alanna and with the gleaming futuristic cities of her world — but the stubborn Zeta-Beam teleporter kept whisking him back to Earth, usually right before he could collect his victory kiss. The vagaries of the Zeta-Beam kept poor Adam from calling any world home.

I culled this story from the DC archives in part because of its novel(ette) format. You're about to read the only Adam Strange tale ever presented in illustrated text form. It has never been reprinted. **—MW**

ADAM STRANGE

WRITER: Gardner Fox ARTIST: Murphy Anderson

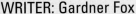

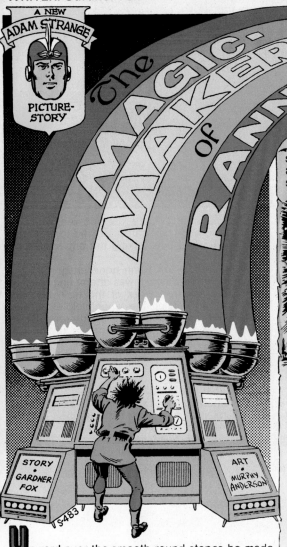

A NEW
ADAM STRANGE
PICTURE-STORY
The MAGIC-MAKER of RANN
STORY • GARDNER FOX
ART • MURPHY ANDERSON
S-483

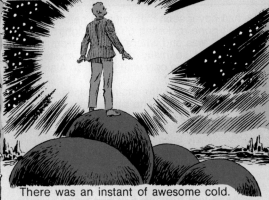

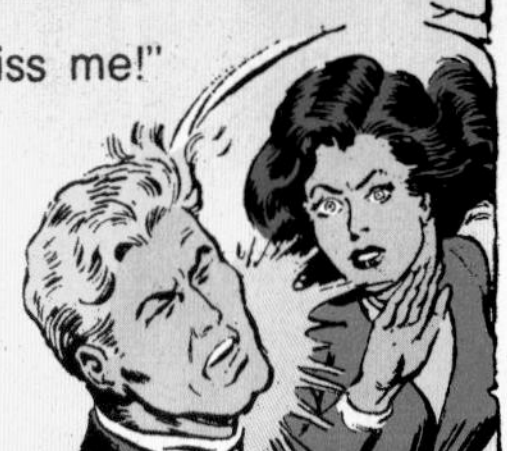

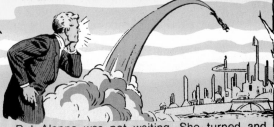

Upward over the smooth round stones he made his way, muscles aching with strain, the cool wind off the Australian Outback pressing his sports jacket and slacks to his tall, powerful body. Only the starry sky was above him as he clambered toward the topmost of these huge rocks known as the **Devil's Marbles** and which are found only in this one spot on Earth.

Adam Strange was not wearing his uniform and rocket jets. When the **zeta-beam** radiation had worn off his body last time he had been on Rann, he had reappeared on Earth along the side of a steep hill. Off balance, he had fallen, heels over head, tumbling so hard to the ground that as his rocket-jet crashed against a rock, it had broken.

There was no way to replace his rocket-jets on Earth, so he had been forced to come here to Australia where the **zeta-beam** was scheduled to hit and seek it out on foot. The beam would be angling in at the topmost rock of the **Devil's Marbles.**

And so as he stood erect on that highest boulder, Adam lifted his arms upward as though reaching to the very stars. He **was** reaching to a star, to **Alpha Centauri,** around which star-sun orbited his beloved planet Rann.

He had not long to wait.

A golden beam flashed from the heavens, splashing across the upright body of the young archeologist. For a breath-taking moment he stood outlined in a brilliant nimbus of yellow radiance.

There was an instant of awesome cold.

Then his feet firmed down on the porla grass of the vast plain before the capital city of Ranagar. Above his head were the familiar green skies, below them—

Alanna of Ranagar, the girl he loved.

His sweetheart was scowling blackly, standing with arms crossed, thin black brows furrowed with fury. A cold chill of deadly premonition stabbed deep inside the Earthman, but he held out his arms.

"Alanna, honey—come kiss me!"

The girl leaped forward, slimly curved in her blue and yellow garb. Her right arm came up. Her palm thudded hard against Adam's cheek in a savage slap that rocked his head back.

"Wha—what's the matter?" Adam gasped in shock. "Why'd you slap me?"

"I never want to see you again, Adam Strange!"

"Whaaaaat? Alanna—wait!"

But Alanna was not waiting. She turned and leaped into the sky, rocket-jets purring to life. Like a frightened cloud she hurtled toward the slender spires and tall towers of the walled city of Ranagar.

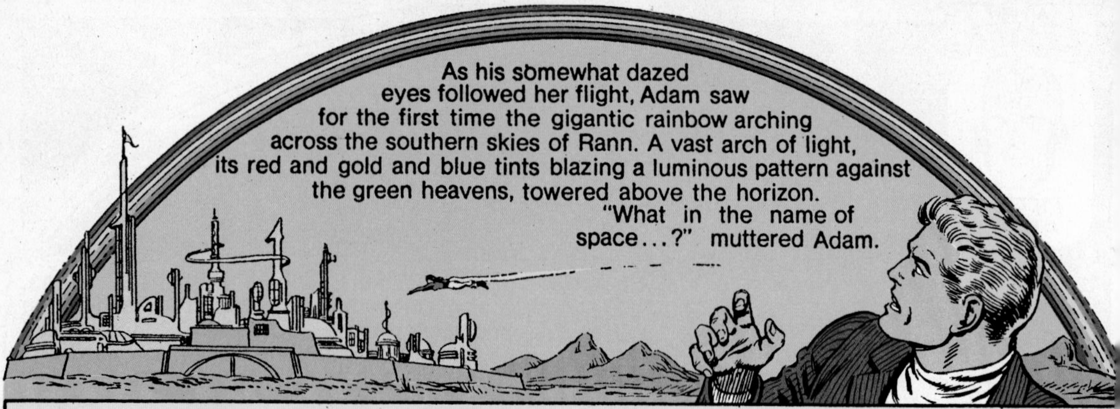

As his somewhat dazed eyes followed her flight, Adam saw for the first time the gigantic rainbow arching across the southern skies of Rann. A vast arch of light, its red and gold and blue tints blazing a luminous pattern against the green heavens, towered above the horizon.

"What in the name of space...?" muttered Adam.

He had never seen that rainbow before. If Alanna hadn't gone rocketing off, she might have told him what it was and where it came from, as she had explained so many of Rann's mysteries in the past. Well, the only way to talk to Alanna was to go after her.

He dashed across the plains grasses, the wind sweet to his nostrils. The porla grass gave off a lemony scent closely akin to Earth sage, mingled with the fragrance from a stand of ulla trees rippling their leafy branches in the breeze. Though the vegetation of Rann was quite different from that of Earth, it was so familiar by now to the young archeologist that he paid little attention to it.

His heart was heavy inside him as he raced toward the walled city. Something was mighty wrong, here. He chuckled through his worry. Every time he came to Rann, something was wrong; it seemed inevitable!

Alanna had long since disappeared when he came to the huge city gates. He slid to an abrupt halt, his shocked eyes raking the city square before him.

Had everybody on Rann gone crazy?

A uniformed patrolman was attempting to direct traffic, but making a mess of the task; his hand was frantically waving the wheelmobiles forward while at the same time his traffic sign read: STOP! Almost beside Adam, two members of the City Guard, good friends both of them and well known to the Earthman, were fighting a savage duel. A mother was belaboring her young son with both hands while tears ran down her cheeks and she shouted that she loved him.

Everywhere he looked he saw evidences that the inhabitants of this city had lost their wits.

"They're all crazy, the lot of them," he muttered, shaking his head in puzzlement. "Everyone seems to be doing the exact opposite of what he should be doing!"

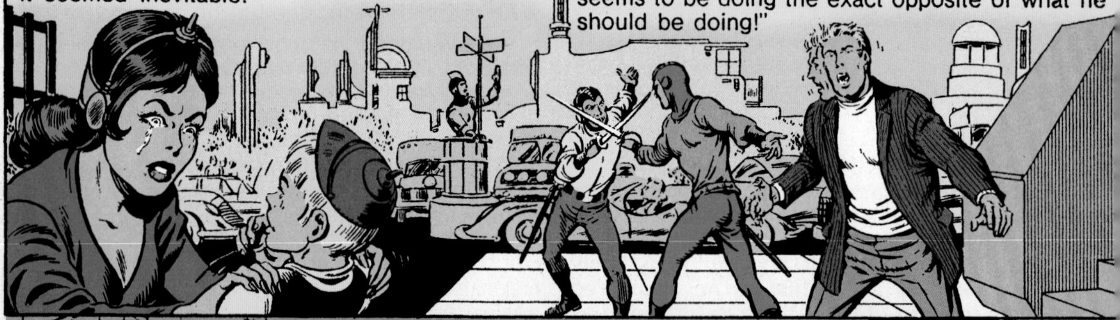

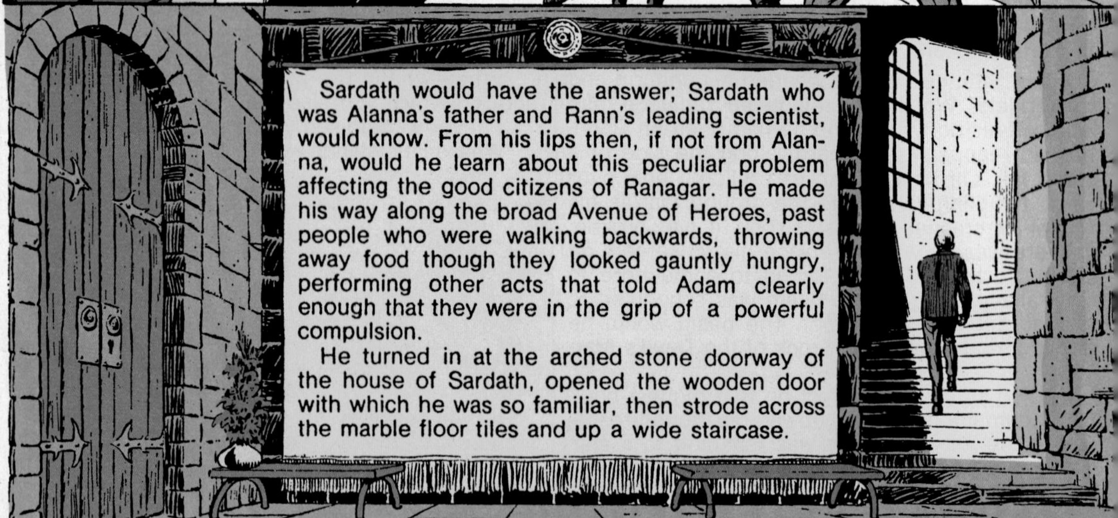

Sardath would have the answer; Sardath who was Alanna's father and Rann's leading scientist, would know. From his lips then, if not from Alanna, would he learn about this peculiar problem affecting the good citizens of Ranagar. He made his way along the broad Avenue of Heroes, past people who were walking backwards, throwing away food though they looked gauntly hungry, performing other acts that told Adam clearly enough that they were in the grip of a powerful compulsion.

He turned in at the arched stone doorway of the house of Sardath, opened the wooden door with which he was so familiar, then strode across the marble floor tiles and up a wide staircase.

Alanna was with her father in his laboratory; he strode past the on-duty guard. Her eyes flashed him a venomous stare, even as she turned her back to the visitor from Earth.

"Sardath," Adam exclaimed, "what in the world is wrong with everybody? Alanna slapped me, I saw men and women acting contrary to their own wishes; I just can't believe my eyes! Is this some new menace on Rann?"

"There is nothing wrong, Adam. Go away!"

Adam glanced about the laboratory. He was getting nowhere. Neither Alanna nor her father were any help. And yet—he was confident he read a mute appeal for help in their eyes. He had faced enough menaces on Rann to know that Alanna loved him and that her father respected and admired him, that both of them would gladly help him—**if** they could.

Something prevented them from talking.

His gaze sharpened when he saw the guard lounging against the wall. He was a big fellow whom Adam knew well. He angled his walk toward the man—

Adam leaped. His right fist came up hard.

The guard staggered against the wall, knocked cold by that terrific blow. His body sagged, slipped down the wall and lay limp on the floor.

The Earthman knew he had to time this just right. If he questioned the guard now, the man would not hear him. If he waited until he became conscious, he could not tell him what Adam desperately needed to know. No, he must ask his questions in those brief moments when the man was coming in, before his conscious mind was in control of his speech, when he could still reach through to his sub-conscious mind.

The fellow stirred. Adam leaned close.

"Felthan, this is your friend, Adam Strange. Why is everyone in Ranagar acting so oddly? Do you know why Alanna slapped me, or why Sardath tells me to go away?"

"They cannot help it. We are all—witches and warlocks. We have been using magic—but because we use this magic...and the more we use it...the more contrary we are compelled to act."

The man was mumbling almost unintelligibly. Adam snapped out his words, fearing that Felthan would recover his wits before he could learn any more. "When did all this begin? And—why?"

"The magic powers appeared simultaneously with the huge rainbow in the southern skies, reaching as far as the distant badlands.

"And with the rainbow—came our magical powers!

"We could do—anything we wanted. I remember I created a beautiful picture just by wishing for it. Then I made myself this mighty new sword. All we had to do was wish—and whatever we wished for, happened...like magic! It was very wonderful. We were all so happy, so excited.

"Imagine! Just by thinking about it, we became great magicians! Sardath theorized that the unusual radiation of the rainbow affected the telekinetic powers of our minds. I'm not too clear about that. It was as if the radiation gave us super-scientific talents.

"For a few days, everything was beautiful. Then the contrariness began. We started to do things we didn't want to do, as if a force inside us were compelling us..."

Adam sat back on his heels, head reeling. What Felthan had said was utterly fantastic! Yet he had faced fantastic things on Rann, before. His problem now was—

How did one go about destroying a rainbow?

He would need his uniform, his ray-gun and the rocket-jets in the guest room where he stayed while on Rann. They were spares he kept always on hand. With those jets strapped to his back—he could follow where the rainbow led. And in the hope that it might prove useful, Adam selected a radiation-absorber from the laboratory of Sardath.

Moments later,

Adam Strange rocketed upward from the flat rooftop of the laboratory, eyes fixed on the eerie rainbow that arched high above the surface of the planet. Higher he went, jets purring with latent power, speeding like a bullet through the air.

He soared into the red band of the rainbow, and was swallowed by a scarlet mist. He fled southward through that brilliant crimson fog, then rose even higher until he was surrounded by a golden glow. Instead of a pot of gold at the end of this thing, he thought, I'm going to find a mess of trouble, if my past experiences on Rann mean anything.

3

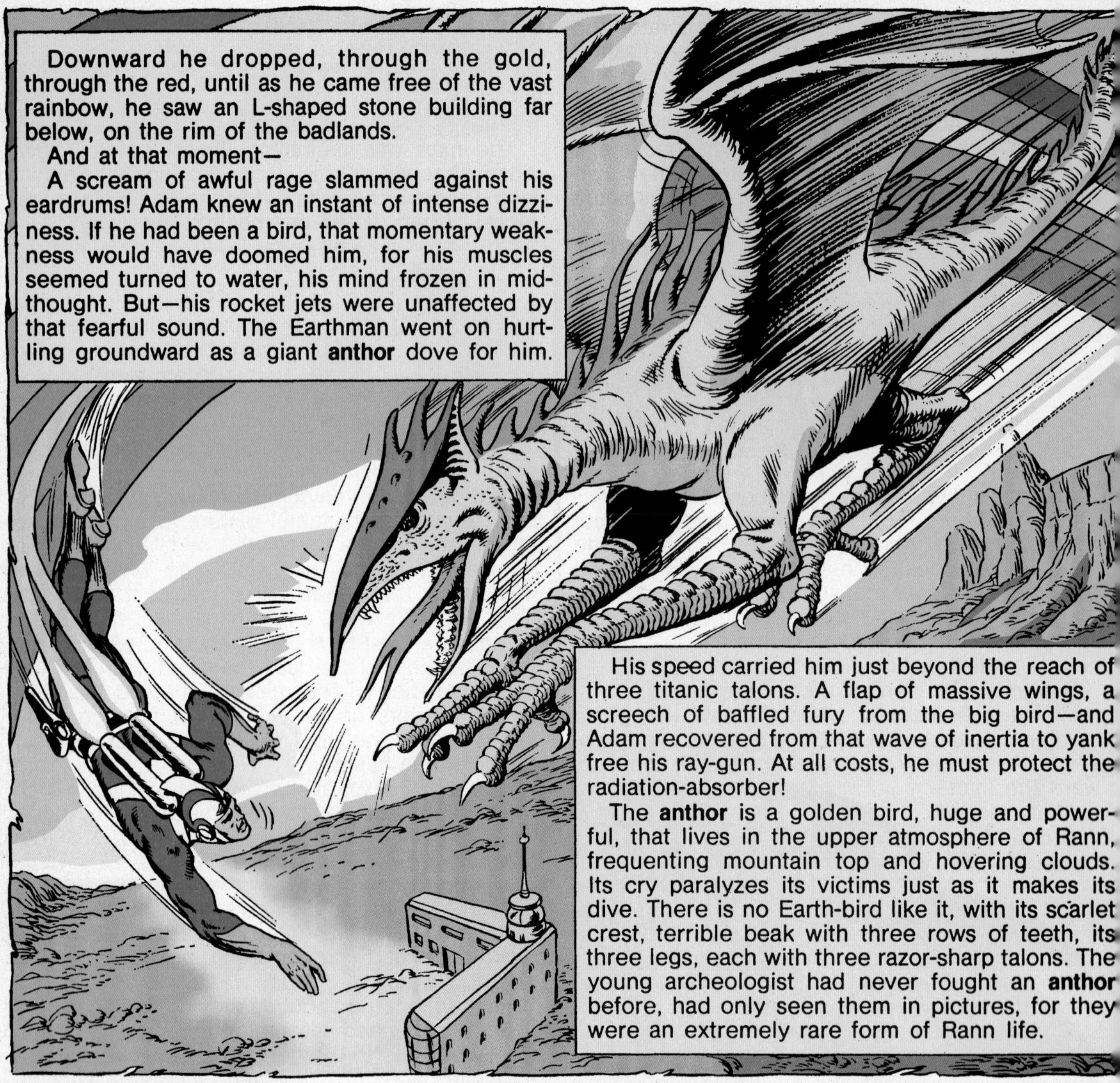

Downward he dropped, through the gold, through the red, until as he came free of the vast rainbow, he saw an L-shaped stone building far below, on the rim of the badlands.

And at that moment—

A scream of awful rage slammed against his eardrums! Adam knew an instant of intense dizziness. If he had been a bird, that momentary weakness would have doomed him, for his muscles seemed turned to water, his mind frozen in midthought. But—his rocket jets were unaffected by that fearful sound. The Earthman went on hurtling groundward as a giant **anthor** dove for him.

His speed carried him just beyond the reach of three titanic talons. A flap of massive wings, a screech of baffled fury from the big bird—and Adam recovered from that wave of inertia to yank free his ray-gun. At all costs, he must protect the radiation-absorber!

The **anthor** is a golden bird, huge and powerful, that lives in the upper atmosphere of Rann, frequenting mountain top and hovering clouds. Its cry paralyzes its victims just as it makes its dive. There is no Earth-bird like it, with its scarlet crest, terrible beak with three rows of teeth, its three legs, each with three razor-sharp talons. The young archeologist had never fought an **anthor** before, had only seen them in pictures, for they were an extremely rare form of Rann life.

The ray-gun hummed. A beam of destructive energy stabbed out. It hit the feathered bulk of the **anthor,** bounced off—right at Adam! The Earthman dove, swung upward in what used to be known on Earth as an Immelmann turn. His curved flight brought him behind the **anthor,** and above it.

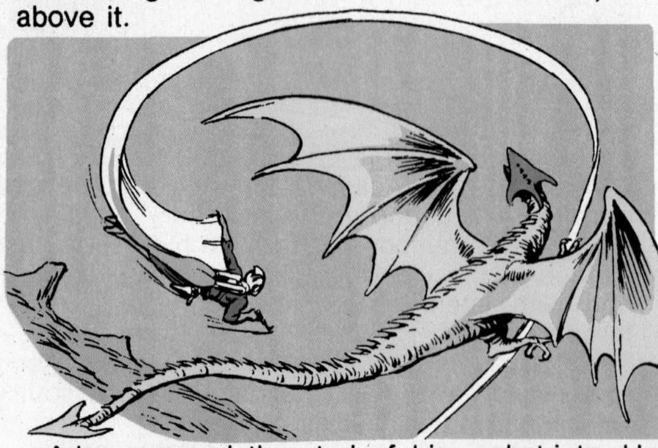

Adam pressed the stud of his rocket-jets. He zoomed downward, landed hard on the back of the bird. With hands and legs he gripped the **anthor,** and swung the rocket-jets over to their last erg of energy. Held fast by the man, the big bird was helpless to fight the powerful jets.

Man and bird dove for the building.

Into the stone wall of that edifice Adam slammed the **anthor.** Through cementwork and the stones from the badlands of which its walls were made, he drove it. Beneath him he felt the quiver which told him the bird was stunned by that fearsome impact. It lay limp, lifeless.

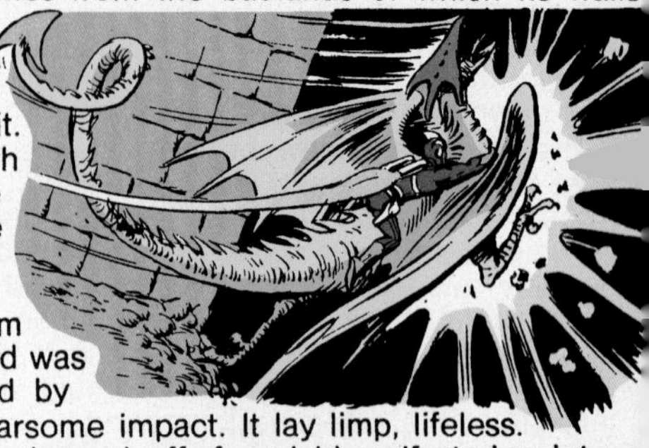

Adam leaped off, found himself staring into a large chamber that seemed part laboratory, part living quarters, through the gaping hole in the broken wall. No time for investigation now! First he must absorb that radiation!

The radiation-absorber was in his hand. He turned its controls. To his surprise, the absorption indicator did not move! How ironic it was that having fought to protect it, it was no good to him!

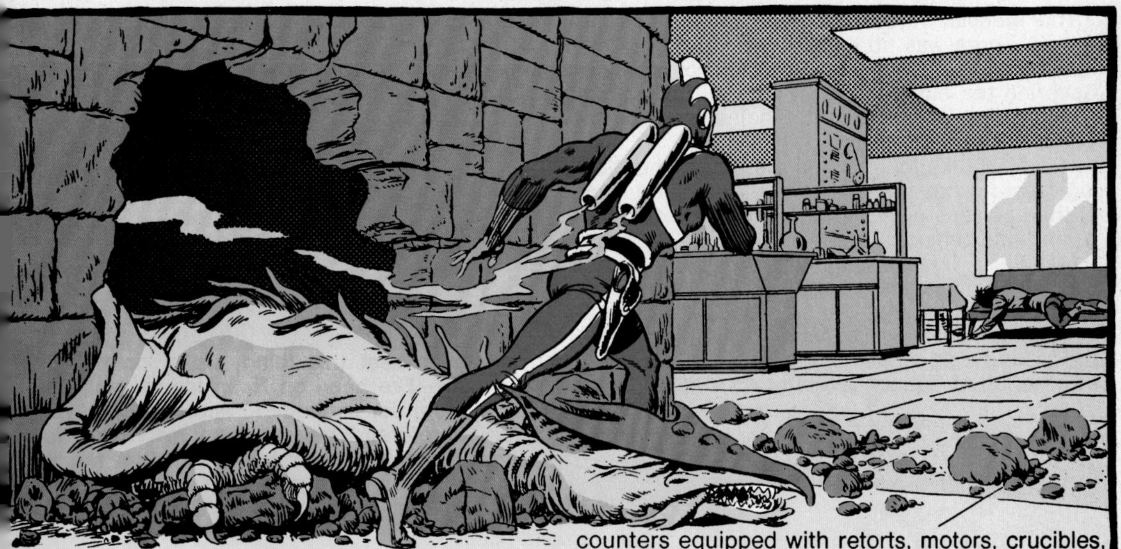

"What's wrong with it?" he wondered, forehead furrowed by a frown. Could the radiation be of a type unknown to Rann science? It must be! Otherwise the absorber would have begun removing it.

He stepped through the hole in the wall, past the body of the **anthor.** Giant computers lined one wall. In the middle of the room were long counters equipped with retorts, motors, crucibles, alembics, all the impedimenta of a fine laboratory. And resting on a couch against the far wall was an old man.

A touch of his hand convinced Adam that the man was dead. If he had created the rainbow and the odd radiation, he could never tell Adam anything about it.

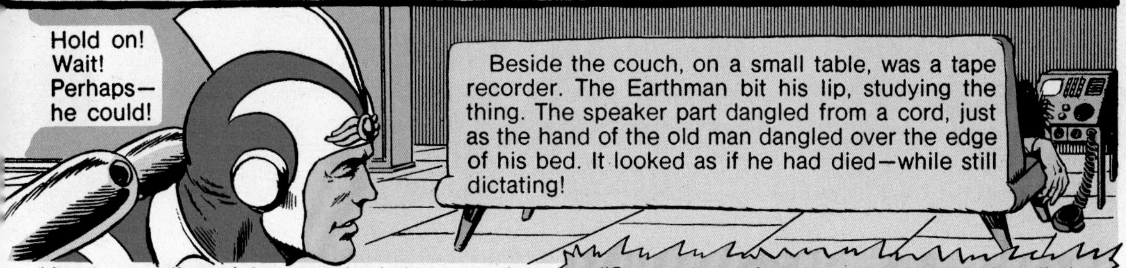
Hold on! Wait! Perhaps— he could!
Beside the couch, on a small table, was a tape recorder. The Earthman bit his lip, studying the thing. The speaker part dangled from a cord, just as the hand of the old man dangled over the edge of his bed. It looked as if he had died—while still dictating!

Heart pounding, Adam touched the reset button, started it up. A faintly metallic voice sprang to life.

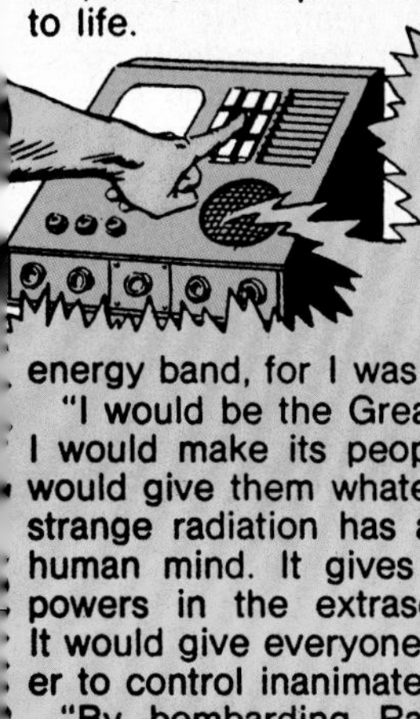

"My name is Thortan Ov. All my life I have been a scientist. Some years ago I began experimenting with an unusual radiation far below the known detectable limits. For years I labored over that energy band, for I was driven by a dream!

"I would be the Great Benefactor of my world. I would make its people healthy and wealthy, I would give them whatever they wanted. For this strange radiation has a wondrous effect on the human mind. It gives the mind super-scientific powers in the extrasensory perception range. It would give everyone on Rann the mental power to control inanimate objects!

"By bombarding Rann with this radiation, I would make every man, woman and child a superbeing, one who might turn a lead bar into gold, a drab garment into a gown of shimmering colors, merely by concentrating on it.

"There would be no more poor people. Nobody would be unhappy, there would be plenty of food and shelter for all. My name would go down in Rann history as its greatest man.

"All this might have happened—

"If it had not been for the meteorite!

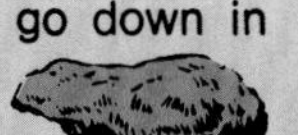

"Some days after I released the **psi** radiation, as I call it, a glowing meteorite curved across the southern skies, blazing red and angry, and landed on the far edge of the badlands with an explosive thump.

"The bright rainbow formed by the psi radiation as a symbol of hope for all Rannkind, became a mockery. For the meteorite absorbed the psi radiation—and **changed** it.

"Also, the men and women of Rann who had been overjoyed by what I had done—though they thought of it as a magic power I'd given them—were changed by that meteorite radiation. They became—**contrary.** They still had their so-called magic powers, but the more they used magic, the more contrary they became. They could not eat the foodstuffs they made, nor wear their lovely clothes. Worse, they turned on those they loved best.

"I tried to destroy the malignant meteorite being that had evolved from a tiny spore inside the metal hulk of the meteorite itself. Instead, I—

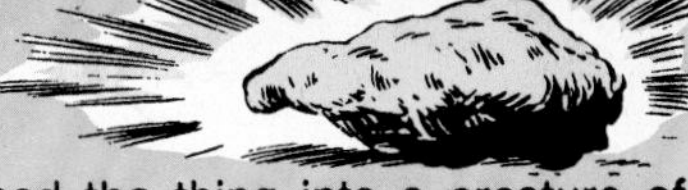

angered it. I turned the thing into a creature of madness, that sought to slay and destroy. Not only was its own peculiar radiation making everyone contradictory, its latent powers became fulfilled—and soon it will be invulnerable to any force on Rann."

The metallic voice died away. Adam Strange sighed. There was no more to do, here. The meteor-being was his enemy, and that of all Rann. Covering the old man with a spread, he stepped out into the Rann daylight. An instant later, he was rocketing southward.

It did not take long to find the thing. The glowing creature was flitting above the tumbled rocks of the badlands not far from a small village which lay in ruins behind it. As he came down out of the emerald sky, he saw something dark blue, flecked with silver lines and shafts of shimmery whiteness, something—that had no shape, for it was always changing. It was as amorphous as an amoeba, as round as a ball, as elongated as an arrow, in a series of sudden alterations. Always, it was in flux.

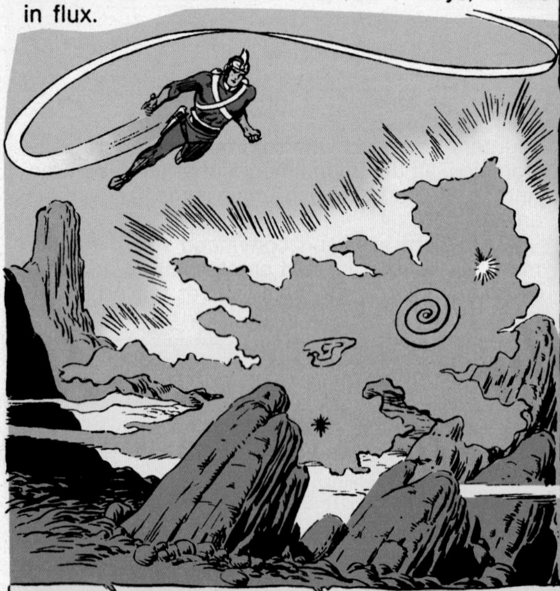

How did he fight such a thing?

He blasted with his ray-gun, sending a beam of awesome power into its middle. And the being swelled—grew! —enlarged as it absorbed the very energy that was supposed to harm it. Mocking laughter erupted in his head.

"Fool! You and your ray-gun cannot bother me. I am invulnerable to any known weapon of yours —and soon I will be invulnerable to everything!"

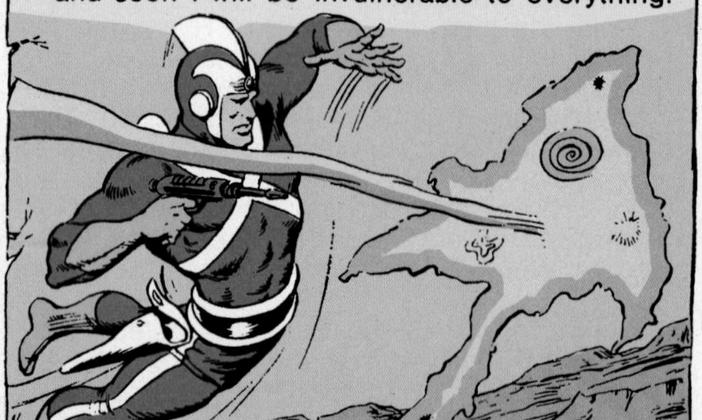

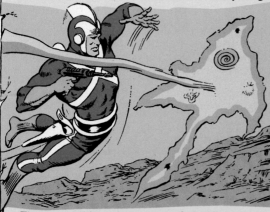

The spore-thing sent a ray of dazzling brightness at him. Adam darted sideways, feeling the terrible heat of that brilliant tendril. Another beam stabbed at him, and another, as the creature rose upward into the air.

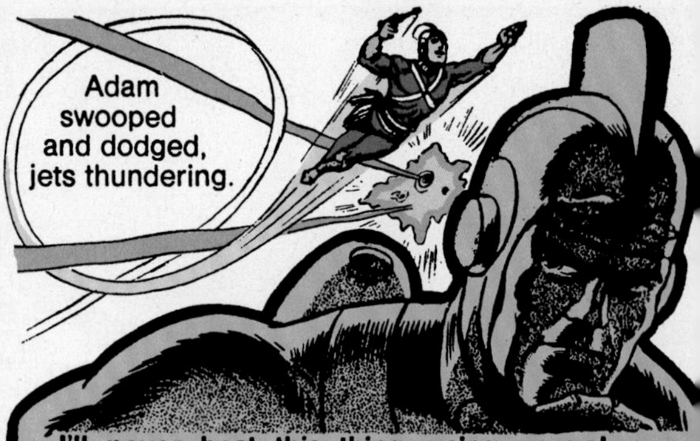
Adam swooped and dodged, jets thundering.

I'll never beat this thing, using normal weapons. But—I've been on Rann for several hours, long enough for my body to absorb the psi radiation. Therefore, I can perform marvelous feats with the mind-over-matter powers that radiation gives me... but at the cost of becoming contrary!

His thoughts were chaotic. Only magic might help him, but if he used magic and failed—his growing contrariness would no longer allow him to fight the thing! His contradictory nature then might make him leap in front of one of those heat tendrils and let it destroy him!

And yet—he must take the risk!

Adam concentrated. Downward from the green sky came a brilliant bolt of lightning—like magic! It hit the spore-being, surrounded it. And the thing from space grew—and grew!

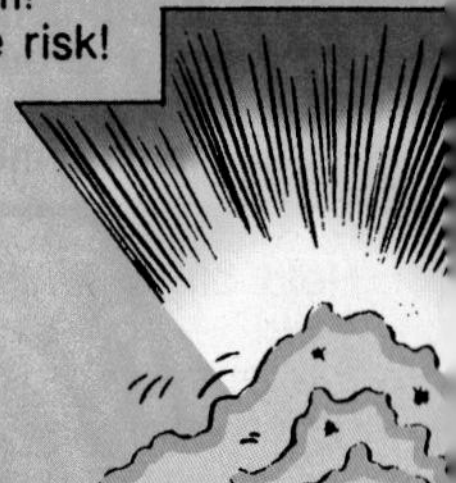

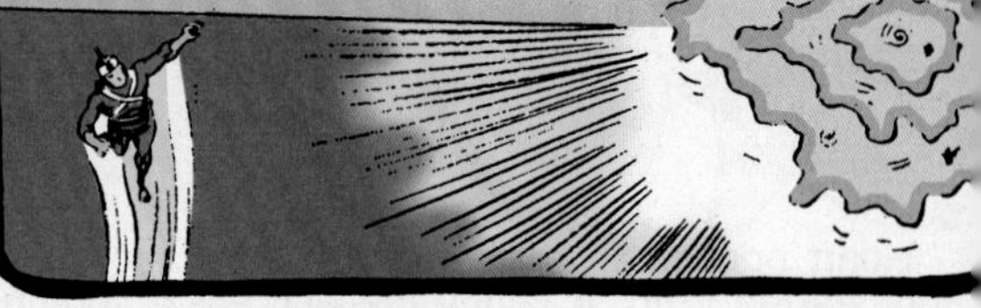

It stabbed a heat-beam at Adam. The Earthman dodged, swooped low over the badland rocks. Ahead of him he saw the faintly glowing meteorite, that had originally held the spore inside it as it sped across the black gulfs of cosmic space.

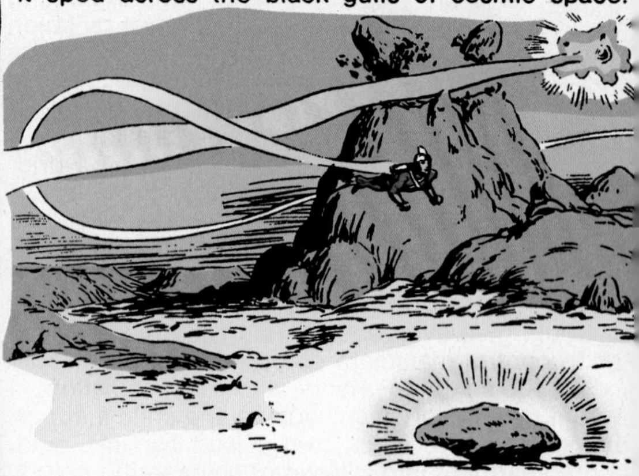

At the same time, the radiation-absorber in his belt began to click, ever so weakly. Adam was too busy keeping out of the way of the spore creature to pay attention to that, right now. For the thing was hurling tiny stars of glittering energy at him and he had to flee lest one touch and destroy him.

His mind worked swiftly. Upward from the rocks it conjured a massive stone hammer that thudded

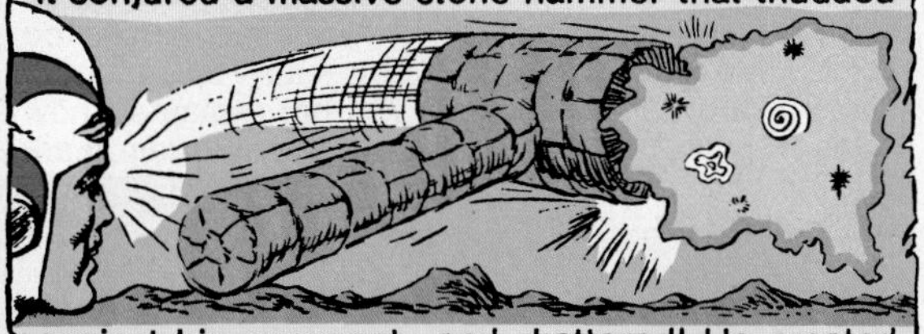

against his opponent—and shattered! He created a white dwarf sun and hurled it. The spore-creature absorbed it, growing even mightier.

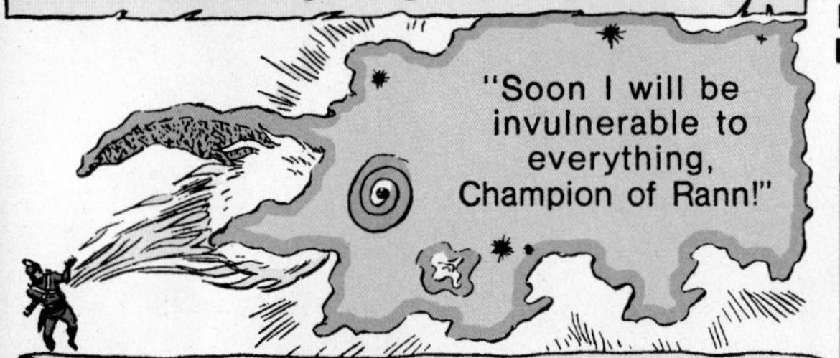
"Soon I will be invulnerable to everything, Champion of Rann!"

It came for him, spreading itself to form a kite-like triangle as it reached with its arms to draw Adam into it. The Earthman darted skyward, bare-

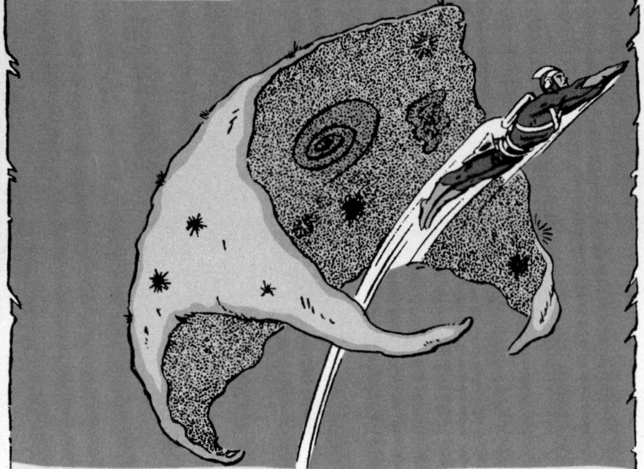

ly eluding that consuming clutch. In return, Adam dug a vast hole in the rocks, caused a mighty hurricane to blow, trying to force the thing into the rock tomb he'd made for it. When the spore-life evaded that, Adam formed a dozen nuclear warheads and hurled them.

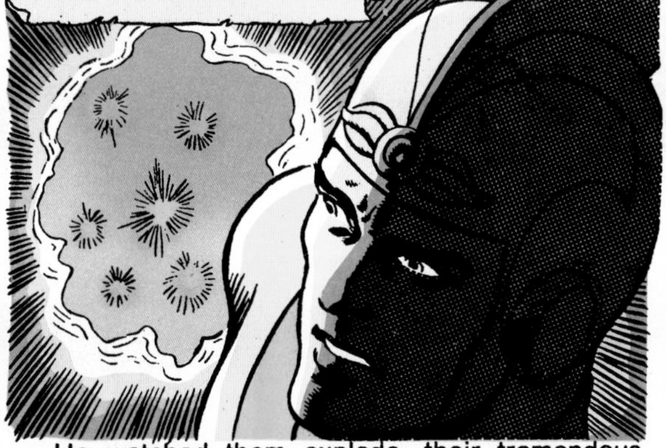

He watched them explode, their tremendous energy swallowed by the thing. A sense of resignation came over Adam. He realized it was the first onslaught of his contrariness. **There's no sense fighting this creature. It doesn't react to anything I do—except to get stronger!**

The more he fought it, the stronger **it** became! The more magic he used to battle it, the weaker **he** became! He wanted to stop, to throw himself at the thing, let it swallow him up as it did his magical weapons.

No! Fight on, fight on! Somehow, in some manner, there had to be an answer. But what could he do? What else was there to do? He had not the slightest clue.

He swept over the badlands, right above the meteorite. This time there was no clicking sound from the radiation absorber. Adam blinked, staring down at the meteorite. It had stopped glowing. It had lost its radioactivity. That meant, it was **lead.**

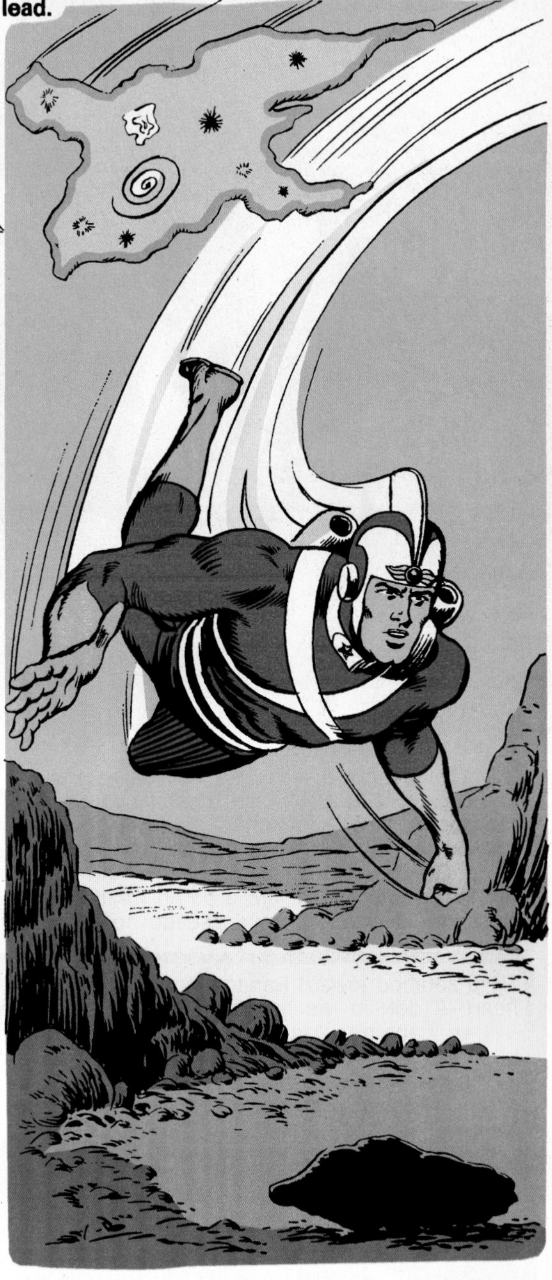

And lead contained any radiation placed inside it! Adam Strange gritted his teeth. He had one last chance to use his magic before the contrariness swept over him. The thing was coming, right behind him. 7

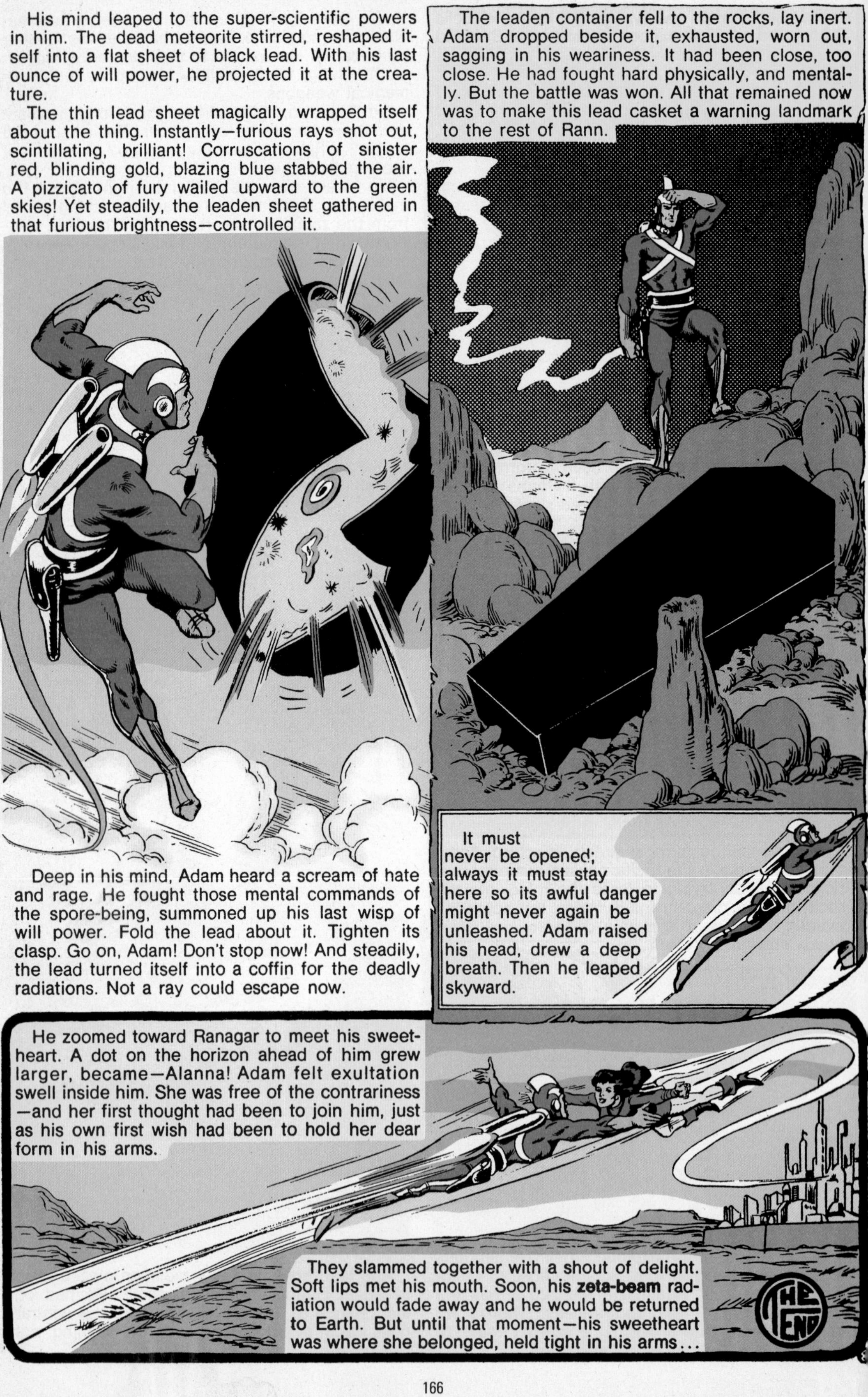
His mind leaped to the super-scientific powers in him. The dead meteorite stirred, reshaped itself into a flat sheet of black lead. With his last ounce of will power, he projected it at the creature.
The thin lead sheet magically wrapped itself about the thing. Instantly—furious rays shot out, scintillating, brilliant! Corruscations of sinister red, blinding gold, blazing blue stabbed the air. A pizzicato of fury wailed upward to the green skies! Yet steadily, the leaden sheet gathered in that furious brightness—controlled it.
Deep in his mind, Adam heard a scream of hate and rage. He fought those mental commands of the spore-being, summoned up his last wisp of will power. Fold the lead about it. Tighten its clasp. Go on, Adam! Don't stop now! And steadily, the lead turned itself into a coffin for the deadly radiations. Not a ray could escape now.
The leaden container fell to the rocks, lay inert. Adam dropped beside it, exhausted, worn out, sagging in his weariness. It had been close, too close. He had fought hard physically, and mentally. But the battle was won. All that remained now was to make this lead casket a warning landmark to the rest of Rann.
It must never be opened; always it must stay here so its awful danger might never again be unleashed. Adam raised his head, drew a deep breath. Then he leaped skyward.
He zoomed toward Ranagar to meet his sweetheart. A dot on the horizon ahead of him grew larger, became—Alanna! Adam felt exultation swell inside him. She was free of the contrariness—and her first thought had been to join him, just as his own first wish had been to hold her dear form in his arms.
They slammed together with a shout of delight. Soft lips met his mouth. Soon, his **zeta-beam** radiation would fade away and he would be returned to Earth. But until that moment—his sweetheart was where she belonged, held tight in his arms...
THE END

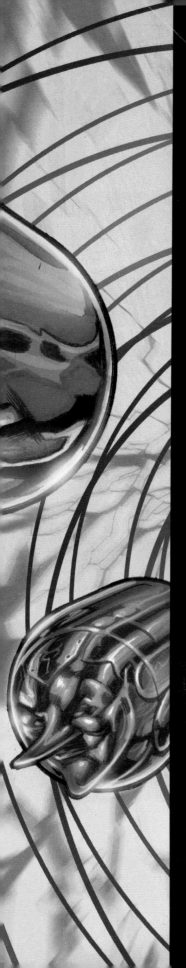

METAL MEN #45

This is the moment when the sunny escapades of the Metal Men began to take a dark and disturbing turn that helped set in motion some of the events that led us to 52.

Doc Magnus's metal band had begun over a decade earlier as a cute, childish take on giant monster movies (they were always fighting a big manta or a massive robot dinosaur) populated by characters of one dimension instead of the then-standard two. Creator Robert Kanigher allowed each of the Metal Men one single personality trait, based on the properties of the metal from which it was built. Mercury was hot-tempered, Lead was strong and steady, Iron was strong and steady, Gold was steady... okay, it gets problematic fast, but the best on the team — and, I'd argue, one of the most inventive DC characters ever — was Tin, the world's first and last super-hero to get through epic after epic without one shred of self-esteem.

In the 1970s, writer Steve Gerber and artist Walt Simonson, working for an older audience, belayed the obvious approach ("Let's give the Metal Men themselves a depth of characterization that would contradict their history!") and instead rode what was there to the limit. The Metal Men were still one-dimensional, but they were growing fearfully aware that the rest of the world wasn't. The big jolt came when the trusted father figure who invented them, Dr. Will Magnus, became dangerously unhinged.

Cartoon characters thrust into a morally grey world is probably the great theme of Steve Gerber's career; before his memorable Metal Men stories, he created Howard the Duck.
                                                              —MW

WILL MAGNUS and the METAL MEN

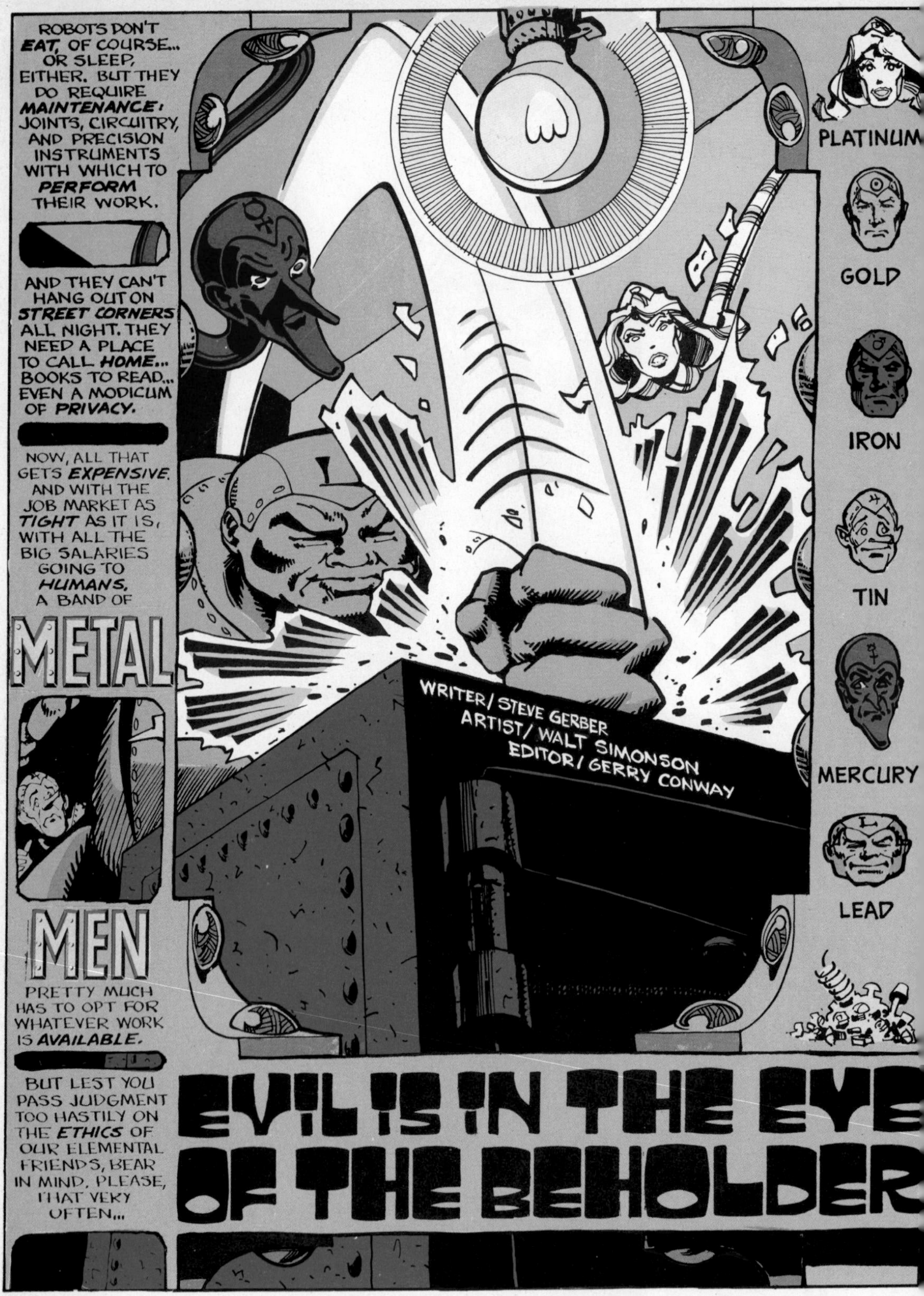
ROBOTS DON'T EAT, OF COURSE... OR SLEEP, EITHER. BUT THEY DO REQUIRE MAINTENANCE: JOINTS, CIRCUITRY, AND PRECISION INSTRUMENTS WITH WHICH TO PERFORM THEIR WORK.
AND THEY CAN'T HANG OUT ON STREET CORNERS ALL NIGHT. THEY NEED A PLACE TO CALL HOME... BOOKS TO READ... EVEN A MODICUM OF PRIVACY.
NOW, ALL THAT GETS EXPENSIVE. AND WITH THE JOB MARKET AS TIGHT AS IT IS, WITH ALL THE BIG SALARIES GOING TO HUMANS, A BAND OF
METAL
MEN
PRETTY MUCH HAS TO OPT FOR WHATEVER WORK IS AVAILABLE.
BUT LEST YOU PASS JUDGMENT TOO HASTILY ON THE ETHICS OF OUR ELEMENTAL FRIENDS, BEAR IN MIND, PLEASE, THAT VERY OFTEN...
PLATINUM
GOLD
IRON
TIN
MERCURY
LEAD
WRITER/ STEVE GERBER
ARTIST/ WALT SIMONSON
EDITOR/ GERRY CONWAY
EVIL IS IN THE EYE OF THE BEHOLDER

I TRIED, GROUP. I GUESS *LEAD'S* TOO *SOFT* FOR THIS KINDA WORK.

IT'S YOUR *HEAD* THAT'S TOO *SOFT*, TUBBY. STAND ASIDE--

--AND WATCH WHAT A *LIQUID METAL* CAN DO!

MERCURY CAN GO *ANYWHERE*-- OOZE RIGHT THROUGH THE SAFE *DOOR!*

HEY! WHAT *IS* THIS?

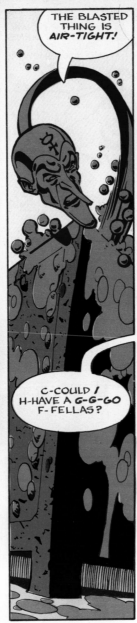

THE BLASTED THING IS *AIR-TIGHT!*

C-COULD *I* H-HAVE A *G-G-GO* F-FELLAS?

ARE YOU *SERIOUS*, TWERP? IF THE HEAVYWEIGHT AND *I* BLEW IT, HOW--?

MERCURY, THAT'S *ENOUGH!* TIN DESERVES A CHANCE JUST LIKE THE *REST* OF US!

TH-THANKS, TINA, I-I'LL TRY NOT TO LET YOU *D-D-DOWN!*

S-S-SEE? W-WE DON'T HAVE TO *B-B-BREAK* IN.

WE JUST N-N-NEED A *K-K-KEY!*

CLIK!

crunch

I W-W-WASN'T *S-S-TRONG* ENOUGH! I G-GUESS I'LL ALWAYS BE JUST A *T-T-TIN* MAN.

DON'T PUT YOURSELF *DOWN* TIN, THE *OTHERS* FAILED, TOO-- AND *YOU* SHOWED US OUR MISTAKE!

M-M-M-ME?

OF *COURSE*, YOU! WE CAN'T *SMASH* IN... OR *SNEAK* IN... WE HAVE TO GO THROUGH THE *LOCK*.

YOU SAW THAT RIGHT AWAY.

NOW, ALL *I* HAVE TO DO IS DRAW MY HAND INTO HAIR-THIN *WIRE*...

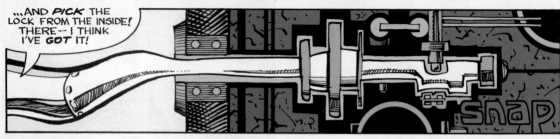

...AND *PICK* THE LOCK FROM THE INSIDE! THERE-- I THINK I'VE *GOT* IT!

snap

NOW CAN WE STOP *QUARRELING* FOR ONCE AND *FINISH* THE JOB? *PLEASE*?

LEAD SMILES, NODS... *MERCURY* GRUMBLES HIS ASSENT... AND *TIN* THROWS HIMSELF ENTHUSIASTICALLY INTO THE TASK...

WITHIN MOMENTS, IT IS COMPLETED, AT WHICH POINT A *SPOTLIGHT* FALLS ON THE METAL BAND...

...AND THE ROOM ERUPTS IN A *CACOPHONY* OF CHEERS, WHISTLES AND *APPLAUSE*!

CHEER!

YAY!

YAY!

WHEET! WHEET!

3

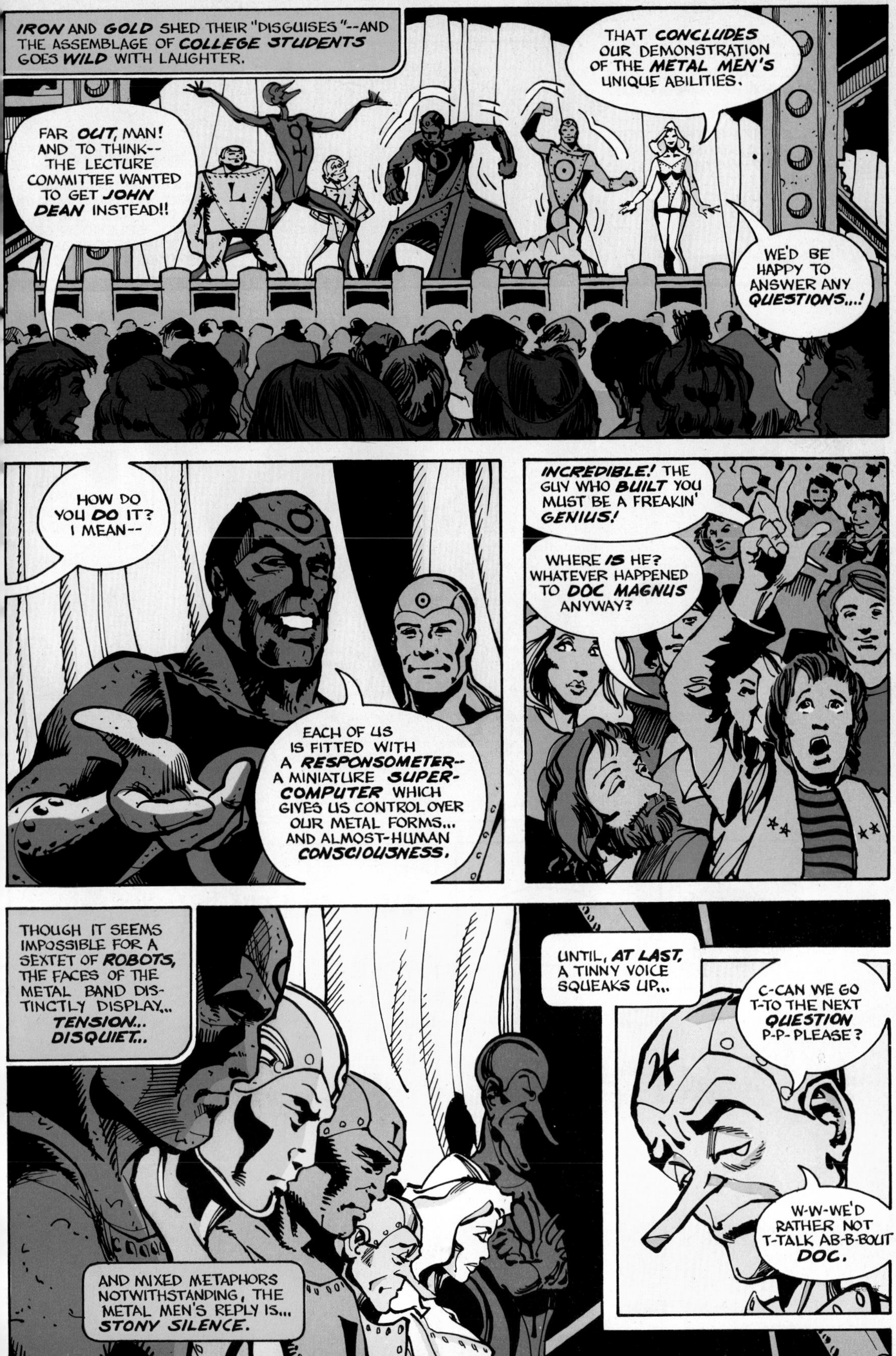
IRON AND GOLD SHED THEIR "DISGUISES"--AND THE ASSEMBLAGE OF COLLEGE STUDENTS GOES WILD WITH LAUGHTER.
THAT CONCLUDES OUR DEMONSTRATION OF THE METAL MEN'S UNIQUE ABILITIES.
FAR OUT, MAN! AND TO THINK-- THE LECTURE COMMITTEE WANTED TO GET JOHN DEAN INSTEAD!!
WE'D BE HAPPY TO ANSWER ANY QUESTIONS...!
HOW DO YOU DO IT? I MEAN--
EACH OF US IS FITTED WITH A RESPONSOMETER-- A MINIATURE SUPER-COMPUTER WHICH GIVES US CONTROL OVER OUR METAL FORMS... AND ALMOST-HUMAN CONSCIOUSNESS.
INCREDIBLE! THE GUY WHO BUILT YOU MUST BE A FREAKIN' GENIUS!
WHERE IS HE? WHATEVER HAPPENED TO DOC MAGNUS ANYWAY?
THOUGH IT SEEMS IMPOSSIBLE FOR A SEXTET OF ROBOTS, THE FACES OF THE METAL BAND DISTINCTLY DISPLAY... TENSION... DISQUIET...
AND MIXED METAPHORS NOTWITHSTANDING, THE METAL MEN'S REPLY IS... STONY SILENCE.
UNTIL, AT LAST, A TINNY VOICE SQUEAKS UP...
C-CAN WE GO T-TO THE NEXT QUESTION P-P-PLEASE?
W-W-WE'D RATHER NOT T-TALK AB-B-BOUT DOC.
4

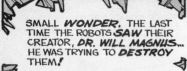

SMALL *WONDER*. THE LAST TIME THE ROBOTS *SAW* THEIR CREATOR, *DR. WILL MAGNUS*... HE WAS TRYING TO *DESTROY* THEM!

BRAINWASHED BY THE DICTATOR OF *KARNIA*, MAGNUS' GENIUS HAS BEEN *TWISTED*... ALL HIS FORMER LOYALTIES *OBLITERATED*... INDEED, HIS *MIND ITSELF* LAIN TO RUIN!

THINGS HAVE *CHANGED* A BIT SINCE THEN. THE PRODIGAL CYBERNETICIST HAS COME *HOME* --AGAINST HIS WILL-- AT THE "SUGGESTION" OF THE *C.I.A.*

AND NOW HE RESIDES *HERE*, OUTSIDE WASHINGTON D.C., AMID THE PASTORAL SPLENDOR OF A GOVERNMENT-OPERATED *MENTAL FACILITY*.

IT'S NOT AN *UNPLEASANT* EXISTENCE. BETWEEN *BRAIN OPERATIONS*, HE PLAYS WITH PUZZLES... COLORS WITH CRAYONS (NO POINTED OBJECTS PERMITTED)... AND TALKS WITH HIS *THERAPIST*, WHO SHOWS HIM PRETTY *PICTURES*.

JUST LOOK AT THE PICTURE AND SAY THE FIRST WORD WHICH COMES TO MIND. *READY?*

YES... NO... I DON'T KNOW...

1361 COLORS

36

LET'S TRY, NOW... WHAT *WORD*--?

TRAMPLE!

RAZE!

ANNIHILATE!

5

FOR LONG MOMENTS, THE SCIENTIST **STARES** WITHOUT SPEAKING. HIS FACIAL MUSCLES GO **TAUT.** FIRST HIS HEAD, THEN HIS ENTIRE BODY **QUIVERS,** ATTEMPTING TO CONTAIN THE **VIRULENCE** RISING WITHIN HIMSELF.

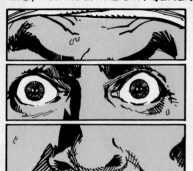

HE **FAILS!**

SHRED!

YOU **SEE,** GENERAL CASPAR? HE'S NOT **READY** TO BE RELEASED!

I TEND TO **AGREE,** DR. ROSEN, BUT--

BUT ACCORDING TO THE **ACCOUNTING OFFICE,** GENTLEMEN, THERE'S NO QUESTION: **HE'S CURED!**

BUDGETS ARE **BUDGETS.** UNLESS MAGNUS CAN **PRODUCE,** WE'LL HAVE TO CONSIDER HIS THERAPY A **FAILURE** AND **SCRAP** THE PROJECT.

YOU'RE TALKING ABOUT A **HUMAN MIND,** WHITTIER--! YOU CAN'T MEASURE HIS PROGRESS IN DOLLARS AND CENTS!

GENTLEMEN, **PLEASE--!**

SURELY WE CAN **COMPROMISE--** ON SOME FORM OF **WORK-THERAPY,** LET'S SAY.

HMMMM, YES, THAT **WOULD** ALLOW HIM TO **PRODUCE...!**

I **STILL** SAY HE'S NOT **READY.** BUT IF THERE'S NO OTHER WAY...!

6

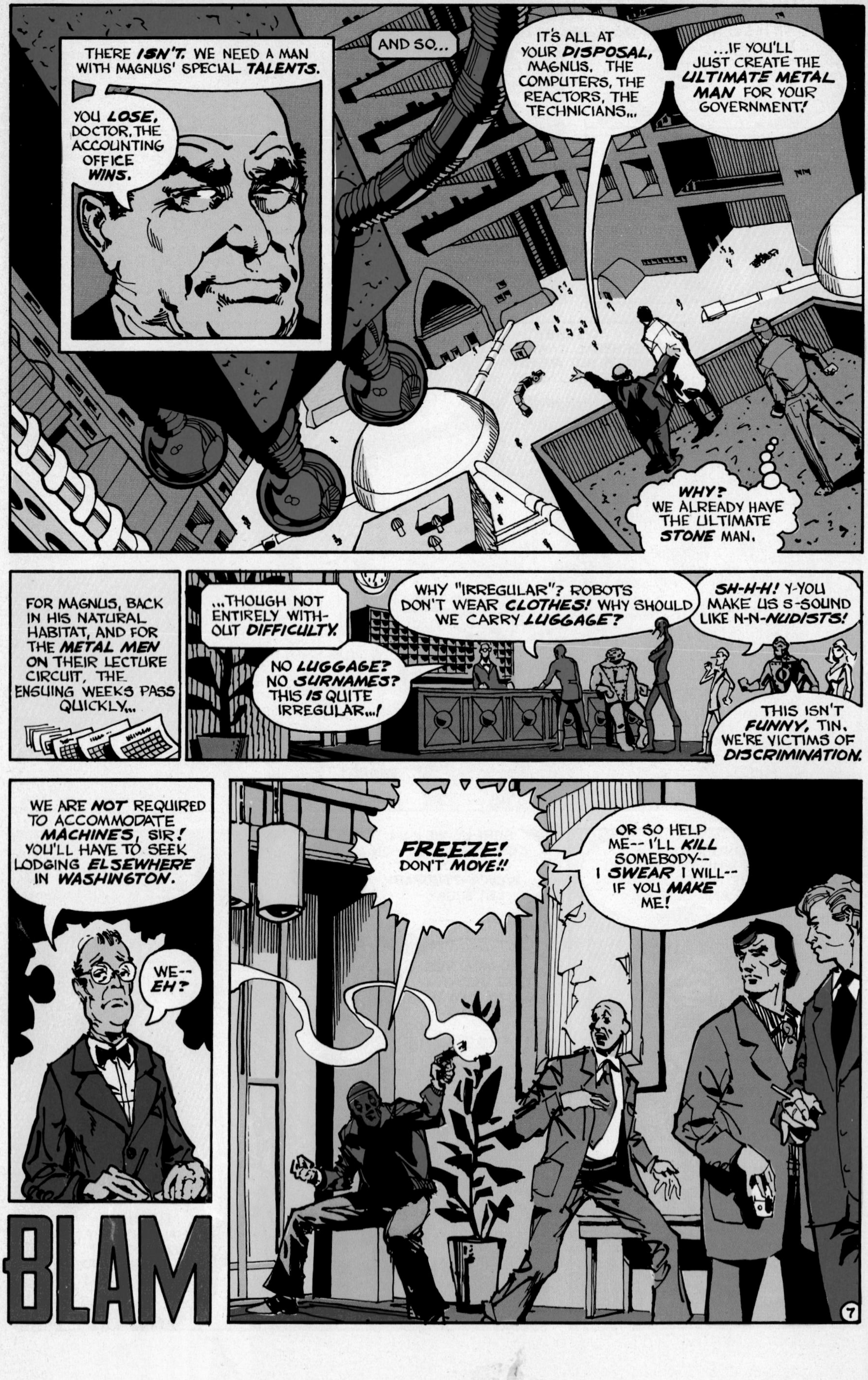

THERE ISN'T. WE NEED A MAN WITH MAGNUS' SPECIAL TALENTS.
YOU LOSE, DOCTOR, THE ACCOUNTING OFFICE WINS.
AND SO...
IT'S ALL AT YOUR DISPOSAL, MAGNUS. THE COMPUTERS, THE REACTORS, THE TECHNICIANS...
...IF YOU'LL JUST CREATE THE ULTIMATE METAL MAN FOR YOUR GOVERNMENT!
WHY? WE ALREADY HAVE THE ULTIMATE STONE MAN.
FOR MAGNUS, BACK IN HIS NATURAL HABITAT, AND FOR THE METAL MEN ON THEIR LECTURE CIRCUIT, THE ENSUING WEEKS PASS QUICKLY...
...THOUGH NOT ENTIRELY WITHOUT DIFFICULTY.
NO LUGGAGE? NO SURNAMES? THIS IS QUITE IRREGULAR...!
WHY "IRREGULAR"? ROBOTS DON'T WEAR CLOTHES! WHY SHOULD WE CARRY LUGGAGE?
SH-H-H! Y-YOU MAKE US S-SOUND LIKE N-N-NUDISTS!
THIS ISN'T FUNNY, TIN. WE'RE VICTIMS OF DISCRIMINATION.
WE ARE NOT REQUIRED TO ACCOMMODATE MACHINES, SIR! YOU'LL HAVE TO SEEK LODGING ELSEWHERE IN WASHINGTON.
WE-- EH?
BLAM
FREEZE! DON'T MOVE!!
OR SO HELP ME-- I'LL KILL SOMEBODY-- I SWEAR I WILL-- IF YOU MAKE ME!
7

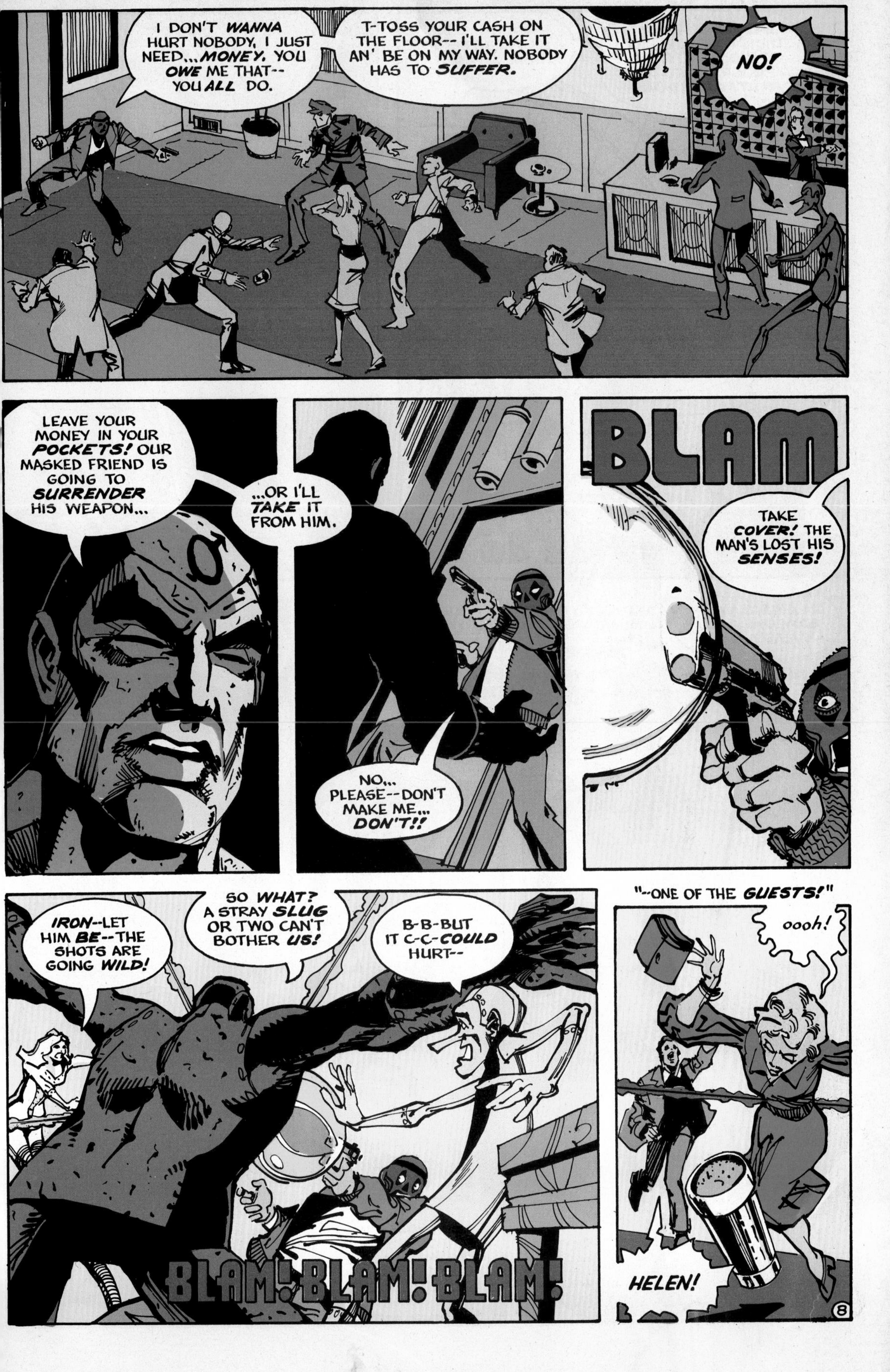
I DON'T WANNA HURT NOBODY, I JUST NEED... MONEY. YOU OWE ME THAT-- YOU ALL DO.
T-TOSS YOUR CASH ON THE FLOOR-- I'LL TAKE IT AN' BE ON MY WAY. NOBODY HAS TO SUFFER.
NO!
LEAVE YOUR MONEY IN YOUR POCKETS! OUR MASKED FRIEND IS GOING TO SURRENDER HIS WEAPON...
...OR I'LL TAKE IT FROM HIM.
NO... PLEASE--DON'T MAKE ME... DON'T!!
BLAM
TAKE COVER! THE MAN'S LOST HIS SENSES!
IRON--LET HIM BE--THE SHOTS ARE GOING WILD!
SO WHAT? A STRAY SLUG OR TWO CAN'T BOTHER US!
B-B-BUT IT C-C-COULD HURT--
BLAM! BLAM! BLAM!
"--ONE OF THE GUESTS!"
oooh!
HELEN!
8

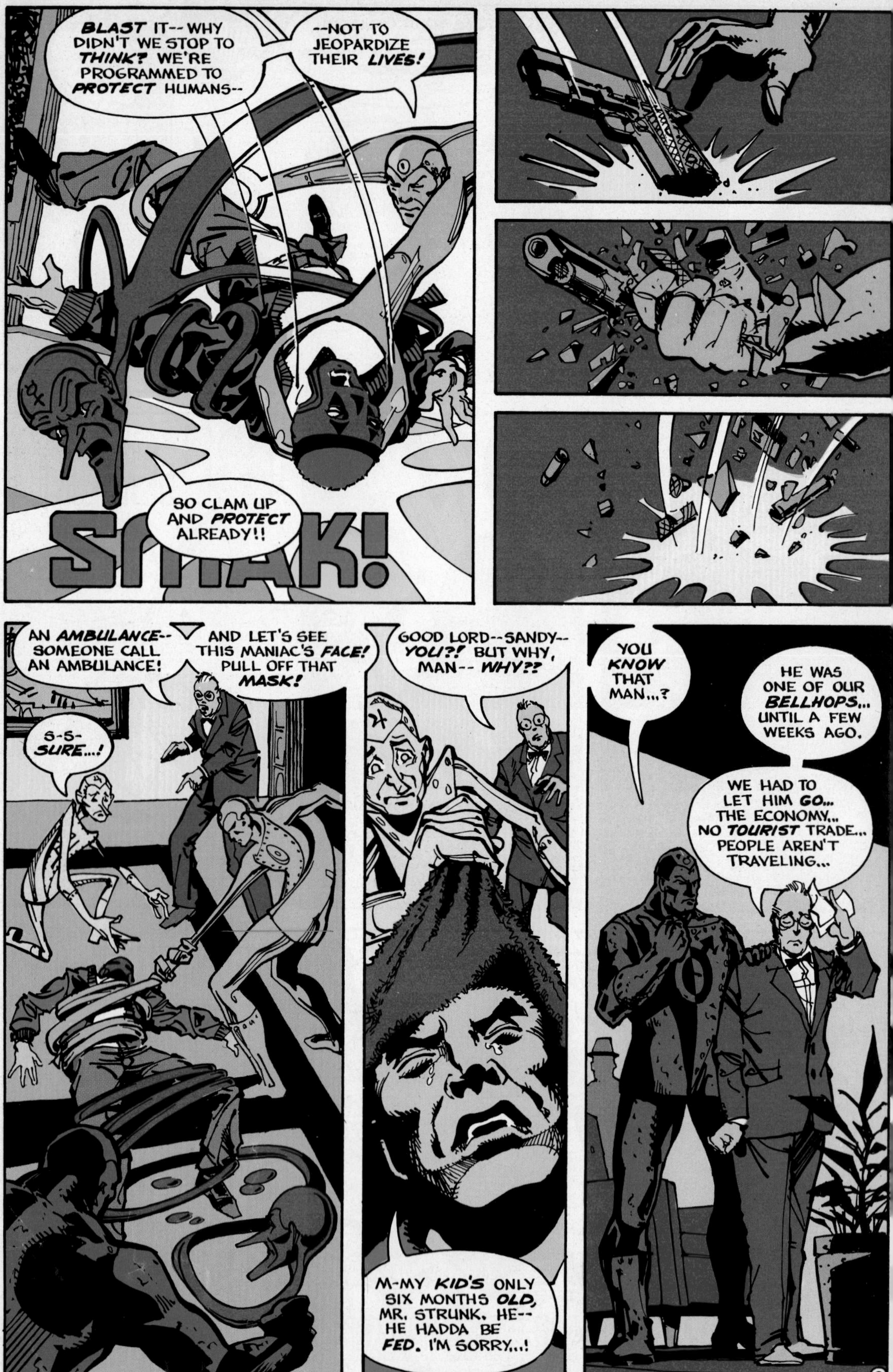
BLAST IT-- WHY DIDN'T WE STOP TO THINK? WE'RE PROGRAMMED TO PROTECT HUMANS--
--NOT TO JEOPARDIZE THEIR LIVES!
SO CLAM UP AND PROTECT ALREADY!!
SMAK!
AN AMBULANCE-- SOMEONE CALL AN AMBULANCE!
S-S-SURE...!
AND LET'S SEE THIS MANIAC'S FACE! PULL OFF THAT MASK!
GOOD LORD--SANDY-- YOU?! BUT WHY, MAN-- WHY??
M-MY KID'S ONLY SIX MONTHS OLD, MR. STRUNK. HE-- HE HADDA BE FED. I'M SORRY...!
YOU KNOW THAT MAN...?
HE WAS ONE OF OUR BELLHOPS... UNTIL A FEW WEEKS AGO.
WE HAD TO LET HIM GO... THE ECONOMY... NO TOURIST TRADE... PEOPLE AREN'T TRAVELING...
9

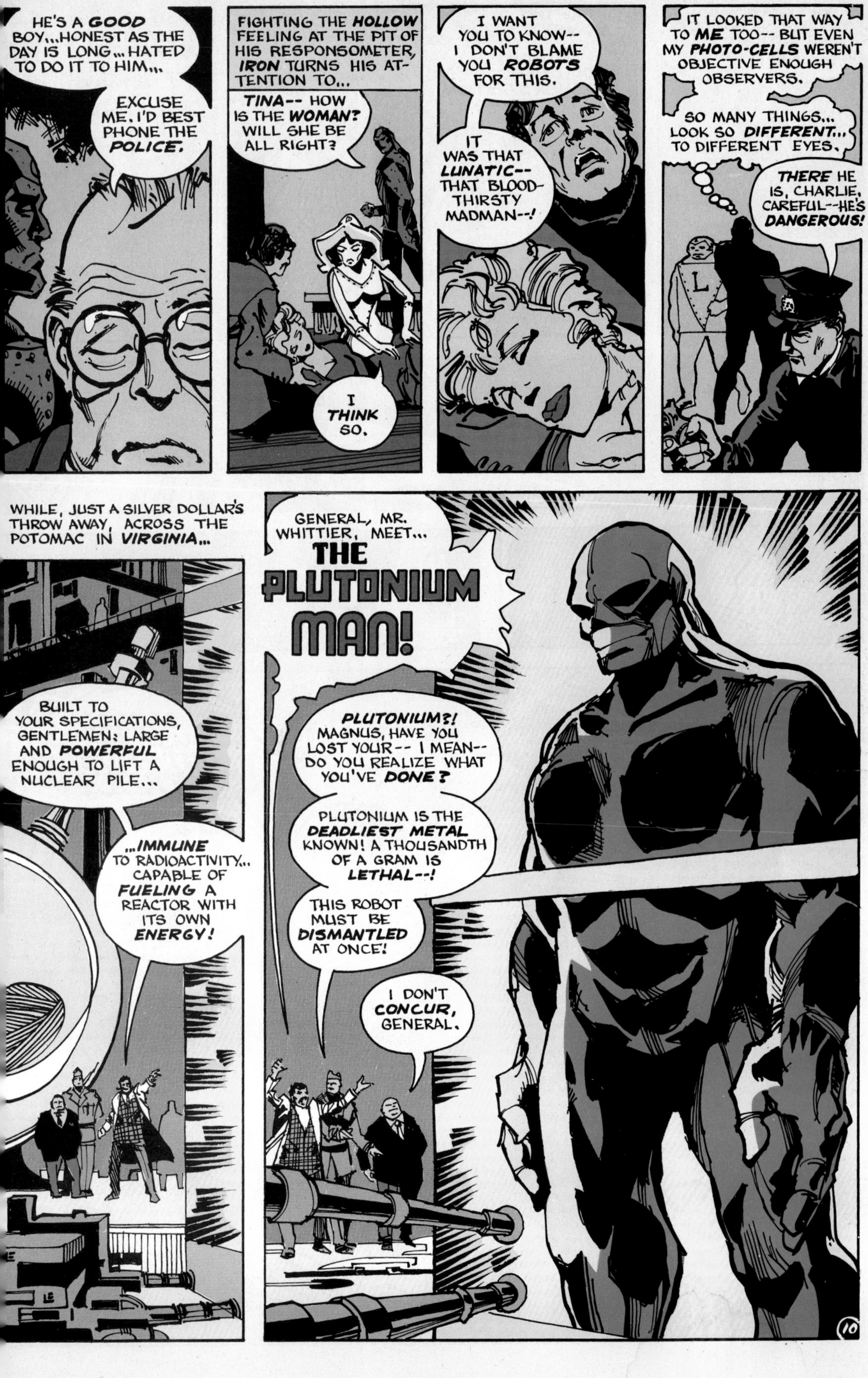
HE'S A GOOD BOY...HONEST AS THE DAY IS LONG... HATED TO DO IT TO HIM...
EXCUSE ME. I'D BEST PHONE THE POLICE.
FIGHTING THE HOLLOW FEELING AT THE PIT OF HIS RESPONSOMETER, IRON TURNS HIS ATTENTION TO...
TINA-- HOW IS THE WOMAN? WILL SHE BE ALL RIGHT?
I THINK SO.
I WANT YOU TO KNOW-- I DON'T BLAME YOU ROBOTS FOR THIS.
IT WAS THAT LUNATIC-- THAT BLOOD-THIRSTY MADMAN--!
IT LOOKED THAT WAY TO ME TOO-- BUT EVEN MY PHOTO-CELLS WEREN'T OBJECTIVE ENOUGH OBSERVERS.
SO MANY THINGS... LOOK SO DIFFERENT... TO DIFFERENT EYES.
THERE HE IS, CHARLIE. CAREFUL--HE'S DANGEROUS!
L
WHILE, JUST A SILVER DOLLAR'S THROW AWAY, ACROSS THE POTOMAC IN VIRGINIA...
GENERAL, MR. WHITTIER, MEET... THE PLUTONIUM MAN!
BUILT TO YOUR SPECIFICATIONS, GENTLEMEN: LARGE AND POWERFUL ENOUGH TO LIFT A NUCLEAR PILE...
...IMMUNE TO RADIOACTIVITY... CAPABLE OF FUELING A REACTOR WITH ITS OWN ENERGY!
PLUTONIUM?! MAGNUS, HAVE YOU LOST YOUR-- I MEAN-- DO YOU REALIZE WHAT YOU'VE DONE?
PLUTONIUM IS THE DEADLIEST METAL KNOWN! A THOUSANDTH OF A GRAM IS LETHAL--!
THIS ROBOT MUST BE DISMANTLED AT ONCE!
I DON'T CONCUR, GENERAL.
10

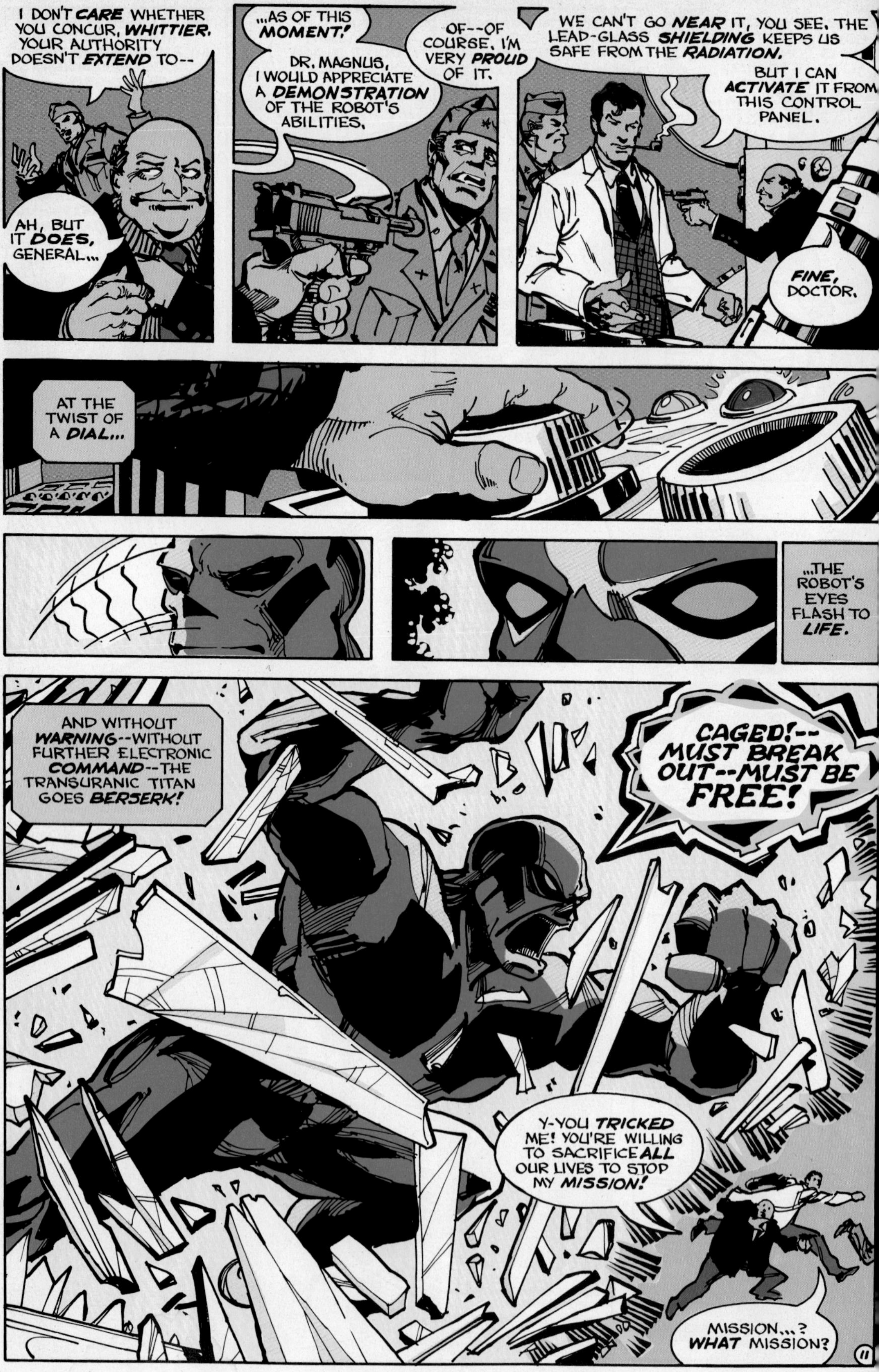
I DON'T CARE WHETHER YOU CONCUR, WHITTIER. YOUR AUTHORITY DOESN'T EXTEND TO--
AH, BUT IT DOES, GENERAL...
...AS OF THIS MOMENT!
DR. MAGNUS, I WOULD APPRECIATE A DEMONSTRATION OF THE ROBOT'S ABILITIES.
OF--OF COURSE. I'M VERY PROUD OF IT.
WE CAN'T GO NEAR IT, YOU SEE. THE LEAD-GLASS SHIELDING KEEPS US SAFE FROM THE RADIATION.
BUT I CAN ACTIVATE IT FROM THIS CONTROL PANEL.
FINE, DOCTOR.
AT THE TWIST OF A DIAL...
...THE ROBOT'S EYES FLASH TO LIFE.
AND WITHOUT WARNING--WITHOUT FURTHER ELECTRONIC COMMAND--THE TRANSURANIC TITAN GOES BERSERK!
CAGED!--MUST BREAK OUT--MUST BE FREE!
Y-YOU TRICKED ME! YOU'RE WILLING TO SACRIFICE ALL OUR LIVES TO STOP MY MISSION!
MISSION...? WHAT MISSION?
11

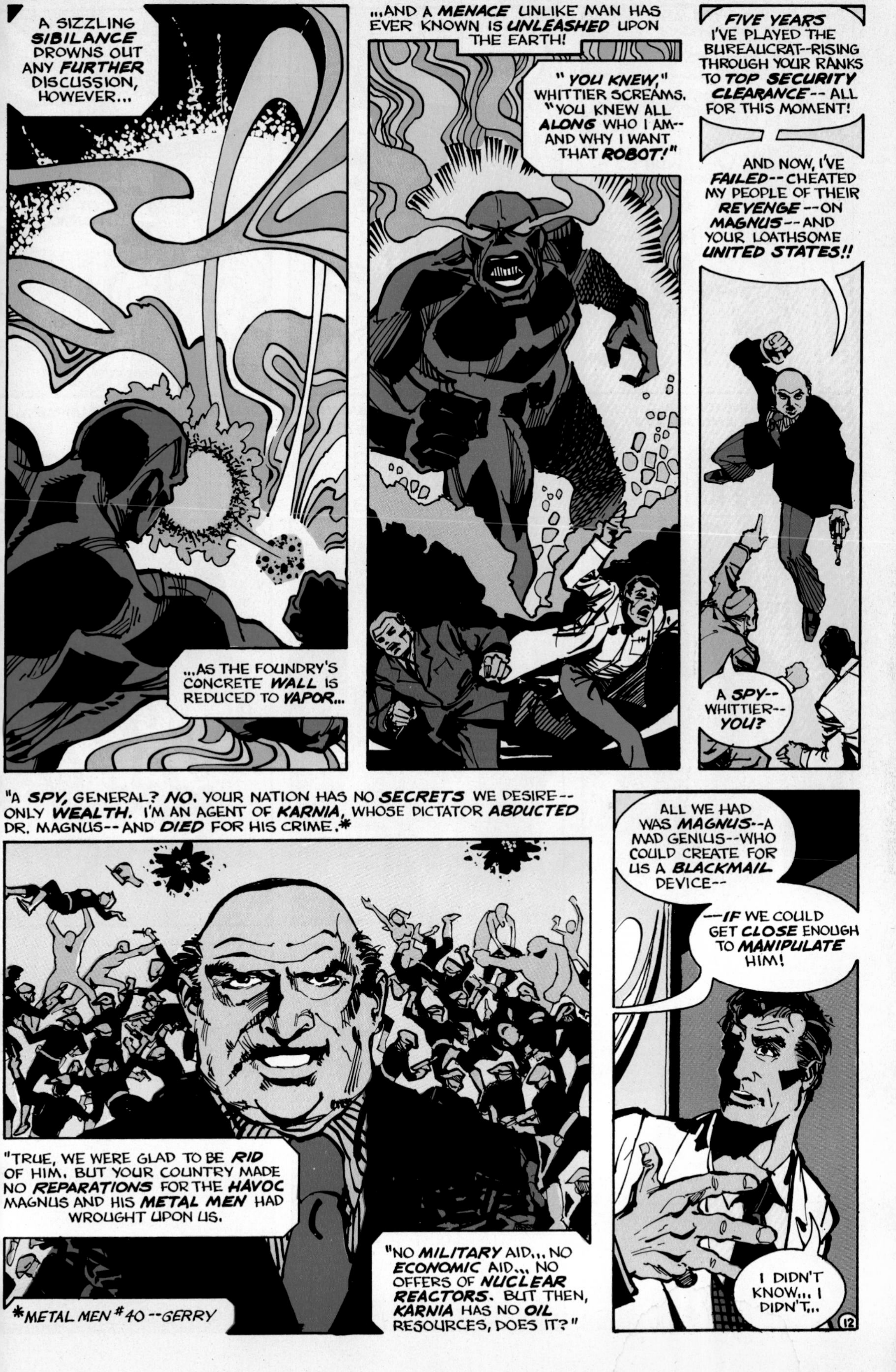

A SIZZLING SIBILANCE DROWNS OUT ANY FURTHER DISCUSSION, HOWEVER...
...AS THE FOUNDRY'S CONCRETE WALL IS REDUCED TO VAPOR...
...AND A MENACE UNLIKE MAN HAS EVER KNOWN IS UNLEASHED UPON THE EARTH!
"YOU KNEW," WHITTIER SCREAMS. "YOU KNEW ALL ALONG WHO I AM--AND WHY I WANT THAT ROBOT!"
FIVE YEARS I'VE PLAYED THE BUREAUCRAT--RISING THROUGH YOUR RANKS TO TOP SECURITY CLEARANCE--ALL FOR THIS MOMENT!
AND NOW, I'VE FAILED--CHEATED MY PEOPLE OF THEIR REVENGE--ON MAGNUS--AND YOUR LOATHSOME UNITED STATES!!
A SPY--WHITTIER--YOU?
"A SPY, GENERAL? NO. YOUR NATION HAS NO SECRETS WE DESIRE--ONLY WEALTH. I'M AN AGENT OF KARNIA, WHOSE DICTATOR ABDUCTED DR. MAGNUS--AND DIED FOR HIS CRIME.*
"TRUE, WE WERE GLAD TO BE RID OF HIM. BUT YOUR COUNTRY MADE NO REPARATIONS FOR THE HAVOC MAGNUS AND HIS METAL MEN HAD WROUGHT UPON US.
"NO MILITARY AID... NO ECONOMIC AID... NO OFFERS OF NUCLEAR REACTORS. BUT THEN, KARNIA HAS NO OIL RESOURCES, DOES IT?"
*METAL MEN #40 --GERRY
ALL WE HAD WAS MAGNUS--A MAD GENIUS--WHO COULD CREATE FOR US A BLACKMAIL DEVICE--
--IF WE COULD GET CLOSE ENOUGH TO MANIPULATE HIM!
I DIDN'T KNOW... I DIDN'T...
12

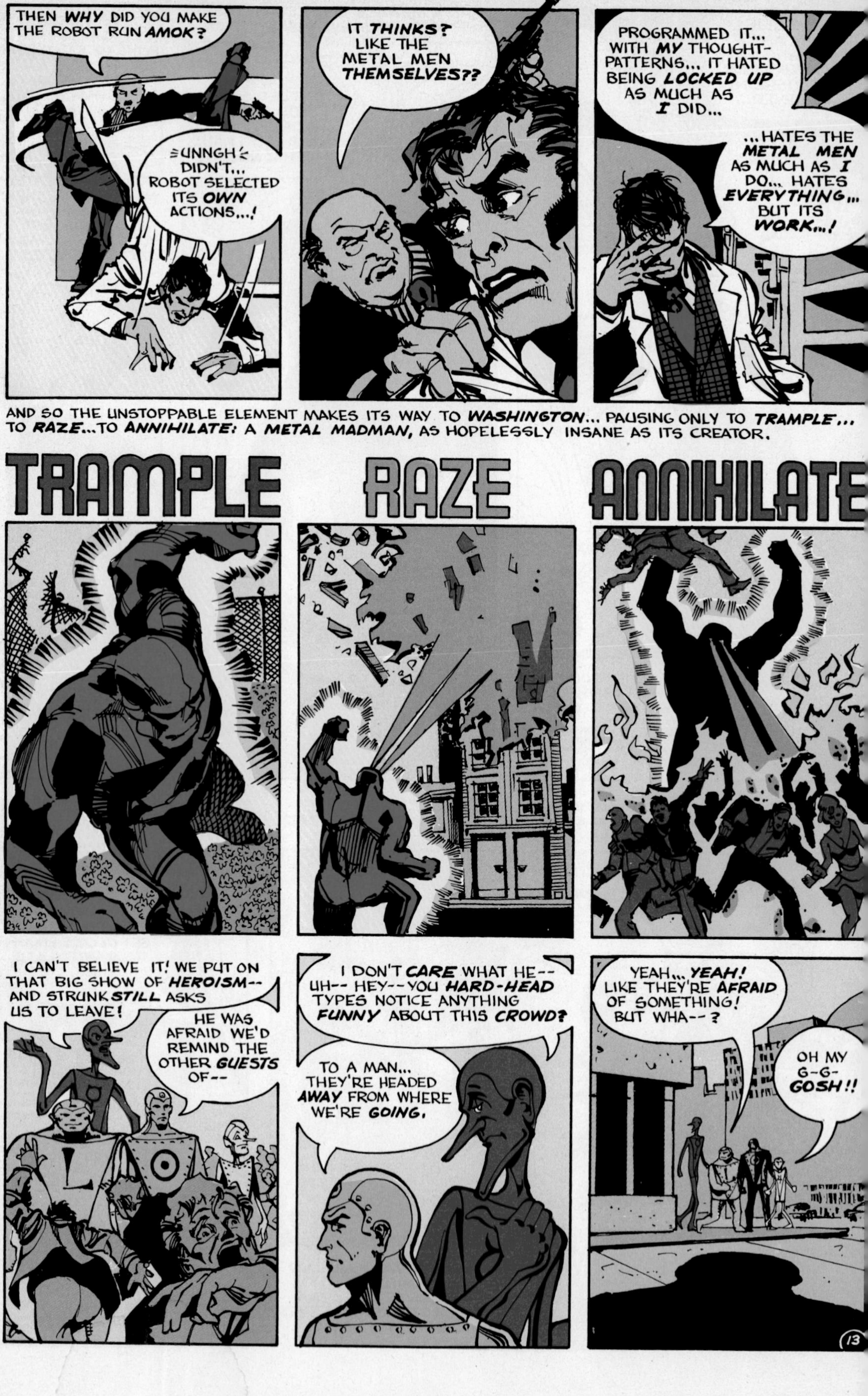
THEN WHY DID YOU MAKE THE ROBOT RUN AMOK?
UNNGH DIDN'T... ROBOT SELECTED ITS OWN ACTIONS...!
IT THINKS? LIKE THE METAL MEN THEMSELVES??
PROGRAMMED IT... WITH MY THOUGHT-PATTERNS... IT HATED BEING LOCKED UP AS MUCH AS I DID...
...HATES THE METAL MEN AS MUCH AS I DO... HATES EVERYTHING... BUT ITS WORK...!
AND SO THE UNSTOPPABLE ELEMENT MAKES ITS WAY TO WASHINGTON... PAUSING ONLY TO TRAMPLE... TO RAZE...TO ANNIHILATE: A METAL MADMAN, AS HOPELESSLY INSANE AS ITS CREATOR.
TRAMPLE
RAZE
ANNIHILATE
I CAN'T BELIEVE IT! WE PUT ON THAT BIG SHOW OF HEROISM-- AND STRUNK STILL ASKS US TO LEAVE!
HE WAS AFRAID WE'D REMIND THE OTHER GUESTS OF--
I DON'T CARE WHAT HE-- UH-- HEY--YOU HARD-HEAD TYPES NOTICE ANYTHING FUNNY ABOUT THIS CROWD?
TO A MAN... THEY'RE HEADED AWAY FROM WHERE WE'RE GOING.
YEAH... YEAH! LIKE THEY'RE AFRAID OF SOMETHING! BUT WHA--?
OH MY G-G-GOSH!!
13

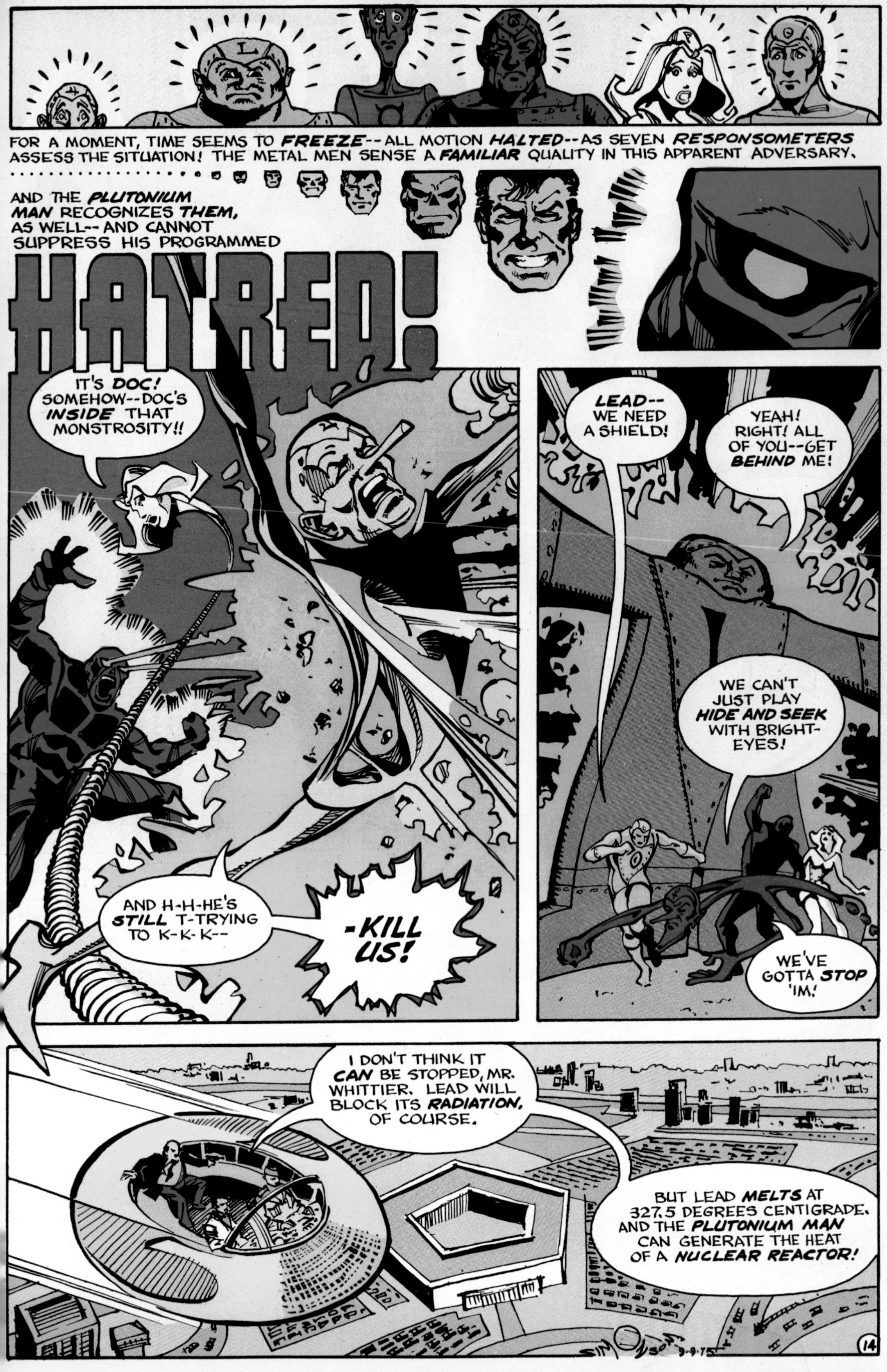
FOR A MOMENT, TIME SEEMS TO FREEZE--ALL MOTION HALTED--AS SEVEN RESPONSOMETERS ASSESS THE SITUATION! THE METAL MEN SENSE A FAMILIAR QUALITY IN THIS APPARENT ADVERSARY.
AND THE PLUTONIUM MAN RECOGNIZES THEM, AS WELL--AND CANNOT SUPPRESS HIS PROGRAMMED
HATRED!
IT'S DOC! SOMEHOW--DOC'S INSIDE THAT MONSTROSITY!!
AND H-H-HE'S STILL T-TRYING TO K-K-K--
-KILL US!
LEAD--WE NEED A SHIELD!
YEAH! RIGHT! ALL OF YOU--GET BEHIND ME!
WE CAN'T JUST PLAY HIDE AND SEEK WITH BRIGHT-EYES!
WE'VE GOTTA STOP 'IM!
I DON'T THINK IT CAN BE STOPPED, MR. WHITTIER. LEAD WILL BLOCK ITS RADIATION, OF COURSE.
BUT LEAD MELTS AT 327.5 DEGREES CENTIGRADE. AND THE PLUTONIUM MAN CAN GENERATE THE HEAT OF A NUCLEAR REACTOR!
SIMONSON 9-9-75
14

SCATTER--LEAD'S GOING UP LIKE BUTTER ON A *GRILL!*

IF THERE'S ANY CHANCE AT ALL TO *BEAT* THIS THING--IT'S THE *DIRECT* APPROACH--

BUT IT *CAN'T* BE TORN APART, GENERAL. OH, POSSIBLY BY *SUPERMAN*... BUT NO ONE ELSE COULD TOLERATE THE *RADIATION LEVEL.*

"EVEN MY *EARLIER* ROBOTS--THEIR RESPONSO-METERS COULDN'T *FUNCTION* PROPERLY...

SKRANG!

--RIP IT OPEN--AND TEAR OUT ITS *CIRCUITRY* WIRE BY WIRE!

"FIRST THEIR PHOTO-CELLS WOULD GO *BLIND*...THEN THEIR *REACTION TAPES* WOULD DECAY...

"THEY'D BE HELPLESS AS A *SIGHTLESS DRUNK* IF THEY TRIED A FRONTAL ASSAULT.

BUT IT COULD BE *BOUND*--IF WE COULD UPSET ITS FOOTING-- AIM ITS BEAMS *UPWARD!*

LEAVE IT TO *ME*, LADY, YOU AND GLAMOR-PANTS GET READY TO DO YOUR *DUCTILITY* ACT!

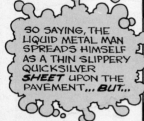

SO SAYING, THE LIQUID METAL MAN SPREADS HIMSELF AS A THIN SLIPPERY QUICKSILVER *SHEET* UPON THE PAVEMENT...*BUT...*

SKLOOSH!

15

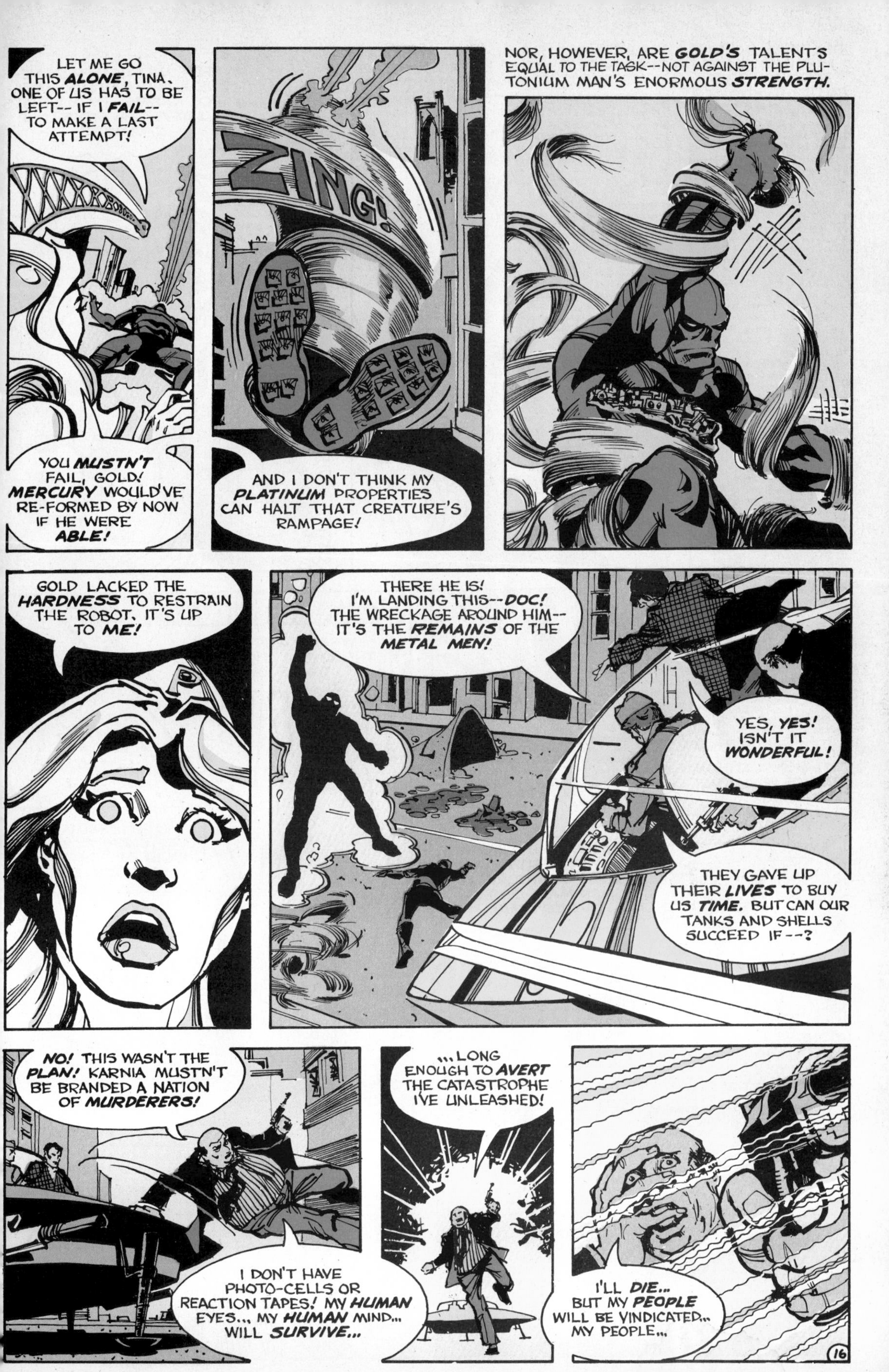
LET ME GO THIS ALONE, TINA. ONE OF US HAS TO BE LEFT-- IF I FAIL-- TO MAKE A LAST ATTEMPT!
YOU MUSTN'T FAIL, GOLD! MERCURY WOULD'VE RE-FORMED BY NOW IF HE WERE ABLE!
ZING!
AND I DON'T THINK MY PLATINUM PROPERTIES CAN HALT THAT CREATURE'S RAMPAGE!
NOR, HOWEVER, ARE GOLD'S TALENTS EQUAL TO THE TASK--NOT AGAINST THE PLUTONIUM MAN'S ENORMOUS STRENGTH.
GOLD LACKED THE HARDNESS TO RESTRAIN THE ROBOT. IT'S UP TO ME!
THERE HE IS! I'M LANDING THIS--DOC! THE WRECKAGE AROUND HIM-- IT'S THE REMAINS OF THE METAL MEN!
YES, YES! ISN'T IT WONDERFUL!
THEY GAVE UP THEIR LIVES TO BUY US TIME. BUT CAN OUR TANKS AND SHELLS SUCCEED IF--?
NO! THIS WASN'T THE PLAN! KARNIA MUSTN'T BE BRANDED A NATION OF MURDERERS!
I DON'T HAVE PHOTO-CELLS OR REACTION TAPES! MY HUMAN EYES... MY HUMAN MIND... WILL SURVIVE...
...LONG ENOUGH TO AVERT THE CATASTROPHE I'VE UNLEASHED!
I'LL DIE... BUT MY PEOPLE WILL BE VINDICATED... MY PEOPLE...
16

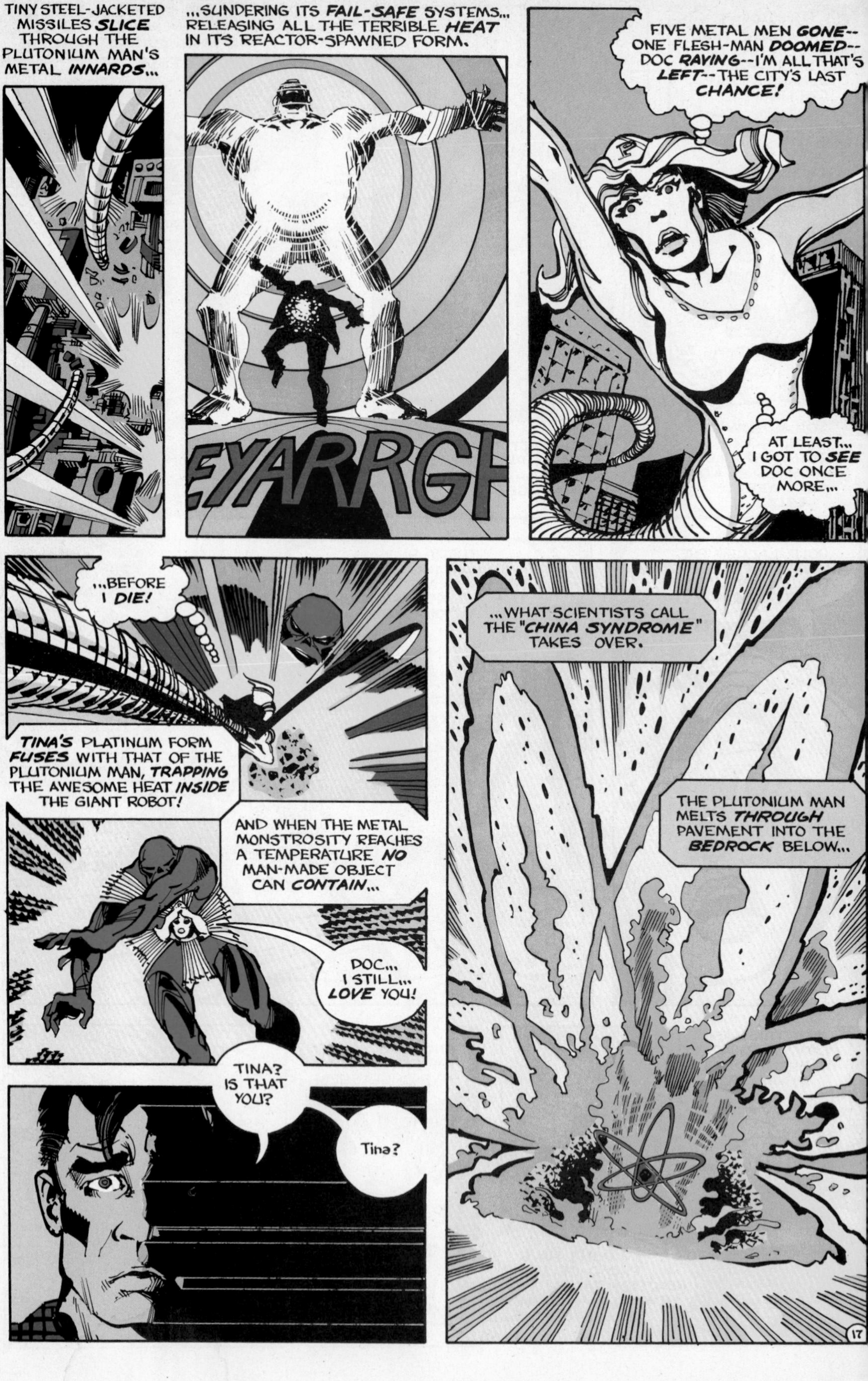
TINY STEEL-JACKETED MISSILES SLICE THROUGH THE PLUTONIUM MAN'S METAL INNARDS...
...SUNDERING ITS FAIL-SAFE SYSTEMS... RELEASING ALL THE TERRIBLE HEAT IN ITS REACTOR-SPAWNED FORM.
EYARRGH
FIVE METAL MEN GONE-- ONE FLESH-MAN DOOMED-- DOC RAVING--I'M ALL THAT'S LEFT--THE CITY'S LAST CHANCE!
AT LEAST... I GOT TO SEE DOC ONCE MORE...
...BEFORE I DIE!
TINA'S PLATINUM FORM FUSES WITH THAT OF THE PLUTONIUM MAN, TRAPPING THE AWESOME HEAT INSIDE THE GIANT ROBOT!
AND WHEN THE METAL MONSTROSITY REACHES A TEMPERATURE NO MAN-MADE OBJECT CAN CONTAIN...
DOC... I STILL... LOVE YOU!
TINA? IS THAT YOU?
Tina?
...WHAT SCIENTISTS CALL THE "CHINA SYNDROME" TAKES OVER.
THE PLUTONIUM MAN MELTS THROUGH PAVEMENT INTO THE BEDROCK BELOW...
17

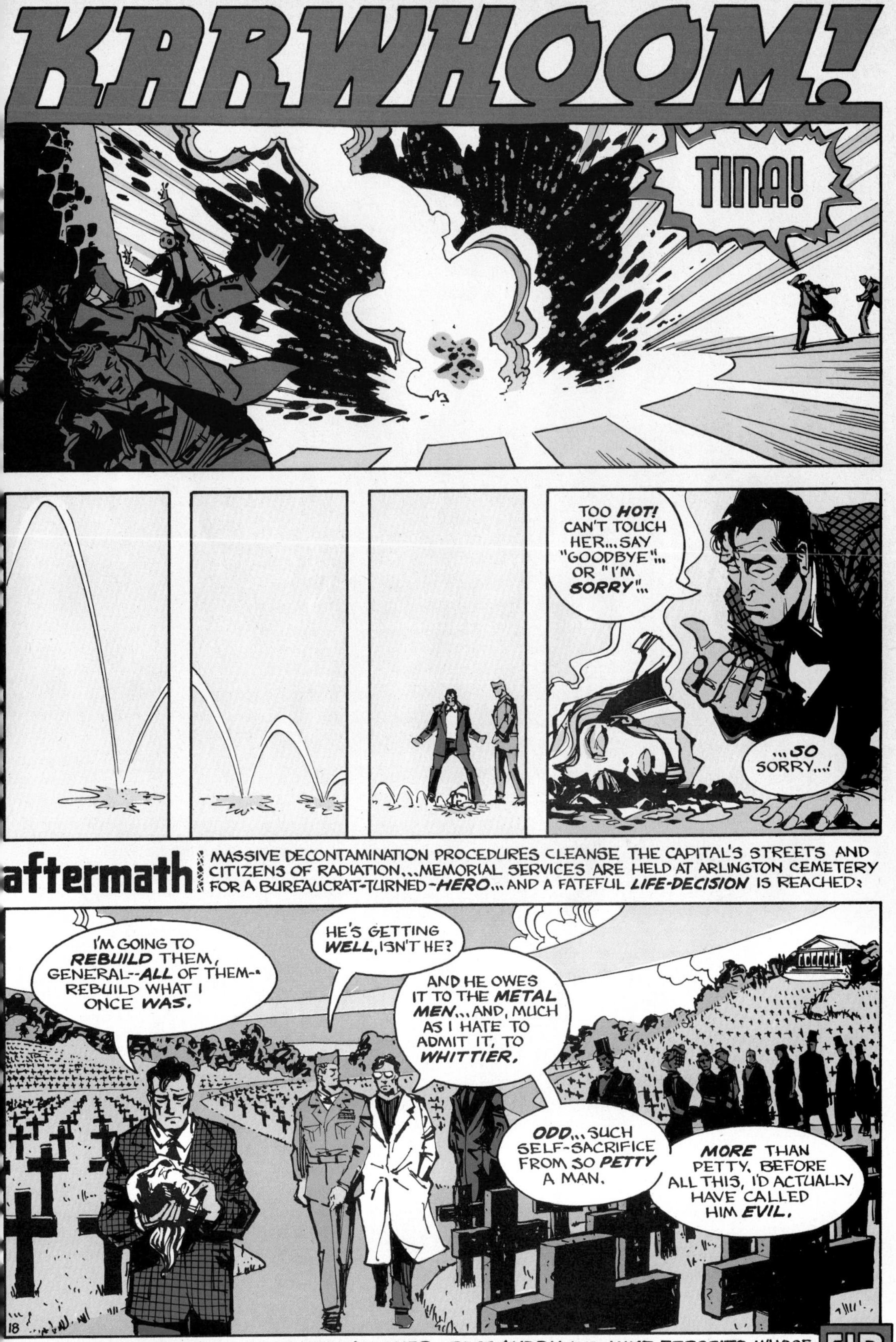

KARWHOOM!
TINA!
TOO HOT! CAN'T TOUCH HER... SAY "GOODBYE"... OR "I'M SORRY"...
...SO SORRY...!
aftermath
MASSIVE DECONTAMINATION PROCEDURES CLEANSE THE CAPITAL'S STREETS AND CITIZENS OF RADIATION... MEMORIAL SERVICES ARE HELD AT ARLINGTON CEMETERY FOR A BUREAUCRAT-TURNED-HERO... AND A FATEFUL LIFE-DECISION IS REACHED:
I'M GOING TO REBUILD THEM, GENERAL--ALL OF THEM--REBUILD WHAT I ONCE WAS.
HE'S GETTING WELL, ISN'T HE?
AND HE OWES IT TO THE METAL MEN... AND, MUCH AS I HATE TO ADMIT IT, TO WHITTIER.
ODD... SUCH SELF-SACRIFICE FROM SO PETTY A MAN.
MORE THAN PETTY. BEFORE ALL THIS, I'D ACTUALLY HAVE CALLED HIM EVIL.
18
THIS STORY IS DEDICATED TO ROBERT KANIGHER, ROSS ANDRU, AND MIKE ESPOSITO, WHOSE CREATIVE FIRES FIRST FORGED THE METAL MEN. -- G.C./S.G./W.S.
FIN

JUSTICE SOCIETY OF AMERICA #43-44

Black Adam was a great find for the 52 writers. Originally created for a Marvel Family story in 1945, he appeared only once before being resurrected in the 1970s as Captain Marvel's archnemesis.

In the pages of DC's JSA series, writers Geoff Johns and David Goyer subsequently turned a one-note character into a tormented, conflicted man with a reason for everything he does, good or bad. In this story, you'll get a glimpse of the harrowing past that formed him and the events that made him the perfect lens through which to view the political climate of DC Earth. **—MW**

PREVIOUSLY IN JSA: After several time-traveling adventures using Black Barax's time cube, JSA members Hawkgirl and Mister Terrific are determined to find their time-lost comrade Captain Marvel — who has been thrust back into ancient Egypt, during the reign of Rameses II.

BLACK ADAM

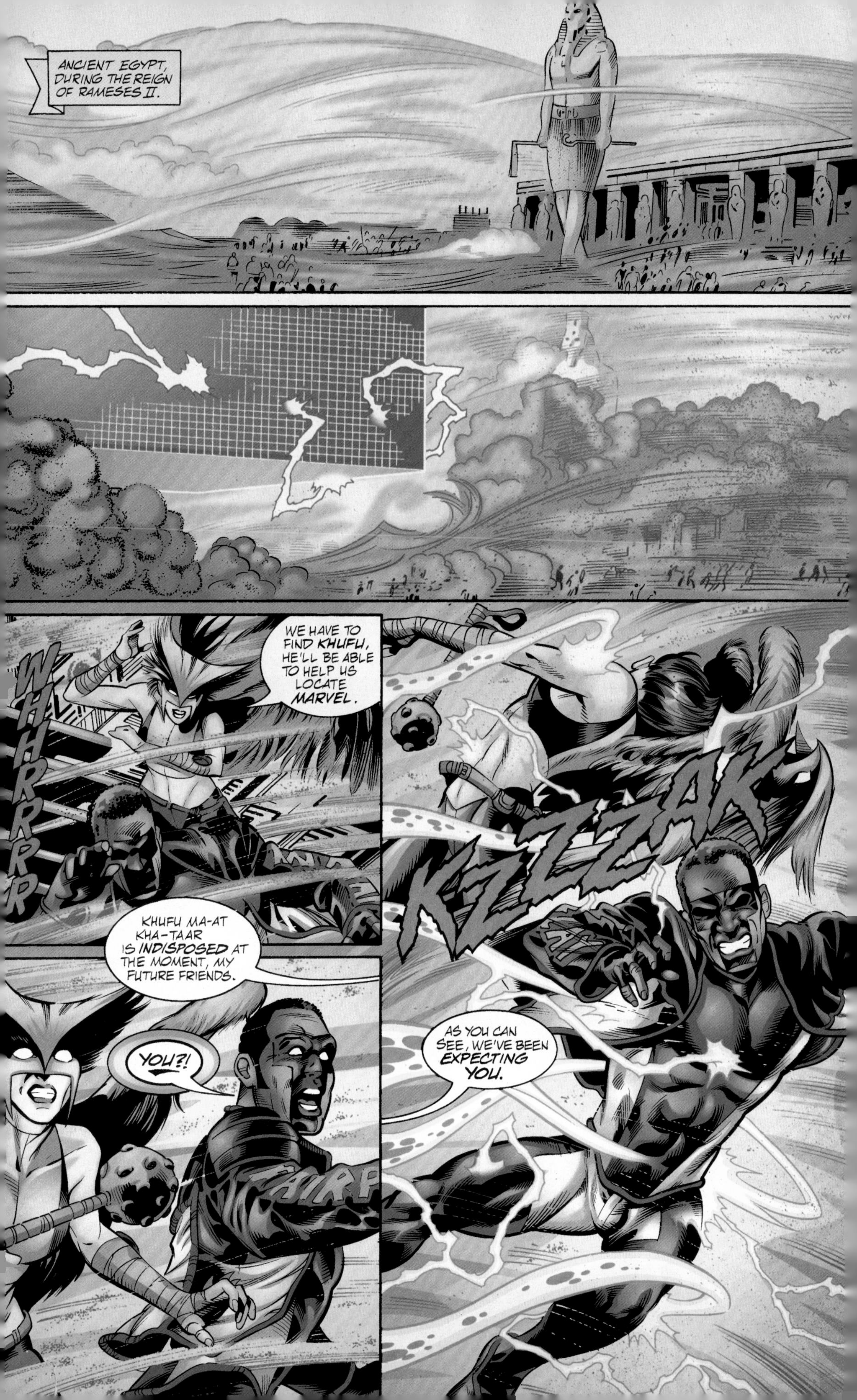
ANCIENT EGYPT, DURING THE REIGN OF RAMESES II.
WE HAVE TO FIND KHUFU, HE'LL BE ABLE TO HELP US LOCATE MARVEL.
WHHRRRRR
KZZZZAK
KHUFU MA-AT KHA-TAAR IS INDISPOSED AT THE MOMENT, MY FUTURE FRIENDS.
YOU?!
AS YOU CAN SEE, WE'VE BEEN EXPECTING YOU.

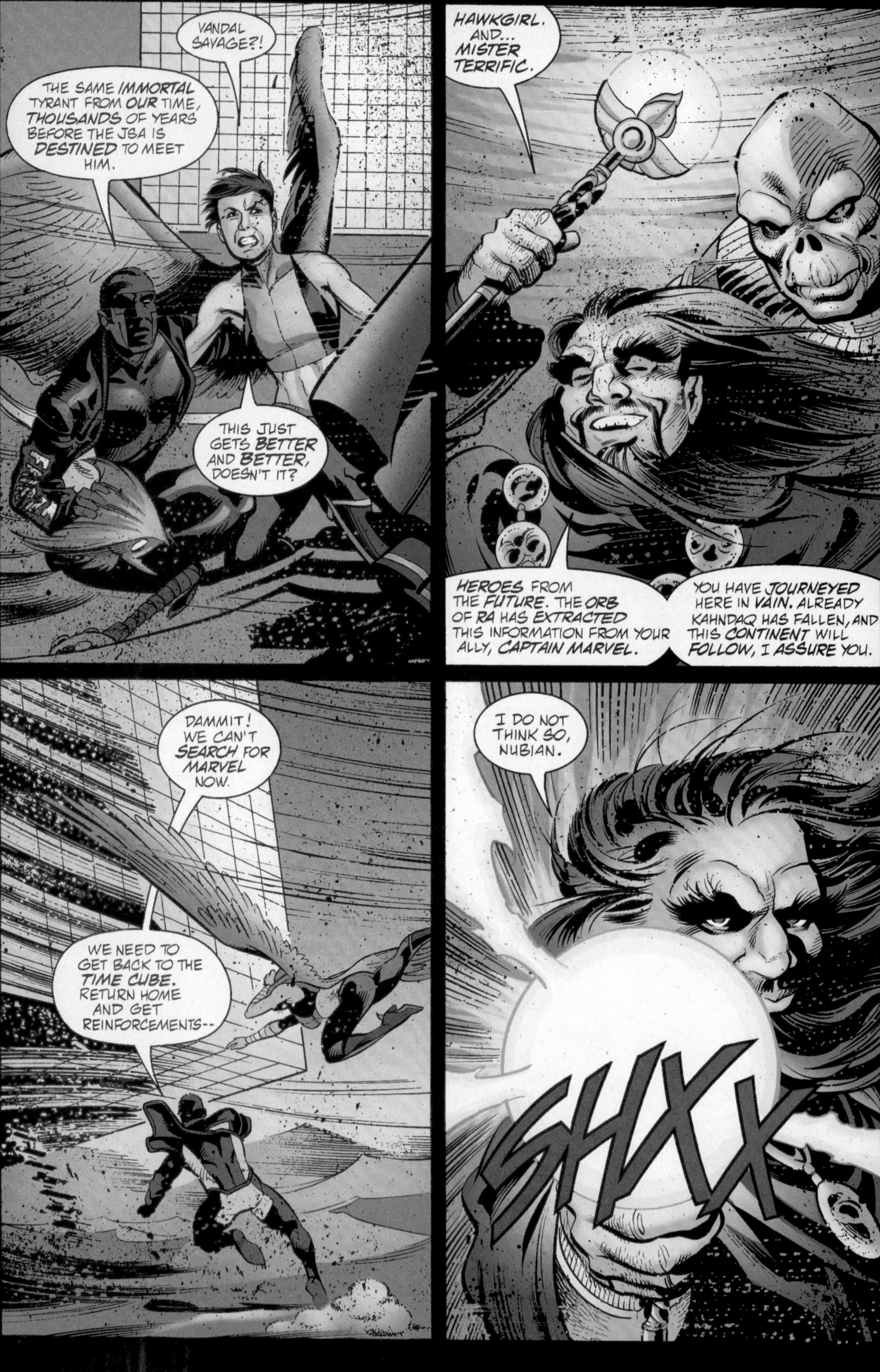
VANDAL SAVAGE?!
THE SAME IMMORTAL TYRANT FROM OUR TIME, THOUSANDS OF YEARS BEFORE THE JSA IS DESTINED TO MEET HIM.
THIS JUST GETS BETTER AND BETTER, DOESN'T IT?
HAWKGIRL. AND... MISTER TERRIFIC.
HEROES FROM THE FUTURE. THE ORB OF RA HAS EXTRACTED THIS INFORMATION FROM YOUR ALLY, CAPTAIN MARVEL.
YOU HAVE JOURNEYED HERE IN VAIN. ALREADY KAHNDAQ HAS FALLEN, AND THIS CONTINENT WILL FOLLOW, I ASSURE YOU.
DAMMIT! WE CAN'T SEARCH FOR MARVEL NOW.
WE NEED TO GET BACK TO THE TIME CUBE. RETURN HOME AND GET REINFORCEMENTS--
I DO NOT THINK SO, NUBIAN.
SHXX

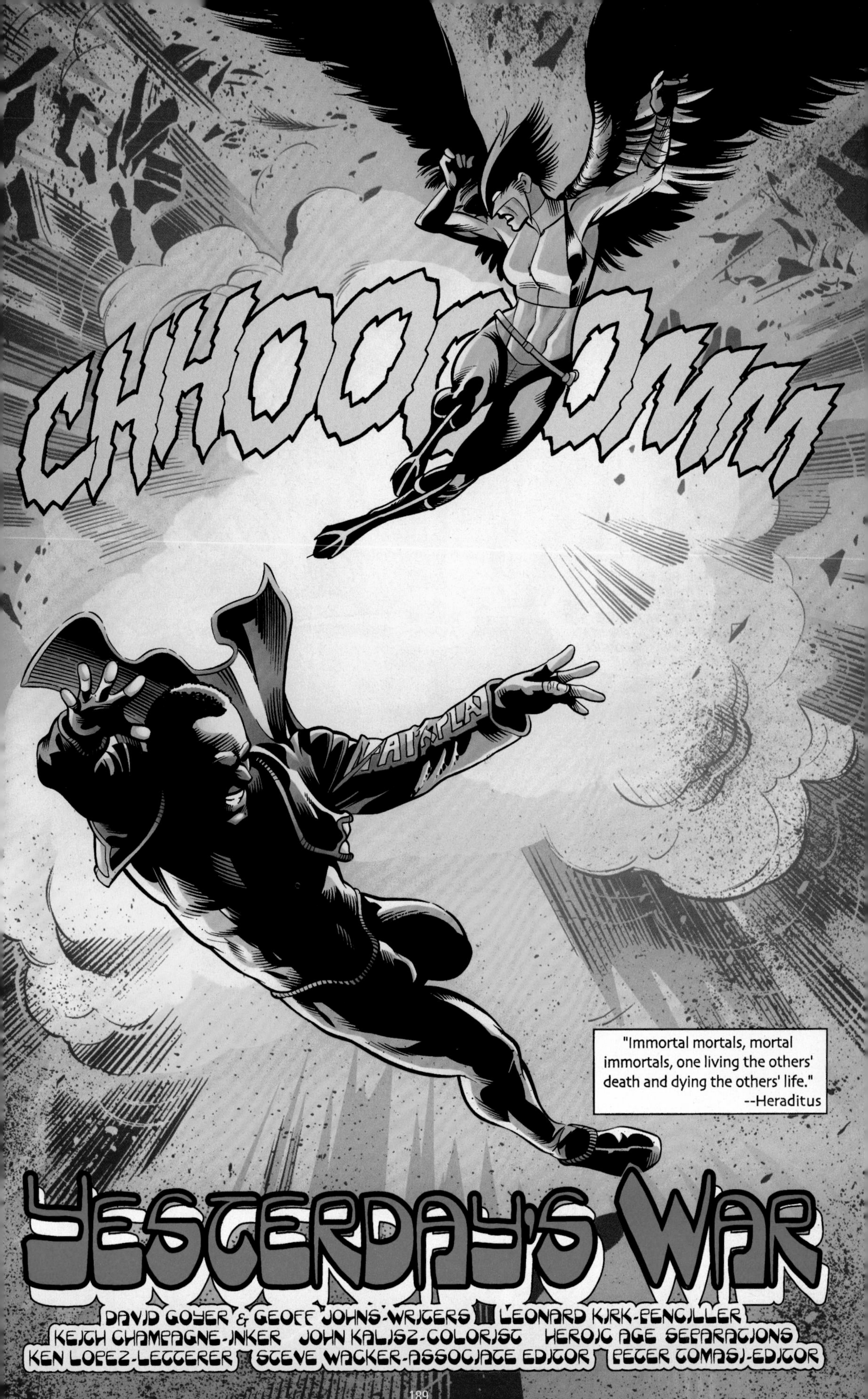
CHHOOOOOMM
"Immortal mortals, mortal immortals, one living the others' death and dying the others' life."
--Heraclitus
YESTERDAY'S WAR
DAVID GOYER & GEOFF JOHNS-WRITERS
LEONARD KIRK-PENCILLER
KEITH CHAMPAGNE-INKER
JOHN KALISZ-COLORIST
HEROIC AGE SEPARATIONS
KEN LOPEZ-LETTERER
STEVE WACKER-ASSOCIATE EDITOR
PETER TOMASI-EDITOR

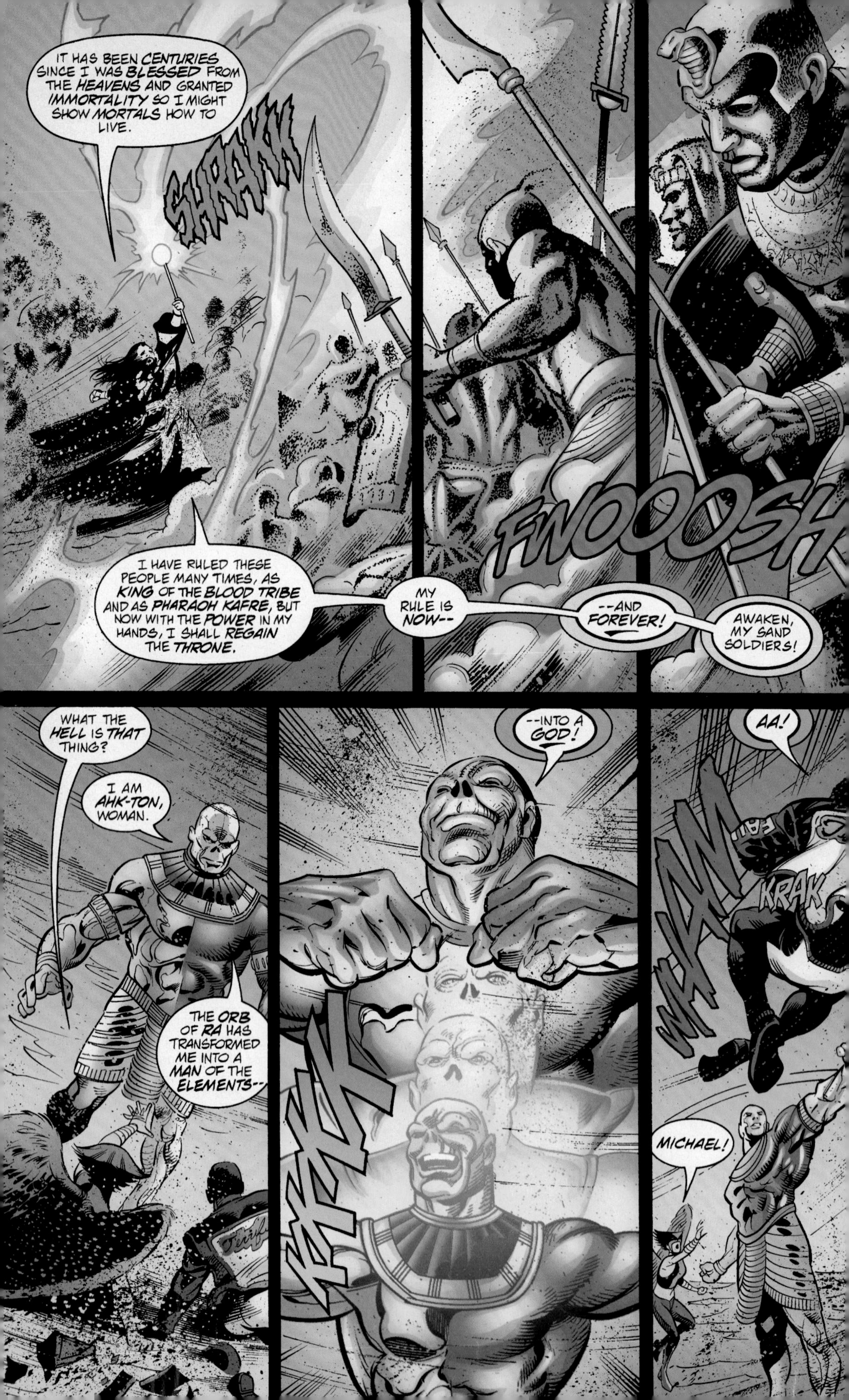
IT HAS BEEN CENTURIES SINCE I WAS BLESSED FROM THE HEAVENS AND GRANTED IMMORTALITY SO I MIGHT SHOW MORTALS HOW TO LIVE.
SHRAKK
I HAVE RULED THESE PEOPLE MANY TIMES, AS KING OF THE BLOOD TRIBE AND AS PHARAOH KAFRE, BUT NOW WITH THE POWER IN MY HANDS, I SHALL REGAIN THE THRONE.
MY RULE IS NOW--
FWOOOSH
--AND FOREVER!
AWAKEN, MY SAND SOLDIERS!
WHAT THE HELL IS THAT THING?
I AM AHK-TON, WOMAN.
THE ORB OF RA HAS TRANSFORMED ME INTO A MAN OF THE ELEMENTS--
--INTO A GOD!
KRAKK
AA!
WHAM
KRAK
MICHAEL!

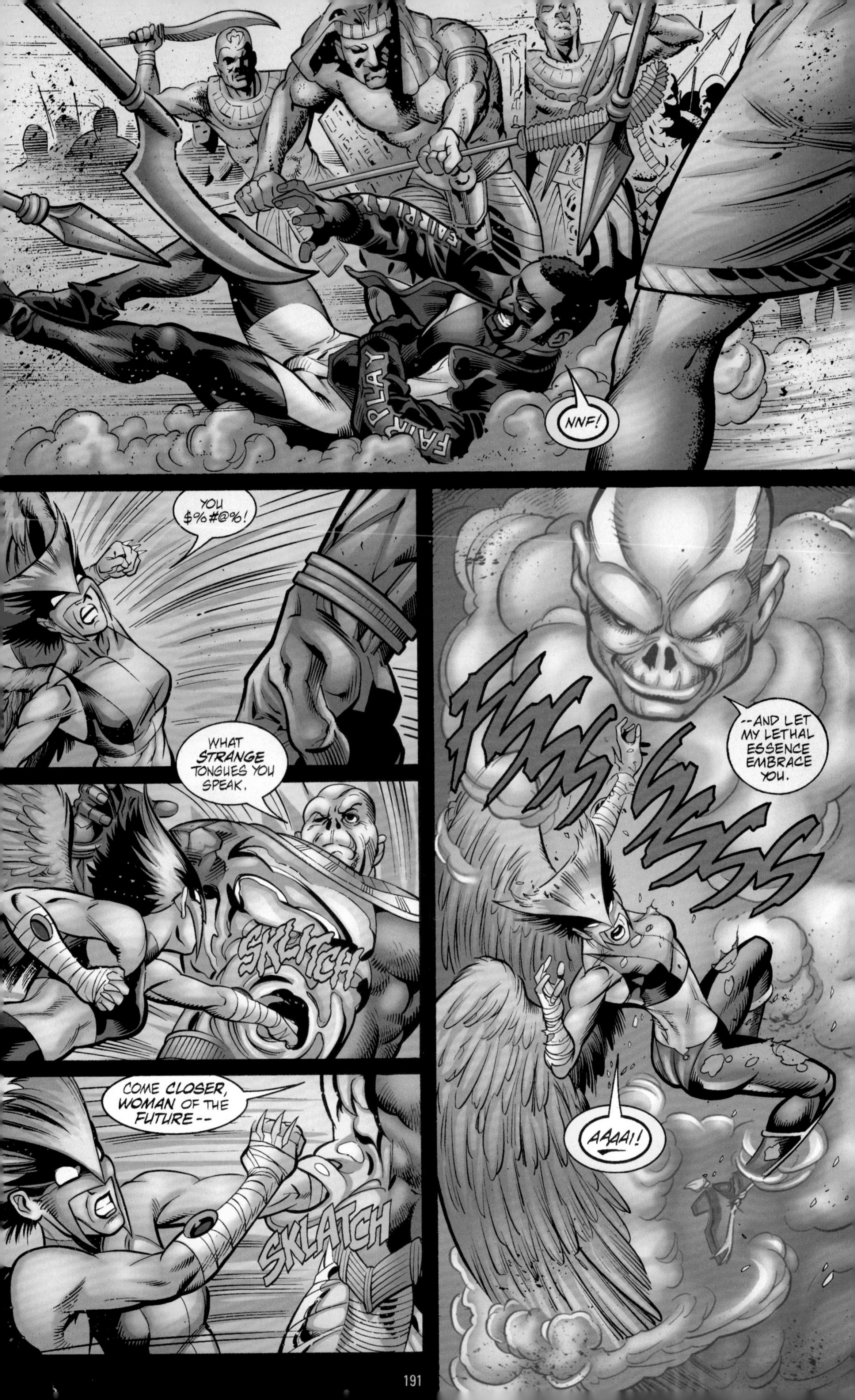
FAIR PLAY
FAIR PLAY
NNF!
YOU $%#@%!
WHAT STRANGE TONGUES YOU SPEAK.
SKLITCH
COME CLOSER, WOMAN OF THE FUTURE--
SKLATCH
--AND LET MY LETHAL ESSENCE EMBRACE YOU.
AAAAI!

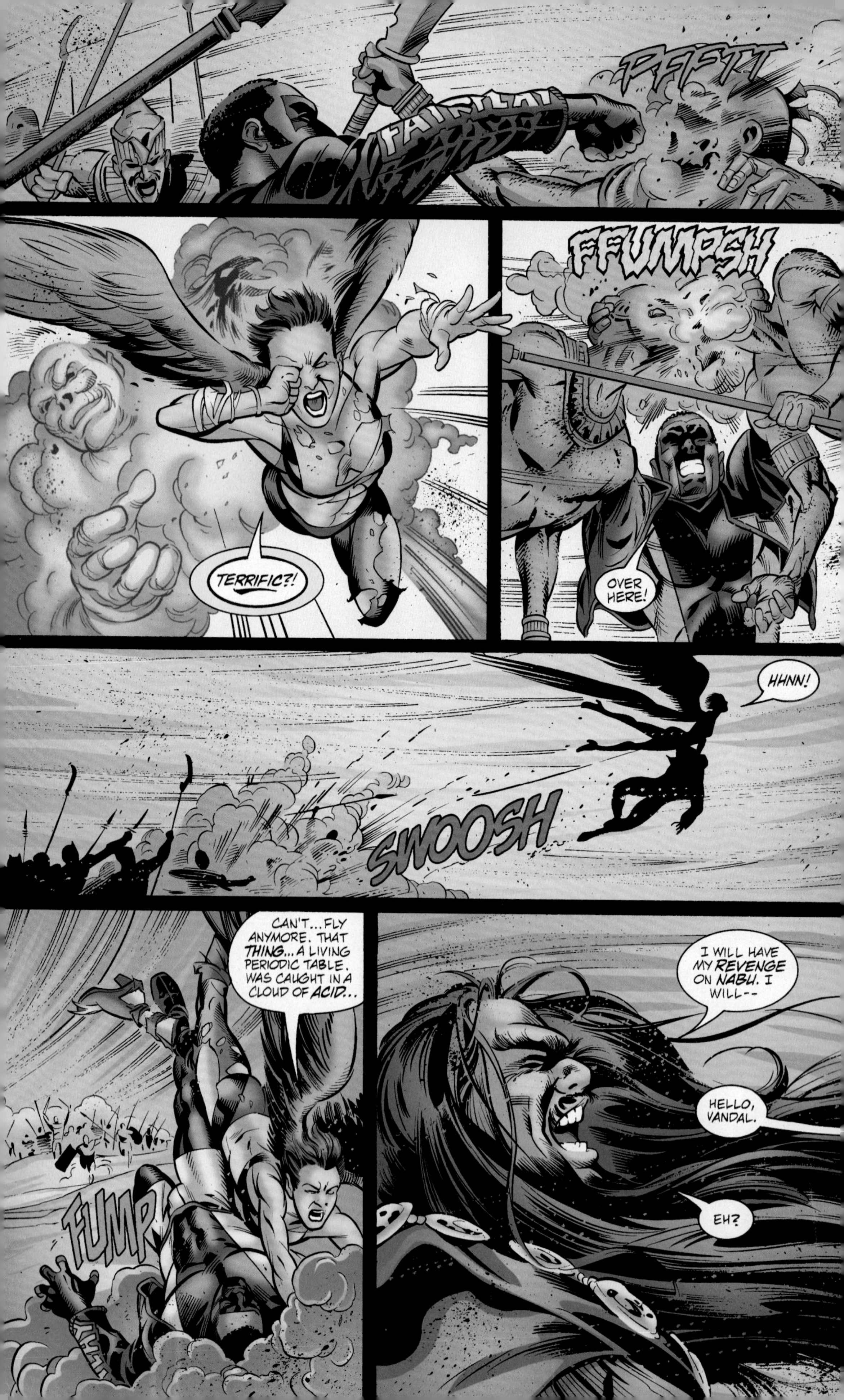
PFFTT
FFUMPSH
TERRIFIC?!
OVER HERE!
HHNN!
SWOOSH
CAN'T...FLY ANYMORE. THAT THING...A LIVING PERIODIC TABLE. WAS CAUGHT IN A CLOUD OF ACID...
FUMP
I WILL HAVE MY REVENGE ON NABU. I WILL--
HELLO, VANDAL.
EH?

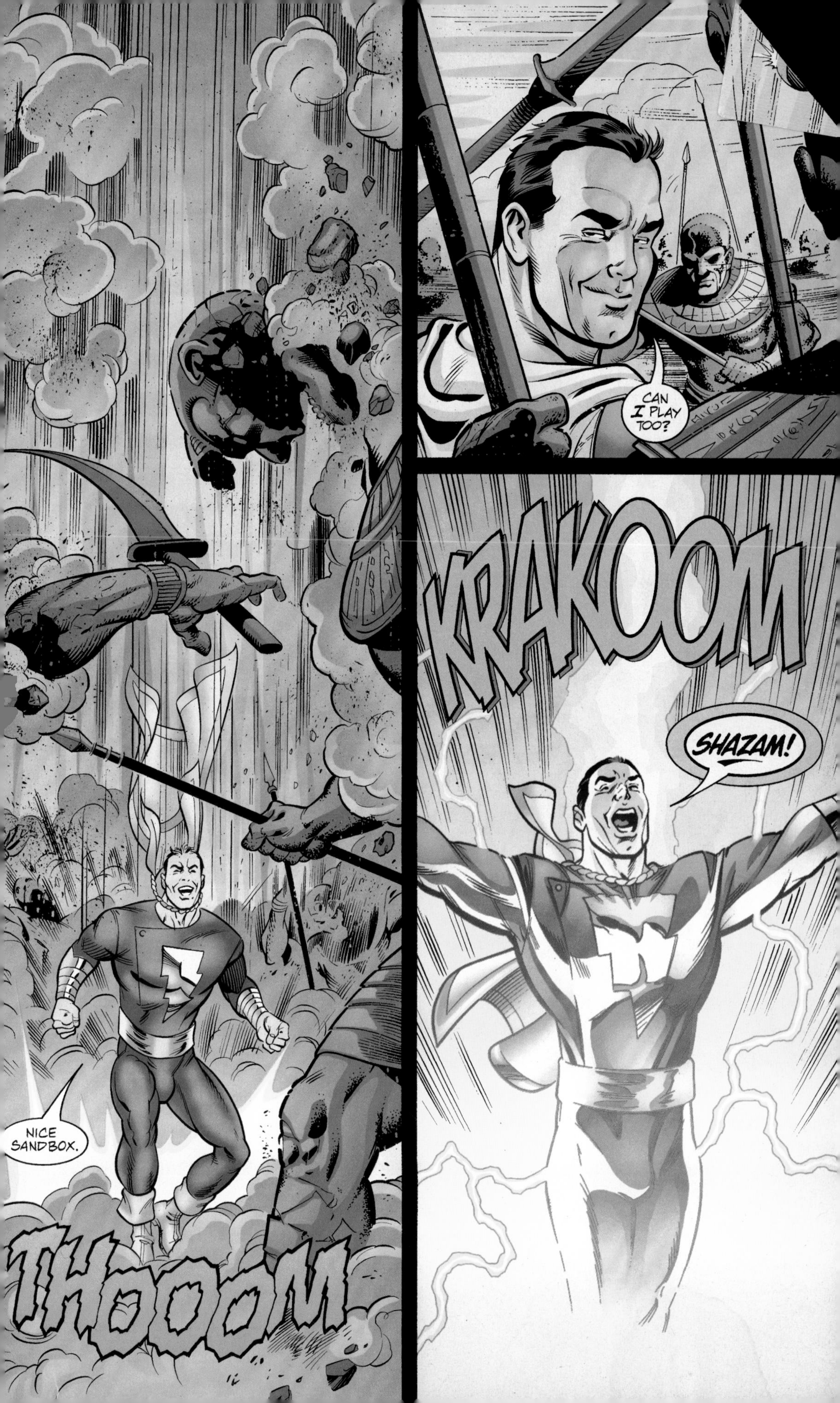
NICE SANDBOX.
THOOOM
CAN I PLAY TOO?
KRAKOOM
SHAZAM!

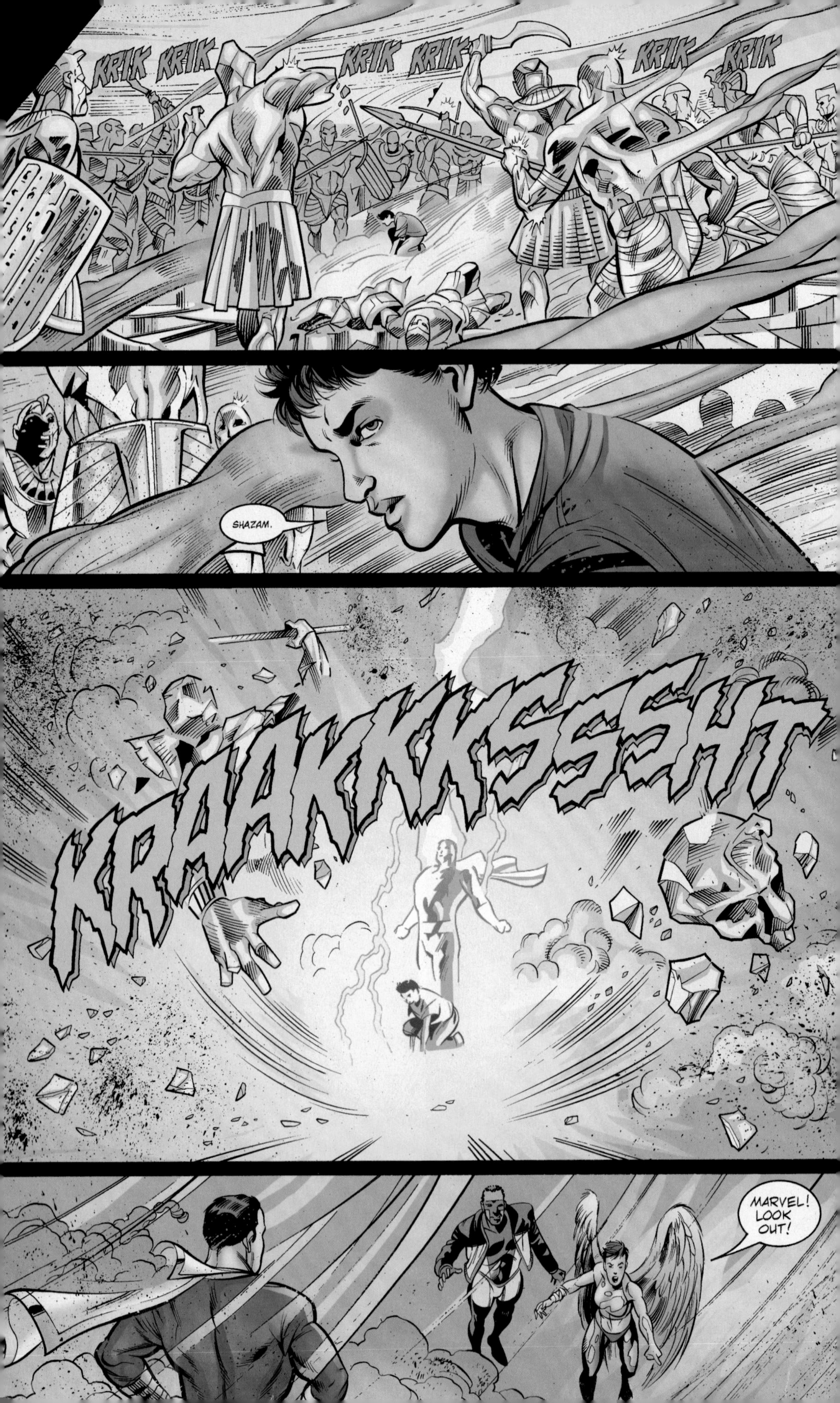
KRIK KRIK
KRIK KRIK
KRIK KRIK
SHAZAM.
KRAAKKSSHT
MARVEL! LOOK OUT!

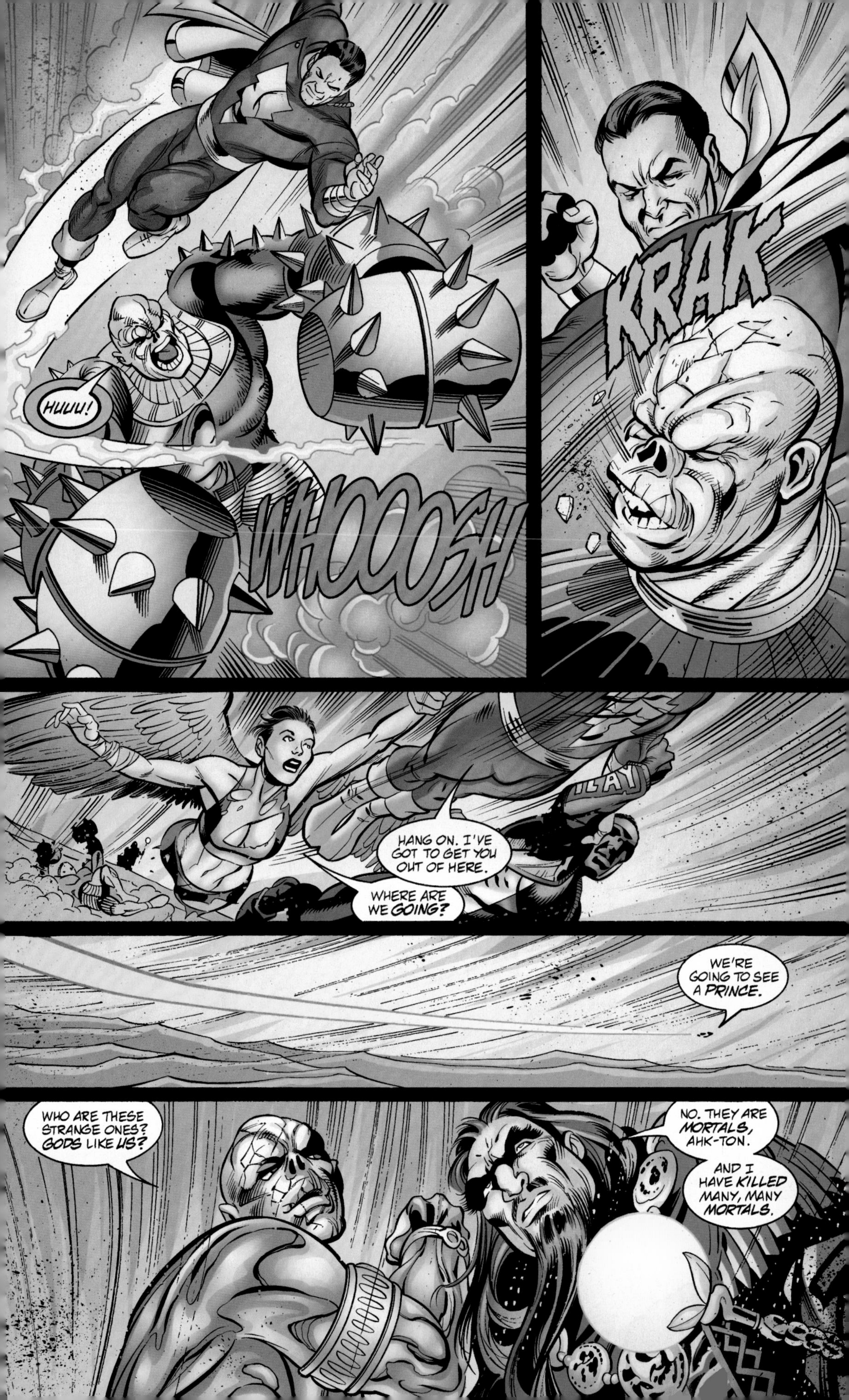
HUUU!
WHOOOSH
KRAK
HANG ON. I'VE GOT TO GET YOU OUT OF HERE.
WHERE ARE WE GOING?
WE'RE GOING TO SEE A PRINCE.
WHO ARE THESE STRANGE ONES? GODS LIKE US?
NO. THEY ARE MORTALS, AHK-TON.
AND I HAVE KILLED MANY, MANY MORTALS.

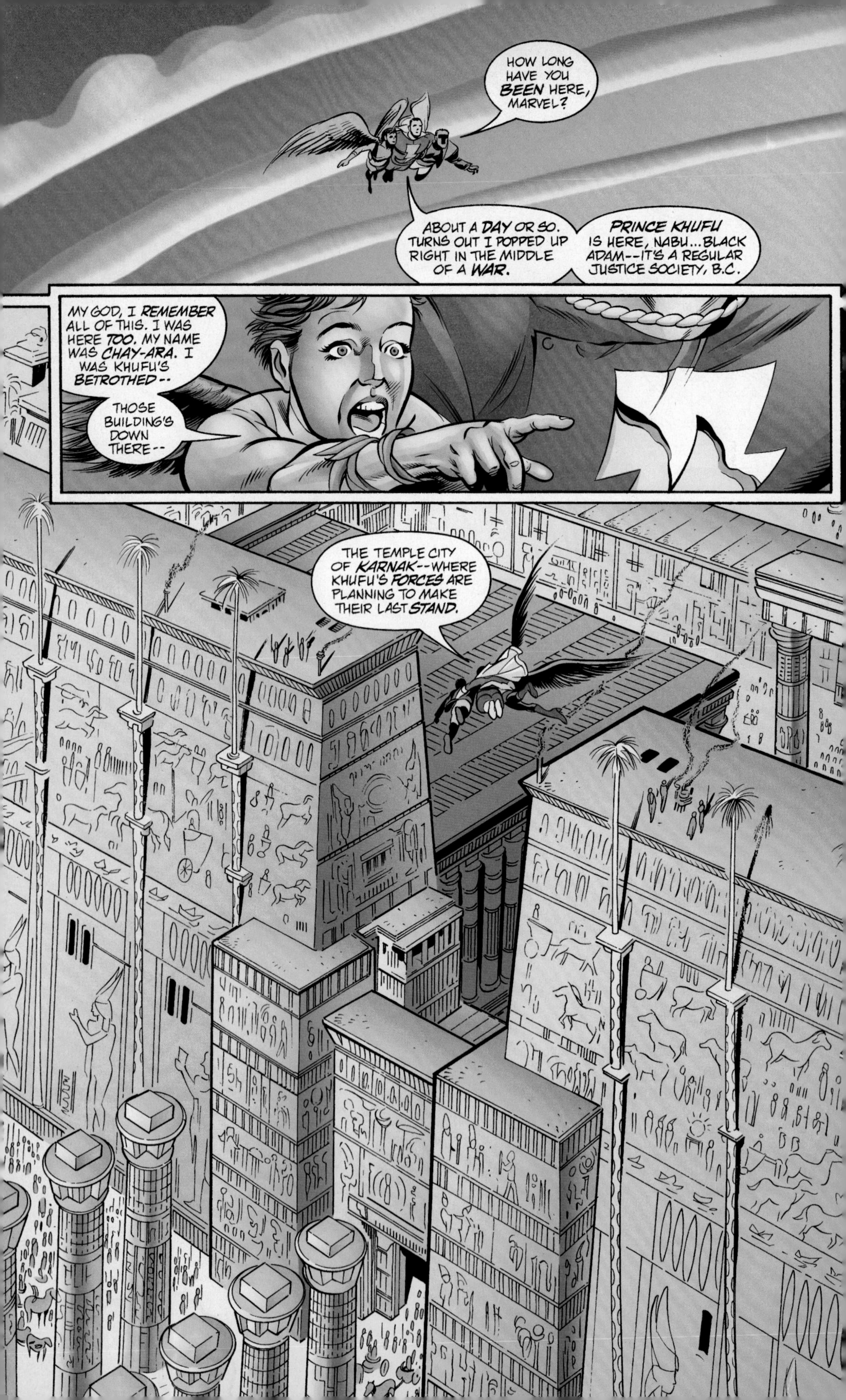
HOW LONG HAVE YOU BEEN HERE, MARVEL?
ABOUT A DAY OR SO. TURNS OUT I POPPED UP RIGHT IN THE MIDDLE OF A WAR.
PRINCE KHUFU IS HERE, NABU...BLACK ADAM--IT'S A REGULAR JUSTICE SOCIETY, B.C.
MY GOD, I REMEMBER ALL OF THIS. I WAS HERE TOO. MY NAME WAS CHAY-ARA. I WAS KHUFU'S BETROTHED--
THOSE BUILDING'S DOWN THERE--
THE TEMPLE CITY OF KARNAK--WHERE KHUFU'S FORCES ARE PLANNING TO MAKE THEIR LAST STAND.

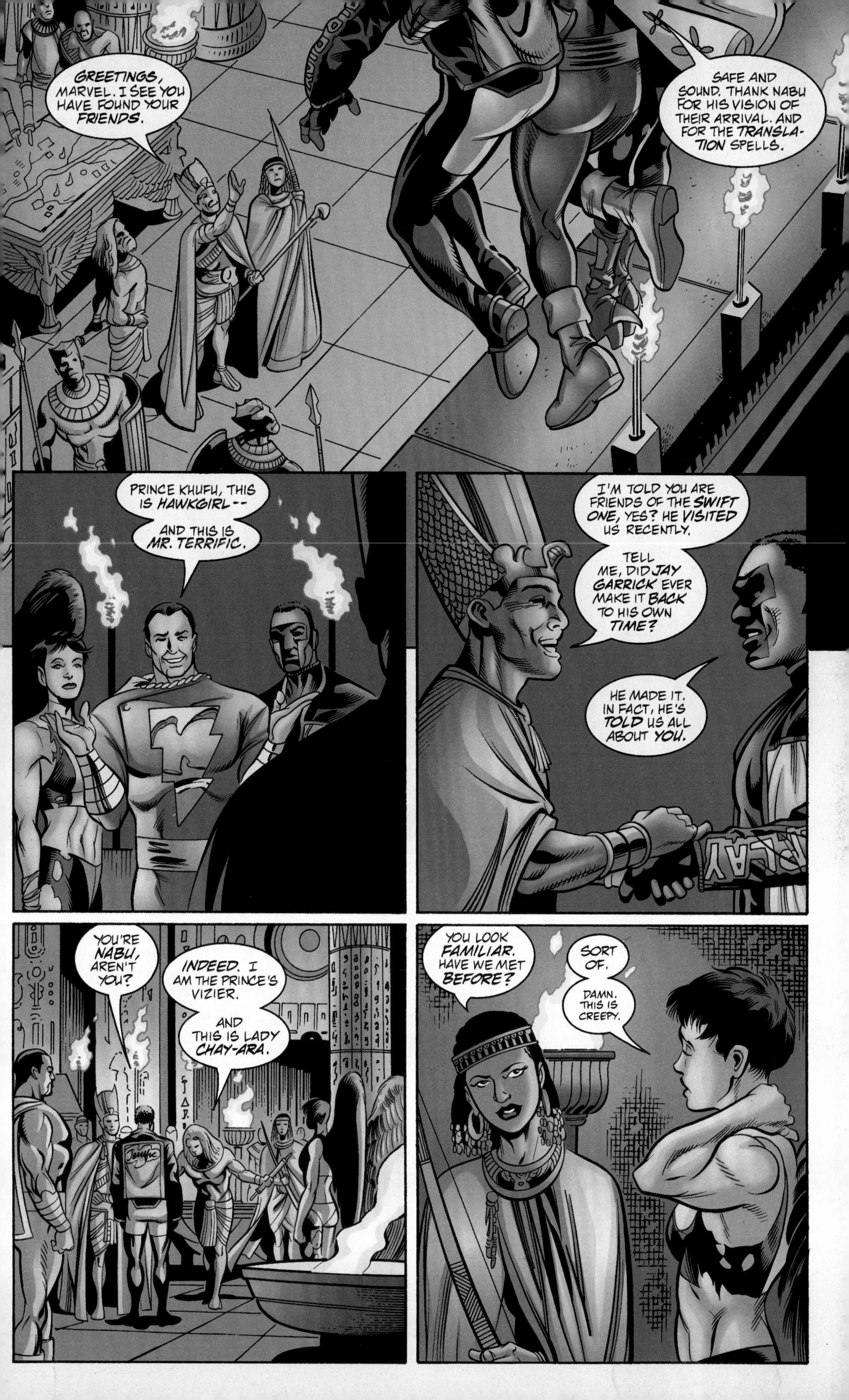
GREETINGS, MARVEL. I SEE YOU HAVE FOUND YOUR FRIENDS.
SAFE AND SOUND. THANK NABU FOR HIS VISION OF THEIR ARRIVAL. AND FOR THE TRANSLATION SPELLS.
PRINCE KHUFU, THIS IS HAWKGIRL--
AND THIS IS MR. TERRIFIC.
I'M TOLD YOU ARE FRIENDS OF THE SWIFT ONE, YES? HE VISITED US RECENTLY.
TELL ME, DID JAY GARRICK EVER MAKE IT BACK TO HIS OWN TIME?
HE MADE IT. IN FACT, HE'S TOLD US ALL ABOUT YOU.
YOU'RE NABU, AREN'T YOU?
INDEED. I AM THE PRINCE'S VIZIER.
AND THIS IS LADY CHAY-ARA.
YOU LOOK FAMILIAR. HAVE WE MET BEFORE?
SORT OF.
DAMN. THIS IS CREEPY.

HOW GOES THE WAR?

BADLY. VANDAL THE SAVAGE AND I HAVE TANGLED BEFORE. BUT WITH THE ORB OF RA NOW IN HIS POSSESSION--

WHAT IS THE ORB?

A POTENT RELIC STOLEN FROM THE TEMPLE OF HELIOPOLIS, CAPABLE OF TRANSMUTING THE ELEMENTS.

SOME SAY IT IS THE HEART OF GREAT SUN-GOD RA HIMSELF.

NONSENSE! RA WOULD NEVER ALLOW HIS GIFTS TO BE DESECRATED IN THIS WAY.

HE IS THE LIGHT-BRINGER, GUIDING HIS NIGHT-BOAT THROUGH THE DARKNESS.

NEVERTHELESS, MY FATHER'S KINGDOM IS ON THE VERGE OF BEING OVERRUN.

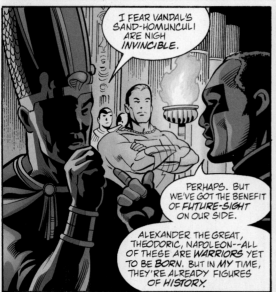

I FEAR VANDAL'S SAND-HOMUNCULI ARE NIGH INVINCIBLE.

PERHAPS. BUT WE'VE GOT THE BENEFIT OF FUTURE-SIGHT ON OUR SIDE.

ALEXANDER THE GREAT, THEODORIC, NAPOLEON--ALL OF THESE ARE WARRIORS YET TO BE BORN. BUT IN MY TIME, THEY'RE ALREADY FIGURES OF HISTORY.

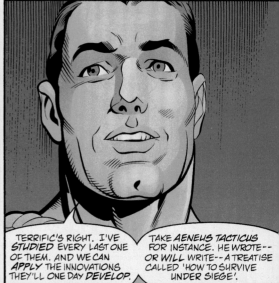

TERRIFIC'S RIGHT. I'VE STUDIED EVERY LAST ONE OF THEM. AND WE CAN APPLY THE INNOVATIONS THEY'LL ONE DAY DEVELOP.

TAKE AENEUS TACTICUS FOR INSTANCE. HE WROTE-- OR WILL WRITE--A TREATISE CALLED 'HOW TO SURVIVE UNDER SIEGE'.

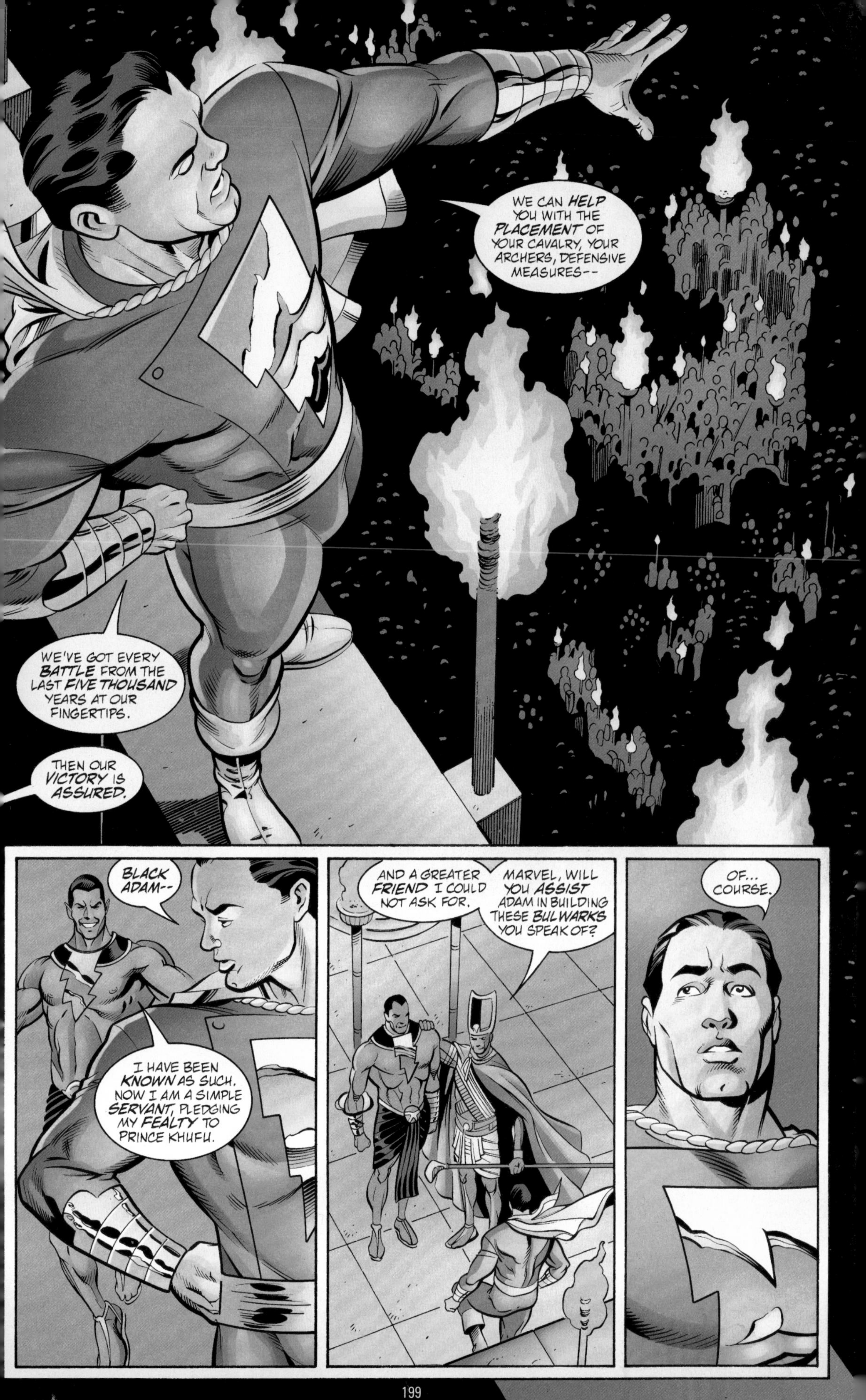
WE CAN HELP YOU WITH THE PLACEMENT OF YOUR CAVALRY, YOUR ARCHERS, DEFENSIVE MEASURES--
WE'VE GOT EVERY BATTLE FROM THE LAST FIVE THOUSAND YEARS AT OUR FINGERTIPS.
THEN OUR VICTORY IS ASSURED.
BLACK ADAM--
I HAVE BEEN KNOWN AS SUCH. NOW I AM A SIMPLE SERVANT, PLEDGING MY FEALTY TO PRINCE KHUFU.
AND A GREATER FRIEND I COULD NOT ASK FOR.
MARVEL, WILL YOU ASSIST ADAM IN BUILDING THESE BULWARKS YOU SPEAK OF?
OF... COURSE.

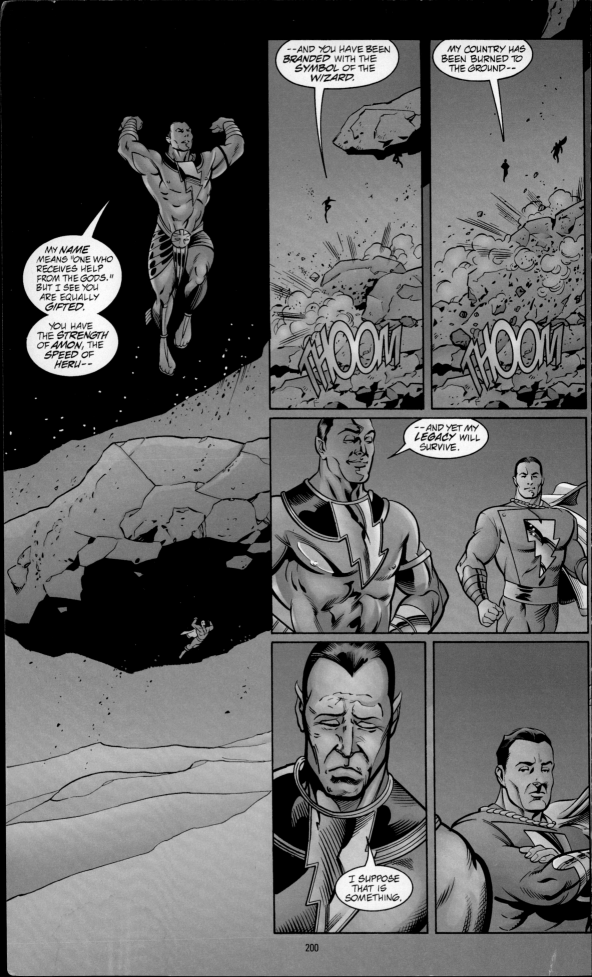

MY *NAME* MEANS "ONE WHO RECEIVES HELP FROM THE GODS." BUT I SEE YOU ARE EQUALLY GIFTED.

YOU HAVE THE *STRENGTH* OF *AMON*, THE SPEED OF *HERU*--

--AND YOU HAVE BEEN *BRANDED* WITH THE *SYMBOL* OF THE *WIZARD*.

MY COUNTRY HAS BEEN BURNED TO THE GROUND--

THOOM

THOOM

--AND YET MY *LEGACY* WILL SURVIVE.

I SUPPOSE THAT IS SOMETHING.

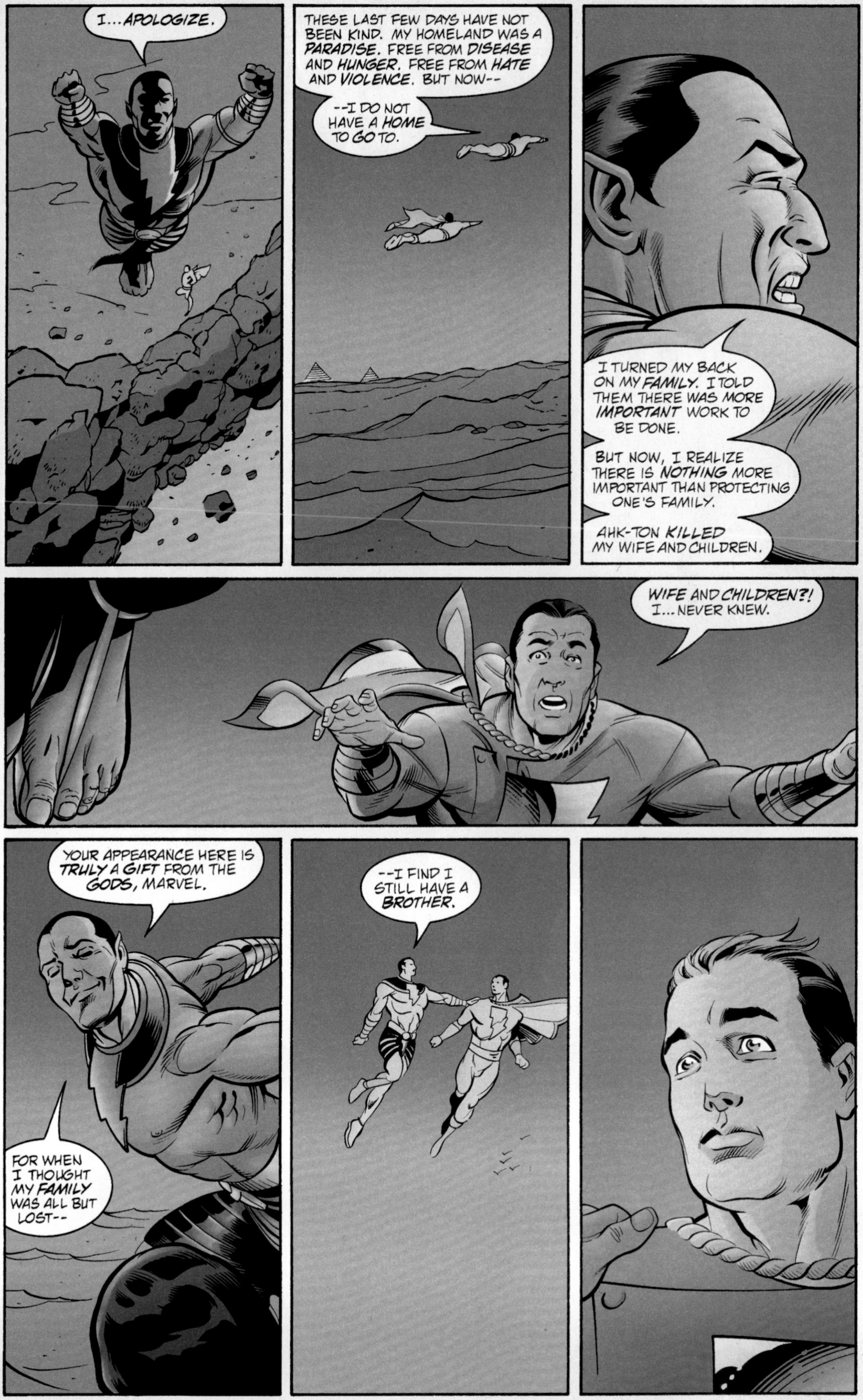

I...APOLOGIZE.
THESE LAST FEW DAYS HAVE NOT BEEN KIND. MY HOMELAND WAS A PARADISE. FREE FROM DISEASE AND HUNGER. FREE FROM HATE AND VIOLENCE. BUT NOW--
--I DO NOT HAVE A HOME TO GO TO.
I TURNED MY BACK ON MY FAMILY. I TOLD THEM THERE WAS MORE IMPORTANT WORK TO BE DONE.
BUT NOW, I REALIZE THERE IS NOTHING MORE IMPORTANT THAN PROTECTING ONE'S FAMILY.
AHK-TON KILLED MY WIFE AND CHILDREN.
WIFE AND CHILDREN?! I...NEVER KNEW.
YOUR APPEARANCE HERE IS TRULY A GIFT FROM THE GODS, MARVEL.
FOR WHEN I THOUGHT MY FAMILY WAS ALL BUT LOST--
--I FIND I STILL HAVE A BROTHER.

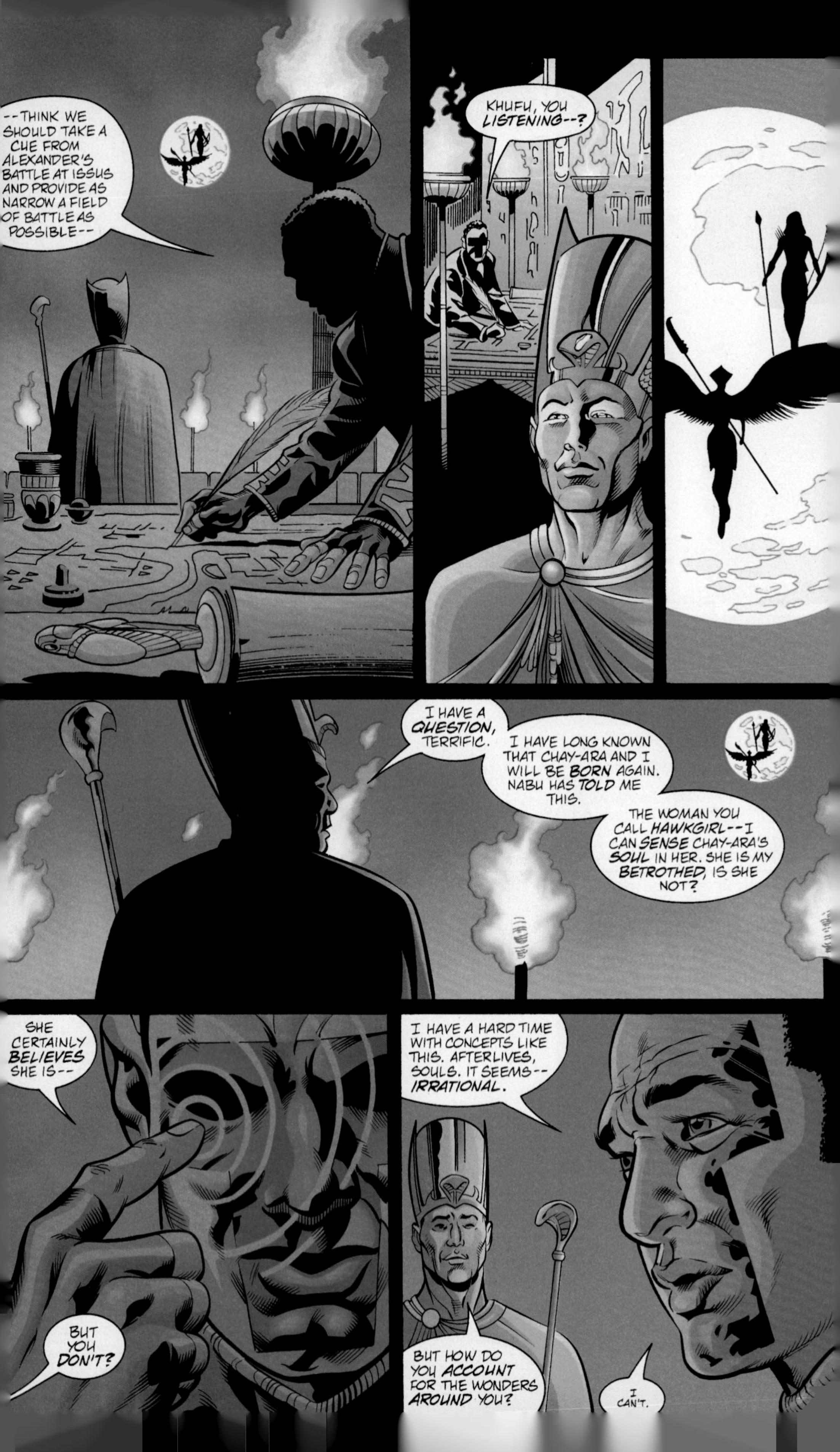
--THINK WE SHOULD TAKE A CUE FROM ALEXANDER'S BATTLE AT ISSUS AND PROVIDE AS NARROW A FIELD OF BATTLE AS POSSIBLE--
KHUFU, YOU LISTENING--?
I HAVE A QUESTION, TERRIFIC.
I HAVE LONG KNOWN THAT CHAY-ARA AND I WILL BE BORN AGAIN. NABU HAS TOLD ME THIS.
THE WOMAN YOU CALL HAWKGIRL--I CAN SENSE CHAY-ARA'S SOUL IN HER. SHE IS MY BETROTHED, IS SHE NOT?
SHE CERTAINLY BELIEVES SHE IS--
BUT YOU DON'T?
I HAVE A HARD TIME WITH CONCEPTS LIKE THIS. AFTERLIVES, SOULS. IT SEEMS--IRRATIONAL.
BUT HOW DO YOU ACCOUNT FOR THE WONDERS AROUND YOU?
I CAN'T.

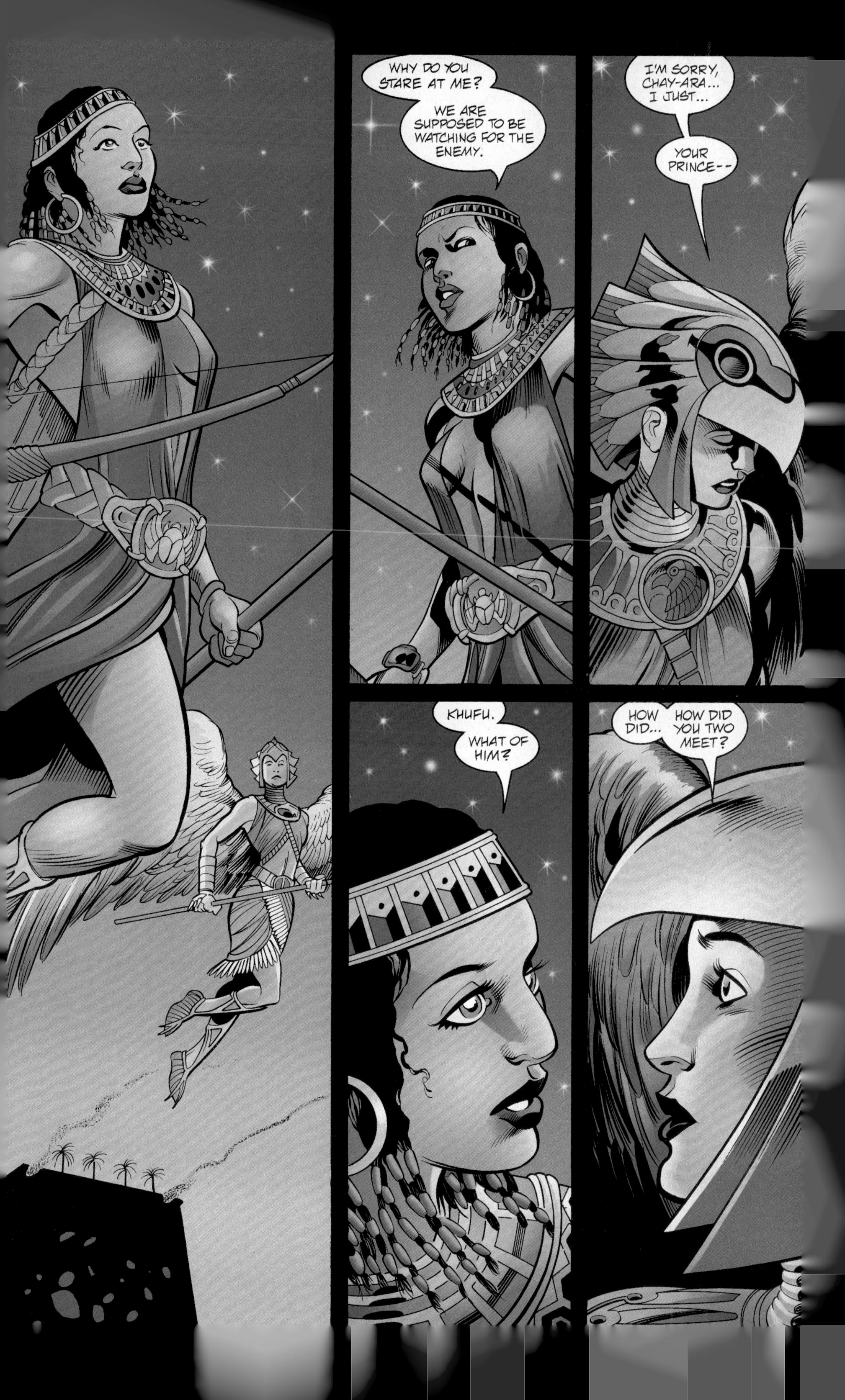
WHY DO YOU STARE AT ME?
WE ARE SUPPOSED TO BE WATCHING FOR THE ENEMY.
I'M SORRY, CHAY-ARA... I JUST...
YOUR PRINCE--
KHUFU.
WHAT OF HIM?
HOW DID...
HOW DID YOU TWO MEET?

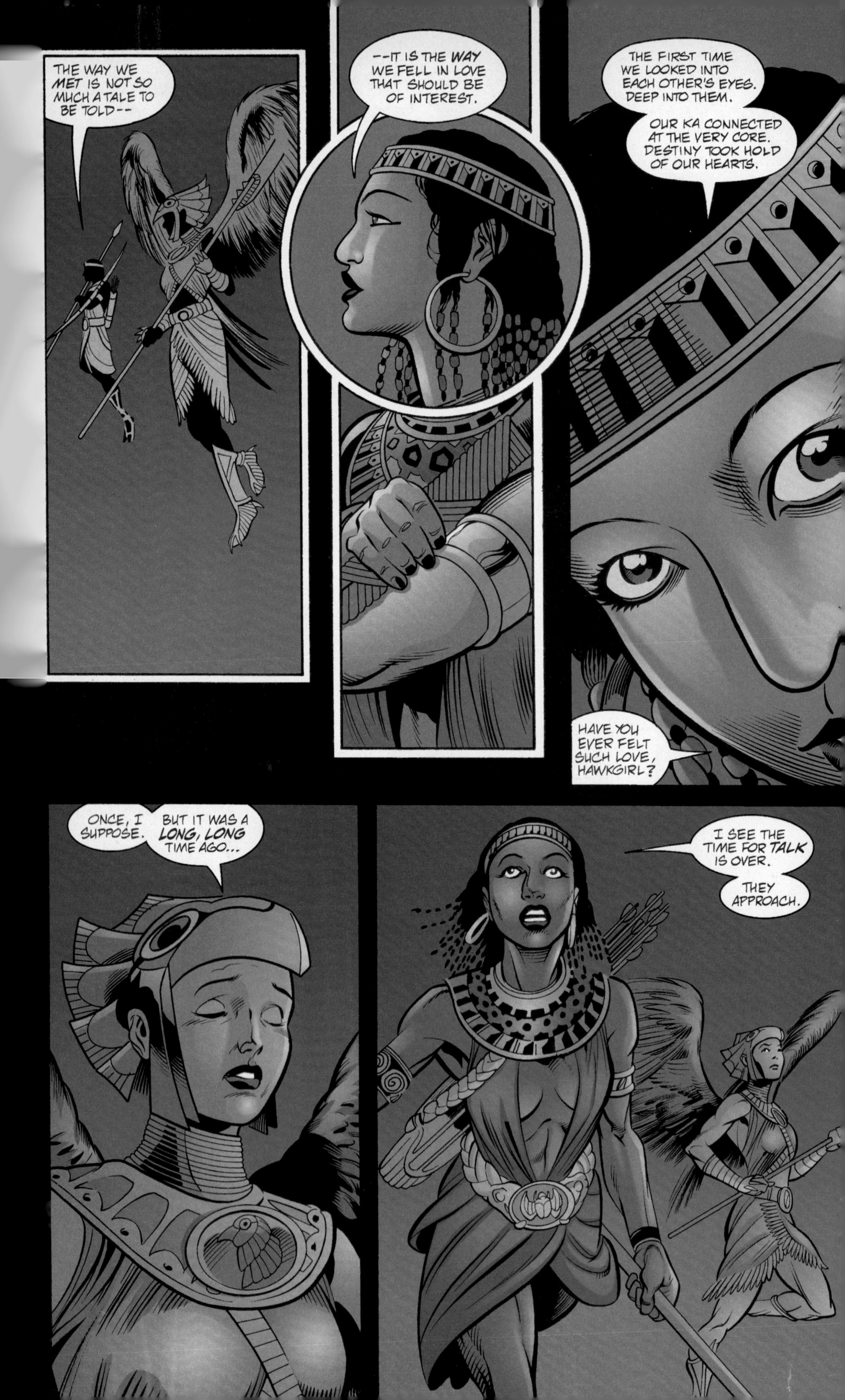
THE WAY WE MET IS NOT SO MUCH A TALE TO BE TOLD--
--IT IS THE WAY WE FELL IN LOVE THAT SHOULD BE OF INTEREST.
THE FIRST TIME WE LOOKED INTO EACH OTHER'S EYES. DEEP INTO THEM.
OUR KA CONNECTED AT THE VERY CORE. DESTINY TOOK HOLD OF OUR HEARTS.
HAVE YOU EVER FELT SUCH LOVE, HAWKGIRL?
ONCE, I SUPPOSE.
BUT IT WAS A LONG, LONG TIME AGO...
I SEE THE TIME FOR TALK IS OVER.
THEY APPROACH.

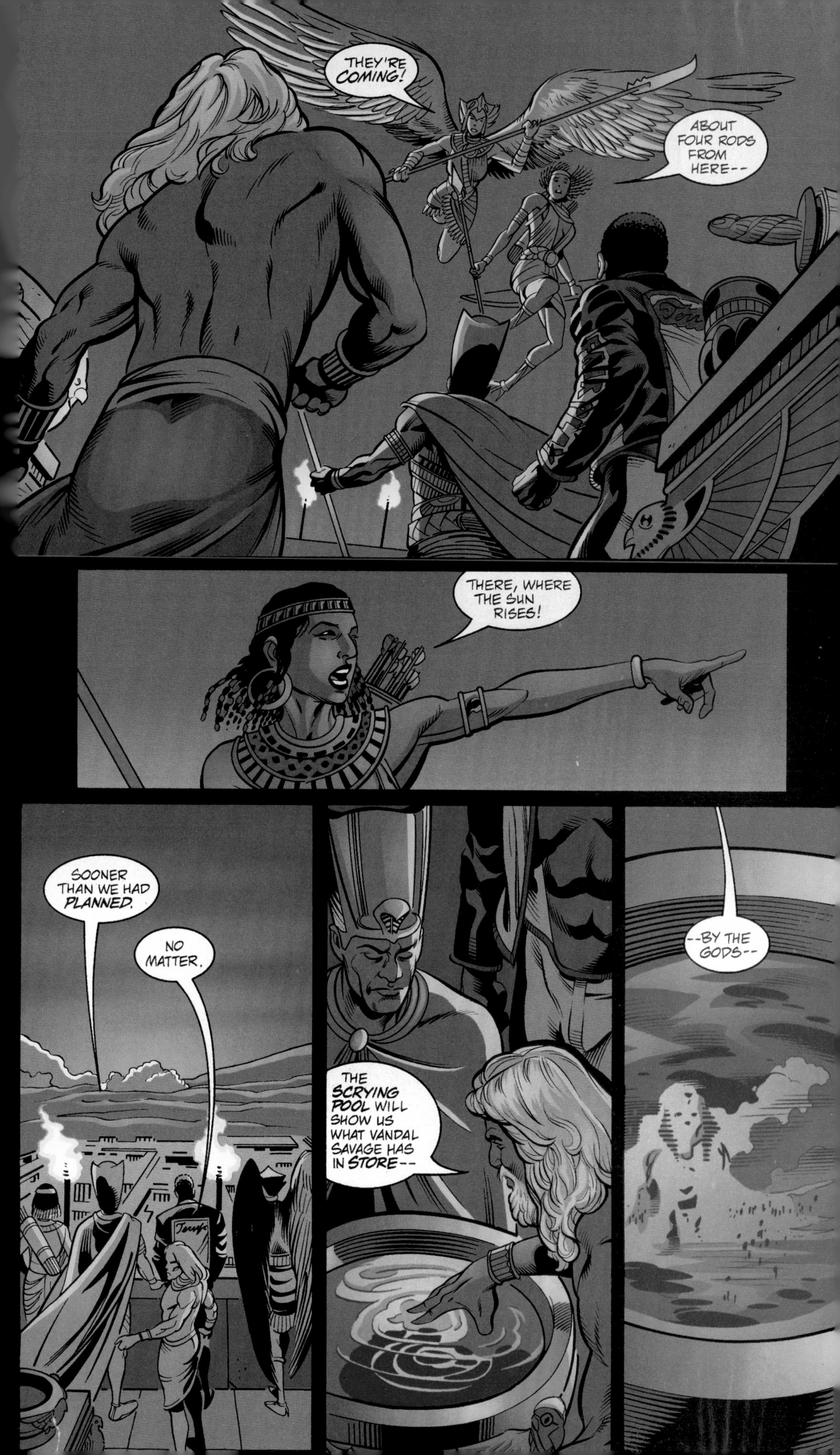
THEY'RE COMING!
ABOUT FOUR RODS FROM HERE--
THERE, WHERE THE SUN RISES!
SOONER THAN WE HAD PLANNED.
NO MATTER.
THE SCRYING POOL WILL SHOW US WHAT VANDAL SAVAGE HAS IN STORE--
--BY THE GODS--

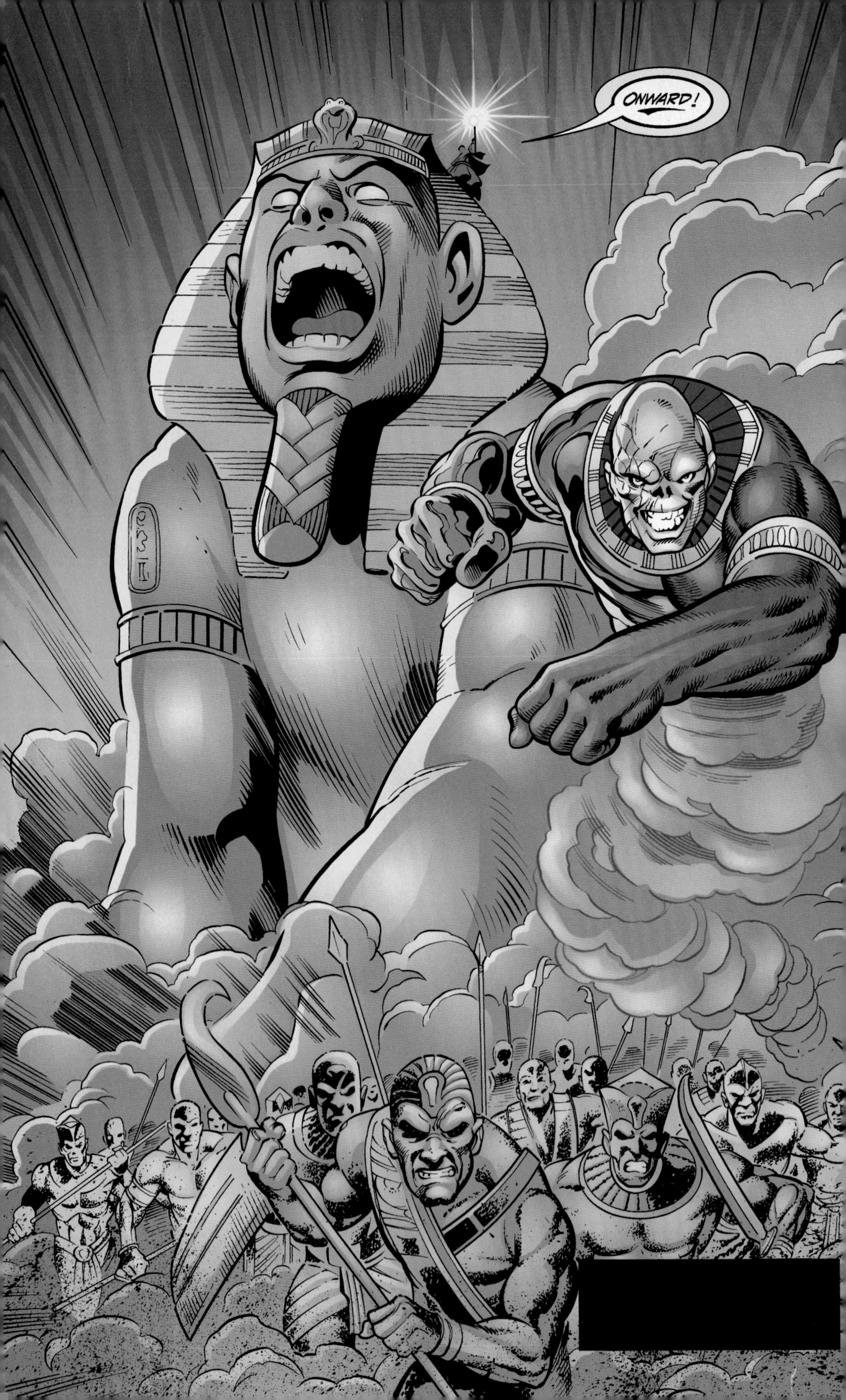
ONWARD!
[redacted]

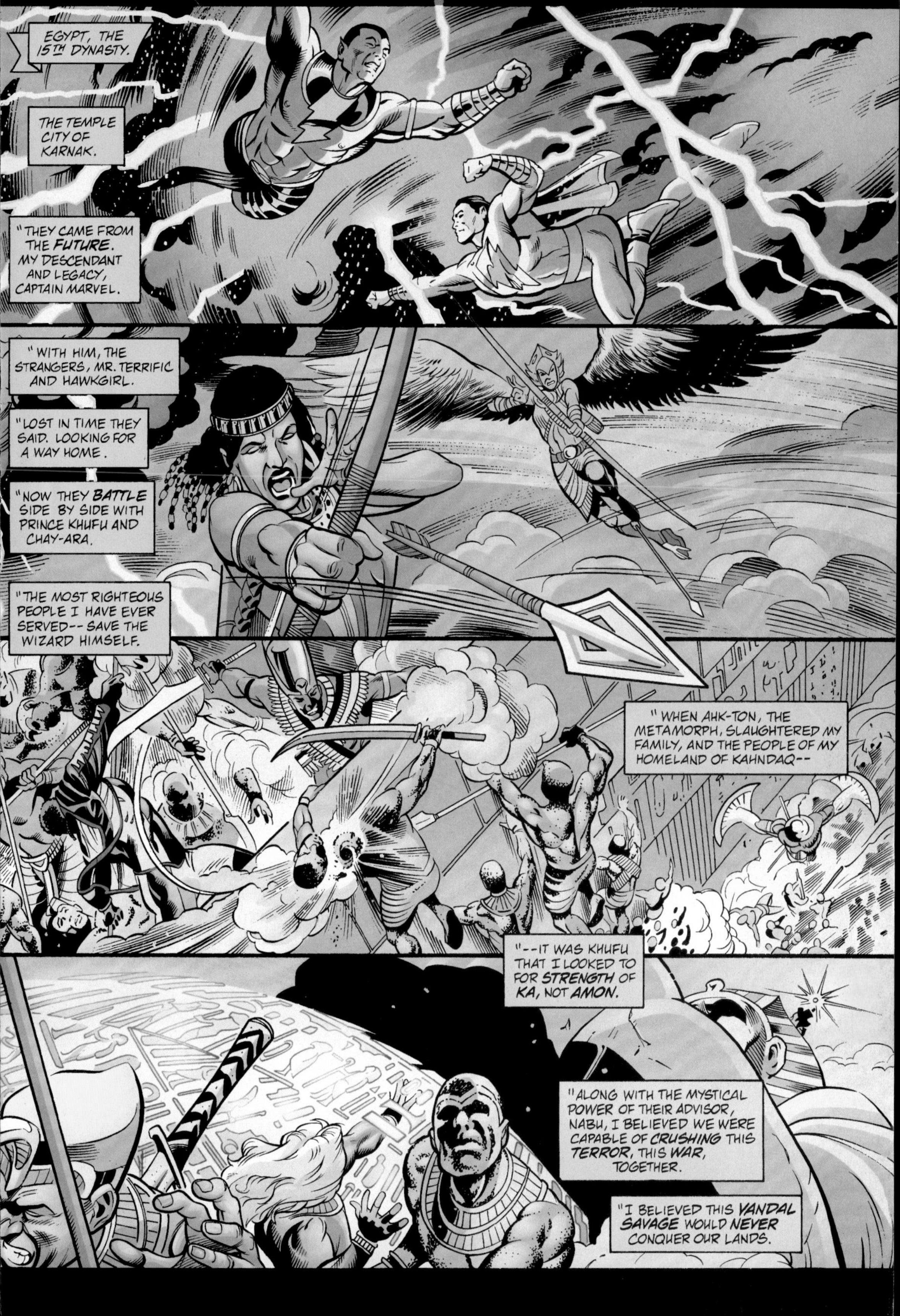

EGYPT, THE 15TH DYNASTY.
THE TEMPLE CITY OF KARNAK.
"THEY CAME FROM THE FUTURE. MY DESCENDANT AND LEGACY, CAPTAIN MARVEL.
"WITH HIM, THE STRANGERS, MR. TERRIFIC AND HAWKGIRL.
"LOST IN TIME THEY SAID. LOOKING FOR A WAY HOME.
"NOW THEY BATTLE SIDE BY SIDE WITH PRINCE KHUFU AND CHAY-ARA.
"THE MOST RIGHTEOUS PEOPLE I HAVE EVER SERVED-- SAVE THE WIZARD HIMSELF.
"WHEN AHK-TON, THE METAMORPH, SLAUGHTERED MY FAMILY, AND THE PEOPLE OF MY HOMELAND OF KAHNDAQ--
"--IT WAS KHUFU THAT I LOOKED TO FOR STRENGTH OF KA, NOT AMON.
"ALONG WITH THE MYSTICAL POWER OF THEIR ADVISOR, NABU, I BELIEVED WE WERE CAPABLE OF CRUSHING THIS TERROR, THIS WAR, TOGETHER.
"I BELIEVED THIS VANDAL SAVAGE WOULD NEVER CONQUER OUR LANDS.

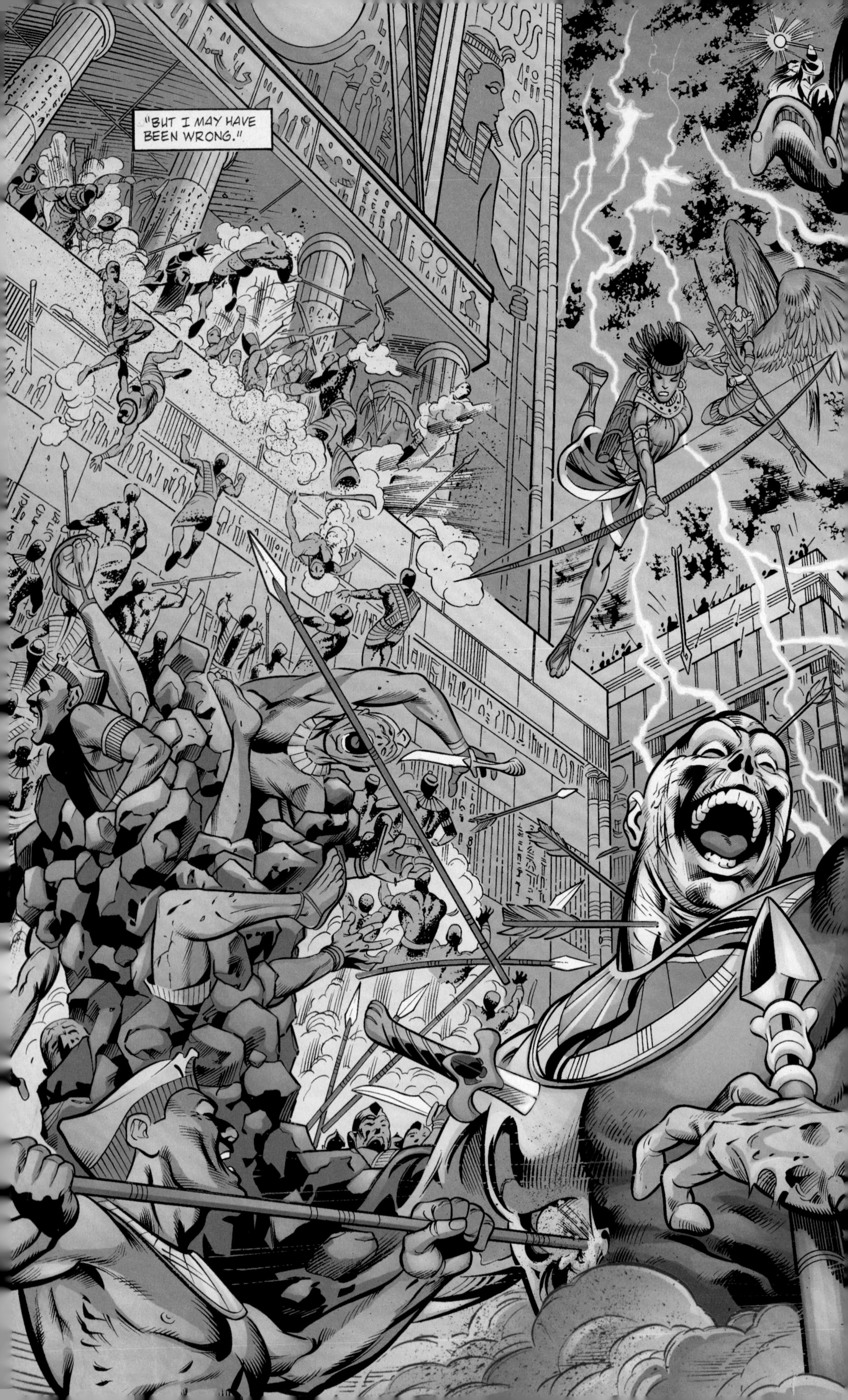
"BUT I MAY HAVE BEEN WRONG."

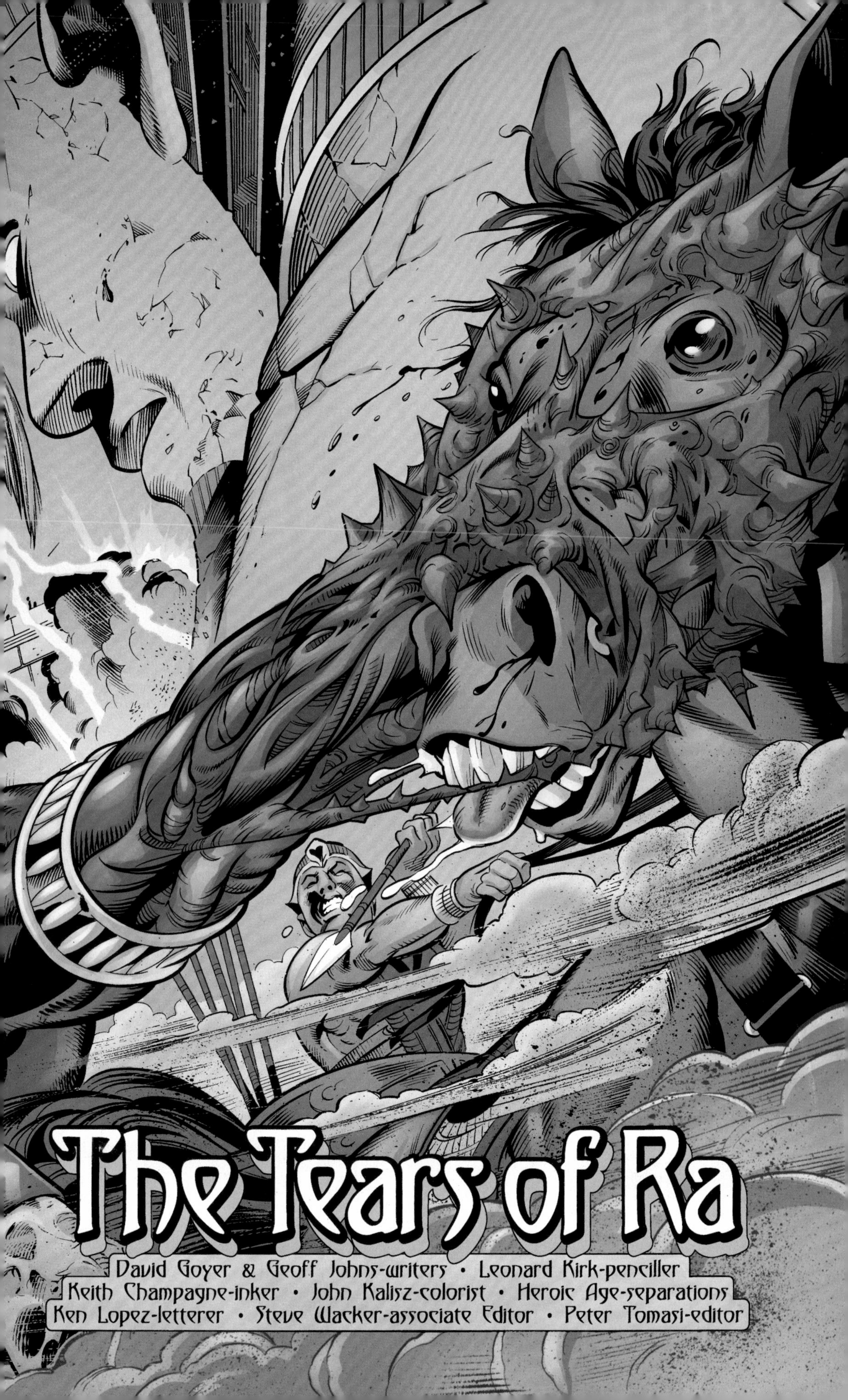
The Tears of Ra
David Goyer & Geoff Johns-writers • Leonard Kirk-penciller
Keith Champagne-inker • John Kalisz-colorist • Heroic Age-separations
Ken Lopez-letterer • Steve Wacker-associate Editor • Peter Tomasi-editor

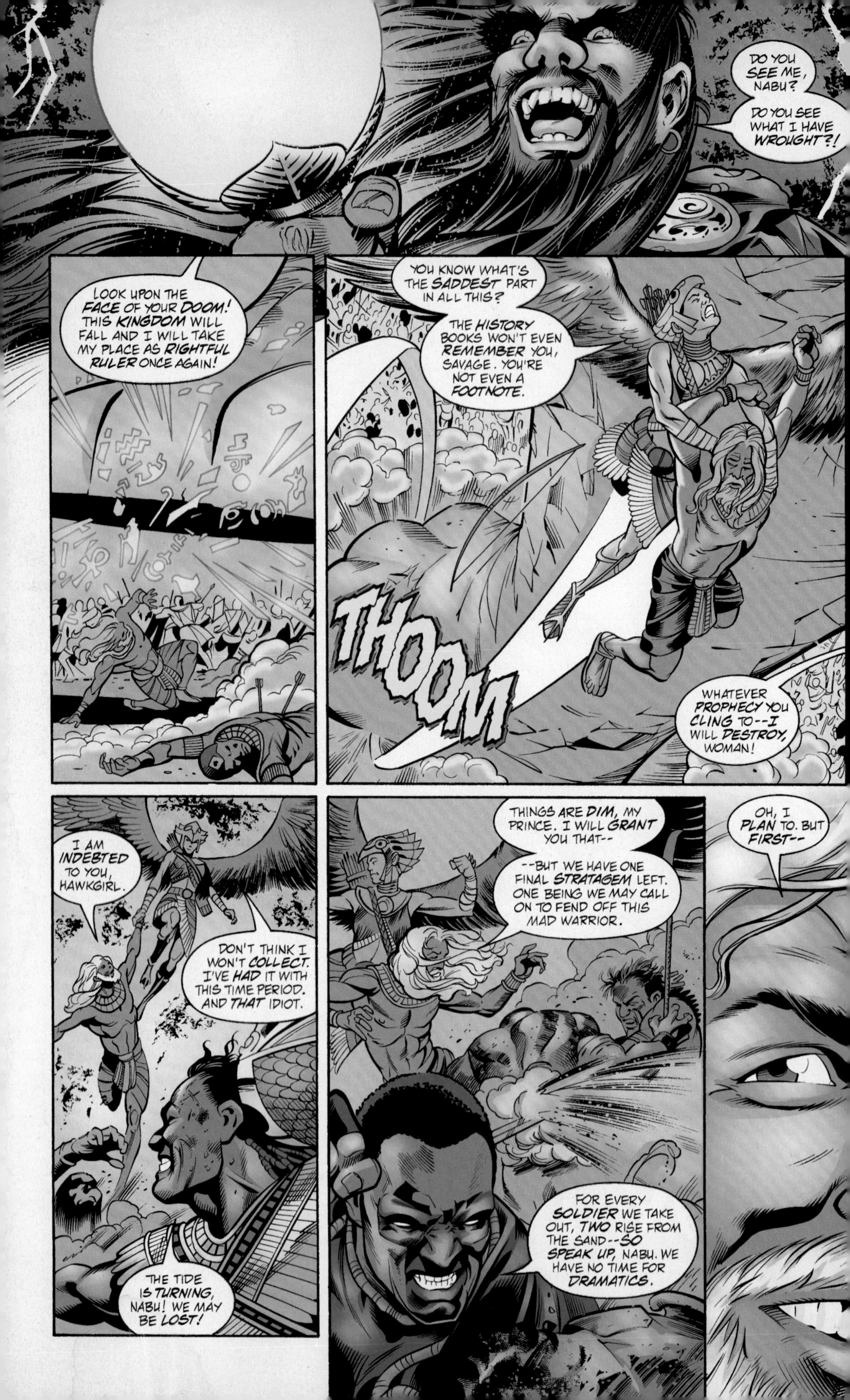
DO YOU SEE ME, NABU?
DO YOU SEE WHAT I HAVE WROUGHT?!
LOOK UPON THE FACE OF YOUR DOOM! THIS KINGDOM WILL FALL AND I WILL TAKE MY PLACE AS RIGHTFUL RULER ONCE AGAIN!
YOU KNOW WHAT'S THE SADDEST PART IN ALL THIS?
THE HISTORY BOOKS WON'T EVEN REMEMBER YOU, SAVAGE. YOU'RE NOT EVEN A FOOTNOTE.
THOOM
WHATEVER PROPHECY YOU CLING TO--I WILL DESTROY, WOMAN!
I AM INDEBTED TO YOU, HAWKGIRL.
DON'T THINK I WON'T COLLECT. I'VE HAD IT WITH THIS TIME PERIOD. AND THAT IDIOT.
THE TIDE IS TURNING, NABU! WE MAY BE LOST!
THINGS ARE DIM, MY PRINCE. I WILL GRANT YOU THAT--
--BUT WE HAVE ONE FINAL STRATAGEM LEFT. ONE BEING WE MAY CALL ON TO FEND OFF THIS MAD WARRIOR.
FOR EVERY SOLDIER WE TAKE OUT, TWO RISE FROM THE SAND--SO SPEAK UP, NABU. WE HAVE NO TIME FOR DRAMATICS.
OH, I PLAN TO. BUT FIRST--

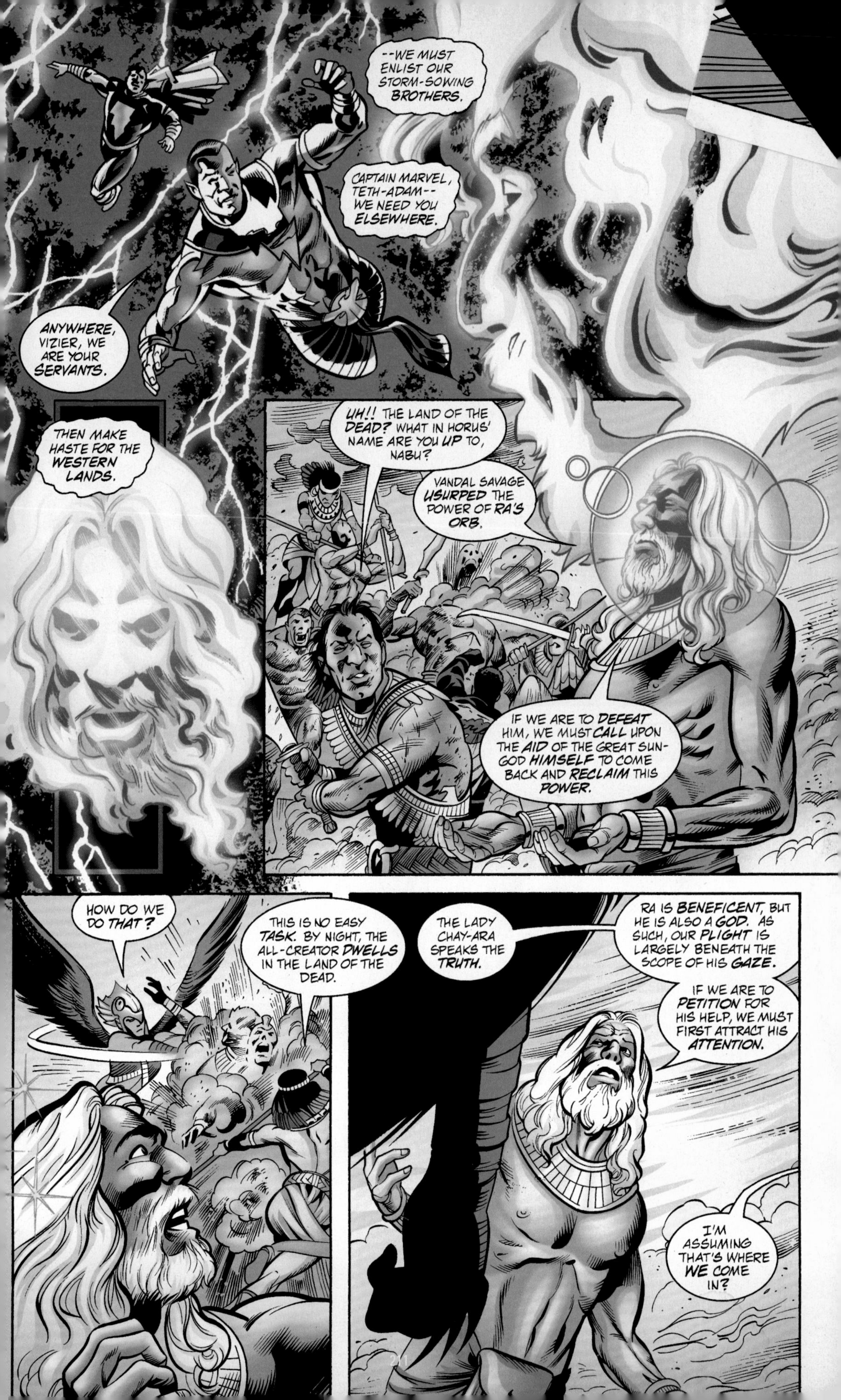

--WE MUST ENLIST OUR STORM-SOWING BROTHERS.
CAPTAIN MARVEL, TETH-ADAM-- WE NEED YOU ELSEWHERE.
ANYWHERE, VIZIER, WE ARE YOUR SERVANTS.
THEN MAKE HASTE FOR THE WESTERN LANDS.
UH!! THE LAND OF THE DEAD? WHAT IN HORUS' NAME ARE YOU UP TO, NABU?
VANDAL SAVAGE USURPED THE POWER OF RA'S ORB.
IF WE ARE TO DEFEAT HIM, WE MUST CALL UPON THE AID OF THE GREAT SUN-GOD HIMSELF TO COME BACK AND RECLAIM THIS POWER.
HOW DO WE DO THAT?
THIS IS NO EASY TASK. BY NIGHT, THE ALL-CREATOR DWELLS IN THE LAND OF THE DEAD.
THE LADY CHAY-ARA SPEAKS THE TRUTH.
RA IS BENEFICENT, BUT HE IS ALSO A GOD. AS SUCH, OUR PLIGHT IS LARGELY BENEATH THE SCOPE OF HIS GAZE.
IF WE ARE TO PETITION FOR HIS HELP, WE MUST FIRST ATTRACT HIS ATTENTION.
I'M ASSUMING THAT'S WHERE WE COME IN?

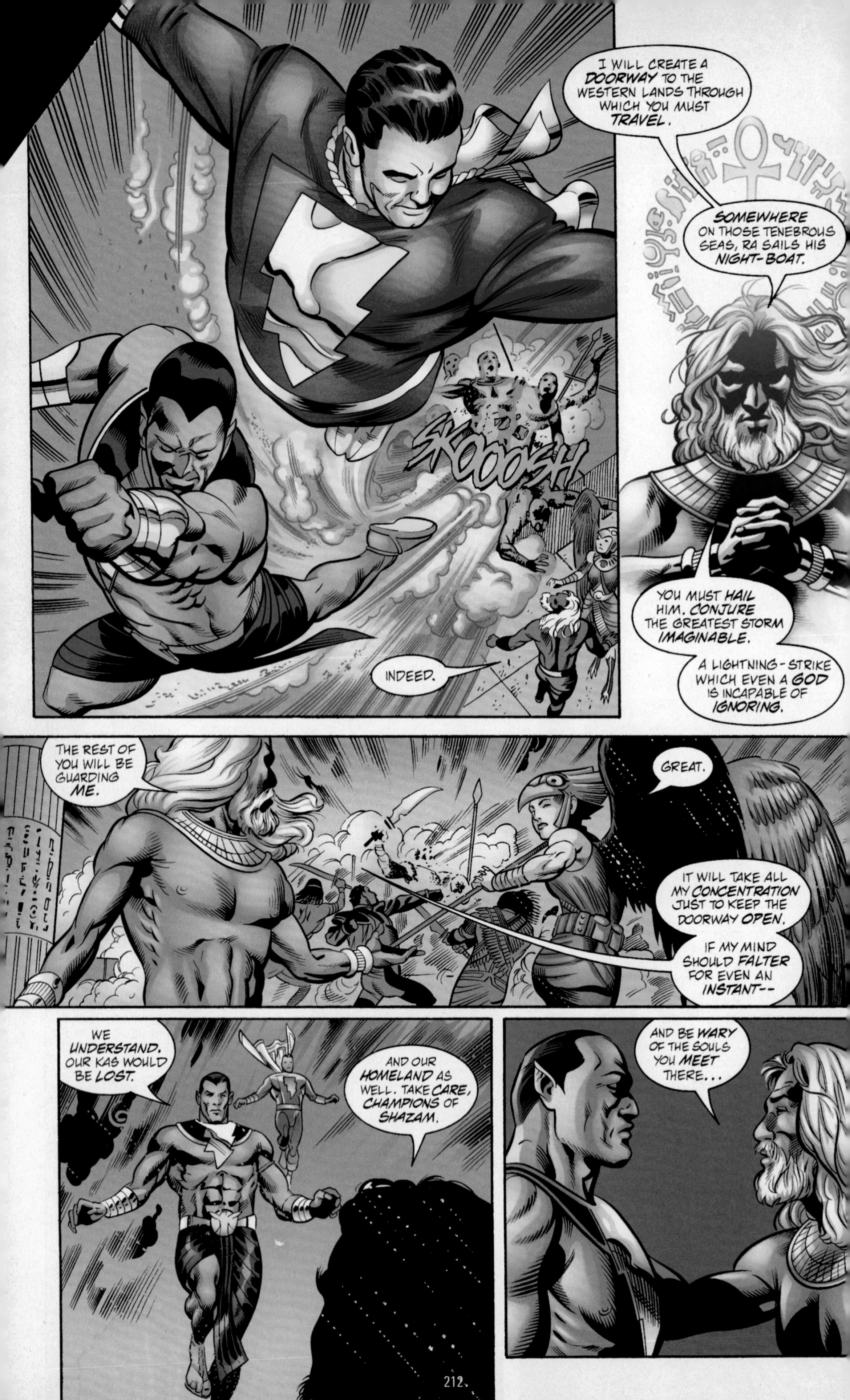

I WILL CREATE A DOORWAY TO THE WESTERN LANDS THROUGH WHICH YOU MUST TRAVEL.
SOMEWHERE ON THOSE TENEBROUS SEAS, RA SAILS HIS NIGHT-BOAT.
SKOOOSH
YOU MUST HAIL HIM. CONJURE THE GREATEST STORM IMAGINABLE.
A LIGHTNING-STRIKE WHICH EVEN A GOD IS INCAPABLE OF IGNORING.
INDEED.
THE REST OF YOU WILL BE GUARDING ME.
GREAT.
IT WILL TAKE ALL MY CONCENTRATION JUST TO KEEP THE DOORWAY OPEN.
IF MY MIND SHOULD FALTER FOR EVEN AN INSTANT--
WE UNDERSTAND. OUR KAS WOULD BE LOST.
AND OUR HOMELAND AS WELL. TAKE CARE, CHAMPIONS OF SHAZAM.
AND BE WARY OF THE SOULS YOU MEET THERE...

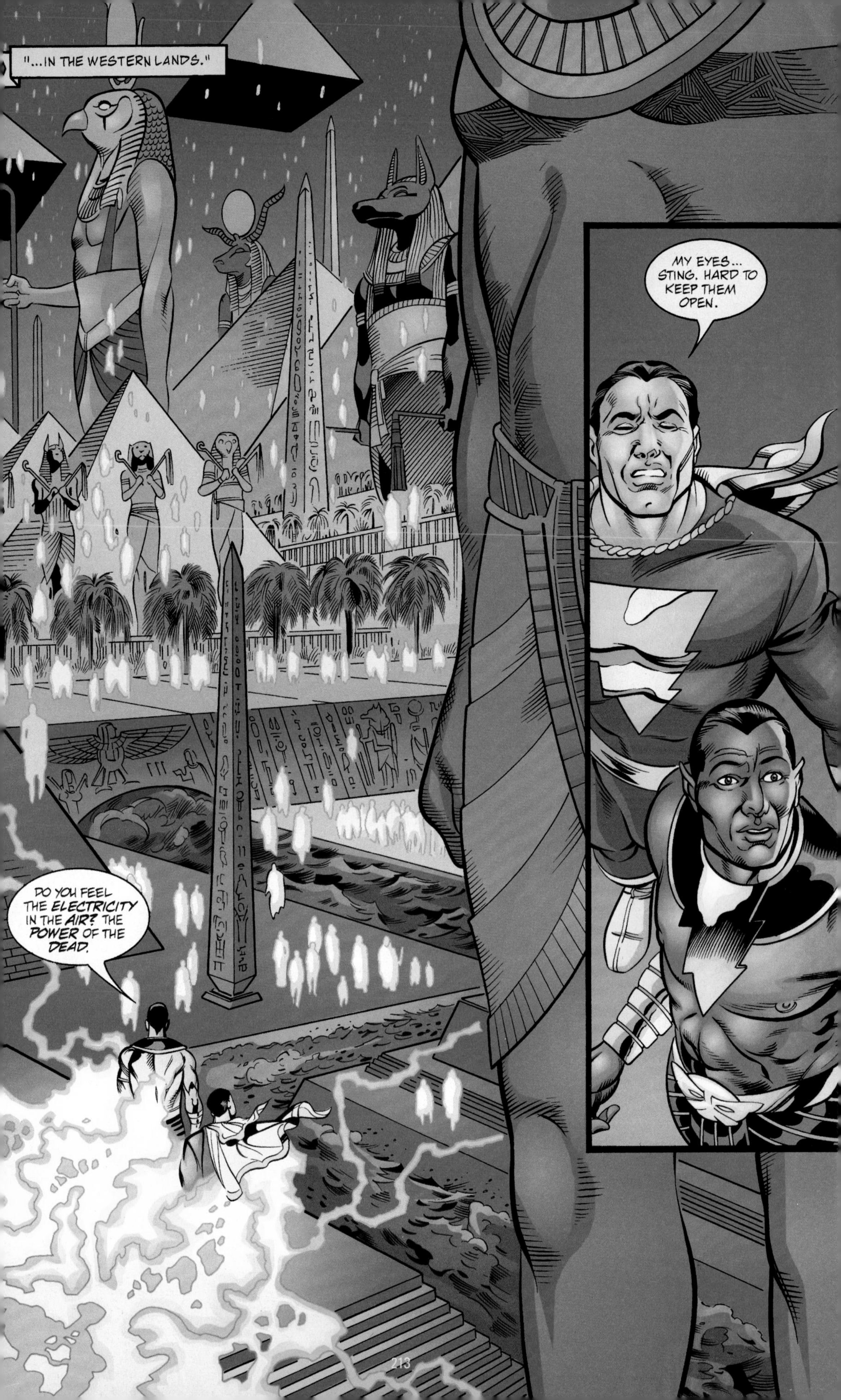
"...IN THE WESTERN LANDS."
MY EYES... STING. HARD TO KEEP THEM OPEN.
DO YOU FEEL THE ELECTRICITY IN THE AIR? THE POWER OF THE DEAD.

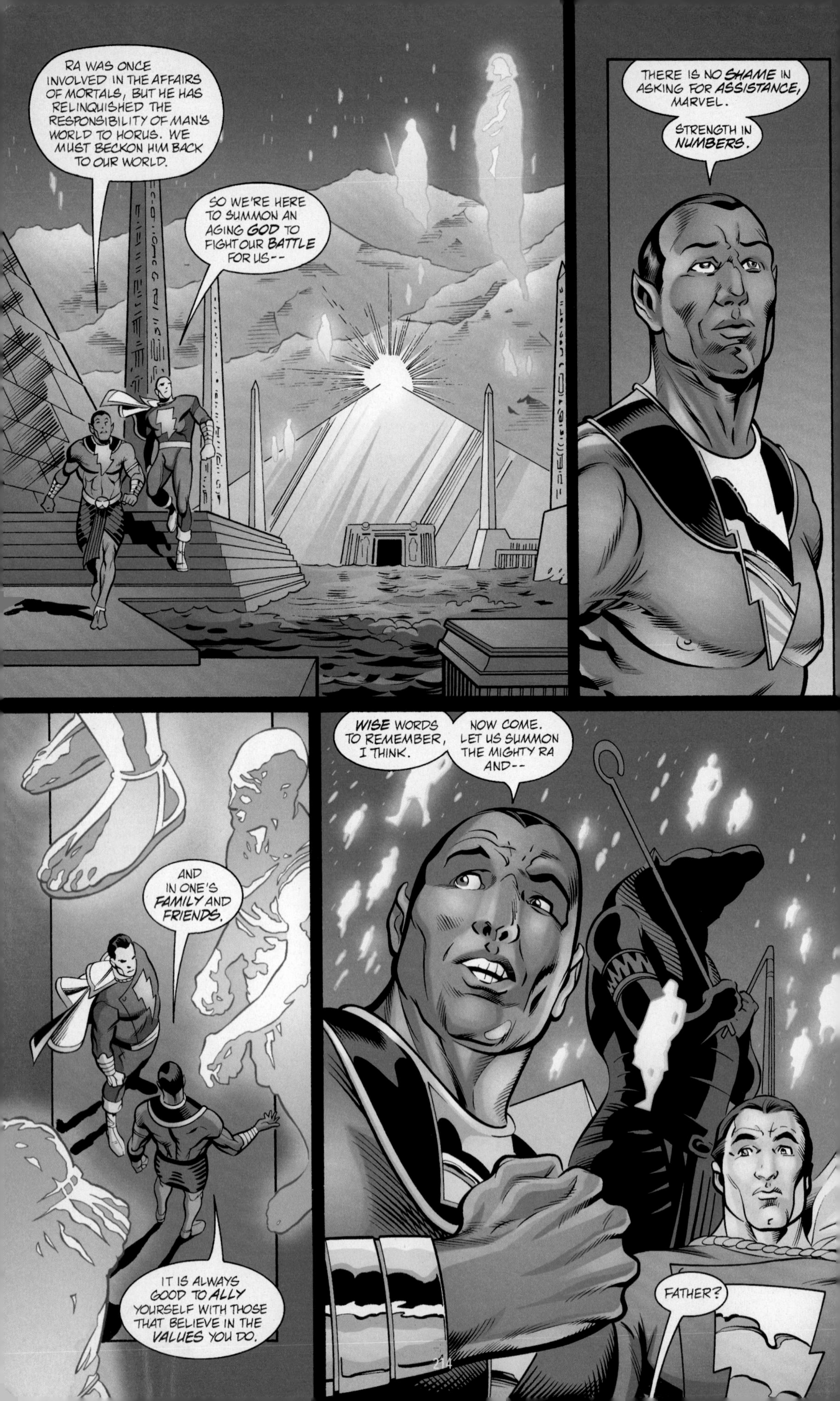
RA WAS ONCE INVOLVED IN THE AFFAIRS OF MORTALS, BUT HE HAS RELINQUISHED THE RESPONSIBILITY OF MAN'S WORLD TO HORUS. WE MUST BECKON HIM BACK TO OUR WORLD.
SO WE'RE HERE TO SUMMON AN AGING GOD TO FIGHT OUR BATTLE FOR US--
THERE IS NO SHAME IN ASKING FOR ASSISTANCE, MARVEL.
STRENGTH IN NUMBERS.
AND IN ONE'S FAMILY AND FRIENDS.
IT IS ALWAYS GOOD TO ALLY YOURSELF WITH THOSE THAT BELIEVE IN THE VALUES YOU DO.
WISE WORDS TO REMEMBER, I THINK.
NOW COME. LET US SUMMON THE MIGHTY RA AND--
FATHER?

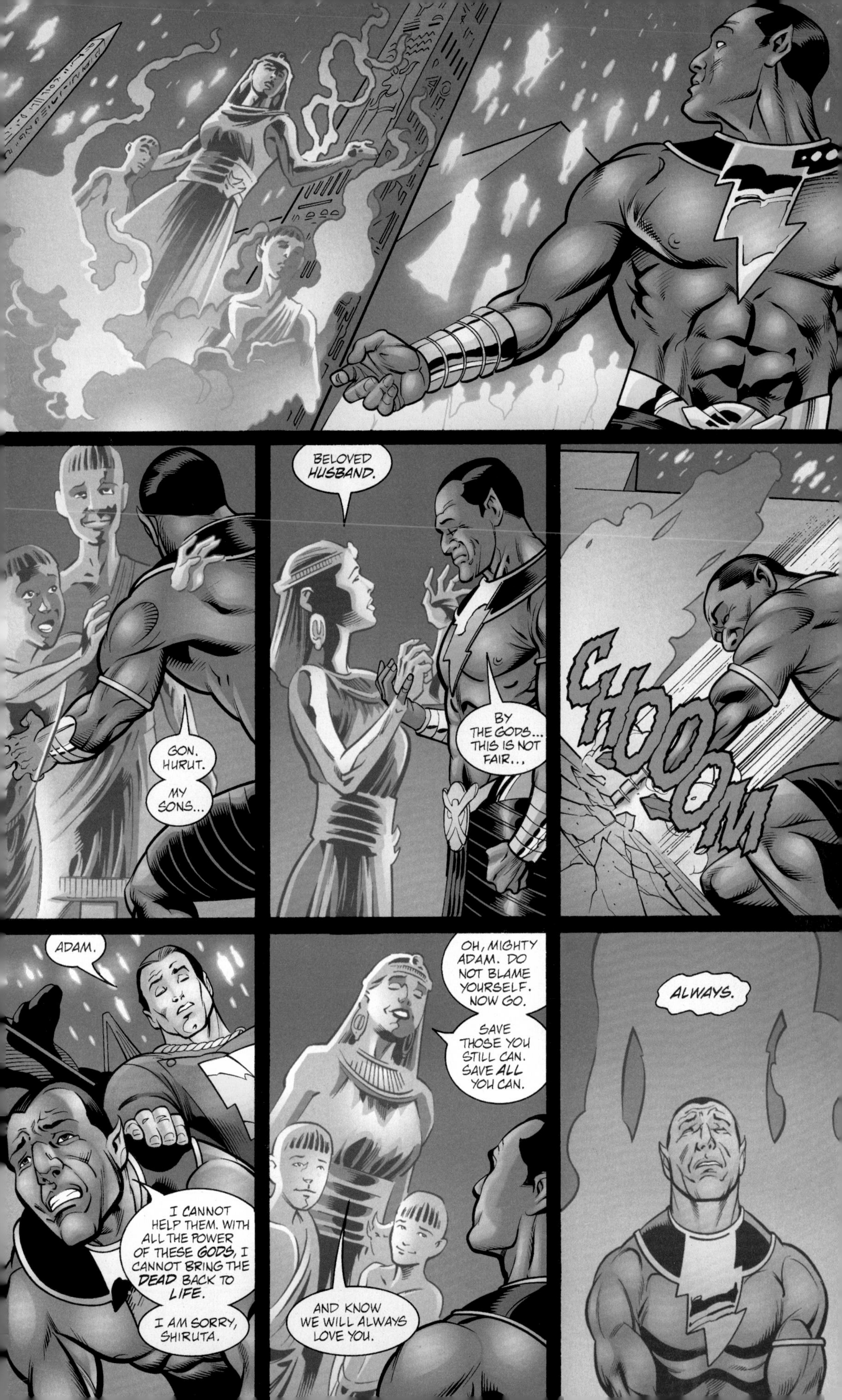
GON. HURUT.
MY SONS...
BELOVED HUSBAND.
BY THE GODS... THIS IS NOT FAIR...
CHOOOOM
ADAM.
I CANNOT HELP THEM. WITH ALL THE POWER OF THESE GODS, I CANNOT BRING THE DEAD BACK TO LIFE.
I AM SORRY, SHIRUTA.
OH, MIGHTY ADAM. DO NOT BLAME YOURSELF. NOW GO.
SAVE THOSE YOU STILL CAN. SAVE ALL YOU CAN.
AND KNOW WE WILL ALWAYS LOVE YOU.
ALWAYS.

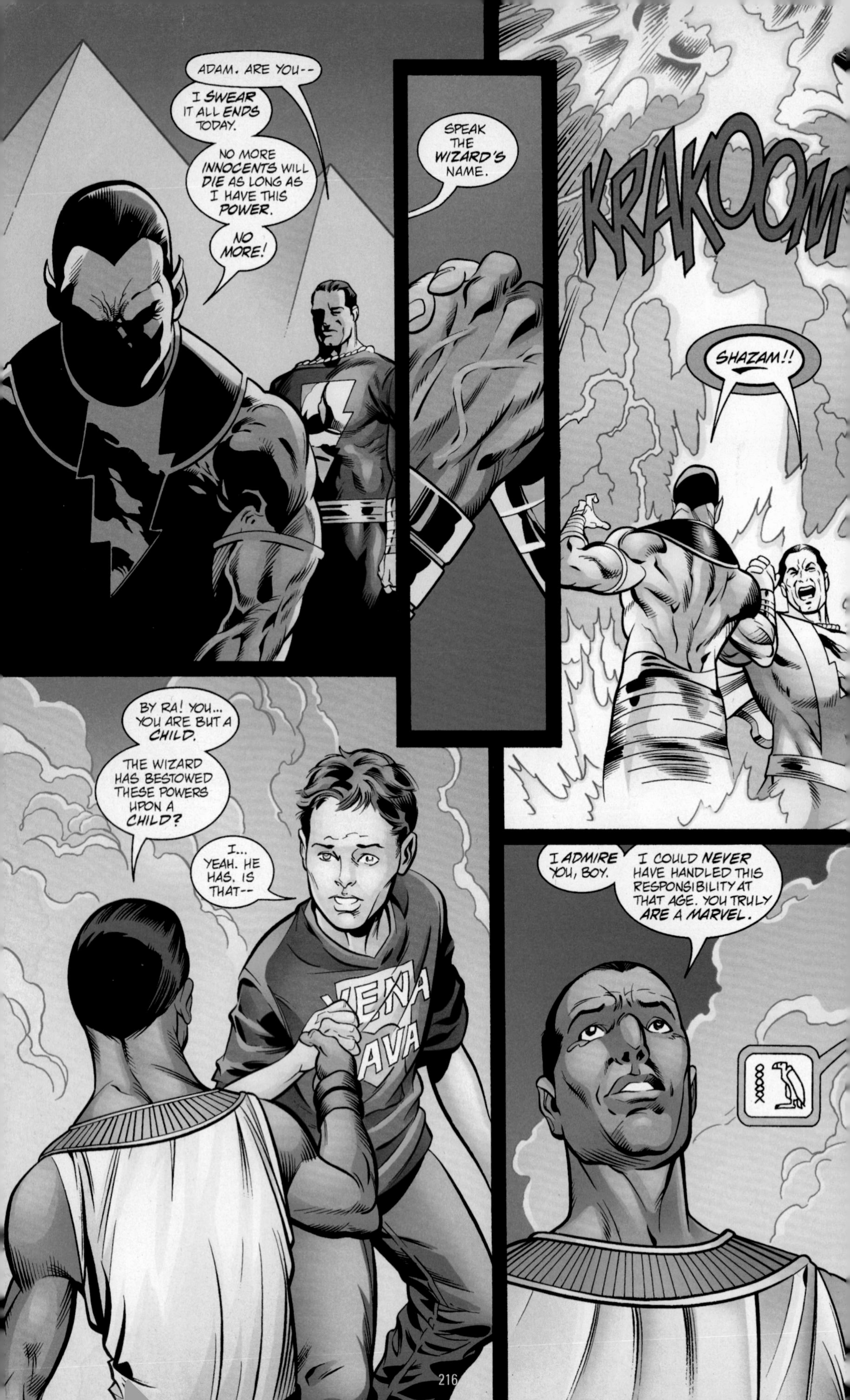
ADAM. ARE YOU--
I SWEAR IT ALL ENDS TODAY.
NO MORE INNOCENTS WILL DIE AS LONG AS I HAVE THIS POWER.
NO MORE!
SPEAK THE WIZARD'S NAME.
KRAKOOM
SHAZAM!!
BY RA! YOU... YOU ARE BUT A CHILD.
THE WIZARD HAS BESTOWED THESE POWERS UPON A CHILD?
I... YEAH. HE HAS. IS THAT--
I ADMIRE YOU, BOY.
I COULD NEVER HAVE HANDLED THIS RESPONSIBILITY AT THAT AGE. YOU TRULY ARE A MARVEL.

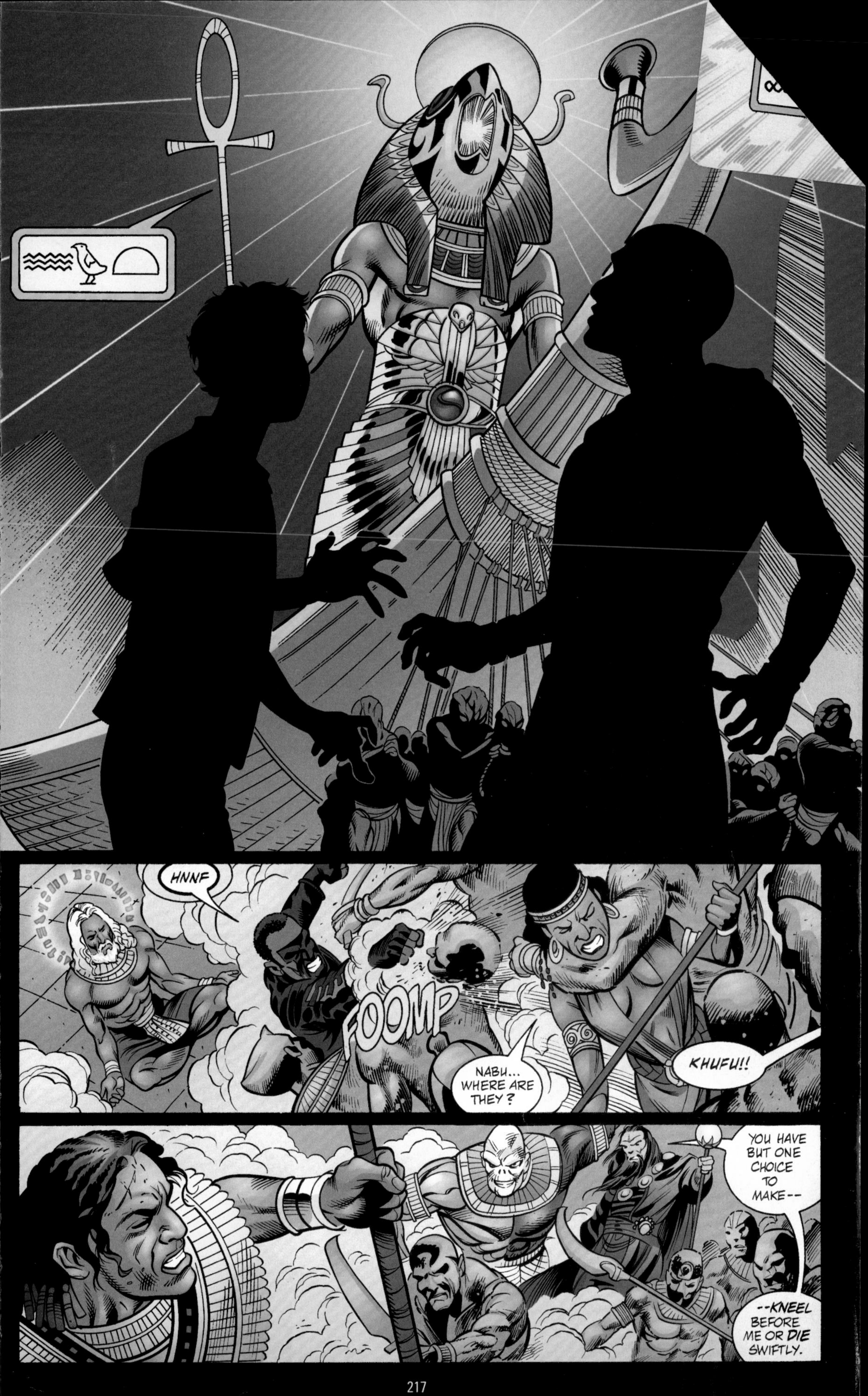
HNNF
FOOMP
NABU... WHERE ARE THEY?
KHUFU!!
YOU HAVE BUT ONE CHOICE TO MAKE--
--KNEEL BEFORE ME OR DIE SWIFTLY.

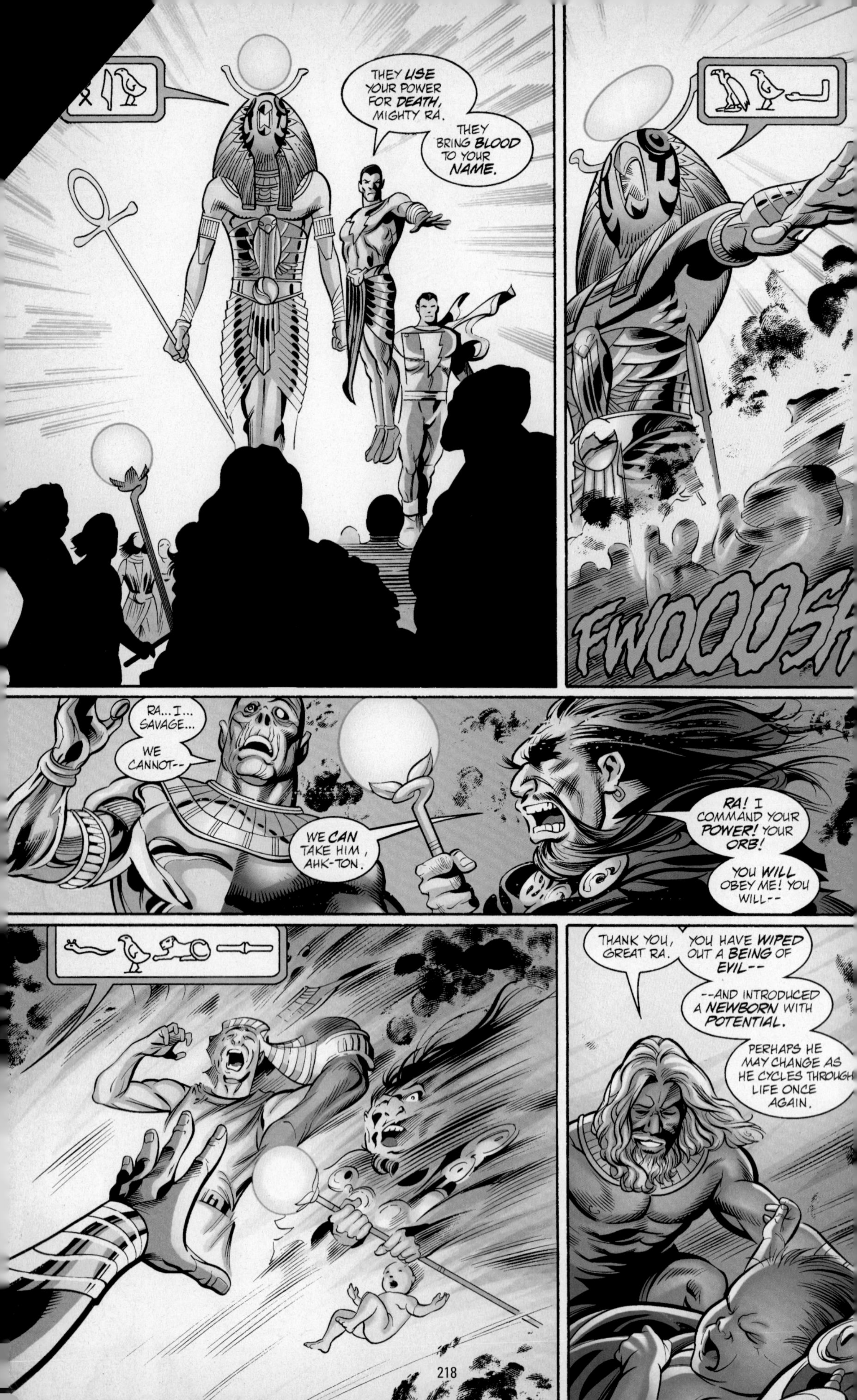
THEY USE YOUR POWER FOR DEATH, MIGHTY RA.
THEY BRING BLOOD TO YOUR NAME.
FWOOOSH
RA... I... SAVAGE...
WE CANNOT--
WE CAN TAKE HIM, AHK-TON.
RA! I COMMAND YOUR POWER! YOUR ORB!
YOU WILL OBEY ME! YOU WILL--
THANK YOU, GREAT RA.
YOU HAVE WIPED OUT A BEING OF EVIL--
--AND INTRODUCED A NEWBORN WITH POTENTIAL.
PERHAPS HE MAY CHANGE AS HE CYCLES THROUGH LIFE ONCE AGAIN.

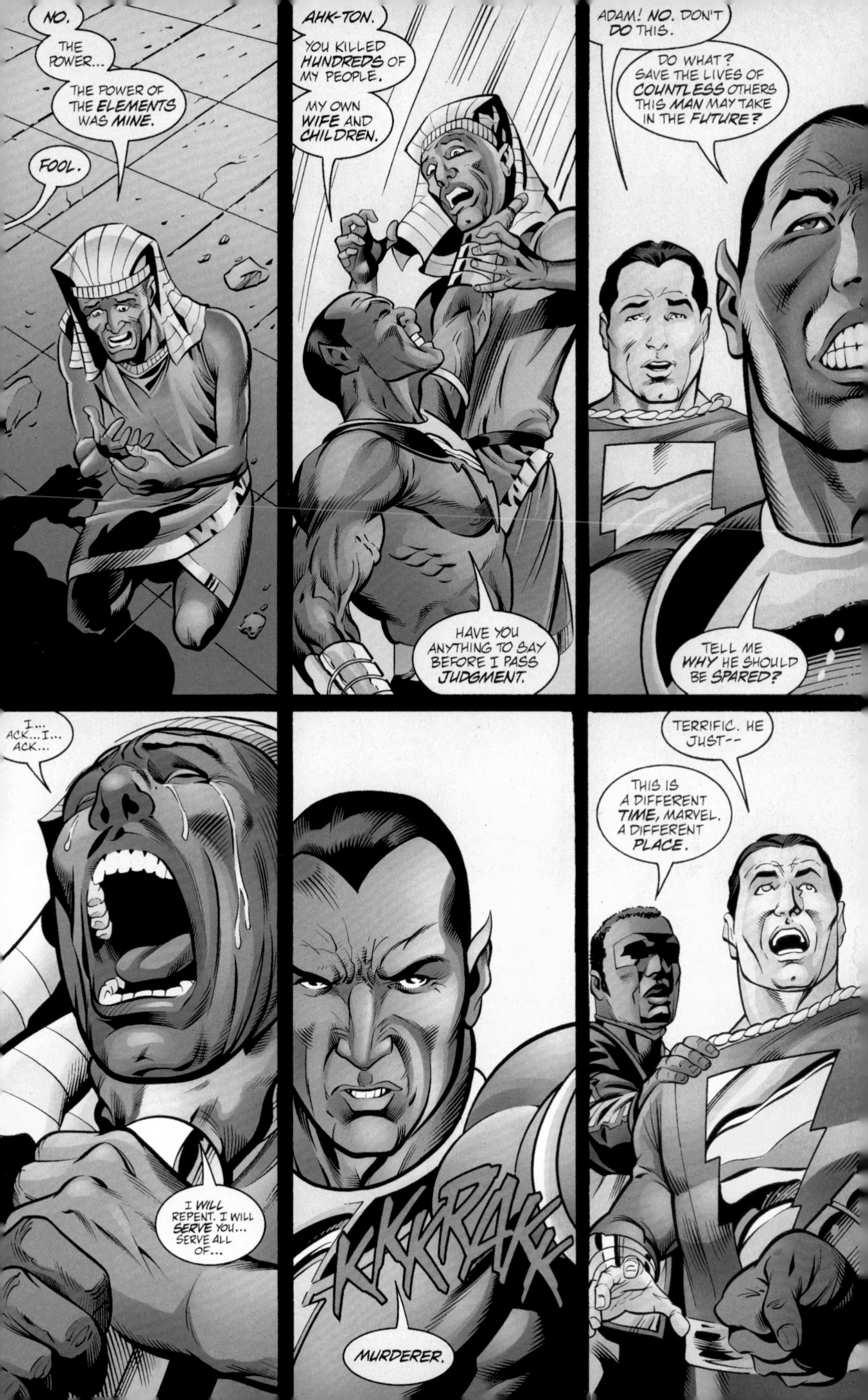

NO.
THE POWER...
THE POWER OF THE ELEMENTS WAS MINE.
FOOL.
AHK-TON.
YOU KILLED HUNDREDS OF MY PEOPLE.
MY OWN WIFE AND CHILDREN.
HAVE YOU ANYTHING TO SAY BEFORE I PASS JUDGMENT.
ADAM! NO. DON'T DO THIS.
DO WHAT? SAVE THE LIVES OF COUNTLESS OTHERS THIS MAN MAY TAKE IN THE FUTURE?
TELL ME WHY HE SHOULD BE SPARED?
I... ACK... I... ACK...
I WILL REPENT. I WILL SERVE YOU... SERVE ALL OF...
SKKKRAKK
MURDERER.
TERRIFIC. HE JUST--
THIS IS A DIFFERENT TIME, MARVEL. A DIFFERENT PLACE.

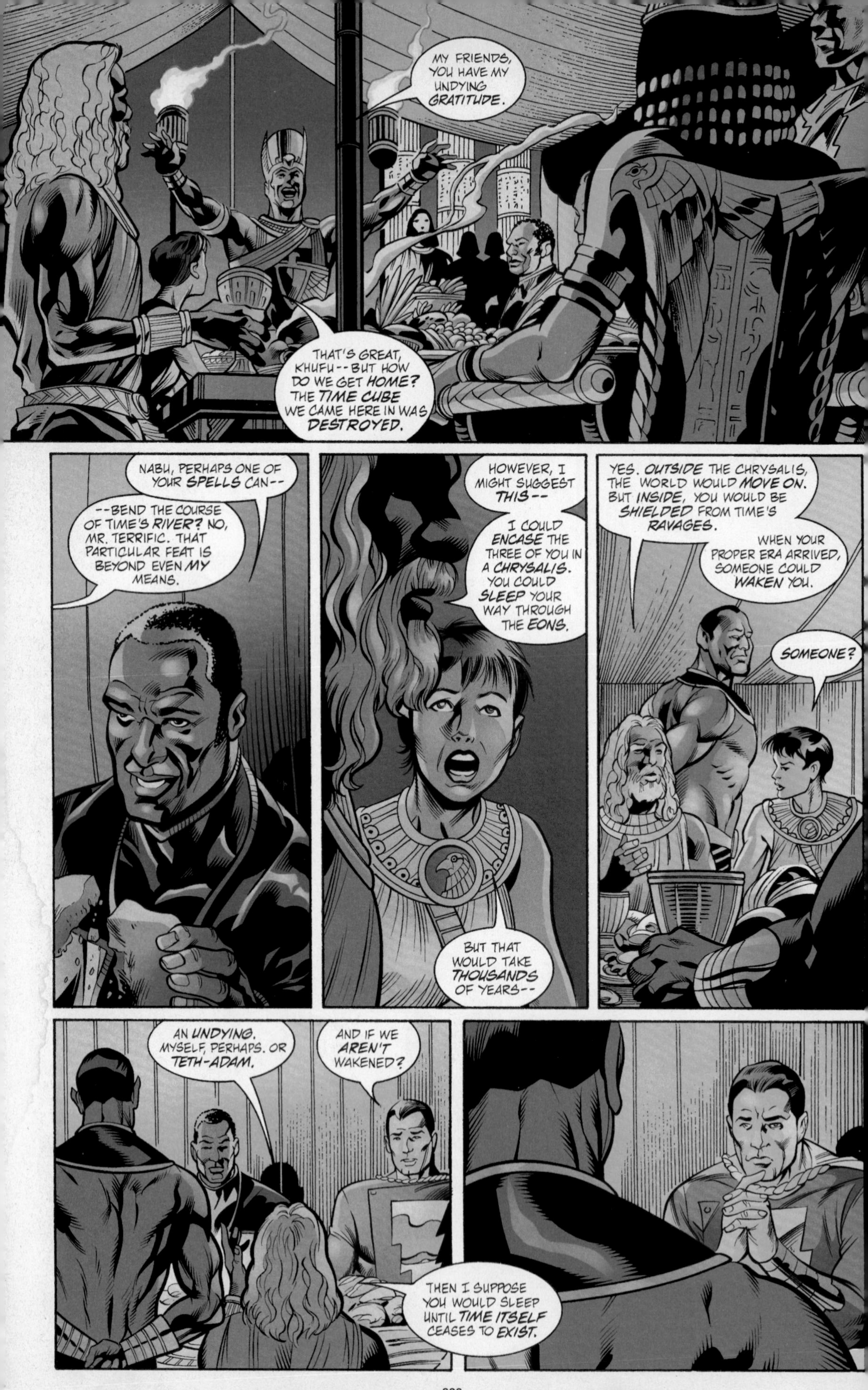

MY FRIENDS, YOU HAVE MY UNDYING GRATITUDE.
THAT'S GREAT, KHUFU--BUT HOW DO WE GET HOME? THE TIME CUBE WE CAME HERE IN WAS DESTROYED.
NABU, PERHAPS ONE OF YOUR SPELLS CAN--
--BEND THE COURSE OF TIME'S RIVER? NO, MR. TERRIFIC. THAT PARTICULAR FEAT IS BEYOND EVEN MY MEANS.
HOWEVER, I MIGHT SUGGEST THIS--
I COULD ENCASE THE THREE OF YOU IN A CHRYSALIS. YOU COULD SLEEP YOUR WAY THROUGH THE EONS.
BUT THAT WOULD TAKE THOUSANDS OF YEARS--
YES. OUTSIDE THE CHRYSALIS, THE WORLD WOULD MOVE ON. BUT INSIDE, YOU WOULD BE SHIELDED FROM TIME'S RAVAGES.
WHEN YOUR PROPER ERA ARRIVED, SOMEONE COULD WAKEN YOU.
SOMEONE?
AN UNDYING. MYSELF, PERHAPS. OR TETH-ADAM.
AND IF WE AREN'T WAKENED?
THEN I SUPPOSE YOU WOULD SLEEP UNTIL TIME ITSELF CEASES TO EXIST.

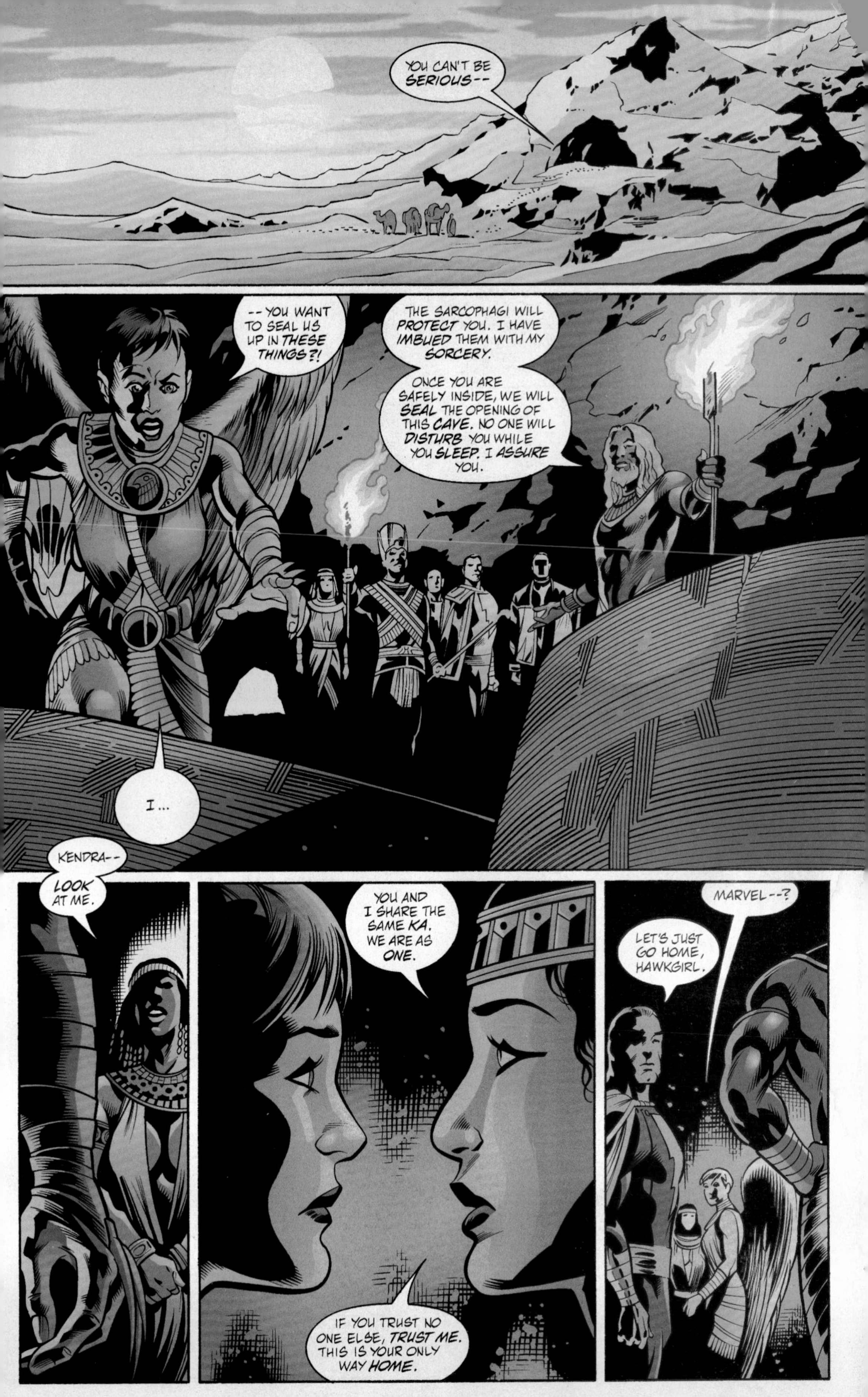

YOU CAN'T BE SERIOUS--
--YOU WANT TO SEAL US UP IN THESE THINGS?!
THE SARCOPHAGI WILL PROTECT YOU. I HAVE IMBUED THEM WITH MY SORCERY.
ONCE YOU ARE SAFELY INSIDE, WE WILL SEAL THE OPENING OF THIS CAVE. NO ONE WILL DISTURB YOU WHILE YOU SLEEP. I ASSURE YOU.
I...
KENDRA--
LOOK AT ME.
YOU AND I SHARE THE SAME KA. WE ARE AS ONE.
IF YOU TRUST NO ONE ELSE, TRUST ME. THIS IS YOUR ONLY WAY HOME.
MARVEL--?
LET'S JUST GO HOME, HAWKGIRL.

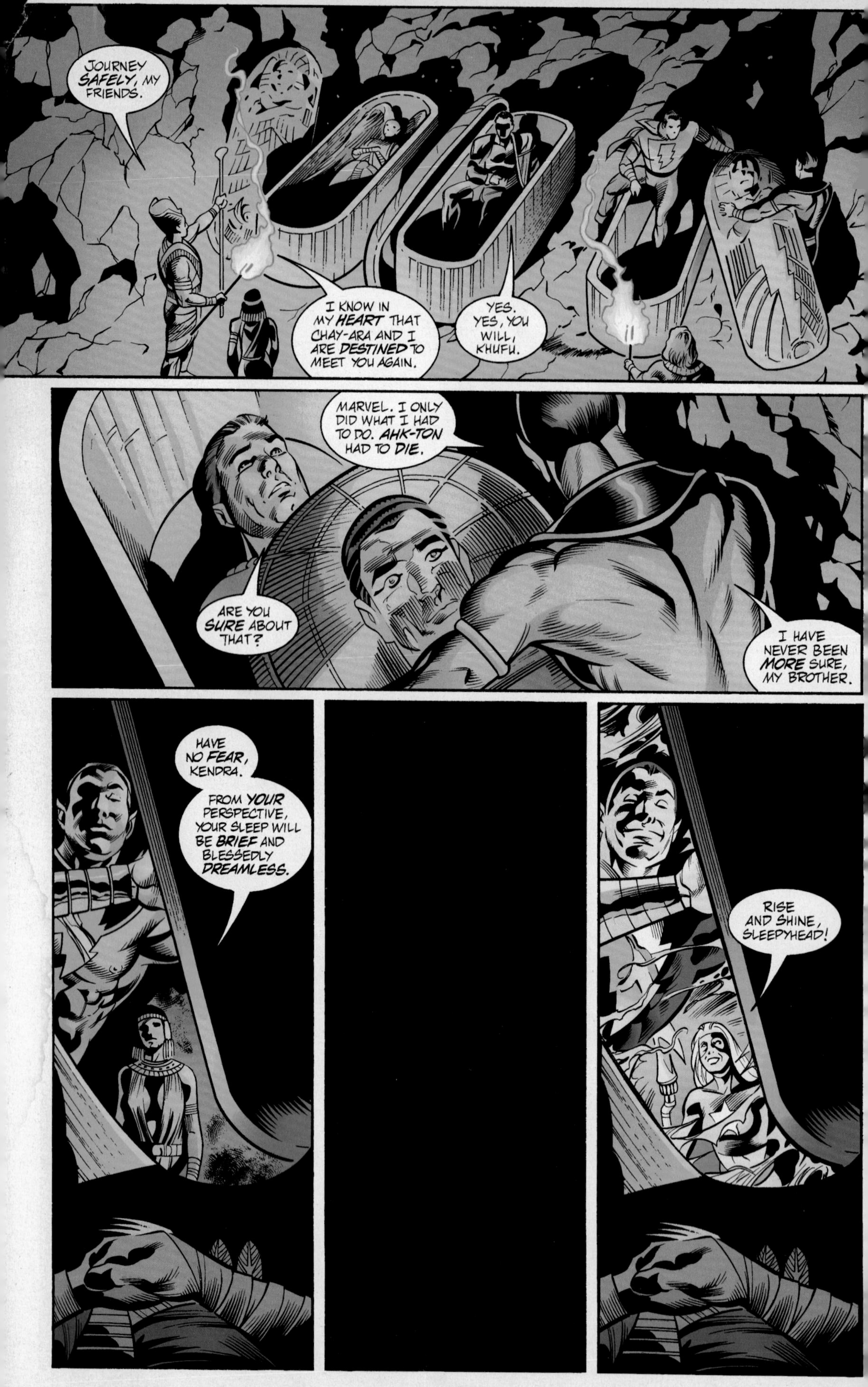
JOURNEY SAFELY, MY FRIENDS.
I KNOW IN MY HEART THAT CHAY-ARA AND I ARE DESTINED TO MEET YOU AGAIN.
YES. YES, YOU WILL, KHUFU.
MARVEL. I ONLY DID WHAT I HAD TO DO. AHK-TON HAD TO DIE.
ARE YOU SURE ABOUT THAT?
I HAVE NEVER BEEN MORE SURE, MY BROTHER.
HAVE NO FEAR, KENDRA.
FROM YOUR PERSPECTIVE, YOUR SLEEP WILL BE BRIEF AND BLESSEDLY DREAMLESS.
RISE AND SHINE, SLEEPYHEAD!

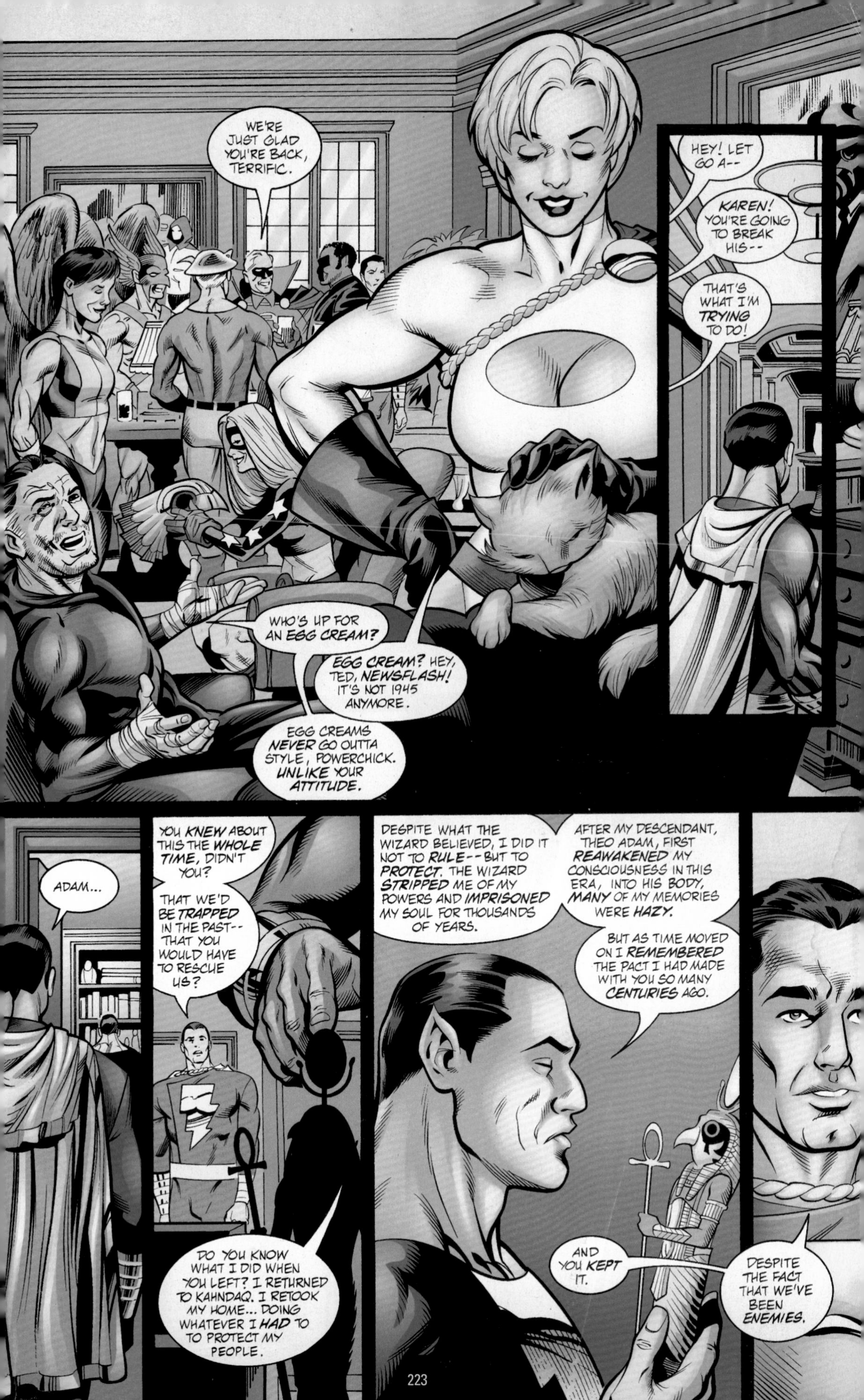
WE'RE JUST GLAD YOU'RE BACK, TERRIFIC.
HEY! LET GO A--
KAREN! YOU'RE GOING TO BREAK HIS--
THAT'S WHAT I'M TRYING TO DO!
WHO'S UP FOR AN EGG CREAM?
EGG CREAM? HEY, TED, NEWSFLASH! IT'S NOT 1945 ANYMORE.
EGG CREAMS NEVER GO OUTTA STYLE, POWERCHICK. UNLIKE YOUR ATTITUDE.
ADAM...
YOU KNEW ABOUT THIS THE WHOLE TIME, DIDN'T YOU?
THAT WE'D BE TRAPPED IN THE PAST-- THAT YOU WOULD HAVE TO RESCUE US?
DO YOU KNOW WHAT I DID WHEN YOU LEFT? I RETURNED TO KAHNDAQ. I RETOOK MY HOME... DOING WHATEVER I HAD TO TO PROTECT MY PEOPLE.
DESPITE WHAT THE WIZARD BELIEVED, I DID IT NOT TO RULE--BUT TO PROTECT. THE WIZARD STRIPPED ME OF MY POWERS AND IMPRISONED MY SOUL FOR THOUSANDS OF YEARS.
AFTER MY DESCENDANT, THEO ADAM, FIRST REAWAKENED MY CONSCIOUSNESS IN THIS ERA, INTO HIS BODY, MANY OF MY MEMORIES WERE HAZY.
BUT AS TIME MOVED ON I REMEMBERED THE PACT I HAD MADE WITH YOU SO MANY CENTURIES AGO.
AND YOU KEPT IT.
DESPITE THE FACT THAT WE'VE BEEN ENEMIES.

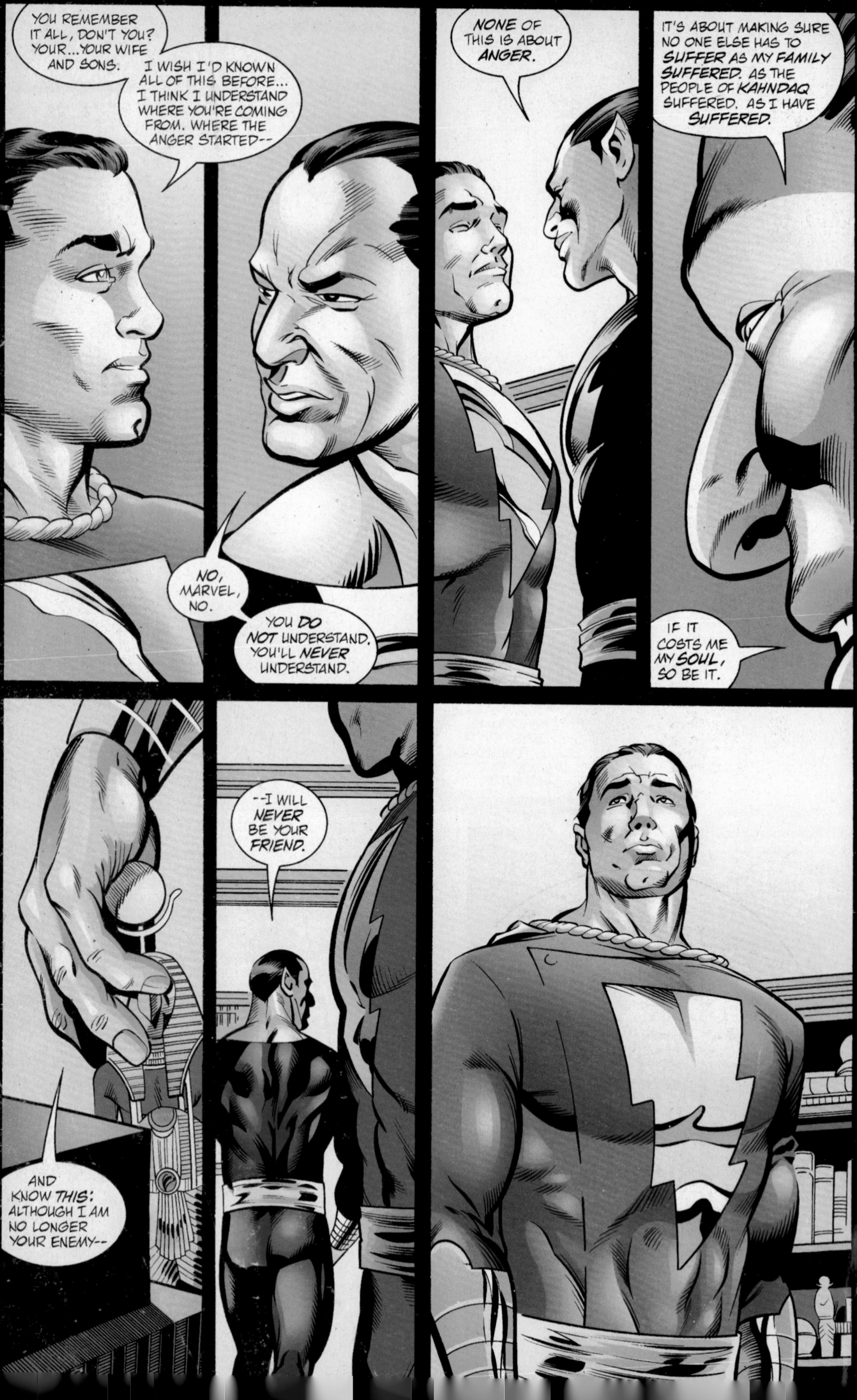
YOU REMEMBER IT ALL, DON'T YOU? YOUR...YOUR WIFE AND SONS.
I WISH I'D KNOWN ALL OF THIS BEFORE... I THINK I UNDERSTAND WHERE YOU'RE COMING FROM. WHERE THE ANGER STARTED--
NO, MARVEL, NO.
YOU DO NOT UNDERSTAND. YOU'LL NEVER UNDERSTAND.
NONE OF THIS IS ABOUT ANGER.
IT'S ABOUT MAKING SURE NO ONE ELSE HAS TO SUFFER AS MY FAMILY SUFFERED. AS THE PEOPLE OF KAHNDAQ SUFFERED. AS I HAVE SUFFERED.
IF IT COSTS ME MY SOUL, SO BE IT.
AND KNOW THIS: ALTHOUGH I AM NO LONGER YOUR ENEMY--
--I WILL NEVER BE YOUR FRIEND.